"When a strong man armed keepeth his palace, his goods are in peace."

LUKE 11 : 21

Books by Robert Leckie

HELMET FOR MY PILLOW

LORD, WHAT A FAMILY

THE MARCH TO GLORY

MARINES!

CONFLICT: The History of the Korean War

THE WARS OF AMERICA: From 1600 to 1992 (in two volumes)

GEORGE WASHINGTON'S WAR: The Saga of the American Revolution

FROM SEA TO SHINING SEA: From the War of 1812 to the Mexican War, the Saga of America's Expansion

NONE DIED IN VAIN: The Saga of the American Civil War

DELIVERED FROM EVIL: The Saga of World World II

OKINAWA: Final Battle of World War II

The United

STRONG
MEN
 ARMED

States Marines Against Japan

R O B E R T L E C K I E

DA CAPO PRESS
A Member of the Perseus Books Group

First Da Capo Press edition 1997
First Da Capo Press paperback edition 2010
ISBN: 978-0-306-81887-5

Published by Da Capo Press
A Member of the Perseus Books Group
www.dacapopress.com
Da Capo Press books are available at special discounts for bulk
purchases in the U.S. by corporations, institutions, and other
organizations. For more information, please contact the Special
Markets Department at the Perseus Books Group, 2300 Chestnut
Street, Suite 200, Philadelphia, PA 19103, or call (800) 810-4145,
ext. 5000, or e-mail special.markets@perseusbooks.com.

To those brave Marines who "foremost fighting fell"

CONTENTS

MAPS

I. Days of Wrath

1

It was the sixth of August, 1942—eight months since Vice Admiral Chuichi Nagumo had swung his aircraft carriers south and sent them plunging through mounting seas toward Pearl Harbor.

Eight months, and during them the power of America's Pacific Fleet had rolled with the tide on the floor of Battleship Row; Wake had fallen, Guam, the Philippines; the Rising Sun flew above the Dutch East Indies, it surmounted the French tricolor in Indo-China, it blotted out the Union Jack in Singapore where columns of short tan men in mushroom helmets double-timed through the streets. Burma, Malaya and Thailand were also Japanese. India's hundreds of millions were imperiled, great China was all but isolated from the world, Australia looked fearfully north to the Japanese bases on New Guinea, toward the long chain of the Solomon Islands drawn like a knife across her lifeline to America.

Eight months, and now an American invasion fleet sailed north to Guadalcanal. Thirty-one transports and cargo ships were stuffed to the gunwales with 19,000 United States Marines and their guns and vehicles. Guarding them were some 60 warships, mostly cruisers and destroyers, one battleship, a few oilers, and that trio of flattops representing all of America's carrier striking power in the South Pacific.

The skies were overcast, as they had been the day before.

As storm and fog had covered the Japanese approach to Pearl Harbor, so low ceilings concealed these Americans in their sweep west and north from the Fiji Islands.

Aboard the troopships it was not only the warm moist air that brought the sweat oozing from the bodies of the men on the weather decks, staining the sailors' light blue shirts as dark as their denim trousers, making blotches on the pale green twill dungarees of the Marines. There was tension in the air. It was almost a living presence. It made voices taut, husky—made the sweat come faster. It was one with the rasp of steel on whetstones, the sound of the Marines sharpening bayonets and sheath knives for the morning's fight. Other Marines squatted on the grimy decks blacking rifle sights or applying a last light coat of oil to their rifle bores. Machine-gunners went over long belts of ammunition coiled wickedly in oblong green boxes, carefully withdrawing and reinserting the cartridges into their cloth loops, making certain that they would not stick and jam the guns. Other men adjusted packs, inspected grenade pins or made camouflage nets for their helmets—those exasperating scoops of steel which banged the back of a man's neck at a walk, bumped over his eyes at a run.

Many of these men wondered silently how they would react next day, in the holocaust of battle. Compassionate Marines suddenly became aware that they had no wish to kill, wondering, as they sat alongside cruel Marines carving X's on bullet ends to make dum-dums of them, if they would actually pull the trigger. Sentimental Marines composing that last letter home for the sixth or seventh time wrote in the grave periods of men already gloriously dead. But some, men such as the lazy Marines who had not cleaned or oiled their weapons, consciously drove the thought of battle from their minds. Others could not grasp its import. "Pogey-bait" Marines stood for hours in line outside the ship's canteen, thinking no further ahead than the next Clark Bar or Baby Ruth. Yardbird Marines—those immemorial dreamers "who never get the word" —were so little impressed by all this martial bustle that one of them could clear out a crowded hold in the *George F. Elliott* by stepping over the threshold with a newly issued hand gre-

4

nade in one hand and a freshly pulled pin in the other, asking shyly:

"What do I do now?"

Kiwi—as Marine yardbirds were now called in honor of that New Zealand bird which also does not fly—Kiwi was marched topside by a gunnery sergeant bellowing, "Grenade! Grenade! Git outta my way—grenade!" It was only after the gunny had cleared the fantail of the ship and had commanded Kiwi to hurl the grenade into the ocean, and had hit the deck alongside him, it was only after this that the gunny turned and booted Kiwi all the way forward and down the hatch to the head.

It was in the heads that the big poker games were played. The money had found its inevitable way into a few skillful hands and the big winners gathered for showdown games in lavatories deep below decks, places in which the air was such a foul compound of the reek of human refuse and cigarette smoke that a man coughing in revulsion blew holes in those blue clouds.

Above decks on one of the transports a young Marine skipped half dollars across the flat gray surface of the sea. A sergeant raged at him and the youth replied with a shrug:

"So what's the use of money where we're going?"

Aboard all the troopships platoons of men attended classes on the subject "Know Your Enemy." For perhaps the twentieth time they listened while lieutenants, few of whom had ever seen combat, read to them from hastily assembled manuals celebrating those qualities which made the Japanese soldier "the greatest jungle fighter in the world." Mr. Moto, said the manuals, could swim miles underwater while sucking air from hollow reeds, he could sneak stealthily through the jungle on split-toed, rubber-soled shoes, and he could climb trees like a monkey, often tying himself to the trunks and fighting from the treetops. He was tricky, capable of booby-trapping the bodies of his friends, and he often cried out in English to lure the unwary into ambush. At night the Japanese soldiers set off strings of firecrackers to simulate numerous machine guns and frighten their opponents into giving away their position, or they signaled to each other by rifle shot. Finally, this strong, stoic Oriental, who tortured and slaughtered in the name of an Emperor he believed to be divine, was also able to march farther, eat less and endure more than any other soldier in the world. Though some of this was true, much of it was hysterical hokum born of the Pearl Harbor psychosis, and because they had been fed it so often and in such large doses, many of these Marines had come to wonder aloud if every last son of Nippon had been suckled by a wolf.

"All right," said a young lieutenant aboard one troopship, "if a Jap jumped from a tree what would you do?"

"Kick him in the balls!" came the answer, almost in concert, and the lieutenant grinned and dismissed his class.

Below decks, many other Marines had joined the sailors in preparing the ships for battle. They sweated in stuffy supply holds, often straining their heads aloft to the open hatches while winches swung the heavy hooks and cargo nets among them, sometimes cursing when beads of sweat which had formed on their eyebrows fell into their eyes, blinding them. Men could be badly hurt by swinging hooks, and one Marine had already been killed by them.

Above the whining of the winches rose the spluttering roar of landing-boat motors being started. Their coxswains were testing them, even as they were being freed of their lashings and swung out on davits. Brassy-voiced bosun's mates shouted at their men, and the harder the sailors worked, the louder the bosun's mates yelled—for it is characteristic of their calling that they sweat only about the mouth.

On the artillery transports, boxes of shells were lifted on deck and placed in readiness to go over the side next day. Seventy-five- or 105-millimeter howitzers were trundled to the gunwales and coils of rope for hauling them inland were looped about their barrels. Winchmen on the assault transports hauled boxes of rifle ammunition, mortar shells, spare gun parts and roll after roll of barbed wire on deck.

So much barbed wire puzzled the men. It was defensive warfare material, and they, as they thought, were strictly offensive troops. Once they had seized Guadalcanal, they would turn it over to a garrison of soldiers and move on to assault

6

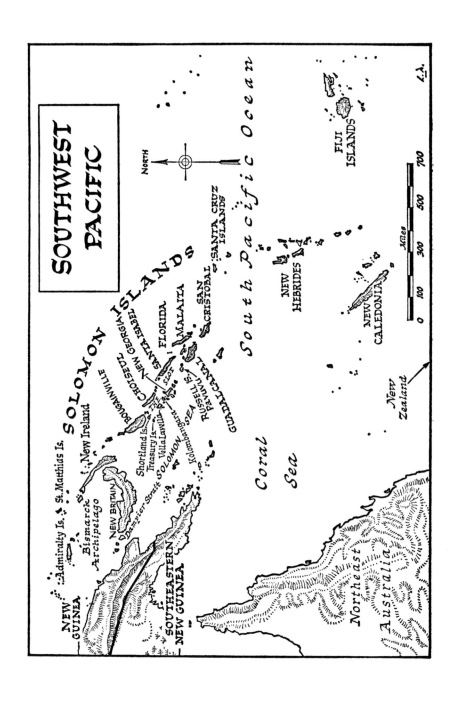

another island. So they had been told, and the great stores of barbed wire bewildered them almost as much as the outlandish nature of the island they were to capture.

"Who ever heard of Guadalcanal?" one of them growled. "Whadda we want with a place nobody ever heard of before?"

It was a common complaint, and it had been raised since July 31 when the troopships had made rendezvous with the warships off the Fijis and the men had been informed of their destination. They had been startled, but their surprise had far from rivaled the astonishment of their commander, Major General Alexander Vandegrift, when he, too, had been abruptly made aware that he was going to Guadalcanal.

When Vandegrift had come to Auckland in New Zealand on June 26, his First Marine Division had already been fragmented by the problem of moving men and munitions across the vast reaches of the Pacific. His Seventh Regiment had been detached from his command and sent to Samoa. His Fifth Regiment was encamped outside the New Zealand capital of Wellington, his First Regiment was sailing from San Francisco for Wellington, the Third Defense Battalion assigned to his division was in Pearl Harbor, his Eleventh Regiment of artillery was divided among these fragments, along with other supporting troops, and the Second Regiment, which would be detached from the Second Marine Division to replace Vandegrift's missing Seventh, was in San Diego Harbor. More gravely, not half the men in this division had been a year in uniform. They were mostly boys in their late teens and early twenties. Though they were high-hearted volunteers, tough and sturdy youths who had flocked to the Marines in the weeks following Pearl Harbor, they were still barely better than "boots." Some had been with their units only a week before departure from New River, North Carolina. They were in great need of training, for all their zest and bounce. So were their junior officers, those "Ninety-Day Wonders" just out of the Officer Candidates School in Quantico. Many of the senior NCO's and officers at company and even battalion level were reservists, men who had trained in armories one night a month and spent an annual two weeks in summer camp. But the division was heavily salted with seasoned NCO's, as well as with many of the battle-blooded officers in the Marine Corps. With these—and with six months' grace—Vandegrift was confident that he could field a fine fighting force in early 1943.

In this mood of confidence, Vandegrift came to Auckland and sat at a table across from Vice Admiral Robert Ghormley, commander of the South Pacific Area. Ghormley handed him a dispatch from America's supreme command, the Joint Chiefs of Staff. It said:

> Occupy and defend Tulagi and adjacent positions (Guadalcanal and Florida Islands and the Santa Cruz Islands) in order to deny these areas to the enemy and to provide United States bases in preparation for further offensive action.

Vandegrift read, deeply interested. Perhaps, when this base was assaulted and secured, he would be able to train his division there.

"Who will do the occupying?" asked the general.

"You," said the admiral.

There was an interval, and then:

"When?"

"The first of August."

If Alexander Vandegrift had glanced at his watch, he could not have been exaggerating the urgency of that moment. August 1! Between the present date and August 1 were thirty-seven days. But it would take six days to sail from New Zealand to the Fiji rendezvous area, and it would take another seven days to sail from the Fijis to the objective in the Solomons. That left twenty-four days in which to await the arrival of troops from California and Hawaii, to reconnoiter the objective, to study its terrain and map it, to get Intelligence working at an estimate of probable enemy defenses and troop strength, to load 31 transports and cargo carriers with 19,000 men and 60 days' combat supply—and then to conduct joint rehearsals before the day of assault. Twenty-four times twenty-four hours to go, and there was not even a battle plan begun. There was not a scrap of information on the objective beyond a Navy hydrographic chart made thirty-two years ago and Jack London's

9

short story *The Red One*, which, though set in Guadalcanal, was already suspect by spelling it Guadalcanar. If General Vandegrift had been asked to land his Marines upon the moon, he could not have had less knowledge of the battleground.

But Vandegrift was a Marine accustomed to adversity and skilled in the art of improvising. In those years between World Wars, when Congress slashed military budgets with a belligerence matched only by the ferocity of its pacifism, he had been among those officers who fought to fulfill a vision of the Marine Corps as a highly trained assault force with a special mission of making ship-to-shore landings on enemy-held terrain. To such professionals, the seeming setback was the normal condition of career. And Vandegrift was a professional, a soft-spoken, tough-minded commander in the mold of Stonewall Jackson. Intelligent enough to be appalled by the task confronting him, sensible enough to mask that dismay before his staff, he set that staff to work at organizing America's first full-scale amphibious invasion—imparting to them some of his own sense of urgency that was the surest guarantor of unpleasant surprise.

It was a surprise to find that the totality of the war did not impress the Wellington longshoremen's union controlling work on the huge Aotea Quay provided by the New Zealand government. The union still believed that the longer a job takes the longer the pay lasts. All cries for speed elicited the scornful rejoinder "Not half!"—and the unloading of ships moved at a crawl. So the union was ignored and the Marines were used as dock-wallopers. Enormous working parties of 300 men each were placed on around-the-clock shifts, unloading and loading their own ships. For the problem was one of *un*loading as well as loading.

Most of these ships had come to Wellington stuffed with supplies for a division assembling for training in a civilized country. But now this division was bound for combat in one of the world's wildest places, a place where priority belonged to bullets, beans and barbed wire, where such niceties as field cots and mattresses landed on the bottom of the heap, beneath drums of gasoline, water cans and mosquito nets. All of these

CENTRAL PACIFIC

NORTH

JAPAN TO
PEARL
HARBOR
Air: 3850 Statute miles
Sea: 3395 Nautical miles

International
Date Line

South Pacific Ocean

.Marcus

.Wake Atoll

MARSHALL
IS.

.Majuro

.Makin
TARAWA
.APAMAMA

GILBERT
IS.

ENIWETOK .

TRUK IS. KWAJALEIN

CAROLINE   ISLANDS

EACH DIVISION IS ONE HUNDRED MILES

Equator

JAPAN

BONIN
IS.
.Chichi Jima
VOLCANO .IWO JIMA
IS.

MARIANAS
IS.

SAIPAN. TINIAN
.GUAM

Sea of
Japan

KOREA

East
China
Sea

Yellow Sea

CHINA

Kerama. OKINAWA
Retto
RYUKYU

SLANDS

FORMOSA

PHILIPPINE
ISLANDS

LUZON

San Bernardino Strait
LEYTE
Sea

Philippine

MINDANAO

Yap Is. .ULITHI ATOLL

.Palau Is.
Peleliu

L.d.

supplies were in bulk lots. They had to be piled on the wharf, classified in the order of their importance and either reloaded or sent inland.

The cold driving rains of the Down-Under winter poured from mackerel skies. Shore winds whipped the rain up and down the great dock in sheets, drenching the Marines in their brown ponchos and tan sun helmets, making a mush of tons upon tons of cornflakes, cigarettes, candy, C-rations—of anything packed in those thin paper cartons that seemed to melt like snow beneath the downpour. Drifts of cornflakes were so deep that the flat-bedded New Zealand lorries could barely butt their way through the mess. Men stumbled or slogged through a churned-up marsh of paper, tobacco and food, sometimes kicking with savage glee at the detested little cans of C-rations which lay glistening in the glow of wharf lights that were seldom doused. Sometimes these Marines drifted to the landward end of Aotea Quay, vanishing in the darkness only to reappear in "browned-out" railroad stations, there to slip off poncho and dungarees covering those neatly pressed green uniforms in which they roamed the steep streets of Wellington, determined that a rain-soaked dock and a mush of ruined supplies would not be the only memory of the first foreign land which most of them had seen. But they came back to join their working parties, and when the division sailed off to battle there were not a dozen deserters among 19,000 men.

At Division Intelligence, meanwhile, that old marine chart and Jack London's short story had been augmented by nothing more than a few oblique aerial photos taken five years before the Japanese occupation, plus a half-dozen postcards made from bad pictures taken years ago by missionaries. True, fliers from the *Yorktown* had photographed the target area in May, but *Yorktown* had been sunk in the Battle of Midway. If the pictures had survived, no one knew anything about them. Worse, the Australian coastwatchers—those intrepid islanders who had remained in Japanese-seized territory to report the enemy's movements—were at present in bad shape on Guadalcanal. The only reliable informant there was Captain Martin Clemens of the British Solomon Islands Defense Force, and he had sprained an ankle and been ordered to hole up in the hills until it healed. Earlier coastwatcher reports had provided an estimate of 1,500 Japanese troops on Tulagi and the twin islets of Guvutu-Tanambogo, and 5,000 more on Guadalcanal. Beyond this, nothing.

It became necessary for Lieutenant Colonel Frank Goettge to fly to Australia in search of those islanders who had fled the Japanese advance. Goettge spent a week in Melbourne and a few days in Sydney, moving from the austerity of military offices to the jolly babble of the pubs to the secrecy of hotel rooms, talking to missionaries, blackbirders, sailboat skippers and one scar-faced giant of a planter named John Mather. They were South Sea characters straight out of a short story by Somerset Maugham, but their memories were all that Goettge had working for him. He brought eight of them back to Wellington with him.

Goettge also requested the Army's 648th Engineer Topographic Battalion, then in Melbourne, to put on a "red-rush" aerial photo-mapping of Guadalcanal. The Army obliged. A photography flight was flown. Then, in the way of every army since Agamemnon's, a transportation officer saw to it that the negatives were delayed ten days in reaching the map plant, after which his naval counterpart had the finished maps placed at the bottom of a steadily mounting pile of boxes in Auckland. The Marines in Wellington never got their maps, making one of their own from such catch-as-catch-can "intelligence" as could be produced during sessions in which anxious Americans prodded amiable Australians with questions and Scotch whisky. At one of the last of these a planter who had lived on Guadalcanal recalled having had to shoot a couple of cows which had fallen into the Tenaru River and could not get back up its steep banks. His appalled interrogator reminded him that he had said earlier that vehicles could cross the shallow Tenaru with ease. The Australian replied that he meant the *mouth* of the Tenaru, never suspecting that any troops would want to cross it upstream. But the Marines *were* crossing upstream and now they would need to bring along bridging material—and that meant unloading and reloading an entire ship.

An aerial reconnaissance made by Lieutenant Colonel Merrill Twining and Major William McKean produced one vital piece of information: that the landing beaches appeared usable. Twining and McKean went aboard an Army B-17 bomber in Port Moresby, New Guinea, and flew to Guadalcanal. A trio of growling float Zeros rose from Tulagi anchorage to welcome them. The Flying Fort's gunners shot two of the Japanese down, but the third badgered the big bomber so persistently that it actually ran out of gas, riding a tail-wind home to Moresby to land with bone-dry tanks.

Yet, the First Marine Division remained confident of its ability to "occupy and defend" the objectives. The plan was to make five landings. The main body—First and Fifth Regiments—would land on the northern beaches of Guadalcanal at a point about 10 miles west of the center of its 90-mile length. Four smaller landings would be made 20 miles directly north. The First Marine Raider Battalion and a battalion of the Second Marines would hit tiny Tulagi, which was almost invisible from northern Guadalcanal for the bulk of Florida looming behind or north of it. A battalion of the Second Marines would secure Florida. The chuteless First Marine Parachute Battalion would hit Guvutu-Tanambogo, twin specks of rock joined by a causeway and lying a few miles east or to the right of Tulagi.

On July 22, eleven days following the arrival of the First Marines from San Francisco, the troopships stood out of the hill-girdled harbor at Wellington and made for the open sea. They reached the Fiji Islands with Vandegrift's staff relieved to hear that D-Day had been pushed back to August 7, but concerned to learn that the Japanese had begun building an airfield on Guadalcanal. General Vandegrift himself was shaken to find that he could not expect Vice Admiral Frank Jack Fletcher to keep his covering carriers in the battle area for more than three days. Fletcher would not risk the Japanese flying down from Rabaul and the upper Solomons. Nor would he stay in waters where five enemy flattops and a force of fast battleships could get at that precious trio of American carriers. The other warships under the over-all expeditionary command of Rear Admiral Richmond Kelly Turner would remain as long as necessary.

At the Fijis also the mass rehearsals were called off when it was found that Koro Island's sharp coral was cutting up the

14

division's landing boats, and it was at the Fijis that the Marines got the last and biggest surprise since Admiral Ghormley had looked at General Vandegrift and said, "You."

Marine officers arriving in the Fijis by plane from New Zealand brought with them copies of the July 4 edition of the *Wellington Dominion,* which carried the following story:

HOPE OF COMING U.S. THRUST
South Pacific Marines
INTENSIFIED RAIDS IN NORTH
(Received July 3, 7 P.M.)

New York, July 2.

Operations to seize Japanese-held bases, such as Rabaul, Wake Island, and Tulagi, are advocated by the military writer of the *New York Herald-Tribune,* Major Eliot. One of the signs which suggest that the United Nations may be getting ready to capitalize on the naval advantage gained on the Coral Sea and Midway battles is the recent American bombing of Wake Island, he says. The other signs include the intensified raids on the Timor and New Guinea areas.

"Bombing alone is not enough, because at best it can only prevent the enemy from using the bases," he continues. "What is needed is to drive the Japanese out of their positions and convert them to our own use. The only way to take positions such as Rabaul, Wake Island, and Tulagi, is to land troops to take physical possession of them."

The *New York Times* suggests that Wake Island may be retaken "not only to avenge the Marines who died defending it but also because if we could take hold of the island our lines would be advanced more than 1,000 miles."

The newspaper adds: "It may also be significant that the censor passed the news of the arrival of the completely equipped expeditionary force of American Marines at a South Pacific port recently, as Marines are not usually sent to bases where action is not expected."

There was more, but the Marines could only think of the earlier phrase: *Rabaul, Wake Island, and Tulagi.* And here they were, sailing to Tulagi, a name which both Japanese and Down-Unders found synonymous with Solomon Islands. It was

15

incredible, but it was not, of course, treachery. It was something equally destructive: stupidity. Still, there was nothing for these Marines to do but to fire off an abundant arsenal of oaths. A few days more, July 31, and the ships weighed anchor and sailed away.

To Tulagi.

2

Daylight of August 6, 1942, had turned to dusk.

Among the ships of the American fleet, the motors of the winches and the landing boats had fallen silent. The open mouths of the hatches made darker pools in the gathering gloom. Men stood at the rails of their ships, talking in low voices, gazing at the horizon where the slender silhouettes of flanking destroyers were rapidly becoming invisible.

"Darken ship. The smoking lamp is out on all weather decks. All troops below decks."

It had come for the last time, this order. It had been heard for many nights, by some men for months of nights, but it had never before possessed such capacity to chill hearts.

They went below, with little of the accustomed horseplay, without the usual ineffectual insults hurled at the bullhorn that had ordered them down. They descended to troopholds far below the water line, where five-tiered bunks were slung from bulkheads and the air could become one with the foul reek of the heads if the blowers should break down. Many of them took showers, in fresh water if they were lucky enough to be aboard a ship that could spare it, but generally in salt water which left their bodies sticky and unrefreshed. Some men gathered at final Protestant services, others went to confessions being heard by Catholic chaplains. Weapons were wiped free of excess oil that might gather sand and clog them. Packs were checked for the last time, filled with mess gear, clean socks and underwear, shaving gear, rations—here a Bible, there a pack of letters-from-home, an unfinished paperback book, a crumpled photo of a pin-up girl—all those individual extras which men put in their packs as whim and character might direct. Now the men were banging the chained bunks down from the bulkheads, crawling into them fully dressed—for no one removed his clothes that night. The showdown games had ended and the ultimate winners were choosing between stowing the money on their persons or sending it home via the ship's post office. Attempts at humor were falling flat and fading into tight-lipped silence, lights were going out below decks, and all was quiet save for the steady throbbing of the ships' motors. Lulled by this and the gentle rise and fall of the ships, the men of the First Marine Division sought sleep.

In the wardrooms above, lights still burned. Shadows formed grotesque patterns on big maps plastered to the bulkheads, and fell in long dark shafts across green-covered tables at which the officers sat with cards and chessboards. Aboard Admiral Turner's flagship *McCawley* both Turner and General Vandegrift were grateful for the darkness closing on them as they reached Guadalcanal's back door. They could not know, but they could suspect, that bad weather during the last two days had grounded enemy seaplanes at Tulagi, allowing them to sail along the southern coast of Guadalcanal undetected.

At two o'clock in the morning of August 7, by the light of a moon emerging just as the American force rounded Cape Esperance at Guadalcanal's northwestern tip, men on the weather decks could make out the bulk of Savo Island rising from the mists ahead.

Because of Savo, a round cone which sat like a brooding sentinel at the western mouth of Sealark Channel, the invasion fleet had to split in two. Ships carrying the main body turned immediately east or right to sail between Savo and Guadalcanal and take up stations off the Guadalcanal beaches. The other sailed north or above Savo before making their eastward turn, moving to stations off Tulagi, Florida and Guvutu-Tanambogo.

17

Both sections were in position before daylight.

Aboard the troopships the men were going to the galleys fully armed. They ate beans for breakfast and climbed the ladders topside. They came on deck, blinking in what was now broad and sunny day, startled to hear the thundering of the American cruisers and destroyers or the crashing of bombs dropped by the warplanes of Admiral Fletcher's carriers.

The bombs fell on those Japanese on both sides of the channel who had awakened in terror to find their waters stuffed with enemy ships. Seaplanes in Tulagi Harbor were caught before they could rise, and were turned into floating torches. One of them tried to take off and was tumbled back into the water by a cruiser's guns. Fires were started on both sides of Sealark Channel. Marines moving to their battle stations gazed with satisfaction at flickering shorelines to north and south. At shortly after seven o'clock the assault troops of both sections were ready to launch simultaneous attacks.

"F Company stand by to disembark. First platoon stand by to disembark."

"All right, you men—down them cargo nets!"

Antlike they went over the side, clinging to the rough rope nets that swayed out and in against the warm steel sides of the ships. They stepped on the fingers of the men below them and felt their own hands squashed by men above. Rifles clanged against helmets. Men carrying heavy machine guns or mortar parts ground their teeth in the agony of descending to the waiting boats with 30 or 40 pounds of steel boring into their shoulders. And the boats rose and fell in the swells, now close in to the ships' sides, now three or four feet away.

The men jumped, landing in clanking heaps, then crouched beneath the gunwales while the loaded boats churned to the assembly areas, forming rings and circling, finally fanning out in a broad line at a few minutes before eight and speeding with hulls down and frothing wake straight for the shores of the enemy.

18

3

It was Tulagi, not Guadalcanal, where the Japanese made their first defensive stand of the war.

Tulagi had been typically British, the seat of the British Solomon Islands with a cricket field, a "Residency" and an Anglican bishop. But now this boot-shaped little island with its magnificent anchorage was Japanese, and its occupants were about to demonstrate that blind bitter tenacity with which they would cling to every fortress across the chain of island empire.

They were dug in on Tulagi, with most of their defenses concentrated at the foot of the boot, the southeastern tip. They were in hillside caves, squeezed into the fissures pocking the island's generous outcropping of rock. Against them came that splendid First Raider Battalion commanded by Lieutenant Colonel Merritt Edson, a short tough man of hard jaw and soft voice, of smiling lips and large cold unsmiling eyes. Red Mike, the men called him, for his thinning wisps of carroty hair.

Tulagi's southeastern beaches were dense with smoke and a small Jap boat blazed against the shore when Red Mike's Raiders leaped from their boats into the surf and charged across a narrow beach into the murk of the jungle. Enemy bullets whispered among them, but no men fell. The Raiders drove swiftly across the island at a point two-thirds up the boot. Behind them came the Second Battalion, Fifth Marines, who turned left and quickly overran the lightly defended northwestern third of the island.

The Raiders wheeled right to drive down the island's spine to the lowlands, working through rocks and trees, keeping clear of shore trails covered by enemy cliffs. They attacked four

19

companies abreast. They began to take a withering sniper fire
—snipers under houses, tied into the tops of trees, dug in beneath those forest giants with huge buttressing roots four and
five feet high. Sniper fire came from the rear too, for the Japanese soldier was already using his trick of lying doggo until the
enemy had passed and he might shoot into his rear. Now the
Raiders on the southern shore of the island were pinned down
by fire from a concentration of machine guns atop a hill. Mortars crunched among them. Caves spat fire. There were casualties, among them a company commander. It took an hour to
get that hill, it took rifles and grenades of the men who inched
forward under covering fire until they had reached the point
when they might come erect and charge the cavemouths. Then
Edson's men moved down to the cricket field set between two
hills, east and west. Here the Japanese fought skillfully from
caves and crevices. Here they could not be budged and the
Marines dug in, for it was now twilight and obvious that the
island could not be taken that day.

That night came the first *banzai* charge.

Marines lying in hastily scooped-out foxholes could hear the
enemy assembling. The Japanese crawled noisily out of their
caves and holes. They came running in scattered bands, their
officers leaping before them and waving long *samurai* sabers.
They howled in their native tongue or shrieked those quaint
English oaths, which, they had been told, would melt the hearts
of the Americans.

"Japanese boy drink American boy's blood!"

"Death for the Emperor!"

The Japanese fired their rifles as they charged, deliberately
trying to draw giveaway fire, but they were met by grenades
spiraling silently through the black to flash among them with
flesh-rending crashes. In twos and threes, they tried to infiltrate in the dark, to close with knives—and where they did
they were met with knives. They punched a hole between two
companies on the southern flank, but were beaten down in
individual combat. They swirled savagely around Marine positions in the center, coming five times against a rise in ground.
Mortar shells thumped and crashed among them throughout
the night, breaking them up as they assembled, driving them

20

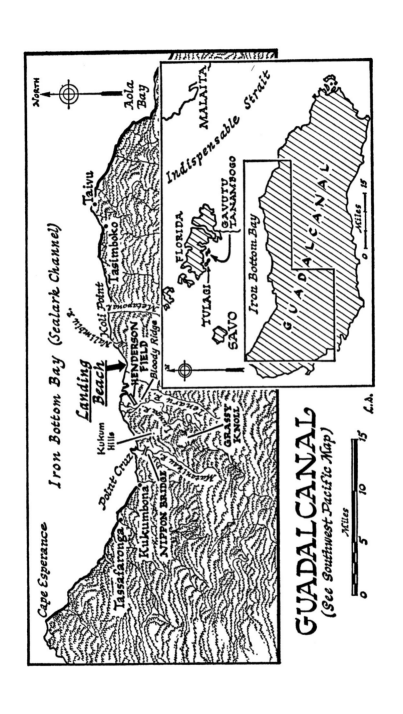

GUADALCANAL

(See Southwest Pacific Map)

into Raider guns. In the end, they failed. In the morning, the Marine counterattack swept forward and squeezed the Japs to death among the limestone hills of the southern third of the island.

Tulagi was taken by nightfall of August 8.

There had been no difficulty in securing Tulagi's western off-shore flank represented by Haleta Village on the southwestern tip of big Florida Island. Company B of the First Battalion, Second Marines, had landed without opposition at twenty minutes before eight o'clock on D-Day morning. Private Russell Miller was the first of these Marines to touch land, becoming the first American to tread Japanese-held soil in World War Two. And Florida fell without a shot fired.

The eastern offshore flank represented by Guvutu-Tanambogo was not so cheaply won. It was not possible to land at more than one or two points on either of these Siamese-twin islets, for both rose steeply from the sea and were ringed with coral. The only landing place on Guvutu, the southernmost or lowest of these two isles connected on a north-south axis, was the seaplane ramp and pier on the northeastern tip. Invaders had to sail around the little islet to get in at it.

At noon of August 7, after Guvutu had been pounded from the sea and sky, Higgins boats carrying the First Parachute Battalion under Major Robert Williams roared straight for the seaplane ramp.

They were struck hard by enemy fire.

The Marines could not land at the ramp, because naval gun-fire had turned it into a jumble of concrete. The boats slanted toward the dock. Out leaped the men, some of them to scamper ashore. But most were pinned down in the lee of the pier. They were like men lined up against a cellophane wall, shot at from both sides. Fire came from trenches behind the pier, from a Guvutu hill to their left and from across the causeway on Tanambogo to their right. One boat ground ashore to the left, bringing a section of mortars to the rescue. Soon the mortar shells were leaving the stovepipes with a metallic *plop,* landing with a *crrrunch-whummp* in the enemy trenches. The assault swept forward again, group after group gaining the pier and charging forward to ram headlong against the steep, cave-pocked defenses of Guvutu.

Then Major Williams was hit and the command passed to Major Charles Miller. Captain Harry Torgerson began lashing sticks of dynamite to the ends of poles, or of strips of planking. Under the protective fire of his men, Torgerson rushed the cavemouths, hurling his explosives like javelins, sometimes stooping to poke them in if the opening was too narrow. Sometimes a bare instant separated his throw and the blast, for these were only five-second fuses. There came a time when an instantaneous explosion sent him rolling down a hill.

"Goddam, Cap'n," yelled an irreverent Marine, "you done lost the seat of yer pants!"

"Screw the pants!" screamed the singed and denuded Torgerson. "Get me more dynamite!"

Thus was born the first of the gloriously raggedy-assed Marines, and thus was Guvutu conquered.

If the Japanese bombers flew to Guadalcanal from the big northern air base at Kavieng on New Ireland, their route would take them over Buka Passage in the Northern Solomons—and there they could be spotted by the Australian coastwatcher, Jack Read.

If they flew from the bigger base at Rabaul, their route took them over Buin—and there they could be seen by the Australian coastwatcher, Paul Mason.

On the morning of August 7 the red-balled bombers rose from Rabaul and went roaring south. They passed over Buin at about half-past ten, the thundering of their motors rousing Mason as he sat in his palm-thatched hideout on Malabite Hill. Mason rushed outside. He counted 24 torpedo bombers, "Kates" as they were called. He ran back inside and flashed his radio message:

"Twenty-four bombers headed yours."

Twenty-five minutes later, aboard the Australian cruiser *Canberra* in the waters between Guadalcanal and Tulagi, an impersonal voice came over the bullhorn:

"The ship will be attacked at noon by twenty-four torpedo bombers. All hands will pipe to dinner at eleven o'clock."

Americans within earshot of that announcement could grin at the suggestion that the Japanese bombers were after "the ship," which was Australian, rather than the convoy, which was otherwise entirely American. But, as the Aussies say, the information was "fair dinkum," and at exactly twelve noon 24 bombers did appear over Sealark Channel. They were met by a roar of antiaircraft fire which put them to flight with only three of their eggs splashing harmlessly into the sea.

The "Bonzer boys" up north had made the first of hundreds of priceless advance warnings.

At a few minutes past six in the evening of August 7, American destroyers ran close to Tanambogo and let go with five-inch guns. A flight of dive-bombers swooped down through gathering smoke to drop their bombs. A Japanese three-inch gun on a Tanambogo hilltop was blown into the air in full view of the Marines coming from Guvutu to attack the island.

B Company of the Second Marines, the outfit which had landed so easily on Florida, was making the assault. Their Higgins boats made a wide swing around the causeway, turning in sharply to a northern beach. The men could see that there was not a tree left standing on Tanambogo. An oil dump was burning furiously beneath a dense cloud of smoke, and the five-inch shells of the destroyers were still wailing over their heads. To the men of B Company, it looked like another holiday.

But it was holocaust instead. A sheet of fire fell on them from the crown of Tanambogo. Private Russell Miller, the first American to land on Japanese soil, fell dead at his Lewis gun.

Then a destroyer shell dropped short and exploded among the Higgins boats.

Shell fragments flew, killing and wounding, striking a coxswain and tearing him from the wheel of his boat. The boat swung sharply around, heading back for Guvutu. Other coxswains, sensing a withdrawal, turned to follow. Only three boats plunged forward through the mounting Japanese fire. In them were Captain Edgar Crane, the mustachioed commander of Company B, and Lieutenant John Smith. The boats lurched to a halt on the sand adjoining a concrete pier.

"Follow me!" cried Lieutenant Smith, darting across the sand and plunging into a thicket.

But his men could not follow. Though Smith had gotten past that crossfire of bullets converging on the three boats, his men could not. They were as though nailed to the beach. They slipped leftward, wriggling through water, until they could link up with Captain Crane at the pier.

Inside the thicket, Lieutenant Smith was all alone. He could hear firing on the beach behind him. He began working back to it, moving from scrub to scrub. He saw someone lying beneath a palm tree. "Come on, Marine," he whispered. The figure came erect, lips parted and bright teeth flashing like his bayonet. Smith shot him dead, whirled, and raced back to the beach.

He returned to a desperate situation. Captain Crane and his men could not fight past the pier. Their machine-gunners had set up to help, but had been silhouetted by the light of the burning oil dump. Jap gunners riddled them. They were forced to withdraw by boat. As night fell, more boats came in to take off B Company's mounting number of wounded. A dozen men hung on at the pier, covering the withdrawal, until darkness came and they slipped across the causeway to Tanambogo.

With that dawn of August 8, the Third Battalion, Second, began the fierce fight which took Tanambogo. First the battalion landed on Guvutu to assist in mopping up that island. Then its companies began the land-sea assault which sent one force advancing across the causeway from Guvutu on foot and the other making a landing from Higgins boats.

The waterborne attack was launched with the support of two tanks commanded by Lieutenant Robert Sweeney. They landed and rolled inland with bullets clanging off their steel sides. Some 50 Japanese came swarming at them, charging with turkey-gobbler shrieks, running low with outthrust pitchforks, with pipes or crowbars which they hoped to ram into the tanks' treads. The tank guns blazed. A few of the Japanese fell. The others came on. Lieutenant Sweeney opened his tank turret to direct fire. He was shot in the forehead. A Japanese thrust a crowbar in the treads of the other tank. It stalled. The Japanese began hurling Molotov cocktails against the tank's side. It began to burn. Tankers came popping out the open turret, jumping through the flames, fighting their way, one by one, through a crowd of knife-swinging, pitchfork-jabbing Japanese.

Marine riflemen were rushing up to take the Japanese under fire. Private Kenneth Koons began picking off enemy soldiers from the throng milling around the other tank, which had become wedged between two coconut trees. He saw one of them slam a pitchfork down its open turret. He saw the Japanese scream and grab his hand where the tank commander had shot him. Koons took aim and finished him off.

Another Japanese jumped on top of the embattled tank. Inside it, Pfc. Eugene Moore aimed his .45 at a round tan face framed like a bull's-eye within the ring of the uncovered turret. He squeezed the trigger. The face flew out of sight. The tank worked free, lurched, and halted. A crowbar had been jammed in the wheelers. Moore seized a tommy gun and poked his head out of the turret and fired.

A hurtling object struck him, fell inside the tank. There was a flash and a roar. It had been a hand grenade. It killed the tank commander. Now Molotov cocktails were bursting on the sides of the tank, setting it on fire. Now Moore's own neck was ablaze. He ducked below.

"Let's get out of here," yelled the driver, and leaped from the turret.

He was shot through the head.

Private Koons was able to kill the driver's killer, but now, as he pressed a fresh clip into his rifle he gaped in astonishment. The last man—Pfc. Moore—was coming out the tank feet first. And the Japanese went wild. They seized him and punched him. They stuck him with pitchforks. They knifed him. They kicked him in the face and in the stomach. They tore the hair from his head. They ripped his pockets apart and took his money. And then, in a final maniacal outburst, unaware of how steadily their numbers had been dwindling under the methodical fire of Private Koons and other riflemen, one of the

26

Japanese grabbed Moore by the feet and another by the arms —and they swung him to and fro against the tank, trying to beat the life out of him until Marine bullets found them and it was they, not Moore, who were dead.

The Japanese died to a man—42 of them—with Koons shooting most of them himself. And Pfc. Moore was hurriedly carried to a battalion aid station, where his numerous wounds and bruises were bandaged and he awoke to hear the news that Tanambogo was also falling.

In late afternoon, while the tankers made their stand just inland of Tanambogo's beaches, the force from Guvutu began advancing across the causeway. A spray of bullets whittled them. They ran forward, some of them falling, at last closing with the Japanese defenders, who jumped from their holes swinging bayonets and brandishing knives. The Marines cut them down and moved on to Tanambogo. By seven o'clock that night the land force had secured the Tanambogo end of the causeway.

By that time also the Marines driving inland from the tank beachhead had captured two-thirds of the islet. Cave after cave fell to the style of attack first improvised by Captain Torgerson on Guvutu. Gunnery Sergeant Orle Bergner earned the nickname of "The One-Man Stick of Dynamite" as he led the way.

Next day mopping-up operations secured the last of the harbor islands. About 750 Japanese had been killed defending them, a score of prisoners had been taken and about 60 more Japanese had escaped by swimming to Florida Island. The islands had been captured at a cost of 144 Americans killed and 194 wounded, an unusually high proportion of dead to wounded which gives testimony to the savagery of the battle. There was also testimony to the spirit which had won it, and this was given by a communications sergeant named Robert Bradley.

Bradley had been perched in a balcony of the Lever Brothers plantation store on Tanambogo. He was a forward observer for a mortar section. Enemy fire pierced his throat, smashing his voice box. Blood gushed from his wound, and as a naval doctor rushed to stop the flow, Bradley began making frantic

writing motions. The doctor gave him a pencil. Bradley wrote:
"Will I live?"

The doctor nodded, and Bradley wrote once more:
"Will I speak again?"

The doctor hesitated, then nodded a second time. Bradley
grinned. Almost with a flourish, he wrote:
"What the hell's the use in worrying!"

That was the sardonic spirit that took Tulagi, and it would
be this—during the four-month ordeal ahead—that would hang
on to Guadalcanal.

4

Guadalcanal.

She was beautiful seen from the sea, this slender long island.
Her towering central mountains ran down her spine in a graceful east-west keel. The sun seemed to kiss her timberline, and
lay shimmering on open patches of tan grass dappling the
green of her forests. Gentle waves washed her beaches white,
raising a glitter of sun and water and scoured sand beneath
fringing groves of coconut trees leaning langorously seaward
with nodding, star-shaped heads.

She was beautiful, but beneath her loveliness, within the
necklace of sand and palm, under the coiffure of her sun-kissed
treetops with its tiara of jeweled birds, she was a mass of
slops and stinks and pestilence; of scum-crested lagoons and
vile swamps inhabited by giant crocodiles; a place of spiders
as big as your fist and wasps as long as your finger, of lizards
as long as your leg or as brief as your thumb; of ants that
bite like fire, of tree-leeches that fall, fasten and suck; of
scorpions without the guts to kill themselves, of centipedes
whose foul scurrying across human skin leaves a track of in-

flamed flesh, of snakes that slither and land crabs that scuttle
—and of rats and bats and carrion birds and of a myriad of
stinging insects. By day, black swarms of flies feed on open
cuts and make them ulcerous. By night, mosquitoes come in
clouds—bringing malaria, dengue or any one of a dozen filthy
exotic fevers. Night or day, the rains come; and when it is the
monsoon it comes in torrents, conferring a moist mushrooming
life on all that tangled green of vine, fern, creeper and bush,
dripping on eternally in the rain forest, nourishing kingly hard-
woods so abundantly that they soar more than a hundred feet
into the air, rotting them so thoroughly at their base that a rare
wind—or perhaps only a man leaning against them—will bring
them crashing down.

And Guadalcanal stank. She was sour with the odor of her
own decay, her breath so hot and humid, so sullen and so still,
that all those Marines who came to her shores on the morning
of August 7 cursed and swore to feel the vitality oozing from
them in a steady stream of enervating sweat.

Vandegrift's main body, some 10,000 men of the First and
Fifth Marines, had hit Red Beach almost at the center of
Guadalcanal's northern coastline. The Fifth landed first, with
two battalions abreast. Unopposed, they jabbed inland, then
wheeled to their right, or west, to work along the shore toward
Japanese installations near the Lunga River. A Japanese labor-
ing force of about 1,700 men had fled when the first of the
American shells and bombs crashed among them as they sat at
breakfast. Marines bursting into their encampment found bowls
of still-warm rice on tables. More important, the Japanese had
abandoned an airfield nearly complete with hangars, blast
pens and a dirt runway 3,600 feet long. This was named Henderson Field after Major Lofton Henderson, who gave his
life crash-diving a Japanese warship at the Battle of Midway.
There was not only Henderson Field but also a complex of
wharves, bridges, ice plants, radio stations and power and
oxygen plants which the Japanese had succeeded in throwing
up since work began July 4. There were tons and tons of rice
—wormy, despicable rice which the Marines spurned but fortunately did not destroy, for it would one day stand between
them and starvation. These were not all discovered the first

day, although the airfield was captured by the First Marines on August 7.

This regiment (Marine regiments are always called "Marines" in the way that Army regiments are known by their arm, as in "4th Cavalry" or "19th Infantry") followed the Fifth ashore. One battalion turned right to overrun the undefended airfield. The other two plunged into the steaming morass beyond or south of it.

All day long the men of these battalions toiled up slime-slick hills and slipped and slid down the reverse slopes, with the machine-gunners breaking the rule of silence by yelps of pain whenever heavy tripods banged cruelly against their necks. They thrashed through fields of sharp-edged *kunai* grass as tall as a man, sometimes shooting at each other. They forded swift cold jungle streams, often stooping to slosh the blessed water against their faces, even lying full-length in the shallows to let it fall into open mouths—ignoring the officers crying, "Don't drink! It may be poisoned!" Back came the unfailing reply: "Fer gawd's sake, lootenant—even the Japs can't poison a whole damn river!"

If there had been an organized enemy in the Guadalcanal jungle that day, there might have been an American catastrophe. For these Marines were far from professionals as they blundered onward toward their objective: a high clear height called Grassy Knoll, or Mount Austen, which commanded Henderson Field from the south.

But if the jungle dissolved Marine discipline, it did not dampen Marine humor. That night, after the men had dug foxholes in the dank earth, they began to ask each other what it was all about. What did General Vandegrift want with Grassy Knoll?

"Maybe," said a private, "it's because it's the only place with a view."

"So?"

"Where else they gonna put the officers' club?"

Then they fell silent, half of them to stand guard in that blind, black whispering jungle, the other half to attempt sleep beneath ponchos that failed to keep out the rain because of the big hole for the head, or behind little veils of mosquito netting that could not keep mosquitoes off because they were plastered to their faces.

They awoke in the morning—puff-eyed, bitten and soaked —and began sloshing south again.

At ten minutes of nine on the morning of August 8, the Australian Jack Read stood on a hill overlooking Buka Passage and counted 45 Japanese bombers flying overhead. They had come from Kavieng. Before the sound of their motors had faded behind him, Read was in his shack and at his radio.

"Forty-five bombers going southeast."

A half-hour later Pearl Harbor again broadcast a warning to the Solomons fleet, and General Vandegrift decided that the noon arrival of the enemy bombers would be just the time to give his beach working parties a rest.

There were just a few hundred of these working-party men, and they were all headquarters troops and specialists. There were no stevedoring battalions to do the job, and Vandegrift dared not risk detaching any combat troops for it. Though the beach was a jumbled confusion of crates and boxes, though he had received the message "Unloading entirely out of hand," though nervous cargo captains were badgering him for more men, Vandegrift would not weaken his line troops. So these makeshift stevedores worked on, sweat streaming from naked torsos, and at noon, with some of them already passed out from exhaustion, they took a break.

Just as half the Japanese bombing force came in low over Florida and went wolfing among the transports.

Then they came in a straight line, torpedo-laden Kates counting on surprise. But they were struck by a storm of sound and flame that obliterated 12 of them. Only one was successful, launching a torpedo which flashed into the hull of the destroyer *Jarvis*, sending her limping from the battle—to be sunk later by Japanese aircraft.

Next the dive-bombing Vals came plummeting down. They too counted on surprise, unaware that fighters from *Wasp* had taken high stations a half-hour before and were now riding them down, risking their own antiaircraft fire polka-dotting the skies with deadly black puffs; unaware, until .50-caliber bullets

31

chopped off their tails, sheared off their wings, set gasoline tanks ablaze, and started them on the long straight fall to oblivion.

Far up north the coastwatcher Read crouched by his radio while an excited voice broadcast the results of his alert: "Boy, they're shooting them down like flies . . . one . . . two . . . three . . . I can see eight of them in the water right now."

But one of them fell in flames into an open hold of the transport *George F. Elliott*. The big ship was set hopelessly afire. She was scuttled at twilight, the first major American ship to rest beneath that body of water which would be known as Iron Bottom Bay for the scores of vessels which would join her on its floor. Fortunately, *Elliott's* troops had gone ashore the preceding day—but she went down with a battalion's supplies.

Night began to fall and General Vandegrift went aboard *McCawley* with a feeling of satisfaction. Though one transport was gone, though one destroyer was apparently only out of action, the Japanese had lost more than three-quarters of their planes, and they had not harmed those piles of precious supplies that were at last beginning to disappear inland. All of Vandegrift's Marines were safely ashore, the airfield was his, the harbor islands were almost secured, and he could count on a few more days of unloading.

But he could not.

Admiral Turner was going to take the supply ships away in the morning.

The powerful Japanese surface force which he and Admiral Fletcher had feared was coming down The Slot.

5

The Slot was the sea corridor running 400 miles from Bougainville to Guadalcanal. It was a watery passage between the Solomon Islands, which faced each other in two near-orderly rows at near-regular intervals of from 50 to 60 miles. Japanese ships based at Rabaul had about 240 miles to go before they reached The Slot's northwest terminus at Bougainville. They entered it at midday, planning to arrive off the southeast terminus at Guadalcanal under cover of darkness.

A task force of seven cruisers led by Rear Admiral Gunichi Mikawa entered The Slot at about midday on August 8. They came down it in column of battle: Mikawa's flagship *Chokai* leading, followed by the heavy cruisers *Aoba* and *Furutaka*, next two more heavies, and then a pair of light cruisers. They were sighted almost immediately by an American search plane. But by half-past eleven on the night of August 8, the search plane's warning had not been received by all of the ships patroling Savo Island.

With their picket destroyers, cruisers *Chicago* and *Canberra* guarded the south gate between Savo and Guadalcanal, while the north gate was held by *Quincy*, *Vincennes* and *Astoria* and their pickets. It was getting on to the midnight change of watches aboard these ships. Weary sailors tumbled out of their bunks, gulped hot coffee and groped their way on deck to relieve the eight-to-twelvers. The new watch could see faint flashes of lightning over the western horizon. A rain squall was making up off Savo. It would work for Admiral Mikawa.

His patrol planes had already been catapulted aloft, prepared to drop illuminating flares. His men were at their battle stations in gun turrets above decks, alongside torpedo tubes below—ready to strike the Allied warships before falling upon the thin-skinned transports at their leisure.

At about eleven o'clock some of the Allied warships began picking up unknown airplanes on their radar. Others actually heard them droning overhead. Some mistook them for friendly aircraft, for the Japanese pilots had boldly turned on running lights. In that confusion which often precedes disaster, the reports were either misdirected, misinterpreted or ignored.

A few minutes before one o'clock in the morning of August 9, Mikawa's lookouts spotted the American destroyer *Blue* off to their right. Some 50 great guns swiveled around in the night and trained upon the little ship. Luckily for *Blue*, unhappily for her sister ships off Savo, neither her lookouts nor her radar had spotted the Japanese.

On went Mikawa's cruisers, hitting 24 knots . . . 26 . . .

At half-past one, Mikawa's lookouts sighted Savo. Three minutes more and Mikawa passed the battle order:

"All ships attack!"

In five minutes, they had gotten the range, had loaded the torpedo tubes. In one more, hissing fish were leaping from the sides of the Japanese cruisers, were cleaving the dark water toward those unsuspecting sentinel ships. Two more minutes, and *Chokai* had closed to within two miles of them, still undetected . . .

Now the warning came. Destroyer *Patterson* had sighted a big ship. The radio alarm was braying:

"Warning! Warning! Strange ships entering harbor!"

It was forty-three minutes past one in the morning of August 9, and it was already too late.

Eerie greenish flares swayed down from the Japanese patrol planes and the harbor rocked to the roaring of the main batteries on *Chokai*, *Aoba* and *Furutaka*. Marines ashore looked fearfully at one another in baleful light filtering down from the blackness above. A dread silence interrupted the Tulagi conference of Vandegrift and Brigadier General William Rupertus. And then two of the Japanese steel fish finished their run by thrusting with cyclonic force into the side of *Canberra*, almost at the same moment that a shower of Japanese shells fell on her decks with merciless precision—and the Battle of Savo Island had begun.

The Japanese torpedoes had already given *Canberra* her mortal wounds, and though she fought back with two fish of her own and a few rounds from her four-inchers, she was done.

Chicago's bow was blown off. She was out of the fight, unable to hinder the enemy cruisers swinging left and making for the northern force, running up on *Quincy, Vincennes* and *Astoria,* switching on their powerful searchlights, taking the stunned Americans under point-blank range and sending them to the bottom. Not all of them sank immediately, but they had taken their death blows.

The Battle of Savo Island, which sailors and Marines more accurately called the Battle of the Five Sitting Ducks, wore on until dawn—when Mikawa took his cruisers out of Iron Bottom Bay and streaked for home. He left the American transports unmolested, but he had sunk four cruisers, damaged a fifth and also damaged a destroyer. His only losses were a direct hit on *Chokai's* chartroom, plus some slight damage to *Aoba.*

After Mikawa left, Admiral Turner also departed with the transports and their escorts.

In the sundown of August 9, men of the First Marines returning to the beaches from their toilsome, useless march inland, saw no ships in Iron Bottom Bay. Only a few blackened, smoking hulls were visible to their left, toward Savo as they faced the water. Otherwise there was nothing.

The Marines were all alone.

The fact of complete isolation had been accepted by Major General Vandegrift as early as the dawn of August 9. In that misty light, in a driving rain, he had assembled his staff officers, his regimental and battalion commanders.

The booming of the big guns could still be heard to the west of the Division Command Post near Alligator Creek. Concussions shook the palm fronds, showering those officers who stood beneath them to avoid the rain. Someone had made coffee over a smoking, sputtering fire. The hot black liquid was passed around in empty C-ration cans.

Offshore, lifting mists revealed the gray truncated shape of a prowless cruiser making slowly eastward between a pair of shepherding destroyers.

"*Chicago*," someone said in awe.

There was a shocked silence, and then Colonel Gerald Thomas, the Division's operations officer, broke the bad news swiftly.

The Navy was going, and no one could say when or if it would return. The Marines could presume loss of the air as well as the sea. They were not only isolated but separated, with nearly half of the combat battalions over on the harbor islands. That very loss of air and sea suggested that there would be no hope of getting these troops over to Guadalcanal. Tulagi had eight days' supplies and Guadalcanal a few days more than that. Reinforcements, resupply, were only a hope. What were they going to do?

They were going to finish the airfield, get the supplies off the beach and dig in. They were going to hold a beachhead, which, when marked off on a map, made an oval shape extending about 3,500 yards inland at its deepest and 7,500 yards from west to east at its widest. Most of the small towns of America are bigger than this beachhead was. But it was all the Marines needed, for it contained the southwest-northern slant of Henderson Field at a point about 2,000 yards inland and equidistant from the eastern and western flanks. These flanks were represented by the Tenaru River on the east or right flank as the Marines faced the sea, and by the Kukum hills on the west or left flank. To the south, behind the airfield, the line was almost made of paper. Here was a series of local outposts, at their strongest as they drew curving back from the Tenaru and ran fairly straight west for about 3,000 yards to the Lunga River. Here, they curved again, following the crooked river line northwest or seaward for 2,500 yards until they ended at the artillery command post and Vandegrift's new headquarters. The gaps to the rear of the airfield were numerous, but between the Lunga and the western hills there was one big gap about 2,000 yards wide. This was to be guarded by constant daily patrols, and to be very loosely "filled" at night by small outposts. The strongest point was the northern or seaward front, where the Marines dug in along the beach to defend against counterlanding.

This was the "perimeter" which was to be held by 10,000 foot soldiers with hand guns, mortars, some tanks and three battalions of light artillery against an enemy who possessed interior lines from Rabaul 640 miles north, as well as all the men, guns, ships and airplanes he needed to press the initiative which was now his. That was the situation which Colonel Thomas outlined to those commanders who stood grim-faced in the rain. And when he stopped speaking and the conference ended, the Battle for Guadalcanal passed from an offensive into a defensive operation.

United States Marines, trained to hit, were now being forced to hold.

Though Vandegrift's commanders tried to keep the bad news to themselves, it was inevitable that the men would soon learn of their perilous isolation. But they only grasped its import gradually. That aching, empty, yearning sense of loneliness that characterized the stand on Guadalcanal would not seize them fully for yet another week. In the meantime, they frolicked.

They found and plundered a warehouse full of delicious Japanese beer and *saki*, a yellowish Japanese rice wine. The day of that discovery Guadalcanal's single coastal road was thronged with dusty, grinning Marines trudging along with cases of beer on their shoulders or pulling captured Jap rickshas piled high with balloon-like half-gallon bottles of *saki*. They buried the loot, out of sight of prying officers, drinking it secretly and sometimes getting in a tipsy state that would account for more than one outburst of "trigger-happy" firing on the lines.

In the morning, the trigger-happy might find that the "enemy" against whom they had battled so valiantly in the dark was one of those blundering mammoth land crabs in which

Guadalcanal abounded or perhaps some scarecrow of a plantation cow.

There was also, in this gay interlude between the real thing of the landing and the impending real thing of the Japanese counterattack, the nightly comedy provided by men who had difficulty pronouncing the passwords.

All of the passwords—"Lallapaloozer," "Lollipop," "Lallygag"—were loaded with L's because the Japanese normally cannot make that sound, turning it into a liquid R instead. But polysyllabic passwords could also tie the tongues of Marines such as the one who had arisen in the night to relieve himself and was having trouble with "Lilliputian."

"Halt!" came the sentry's cry.

"Fer Gawd's sake, don't shoot. It's me, Briggs."

"Gimme the password."

"Lily-poo . . . luly . . ."

"C'mon, c'mon! The password, or I'll let yuh have it."

"Luly-pah . . . lily-poosh . . ." Silence, and then, in outrage: "Aw, shit—shoot!"

Of course the sadistic sentry did not shoot, for he and all the men around him were already collapsed with laughter, a bawdy mirth that continued throughout that naïve week until Lieutenant Colonel Goettge led out a patrol to accept a Japanese surrender and was ambushed and massacred.

It was Goettge who had organized the helter-skelter gathering of information prior to the landings. He was a man of great vigor and daring. He was also a man of compassion, and this, when offered to an enemy as compassionate as a crocodile, was a fatal virtue.

On August 12, a Japanese naval rating had been captured behind the western lines. He was questioned. He was a sour little crab-apple of a man, making his answers sullenly and with great reluctance. But he admitted that many of his fellows west of the Matanikau River—a stream lying a few miles to the west of the Kukum Hills line—were sick and starving, and that they might be persuaded to surrender. To this was added a patrol report of a "white flag" flying at a Japanese encampment west of the Matanikau.

Hearing this, Goettge was moved. He took personal charge

of a patrol that was to have scouted the Matanikau that day. He included in this patrol the Fifth Marines' surgeon, Lieutenant Commander Malcolm L. Pratt, and Lieutenant Ralph Cory, an interpreter. Goettge cleaned out the Division Intelligence Section and borrowed veteran NCO's from its regimental counterpart in the Fifth. After dark, under a moonless, starless night, leading the ill-natured Japanese by a rope, Goettge and 25 men left by Higgins boat for the "surrender area."

They landed opposite Matanikau Village. They moved quickly inland about 20 yards, halting before a cluster of grass huts set in a fringing wood. They built up a perimeter. Goettge and a few men went forward to reconnoiter and were struck to the ground by converging streams of rifle and machine-gun fire. Goettge was killed instantly, shot in the head. The Japanese fire rose in fury. Commander Pratt was mortally wounded. A sergeant with the prophetic name of Custer was shot in the arm, then killed.

The Marines were pinned down, unable to move, firing back blindly while the enemy fire raked them mercilessly. The Japanese were so close that the Marines could feel the hot air of their muzzle blasts. But the enemy did not approach. He was content to toy with this rainbarrel full of fish.

At one in the morning Sergeant Monk Arndt was ordered to swim back for reinforcements. He stripped. He crawled back to the water, naked but for shoes and helmet, under which he had tucked his pistol, hooking its butt on the chin strap. He swam breaststroke along the beach. The Japanese fired, raising little spurts of water all around him. Arndt felt foolishly exposed, as though his nakedness had left him without armor. He swam out to sea, crawling over the cruel subsurface coral that tore and tattered his flesh like pinking shears. He turned shoreward again. He found a beached native boat. One end was riddled with bullet holes. He pushed the boat out and got in the other end, paddling with a plank lying on its bottom. He paddled past the Marine lines, shouting "Million! Million!" for though he had forgotten the password, he knew that million had a million L's. As dawn came and the mists swam up from the sea, Arndt had reached the Marine boat base. He waded ashore, the red of his blood streaming from multiple slashes below the hips, the knucklebones of his fingers laid bare. But Arndt had arrived too late. It was already all over for the patrol to the west. Two other Marines escaped, swimming east to safety. One of them who left just before daybreak turned for a parting look as the sun came up. He saw sabers flashing in the sun.

Sabers flashing in the sun.

It ran like a rallying cry all along the Kukum ridges, sweeping east through the coastal gunpits and foxholes, turning right to race up the barbed-wire line of the Tenaru, bursting in the ears of the airfield outposts, among the artillerymen, the amtrack drivers, the tankers, and the engineers grimly bulldozing the airstrip which only the day before had received its first American plane. It had the power to chill hearts, but on Guadalcanal those hearts were swelling with rage. The Marines could not have known that the "surrender flag" was actually a Japanese battle flag accidentally hanging limp and thus obscuring its red center, or that the Goettge mission was conceived in an error compounded by compassion. They only knew that Marines had risked their flesh to help the enemy and had been slaughtered in reward.

All light bantering ceased. Timid patrols turned aggressive and savage. Marines hoped openly for battle, and because they had also not yet known it, talked loudly of wanting the enemy to come because they wanted to kill him and chop him up with his own sabers. There would also come a time when these same men would dread recurrent battle, but now, after the Goettge patrol, they wanted it.

They would get it. It came, at first, down The Slot. Destroyers, sometimes cruisers, sneaked into the bay during darkness to pound the airfield or the men crouching in pits, turning at dawn to streak back to Rabaul. Submarines surfaced between Guadalcanal and Tulagi, firing deck guns to sink every small American ship in sight, chasing Higgins boats back to the anchorage. Sometimes the Marines dueled the enemy warships with their puny 75-millimeter pack howitzers or with the .75 rifles mounted on half-tracks run down to the water. Once the celebrated Gunnery Sergeant Lew Diamond offered to take an 81-millimeter mortar aboard a Higgins boat and go after a submarine which was shelling Guadalcanal with five-inch guns. The offer was declined. But Gunny Lew's proposal was reflective of the new aggressive spirit which had seized Vandegrift's Marines after the Goettge patrol, and which kept them on their guns even as the bombs came wailing and crashing down on Henderson Field during increasing aerial bombardment of Guadalcanal.

Lieutenant General Haruyoshi Hyakutate, then assembling his 17th Army at his headquarters in Rabaul, was of one mind with Imperial Headquarters in its conviction that the Americans would tire quickly of war. To this end Admiral Nagumo had sailed to Pearl Harbor. Strike the Americans hard, set them back so far that by the time they had changed from the manufacture of playthings to the making of munitions the resource-rich booty of the Southwest Pacific and Southeast Asia would have been consolidated under the Reign of Radiant Peace. Then, when the Americans attempted to come back, Japan would make it so costly that they would quit the war in a negotiated peace.

Until recently, General Hyakutate's mission in the over-all scheme of conquest laid down by the militant Premier Hideki Tojo had been to capture Port Moresby in New Guinea, which was just to the north of Australia. But then Port Moresby was given to the 18th Army while Hyakutate's 17th was told to recapture Guadalcanal. The change annoyed General Hyakutate. Port Moresby seemed by far the more important operation. Nor was the general—a small, thin, testy man—pleased with the army which Imperial Headquarters had given him to do the job at Guadalcanal. As so often happened with the Japanese military, the 17th Army's 50,000 men had been given to Hyakutate unassembled. The famous 2nd Division—called the Sendai after the city near Tokyo from which most of its men were recruited—was in Java and the Philippines; the 38th Division was in China, along with 17th Army antitank units as far away as Manchuria; the Kawaguchi Brigade, actually close to a division, was in the Palaus; and the Ichiki Detachment was on Guam.

The Ichiki Detachment, which, in the Japanese manner, took the name of its commander, Colonel Kiyono Ichiki, was a reinforced battalion with a strength of about 2,000 men. General Hyakutate decided to use this unit to deal with the annoyance —for such he still regarded it—at Guadalcanal. Though there were but 2,000 Ichikis to hurl against an enemy force his intelligence had estimated at 10,000 men, were these enemy troops not, after all, Americans?

General Hyakutate lost some of his irritation in contemplating a bold stroke that would at once regain Guadalcanal and its vital airfield, would gratify Imperial Headquarters and would also respectfully suggest a measure of his contempt for the new assignment.

Hyakutate ordered Colonel Kiyono Ichiki to move. The Ichikis sailed from Guam to the great naval base at Truk. On August 16, Colonel Ichiki led some 900 storm troops aboard six fast destroyers and shoved off. Behind them came a cruiser and a destroyer escorting two transports carrying the remainder of Ichiki's troops and his supporting arms.

Ichiki's destroyers sped swiftly down The Slot, rapidly leaving the slower transports behind. The colonel was in a hurry, for one of the Army's battle reports on American capabilities said: "It can be seen that when they are pressed for time, the American dispositions and especially their organization of fire are not coordinated. Therefore we must not fail to move fast and attack quickly, giving them no time in which to prepare their positions."

But the Marines were already prepared and there was aerial reinforcement on its way.

She had been the merchant ship *Macmormail*, but now she was the *Long Island*. With her flight deck topside and a few guns she had been turned into a makeshift aircraft carrier, dignified in that status with the name of an American battle, and sent into the Pacific.

On August 20 she reached the southern Solomons and flew off 19 Wildcat fighters and 12 Dauntless dive-bombers to the embattled Marines on Guadalcanal.

The planes came skimming over the coconuts, and the men

below glanced up nervously to hear the hum of motors. But then they saw the Yankee star on the wings and they shouted in jubilation. Two of the planes deliberately circled Henderson Field for all to see, and the men ran along the ridgesides and riverbanks and beaches, throwing helmets in the air, punching each other gleefully, cheering and crying for joy.

The first relief had come.

Colonel Kiyono Ichiki was a military man. His carriage was stiff, his jaw square, and his glance struck straight from narrowed eyes. His habit of courage was matched by a habit of thought as clipped and uniform as his military mustache.

He had landed his 900 men on August 18 at Taivu 20 miles to the east of the Tenaru River and he had decided not to wait for the following troops. Nine hundred men such as his—big, strong fellows among the very best troops in the Empire—were surely sufficient to overrun the American defenses and seize the airfield.

Next day, Colonel Ichiki wrote in his diary: "18 Aug. The landing. 20 Aug. The March by night and the battle. 21 Aug. Enjoyment of the fruits of victory."

True, it was only 19 Aug.—but Colonel Ichiki foresaw the chance that he might die before he could make this entry. So he inscribed the inevitable, postdated it for posterity, and then he sent out a large party to lay communications wire.

Captain Charles Brush was not a military man. His shoulders slumped, his gait was shambling and his sideways glance was of an accusing character calculated to cause respect among the troops, but which actually only confirmed their suspicion that the skipper had quit teaching high school to take a small revenge on the schoolboys who would follow him into service.

On the morning of August 19, leading a patrol of roughly 80 men, Captain Brush shuffled eastward from the Tenaru. Some time after noon, his advance scouts caught sight of the Ichiki wiremen moving slowly westward. Brush attacked.

Part of his patrol drove straight ahead while a platoon swung to the right to get behind the Japanese. In a fight lasting nearly an hour, 31 of the Japanese were killed and three others escaped into the jungle. Three Marines were killed and three wounded.

It might have been put down as another jungle skirmish, except that the patrol was unusally large for the supposed remnant of laborers left on the island. Moreover it had been led by four officers of surprisingly high rank, the uniforms of the dead soldiers were new—and they had been laying communications wire when attacked.

Brush quickly stripped the dead of maps and documents and sent these back to the perimeter.

Marine intelligence officers were disturbed by the maps. They were accurate, with all of the weak points along the Tenaru carefully marked.

Lieutenant Colonel Al Pollock pulled some of the machine-gunners of his Second Battalion, First, off the beach line and sent them south along the Tenaru to extend his right flank. On the left where a sandspit kept the green sluggish Tenaru from reaching the sea, Pollock had placed his heaviest concentration—machine guns, riflemen and a 37-millimeter antitank gun, all dug in behind a single strand of barbed wire running across the sandbar.

The sandpit was as good as a bridge across the river. Pollock placed outposts beyond it, west of it, in the coconut grove across the river.

Night fell swiftly, as it does in the jungle. A few stray shafts of light seemed to linger, as though trapped between jungle floor and jungle roof, and then it was black and silent except for the stirring of those creeping, crawling things that move by night. Men crouched along the Tenaru peered at the narrow dark river gleaming wickedly in the faint starlight and felt all those atavistic fears flowing formlessly around their hearts. The crocodiles were out, their noiseless downstream swimming marked by the gradually widening V of their wakes.

Down at the sandbar there was movement opposite the outposts. A marine fired at the sound.

"No, no! Me Vouza. Me Sergeant-Major Vouza."

A short powerful figure stagged out of the darkness. Blood streamed from his naked chest, from his throat. He was a fuzzy-haired Melanesian, he was Sergeant-Major Vouza of the Solomons Island Police and the Japanese had caught and tortured him. He was taken to Pollock's command post, and there, with blood still dripping from his wounds, he began to speak.

"I was caughted by the Japs and one of the Jap naval officer questioned me but I was refuse to answer. And I was bayoneted by a long sword twice on my chest, through my throat, and cutted by side of my tongue. And I was got up from the enemies and walked through the American front line."

"How many Japs?" Pollock asked sharply.

"Maybe 250, maybe 500."

Pollock had heard enough. He called Division to come for Vouza. He glanced at his watch to mark the time at eighteen minutes past one in the morning, and at that moment a green flare rose from the coconut grove, a Marine sentry fired a shot —and the charge of the Ichikis began.

They came flowing across the sandspit, sprinting, hurling grenades, howling. They came blundering into that single strand of barbed wire, and there they milled about in a jabbering frenzy. They hacked wildly at the wire with bayonets, they tried to hurdle it, and they slung long thin lengths of explosive-packed pipe under it in hopes of blowing gaps in it.

Then the Marines opened fire, the flare-light faded and the re-enveloping night seemed to reel with a thousand scarlet flashes. Machine guns chattered and shook. Rifles cracked. Grenades whizzed and boomed. Fat red tracers sped out in curving arcs and vanished. Orange puffs spat from the mouth of the antitank gun. Howitzers bayed in the rear distance and their whistling shells crashed and flashed among the coconuts where mortar missiles had already described their humming loops and were falling with that dull *crrrunch* that tears and kills.

Private Johnny Rivers unclamped his heavy machine gun to spray a hosing fire. Across the river a Japanese machine-gun section jumped into an abandoned amtrack to set up a crossfire on Rivers' pit. Their bullets crept up the riverbank, ate their way down the water-jacket of Rivers' gun and found his heart. Rivers froze on the trigger. Dead, he fired 200 more rounds. Private Al Schmidt jumped on the gun, fed it another belt, resumed the fire. A grenade sailed into the pit. It exploded. It knocked out the gun. It blinded Al Schmidt. He lay in the darkness while the battle swirled around him.

Downstream the barrel of the antitank gun glowed red in the dark. It was firing point-blank at the charging foe, spewing a hail of cannister shot that sometimes struck them down in squad groups. Another grenade somersaulted through the night. It fell hissing into the antitank dugout and filled it with roaring light and death. Riflemen jumped into the dugout and the 37 glowed red again.

The Ichiki charge rose in fury. Squad after squad, platoon after platoon, burst from the covering darkness of the coconut grove to dash against the line. They broke it. They came in on holes and gunpits, running low with bayoneted rifles outthrust for the kill. At a gap in the leftward wire, three Japanese rushed for big Corporal Dean Wilson in his foxhole.

Wilson swung his BAR toward them. It jammed. The Japanese rushed onward, screaming "Marine you die!" One of them drove downward for the thrust. Wilson seized his machete and slashed. The man sank to the ground, his entrails slipping through his clutching fingers. The others slowed. Wilson leaped from his hole and attacked, hacking them to death with his thick-bladed knife.

There was a Japanese inside Corporal Johnny Shea's hole. His bayonet was into Shea's leg, out again, in again—out and slashing upward. Shea kicked with his right foot, slamming the Japanese against the foxhole side while he yanked desperately at the bolt of his jammed tommy gun. The bolt snicked free and Shea shot his assailant to death.

There were hurrying squat shapes swarming around the foxhole where Lieutenant McLanahan lay with wounds in both arms, in his legs, in his buttocks—loading rifles and clearing the jammed weapons of those men who could still fire.

There were tall shapes mingling with the short ones, figures that closed, merged, became as one grotesquely whirling hybrid of struggling limbs, for now the battle had become that rarity of modern war, the close-in fight of clubbed rifles and thrusting blades, of fists and knees and gouging thumbs. Now there were more tall shapes than short ones, for Pollock had

46

thrown in a reserve platoon, and the guttural cries of "Banzai!" were growing fainter beneath the wild keening of the battle, the crackling of rifles, the hammering of machine guns, the gargling of the automatics, and the jumping *wham* of the 37.

The Ichikis were stumbling now over heaps of slain comrades strewn along the sandbar. They were themselves slumping into loose ungainly death, for the Marine fire had been multiplied from upriver where the guns had been swung seaward and trained on the sandspit. The last of the Ichikis were trapped. Marine mortars had drawn a curtain of fire behind them. Bullets ahead, shell-bursts behind—forward or backward was to die.

Some chose the river, where American bullets still sought and found them and where crocodiles found them in the morning. Some chose to run the gantlet of guns along the shore, peeling off to their right at the barbed wire, dashing through the surf only to be dropped where the incoming tide would roll their bodies and cover them with sand. Others chose the sea. They plunged into the water. They tried to swim back to the east, but it was now dawn and their bobbing heads were visible targets for those Marine riflemen who had left their pits and had thrown themselves flat to fire from the prone position.

"Line 'em up and squeeze 'em off!" roared Pollock, striding among his men. "Line 'em up and squeeze 'em off!"

The remainder of Colonel Ichiki's elite was being wiped out within the coconuts.

"Cease fire!" came the order, up and down the line. "Hold your fire, First Battalion coming through!"

Over the river, green-clad men were flitting through the coconuts. The First Battalion, First, had crossed the Tenaru upriver and had fanned out into a flanking skirmish line. Now they were working seaward.

Downstream, Marine tanks rolled slowly over the sandspit. They reached the coconut grove and turned right.

By nightfall more than 700 Japanese bodies had been counted. There were 34 dead Marines and 75 wounded. The surviving Japanese had sought the treacherous sanctuary of the jungle, there to endure hunger, black nights and the slow dis-

47

solution of the rain forest. They wandered leaderless, for Colonel Kiyono Ichiki had already tasted "the fruits of victory." He burned his colors and shot himself through the head.

7

In all the Imperial Army there was no commander who could surpass Lieutenant General Haruyoshi Hyakutate in the peculiar Japanese custom of celebrating defeat with a loud cry of victory. General Hyakutate knew all those euphemisms whereby a setback became "a valiant advance" or the report of a rout reached the ears of the Emperor as "a glorious withdrawal of unshaken discipline."

But the affair of the Ichikis was unique. There was no euphemism at hand to describe annihilation. Undaunted, General Hyakutate sent Tokyo this message: "The attack of the Ichiki Detachment was not entirely successful." Then he drew up a plan for another attempt at recapturing Guadalcanal.

This time he would use the surviving rear-echelons of the Ichiki Battalion—around 1,100 men—together with the 6,000-man brigade commanded by Major General Kiyotake Kawaguchi (the Japanese have no rank of brigadier general). This force would land on Guadalcanal supported by planes and ships of the Combined Fleet. The fact that it was still outnumbered by the 10,000 enemy troops to the south did not deter Hyakutate. He still refused to accept the Americans as worthy foemen. He believed the battle report that stated: "The American soldiers are extremely weak when they lack support of fire power. They easily raise their hands during battle and when wounded they give cries of pain." So General Hyakutate ordered 5,000 Kawaguchis to join the remaining Ichikis on one of those nightly runs down The Slot which the Marines were already calling the Tokyo Express. He sent them south with the battle cry:

"Remember the Ichiki suicide!"

And they had to turn back.

On August 25, the day after the Japanese Combined Fleet met Admiral Fletcher's carriers in the Battle of the Eastern Solomons, the Japanese convoy was sighted north of Guadalcanal by bombers from Henderson Field. A Dauntless piloted by Lieutenant Larry Baldinus dove down to plant an egg forward on the big escort cruiser, *Jintsu*. She went staggering home, asmoke and afire, while a Navy dive-bomber and other Marines fell on the transport *Kinryu Maru*. They stopped her dead in the water, and when destroyer *Mutsuki* went to help her, they stopped *Mutsuki* to—leaving both ships to await the obliterating bombs of a flight of Flying Fortresses which followed up their attack. The remaining Japanese ships turned north and sailed to the Shortland Islands, where the soldiers debarked to board barges for a less ostentatious trip south.

Henderson Field, meanwhile, had withstood the aerial assaults which had been planned to make way for these troops. On August 24, the Marine fighter pilots shot down 11 Zero fighters and 10 bombers at a loss of three of their own planes. That date marked the beginning of the long epic defense of Guadalcanal's skies, which was to match the stand being made on the ground. From August 24 onward, Marine fliers began shooting down Zeros and twin-engined Betty bombers at a rate of from six to eight kills for every one of their own men lost. They fought, of course, with the almost invariable assistance of Navy and Army airmen—but the Guadalcanal aerial war was in the main a Marine affair, fought by the self-styled Nameless Wonders of the Bastard Air Force. These men were galled almost nightly to hear the San Francisco radio speak of "Navy fighters" or "Army bombers" while only the enemy might know who rode the cockpits of "American aircraft" or "Allied planes." And it was a Bastard Air Force, for if aerial combat is a gentleman's war, if it is clean, quick and sporting to fight in the clouds with hot meals and soothing drinks and laundered bedsheets awaiting the survivors, this was not so on Guadalcanal. Here the fly-boys were like the foot-sloggers.

49

They lived next to Henderson Field, in the very center of the Japanese bull's-eye. They rose an hour before dawn. If they cared to eat that common gruel of wormy rice and canned spam that passed for meals on Guadalcanal, they ate it standing up, spooning the detestable slop out of borrowed mess gear. They gulped hot black coffee from canteen cups while bumping jeeps drove them through the darkness to the airstrip, where they warmed up planes that had to be towed from revetments by tractor. Then it was dawn and they were roaring aloft, climbing high, high in the skies, sucking on oxygen. They went to battle in a sort of floating world where the only sounds were the roaring of their own motors and the hammering of their guns; where all the sights were the blind white mists of engulfing clouds, the sudden pain of reappearing sunlight bursting in the eyeballs, the swift dread glimpse of the red balls streaking by.

If the Japanese patrol planes which came over at night and were called Washing-Machine Charley for the uneven beat of their motors failed to kill many of these pilots, they succeeded in keeping them awake. They circled the night sky for hours. When their gas was low and the patience of their victims nearly exhausted, they dropped their eggs and sauntered home.

To be replaced by another Charley, or far, far worse, to be supplanted by Louie the Louse. This was the name for all those scouting aircraft whose swaying flares heralded the arrival of the Tokyo Express off Guadalcanal. Louie's droning motors and his flares were all the warning given. Then the sea-lying darkness flashed and the great naval shells wailed overhead and these pilots who were the very targets of the Japanese ships were flung gasping out of their cots while the roaring air squeezed their bodies like rubber dolls in the hand of a giant.

Only after the warships were gone, could the fliers of the Bastard Air Force sleep.

But they would rise again at dawn, greet the first light with scalding hot coffee to dissolve the rice lying in the belly like stones—greet it with the barely comprehended news of more men killed, more men wounded, and the wreckage of their tiny air force strewn up and down their mangled airstrip.

Still they flew on, taking to the skies in patched-up aircraft, flying wing-to-wing in that technique of fighting by pairs which they would bring to perfection. Within a week of their arrival, some of them were aces. By August 30, Major John Smith had five little red balls painted on his Wildcat fighter. By nightfall, there were four more.

August 30 was one of those rare days when only the Zeros came down to strike at Henderson Field. Major Smith shot one of them to earth quickly, coming in on the enemy pilot's rear and killing him in his cockpit before he knew he was under attack. Then Smith banked toward a Zero attacking his wingman. The red ball flashed full in Smith's sights. He pressed the button. The Zero flamed and crashed. Now a third Japanese fighter was coming up under Smith. His bullets were sewing stitches up and down his fuselage. Smith nosed over. He came at the Japanese head-on. A bullet struck Smith's windshield and whined past his ear. He kept his thumb on the button. The Zero was coming apart in chunks. The two planes roared toward collision. They tore past each other not 15 feet apart.

Over his shoulder Smith could see the Zero spinning down, and its pilot bailing out. Then there was no time to watch for the flowering of the parachute, for Smith, running low on gas, had only a few rounds of bullets left for those six wing guns and here he was coming down on top of a fourth Zero hedge-hopping along the shore.

Smith skimmed over the coconuts with all guns blazing and the Zero fell into the sea in flames.

So it went into September, while the Bastard Air Force's collective total climbed toward 100, while its fighters also flew the cover under which Major General Vandegrift withdrew the Raiders and other troops from Tulagi to meet a fresh emergency.

The Kawaguchis had slipped into eastern Guadalcanal by night barge and were marching through the jungle toward the gaps behind Henderson Field.

8

Major General Kiyotake Kawaguchi had brought his dress whites to Guadalcanal with him. He had them in a trunk when his brigade landed at the village of Tasimboko, a mile or so west of the same Taivu area where Colonel Ichiki had landed. Kawaguchi had stowed the whites among his brigade's supplies at Tasimboko against that day when, with the Rising Sun again waving above the island airfield, with his silk uniform facings gleaming in the sun, his braided cap clapped over his balding head, his handlebar mustache ends twisted briskly to attention, he would turn his face toward the Emperor and the photographers.

That had been September 6. Next day, after posting a rear guard of about company strength in Tasimboko, General Kawaguchi strode off into the jungle in khakis, confident that his men had landed undetected, assured that Japanese air and sea power would keep the Americans engaged until he had slipped into position to spring his surprise attack the night of September 12. By that time, too, his rear-guard would have joined him with his supplies, his remaining guns, and, of course, the whites.

Red Mike Edson and about 850 Raiders came ashore near Tasimboko at dawn of September 8. They landed a mile west of the village supported by the shelling of destroyer-transports and the strafing of Army P-400's. They turned right to the village, dueled briefly with gunners of Kawaguchi's rear-guard —and then swept through Tasimboko on the heels of an enemy broken on the anvil of encirclement. They killed 27 Japanese at a loss of two of their own killed, six wounded—and now they had the village.

They broke into a beer warehouse only to find that the last bottle had been issued the day before. Whereupon they burned the warehouse down and the village with it. They towed a battery of Kawaguchi's guns into the sea, hurling the breech blocks into the water. They blew up supplies. They committed those unspeakable movements of spoliation upon the food which caused one Japanese diarist to write: "It is maddening to be the recipient of these insulting attacks by American forces." And then Red Mike Edson's Raiders found the fancy pants of Kiyotake Kawaguchi and carried them back to the airfield in triumph. Two days later they were climbing a ridge to plug one of the gaps behind Henderson Field.

That was where they were on the night of September 12 when Kiyotake Kawaguchi came furiously against Henderson Field, doubly determined to save his face, now that he had lost his pants.

Bald but for its *kunai* grass, nameless and bumpy, the ridge rose like a long thin island from the dark green sea of the jungle. It lay a short mile south of Henderson Field. It stretched perhaps a thousand yards on a northwest-southeast slant. It could be bombed and shelled, it could be easily approached, it could be turned, be overrun, cut off—but whoever held the ridge commanded Henderson Field, and whoever held the airfield held Guadalcanal.

It was here that Red Mike Edson brought his Marines on September 10, after General Vandegrift received reports which told him that the payoff battle was impending.

To the east of the Tenaru, patrols had found emplacements of Japanese mountain guns. They were carefully sighted in on the Marines' defenses and thoughtfully smeared with grease against the corrosion of the jungle. They were left unguarded or only protected by a single soldier. But Vandegrift had learned not to be baffled by the enemy's ways. He could judge now between what mattered and what seemed to matter. It mattered that these guns were new, not that they were undefended; that their sentries were well fed and well equipped, not that they were solitary. It mattered that the dump which Edson had destroyed at Tasimboko had been large, not that it was lightly guarded. It mattered that the Melanesian natives now swarming to the sanctuary of his perimeter were terribly frightened, not that their estimates of Japanese numbers were as usual unreliable; that they babbled of gun-point forced labor on a "tunnel" southwest through the jungle, not that they had actually seen or had not seen the torture and murder of missionary priests and nuns.

Vandegrift could now judge with certainty that the enemy had returned to Guadalcanal in force, that he was heavily armed, that he had lost his supplies and must therefore attack quickly, that he had disappeared to the southwest and was probably looking for a route to the airfield through one of the gaps behind it. That was why, on the tenth, Vandegrift sent Edson up to that ridge to plug the biggest gap. Also on the tenth, Vandegrift took the mounting fury of Japanese aerial bombardment to be one of the surest signs of approaching battle. But then, having judged the situation, he could not act.

He could not maneuver, for he had only a single battalion in reserve. He could not reinforce Edson or plug other gaps, for his specialists, truck drivers, pioneers and amtrack men had already been formed into rifle battalions and sent to hold isolated strong points. Nor dared he strengthen the ridge by weakening other points already spread disastrously thin and held by troops already melting away with malaria.

Next day, the eleventh, there was help. Twenty-four Navy fighters flew into Henderson Field, and rarely before had sailors been so warmly welcomed by Marines. There had been

46 Japanese bombers and fighters over the airfield that day and the Marines were down to 11 planes.

On the eleventh, Major General Kawaguchi decided that the guns lost at Tasimboko meant that he would cancel a thrust at the Tenaru scheduled to coincide with his surprise attack. Otherwise, he would go ahead and surprise the Americans whom his scouts had sighted on the ridge.

On the eleventh, the Marines on the ridge had their first mail call in two months. Major Kenneth Bailey, hardly recovered from his Tulagi wound, had gone over the hill from the hospital in New Caledonia and brought the outfit's mail with him. There were bundles of letters, hometown newspapers, food packages from home. The men grinned happily. At last they were getting a rest. They could read letters, munch pogey-bait, loaf, or perhaps stroll up to the ridge crest to enjoy the spectacle of fierce dogfights growling over the airfield. They scattered when the Zeros sighted them and came snarling down with bullets digging up dirt, their empty cartridges tinkling to earth in a chilling fugue.

Also on the eleventh, Colonel Red Mike Edson scouted the jungle to his front and became alarmed at signs of an enemy build-up. On the twelfth he was among his men, softly urging them forward on the ridge, ordering them to stow their mail, dig in, string barbed wire, for this was it as it had never been before.

Red Mike could guess that his men were bitter. They had fought at Tulagi, patroled Savo, fought at Tasimboko. They had gambled against the law of averages, the only law that bound them, and had survived that awful lottery. Now, seeking the respite in which they might forget the mounting odds, they were being asked to toss their numbers in again. *Their* numbers. Not those of the other outfits below them, fresh outfits, fat outfits, outfits that had yet to risk the odds—but the Raiders again, the Paramarines again. They cursed Red Mike for a "glory hound." They muttered that he hung around Division to hunt up new assignments for the outfit, more medals for himself. But they dug.

Soon only a singularly stupid man wasted his breath cursing the brass. He saved it for the moment he had struck his pick mattock on the ridge shale and the frail tool snapped in his hands, or when the barbed wire tore his flesh and left it festering and unbandaged, for no adhesive tape would stick to bodies slippery with sweat.

They fortified the southern nose of the ridge where it sank into the jungle between steep wooded ravines falling away to right and left. In the right ravine a company was strung out a half-mile west to the Lunga River. On the left another line stretched east a similar distance and ended with an exposed flank in the jungle. The men in the ravines cut fields of fire, strung single strands of wire from tree to tree. On the ridge, artillery observation posts were set up, machine guns emplaced, reserve companies put into position.

The aerial battle began over Henderson Field again, and the shriek of diving airplanes, the sharp cracking of the antiaircraft bursts, the hammering of guns and wailing of bombs took on dread significance for these Marines: the Betty bombers laid sticks of eggs all down the long axis of their ridge.

Then the clamor of aerial battle ended and the ridge became silent but for the clinking of picks, the rasping of shovels, the soft urgent calls attuned to gathering dusk. Men straightening on the ridge could see the last flights of parakeets skimming over the jungle roof, the brilliance of their plumage vanishing with the fading light. Night came clear and moonless. The jungle seemed to flow around the ridge like a silent dark sea. Men in the ravines squeezed their eyes tight shut to accustom them to the night, and were startled to hear the cry of the bird which barked like a dog, the *crrrack* of the bird whose call was as the clapping of wood blocks.

The ridge was ready.

At nine o'clock that night a green flare fell from a Japanese patrol plane droning over Henderson Field. A half-hour later a Japanese cruiser and three destroyers stood off the mouth of the Lunga to pound the ridge with eight- and five-inch shells. In twenty minutes more a rocket rose in front of the Marines on the right or Lunga side of the ridge.

Firecrackers exploded, random shots rang out, mortars fell and the Kawaguchis struck with a howl.

They had marched down the bank of the Lunga, swung right toward the ridge, and then, silhouetted in the swaying light of their parachute flares, had come sprinting on in waves. Grenadiers first, riflemen, light machine-gunners, coming in columns stretching as far back as the Marines could see, they came on to a cadenced slapping of rifle butts, a rising, rhythmic chant:

U. S. Marines be dead tomorrow.
U. S. Marines be dead tomorrow.

They drove the Raiders back. In the blackness that followed the dying flares, they split the center of Edson's lines, sliced off a platoon to the far right flank, cut communications wire, and moved down the Lunga to attempt an encirclement. If General Kawaguchi had chosen to follow quickly upon that first shattering rush, he might have overwhelmed the ridge. But his men merely flowed up against its right side, thrashing about in the jungle that had engulfed them, tripped them, confused them, once they had left the straight going of the riverbank. The battle that had been joined so swiftly became fragmented almost immediately.

Groups of Marines struggling to restore their lines blundered into groups of Japanese milling about trying to cut fields of fire in the undergrowth. The shooting was wild, the grenades fell among friend as well as foe, the bayonet jabbed against the sound of a strange tongue and found only air. It was a battle fought beyond the direction of either commander. Even a fresh Japanese naval bombardment after midnight did not drastically alter the deadlock established after the first fierce charge. It smoldered on until daybreak, a mindless fight, but it ended in a victory for General Kawaguchi.

His men had cut communications between the Marine companies and forced them back. They spent the daylight of the thirteenth fortifying their positions for the final blow that night.

Red Mike Edson's men were stunned. They stumbled as they walked, lifting their feet high as though fatigue had weighted them with lead. They mumbled as they talked, licking cracked dry lips with swollen tongues. They had been thrown back, and they did not like to remember it. They had attempted to drive off the Japanese with a morning counterattack, but they had failed again. They had expected to be relieved or reinforced by the Second Battalion of the Fifth Marines, but intermittent attacks on Henderson Field had kept this force under cover. The men of the Fifth could not reach the ridge until dusk, after the dogfights over Henderson Field ended and enemy guns from land and sea had fallen silent. Even then they would only be able to take up supporting positions.

It was up to 400 men holding a shortened line 1,800 yards long against 4,000 Japanese—one man every five yards against 10 of the enemy. Red Mike Edson gathered a small group of men in late afternoon, a few minutes after they had eaten their first food since the day before, and he spoke to them like a professional.

"This is it," he said softly. "It is useless to ask ourselves why it is we who are here. We are here. There is only us between the airfield and the Japs. If we don't hold, we will lose Guadalcanal."

The men returned to their gunpits. But this time there was no cursing.

Major General Kiyotake Kawaguchi had lost more men than he had anticipated, but he had successfully forced his way past that deadly American firepower. He was in close, where the "spiritual" power of *Bushido* was unstoppable. His men had been pleased to hear the sound of friendly bombs falling upon the Americans. Tonight, he would attack earlier than usual. He wanted to have the airfield cleared of Americans before Admiral Mikawa's cruisers arrived at midnight. Then the honor of retaking Guadalcanal would belong to the Army. Also, he had ordered the Ishitari Battalion then east of the Tenaru to strike the river line at midnight. Then, he, Kiyotake Kawaguchi, would wheel his three battalions right or east from the airfield and crush the Tenaru Americans from the rear.

General Kawaguchi sent a radio message to Tokyo. It was not as premature as had been the diary entry of Colonel Ichiki, but it did suggest that if Radio Tokyo were to announce the recapture of the airfield, Major General Kiyotake Kawaguchi would back them to the hilt on it.

At half-past six that night he attacked.

"Gas!"

Smoke rolled over the Marine right. Again the flares, again the jabbering, and again that voice, precise and un-American:

"Gas attack!"

But there was no gas, it was only smoke, only another Japanese trick, and the Marines held to their holes until more flares had made a ghoulish day of the night and from 75 yards away the jungle spewed forth platoon after platoon of short tan shapes. But now the Marines were screaming their own coarse epithets at the onrushing enemy. They were firing. The Japanese were falling. Still they came on, a full battalion rushing a right flank held by less than a hundred Marines, and this time they were shooting from the hip as they came.

Again the Japanese closed and fragmented that right flank. Quickly they cut off a platoon and surrounded it. The Marines fought back individually. Pfc. Jimmy Corzine caught sight of four Japs setting up a machine gun on a commanding knob. He rushed them. He bayoneted their leader and as the others fled, turned the enemy gun on them, killed them, and fired on until he himself was killed.

Edson's right was in serious trouble. Captain John Sweeney's Company B had been cut into small pockets among a surging sea of enemy. He had lost his right flank platoon, he was down to less than 60 men, and on his left a mortar barrage and another headlong rush of the Kawaguchis had driven the Paramarines back.

Captain Torgerson took command of the retreating Paramarines. He rushed among the knots of men drifting back along the ridge spine. He held roll call. He singled the men out by name, he taunted them to go forward—and they did. They drove out through a rain of Japanese hand grenades, throwing themselves on the bare slopes to fire, to set up machine guns. The Japanese singled out the Marine machine guns, dropping grenades on them from the little launchers or "knee mortars"

59

they carried forward strapped to their legs. Sergeant Keith Perkins scurried over the ridge, hunting grenades and ammunition for his two machine guns. One by one, his gunners fell or were wounded. Perkins jumped on his last gun. He fired. He was killed.

The Paramarines were hanging on to what remained of the left flank as Red Mike Edson came forward on the ridge and tried to make telephone contact with Captain Sweeney's Company B alone on the right. A voice came through.

"Our situation here, Colonel Edson, is excellent. Thank you, sir."

Edson swore softly. It was a Japanese. They had cut his wire. How to reach Sweeney? Edson seized a brass-lunged corporal and spoke rapidly. The corporal darted forward on the ridge. He cupped his hands to his mouth and bellowed:

"Red Mike says it's okay to pull back!"

Sweeney heard and gathered the remnant of his company. Slowly, taking a raking fire, grenades, they fought back to the ridge.

On top of the ridge Edson and Major Bailey were rallying their men with insults and taunts, trying to drive them forward with those irrational shouts which often halt those rational drifts to the rear. Edson was now within 10 yards of his foremost machine gun. He lay on his belly with his arm curled around his hand telephone, sometimes lifted and slammed to earth by the force of enemy mortar blasts. He saw a knot of men milling around aimlessly. He rose and rushed at them, screaming as he pointed toward the Japanese: "The only thing they have that you don't is guts!" He led them to new positions, for he was shortening his lines, while Bailey ran among other reluctant Raiders, seizing them individually by the arm. "You," he snarled, "do *you* wanna live forever?" It had been said by Dan Daly in Belleau Wood and had been mocked by a generation, but now it was being flung in American teeth once more and it could still sting.

They went forward again, to dig in, to hurl the grenades rushed to them by Bailey, to draw a shallow horseshoe on the center of the ridge and await the full fury of the Kawaguchi Brigade now massing for the final rush.

Red Mike Edson had called for artillery; with him to spot the enemy was a private named Watson. He would be Second Lieutenant Watson in the morning in reward for that hell he called down from the heavens. The shells came whistling in from the Eleventh Marines' 105-millimeter pack howitzers a half-mile back. They fell in a curtain of steel not 200 yards from that desperate last horseshoe of defense. They shook the Marine defenders, squeezed their breath away, but they made a flashing white slaughter among the Kawaguchis.

When the Japanese commanders fired rocket signals for attack, Watson marked them and directed redoubled shelling on the enemy breaking for the ridge. They were blown apart. The night was made hideous with their screams, and those who passed that dreadful line were either cut down by Marine fire or beaten to the earth by clubbed rifles and bayonets.

It was now half-past eleven and Red Mike Edson had contacted his general and told him he would hold.

Just before midnight Admiral Mikawa's warships reached Guadalcanal. They heard firing to the south of the airfield. They began cruising about, awaiting General Kawaguchi's flare signaling recapture of the airfield. Then they heard firing to the east.

The Ishitari Battalion had attacked the Tenaru. They struck through a field of *kunai* grass against the weapons and barbed wire of the Third Battalion, First Marines. They were caught halfway across by the massed firing of Marine 75-millimeter howitzers. The Ishitaris were broken. They reformed and came again. The guns roared. Marine tanks joined the riflemen. The Ishitaris were driven off.

Admiral Mikawa was bewildered. The firing to the east had subsided. There was only a fitful crackling of gunfire in the southern hills. There was still no flare, and it was getting dangerously close to the dawn that would make him visible to American bombers. Admiral Mikawa gave up and sailed home.

It was daybreak on the ridge. A rosy sun was rising almost directly to the left of the Marine front, lighting the battle that was now over. There was only an occasional shot, the boom of a grenade on a boobytrapped body. Six hundred Japanese lay sprawled on the ridge slopes or were faintly visible in the ravines below. Souvenir-hunters were already moving warily among the bodies. Major Bailey was receiving treatment for another wound. Red Mike Edson's men were being relieved by the Second Battalion, Fifth. Slow-flying Army Airacobras rose from the airfield to harry the retreating enemy. Mopping-up began in the jungle and far to the Marines' rear among those Japanese who had infiltrated. Four of these infiltrators rushed into General Vandegrift's headquarters with a cry of "*Banzai!*" They were shot down, but only after a Marine sergeant had died of a sword thrust.

There was also a brief flare-up to the west, where a Japanese daylight attack across the Matanikau River was hurled back.

By daybreak the main battle, that which the Marines were already calling Bloody Ridge, was over. There were 40 dead Marines and 104 wounded, against a Japanese toll which would rise far above the 600 dead at Bloody Ridge, the 250 who fell at the Tenaru, the 100-odd destroyed at the Matanikau. For General Kawaguchi had already begun a cruel march south through the jungle, a terrible red-trailed retreat of which one of his officers wrote:

"I cannot help from crying when I see the sight of these men marching without food for four or five days and carrying the wounded through the curving and sloping mountain trails. The wounds couldn't be given adequate medical treatment. There wasn't a one without maggots. Many died."

And yet, Bloody Ridge marked only the end of the beginning—a fact made plain to the Marines by a Japanese prisoner who stood among his slaughtered countrymen and said:

"Make no matter about us dead. More will come. We never stop coming. Soon you all be Japanese."

10

September 15—the day after the Battle of Bloody Ridge—gave proof that the high superiors of that Japanese prisoner were truly determined to keep coming.

On that day an American fleet was hit hard in "Torpedo Junction," a 640-mile stretch of the Coral Sea between Guadalcanal and Espiritu Santo which abounded in Japanese submarines.

The Japanese subs attacked the carriers *Wasp* and *Hornet*, the fast new battleship *North Carolina*, seven cruisers and 13 destroyers—in effect the American Pacific fleet. Fortunately, a prudent decision by Vice Admiral Richmond Kelly Turner deprived the Japs of juicier prey: the six transports carrying the Seventh Marine Regiment from Espiritu to Guadalcanal. The day before, a big Kawanishi flying boat was spotted tracking the task force. Turner sent the transports back to Espiritu that night.

Next day, the fifteenth, a blue, cloudless, tropic day, the red-balled Japanese subs struck at the Americans sailing in two sections about a half-dozen miles apart.

Mighty *North Carolina* shuddered as a Japanese fish smashed her side. She turned and went streaking south. Little *O'Brien* staggered after her, only to fall apart and sink before she could reach port. *Hornet* and the others got away, but *Wasp* took three torpedoes. She burned brightly beneath the red glow of twilight on September 15, and then she went under.

Beneath the same red sky in Tokyo, high-ranking officers of the Imperial Army and Navy reported the results to cheering thousands in Hinomiya Stadium. They also reported the news

63

of the "recapture" of the Guadalcanal airfield, and then, to bursts of thunderous applause, came this announcement:

". . . and the stranded 10,000 Marines, victims of Roosevelt's gesture, have been practically wiped out."

It was a great day in Tokyo, and at Rabaul, Lieutenant General Haruyoshi Hyakutate, gratified to hear that his humble part in the victory had not been overlooked, turned to tidying up his triumph.

Hyakutate was going to use all the 20,000 soldiers then available to him to dispose of the remaining Marines. He would be sure this time, for reports filtering back to Rabaul from the Kawaguchis suggested that these Marines did not conform to the Imperial Staff Manual descriptions of Americans. They were beasts, the refuse of jails and insane asylums. They drank blood. They cut off the arms of their prisoners and staked their bodies to the earth. Then they drove over them in steamrollers.

No, Hyakutate would not gamble again. He would send all the Sendai Division. Advance units would go down The Slot in fast destroyer-transports. They would be followed by the Sendai's commander, Lieutenant General Masao Maruyama, then the main body aboard slower transports, next the combined aerial and sea power of the Imperial Navy—and finally by Lieutenant General Haruyoshi Hyakutate, who would sail down in October in time to accept the American surrender.

In the third week of September the Tokyo Express began running troops to Guadalcanal again.

There were now 23,000 Marines on Guadalcanal, for the Seventh Regiment had come in.

Becoming bold in the wake of the Torpedo Junction disaster, Kelly Turner had turned the six transports around while still at sea and started them for Guadalcanal again. Under cover of hazy skies, assisted by the plastering of Rabaul by Army bombers, the transports sailed through Torpedo Junction on the sixteenth and seventeenth and arrived off Lunga Roads at Guadalcanal before dawn of September 18. At a few minutes before six the men of the Seventh began coming ashore.

Now, bolstered by 4,262 fresh men, and more of his combat

troops coming over from Tulagi, Major General Alexander Vandegrift changed his style of defense.

The system of strong points with artillery covering the gaps was abandoned in favor of a ring around Henderson Field and the new fighter strip. It meant spreading a lot of men thin. It meant defending every point, but weakly, as opposed to defending some vital points, but strongly. And thus it would also mean that wherever the enemy attacked he would be hitting with the most against Vandegrift's least. It was an old-fashioned defense, as surely outdated by artillery as the long bow had made an anachronism of mounted knights. But the Japanese artillery had been as ineffectual as the Marines' had been superb.

So Vandegrift drew his ring around Henderson Field. With barbed wire, axes, shovels, sandbags, machetes and bulldozers now in abundance, his men began building a tight bristling defensive ring which would lead one Japanese officer to snort that U. S. Marines were actually not true jungle-fighters because "they always cut the jungle down." The cordon followed approximately the same oval-shaped dispositions as the old beachhead line 3,500 yards deep and 7,500 yards wide, but all the gaps were plugged—especially the big ones to the south of the airfield.

Coconut groves rang to the strokes of the axe. Big trees came crashing down, were chopped into sections and dragged over wide sandbagged holes. More sandbags went atop the logs and over this were planted clumps of grass. In that lush-growing moist heat, the grass quickly took root and the rough-hewn pillboxes took on the appearance of low hummocks. Fields of fire—that is, cleared lanes between the guns and the enemy— were burned out in the grass or hacked out in the jungle. Apron after apron of barbed wire was strung until many of the Marine fronts were as wicked laceworks of glittering black wire and tan, charred grass. Riflemen learned to dig Japanese spider-holes, those vertical foxholes in which a man could stand to fight. Mortarmen sandbagged their heaps of shells. Booby-traps were fashioned of hand grenades with partially loosened pins attached to trip wires. Machine-gunners set up interlocking crossfires or registered their guns for night firing. Artillery-men plotted the fronts, registered the trails, marked the likely assembly areas. As the men worked, barely nourished by two daily meals of wormy rice, daily patrols went winding into the jungle.

Patrols were the eyes and ears of that line of defense, the feelers that went out daily—east, south and west—probing for the presence of the enemy. They went out in groups of a dozen men, occasionally in company strength. They were lightly armed. The men carried only a canteen of water. They fastened their gear tight to prevent tell-tale clinks, they daubed their faces with mud, adorned their blouses and helmets with branches—and moved out slowly, hugging the trails to right and left with intervals of a dozen feet between them, listening for the sudden cry of birds that might betray a lurking enemy, moving at a crawling, crablike rhythm, at a pace so madden-ingly slow that tension became multiplied, all the sounds so magnified that the rustling of a lizard might echo in helmet-muffled ears like the movement of a human body.

Patrols moved warily because ambushes were frequent dur-ing September. On one of them a company scouting the Lunga south of the perimeter was struck by a sudden storm of fire. Men could hear Japanese calling from the jungle, "Come here, please. Come here, please."

Private Jack Morrison saw Marines slump to earth around him. He felt white-hot pain sear his arm and his chest. He shouted in agony and toppled into a bush, his body obscured by undergrowth, his feet sticking out over the trail. To his right along the riverbank a Marine had fallen behind a log. He was moaning aloud. Behind him, hidden in a foxhole, was another Marine. He was Pfc. Harry Dunn. He was not wounded. He was playing dead. For in the complete surprise and success of that assault, the ambushed company had pulled back down the trail.

It was late afternoon and Morrison lay in the bush listening to the Japanese running about, jabbering to each other as they hunted down the wounded and bayoneted them. Great retch-ing waves of pain swept over his body, but he ground his teeth and kept silent. He had heard the Marine behind the log moan.

66

He had seen the Jap jump over the log with upraised bayonet, had seen it slammed down—once, twice—and had heard no more moaning.

Sometimes a merciful blackness engulfed Morrison. He would pass out, returning to the agony of consciousness, pass out again. He could feel the blood oozing from his wounds, sense the strength leaving him. His thirst was a torment. Still he dared not move—not even after night had fallen, for the enemy was still active.

Toward midnight he felt a presence alongside him. A hand came over his mouth. He stiffened in terror, then relaxed to hear the voice whisper in his ear, "It's all right. It's me—Harry Dunn." Slowly, gently, Dunn pulled Morrison away from the trail and into a thicket. He took off the wounded youth's shirt and tried to bind his wounds. But there was so much blood the shirt became soaked and was useless. Dunn threw it away.

Dunn crept out of the thicket in search of water, for both men's canteens were empty. He crawled to the dead Marine behind the log. But the body had been completely looted. Helmet, weapon, belt, canteen, all were gone. Dunn looked to his right. He could see the Lunga gleaming darkly, could hear the wavelets lapping her shores. But he dared not break for it. He would have to cross a clearing in full view of the Japanese, still moving around the riverbank, still calling out loudly to one another.

Dunn crawled back to Morrison in the thicket. They lay there, through the night, through the entire next day, among swarming mosquitoes and crawling ants while the terrible sweet stench of decaying flesh rose from the lumps that had been their comrades, while their tongues swelled in their mouths, and while Morrison burned in the fire of his pain and Dunn kept his hand clamped over his mouth to stifle his groans.

At last it was night again and the Japanese had moved up-river. Dunn dragged Morrison down to the river. He pulled him behind a log caught in the shore underbrush and lowered him gently into the water. Then he lay down and rolled over, opening his mouth, allowing the river water to caress his burning palate. Morrison drank, too, for the first time in two days.

Now Dunn had Morrison on his back. He was crawling down the riverbank toward the sea and the Marine lines, keeping well inshore for fear of the crocodiles prowling the Lunga, yet shying clear of the enemy-infested jungle. He stopped frequently to rest, and crawled on again. Sometimes Morrison mumbled wildly in his delirium, sometimes he sank into unconsciousness. Occasionally Dunn would also lose his senses. But he would awaken and crawl on.

At daybreak they reached the Marine lines. Still bleeding, Morrison was rushed to the airfield and quickly evacuated to a base hospital. Dunn was taken to a field hospital, carried there—for he had passed out from exhaustion.

It was no longer the Bastard Air Force but Cactus Air Force, so called after the code word for Guadalcanal. It was under the command of a grizzled white bear of a brigadier general named Roy Geiger. He was a flying general, a pioneer of Marine aviation who had flown as a captain in World War One. General Geiger was also a student of land warfare. On Guadalcanal, he consistently visited the front lines to study Vandegrift's dispositions. Geiger would one day become the only Marine to command an American army, but in those late September days on Guadalcanal he was still bringing Marine air power to its maturity.

Geiger came into Guadalcanal September 3 on the first transport plane to reach Henderson Field. Shortly afterward he was promoted to major general. He took up headquarters in a wooden shack called "The Pagoda" and located only 200 yards from the main runway. He quickly became known as The Old Man to that youthful flying fraternity which made up his command. For Cactus Air Force was actually a band of brothers who looked so much alike on the ground—the faces of each obscured in the shadow of identical long-billed blue baseball caps, the left breast of each bulky with the same automatic pistol stuffed into the same shoulder holster . strapped over identical faded khaki shirts—that it was not surprising to see them fighting like wing-joined twins in the skies.

Geiger's men had learned never to dogfight a Zero. The Japanese fighter planes were too fast, too maneuverable. They would be in on the Wildcat's tail and firing away. But the Wildcats had the armor and the firepower, and if one of them was no match for one Zero, two of them fighting together could take on five enemy. They watched each other's tails, firing quick six-gun bursts at the attacking Zeros—and because the Japanese planes had thin skins and no self-sealing gas tanks, they flamed easily. The Marines had learned other things, among them the necessity of wiping their guns free of oil lest they freeze at altitudes above 25,000 feet, and the danger of coming in behind a bomber's tail guns. They contented themselves with making overhead passes at the bombers, flashing past protecting Zeros with quick bursts, then diving for safety and a pull-out.

And while the Wildcats were mastering the Zero which had once been the scourge of the Pacific—slaughtering the Marine Buffaloes at Midway—Cactus Air Force's Dauntless dive-bombers and Avenger torpedo-bombers ranged up The Slot to fulfill Vandegrift's requests for strikes on the Tokyo Express.

On September 21 Lieutenant Colonel Albert Cooley led the bombers against the destroyer *Kagero* while she landed troops at Kamimbo Bay, a point roughly 30 miles west of the Marine perimeter.

On September 22 the bombers hit the Japanese massing-point at Visale, a few miles north of Kamimbo Bay. One of the dive-bombers was flown by fifty-seven-year-old Roy Geiger. He had become angered when his men complained that the runway was so pocked with bomb-blasts they could not take off safely. He lumbered from The Pagoda, squeezed his bulk into a Dauntless cockpit and roared north to drop a thousand-pounder on the enemy. That same date more bombers went after destroyer-transports in a night attack.

On September 24 Cooley's planes bombed and strafed destroyer-transports *Kawakaze* and *Umikaze* in Kamimbo Bay.

But the troops were getting ashore, and this, together with patrol reports of increasing build-ups to the west, convinced General Vandegrift that before the Japanese could gather all their strength he had better break them up.

He attacked.

★

Vandegrift had two reasons for striking the Japanese west of the Matanikau River. He wanted to break them up before they could cross to the east bank, from which they could punish Henderson Field with their artillery and prepare an assault on his line at Kukum, and he wanted to occupy the east or inner bank of the river himself.

On September 23 Vandegrift ordered the famous jungle-fighter, Lieutenant Colonel Lewis Puller, to take his First Battalion, Seventh Marines, on a reconnaissance-in-force into the hills south and west of the perimeter. The scouting expedition was to end by September 26, on which date the Raider Battalion, now under Lieutenant Colonel Samuel Griffith, was to cross the Matanikau River at its mouth and march about 10 miles farther west to the village of Kukumbona. The idea was that the Raiders could set up a patrolling base at Kukumbona. All this was to be preliminary to Vandegrift's attack.

Nothing was heard from Puller until, on the night of September 24, he reported meeting the enemy near Grassy Knoll, about four miles south of the western half of the perimeter, and losing seven men killed and 25 wounded in the fight that followed. Because of rugged terrain, it required four men to carry back each of the stretchers on which the 18 seriously wounded lay. Vandegrift sent Puller the Second Battalion, Fifth Marines, and told him he was on his own as far as continuing his mission or withdrawing was concerned.

The wounded were placed in the care of two companies from Puller's own battalion under Major Otho Rogers. Then Puller led the rest of his force west of the Matanikau.

The night of September 24 Puller's force bivouacked just short of the Matanikau's east bank. Next morning the Marines reached the river and turned right, or north, to work down its east bank to the sea. In early afternoon, still several hundred yards short of the rivermouth, mortar shells fell on them from enemy positions across the river and near the coast. The Marines took cover and gradually crept down to the mouth of the Matanikau. But every attempt to cross the river was repulsed.

And now the Raiders who were to cross the Matanikau on their march to Kukumbona that very same day were obviously unable to do so. Vandegrift sent them up the east bank of the river. They were to move inland, or south, about 2,000 yards until they came to a log-crossing just beneath a fork in the river. They would cross there and come down on the Japanese right flank. This action was to begin the following day, September 27, with support from the air and from Marine artillery.

It began, but as the Raiders approached the log-bridge they were pinned to the ground by Japanese who had crossed the Matanikau at that point during the night and had occupied the east bank. The gallant Major Bailey was killed here and the Japanese kept the Raiders pinned down and cut them up with mortars.

Back at his headquarters, Vandegrift was under the impression that the Raiders had crossed the river and were now engaging the enemy on the *west* bank. He thought his planned strike at the Japanese right flank was taking place. So he sent the companies under Major Rogers on an amphibious thrust at the Japanese left. They were to go west to the Kukumbona vicinity by boat that same day. They were to land there and cut off the "defeated" enemy's retreat.

The Marines under Major Rogers shoved off just as the first of three waves of Zeros and bombers swept overhead. Destroyer *Ballard* which was to deliver supporting fire was forced to flee. Still the Marines went west, but when they came ashore they were far short of Kukumbona. They were at Point Cruz, a small peninsula just west of the Matanikau and just north or behind the Japanese left.

The Marines went in without radio, without naval gunfire, and before they had gone 500 yards they were blasted by Japanese mortars and Major Rogers was killed. An enemy column came from the Matanikau's west bank and struck them. The Marines took refuge on the top of a ridge, and the Japanese moved in between them and the sea and began pounding them with mortars.

Now Vandegrift had three battalions in trouble and the last one was out of contact.

H-E-L-P

Lieutenant Dale Leslie could not be sure. He was flying his Dauntless west of the Matanikau, on station for the aerial support planned against the Japanese there, and this could be another enemy trick. Leslie peered over the side of his plane. There it was—H-E-L-P—spelled out with something white, maybe T-shirts.

Leslie passed the word to the Fifth Marines, with whom he was in radio contact. The Fifth contacted Vandegrift and a rescue by sea was set in motion.

Ballard went west along the coast again. She stood off Point Cruz. Her officers saw a Marine leap up on a ridge about 500 yards inland. He was waving his arms, making semaphore signals.

The waving Marine was Sergeant Robert Raysbrook, standing erect amid Japanese bullets. His signals told *Ballard's* officers that the Japanese stood between the Marine ridge and the beach. *Ballard's* five-inchers boomed, striking the Japanese, cutting a swath of safety for the Marines. One of the batteries of Marine artillery which was to support the attack at the rivermouth raised sights and battered the nose of Point Cruz, which jutted into the water east of the besieged ridge and which could hold enemy gunners.

The Marines came down the ridge, taking heavy enemy fire. The Japanese rushed to close. Sergeant Tony Malinowski turned to cover his company's withdrawal. He took on the onrushing Japanese with his BAR. He was never seen again.

But his comrades got down the hill. Now they were at the beach. The Japanese set up an interlocking fire of machine guns. They swept the beach. Casualties mounted. The Marines threw up a defensive perimeter while a Coast Guardsman named Donald Munro led the first wave of boats through the surf. They got in, though Munro was killed—winning a posthumous Medal of Honor. But the second wave hesitated.

Lieutenant Leslie nosed his Dauntless down again. He came in with a roar, flying low, shepherding the faltering boats shoreward, spraying bullets as he banked to climb for the return swoop. The Marines got out, with all of their 23 wounded, but not all of their 24 dead.

It was a daring rescue compounded of ingenuity and courage, and it served to take some of the sting out of the Marines' defeat at the Matanikau.

Defeat it was, for Vandegrift shortly afterward called all his forces back from the river. He had lost 60 dead and 100 wounded and his repulse had been the result of bad intelligence and piecemeal commitment of forces, tactics that had heretofore characterized only Japanese operations.

But Cactus Air Force was still master of the aerial enemy. By the end of September General Geiger's flyers had 171 Japanese kills to their credit. There were 19 little red balls painted on Major Smith's Wildcat and "Smitty" had won the Medal of Honor. So had Major Bob Galer, who shot down 13 enemy planes, who might have destroyed more if he had not been knocked down three times himself. Captain Marion Carl's string had been run up to 16, after the interruption of a jungle crash.

So the second month on Guadalcanal ended with the Marines on the ground bruised but still capable of more battle and with those in the skies steadily whittling enemy air power.

And then it was October.

11

October was the month of the dreadful rains, the month of decision, of change, of unending battle between men and ships and airplanes—the month of the Night of the Battleships, of Dugout Sunday, of Pistol Pete—the month when Americans on Guadalcanal were still hanging on while other Americans in Washington were backing off.

By day the Marines strengthened their lines, sent out patrols, rushed in supplies and troops or flew from the airfield to break up those aerial attacks which the enemy launched by day to clear the way for his movement at night. At night the Marines lay still in their holes, peering into the rain-swept darkness, knowing that destroyers were disgorging troops to the west, or that great dark shapes were gliding into the bay and that at any moment the silence might be shattered by the thundering of guns and the yelling of a new attack.

On each of those early October nights, the Tokyo Express brought an average of 900 troops to the island. On the night of October 4, they landed Lieutenant General Masao Maruyama.

Maruyama was a disciplinarian. He was a proud man, with haughty chin and an aristocratic nose beneath which ran a thin line of mustache as supercilious as a raised eyebrow. He was easily irritated, and he was displeased with what he found on Guadalcanal. Colonel Akinosuke Oka should not have allowed the American Marines to get away so cheaply on September 27. More, he should not have permitted the Ichiki and Kawaguchi survivors he commanded to mingle with the men of the Sendai's fresh 4th Regiment and spread their tales of horror among them.

The 4th had arrived first from Rabaul. It had come ashore on Guadalcanal and reached Kukumbona, Maruyama's headquarters, with its men full of vigor and splendidly equipped. Apart from his weapon, each man was supplied two pairs of trousers, two shirts, gloves, camouflage helmet-cover and split-toed shoes. His pack bulged, not with uncooked rice, but with canned fish or beef, canned vegetables—even a ration of hard candy. None of the "Old Whisky" looted from the Philippines had yet come down to Guadalcanal for the troops, but there would certainly be beer for them later and *saki* for the officers.

But Oka had allowed these excellent men to mingle with the scarecrows bequeathed him by General Kawaguchi. Those who were not prostrate with malaria or malnutrition had been telling horrible stories of Guadalcanal to the men of the 4th.

On October 5, General Maruyama received a letter written by a soldier of the 4th and intercepted by his commanding officer. It said:

> The news I hear worries me. It seems as if we have suffered considerable damage and casualties. They might be exaggerated, but it is pitiful. Far away from our home country a

fearful battle is raging. What these soldiers say is something of the supernatural and cannot be believed as human stories.

Lieutenant General Masao Maruyama issued a general order, which said:

> From now on, the occupying of Guadalcanal Island is under the observation of the whole world. Do not expect to return, not even one man, if the occupation is not successful. Everyone must remember the honor of the Emperor, fear no enemy, yield to no material matters, show the strong points as of steel or of rocks, and advance valiantly and ferociously. Hit the enemy opponents so hard they will not be able to get up again.

Then, while awaiting the arrival of his other troops—the 16th and 29th Regiments, his heavy artillery and a few thousand men of a Naval Landing Force Brigade—General Maruyama went to work planning an advance across the Matanikau. He, too, had seized the importance of the east bank. He would need it to gain room for the jumping-off of his main attack. He ordered Colonel Juro Nakaguma to take the 4th across the river in the early-morning dark of October 7.

Then Maruyama began searching his maps for that point most suitable to receive the surrender of the American General Vandegrift.

Although the detail of a surrender point escaped him, Alexander Vandegrift also studied maps of the Matanikau that afternoon of October 5.

He still believed that he could not allow the Japanese west of the river to build their forces unmolested. His earlier setback had only impressed upon him the need of using a force large enough to destroy the enemy. He decided to use five full battalions led by Red Mike Edson, now commander of the Fifth, and Colonel Wild Bill Whaling of the special Scout-Snipers group.

They would attack on October 7.

On October 6 the Japanese 4th Regiment's approach march from Kukumbona to the Matanikau was broken up by Marine aircraft. The men took cover. At night Colonel Nakaguma ordered them forward to the west bank of the river. They dug in. They would cross in the early morning. Meanwhile, Nakaguma sent three of his companies downstream to the rivermouth. They crossed there.

On October 7 Colonel Edson's force reached the east bank of the Matanikau mouth. The Third Battalion, Fifth, joined battle with Nakaguma's three companies which had crossed to the east bank. The Marines pressed the Japanese back, slowly containing them. Edson asked for reinforcements. Vandegrift sent the Raiders into their last battle. Commanded by Major Silent Lou Walt of the Fifth Marines, the Raiders helped push the enemy into a pocket. During the night the Japanese attempted to break out. They were destroyed.

Upriver on October 7 Colonel Whaling's men were unable to cross until nightfall, at which time they turned right to face the sea themselves on the west bank, the Edson forces on the east bank.

On October 8 it rained. Water poured from skies so dark that the jungle became a murk of gloom. Both sides were mired in a slop of mud.

On October 9 the coastwatchers up north sent word of a great invasion force making up in Rabaul. Vandegrift was forced to shave his ambitions. Even though Whaling's men had begun to make good progress seaward that day and Edson was across the Matanikau, Vandegrift decided that he would not strike at Kukumbona but be content with battering the enemy in the Point Cruz-Matanikau Village area before withdrawing to the east bank of the river and fortifying it.

It was then that the First Battalion, Seventh, was ordered out on reconnaissance again.

Lewis Burwell Puller was the battalion commander's full name, but he was simply "Chesty" to his men. This was the famous Chesty Puller who had already blooded his battalion in the Matanikau defeat and who had chafed at the order to withdraw. He was a man of only five feet six inches in height, but with an enormous rib cage stuck on a pair of matchstick legs—the barrel chest crowned by a great commanding head with strong outthrust jaw. At forty-four Puller was only a "light" colonel, for in him there was none of the guile that slips up the ladder of promotion. Chesty had become notorious among brother officers for insisting that regimental staffs were too large and the distance between command posts and front lines was too long. When he came to Guadalcanal leading the First Battalion, Seventh, he was already legendary for battles which had won him two Navy Crosses and for a salty tongue which had won him the affection of his men. Asked why Nicaragua patrols were slow, he had snapped: "Because of the officer's bed roll!" Shown his first flame-thrower, he had growled: "Where do you fit the bayonet on it?" Flunked out of Pensacola flying school on the unique report, "Glides too flat, skids on turns, climbs too fast," he had merely been relieved that he might return to the riflemen where "all the fightin's on foot."

And now he was on foot again during the afternoon of October 9, leading his battalion over a series of grassy ridges west of the Matanikau near the coast. Atop a high ridge Puller saw that a ravine below him was swarming with Japanese. At the same moment he received orders to scout the coastal road toward Kukumbona and to avoid combat. He asked and obtained permission to stay where he was for he had found a whole battalion under his guns.

The ravine became a slaughter-pen.

Marine mortar shells fell with dreadful accuracy. Death swept suddenly and invisibly among those Japanese, devastating them. They swarmed blindly up the hill against Puller's men. They were raked with small arms. They fled back down into the ravine, rolling down the slope, sprinting in terror through that hell of mortar fire and up the side of an opposing ridge, only to re-emerge on the crest in full view of Puller's Marines. They were riddled.

Again they fled down into the ravine, again they tried to come up through Puller's men again, were halted, turned, and sent through the reverse gantlet once more—and now the carnage was multiplied by the aerial bombs and artillery shells which Chesty Puller had called down into the ravine.

There were few Japanese who survived.

Seven hundred fell in that awful trap, and Lieutenant

77

General Masao Maruyama's attempt to seize the east bank of the Matanikau met with disaster. For there were roughly 200 more casualties inflicted on the 4th Regiment as the converging Whaling and Edson forces drove briskly into Point Cruz-Matanikau Village. The 4th was shattered and now Nakaguma's men had terrifying tales of their own to spread among comrades sailing south to the place they would call Death Island.

Marines withdrawing east from the river, bringing back their 65 dead and 125 wounded, heard the welcome roar of massed motors overhead. Major Leonard (Duke) Davis was leading Squadron 121 to the Cactus Shivaree.

Riding the cockpit of one of those 20 Wildcats was a cigar-smoking, blunt-featured, high-spirited Marine captain by the name of Joseph Jacob Foss.

12

It was clear that the Matanikau had eclipsed the Tenaru in importance. The Japanese no longer landed on eastern Guadalcanal but came ashore in the west. It was vital that the Marines' western boundary be extended to the east bank of the Matanikau River to stop the inevitable thrust from the west.

Because he had not enough men to hold all the river line, Vandegrift decided to defend the two main crossings—at the mouth of the river and at the upriver crossing which the Marines called Nippon Bridge from the Japanese characters *ippon-bashi,* meaning "one-tree bridge." This was about 2,000 yards inland, just below the fork in the stream.

The river block became a shallow horseshoe. Fortifications at the mouth "refused" the right flank, that is, exposed it in a backward curve to the beach behind it. Then the line ran slightly more than 2,000 yards along the river past Nippon Bridge to refuse the left flank, which was drawn back across a ridge and down into the jungle and allowed to dangle there. Vandegrift knew it was possible to cross the river at other points farther inland than Nippon Bridge. But he was making shift with what he had. He could spare two battalions. The Third Battalion, Seventh, went in line on the left and the Third Battalion, First, on the right. They could be reinforced and supplied along the coastal road connecting them with the original perimeter still held intact a few miles back east. Artillery was placed in support.

All this was done in the few days following the victory gained across the Matanikau October 7-9, done while that big invasion force of which the coastwatchers had sent warning was sailing down The Slot.

The Japanese ships were bringing Pistol Pete to Guadalcanal.

This was the collective nickname which the Marines were to bestow on those 150-millimeter howitzers with which General Maruyama hoped to chew up the runway at Henderson Field, as well as to batter the American lines.

On October 10 four of these big guns went aboard a sea-plane tender at Rabaul.

Next day they sailed south in that task force which included destroyer-transports bringing more of the Sendai Division to Guadalcanal, cargo ships, a protecting screen of destroyers and a division of cruisers to shell Henderson Field while guns, men and supplies were being put ashore.

Waiting for them off Cape Esperance was Rear Admiral Norman Scott with four cruisers and five destroyers of his own.

Again the island of Guadalcanal was quivering like a live thing. Once more the night glowed with the glare of burning ships while concussions rolled unimpeded over blackly gleaming water. Marines ashore were throwing aside ponchos and blankets and rushing for their holes in frantic, jostling groups. And Alexander Vandegrift was entering his headquarters tent to sit in battle vigil beneath the light of a single blue electric bulb.

The Battle of Cape Esperance had begun.

Pistol Pete and the bombardment force coming down had collided with Rear Admiral Norman Scott's cruisers and destroyers coming up. And Scott "crossed the T." He swung wide of western Guadalcanal to cover the Savo Island water gate and at midnight his ships were standing broadside to the Japanese, all their guns swiveled and trained starboard upon the perpendicular of an enemy column "now visible to the naked eye."

Heavy *Salt Lake City* hurled ten swift salvos into cruiser *Furutaka*, broke her in two, sank her. Heavy *San Francisco*, the lights *Boise* and *Helena*, and the five destroyers, shot off shell after shell into the others. Big *Aoba*, Rear Admiral Aritomo Goto's flagship, took 40 hits. She staggered out of the battle, Goto dying on his bridge, half of the crew dead. The big destroyer *Fubuki* went down. Destroyer-transports hit bottom. In the morning, planes from Henderson boiled out to finish big destroyers *Natsugumo* and *Murakamo*. By then the American destroyer *Duncan* was also gone—shot at by both sides—and *Boise* had two gun turrets burned out. But before morning Alexander Vandegrift's vigil had ended in jubilation. Colonel Thomas had rushed into his tent to tell him that Norman Scott had squared accounts for the Battle of the Five Sitting Ducks. Iron Bottom Bay was no longer a Japanese lagoon. The Navy would be coming back, and there would be reinforcements.

But a dozen miles west to Kukumbona, General Maruyama gave orders for the emplacement of four big guns with their tractors. If many ships and men had not survived the crossing of the T—Pistol Pete had.

> *We asked all the Doggies to come to Tulagi*
> *But General MacArthur said "No."*
> *When asked for his reason—*
> *"It isn't the season.*
> *"Besides you have no U.S.O.!"*

There was a refrain, beginning with the uncomplimentary and unjust sobriquet "Dugout Doug." The Marines knew that

General Douglas MacArthur was a brave man, but this did not deter them from singing their derision of the Army Dogfaces who had still not arrived on Guadalcanal. The Marines had given up hope—not of victory, but of help—and had turned to mocking the Doggies.

So they were astonished, almost resentful, to find on the morning of October 13 that the Doggies had actually come to Tulagi. The Army's 164th Infantry Regiment had arrived from Noumea, just in time for a fiery baptism which not even the Marines had experienced.

For the thirteenth was also the day on which Australian coastwatchers in Bougainville were fleeing Japanese patrols and keeping radio silence. There were no advance warnings of the three Japanese aerial formations that struck so savagely at the island. At noon, 24 twin-engined bombers and escorting Zeros flew over Henderson Field before the Marine Wildcats could climb to intercepting stations. They let loose a rain of bombs and incendiary bullets that set stores of aviation gasoline blazing. Two hours later 15 more bombers pounced, multiplying destruction. Captain Joe Foss shot down one of the escorting Zeroes—his first—took a bullet in the oil pump of his engine and came rocketing down from 22,000 feet to a deadstick landing while a trio of Zeros rode his tail. But the rest of the attackers escaped. And then the third Japanese formation struck, bombing the coconut groves where the 164th was bivouacked.

The Doggies had been blooded.

It was dusk and Sergeant Butch Morgan was preparing the evening meal for General Vandegrift. He was frying meat on a Japanese safe that had been upended and made into a griddle.

Pistol Pete spoke.

His first shell screamed over Division Headquarters and struck the airfield with a crash. Sergeant Morgan grabbed his helmet and raced for his air-raid hole. Another shell screeched overhead. Sergeant Morgan held his helmet down tight and ducked.

Crrrrrash!

Alexander Vandegrift looked up in surprise. He glanced thoughtfully overhead.

"That wasn't a bomb," he called. "That's artillery."

Sergeant Butch Morgan was embarrassed. He glanced about him, shamefaced, hoping that no boot had seen his flight—for Sergeant Morgan was an Old Salt who had fought in France and knew something of artillery.

"Aw, hell," he muttered, taking off his helmet. "I mean, only artillery . . ."

If it was "only artillery" it was the first with enough authority to reach the airfield. And now Pistol Pete was pumping them out, ripping up the big strip with a thoroughness that would make night flight impossible, shifting to hammer the perimeter, swinging to Kukum to blow up naval stores—and finally falling among the men of the 164th with such rending red terror that a sergeant crawled about begging his men to shoot him.

And then the same terror came upon all the island.

Red flares shot up from the jungle, Pistol Pete roared and roared, enemy aircraft circled overhead—drifting in and out of the crisscrossing searchlight beams that sought them, eluding the flak and dropping bombs—and men stumbled into foxholes, climbed out of them, ran back to them, bracing in expectation of they knew not what.

At half-past one in the morning Louie the Louse planted a green flare over the airfield and the Night of the Battleships began.

Mighty *Haruna* and *Kongo* had steamed down from Rabaul. Cruisers and destroyers came with them, some to join the airfield bombardment, others to protect seven transports loaded with General Maruyama's remaining troops.

They slid into the bay, screened by cruiser *Isuzu* and eight destroyers. They awaited the flares of the ground troops, the patrol plane's green light. Then: "Commence firing!"

Star shells rose, horrible and bright, scarlet with the fat red beauty of Hell, exploding like giant ferris wheels to shower the night with streamers of light. And then, the 14-inchers of the battleships, the eight-inchers of *Isuzu,* the five-inchers of the destroyers . . .

Pah-boom, pah-boom. Pah-boom, pah-boom, pah——

Men in their holes could hear the soft hollow thumping of the salvos to seaward, see the flashes shimmering outside the gun ports, and then the great airy boxcars rumbling overhead, wailing and straining—*hwoo-hwooee*—seeming to lose breath directly overhead, to pause, whisper, and go on. Then the triple tearing crash of the detonating shells and the bucking and rearing of the very ground beneath them.

American troops had never before been exposed to such cannonading and would never be so again. Even the great naval shellings that would one day fall upon the Japanese would not be comparable, for the Japanese would be in coral caves or huge pillboxes of ferro-concrete, while these Americans crouched in dirt holes, within shelters of mud and logs.

Henderson Field's bombers were blown to bits, set afire, crushed beneath collapsed revetments. Shelters shivered, sighed and came apart. Foxholes buried their occupants. Men were killed—41 of them, among them many pilots—and many, many more men were wounded. But the over-all effect upon men's souls was devastating.

In that cataclysm, when every shell seemed to explode with the pent-up flame and fury of a full thunderstorm, some men might glance at their buddies and see in horror how their features had dissolved in a nerveless idiot mask. Men whimpered aloud. Others burst into sobs and rushed from the pits rather than betray their weakness, if such it was, before comrades. There were Marines who put their weapons to their heads. Men prayed with lips moving silently across the backs of others against whom they lay huddled, prayed in confusion —mentally murmuring Grace or a childhood refrain as though it were the Lord's Prayer—prayed for the strength to stay where they were, to suppress that nameless thing fluttering within them.

The bombardment lasted an hour and twenty minutes, and then *Haruna* and *Konga* and their nine sister furies masked their guns and sailed north.

The bombers remained until dawn.

And at dawn Pistol Pete resumed action.

But the Marines and soldiers came above ground anyway. There had been no attack, and who would fear a six-incher after having felt the lash of 14-inch naval rifles?

They were dull-eyed and dazed, but they were already pluming themselves on having "really had it rough," already forgetting the fierce vows of the night in the profane oaths with which they asked God to take a look at the size of those 14-inch base plates and enormous shell fragments that were displayed to them by day.

The airfield was a shambles. The main strip was unusable. Of 38 bombers, only four survived the shelling. But these four went roaring skyward from Fighter Strip One to strike at the Japanese transports which had put Maruyama's troops ashore during the night. They sank one, and flew back to an airfield where Marine engineers and Seabees were already hauling fill to the big strip. Bulldozers were butting earth into yawning shell-craters and anxious squadron commanders were conferring with repair officers on the chances of getting airborne.

"What's left, Lieutenant?"

"You'd need a magnifying glass to find it, Colonel."

"Well, start using one then. How about Number 117?"

"*Her?* Oh, she's great—wasn't even scratched. Except that she needs an engine change. Other than that, all she needs is both elevators, both stabilizers, the right auxiliary gas tank, right and center section flaps, right aileron, windshield, rudder, both wheels and the brake assembly. But she's still in one piece, sir, and I guess we can get her up in six days."

"Six days!"

"Dammit, Colonel, back in the States it'd take six months to do it!"

"All right, all right—but let's keep those junk-pickers of yours busy."

They patched together ten more bombers that day. They filled gas tanks by hand, hauled bomb trailers by hand, and lifted the big eggs into the racks with straining, sweating bodies. They did this while Japanese bombers swept over Henderson Field again and again, for Cactus Air Force must be ready to go by the next day, when the remaining Japanese

84

cargo ships would surely return to unload General Maruyama's supplies.

And then it was discovered that they were running out of gasoline.

Not even the arrival of six more Dauntlesses that afternoon of October 14 raised the drooping spirits of men who heard that news.

General Geiger began issuing orders. He sent a flight of Army B-17's back to Espiritu Santo, for the Flying Fortresses drank too much gasoline. He ordered the tanks of wrecked planes drained. He sent out a search party to find a cache of 400 drums of gasoline which had been buried outside the airfield in the early days. He instructed Marine air transports to fly in nothing but gasoline. He got fast destroyers headed toward Guadalcanal with more drums lashed to their decks. He called off individual fighter sallies to husband his strength, for he wanted to use all that he had at dawn the next day.

But during the night the big cruisers *Chokai* and *Kinugasa* sped down The Slot to enter the Bay and hurl 752 eight-inch shells into Henderson and its defenders. At dawn, Marines standing atop the southern ridges looked westward to a place called Tassafaronga to contemplate the chilling spectacle of six squat Japanese ships calmly going about the business of unloading supplies.

Behind them on the battered airfield there were but three Dauntless dive-bombers able to fly.

"Always pray, not that I shall come back, but that I will have the courage to do my duty," wrote Lieutenant Anthony Turtora to his parents on a day before his squadron came to Guadalcanal.

In the daylight of October 15, Lieutenant Turtora climbed into the cockpit of his patched-up Dauntless and flew down to Tassafaronga to do his duty. He did not come back. But he and many others of the same spirit did what they set out to do.

By ten in the morning, after a flurry of single-plane sallies, the patchwork, ragtag Cactus Air Force was rising to the attack. It was incredible. They had no right to be airborne. Departing *Chokai* and *Kinugasa* had assured the transports that American airpower was now as defunct in fact as in the communiqués of Imperial Headquarters. But here they were coming with the sun glinting off their wings—Wildcats, Dauntlesses, Avengers, Army P-39's and P-400's, and later Flying Forts from Espiritu. Henderson mechanics had not slept for three days but they had made good their vow to salvage all but bullet holes. Thousand-pound and 500-pound bombs fell among the Japanese ships and beached supplies, bullets flayed and scattered enemy shore parties—while Marines on the ridges wildly cheered the Tassafaronga parade. And then, a great shout of delight broke from their throats to see a clumsy Catalina flying boat lumber into the air with two big torpedoes under her wings.

It was the *Blue Goose*, General Geiger's personal plane.

Mad Jack Cram was at the controls. Major Cram had never heard of a PBY making a daylight torpedo attack before, nor had he ever fired torpedoes. But he had flown into Guadalcanal at dusk of the preceding day and been told that there were no Avengers to use the big fish nestled beneath his wings. In that case, he replied testily, he would launch them himself. He had received five minutes' instruction from a fighter pilot whose brother flew a torpedo bomber, and then, gathering his crew, had climbed into the big Cat.

Now Cram was nursing his ship up. He made for a rendezvous with eight fighters and a dozen Dauntlesses a few miles east of Henderson, far from 30 Zeros flying cover for the ships. Major Duke Davis' Wildcats were roaring down the runway behind him, taking off even as Pistol Pete ripped at the field again.

The Dauntlesses were at 9,000 feet. They were going over. The lead plane rolled over on its back, flashing down. The Zeros above them began peeling off, riding them down. Flak rose from Tassafaronga. The *Blue Goose* was going over. She was almost vertical, going for a Japanese transport a mile away. Cram rode the controls with his eyes devouring the speedometer needle. A Catalina was built for 160 miles an hour. *Blue Goose* was coming down at 270. Her great ungainly wings wailed and flapped in an agony of stress. She would surely come apart.

Cram hauled back on the stick. *Blue Goose* began to level off at 1,000 feet. Cram went over again. *Blue Goose* came screaming in at 75 feet, flashing past two transports, shuddering at the antiaircraft burst that knocked off her navigation hatch. Now Cram was sighting off his bow at a third transport. He jerked the toggle release. The first torpedo splashed in the water and began its run. Cram yanked again. The second fell, porpoised, righted—and followed the first into the transport's side.

Five Zeros quit the dogfight to go after *Blue Goose*. Cram stood the plane on its wing and banked for Henderson Field. Behind him the transport was sinking. But the Zeros were around him, taking turns at making passes at his tail. Cram roller-coasted his ship, diving and rising, diving and rising, while the Zeros raked him homeward. *Blue Goose* was over the Henderson main strip, but Cram was going too fast to get down. He made for Fighter One, *Blue Goose* now wheezing through a hundred holes. Still the Zeros struck at his tail.

Cram began putting *Blue Goose* down. A Zero climbed his tail, just as Lieutenant Roger Haberman was also bringing his smoking Wildcat into the landing circle with lowered wheels.

Wheels still down, Haberman completed his turn, came in behind the Zero and shot it down.

Blue Goose ploughed up the strip in a glorious pancake landing. Mad Jack Cram and his crew emerged unharmed, though it would take much skill and patience to pull *Blue Goose* together again.

She had accounted for one of the three lost Japanese transports, and helped to drive the others away from Guadalcanal. The Tassafaronga tally-ho had struck a grievous blow at Lieutenant General Masao Maruyama. He had 20,000 men ashore, but he had lost most of the shells for his big guns, much of his food, and nearly all his medical supplies. The last was the worst of all, for beriberi and malaria had already begun to sweep among Maruyama's earlier arrivals and one of those

87

inveterate Japanese diarists was already setting down his lament:

> The lack of sympathy by the headquarters is too extreme. Do they know we are left on the island? Where is the mighty power of the Imperial Navy?

It was coming down The Slot again.

Once again the flares, the night aglow with muzzle blasting, the long sleek shapes in the lagoon, American feet pelting madly in the darkness—and 1,500 shells raining in upon Henderson and the perimeter from the heavies *Myoko* and *Maya*.

It went on for an hour, and then there was silence. Fearfully at first, then with growing confidence, weary Marines climbed out of their pits and foxholes and stumbled to rearward sleeping holes that were only better in that they had ponchos drawn across them. Along the airfield the pilots dragged themselves to tents and cots. Among them was Major Galer. He looked around for his friend, Major Smith. He had been talking to him when the shelling began, and they had raced for the dugout together. Galer was worried. He went outside the tent and began calling:

"Smitty? Smitty? Where are you, Smitty?"

There was a momentary silence and then, faintly, from the airfield dugout came the infuriated voice:

"Here I am, dammit! Somebody bring me my shoes, will you? I'll be damned if I'm going to walk barefooted over all those sharp-assed stones!"

There was another silence, and then, snickering, from Major Galer this time:

"How the hell'd you get out there, Smitty?"

At daylight of October 16, General Geiger calculated that he had lost 41 bombers and fighters to Japanese guns in the past three days, plus 16 more aircraft damaged. He had 25 bombers left in flyable condition, once repairs were made to the victims of *Myoko* and *Maya*, but he had only nine fighters. Geiger signaled Efate in the New Hebrides for hurry-up help.

In came 19 Wildcats and seven more Dauntlesses, led by

Lieutenant Colonel Harold (Joe) Bauer—rugged Joe Bauer who had shot down five Japanese aircraft while "visiting Guadalcanal." Bauer's Squadron 212 came in just as the Japanese launched a savage dive-bombing attack on the field and the American ships in the Bay. Bauer's gas tanks were nearly empty, but there were eight enemy Vals plummeting down on a wildly zigzagging destroyer.

Bauer went after them alone. He pulled back on the stick and went slashing up through his own antiaircraft fire and then came snarling down again. He shot down four Vals before he landed and he saved the destroyer. It was swift, as aerial combat goes, but it was then, and has remained, the most extraordinary feat of individual heroism among the Henderson airmen, men who already acclaimed Joe Bauer as the best fighter pilot the Marines had produced. Bauer got a Medal of Honor for it, and it boosted his individual score to 11.

So ended the six-day ordeal begun with the arrival of Pistol Pete. But Pistol Pete was losing his voice. The airmen had put his shells on the bottom, and this would matter greatly in the tide of battle now flowing back to land.

13

By mid-October of 1942 the struggle for Guadalcanal had become the preoccupation of the Empire. It had long since overshadowed the offensive against Port Moresby in New Guinea, where, in fact, the Australians had not only held but had pushed the Japanese 18th Army back, and had finally been joined by American soldiers in a drive on Buna-Gona.

It was now the 17th Army of Lieutenant General Haruyoshi Hyakutate which was receiving most of the men, munitions, airplanes and ships. At the conference which Fleet Admiral

Isoroku Yamamoto had called at Truk, General Hyakutate was assured that he would receive the support of the Combined Fleet. Yamamoto was giving him four aircraft carriers, four battleships, eight cruisers, twenty-eight destroyers, four oilers and three cargo ships under the divided command of Vice Admirals Chuichi Nagumo and Nobutake Kondo. Haruyoshi Hyakutate was no longer displeased with the southern Solomons assignment, when, on the night of October 17, a lighter brought him to Guadalcanal to take personal charge of the campaign.

The general landed near Kukumbona and made straight for Maruyama's headquarters there. He asked Maruyama for his battle plan. He read it carefully. In the dim light, with his thin face and great round eyeglasses, Hyakutate looked something like a lemur.

Maruyama's plan was a good one. It dovetailed with the Truk strategy whereby the Army would capture the airfield, while the Combined Fleet swept the waters clear of Americans and flew off aircraft to occupy Henderson Field. Maruyama planned three thrusts, two from the vicinity of the Matanikau and a surprise attack from the south.

On October 20 Colonel Oka's force was to cross the Matanikau far above Nippon Bridge and work down the east bank to be in position to drive behind the exposed American left flank on the night of October 21.

On that same night the remainder of Colonel Nakaguma's 4th Regiment was to cross the sandbar at the mouth of the Matanikau behind 11 tanks. The armor, drawn from the 1st Independent Tank Company, was already hidden in a tunnel cut in the jungle on the edge of the sandbar. When the order came, the tanks would crash through the last few feet of underbrush like metal monsters bursting paper hoops.

On the following night, October 22, with the tanks safely across the river and firing at the Marines in the southern hills, with Oka sweeping around the American left to the airfield, General Maruyama would deliver the surprise crusher from the south.

He had already assembled his main body—the 16th and 29th Regiments of his own Sendai Division, plus part of the 230th Regiment from the 38th Division, some dismounted cavalrymen and a battery of mountain guns—and sent them to the headwaters of the Mamara River, which was about 10 miles south and a bit west of Kukumbona. From there they would march almost directly east until they were opposite the Marines in the hills behind the airfield. Then they would slip left or north to steal up on the Americans undetected. Engineers had already gone ahead of the foot troops to hack out the 35-mile jungle passage which the Sendai commander was already calling the Maruyama Road. The march was expected to take five days. Aerial photographs had shown no difficulties of terrain, and men as tough as the soldiers of the 29th—who had once marched 122 miles in three days, double-timing at the end—should be able to cover the distance easily.

General Maruyama not only counted on surprise but also hoped to pierce the enemy line without a fight. The Sendai intelligence officer, a Lieutenant Colonel Matsumoto, having failed to obtain intelligence of the enemy by torturing a captured Marine, had beheaded the American in the honorable way and turned to searching enemy bodies. He had found an American operations map which showed many gaps in the enemy's southern line. The map had been reproduced for the Sendai's officers.

Lieutenant General Hyakutate was pleased. He agreed, also, that the American, Vandegrift, should surrender his sword at the rivermouth.

Maruyama bowed and strode off to join his main body.

The following day, October 18, far to the southeast in New Caledonia, a stocky American admiral with a bulldog face led a force of carriers into the harbor of Noumea. The great ships dropped anchor. A whaleboat drew alongside the admiral's flagship. A naval officer came aboard and handed the admiral a manila envelope. Inside it was another marked SECRET. The admiral ripped it open. It was from Admiral Chester Nimitz, the commander-in-chief of the Pacific. It said: "You will take command of the South Pacific Area and South Pacific forces immediately."

"Jesus Christ and General Jackson!" the admiral swore. "This is the hottest potato they ever handed me!"

91

William Frederick Halsey was taking over—old Bull Halsey of the craggy bristling jaw, the creed of attack and the undying hatred of the enemy. The Marines on Guadalcanal now knew they had a fighting sailor behind them.

The day after Halsey took command in the South Pacific, Secretary of the Navy Frank Knox held a press conference in Washington to discuss the perilous situation on Guadalcanal. There was a direct question: Could the Marines hold?

"I certainly hope so," the secretary replied. "I expect so. I don't want to make any predictions, but every man out there, ashore or afloat, will give a good account of himself."

Those Marines on Guadalcanal who had been jubilant to hear that Old Bull was taking over received the secretary's shy little pep talk with the wonderful bad grace which would always sustain them.

"Didja hear about Knox? It was on the 'Frisco radio. He says he don't know, but we're sure gonna give a good account of ourselves."

"Yeah, I heard—ain't he a tiger?"

The Maruyama Road had run into unexpected roadblocks. Captain Oda's engineers had slashed easily through the foothills of the Lunga Mountains, but then, three days and about 20 miles out, they had blundered into a maze of steep cliffs and a clutter of jungle-tangled ravines and gorges. General Maruyama chafed at the delay, but there was nothing he could do. A patrol might have moved along the Maruyama Road, but not almost a division of troops loaded down with burdens of 50 pounds each. Each man carried an artillery shell in addition to his own equipment. They had to cut footholds in the cliffs, haul the guns up by ropes. Rain fell constantly. Advance troops churned the underfooting into a mush which slowed the steps of following soldiers. Maruyama had to call repeated halts to close the gaps. His men were weakening, for Maruyama, having lost much food, had been forced to put them on one-third rations.

By evening of October 20 the Sendai was still far short of its intended position to the south. General Maruyama signaled his superiors by portable radio. Would the Navy hold off its sweep until October 26? The photographs made by the naval fliers had been imperfect. There *were* difficulties of terrain. Also, had he remembered to point out to General Hyakutate that General Vandegrift's surrender offer must be accepted at once, that he must come from his headquarters alone but for an interpreter?

Alexander Vandegrift was not at his headquarters that evening. He was in Noumea, conferring aboard the U.S.S. *Argonne* with Bull Halsey, Major General Millard F. Harmon, the Army's South Pacific commander, and Major General Alexander M. Patch, who would one day relieve Vandegrift. Even the commandant of the Marine Corps, Lieutenant General Thomas Holcomb, was present at this dramatic shipboard conference.

Vandegrift told his story. The facts marched forth as gaunt and unpolished as his Marines. Halsey asked:

"Are we going to evacuate or hold?"

"I can hold," Vandegrift said. "But I've got to have more active support than I've been getting."

Rear Admiral Richmond Kelly Turner was stung. He commanded the Amphibious Forces Pacific, and Kelly Turner could not accept that Marine rebuke without reply. He spoke quickly in the Navy's defense. There were getting to be fewer transports and cargo ships, fewer warships to protect them. There were no sheltering bases at Guadalcanal, and the Solomons' landlocked waters were too narrow for maneuver. There were enemy submarines.

Halsey heard him out. But he had made up his mind.

"All right," he told Vandegrift. "Go on back. I'll promise you everything I've got."

Even as Vandegrift flew back to Guadalcanal, Lieutenant General Hyakutate had decided to press the attack on the Matanikau. His irritation had not been mollified by Maruyama's nice touch about the surrender. The Navy had grown churlish. Kondo and Nagumo were badgering him: would soldiers never learn that ships sail on oil? The Combined Fleet could not remain much longer at sea. Hyakutate had better get on with it.

He did. On the afternoon of October 21, he ordered Pistol Pete to begin pounding the Third Battalion, First Marines, atop the ridges overlooking the sandbar at the rivermouth. With night, the tanks would roll.

But that afternoon Pistol Pete found himself in a fight with the five-inch rifles of the Third Marine Defense Battalion. Two of the Japanese 150's were silenced, and the others were forced to change position.

When Colonel Nakaguma's 4th Regiment came at the Marines that night with their tanks and their gobbling cries of death, the big howitzers joined the lighter ones to destroy the lead tank and send the remaining ten rumbling back into the jungle with the 4th's infantrymen swarming after them.

The Japanese repulse was so swift, the flare-up so brief, that General Vandegrift considered the entire engagement a patrol action.

It had not been, of course, it had only been Colonel Oka again. Not ten minutes after the tanks had rolled, Lieutenant General Hyakutate had learned that Oka was twenty-four hours behind schedule. He not only had not gotten into position east of the river upstream, he hadn't gotten over the river.

Hyakutate quickly called off the attack.

Next day the commander of the 17th Army arrived at the Matanikau front in a rage of command. He signaled Oka and told him that he had better get across the Matanikau and be prepared to attack the exposed left flank of the Marine line by the night of October 23. Men who malingered were to be dealt with ruthlessly.

The assault was going to be made the night of the twenty-third no matter what, and with any luck, it might just happen that Maruyama—from whom nothing had been heard since October 20—would strike at the same time.

But General Maruyama had not yet reached his point of attack on that black night of October 23, and Colonel Oka was still dragging his feet. Only Colonel Nakaguma attacked, and it would have been better for the Japanese cause if he had not. For Nakaguma was another of those Japanese officers who pressed home attacks that were no better than massed deathswarmings. They could not fight and run away, these commanders. They would not fight another day. They would look on death before defeat.

The 4th Regiment rushed into the massed fire of 10 batteries of Marine artillery, into the murderous interlocking fire of machine guns, rifles and automatic weapons. They were like moths, seeking to obliterate the light with their exploding bodies. They matched flesh against steel and were torn apart.

Only one of Nakaguma's 10 medium tanks succeeded in crossing to the east or Marine bank. It held the tank company leader, Captain Maeda. It raced over the sandbar, rolled over the barbed wire, crushed a pillbox and swung right to come clanking down on a foxhole held by Private Joe Champagne.

Champagne ducked. He fumbled for his grenade. The tank's underbelly blotted out the night. Champagne reached up, slipped the grenade into the tank's treads. He huddled down again.

Wham!

Captain Maeda's tank sloughed around out of control. A Marine half-track rolled out on the sandbar. Its 75-millimeter rifle flashed. Maeda's tank lurched. The half-track fired again.

A sheet of flame gushed from Maeda's tank. The half-track had hit the ammunition locker and the tank was blown 20 yards into the sea, where it was finished off.

Now, one by one, Marine half-tracks rolled down to the sandbar and destroyed the remaining tanks.

The attack which had begun with dark was over by ten o'clock in the night. Morning revealed a hideous spectacle on that sandbar. Nothing moved among jagged coconut stumps, twisted blackened tanks, whole tops of trees lying in brokenheaded ruin among the heaps of dead—nothing moved but the bloated crocodiles swimming lazily downstream.

14

The day after the 4th Regiment met *zemmetsu* or annihilation on the Matanikau, Colonel Akinosuke Oka explained his own unit's failure to attack with this report:

"The Regiment endeavored to accomplish the objective of diverting the enemy, but they seemed to be planning a firm defense of this region."

It was not true, there was no defense on the left of the Marines opposite Nippon Bridge, and Lieutenant General Hyakutate could not accept Oka's alibi. The colonel had again played the part of Ferdinand the Bull. But by late afternoon of October 24 the general was at last able to goad Oka into getting across the river and moving down toward that exposed left.

Oka did and moved too far.

Men of the Third Battalion, Seventh Marines, on top of the ridge where the Marine left was refused spotted Japanese soldiers moving across a lower ridge to their left. They reported it to headquarters.

General Vandegrift acted quickly. The Second Battalion, Seventh Marines, was even then moving out of reserve to relieve the Third Battalion, First, which had fought at the rivermouth the night before. Vandegrift turned this battalion south and sent it up to the undefended high ground lying about 1,000 yards east of the refused left flank.

The Marines of the reserve began moving south just as the sun began to fade from the sky to their right.

The dying sun of October 24 was on the left of Lieutenant General Maruyama's main body as it at last moved north on its march to battle. Maruyama's men had made their left turn, had quit the tortuous ravines, and were coming in undetected on the Marines who held the hills between them and Henderson Field. They could hear their own bombs exploding within the Marine perimeter a few miles in front of them. Maruyama was pleased that radio contact was being renewed with Hyakutate and that the naval liaison officer present at the Kukumbona headquarters would be able to relay news of the airfield's capture to Admiral Yamamoto, thus sending the Combined Fleet into action.

General Maruyama was confident of victory. Like Colonel Oka, he believed that he was moving on a weak point in the enemy lines. He trusted in the map provided by Matsumoto. There was no reason not to. How could Maruyama know that the map taken from the dead Marine was an American copy of a map taken from a dead Japanese early in August? How could he suspect that the American lettering on it marked positions held by the Japanese prior to the Marine landing?

Maruyama, like Oka, was not moving against a gap. He was approaching the low-lying jungle to the east of Bloody Ridge, a point held by the battalion commanded by Chesty Puller.

The sun was down.

It was dusk of Saturday night, October 24.

A young Marine on patrol outside Puller's line in the southern hills stopped dreaming of the delights of Saturday night back home and hurried to catch up with comrades who had left him behind. He paused. Behind him, just silhouetted on a low ridge, he could see a Japanese officer studying the line through field glasses. The officer disappeared. The Marine rushed on to report to his patrol leader.

Japanese south of the airfield?

Vandegrift was uneasy. He had just strengthened the Matanikau left with all he could spare from his reserve. What would he do if Puller got hit hard back there?

Probably, he thought, he would have to use the soldiers. There was a battalion of the 164th in bivouac behind the Tenaru.

The men of the U.S. 164th Infantry Regiment were sulking. They were sick and tired of being an orphan outfit, being pushed around. They had been squeezed out of their own division—the 41st—when the old National Guard "square" divisions were made "triangular," that is, cut from four to three infantry regiments. They had been tossed into another orphan outfit with the bastard name of Americal Division—not even a number!—and been pushed around the Pacific. They had landed in dismal Noumea, which was bad enough, being an oversized hatrack for Navy brass, but which was also worse with those snooty French colonials frosting the doughfoots and the fact that if there was so much as a single native girl to go skylarking with she'd surely be found doing some shavetail's laundry.

Then they were detached again and handed over to the Marines!

They had been bombed and shelled and shot at and put on the Tenaru and then been made to suffer the indignity of having fresh-faced kids five and six years their junior tell them they should have been on Guadalcanal "when it was *really* rough." Kids that couldn't grow beards, and they'd come around with their notched rifles and try to swap souvenir battle flags for the candy the 164th still possessed or for wristwatches that had not yet rusted in the jungle. Japanese "battle flags"! Even the men of the 164th knew that the Marines made them by pounding red match tips onto the center of white handkerchiefs.

The men of the 164th were sore, nor did they feel any better when they heard the rumor that they had been alerted to stand by for action in a battle expected that night.

At seven o'clock on that night of October 24, Platoon Sergeant Mitchell Paige crawled forward to the nose of the ridge position which was then being occupied to nail down the Matanikau left flank. Paige's men had reached their position in darkness. Now the sergeant was feeling around him with his hands, searching for a good position for the guns. He felt the ridge fall away sharply to either side.

"Here," he whispered to the men of his machine-gun platoon. "Put the guns here."

They set them up, moving stealthily, careful not to stumble in the mud, careful to slip the gun pintles into tripod sockets without a telltale clink of metal.

"Chow time," Paige whispered. "Where's the chow?"

They had one can of Spam and also a can of peaches "borrowed" from a rear-echelon galley on their march south to the ridge. The man carrying the peaches mumbled that he had dropped the can and it had rolled down the ridge into the jungle. There were fierce coarse things hissed in the dark and it was well for the loser of the peaches that the night veiled his face. Paige opened the Spam, tore the soft meat in pieces and pressed them into outstretched hands. The men ate.

They took up watches on their guns. It began to rain. Suddenly, after midnight, from far to their left, they heard the sound of battle.

At half-past midnight Sunday morning, October 25, the rain was coming down in a torrent, and a torrent of Japanese soldiers was washing against the line held by Chesty Puller's Marines.

Their attack came at a point perhaps 2,000 yards south of Henderson Field, and a little less than five miles to the east or left of the newly fortified ridge where Sergeant Paige and his men sat.

The Japanese came by the thousands, so many of them rushing and shrieking that the soggy ground shook beneath their feet. They hit the barbed wire even as the Marine guns erupted, and some of them came through it, using the bodies of fallen comrades as ladders over and bridges through the wire.

These were soldiers of the 29th Regiment led by the shouts of their commander, Colonel Masajiro Furumiya, inspired by the dashing sight of the 7th Company—the color company streaking through a rent in the barbed wire and charging toward the line of American pits and holes.

A few feet behind that line Chesty Puller bellowed at his

men, directing counterfire. He found one Marine lying in the tall grass. He stooped, seized him, booted him in the behind, and snarled: "Get the hell up theah, an' doan lemme se youah shirttail touch youah ass until you do!" The Marine ran forward to fight—to fight and live to boast of how old Chesty gave him a good one right between the cheeks.

Now that gap in the wire was being closed as Marine riflemen and machine-gunners opened up in concert. Colonel Furumiya and the men of the color company were cut off between the wire and the Marine foxholes. The two guns under Sergeant John Basilone—Manila John they called him—were firing full trigger, piling up bodies as the bullets streaked out at a rate of 250 rounds a minute. Soon Basilone's guns were out of ammunition. Manila John ducked out of his pit and ran to his left to get more belts. As he did, Furumiya's men, drifting to the west, overran the section of guns at Basilone's right. They stabbed two of the Marines to death and wounded three others, driving on farther to the rear after the American guns jammed when the Japanese tried to turn them on the Marines.

Basilone returned to his own pit just as a runner came up gasping: "They've got the guys on the right." Basilone raced up the rightward trail. He blundered into a barefoot private named Evans—"Chicken" they called him because of his tender eighteen years—and the Chicken was firing his rifle and screaming at the enemy: "C'mon, you yellow bastards!" Basilone ran on, jumped into the silent pit, and found that the guns were jammed. He ran back to get one of his own guns.

At his own pit, Basilone seized a machine gun and spread-eagled it across his back. He shouted at half of his men to follow him and ran back up the trail to his right. The men ran after him, overtaking him just as he reached a bend in the trail. Around the bend were half a dozen Japanese infiltrators. The Marines killed them and ran on.

Now they were in the fallen pit and the men were firing the gun Basilone had brought, while Manila John himself lay in the mud working to unblock the jammed guns. The Japanese were forming again outside the wire, gliding through the rain in bunches. Now Basilone had the guns fixed. They were set up. The men were frantically scraping mud from machine-gun belts they had dragged uptrail. Then they were firing again, and Basilone was rolling from gun to gun, shooting up each successive belt as soon as it was fed into the breech and snicked into place.

Now it was half-past one in the morning and still the men of the Sendai were rushing, while their commanding general made a jubilant report of victory back to Hyakutate. And the Sendai were falling even as the naval liaison officer back at Kukumbona relayed the message to Admiral Yamamoto and the Combined Fleet in these words: *"Banzai!* Occupied airfield."

During the next half-hour the Japanese began to falter under rising American fire. They still rushed at the wire, but when they reached that point where the bullets crisscrossed with an angry steady whispering, they began to peel off in groups, flitting through the rain-washed illumination of the shell flashes to throw themselves down in the darkness and crawl toward the Marine lines on their bellies. Sometimes Basilone and his men turned their pistols and rifles around to take on the infiltrators.

In that half-hour, it became clear to General Maruyama that his first two thrusts had failed and he had better regroup and try again. The earlier optimism must be toned down and he sent off a report to Hyakutate that the fighting was still going on. The naval officer transmitted the message to Yamamoto.

It was now a little after two in the morning and the firing had begun to die down.

At shortly after two in the morning, Sergeant Mitchell Paige and his men heard firing to their right. Unknown to them, a party of Colonel Oka's men had slipped through a draw between their right and the left of the Third Battalion, Seventh, and had overwhelmed an observation post.

Paige crawled forward on the ridge. He heard low mumbling in the jungle below. There were Japanese down there. Paige decided to force them to attack before they could discover his position. He pulled the pin from a hand grenade. His men, hearing that snick, pulled their own pins. Paige threw.

The men handed him their primed grenades and he threw these too. There were explosions, flashes—screams.

Paige's men scuttled back to their guns, bracing.

But no one came.

At half-past three in the morning the Sendai came rushing again at Lieutenant Colonel Puller's line, and at that time also the men of the 164th Infantry went into battle with the Marines.

Led by Lieutenant Colonel Robert Hall, the regiment's Third Battalion had marched from bivouac behind the Tenaru to Puller's battlefront to the southwest. They came sloshing in through the darkness, guided by the yelling and jabbering and hammering of the fight. Lieutenant Colonel Hall quickly found Lieutenant Colonel Puller, who was brief.

"I'm in command here," Chesty snapped, "and I'm feeding youah men in piecemeal whether you like it or not."

Hall had heard of Puller and this was obviously not the moment to quibble over seniority.

"Go ahead," Hall said, and the 3rd Battalion, 164th, went into line.

The soldiers went in by squads, moving in alongside squads of Marines, sometimes having to be led by hand, it was so dark, the ground was so slippery. They also held, helping to halt and shatter that third and final onslaught of the Japanese.

By seven o'clock in the morning the Sendai stopped coming, and Admiral Yamamoto's aide had flashed the word that the airfield was still American. By then also the rain had stopped.

The sun was out, falling with ghastly illumination on the sodden heaps of lifeless flesh lying sprawled before Puller's lines, warming the Marines and soldiers, setting the jungle steaming.

It was Dugout Sunday.

That thundering sabbath of the twenty-fifth of October, during which only stretcher-bearers, ammunition-carriers or airfield crews dared stay long erect, was set in motion by that prematurely jubilant *"Banzai!"* which the naval officer at

102

Kukumbona had flashed to Yamamoto at half-past one in the morning.

His subsequent messages were vague. Before he could send off the seven o'clock admission that the airfield was still American, the Japanese Combined Fleet had begun its end of the coordinated land-sea-air attack which was to crush the Americans.

Carriers flew off airplanes to obliterate remaining American air strength on Henderson Field and to sink whatever ships were found in Iron Bottom Bay. A cruiser-destroyer force made for a point behind Florida Island to enter the battle on call. Three big destroyers—*Akatsuki, Ikazuchi* and *Shiratsuyo*— sped down The Slot to shell the Guadalcanal shore and to attack shipping. And then, as the liaison officer began tempering his original jubilation, Yamamoto kept the remainder of the Combined Fleet sailing a circle 300 miles north of Guadalcanal. The situation had not only become unclear, the Japanese admiral had received reports indicating that American carrier and surface forces were coming up to Guadalcanal from southern bases.

Dugout Sunday's services began at ten in the morning, which was when *Akatsuki, Ikazuchi* and *Shiratsuyo* showed up. They steamed into the Bay with all guns going and pounded Marine coastal installations. They sank the tugboat *Seminole* and made wreckage of other little harbor craft. They looked hungrily about for other victims, and then, to their great surprise, geysers of water rose around them.

Gunners of the Third Marine Defense Battalion were blasting at the Japanese destroyers with five-inch rifles. They were scoring hits. Soon black clouds were boiling off the destroyers' sterns. Sending up a screen of smoke, *Akatsuki, Ikazuchi* and *Shiratsuyo* streaked for home.

The airplanes arrived at half-past two.

The Japanese pilots attacked thinking the airfield had been knocked out. If they had come in the morning their belief would have been correct, in effect, for the rains of the preceding night had made a mire of both runways. But General Geiger put his repair crews to work while placing a call for help with American air bases in the south, and the Seabees and engineers, aided by a hot, drying sun, had the runways operable by midafternoon. Then there began that daylong jolting rhythm of flying, fighting, landing, refueling, rearming —and flying again.

Captain Joe Foss and Lieutenant Jack Conger were among those Marine fighter pilots who struck ferociously at the first Japanese flight of 16 heavy bombers, plus escorting Zeros. Foss had been on Guadalcanal only 16 days and he was already a legend. He had shot down 11 enemy planes—had flamed four bombers on October 23 alone—and now on Dugout Sunday, riding his cockpit with a dead cigar stub clenched in his teeth, he was climbing aloft to duplicate that feat. In the first scramble Foss and three others took on six Zeros. Foss got two of the three knocked down. But his Wildcat was so riddled by bullets he had to go down for another one, bringing his pilots down with him to refuel. They went back up to close with nine of the dozens of Zeros leading a fresh formation of bombers over the field. Foss shot down two more, and dove for home again, just one plane shy of a kill for every day he had spent on the island.

Lieutenant Jack Conger fought until he ran out of ammunition. He had escorted a crippled comrade back to Henderson, fighting off Zeros all the way. He shot one down, but now, as he turned and screamed up toward an enemy fighter, the pressure of his thumb on the gun button brought no response from his wing guns. Still he flew upward at the Zero. He brought his whirling propeller blades under its tail. The Zero turned frantically, and broke in two.

Conger's plane was also staggered. It was going over, falling. Conger couldn't bring it out. That huge obliquely-sliding mirror which was the surface of Iron Bottom Bay seemed to flip up toward him. Conger strained at his escape hatch. He couldn't get out, he thought he would never get out, and that monster mirror was about to slap him. With a great wrench, Conger was free. He was barely 150 feet above the water when his parachute billowed, jerking him. He could see his plane plummet down among the coconuts, then he was into the mirror, jolted and jarred as though it possessed the very density and opaqueness of glass.

104

Conger surfaced, treading water. He slashed at the smothering shroud of his parachute. He glanced up to see another Zero falling in flames. He gaped in astonishment as its pilot floated down to water not 20 feet away from him.

Now there was a rescue boat speeding toward Conger. It came alongside, its exhaust putt-putting hollowly in the swells. Conger was hauled aboard. The boat slewed around and made for the Japanese pilot. Conger called to him, made surrender motions. The flier dived under. He came up beside the boat, kicked with both feet against its hull, and tried to swim away. The boat pursued. Conger grabbed a boathook and caught the flier by his jacket. The man struggled. Conger leaned forward. They contemplated each other, warbirds of East and West, the one rescuing, the other refusing—and the Japanese pulled out a Mauser pistol, pressed it against Conger's face and pulled the trigger.

Click!

Conger sprawled backward. *I'm dead!* he thought. But he was not, nor was the Japanese pilot, who, failing to return death for life, had placed the pistol to his own head and produced another *click*. Conger seized a water can and slammed it down on the flier's head. Limp and unconscious, the Japanese was hauled into the boat.

In all, 26 Japanese planes fell to Marine fighters and antiaircraft gunners. Marine bombers went up too, and from the hilarious shouts of their returning pilots, even the imprisoned little flier might have guessed that they had caught the Japanese ships behind Florida and left a cruiser sinking.

And yet, the flier's confusion could never match the consternation of that naval liaison officer then composing a fourth report for Admiral Yamamoto. The Army's night attack had failed. There had been "difficulty in handling the force in the complicated terrain," he reported, but General Hyakutate was going to try again that night. The Army was ready.

The Army had *better* be ready, the Navy thundered. There was a naval battle making up northeast of the Solomons and the Army must have possession of the airfield before it began.

Down the chain of command went Hyakutate's frustration. Colonel Oka had *better* attack tonight. Maruyama's Sendai had better keep faith with its motto: "Remember that Death is lighter than a feather, but that Duty is heavier than a mountain."

But heavier than duty was that mountain of despair weighing upon the men of the Sendai this night of October 25. They munched their meager ration, stunned, dispirited and wet—for the jungle continues to drip long after the sun comes out. Their officers were not sure of their position; Matsumoto's map had caused them to blunder into the Marines the preceding night. The men were still mindful of that hideous firepower which had nearly made *zemmetsu* of the 29th Regiment. What had happened to the 29th? Was it true that they had lost their colors? Where was Colonel Furumiya?

He was trapped behind the enemy lines.

The 7th Company which had carried the 29th's colors through the Marine wire had been annihilated. Only Colonel Furumiya and a staff officer had survived. Throughout the night they had blundered through the dark, hoping to rejoin their regiment. They had become lost. With day, they had gone into hiding, for the colors were wound around the waist of Colonel Furumiya. Loss of the regiment's colors to the enemy meant that the 29th would be struck from the lists in disgrace. Rather than risk exposing them to capture, Colonel Furumiya decided to lie low and await Maruyama's inevitable night attack.

The inevitability of an attack that night of October 25 was also evident to Sergeant Paige's platoon of machine-gunners, men with names like Leiphart, Stat, Pettyjohn, Gaston, Lock, McNabb, Swanek, Reilly, Totman, Kelly, Jonjeck, Grant, Payne, Hinson.

They had found their can of peaches in the jungle and had opened it with a bayonet—Guadalcanal's all-purpose instrument—and eaten. Then they dug in, certain of an attack from the fact of the myriad winking lights they had seen in the jungle. They knew these were not fireflies but the colored flashlights which the enemy used for signaling.

★

106

Lieutenant Colonel Chesty Puller was also ready, though the fury of Dugout Sunday had not given his men much time to improve their positions; there had been time to resupply the 81-millimeter mortars, those unlovely stovepipe killers of which their gunners sang:

We have a weapon that nobody loves,
They say that our gun's a disgrace,
You crank up 200, and 200 more—
And it lands in the very same place.
Oh, there's many a gunner who's blowing his top,
Observers are all going mad.
But our affection has lasted,
This pig iron bastard
Is the best gun this world ever had.

Proof of the last line was to be given shortly. At eleven o'clock that night the men of the Sendai Division came padding up the narrow jungle trails into assembly areas south of Puller's lines. Officers began to whip them into frenzy. Soon they were chanting, "U. S. Marine you going die tonight, U. S. Marine you going die tonight."

Marine mortars began falling among them. Shells flashed along the trails. The Japanese charged and the mortars stayed with them, whittling this heaviest of all Guadalcanal charges before it reached the wire. Soon the howitzers to the rear were booming.

And the Sendai Division still charged.

Colonel Oka's men had at last made a direct attack.

They struck heaviest at the ridge nose held by Sergeant Paige and his men. At two in the morning, Paige again heard low mumbling. It was much closer than the night before. The Japanese were floundering about in the bushes with less than Oriental stealth. Paige passed the word:

"Use grenades. Don't let 'em spot the guns. Fire only when you have to."

They pulled pins and threw. They grasped grenades in both hands and tore out the pins with their teeth and rolled the yellow pineapple bombs down the slopes.

107

Oka's men came bowling up at them.

"Fire!" Paige bellowed, but he needn't have, nor could he have been heard above that sudden eruption of sound and light. All of his guns were hammering, spitting orange flame a foot beyond the flash-hiders. But the enemy was swarming in. It was hand to hand. Paige could see little Leiphart down on one knee, wounded, trying to fight off three charging shapes. Paige shot down two of them with his rifle. The third bayoneted Leiphart, killed him, and Paige killed his killer. Pettyjohn was shouting that his gun was out of action. Gaston was battling a Japanese officer, blocking with his rifle while the officer swung a saber, kicking wildly after the rifle had been cut to pieces. Now part of Gaston's leg was gone. He kicked again. His foot slammed up under the officer's chin and broke his neck. Now it was fighting without memory of a blow struck, a shot fired, a wound received; now it was mindless, instinctive, reflexive; the shapes struggling on the slopes, the voices hurling wordless atavistic battle shouts, "Aaa-yeee!"; the voices crying, "Kill! Kill!" and *"Bonnn-zahee!"*; the voices hoarse with death, shrill with pain—and beneath it all ran the cracking booming chorus of the guns.

Then the attackers flowed back down the hill and vanished. The first wave had been shattered.

Paige knew they would come again, and ran quickly to Pettyjohn's disabled gun. He worked to dislodge a ruptured cartridge. He pried it free, slipped in a fresh belt of ammunition—and hot pain seared his hand. A Japanese light machine-gunner had fired a burst into the gun and wrecked it. With that burst came the second wave.

Oka's men flowed upward in a yelling mass. Grant, Payne and Hinson held out on the left, although they were all wounded. In Paige's center, Lock, Swanek and McNabb were hit and carried to the rear by corpsmen. The Japanese moved into the gap in the center. Paige ran to his right, hunting for men to counterattack the Japanese, for another gun to put back in the center. He found the machine gun manned by Kelly and Totman. They were protected by a squad of riflemen. Paige ordered the machine-gunners to break down their gun, told the riflemen to fix bayonets, and then, with the cry

"Follow me!" he led them back to drive the enemy out of the center. Paige set the gun up. He fired it until dawn, while Kelly and Totman fed it ammunition. At dawn, Sergeant Paige saw another of his platoon's machine guns standing unattended on the forward nose of the ridge. There were short men in khaki and mushroom helmets crawling toward it. Paige got up and ran forward. . . .

To the left of Paige's position, where the second wave of Oka's men had made a penetration, the fight had gone badly for F Company of the Second Battalion, Seventh. Oka's men had forced F Company back and captured a ridge on the extreme left of the Second Battalion's line. They put 150 men in position. They set up two heavy machine guns. They began raking the Marines from the flank.

In that early-morning light in which Sergeant Paige had spotted the machine gun, Major Odell (Tex) Conoley could see vapor rising from the Japanese machine guns as the hot steel condensed the jungle water on the barrels. Conoley realized that the Japanese now had a strong penetration which could be built up for a breakthrough. He was the battalion executive officer, and only a few of the men around him were riflemen. But there were also at hand a few bandsmen serving as litter-bearers, a trio of wiremen, a couple of runners and three or four messmen who had brought up hot food the night before and had stayed. There were 17 in all. Tex Conoley formed this bobtail band and charged.

They went in hurling grenades. They knocked out the machine guns before the Japanese could fire at them and they came in with such sudden force that they routed the startled defenders of the ridge crest. And then the mortarmen shortened range to draw a curtain of steel across the forward slope of the ridge while Conoley consolidated and received reinforcements.

Daylight of October 26 lighted the destruction of the Japanese 2nd or Sendai Division.

The assault against Puller's lines had gone on all night, but it had produced not a single penetration. It ended at dawn with Japanese losses in proportion to the fury of their charge. It was the most savage assault, it became the most stunning defeat.

The Sendai could not fight again as a unit on Guadalcanal.

Sergeant Paige got to the gun first. . . .

He dove for the trigger, got it, squeezed it—and killed the crawling Japanese. A rain of enemy fire came down on Paige. Bullets spattered off the ridge shale, spurting, squealing away in richochet. Paige kept firing. Three men ran to him with ammunition belts—Stat, Reilly and Jonjeck. Stat went down with a bullet in the belly. Reilly reached the gun, took a bullet in the groin, and went down kicking—nearly knocking Paige off balance. Jonjeck came in with a belt and a bullet in the shoulder. As he stooped to feed the gun, Paige saw a piece of flesh go flying off Jonjeck's neck.

"Get the hell back!" Paige yelled.

Jonjeck refused. Paige hit him on the jaw. Jonjeck obeyed.

It was full light now, and Paige was scurrying back and forth, moving his gun to avoid the inevitable rain of grenades greeting each burst. In the tall grass below the ridge some 30 Japanese sprang erect. One of them put field glasses to his eyes. He signaled a charge.

Paige triggered a long searing, sweeping burst and the Japanese vanished from sight like puppets pulled on a string. Then Sergeant Mitchell Paige charged himself. He called to his riflemen. He slung two belts of ammunition crisscross over his shoulders. He unclamped the gun, yanked it from its cradle and cradled the burning-hot water jacket across his left arm.

"Let's go!" he yelled.

Straight downhill they charged, screaming their rebel yells —"Ya-hoo! Yaaaa-hoo!"—firing from the hip as they went, obliterating all before them while Paige aimed a disemboweling burst at the enemy officer who had popped up out of the grass. And then they were in the jungle and it was strangely quiet.

It was the hush that comes upon the end of battle, as eerie

as that long white snakelike blister that ran from the fingertips to the forearm of Platoon Sergeant Mitchell Paige.

15

On October 26, while land fighting sputtered out on Guadalcanal, the naval battle which Admiral Yamamoto expected was fought in waters roughly 300 miles to the east.

Yamamoto, who had always sought a major engagement with the American fleet, hurled his forces into the fight as eagerly as Bull Halsey, who sent Rear Admiral Thomas Kincaid into action with the signal: "Attack! Repeat—Attack!"

But the air-sea engagement known as the Battle of the Santa Cruz Islands fell short of a clear-cut decision. The Americans lost the carrier *Hornet* and a destroyer to submarine attack, and 76 American planes went down. The unsinkable *Enterprise* was again hit. The Japanese suffered severe damage to two carriers and a heavy cruiser and lost 100 aircraft. Minor damage was about even.

Santa Cruz was a disappointment to both sides, but neither side allowed the stand-off to weaken its resolve to fight on for Guadalcanal.

Already, in the final days of October, while the surviving ships of both nations steamed north to Truk and south to Noumea, the Americans were sending more ships to the South Pacific area and Marine and Army units were under orders for movement to the island.

Up in Rabaul, Lieutenant General Hyakutate was taking the last shot from his locker. He was calling on the 17th Army's reserve division, the 38th. Hyakutate had already fed in the Ichiki Detachment, the Kawaguchi Brigade, the Sendai

Division, and a handful of lesser units. Now he would send roughly 15,000 troops down The Slot, the bulk of that 38th or Nagoya Division commanded by Lieutenant General Tadayoshi Sano.

On Guadalcanal itself in the final days of October, the broken remnants of the Sendai Division, together with the survivors of all those other units which had come to the island since early August, were streaming westward through the jungle. They were disorganized, starving, wounded and sick. Some 5,000 Japanese died beneath Marine guns in those attacks which began on October 21, and which, after Maruyama's main thrust was shattered on October 24-26, erupted sporadically in small local actions or jungle skirmishes until the month ended.

Among these dead was Colonel Furumiya. He and his staff officer had not been able to find their way back to the jungle south of the American lines. They had not eaten for days. They had barely enough strength to tear the 29th's colors into bits and grind them into the mud with their feet. They had not burned the flag because the smoke might give them away. Then Colonel Furumiya wrote a letter which the staff officer was to deliver to Maruyama, although it would actually be taken from the officer's dead body by the Marines who killed him. Furumiya wrote:

> . . . I do not know what excuse to give . . .
>
> I am sorry I have lost many troops uselessly and for this result which has come unexpectedly. We must not overlook firepower. When there is firepower the troops become active and full of spirit. But when firepower ceases they become inactive. Spirit exists eternally.
>
> I feel sleepy because of exhaustion for several days.
>
> I am going to return my borrowed life today with short interest.

Colonel Furumiya straightened. He placed a pistol to his head. He bowed in the direction of Tokyo and the Emperor, and the staff officer pulled the trigger.

★

112

Chesty Puller was also writing a letter, composing it mentally while he lay on a hospital cot with seven pieces of shrapnel in his legs.

Puller had been helping wiremen repair communications wire in a patrol to the east of the Tenaru when an enemy shell burst among them, wounding Puller. A Navy corpsman quickly gave him aid and began to write out an evacuation tag.

Chesty tore it from the corpsman's hand and flung it at him. "Go label a bottle with that goddam tag!" he roared.

But Puller had been forced to accept hospital treatment. Now he lay on his cot, thinking. He had had a close call with the corpsman. He could have been evacuated and sent Stateside, out of the war. Automatically, the words of a request to Headquarters began forming in his mind: ". . . therefore I respectfully request . . . duty overseas with a combat unit . . . for the duration of the war . . ."

He would write it as soon as he returned to his men, with all but one of the shrapnel pieces pried from his legs, which would be at the end of that dreadful black month of November.

16

It was in November that the Marines of Major General Alexander Vandegrift came close to losing their minds.

A bitter aching fatigue had come upon them. They had met the enemy on the beaches, in caves, atop the hills, down in the jungle swamps—and they had defeated him. They had been battered by every weapon in the arsenal of modern war. They had been blown from their holes or been buried in them. They had not slept. They had been ravaged by malaria, weakened by dysentery, nagged by tropical ulcers and jungle rot, scorched by the sun or drenched by the rain. They had met each ordeal with the hope of victory, and had survived only to prepare for greater trial. They had come to Guadalcanal lean and muscular young men, and now there was not one of them who had not lost twenty pounds, and there were some who had lost fifty. They had come here with high unquenchable spirit, but now that blaze of ardor was flickering low and there was a darkness gathering within them and their minds were retreating into it.

All the world was circumscribed by their perimeter. Guadalcanal had become Thermopylae multiplied by ninety days. There might be ninety more, for all they knew, for there seemed no way out, around or through. This was that "feeling of expendability" of which so much has been written, but which, like a toothache, can never be understood but only felt. It was a long shuddering sigh of weariness with which men rehearsed in their minds what had gone before, wondering dully, not that it had been sustained, but in what new hideous shape it would reappear. It was a sense of utter loneliness made poignant by their longing for encouragement from home, which never seemed to be forthcoming, by their hope of help, which was always being shattered. It seemed to these men that their country had set them down in the midst of the enemy and left them there to go it alone. They could not understand—had no wish to understand—that high strategy which might assign a flood of men and munitions to another theater of war, a trickle to their own. They reasoned only as they fought: that a man in trouble should get help, and here they were alone.

So they turned in upon themselves. They developed that vacant, thousand-yard stare—lusterless unblinking eyes gazing out of sunken, red-rimmed sockets. They drew in upon themselves in little squad groups, speaking constantly in low voices to each other, rarely to men of other units. They avoided those top NCO's and officers who might put them on working parties unloading ships. They were not shirking duty, they were saving strength—for the daily patrols, for the ordeal of the night watch with its terrors of the imagination, terrors fancied but real. Some of these men had not the strength to go to the galley to eat, for galleys usually lay in the lowlands behind the lines. Weakened men might get down to the galley, but they could not get back up. Their friends brought them food, just as men brought food to buddies sickened by malaria but not sick enough to occupy a precious cot in the regimental sick bays. Men with temperatures a few points above 100 were not regarded as bona fide malaria cases. There had been only 239 of these in September, there had been 1,941 of them in October—and before November ended there would be 3,200 more.

So these men faced the month of November, forgetting the outside world, forgetting even that they were Americans— mindful only that they were Marines and trying always for those flashes of rough comedy which could nourish their spirit.

Sometimes men stood on the hills and shouted insults at an unseen or nonexistent enemy in the darkened jungle. They called Emperor Hirohito "a bucktoothed bastard." They dwelt at loving length on the purity of his lineage. They yelled unprintables at Premier Tojo while ascribing to him every vice in the book of human depravity. And there came an astonishing night when a thin reedy voice shrilled up at them in outraged retaliation:

"F—— Babe Ruth!"

So went November on Guadalcanal, the month which General Vandegrift began with another offensive west and a counterinvasion move east.

On November 1 a force of roughly 5,000 Marines moved across the Matanikau. Vandegrift was again hoping to prevent an enemy build-up to the west, as well as to destroy the disorganized survivors of the October battles. He hoped also to raise morale with a successful offensive and to knock out Pistol Pete, now firing again, and all other enemy artillery to the west. The western force moved cautiously at first, striking along the coast toward Kukumbona.

On the same day another force of Marines was trucked to the Tenaru preparatory to crossing the river next day. Admiral Halsey had already notified Vandegrift that Koli Point, about a dozen miles east of the Tenaru, was probably going to be the next enemy landing place. Halsey was also worried about the security of Aola Bay, 18 miles east of Koli Point, where he hoped to build another airstrip and where engineers and the newly arrived Second Raider Battalion were to land on November 3. An enemy unit at Koli Point could cut communications between the perimeter and the Aola Bay force. So Vandegrift was sending troops east to prevent a Koli Point landing.

The eastern force was the same Second Battalion, Seventh Marines, which had stopped Oka. It was led by Lieutenant Colonel Herman Henry Hanneken, the "King of the Banana Wars" who had fought as a sergeant in Haiti, meeting the Caco leader, King Charlemagne, in personal combat and killing him.

The next morning, November 2, Hanneken's battalion crossed the Tenaru and began a forced march to Koli Point. They reached it before dusk, crossed the Nalimbiu River which cuts through it, and then also crossed the Metapona River another few miles east. They set up a coastal defensive perimeter on the east bank of the Metapona. And then, in the fading light of day, they saw three Japanese ships slip into the lee of the coast another mile east and begin unloading troops. Hanneken watched helplessly. Rain had put his radios out of commission, and he had strung communications wire no farther east then the Nalimbiu.

In three hours, the 230th Infantry Regiment, vanguard of the 38th or Nagoya Division, came ashore with supplies and guns—and the cruiser, destroyer and transport which had brought them sailed away.

Next morning, Hanneken decided to attack. His mortars opened up. The Japanese replied with an artillery barrage and themselves began attacking. They came down the beach in superior force and Hanneken withdrew. He got back behind the Metapona, set up, and was attacked again.

A destroyer had put a Japanese landing party ashore in front of Hanneken's Marines.

At about the same time west of the Matanikau, the Fifth Marines closed in on a few hundred Japanese caught in a trap around Point Cruz and destroyed them with bayonets. Next day the Fifth was to sweep on to Kukumbona.

116

But they would not. That night they were under orders to return to the perimeter next day, for Lieutenant Colonel Hanneken's radios had at last begun to function and the beleaguered commander had asked for reinforcements. Vandegrift was calling off his western offensive again, and planning a trap for the Japanese 230th Infantry.

The Marine general ordered the First Battalion, Seventh, east by boat to reinforce Hanneken, who was even then successfully forcing his way west of the Nalimbiu River. The unit which landed in front of him was not large enough to contain him. Hanneken set up a beachhead 400 yards wide and 300 yards inland and at midnight the reinforcing battalion arrived and joined his defense line.

Next Vandegrift ordered his air to strike everything the Japanese had in the east, especially with an eye toward protecting the Aola Bay airfield-construction force which had also landed November 3.

Finally, he sent the 164th Infantry Regiment on a march southeast. This was begun November 4, even as Hanneken's force attacked eastward again and recrossed the Nalimbiu. When the 164th was far enough southeast, or behind the Japanese, it would wheel and face north to the sea. Hanneken, meanwhile, would turn the enemy inland. Thus, the soldiers of the 164th Infantry would become the anvil on which the hammer blows of the Seventh Marines would shatter the enemy.

As a final touch, to cut off and annihilate any Japanese who might burst out of the trap, Vandegrift was going to place another force still farther south. He had just the outfit to do it.

Carlson's Raiders.

They specialized in private wars, these men of Carlson's. They had made the hit-and-run raid on Makin Island on August 25, and though they had been wildly acclaimed in the States, their score of roughly 100 enemy dead had failed to impress the dogged, sardonic defenders of Guadalcanal. For the "Gung Ho Boys" of Evans Carlson were not popular with brother Marines. They regarded themselves as an elite of an elite, they had volunteered for the Raiders' special mission of staging commando-style raids, they had all answered "Yes" to their commander's unique question, "Could you cut a Jap's throat without flinching?"—and because of this, because of Makin, because they could march and fight on an unchanging ration of rice, tea and bacon, they thought themselves tougher than the ordinary Marine.

But the "ordinary" Marine, if such exists, could not agree. They now knew to the last cruel degree of adversity the difference between the unromantic foot-slogger who hits-and-holds and the dashing beach-leaper who hits-and-runs. Even the Raiders' motto of "Gung Ho"—the Chinese phrase for "Work Together" which Carlson had learned during his prewar service with the Chinese Eighth Route Army—was not likely to thrill or awe these ordinary Marines. It was more likely to call forth sarcasm. If the Marine Corps' own slogan of "Semper Fidelis" was often interpreted to mean "I got mine, how'd you make out?" the Raiders' flamboyant "Gung Ho!" could receive the sneering twist, "Which way's the photographers?"

Carlson's Raiders were now at Aola Bay. On November 5 they moved west toward the Japanese who had attacked Hanneken. They sloshed up the trails following that tall, lean, long-nosed, passionate man who had given them their individuality and their battle cry, unaware, as he was unaware, that "Gung Ho!" now must prove itself beneath the eyes of the most critical audience they knew—the ordinary Marines of Guadalcanal.

On November 8, while Vandegrift's eastward forces were still maneuvering to spring their trap, Vice Admiral Halsey came to Guadalcanal.

He came in without fanfare. He put on Marine dungarees and boondockers and rode in a jeep around the perimeter. His staff officers begged him to stand up, to wave, to do anything that would let the men know that Bull Halsey was there. He refused.

It would be "too damn theatrical," he said, it would be an affront to the weary men who had held this island for three months.

At noon Halsey went to Vandegrift's headquarters for lunch.

118

It was a surprisingly good meal. There was even apple pie. Admiral Halsey was so impressed that he wished to compliment Vandegrift's cook.

"Sergeant," Vandegrift called, "the Admiral would like to speak to you."

Butch Morgan came out of his tent-galley. He drew a tattoed forearm across his glistening handlebar mustache and grimy stubble of beard. He carefully wiped his hands on his T-shirt.

"Sergeant," Admiral Halsey said grandly, "I want to compliment you on your cooking. Especially the apple pie. It was terrific!"

Sergeant Morgan shifted his feet sheepishly while that awful thing called a blush colored his wrinkled, weather-leathered face. He looked at his general in agony, and then he burst out:

"Oh, bullshit, Admiral—you don't have to say that!"

The admiral and the general exchanged glances, and the sergeant was mercifully dismissed. The next day Bull Halsey flew back to Noumea, heartened to hear that Archie Vandegrift still thought he could hold, convinced that men fed by such cooks could never be defeated.

One day later, November 10, those men of Alexander Vandegrift had pulled the string on the Japanese to the east. They killed 350 of them, against their own losses of 40 dead, 120 wounded. They captured 15 tons of rice, 55 boats and much of the enemy's artillery. But most of the 230th escaped, pouring through a gap blasted in the inland line held by the 2nd Battalion, 164th. They fled westward toward Hyakutate's reorganizing remnants, moving over the trail which the Kawaguchi Brigade had cut around the Marine perimeter in September. Following them like a scourge came Carlson's Raiders.

Another private war had begun. With only an occasional air-drop of ammunition and rice, disdainful of help or the barest report which might acknowledge the fact of the larger war raging seaward, Carlson's Raiders began to whittle the retreating 230th Regiment.

They struck the Japanese column twelve times, falling savagely on the flanks and rear, vanishing almost as suddenly as they had appeared—employing that simple guerrilla tactic which Carlson had learned from the Chinese. The Raider main body marched in a line parallel to the retreat of the Japanese main body, sometimes on the right side, sometimes on the left. Directly behind the Japanese came Raider patrols. Each time the patrols ran into large numbers of Japanese they opened fire. Whereupon the enemy would begin to rush reinforcements to his rear. As he did, Carlson's main body struck from the flank with concentrated firepower.

Carlson's Raiders killed 500 men of the 230th Regiment with this tactic, and when they returned to the Marine lines 30 days after they had set out from Aola Bay, with only 17 of their comrades fallen, they found that "Gung Ho!" was no longer a cry of derision among their brother Marines. They also found that their private war had run concurrently with the general war they had left—for the tide of battle on Guadalcanal had at last turned.

And it turned at sea.

17

"Commence firing!" Rear Admiral Daniel Callaghan shouted. "Give 'em hell, boys!"

Callaghan's little stopgap fleet drove ahead; his ships plunged straight into the flaming guns of the mighty Japanese fleet which had come south to pulverize Henderson Field. Guns roaring, sterns down, keels carving hard white wakes in the glittering obsidian waters of Iron Bottom Bay, they rushed on to destruction—to the fiercest surface battle of the war.

Callaghan's fleet had come north to escort the Army's 182nd Infantry Regiment to Guadalcanal. There were his own flagship, the cruiser *San Francisco*, the other cruisers *Atlanta*—with Rear Admiral Norman Scott aboard her—*Portland*, *Helena* and *Juneau;* and the destroyers *Laffey, Cushing, Sterrett, O'Bannon, Aaron Ward, Barton, Monssen* and *Fletcher.* They covered the 182nd's landing November 11, and when 32 Japanese torpedo bombers and fighters came winging over The Slot the afternoon of November 12, their antiaircraft guns joined Henderson's fighters in knocking all but one of them from the skies.

In the afternoon succeeding that fifteen-minute flurry came word of the Japanese bombardment fleet sweeping down from the Shortlands: the battleships *Hiei* and *Kirishima,* the cruiser *Nagara,* and 14 of those big Nipponese destroyers.

To stop them Admiral Turner had only Uncle Dan Callaghan and his five cruisers and eight destroyers. He ordered Callaghan to attack.

Admiral Kondo had to be held off for at least one night, for mighty *Enterprise* had been repaired and was tearing north with a load of warplanes to hunt out the Japanese transports bringing the rest of the Nagoya Division to Guadalcanal. The planes would need to land at Henderson Field. Therefore Henderson must not be bombarded.

Turner's decision was made after the twilight in which Callaghan's ships stood out to sea. They returned at midnight. At a quarter of two in the morning of November 13 Callaghan stood on *San Francisco*'s bridge and shouted his rallying cry and the battle was joined.

It was as though the world were being remade. It was cataclysm ripping matter apart like paper. Searchlights slashed the star-shell-showered night. Gunflashes flitted like bolts of summer lightning. The wakes of speeding ships were crisscrossed by the thin foaming lines of racing torpedoes, blotted out by the flaming geysers of their collision. And above the smoking roar of battle, Admiral Callaghan was crying over the Talk Between Ships:

"We want the big ones, boys, we want the big ones!"

Little *Laffey* took on a big one. She ran in under great *Hiei*'s mighty 14-inch turrets and peppered her bridge. She was so close that *Hiei*'s pagoda silhouette seemed to sway above

121

her. *Hiei* thundered and *Laffey* lurched and began to burn. *San Francisco* was dueling *Hiei*, hurling salvo after salvo into her superstructure. *Hiei* thundered again. A full salvo of 14-inchers tore into *San Francisco's* bridge, killing Callaghan and every other man there. *San Francisco's* gun turrets began firing on local control, and her salvos were rocking crippled *Atlanta*. Admiral Norman Scott was dead; the commander who had won the Battle of Cape Esperance had fallen from our own fire. Silhouettes plunging in and out of smoke were difficult to determine. American fired on American, Japanese on Japanese—and every ship but *Fletcher* was hit. *Barton* blew up. *Monssen* sank. So did *Cushing, Laffey*—and the cruisers *Juneau* and *Atlanta*.

But the Japanese were running. Every one of them had been staggered. Destroyer *Yudachi* was going down. So would *Akatsuki*. Admiral Kondo's ships were streaking north, and limping behind them, rudderless, her hull rent with jagged holes from the twin torpedoes of little *Sterrett*, her superstructure a mass of wreckage from 85 shell hits, came great *Hiei*.

After her came the fighters and bombers from Henderson Field. Though Callaghan and Scott and many of their men had died, though the Americans had lost six ships, Henderson had not been scratched. The battle which Fleet Admiral King called "the fiercest naval battle ever fought" had served its purpose, the preservation of the airborne Marine fighters and bombers that were now coming to kill *Hiei*. They slashed down on the eight Zeros sent south to cover her and shot them down. Major Joe Sailer planted a bomb on *Hiei's* remaining antiaircraft turrets and knocked them out. Captain George Dooley's quartet of Avengers sent another torpedo flashing into the great ship's hull. Seven Dauntlesses fell upon her with thousand-pounders. Nine Avengers from *Enterprise* joined the assault, and full five more attacks were made on *Hiei* that day. Still the great sea monster wallowed in the swells, glowing cherry red, sailing an aimless circle, now making for Guadalcanal, now drifting north again—refusing to go under.

At night the Japanese scuttled her. By morning only a shining oil slick two miles long marked the sun-dappled seas off Savo, marking the place where great *Hiei* sank.

122

But before that morning, the Japanese Navy again came to Henderson Field. Gunichi Mikawa, who had won the Battle of the Five Sitting Ducks three months before, led six cruisers and six destroyers down to Savo again. They arrived at midnight. Standing off the island's cone, Mikawa sent in *Suzuya* and *Maya* while his flagship *Chokai* and the others covered for them. The two heavies hurled 1,000 shells into the island. They would have hurled more, but six little torpedo boats crept from the creeks and coves of Tulagi Harbor and came with a roar at the big ships. They loosed a spread of torpedoes, hit cruiser *Kinugasa* and drove the rest away.

Gunichi Mikawa, who had passed up the chance to sink the American transports three months ago, sinking their escorts like a wolf killing the dogs and letting the sheep go, was once again departing Savo Island with that high speed which the exultant torpedo-boaters described as the act of "hauling ass."

Then it was full morning, and in the daylight of November 14 the Wildcats and Dauntlesses and Avengers were up early to hunt out Mikawa's force. The Japanese shelling had destroyed only two planes and damaged 16 others, and Fighter One had been manhandled swiftly into shape.

The Marine fliers found Mikawa's ships under a cover of fleecy clouds. They put torpedoes into crippled *Kinugasa*, planted bombs on two more cruisers and a destroyer—and then, calling for *Enterprise*'s fliers to come north to finish *Kinugasa* and batter the others, they flew back to Guadalcanal in time to launch the slaughter of the Nagoya Division known as the Buzzard Patrol.

Commander Tadashi Yamamoto stood on the bridge of his destroyer *Hoyashio* as it plunged south under empty blue skies. It looked as though the convoy was going to make it undetected. There were no enemies aloft and none over the horizon. Eleven transports stuffed with about 12,000 men, plus 12 escorting destroyers, seemed destined to arrive safely off western Guadalcanal that night.

It had been so predicted. Admiral Mikawa had radioed the utter destruction of Henderson Field and reported the absence of enemy surface ships.

This was well. Even Commander Yamamoto, accustomed to his nation's indifference to the comfort of its soldiers, felt uneasy at the sight of those troopships looking like drifting logs aswarm with ants.

It was a little after noon. There were less than six more hours to go. And then Yamamoto heard the motors.

The Americans came hurtling down from the skies, every last precious airplane which Henderson Field could put aloft. Major Joe Sailer, Major Bob Richard and the Navy's Lieutenant Al Coffin were among the first to strike. Thousand-pound eggs tucked beneath their Dauntless bellies fell away, described that dreadful yawning parabola—and exploded on crowded decks in leaping sheets of flame and flying steel. Two such bombs gave one of the transports its mortal wounds, six more left another troopship dead in the water, two others crippled a destroyer.

Flights now came from everywhere, from *Enterprise*, from Espiritu Santo, from the Fijis. They flew in, dropped their bombs, launched their torpedoes, strafed and flew away—sometimes to their own base, sometimes to Henderson for rearming. Zeros roared down from Rabaul to intercept them, but there were Marine fighters such as Captain Joe Foss and Lieutenant Colonel Joe Bauer flashing among them, shooting them down or driving them away from the diving Dauntlesses or skimming Avengers. Nor could the Zeroes tarry long. The range was now in the Americans' favor. When they left, Marine and Navy pilots, the Army Lightning fighters lately come to Guadalcanal, swooped down at masthead level to rake decks already slippery and running red with blood.

Even the sea about those listing, settling, burning transports was incarnadine with Japanese blood. The water was dotted with thousands of bobbing heads—men blown overboard, men who had jumped to flee the fires only to feel the bullets sting and sear among them. It was merciless, it had to be merciless. Every Japanese safely ashore on Guadalcanal was another soldier a Marine must kill. Men vomited in their cockpits to see the slaughter they were spreading. They dove and saw with horror how the decks and bunks and bulkheads

124

visible through jagged, gaping holes were glowing red with heat.

It went on until nightfall, until seven of the transports were sunk or sinking. The remaining four staggered shoreward in flames to beach themselves near Kukumbona, putting a few hundred leaderless soldiers ashore before they were destroyed by Marine fliers, the destroyer *Meade* and the five-inch batteries of the Marine Third Defense Battalion. Of the 12,000 men of the Nagoya Division who sailed south, something less than 5,000 survived the scourging of the Buzzard Patrol. Most of these were taken aboard the destroyers and carried north. Some reached Guadalcanal by boat. Others were scattered in ragged dispirited groups throughout the Central Solomons. And of all the supplies which General Hyakutate sent south, only five tons got ashore.

It was a stunning victory, almost absolute, but for the loss of the incomparable Joe Bauer, who was shot down and never seen again.

To Vandegrift's Marines it seemed that they had been saved.

The great enemy convoy had been destroyed at sea. They would be reinforced, they would be relieved, they would sling their rotted field packs on their shoulders, seize their rusted rifles—and sail away from this horrible island forever.

But not yet.

If the virtue of the Japanese warrior was his tenacity, as it was, then the defect of that virtue was his inflexibility.

Among those admirals whom the great Admiral Yamamoto had sent to reinforce Guadalcanal or to knock out Henderson Field, none was more tenacious than Vice Admiral Nobutake Kondo. Nor more inflexible.

Kondo's plan had called for the shelling of Henderson on three successive nights. The first night, November 12, had been a failure ending in disaster—the loss of *Hiei*. The second night had been better, but no success when balanced against the daylight bombing of Admiral Mikawa's bombardment group and the calamity befalling the ships and men of the Nagoya Division.

Now it was the third night, that of November 14. Nobutake Kondo kept to his plan. He was headed for Henderson Field with battleship *Kirishima*, heavy cruisers *Atago* and *Takao*, two light cruisers and a flock of nine destroyers. He was loaded for bombardment, and he was not expecting a fight. Only those tiny torpedo boats which had buzzed Mikawa the night before might stand in his way, and the destroyers would make *sukiyaki* of these.

Even if the Americans had capital ships available, he was sure they would not dare risk them in the narrow waters of Iron Bottom Bay.

It was getting on to midnight as a trio of torpedo boats slipped out of Tulagi Harbor. They took up station at Savo's north gate. They believed themselves to be all that was left to defend Henderson Field against the great fleet coming down. The sea was calm, the night air soft and fragrant. A first-quarter moon had set behind Cape Esperance. The pale gold gleaming beneath the violet vault of the heavens had vanished from the surface of the sea, and the lookouts peered anxiously into the dark.

They stiffened. Two great shapes came gliding toward them.

The Americans did have big ships and they were risking them in the narrow waters of Iron Bottom Bay.

Bull Halsey had sent Rear Admiral Willis Augustus Lee charging north from Noumea with the new 16-inch-gunned *South Dakota* and *Washington* and a hastily assigned screen of four destroyers. Lee had no battle plan or radio call-signal, and he had very little information other than that the Japanese heavies were coming down.

Admiral Lee was hungering for intelligence as his ships swept west of Savo, turned north, swung east and put the hulking island off to the right, unaware that he had also put two little torpedo boats to his left. Admiral Lee signaled Guadalcanal, using the code word, "Cactus." Back came the exasperating reply:

"We do not recognize you."

Admiral Lee decided to play it by ear. Archie Vandegrift was his personal friend. He would remember Lee's Annapolis nickname.

"Cactus, this is Lee. Tell your big boss Ching Lee is here and wants the latest information."

Silence.

And then, over the Talk Between Ships from the softly chatting torpedo boat skippers, came this:

"There go two big ones, but I don't know whose they are."

Unrecognized to his right, suspected to his left, Admiral Lee quickly called Guadalcanal.

"Cactus, refer your big boss about Ching Lee. Chinese, catchee? Call off your boys!"

Guadalcanal replied: "The Boss has no additional information," and Admiral Lee took his battleships into the Bay. He about-faced and sailed west again. It was close to midnight when he addressed the startled PT-boat skippers:

"This is Ching Lee. Get out of my way. I'm coming through!"

The little boats scurried aside and the battleships went through.

At sixteen minutes past one in the morning, Lee's radar screens were covered with approaching pips and there was a babble of Japanese voices on the radio-telephone.

It went hard at first for the Americans. *Preston, Benham* and *Walke* took the full brunt of shoals of Japanese torpedos and were sunk. *South Dakota* was pinioned like a big bug on the cold white shafts of enemy searchlights and was shuddering under the impact of their shells. But Lee's flagship *Washington* had tracked mighty *Kirishima* and her terrible sixteen-inchers were tearing her apart. *Kirishima* was a mass of flames topside, and would soon join her sister *Hiei* on the bottom of the sea. And now *South Dakota* was helping *Washington* batter the heavy cruisers *Atago* and *Takao*. Her great guns flashed and smoked above the litter of dead and wreckage topside. The Japanese heavies dragged themselves out of the fight. They would not see action again for many, many months. The destroyers and lights fled after them.

127

It was quiet on the Bay.

Ching Lee sailed back to Noumea with triumphant *Washington,* with valiant *South Dakota,* with lucky little *Gwin.*

Never again would Japanese battleships come out to fight until they sailed to their fiery *Götterdämmerung* in the narrow seas of Surigao Strait two years hence. The three-day Naval Battle of Guadalcanal was over.

The Marines had held, and now they were truly saved.

18

It was December 9 and command of Guadalcanal was passing from the Marines to the Army.

Major General Vandegrift had again put together an offensive to the west and had finally seized the high ground he wished to hold. The Army would direct the clean-up of the island.

The last weeks of November and early days of December were relatively quiet, though the enemy continued to sneak in a few thousand troops by barge. On November 30 Japan sent down the last supplies by sea, and won the Battle of Tassafaronga when the torpedoes of eight of her destroyers drove off the American force trying to intercept them.

Aerial battles sputtered sporadically, there were infrequent bombings, but Henderson Field was gradually shaping up as the great forward bastion of American air power in the Pacific. From the 31 Marine aircraft with which Cactus Air Force was launched on August 20, Henderson's strength had slowly risen through September, had sunk to that disastrous low of 14 after the Night of the Battleships, and was now climbing toward 150.

Troop strength had increased concurrently. Vandegrift now commanded his own First Marine Division as well as all but one infantry regiment of the Second Marine Division and the

Army's American Division. With these went supporting troops and specialists.

As Major General Alexander Vandegrift handed over command to Major General Alexander Patch on this day of December 9, the men who had done so much to make the Rising Sun stand still—the men of Vandegrift's First Marine Division —were coming down from the hills.

Some of these Marines had spent as many as 122 consecutive days on the lines without relief. They gaped in astonishment at the mountains of food heaped within supply dumps behind their perimeter, for they had only dreamed of this while their sodden bellies growled with rice and Argentine corned beef. They saw big trucks raising clouds of dust along the coastal road, great four-engined bombers roaring off the airfield, ships of all sizes in the Bay. They saw the new cemetery, serried ranks of white crosses broken here and again with stars of David. They were astounded to hear that there was an open-air movie near the airfield, and most of them refused to go—for they wanted nothing of a luxury that belittled their own hard memories of this island.

Then they marched down to the beach to take ship. The Fifth Regiment left first on December 9, the First Marines by December 22, the Seventh Marines before January.

But they could not really march. They stumbled. They were ragged, bearded, sick, emaciated. They had not the strength to climb the cargo nets. Sailors had to pull them over the gunwales, fish them out of the water where they had fallen—doing it gladly and with open tears. They were sticks of men and their sunken eyes stared wonderingly at that island they were leaving, where General Vandegrift, Manila John Basilone, Red Mike Edson, Mitchell Paige and the fallen Major Bailey had won Medals of Honor; where 621 of the Division's men died, where 1,517 more were wounded and another 5,600 had been stricken with malaria. It seemed such a small cost to balance against the 30,000 soldiers Japan lost at Guadalcanal. But who would count that other cost, that toll of suffering and sacrifice told in shrunken necks and knobby joints and stark rib cages and faces made of bone and parchment flesh?

They couldn't tell. They could only go below to the Marine's reward of a hot meal and a clean bunk, while the great ships shuddered and made for the open sea.

Behind them, General Patch's soldiers and Marines were already moving against General Hyakutate's remnant, men now scourged beyond belief by malaria and beriberi, men who were now clinging, as the Marines had clung, to the hope of reinforcement. It had been often promised in propaganda leaflets tucked inside those pitiful few sacks of rice or cases of bullets air-dropped to them from the skies:

"The enemy is collapsing before your eyes."

"We are convinced of help from Heaven and Divine Grace. Respect yourself and by no means run away from the encampment."

"We, too, will stick to it."

But they did not. Though there had been bitter conferences between the Army High Command and the War Ministry, though staff officers came to blows in the quarrel over whether Guadalcanal should be reinforced or evacuated, it was the War Ministry's resolve to evacuate that carried.

Once again swift destroyers swept down The Slot. On three February nights 20 destroyers skillfully took off Haruyoshi Hyakutate and most of the 13,000 men remaining in his 17th Army. On the afternoon of February 9, 1943, at a village west of the Tenamba River, a patrol of soldiers from the 132nd Infantry joined with another patrol from the 161st Infantry. They had reached the island's west coast and found no enemy.

Guadalcanal was secured.

But not until October 27, 1947, did the last of those most tenacious Japanese soldiers surrender. He came out of his cave, his hair long and matted, his uniform in tatters, a broken Australian bayonet stuck in his belt, a shovel in one hand, a water bottle in the other. His feet were bound in rags and wire, and as he approached a member of the British constabulary, he bowed deeply from the waist.

He inquired about the war and about the Americans, those ferocious Marines whom Tokyo Rose always called "the butchers of Guadalcanal." He was told that they had sailed away nearly five years ago.

And gone charging on to westward.

II. All Their Blood

Song for a Pilot

Who plows the sky, said a wise man,
  Shows himself a fool;
But he went out to plow it—
  Taught in a different school.

Who sows the wind, says Scripture,
  Must reap and reap again;
But he went out to sow the wind—
  And reaped the bitter grain.

He took his death like charity,
  Like nothing understood;
He freshened all the oldest words
  With all his blood.

—Captain Richard G. Hubler

1

Once a jolly swagman camped by a billabong
Under the shade of a coolibah tree.
And he sang as he watched and waited till his billy boiled,
"You'll come a waltzin' Matilda with me."

It was a great tune to march to, a rollicking one to bellow at top voice while rolling merrily home through the quiet broad streets of Melbourne—that spacious airy Australian city where the First Marine Division had begun to recuperate from Guadalcanal.

The Marines arrived in Melbourne in early January, 1943, and were at once clasped to the hearts of its people. They were looked upon as the saviors of Australia, for they had preserved the country's lifeline to America. They were treated as saviors, in spite of their being men of another nation as well as mere human beings inclined to take advantage of the savior status. But there seemed to be nothing that these Marines could do to outrage their hosts, and gradually, after the Marines' inevitably exuberant response to the delights of civilization became contained, there developed between host city and guest army a friendship so warm and understanding as to be unique.

Australian soldiers or "Diggers" who might have been miffed, at first, to find the pubs closing early a few times weekly because the Yankee Marines had again drunk the town dry, also

133

found that they were perpetually welcome at the wet canteens or "slop-chutes" of the Marine camps. Complaints that the Americans' voracious appetite for steak-and-eggs was making beef hard to come by were tempered by the realization that the Yanks were generous with their coveted cigarettes and that they frequently arrived at Australian homes bringing a pound of precious butter. Soon the Aussies were saying "okay" for "good-o" and their movie theaters played "The Marines' Hymn" as often as "God Save the King," while over in the Marine camps—where the band often played "Waltzin' Matilda" on ceremonial parade—the Yanks called their friends "cobber" and spoke of riding a "tram" to keep a date with some "shiela." Before the division departed Melbourne there was many a Yankee ring on an Australian finger, and during the nine months of that truly remarkable rest the Marines thought less and less of the alternating hell of fear and fire which they had left behind them, remembering it only when a comrade looked up from a Melbourne newspaper account of the war in North Africa or New Guinea and exclaimed:

"I wonder what it's like back on the 'Canal?"

Back on the 'Canal in that early January of 1943 the war had lost its spectacular quality. Over at Tulagi there was a sign which, in letters two feet high, proclaimed Bull Halsey's battle creed: KILL JAPS, KILL JAPS, KILL MORE JAPS. But most of the killing would have to be done farther north, for Hyakutate's men had already pulled back preparatory to their evacuation and Japanese naval strength no longer ventured south.

The coastwatchers who occupied the lonely high peaks of Guadalcanal were being called in. Among them was the erstwhile planter K. D. Hay, a veteran of World War One and easily the fattest man in the South Pacific. Yet he had hung on to his station at the mountain mining camp known as Gold Ridge. But now, in January, he was coming down, bringing with him the aged nun who was the sole survivor of a Japanese mission massacre and whom Hay had cared for. Melanesian bearers brought the nun down. Hay made his own panting descent. By the time he had reached the coastal road he was near collapse. He sent word to the Americans requesting a jeep. He explained that he was "knocked up," innocently unaware that the Australian slang for being exhausted was also American slang for being pregnant.

A puzzled U. S. Army officer drove up the road. He saw Hay. He saw his belly. He clapped his hand to his forehead and swore:

"My God, it's true!"

In mid-January Japanese aerial attacks on Henderson Field began to increase, giving Captain Joe Foss his chance to break Captain Eddie Rickenbacker's record.

Foss was back on Guadalcanal. He had recovered from the malaria which had stricken him November 24, the day after he had shot down his twenty-third plane. He had been evacuated to Sydney, but now he was back with Squadron 121 with only a few weeks to go on his tour of duty. And all the talk was whether or not Joe would equal the 26 kills which had made Rickenbacker the American ace-of-aces in World War One.

On January 15 Captain Joe Foss became the ace-of-aces in the new war. On that day he tore into a formation of Zeros and shot down three of them. Foss's score stayed at 26, while his squadron went on to record 164 kills against 20 of its own pilots lost. At the end of January Joe Foss's tour of duty was over.

He went home to receive the Medal of Honor, the path of his homegoing convoy crossing that of those carriers and convoys coming out with a new weapon and a new outfit for the Marines' war against Japan: the peerless Corsair fighter and the Third Marine Division.

The first of the Corsairs arrived at Guadalcanal on February 12. They came to Henderson Field with a bad reputation, for many Navy pilots swore they were "full of bugs" and at least one carrier commander refused to permit them aboard his ship. But the Marines made the Corsair their own, forgetting the stubborn Wildcat which had won the air battle of Guadalcanal in their jubilation at the range and staying power of this gull-winged, paddle-bladed killer. The big Corsairs could

135

fly faster than anything Japan had, could climb nearly 3,000 feet a second, and range twice as far as the Wildcats. If they were difficult aboard ship they were not so ashore—and the Marine fliers would be landlocked for most of the rest of the war.

The Third Marine Division which entered the Pacific Theater almost simultaneously with the Corsair was not only new but also novel. It was a weld of raw recruit and battle-blooded veteran. It made manifest the fact that the rewards of the Solomons offensive were not all strategic. Unlike Guam, Wake or the Philippines, Guadalcanal had ended in a victory that produced thousands of veteran warriors to drill and lead America's cadres. Even the lowest ranks of the Third Division included men who had fought the Japanese on Guadalcanal. Having recovered from the wounds or malaria which had brought them home, they had been assigned to the Third. Many of the new division's officers and top NCO's were also veterans. They had been promoted and detached from the First to command in the Third.

Never again would a Marine division go into battle as green as the First had been at Guadalcanal. Every outfit would have its heavy quota of officers and men who knew the difference between the myth of the superman of the jungle and the fact of the tenacious enemy who fought so much with his heart, so little with his head. They could tell the boots and Ninety-Day Wonders of the Third that though the enemy was indeed "a tricky little bastard," his tactics were so tied to trickery that he sometimes confused his means for his ends.

By April all of the Division's units—the Third, Ninth and Twenty-First Marines, the Twelfth Marine Regiment of artillery, the Nineteenth of engineers—had been assembled in New Zealand. They began training at twenty-two separate camps in the vicinity of Auckland.

South of them, down at the capital of Wellington, was that older brother division, that angriest and most stridently warlike of all Marine divisions—the Second.

★

The Second Marine Division had come to Wellington from Guadalcanal with a chip on its shoulder. The chip was there for the First Marine Division to knock off. For the Second was sore. Its Second Regiment had been at Tulagi-Guadalcanal since the August 7 landings, had in fact been the first unit to take enemy soil in World War Two, and though it had not been in the thick of it thereafter, it had been forced to stay on Guadalcanal for more than a month after the glory-hounds of the First Division shoved off. The Eighth Marines and Tenth Marine Artillery had come onto the island in November. The Sixth had arrived in January. All had joined General Patch's offensive without benefit of publicity, for no newspaper in the States seemed to have heard of the Second Marine Division. It was always the First that got the headlines.

So the Second Marine Division was sore and it was going into training to prove its superiority to those headline-hunters up in Australia. Its men were also determined to "pitch a liberty" that would even outdo what was already being called "The Battle of Melbourne."

What Melbourne already was to the First, Wellington was becoming to the Second. It was another love affair, the only variations being Maori music supplanting "Waltzin' Matilda" and the steep hills and canyons of North Island substituting for the featureless Victorian plain. In Wellington there were also steak-and-eggs and long-haired girls learning to jitterbug to an American beat—and there were also marriages. And though both New Zealander and American would exchange monuments and plaques on Aotea Quay after the war, the bond that now existed would be manifested by that odd tradition with which United States Marines would henceforth memorialize the people of the Antipodes. Hereafter they would go into battle on a breakfast of steak-and-eggs.

So the Marine Corps took a deep breath in the first quarter of 1943 while the war rolled elsewhere, while Australian and American soldiers drove the Japanese invaders north and west up the New Guinea coast, while the Allies in North Africa began the offensive which doomed Germany's Afrika Korps, while the Third Reich caught its mortal cold in the Russian snows—

and while Fleet Admiral Isoroku Yamamoto plotted a flaming revenge for the loss of Guadalcanal.

2

It was called the "I" operation. It was intended to blast American bases to rubble, to sink American shipping, to set the American land forces back on their heels while the Japanese strengthened their defenses in the upper Solomons, New Guinea and New Britain. And it was meant to console Emperor Hirohito for the loss of Guadalcanal.

At the end of March—about a month after the Third Marine Raiders and Army units had moved into the undefended Russell Islands about 60 miles northwest of Guadalcanal—Admiral Yamamoto came down to Rabaul to put "I" into effect. He assembled 96 fighters, 65 dive-bombers and a few torpedo bombers aboard four carriers, and to this he added a land-based force of 86 fighters, 27 dive-bombers, 72 twin-engined bombers and a few more torpedo bombers. That was roughly 350 planes—a big force even by the standards of 1945, by those of 1943 enormous.

Yamamoto was going to hurl this thunderbolt at Guadalcanal, where his scout planes reported growing naval strength, and later at New Guinea. During the first week of April the land-based forces were built up at Rabaul and the carrier planes fleeted down to Buka, Kahili and Ballale in the Bougainville area. On April 7, with an early-morning report that four American cruisers, seven destroyers and 14 transports were in Iron Bottom Bay, Yamamoto let fly.

The first of four waves of Vals and Zeros roared aloft from Rabaul. Coastwatchers spotted them and flashed the word. At noon the task force standing out of Tulagi heard the warning and went streaking for the open sea at full steam ahead. But more than 30 smaller vessels were still in the Bay.

By one o'clock the planes from Rabaul had been augmented by three other waves and there were now 67 Vals and 100 Zeros roaring over The Slot. On Segi Point in New Georgia the coastwatcher Kennedy, the man who had rescued Joe Foss and many others, gaped in astonishment at their numbers. He couldn't count them all. He could only signal "hundreds headed yours."

By two o'clock the massive Japanese aerial armada was thundering over the Russells, turning the radar screens milky with pips, changing the earlier warning of "Condition Red" to an alert never made before or since.

"Condition *Very* Red!"

And then the Japanese swept over Tulagi, the dive-bombers making for the ships in the harbor, the fighters taking on the 76 Marine, Army and Navy planes that had been scrambled aloft in readiness. Among them was a Marine boot pilot named Jimmy Swett, the most amazing greenhorn of World War Two.

Twenty-two-year-old Lieutenant Swett had never been in combat before. At three o'clock that afternoon, he and three comrades flew their Wildcats toward Tulagi, their own yelps and rebel yells contributing to that crackling cacophony of "Heigh-ho Silver!" or "Tally-ho!" then drowning out the fighter director's frantic plea of "Protect your shipping!—Protect your shipping!"

Fifteen minutes later Jimmy Swett had shot down seven enemy bombers. He flamed them so fast he had no recollection of their destruction. He shoved his Wildcat over and dove into the storm of antiaircraft fire flowing up from Tulagi and shot down three Vals at three separate levels of his dive. He cut down to pick-up speed, climbed, and roared after four more Vals and blasted them into the treetops of Florida Island. Then, with his cooling system destroyed, his face bloodied by flying bits of glass from his shattered windshield, he crash-landed in the Bay.

Swett was rescued. He received the Medal of Honor, and

the nickname "Zeke," for this is what Zeros were now being called since the cataloguing of enemy fighters with male nicknames, bombers with female ones. He would fly again, but in the cockpit of a Corsair, and he would shoot down seven more planes before he was through. But on that afternoon he had done more than anyone else to stagger Fleet Admiral Yamamoto's "I" operation, and henceforth all boot Marine pilots would fly out to maiden combat determined "to do a Jimmy Swett."

In all, 39 Japanese planes were shot down that wild afternoon of April 7, and 28 of these were destroyed by Marine flyers at a cost of seven of their own aircraft, with no pilots lost. In their elation, pilots of all services claimed kills all over the lower Solomons, and many of the antiaircraft gunners on those little merchant ships were already proudly painting red balls on their gun mounts, their prows, their sterns, so that all claims taken together would surely have meant the destruction of more planes than Yamamoto possessed.

The Americans were not the only Munchausens abroad in the Solomons that day and the next, when the "I" armada thundered over New Guinea. Japanese pilots, having sunk only a destroyer, a tanker and a corvette at Guadalcanal and a small Netherlands transport in New Guinea, returned to base with such glowing reports of success that Yamamoto put an end to "I" and sent the carrier pilots back to their ships.

The Marine air arm thereupon countered with an offensive of its own, striking at Munda Airfield on New Georgia about 190 miles up the Solomons ladder. The field had been cleverly hidden beneath a fake forest. The Japanese had cut away trees but had kept the treetops in place with wires. Beneath them they had built the base which became a thorn in the side of the Americans.

On April 13, 16 Corsairs left Guadalcanal to escort 12 Avengers on a strike at Munda Airfield. Young Bill Coffeen flew one of the Corsairs. He was that rarity in air combat, a flying staff sergeant. He was also a veteran, and when he took off that early morning, nearly blinded by a guide light at the end of the runway, narrowly missing the trees at the edge of the airfield, he guessed that he had begun a bad day.

By the time he had passed over Munda and the Avengers had flashed down, Coffeen's engine was smoking and his oil line leaking. He was losing altitude rapidly, coming down very fast over The Slot between Choiseul and Kolombangara. At 3,000 feet his motor was so hot he feared it would explode. Coffeen jumped. His parachute opened.

A few seconds later he had slammed into the water. He surfaced and pulled the cord on his life jacket, his "Mae West." It had a hole in it and could not be inflated.

He pulled out his rubber raft and inflated that. The paddle was missing.

Then a storm broke over The Slot and a wave capsized Coffeen's rubber boat, carrying off his shoes, his medical supplies, his food. Coffeen now had his rubber raft, the clothes he wore, a hunting knife and a pistol—but he also had hope, for he had heard the sound of approaching motors.

It was his flight returning to Guadalcanal. Coffeen waved the raft's white sail happily. The planes flew on. He fired his pistol. Two Corsairs came in low. Coffeen fired again and waved the sail. The Corsairs flew on. They had not seen him. There were shark fins sliding by and it was getting dark on the waters of The Slot.

The Americans had broken the Japanese code and they had discovered that Fleet Admiral Yamamoto was preparing to visit bases on Bougainville.

Intelligence was queried: Would it be wise to kill Yamamoto? Would his death hurt Japan or would it make room for a commander better than he? The answer was that Isoroku Yamamoto was the best military mind in Japan, and so his doom was sealed.

On Henderson Field, Rear Admiral Marc Mitscher, air commander for the Solomons, rounded up a squadron of triggermen. He chose the Army Air Corps for the job, for their twin-tailed Lightnings were the longest-ranging things aloft. Sixteen pilots of the 339th Squadron under Major John Mitchell were alerted for the day of Yamamoto's departure from Rabaul on April 18.

★

On April 18 Sergeant Bill Coffeen decided that if he stayed where he was he would die.

He had spent two days paddling by hand, burned by sun and salt. He had spent two nights sleeping upright for fear of falling, for fear of sharks. At last he paddled to a tiny island. It was uninhabited. It had no fresh food, no water—only coconuts. After three days of eating coconuts, with the growling of approaching dysentery already audible within his stomach, Coffeen looked at a larger island in the distance and made up his mind to try for it.

He floated his boat. He got in, pulled out his automatic pistol, found it rusted beyond use—and threw it away. With a stick for a paddle, he moved out on The Slot. He paddled and rested, paddled and rested, judging the time and his progress from the position of the sun. At somewhere around nine o'clock he rested and heard the sound of motors. He glanced up eagerly.

They were too high, much too high to see him. They looked like Lightnings.

There were 16 of them.

At thirty-five minutes after nine o'clock on the morning of April 18, two twin-engined Betty bombers arrived over Kahili airdrome. They carried Fleet Admiral Yamamoto, his chief of staff, Vice Admiral Ugaki, and the most important officers of his staff. It was as though Admiral Chester Nimitz had flown up to Guadalcanal from Pearl Harbor, collecting Bull Halsey and other top aides along the way.

A cover of nine Zeke fighters patrolled the skies above the Bettys, watching them drop down to land. Just as the Zekes turned for home, 12 white-starred, twin-tailed killers struck at them from above. Four more Lightnings went flashing down on the helpless Bettys.

Captain Tom Lamphier shot one of the bombers down in the jungle. Lieutenant Rex Barber sent the other spiraling into the sea.

Up above, Major Mitchell's covering Lightnings shot down three of the horrified Zekes who had wheeled to slam the door left so helplessly open. Only Lieutenant Raymond Hine was lost.

The remaining 15 triggermen flew back to Guadalcanal to make the report which would send wild but highly-secret elation sweeping eastward over the Pacific until it spread through the offices of the Pentagon. But the jubilation had to remain guarded; it would be foolish to let the enemy suspect that his cipher had been cracked. Thus such cryptic vaults as Bull Halsey's message to Marc Mitscher: "Congratulations to you and Major Mitchell and his hunters. Sounds as though one of the ducks in their bag might be a peacock."

It was. On May 21 Tokyo announced that the great Yamamoto was gone. He had been in the plane which Lamphier sent crashing into the jungle and he had been killed with a half-dozen staff officers. Admiral Ugaki had been badly hurt, but he had survived.

That brilliant proud leader who had arrogantly told the world of his intention to dictate peace terms in the White House, the Emperor's "one and only Yamamoto," was now dead.

Bill Coffeen knew that he was dying.

He had reached that larger island two days after he had seen the returning Lightnings flying high above him and had noticed that there were only 15.

But the larger island had no food or water either. Nor did a third island to which he had made a laborious three-day voyage.

A mosquito bite on his left hand had become infected. A red streak ran from the hand to his shoulder. On the morning after he had reached the third island, Coffeen's arm was twice its normal size. He seized his knife and cut open the festering sore which was poisoning his blood. He bathed the wound in sea water, and discovered that his right foot was also infected.

He moved on to another island.

He paddled on, coming ashore on another lifeless rock, eating coconuts, sleeping on beaches, scratching in the sand for anything edible, moving on repeatedly while the weeks turned two and moved toward three.

Around the twentieth day he saw a red-roofed house a mile or more ahead of him on the shore of the island he was coasting. But Coffeen was too weak to paddle farther. He went ashore to rest through the night, hoping to reach the house next day. Beaching his raft, he found that he had stumbled on an abandoned copra plantation. There were outbuildings. But he saw no sign of life or food. Then he heard the cackling of a hen.

He staggered toward a rotting henhouse. He found an aged hen nesting inside. He poked her with a stick. She clucked in outrage and scampered away—exposing twelve beautiful white eggs to the starving eyes of Bill Coffeen. He broke them open and gulped them down. He found some little tropical limes and squeezed the tart juice into his mouth.

He felt certain that he would live and he refloated his boat and made it to the plantation house in another day. He lay on the floor that night and prayed to God for the strength to keep him going.

In the morning he was paddling again, keeping carefully close to the shoreline. At dusk four days later a storm broke over The Slot and swept his raft out to the open sea.

Night fell. Black water swept over Coffeen's burning flesh, and it was then that he began to scream.

It was mid-May. The campaign in North Africa had ended in victory. The new-style landing boats that had brought the soldiers ashore at Casablanca and Oran were now coming to the Pacific in great numbers.

The old wooden Higgins boats from which the Marines were accustomed to leap into boiling surf were now discarded. Replacing them were the new LCVP's (Landing Craft, Vehicle, Personnel) which the Marines would simply call "landing boats." They were 36 feet long, could move at nine knots and could carry 36 Marines or a three-ton vehicle or 8,000 pounds of cargo. They had ramps which were lowered at the moment of impact with the beach, enabling the Marines to run ashore and make one of those ladylike "dry landings" for which they

144

were forever ribbing the dogfaces. Many months later, when the Marines saw the famous pictures of General MacArthur wading ashore on his return to the Philippines, they hooted in wild derision, for they knew nobody need wade with a landing boat around.

There was also the landing boat's big sister, the LCM (Landing Craft, Medium) which would always be called that. It was 50 feet long and 14 feet wide, and could carry a Sherman tank or 30 tons of cargo or 69 men. The LCM's were ideal for small forays. They mounted a pair of 50-caliber machine guns and the ramp could be lowered just enough to allow the Sherman's cannon to fire. Roaring inland, with this armament blazing, the LCM's were a terrifying sight for enemy riflemen to behold and they could provide excellent supporting fire for those Marines swarming down the ramp.

And the old amtrack was coming into its own. The Marines had had the LVT (Landing Vehicle, Tracked) at Guadalcanal and called it the Alligator. Excellent though it was for crossing swamps or sailing up navigable jungle rivers, it had been erratic in salt water. The tracks corroded and became stuck. Now there was an improved amtrack coming out to the Pacific, and soon there would be amtracks with ramps to the rear, amtrack tanks—or amtanks—and even amtracks mounting flame-throwers which could spew tongues of liquid fire a hundred feet long.

There were bigger boats, such as the bargelike LCT (Landing Craft, Tank) which was 122 by 32 feet and could carry four Shermans or 150 tons of cargo. There was also the LCI (Landing Craft, Infantry), a sleek, swift little ocean-going troop-carrier. The diesel-powered LCI's were 148 feet long and could hit 16 knots and cruise for 8,000 miles. They had quarters for nine officers and 196 men, with cargo capacity of 32 tons. When the boat beached, twin ramps to either side of the bow could be lowered for the Marines to run ashore. The LCI's were eventually converted into rocket ships, for which purpose they were admirably suited, and the Marines were not sorry to see them go. They were hot, airless and crowded, with the most rudimentary provision for washing and eating, and they were far from stable.

145

The LST (Landing Ship, Tank) was stable. Many Marines said that LST stood for Large Stationary Target, for these pin-headed monsters were indeed slow and indeed large. The LST was 328 feet long and could carry 2,100 tons. Her most unusual feature was the enormous high bow composed of two huge doors which swung open the moment the shallow-draft LST's ran up on the beach, or which could be opened at sea to allow amtracks to roll down a ramp into the water. Through these great yawning jaws ran, rode and rolled all the men and munitions of Mars. To sit in the cavernous belly of an LST on the morning of battle was to be sailing to war within the Lincoln Tunnel—trucks, jeeps, tanks, field guns, ambu-lances, amtracks, everything wheeled or tracked was lined up nose-to-end behind hundreds of combat-loaded Marines crouching forward for the moment when the doors swung open to reveal the forts of the enemy.

The Marines hated their LST's with a flippant fierce hatred. Very few men enjoyed the luxury of sleeping in the bunks pro-vided for them below. Most of them slept on deck, usually on field cots placed underneath LCT's lashed to the deck on blocks so they could be launched over the side on D-Day. Be-ing nine-knot cows, LST's had to leave for combat earliest, for they took the longest, and this meant that the chances of their being bombed, torpedoed or shelled were more prolonged, and that their food supply would inevitably give out, along with the fresh water, forcing the troops to live off the rations in their packs and to wash in salt water.

No, the LST's were not popular, any more than had been the M-1, or Garand, semiautomatic rifle when it was first issued. The Marines had fought with the bolt-action, five-shot Springfield rifle on Guadalcanal. This was the famous '03 which had made the United States Marines the sharpest shoot-ers in the world. They hated to exchange it for the less-accurate M-1, even though the Garand fired an eight-round clip as fast as a man could pull the trigger. Burning powder gases operated the M-1's loading mechanism, thus providing the greater firepower, to which the Marines reluctantly yielded.

But at least they had gotten rid of the Reising gun, that slovenly substitute for a Thompson submachine gun which they had taken onto Guadalcanal. The Reising gun was useless, and the Marines swore that the only Japanese hurt by them were those hit by the ones being thrown away. In the Reising's place came the tommy gun, firing 20- or 30-round clips. For officers and machine-gunners and other Marines assigned to crew-served weapons there was the new M-1 carbine. It was light, firing a clip of 15 .30-caliber bullets at semi-automatic. It provided firepower, but it wasn't tough enough to withstand the corrosion of the jungle. It would break down when fired too long, and then anyone who carried a carbine would search frantically for a rifle—still the best gun to have around when things were getting sticky.

There was also the bazooka, that long-tubed rocket-launcher which a man rested on his shoulder and fired like a rifle, and there was the flame-thrower. Both were new and untried.

They would soon be tested, however, as would all those other weapons and ships now flowing to the three Marine divisions training in the Antipodes and to the Raider battalions on Noumea in mid-May of 1943.

It was May 15 and Bill Coffeen had the foolish notion that someone was cradling him like a baby.

He opened his eyes. He *was* being carried. He was in the arms of a husky Melanesian and he was being lifted from his raft.

"You allasame 'Merrican?" the man asked, "or you allasame Jap?"

"I'm American," Coffeen gasped.

The Melanesian's white teeth flashed in his dark face.

"'Merrican good fella," he said, and gathered Coffeen in his powerful arms and took him to a village inland from the beach. Coffeen was puzzled at first over how the Melanesian could mistake a tall Westerner for a short Japanese. But then he understood. He had shrunk to a hank of bone and shriveled skin, his flesh was like burnished copper, his head was a mop almost as fuzzy as his rescuer's, but plastered down with dried salt, as was the heavy beard covering half his face.

At the village, Coffeen ate. He was saved. Next day his infected foot was lanced, the ulcers covering his body were bathed in an antiseptic—and then Coffeen fell ill with malaria.

There were now four airfields on Guadalcanal and Fleet Admiral Mineichi Koga was determined to succeed where his predecessor, Yamamoto, had failed. He was going to destroy Guadalcanal air power.

In mid-May he shifted his aerial strength from Truk to Rabaul and in early June the Zekes and Vals and Bettys swept south again.

On June 7, 112 of them collided with American and New Zealand planes high above the Russell Islands in one of the Solomons campaign's biggest dogfights. At 22,000 feet, Lieutenant Sam Logan's Corsair was turned into a torch by the 20-millimeter cannon of a Zeke.

Logan bailed out. His parachute opened and he began to float seaward.

The Zeke returned. Its pilot made pass after pass at the helpless Logan, and then, failing to hit him, drove at him with whirling propeller blades in an attempt to chop him to pieces. He had cut off part of Logan's right foot and left heel and was coming again to finish the job when a New Zealand pilot drove him off. Logan hit the water and was rescued. But his right foot had to be amputated. Even so, Logan flew again, for this indomitable Marine was the first American to receive permission to continue to fight and fly with what the Marines called "a store leg."

So also would Lieutenant Gil Percy live to fight again, even though on that same afternoon of June 7 he had fallen into the sea from a height of 2,000 feet. Percy's elevator control and wing tanks were shot out when he was flying at that altitude. He leaped from his cockpit and pulled the parachute cord. The chute didn't open. It merely trailed after him to mark his plunge. Percy was certain he was dead in that obliterating instant when life seemed to be blotted out, but then he tasted salt water. He opened his eyes. There were bubbles all around him and then his head had burst into the light of day and the only things he had to worry about now were sharks and how to swim to a nearby island with a broken back, two sprained ankles and cannon wounds in one arm and both legs.

He began back-stroking toward an island a mile distant. Three hours later he reached an offshore reef. He dragged himself up on it and lost consciousness. At dawn the tide floated him into shore and he crawled up on the sand to be found by three Melanesians. One of them stood guard over Percy while the others went for help. Soon a motor launch with two doctors aboard came to the island. Percy went back to Guadalcanal, and then to a hospital in Auckland. One year later he was back in action.

Admiral Koga lost 23 pilots that day of June 7, and he lost 107 more when he sent 120 planes south on June 16. After the sixteenth, Guadalcanal was never again attacked by daylight.

The Japanese had had enough of Captain Donald Kennedy.

Among the most daring of all the coastwatchers, Captain Kennedy had kept most of the Melanesians on New Georgia hostile to the Japanese, using them to hide downed American flyers while he signaled for small boats or the big flying ships called Dumbos to come get them. Kennedy had also harried the Japanese on New Georgia incessantly—bursting from his mysterious jungle lair to strike swift blows, then melting back into the green tangle again—and he had repeatedly waylaid barges loaded with Japanese soldiers and massacred them.

Kennedy had only attacked when it became likely that Japanese patrols or barge movements might stumble on his Segi Point hideout and thus reveal the entire coastwatching apparatus, of which the Japanese still had no suspicion. Though he had only killed to keep his secret, he had done so with customary vigor and efficiency. Now Colonel Genjiro Hirata was going to use the entire First Battalion of his 229th Regiment to get rid of him.

Kennedy ambushed the first force sent against him and captured the inevitable diary describing Colonel Hirata's plans for Captain Kennedy. Kennedy called for help.

At dusk of June 20 two companies of the Fourth Raiders boarded the destroyer-transports *Dent* and *Waters* and sped from Guadalcanal to New Georgia. By dark the two ships

149

were gingerly picking their way through the shoal-filled channel to Segi Point. Kennedy lighted bonfires ashore to guide them in and cheerfully radioed, "Okay here." It was not quite okay in the channel, for both ships had scraped bottom. But they worked free, and in the morning the Marines came ashore to seize the beachhead which opened the campaign in the Central Solomons. The long breathing spell between the end of fighting on Guadalcanal and the resumption of the American offensive was ending.

It was June 25 and a Dumbo had come for Staff Sergeant Bill Coffeen. The big PBY landed offshore from the native village and Coffeen went out by canoe to climb aboard.

The Melanesians had saved his life. They had nursed him through malaria. Their food had restored half of the roughly 40 pounds Coffeen had lost during the thirty-two days he had paddled about The Slot on his raft. They had even given the young American a pet parrot to take back to Guadalcanal with him. Coffeen waved his farewell and they waved back gaily, smiling warmly.

Then Bill Coffeen flew back to Guadalcanal, only to start "beating his gums" not ten minutes after his return.

It was not that Bill Coffeen was not grateful for his life, not that he minded the hunger or ulcers or sunburn or malaria so much, it was only that while he had been 72 days missing in action his buddies of Squadron 213 had finished their tour of duty, had "pitched one helluva liberty" in Sidney, and were now back on the 'Canal ready to start their second tour with good old Bill Coffeen back aboard.

"We told the Aussie gals all about you, Bill," his buddies said solemnly. "Usually while we were walking down to the pub."

3

Take me somewhere east of Ewa
Where the best ain't like the worst,
Where there ain't no Doug MacArthur
And a man can drown his thirst—
Where the Army gets the medals
And the Navy gets the queens,
But the boys who get the rookin'
Are United States Marines.

It was the song of the Solomons and it had a chorus descriptive of the changed character of the aerial war against Japan. It went:

Hit the road to Gizo Bay
Where the Jap fleet spends the day.
You can hear the duds a'clunkin'
From Rabaul to Lunga Bay.
Pack your load up to Rekata,
Where the float-plane Zeros play,
And the bombs come down like thunder
On the natives cross the way.

For it was now the American bombers which went sweeping *up* The Slot. Marine airmen who roared that sardonic ditty while gathered at the Hotel De Gink for a convivial canteen cup of medical alcohol cut with grapefruit juice were bellowing their displeasure with the daily bombing missions aimed at knocking out the Bougainville airfields while the New Georgia offensive slugged ahead. That the De Gink—Guadalcanal's famous shack for itinerant pilots—now resounded to the singing of a bombardier's ballad was indicative of the

151

change. Even the De Gink was new, for the old one had been destroyed in one of those shellings during the days when the fighter pilot was the photographer's darling.

By the end of June the hot pilot was in demand again. The Army's 43rd Division landed at Rendova while Marines and soldiers landed at Vangunu east of Munda, and the enemy's attempts to get at the transports brought 170 Allied fighters swarming aloft to intercept 130 Japanese invaders. Dogfights swirled all over the Central Solomons in a wild, far-ranging struggle during which 100 enemy aircraft were shot down, as opposed to 14 American, and a new brood of Marine Corsair aces was born. Among them were Lieutenant Ken Walsh and Lieutenant Alvin Jensen, and a wisecracking, cigar-smoking fly-boy with the fanciful name of Murderous Manny Segal.

Like Walsh and Jensen, Lieutenant Segal had been a former enlisted naval pilot. Now he was a Marine officer, flying wing off the famous Zeke Swett as the Fighting Falcon Squadron helped to cover the Rendova landing. At noon Murderous Manny Segal heard someone yip, "There's a big fight going on downstairs!"

"This I gotta see," Segal murmured, and went nosing over as Swett led the division down. Segal was momentarily startled. Swett was leading the Corsairs around and beneath the dogfight. Then he saw the bombers with their "big angry meatballs" on the fuselage and he understood. Murderous Manny Segal worked up on one of the Bettys in a high side run. He fired. He could see his tracers flowing into the bomber's starboard engine. It burst into flames. Hypnotized by his first taste of combat, Segal nearly flew into the wreckage. He was awakened by the blasting of antiaircraft shells from an American destroyer. His Corsair was all but thrown back on its tail and his cigar flew from his mouth. Groggy, he pulled back on the stick and climbed to safety.

Up high again, Segal saw a Zero riding the tail of a smoking Wildcat. He chased the Zero all the way up to the next island, Kolombangara, where a single sharp burst blew it up. He had two planes to his credit on his first flight, and within another two weeks he was an ace.

On July 11, with Segal again flying wing for Swett, eight of the Fighting Falcons took off for a patrol over Rendova. Six turned back because of engine trouble. Swett and Segal were alone. They heard from the fighter director that there was "a big bogey" coming down The Slot: 30 Bettys with a cover of 20 Zeros flying at 18,000 feet. Swett and Segal nosed over from 26,000 feet and went slashing among them. They broke up the formation. Swett missed on his first pass, but Manny Segal shot down the Zero that went for Swett's tail. Three more eased in behind Segal, and Swett obliged by shooting one of them down. Then the two Marine fliers became separated. They were no longer able to protect one another, but Segal shot down two more planes, and Swett sent a bomber plunging into the ocean with such impact that water swept skyward in a plume so high it doused his Corsair.

And then Segal and Swett were shot down.

Swett's Corsair smacked the water in a dead-stick glide. It remained surfaced for some time, giving Swett protection from the pair of Zeros which strafed him. He was finally rescued by Captain Donald Kennedy's smoothly-functioning organization at Segi Point.

Murderous Manny Segal also survived. His face smashed and bloodied from the impact of his watery crash, Segal paddled about The Slot for twenty-three hours until an American destroyer spotted him and threw him a line. He was hauled aboard. The sailors rushed forward to help him, and Segal waved them weakly away.

"Don't worry, boys," he gasped—"things are bad all over."

On July 28, soldiers of the Fourteenth Corps, spearheaded by Marine flame-throwers mounted on tanks, struck at the Munda Airfield's labyrinthine defense. They pushed through a gaunt no man's land where not a tree had been left intact. By August 5 they had taken the airfield. Ten days later the strip was in use and Lieutenant Ken Walsh was fireballing a Corsair down the strip. He roared up to Vella Lavella, shot down a fighter and then launched a lone attack on a formation of nine Vals. He shot down two of them and came in to Munda with two cannon holes in his right wing, his hydraulic line cut, his horizontal stabilizer punctured and his right tire blown. But he made a perfect landing and was actually cheered by the ground crews.

Fifteen days later Walsh was again demonstrating his superb flying skill. He flew to Kahili, developed engine trouble and returned to get another Corsair. He took off again and tore north to take on 50 Japanese fighters by himself. He shot down four. Walsh was awarded the Medal of Honor for both these actions, and before he left combat he had shot down 21 planes.

During that same period of fighting in the Central Solomons, Lieutenant Jensen destroyed 24 parked enemy planes in one of the Pacific's freak feats of combat.

During a storm which burst suddenly over Kahili on August 28, Jensen found himself separated from his comrades. He flew down through the storm. To his great surprise he emerged from it upside down and directly over the enemy airfield. Jensen twisted his Corsair right side up while roaring to one end of the airport. He banked around and came skimming over the runway with all guns hammering, turning eight parked Zekes, four Vals and 12 Bettys into flaming heaps before the stunned Japanese had a chance to raise a hand against him.

Such was the heat of the aerial warfare, matching the bitter savagery of the Central Solomons ground fighting, during that August when the armed forces of both nations seemed to be marking time.

But August also marked the end of that seeming lull, for in Quebec the Quadrant Conference between President Roosevelt and Prime Minister Churchill had already marked out the specific routes for the march on Japan. General MacArthur would still strike through the Bismarcks to the Philippines, and the Marines would fight twice more in the South Pacific. But Quadrant was also shifting emphasis to the Central Pacific, to the chain of island fortresses that ran like steel-sheathed stepping stones to the very heart of Japan.

In that same month of August a Japanese rear admiral named Keiji Shibasaki came out from Japan to the Central Pacific to direct the defense of the Gilbert and Marshall groups which were the foremost of these islands, the outer glacis of Fortress Nippon. Shibasaki was particularly anxious to fortify an island shaped like an upside-down parrot. The Gilbert Islanders called it Betio, the Japanese renamed it Bititu and the world would know it as Tarawa.

4

Major Gregory Boyington was called "Pappy" because he was already a venerable thirty-one years of age when he burst upon the South Pacific with all the ungentle force of his brash, boisterous, belligerent character. His men called themselves "Black Sheep" because they were a collection of replacements, rejects and loners turned over to Boyington as much to squelch his demands for a squadron as in hopes that he would put one together.

He did put together a squadron, a unique one, and he did it in hardly a month of training on Espiritu Santo in the New Hebrides. For the captain had found the men, and the men their captain. It was as though mavericks had actually gathered to elect a leader, and then, having asked themselves who among them could shoot fastest, drink most, care less, fly highest and make more enemies in high places, had chosen Boyington.

Boyington was a veteran long before World War Two broke. He had left the Marines to join Claire Chennault's Flying Tigers in China and Burma. He had shot down six Japanese planes there. After Pearl Harbor he returned home and requested reinstatement in the Marines. But Boyington was considered to be in disgrace for "having left the Corps in a time of national emergency." After three months of rebuff he at last sent off a desperation telegram to the under secretary of the Navy and was returned to duty.

He left off parking cars in a Seattle garage and came out to Guadalcanal. With prompt perverseness he broke his ankle playing a sort of nocturnal leapfrog. It seemed that much that had been said about Boyington's off-duty habits might be true, and it was after this episode that Boyington was given his last chance to deliver.

By September he had trained his Black Sheep to fly the big Corsairs and had brought them to a base in the Russells.

By September 16 they roared aloft on their first mission.

They were assigned to cover a formation of bombers headed for Ballale Airfield off the southern tip of Bougainville. The clouds over Bougainville were thick. Boyington and his 19 comrades didn't anticipate interception from that direction while the Dauntlesses and Avengers dove and slashed at tiny Ballale, raising puffs of dirt and smoke. The Black Sheep started down. They flew right into a formation of 40 Zeros coming up.

One of them tore past Boyington's right wing and wobbled his wings as though to say "Join up." The American pilot pressed his gun button and found he had been so absorbed in the bombing display he had forgotten to turn on his electric gunsight or his gun switches. He had not even charged his guns. But Boyington quickly corrected the oversight and "joined up" with the Japanese, firing into the unsuspecting Zero's tail and sending it spiraling down in flames.

Streaking down to the water where the bombers were re-forming for the homeward flight, Boyington flashed by another Zero. He aimed a burst at the cockpit and the plane gushed flame and smoke and vanished, some of its parts striking Boyington's plane.

Boyington was alone. The American bombers had gone home. Boyington turned to wolfing among the remaining Zeros. He struck down on a Zero flying low over the water, sensed a trap, eased up—and caught the bait Zero's triggerman coming at him head-on. Boyington's bullets tore apart the Zero's underbelly. It fell into the sea, smoking.

Now Boyington pointed his Corsair in the direction of the retreating American planes, and found himself above a Zero racing homeward. It was low over the water. A single burst sent it in.

It had been an impressive first mission. Boyington was satisfied to call it a day and head for Munda, for he had not enough gas to reach the Russells. Nearing the new airstrip he came upon an oil-smeared, shell-riddled Corsair flying low over the water while a pair of Zeros harried its tail. Boyington roared down behind the closest Zero, his guns chattering. The Zero stood on its tail. Boyington hauled back on the stick and fell into a spin just as the Zero burst apart in flames.

The other Zero fled and the Corsair vanished. Boyington never saw it again, and there was no time to search. He came into Munda with his tanks dry and but 30 rounds of ammunition left for his guns.

He had shot down an ace's portion on his squadron's first mission and his men had added a half-dozen kills of their own to the score.

Soon the *baaing* of the Black Sheep would be heard over all the South Pacific.

Kennedy the coastwatcher had at last been persuaded to come to Guadalcanal. New Georgia had been secured, the entire Central Solomons campaign had been victoriously concluded on September 25, and now, in the final days of September, the Americans were insistent that Captain Kennedy come south to his just reward.

"Captain Kennedy," the general said, "we would like to present you with a medal."

"Thanks, no—give the medals to the chaps doing the flying."

"Captain Kennedy," the general continued, "there must be something you want."

"If you really insist on wanting to know, then I guess I'd better tell you."

"Captain Kennedy," the general said gladly, "what would you like?"

"After thirty-six months in the bush I would like to have thirty-six beautiful chorus girls arguing over my drunken carcass."

The Black Sheep were coming up to Kahili, the formidable air base on the southern tip of Bougainville. This was the base which had to be smashed to make way for two of the three Marine offensives preparing that October. It had been struck repeatedly by Marine aircraft from the Russells and from Munda, where the Black Sheep were now based. On this flight the Black Sheep were escorting bombers, but the weather was bad for bombing and the Avengers flew home. The Black Sheep hung around. Suddenly, in a voice with no trace of accent but too precise to be true, the radio crackled with the question:

"Major Boyington, what is your position?"

Boyington grinned. It was the Japanese ground-control director pretending to be an American pilot.

"Over Treasury Island," Boyington lied, immediately beginning to climb, for the next question would concern his "angels" or altitude. It came:

"What are your angels, Major Boyington?"

"Twenty angels, repeating, twenty angels."

"I receive you, five by five," the Japanese concluded with prim efficiency, and by then the Black Sheep were already up to 21,000 feet—and streaming up below them, coming out of a white cloud, was a formation of 30 Zeros.

It was over in less than a minute. The Black Sheep struck out of nowhere, with the bright sun at their back to blind their enemies, and they continued their downward flight through the exploding wreckage of a dozen downed planes. Boyington got three of them himself. A few days later he and his Black Sheep again beguiled the enemy by flying high over Kahili in a V of V bomber formation, luring the Japanese into the swift onslaught and massed firepower of fighters.

For such exuberance in aerial combat—and for off-duty exuberance which was the inevitable consequence of Boyington's unrivaled ability to draw large issues of medical brandy— the Black Sheep became the toast of the Marine air arm. And they had taken to toasting their leader in a serenade adapted to the Yale "Whiffenpoof Song." It went:

To the one-arm joint at Munda,
To the foxholes where we dwelt,
To the predawn take-offs that we love so well,

Sing the Black Sheep all assembled,
With their canteens raised on high,
And the magic of their singing casts a spell.
Yes, the magic of their singing,
And the songs we love so well,
Old Man Reilly, Mrs. Murphy and the rest,
We shall serenade our Gregory
While life and voice shall last—
Then we'll pass and be forgotten with the rest.

They were indeed "poor little lambs off on a spree," for in a single month of combat they had damned 57 enemy pilots "from here to eternity" while losing but two of their own.

5

In mid-October of 1943 the First Marine Division had said farewell to Melbourne and its units were sailing to staging areas in New Guinea and Goodenough Island. The Third Marine Division was on Guadalcanal, completing jungle training, and the staff of the Second Marine Division was busy on plans for the seizure of Tarawa. In that same month General MacArthur and Admiral Halsey agreed on the first step in the drive to reduce Rabaul.

Rabaul was at the center of things in the South Pacific. So long as Japan possessed this great air-sea-troop base on the northeastern tip of New Britain, she could move south to the Solomons or strike west to New Guinea. She could send her bombers northeast to the Gilberts and Marshalls.

Deny Japan the use of Rabaul, and General MacArthur could drive up the New Guinea coast with his seaward flank secure and the assault in the Central Pacific could begin without fear of Rabaul's bombers.

But to get at Rabaul required an air base closer to it than Munda on New Georgia. Such a base could be on any one of a number of islands in the Northern Solomons. General Mac-Arthur and Admiral Halsey agreed that it should be Bougainville.

Bougainville was assaulted by the Third Marine Division, with the Army's 37th Infantry Division in reserve. Both units were part of the First Marine Amphibious Corps, commanded by Alexander Vandegrift, now a lieutenant general. With three stars on his shoulder, Vandegrift now outranked his old opponent, Haruyoshi Hyakutate.

Lieutenant General Hyakutate still commanded the 17th Army. He had been placed in charge of the Northern Solomons by General Hitoshi Imamura, whose 8th Area Army command included the Bismarcks (New Britain and surrounding islands), New Guinea and the Northern Solomons. Hyakutate expected the Americans to strike at Bougainville, probably at Kahili Airfield on the southern tip.

Guessing that the Japanese strength was concentrated at Kahili, Vandegrift had to pretend that he was going there while he was actually going somewhere else.

He was going to land at Empress Augusta Bay halfway up Bougainville's 130-mile west coast. The landing place would be immediately west or left of Cape Torokina, which formed the Bay's upper hook. Cape Torokina's beaches were known to be lightly defended. Its central location suggested that it would take the Japanese months to mount a massive counter-attack against it.

But the 20,000 men of the Third, with the attached Second Raider Regiment, would not sail straight for Torokina. Their convoy would rather make straight for Kahili. After having been seen, the convoy would sneak west and north under cover of night to effect the dawn landing at Torokina.

This ruse would also be preceded by a hard jab to the left of Kahili and a feint to the right. On October 26 a brigade of New Zealanders were to occupy the Treasury Islands just below and left of Bougainville. This would strengthen Japanese suspicion of an impending assault on Kahili, while providing a forward staging base for Torokina.

The following night Lieutenant Colonel Victor Krulak's Second Marine Parachute Battalion was to land at Choiseul, below and to the right of Bougainville. They would come ashore loudly rattling sabers and making very much smoke from very little fire. For though there were only 725 of them, Vandegrift had told Krulak on October 25:

"I want an immediate and credible appearance of a large force."

By that time Hyakutate was ready with new troops and an old plan.

The remnants of those 17th Army units cut up at Guadalcanal had been sloughed off on Major General Noboru Sasaki in the Central Solomons. While Hyakutate had been up in Rabaul raking in the fresh 6th and 17th Divisions to replace them, the luckless but able Sasaki had been down in New Georgia conducting a brilliant delaying campaign with such men as those Nagoya unfortunates who had arrived in his command swimming. By the time of Sasaki's defeat in early October, Hyakutate's 17th Army was again up to 50,000 men.

Some 40,000 of them were in the Bougainville area, and most of them belonged to the 6th Division—the infamous 6th which had raped Nanking—commanded by Lieutenant General Masatane Kanda. Again, as much because of the inflexible Hyakutate's notions of how to defend against amphibious attack as because of Bougainville's extensive coastline, these troops were strung out. There were some 5,000 in the north, another 5,000 on the east coast and about 25,000 around Kahili to the south and those island airfields off the southern shore.

There were only 300 at Cape Torokina, but Hyakutate was confident of his ability to repulse the enemy no matter where he landed. He still believed that counterattacks or counterlandings with reinforcements from Rabaul would destroy the enemy, despite the fact of what had happened to such attempts at Guadalcanal. He still relied on the sea and air power of the Japanese Navy to make such troop movements possible, despite the fact of what had been happening to that Navy since Ching Lee took the battleships through. He still regarded the jungle as an excellent cover for the maneuvering of troops, despite the fact of how cruelly the jungle had scourged the Kawaguchis and the Sendai.

By October 26, the day the New Zealanders occupied the Treasuries, Hyakutate was more certain than ever that the invasion would be at Kahili. But next day he was startled to receive reports of "large forces" landing at Choiseul. The Treasuries had held down Bougainville's eastern flank. Choiseul still guarded the west. Should he join the battle at Choiseul?

Victor Krulak was called "Brute," as all the coxswains of Annapolis crews are called. In the Marine Corps the nickname stuck for other reasons. The short, blond Krulak could take it.

He could also move with great speed. Hardly six days after Lieutenant General Vandegrift had told him, "Take immediate action. Get ashore where there are no Japs," Krulak had brought his Second Parachutists ashore on Choiseul at a place called Voza.

They boarded the destroyer-transports *Kilty, Ward, Crosby* and *McKean* late in the afternoon of October 27, sped up The Slot through inaccurate bombing of Japanese night prowlers and began landing a half-hour before midnight.

Next day they hid themselves. They set up a dummy beach far away from the point at which they had actually landed. After they dispersed in the jungle some 80 Melanesian bearers carefully brushed out all their footprints in the sand. They spent the day marking time until Admiral Halsey's announcement that "strong American forces" had landed on Choiseul.

At dawn the next day Krulak's men went out to raise deliberate hell on Choiseul's southwest coast. One patrol moved noisily into the mountains. Another led by Krulak moved right or southeast toward the Japanese base at Sangigai. The Marines spotted about 15 Japanese soldiers unloading a *daihatsu* landing barge. Krulak gave orders to fire, but to be sure not to kill more than half of them so that word of the enemy would get back to Sangigai.

Three light machine guns were set up on a rock cliff overlooking the beach and the Japanese 150 yards away. They fired. They killed three Japanese instantly and shot down four more of those who ran down the beach. They let the rest of them go, destroyed the barge, and while word of the appearance of the Americans was signaled to Hyakutate in Rabaul, Krulak's patrol began sketching the enemy's position at Sangigai in preparation for an attack next day.

On that day, Krulak split his forces. One half moved downcoast to assault Sangigai from the west. The other half, under Krulak, marched up the Vagara River, crossed and came down on Sangigai from the northeast.

It was a toilsome march, for the Japanese rarely cut roads into the interior of the jungle and they slashed out trails to their own scale. The Marines moved through swamps, fording the snakelike Vagara at twelve different points. And when most men moved through water up to their chest, the Brute was immersed up to his neck. There was no time to rest; the coastal force had been instructed to attack two hours after Krulak's men marched off.

Shortly after two that afternoon the coastal force pounded Sangigai with rockets and mortars. The men of Company E charged into the town and found it deserted. The Japanese had taken Admiral Halsey at his word and had already retreated into the hills, where they were already colliding with Krulak.

About a half-hour after the beach barrage began, the Marines in the mountains heard jabbering in the jungle not 20 yards ahead. They dropped to the ground and began hastily building up a front, just as the Japanese popped into view 10 yards off.

The fight lasted an hour. First the Japanese closed with yells and rifle shots, and the Marines repulsed them. One machinegunner, unable to wait for his buddy to bring up the gun's tripod, fired with the butt braced against his right leg and the barrel clasped in his left hand. By the time the tripod arrived and he withdrew his hand, much of its flesh was left on the barrel. Another gunner fired while a rifleman dueled a sniper in the foliage of a huge banyan tree. The sniper fell

163

alongside the machine-gunner. He was wounded in the hip. The gunner pulled out his knife, killing the sniper with his right hand while continuing to fire with his left.

The enemy pulled back to a system of burrows and bunkers dug underneath those enormous banyans while snipers left behind in the treetops raked the Marines, wounding Krulak in the face. Marine demolition men crawled forward toward the bunkers. One of them reached into his kit for a six-block charge. It wouldn't come free. He tore at it and the entire kit of twenty-four blocks came loose. The Marine shrugged, stuck in a fuse, lighted it and hurled it beneath the banyan. There was a rocking explosion. The great tree jumped in the air, toppled and crashed against another forest giant.

The fight ended with the customary *banzai.*

The Japanese crawled out of their holes and came rushing at Krulak's Marines. They got among them, but were killed in hand-to-hand fighting. Immediately Krulak ordered a platoon forward in a counterattack.

The Marines rushed at the shrieking Japanese with wild yells of their own, and as they broke them and sent them fleeing into the jungle, an outraged BARman raised his head above the edge of his foxhole and bellowed:

"For God's sake, shut up! Us bastards are mad enough already!"

In a few more moments all was quiet but for the muffled explosions coastward, where E Company was methodically blowing up the Japanese headquarters, turning ammunition dumps into miniature volcanoes and cheering with delight to see the explosive gala provided by the detonated medical supply dump, where the sky was filled with flaming fragments of wood and metal crisscrossed by long white ribbons of the bandages unrolling in flight.

Krulak's men made more smoke for General Vandegrift before they were withdrawn by LCI at midnight of November 3. By that time they had accomplished their mission. General Hyakutate had already begun to move Bougainville troops south to Choiseul by barge. On November 1 he sent 60 bombers and escorting fighters against the "force of 20,000 men" which Radio Tokyo said was then ashore on Choiseul.

The Japanese aircraft were bombing the bait even as the Third Marine Division commanded by Major General Allen Turnage hit the narrow beaches of Cape Torokina.

6

November 1, 1943, was clear and bright, a tropic day when the air is soft and aromatic, when the sea is all silvery and glittering in the light of the rising sun. At a quarter after six Marines crowding the rails of their transports could see the sun standing clearly above the bleak blue line of the Bougainville mountains, a thread of smoke from the crater of Mount Bagana trailing across its face. The Marines also saw the shell-smoke rising from Cape Torokina and from the island of Puruata, 1,000 yards offshore and about the same distance to the left or west of the Cape. American cruisers and destroyers had begun a bombardment. In another hour the landing boats churned shoreward and the naval gunfire lifted.

At that point, 270 soldiers of the 2nd Company, 1st Battalion, 23rd Japanese Infantry, began fighting to hold the landing beaches west of the Cape. Snipers on Puruata poured rifle fire into the boats rounding the island, and from 18 big pillboxes on the right or east flank came the bullets of automatic weapons and the shells of a 75-millimeter field piece.

The Japanese gun whanged from within a concealed emplacement of coconut logs and sandbags. Before it fired 50 shells it had sunk four landing boats and damaged 10 others carrying the men of Major Leonard (Spike) Mason's First Battalion, Third.

Sergeant Robert Owens, among the first men to land safely, spotted the emplacement from which the gun poured its terrible fire. He crawled toward it. He posted four men to pin down the two rifle bunkers which covered the approach to the gun. Then he jumped to his feet and charged. He was hit repeatedly on his way in, but he kept on. He dove straight through the gun port. He killed the gunner and drove the other crewmen out the rear entrance, where they were cut down by his companions. Then Owens sank to the ground, dying. His charge had won the Medal of Honor and also had destroyed the most formidable obstacle on the Torokina beaches.

With the gun knocked out, Major Spike Mason could continue his reorganization of the assault on the pillboxes. One by one they fell, while Mason's Marines and the Second Raider Battalion of Lieutenant Colonel Joseph McCaffery darted low through enemy small-arms fire, running in close to the hulking pillboxes to hurl the grenades that flushed the enemy into the open. At one pillbox Platoon Sergeant Bill Wilson began firing at 15 enemy soldiers dashing from an exposed trench for the security of a pillbox. He was joined by another Marine. They killed them all and advanced on another bunker. As a terrified Japanese burst from its entry Wilson leaped on his shoulders and finished him with a knife thrust.

It was that kind of fighting—savage, close, primitive. For the first time the Marines were meeting an organized beach defense, and they were taking casualties. McCaffery fell, mortally stricken. Mason was wounded. He refused evacuation, for he feared a counterattack and had no wish to be the living commander of a lost battalion. He turned command over to his executive. "Get the hell in there and fight!" he swore, and the assault swept on until the smoke and yells and roar of battle had faded by noon and most of the 270 Japanese who had fought so hard to hold the Cape were dead.

On the west or left flank it was not the Japanese but the sea that was the enemy. The Ninth Marines came in unopposed, but their beaches were too steep for the landing boats to ground along the full length of their keel. They were upended. They were swamped or they filled at the stern and slid off the beach to sink in deep water. Sixty-four landing boats and 22 LCM's were broached before the troops came ashore.

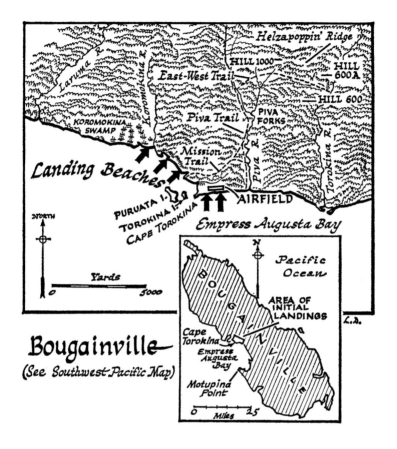

Bougainville
(See Southwest Pacific Map)

But by noon, more than half the Third Marine Division had been landed and destroyers were heading south for Guadalcanal to escort the second echelon north. Over at Puruata the Third Raider Battalion was mopping up the Japanese snipers. And the 30 Japanese fighters and bombers which had been gulled down Choiseul way had at last found the true target and were roaring in to strike it.

The red-balled planes arrived at forty minutes past noon, making for the troops ashore and the transports out in Empress Augusta Bay. Dropping down from the clouds to take on eight of them came five Marine Corsairs led by Lieutenant Colonel Herbert Williamson. Among them was Butcher Bob Hanson, the youthful, India-born lieutenant who was to have one of the most brilliant—and meteoric—careers of all American fliers.

While his comrades knocked down two of the enemy aircraft, Hanson made three quick high side passes at a trio of low-flying Kates and shot down all of them. But the bullets of a Kate rear-gunner shot down Hanson. He crashed safely, got out, inflated his rubber boat until he sighted the destroyer *Sigourney* in the Bay. He paddled toward it, hopefully singing "You'd Be So Nice to Come Home To," and *Sigourney* obligingly came about and picked him up.

Except for slight damage to destroyer *Wadsworth*, where two sailors were killed and five wounded, the Japanese attackers caused little damage. They lost 22 planes while shooting down four Americans, and they had not killed a single Marine.

It had not been thought possible that the swamps and steaming jungle of Guadalcanal could be anywhere exceeded. These men had trained on Guadalcanal and had learned how to live in the rain forest. After Guadalcanal they thought of themselves as jungle-fighters, but they had not been on Guadalcanal during the rainy season.

Before dusk the rain began to fall. Marines sloshing inland discovered that the difference between Guadalcanal and Bougainville was that Bougainville was all jungle. There were no lovely white beaches, only a streak of sand separating sea from forest. There were no pleasant groves of coconuts, for dark and wild Bougainville had never attracted planters.

In the rains falling that dusk of November 1, wiremen found that it was taking them an hour to move a hundred yards. It was hard to move supplies, except by hand or amtrack. Anything wheeled was useless. Because of this it was not until nightfall that Major General Turnage had established his beachhead perimeter.

This was an area about 5,000 yards in width on an east-west axis, and 1,000 yards at its deepest. Protecting it against the

Japanese 23rd Regiment then assembling inland was a road-block which a battalion of Raiders had set up along the Mission Trail. The trail ran into the jungle from roughly the center of the perimeter, slanting right or east. The Raider road-block was placed across it at a point about 2,000 yards outside the perimeter. This was to stop, or at least check, the night's inevitable Japanese counterattack.

But it never came.

Marines sitting up to their waists in water heard nothing but the blundering of an occasional wild pig, or, more infrequently, the thrashing of one of those Japanese soldiers who had infiltrated with no notion of what he would do once he had pierced the line. One of these fell into a water-filled hole occupied by a Marine rifleman.

"I'm too young to die," he cried in impeccable English.

"So am I," the Marine yelled, and killed him with his knife.

Otherwise, the lines were quiet. There was only the steady drumming of the rain. Back in Division headquarters it seemed strange that the enemy did not strike.

Then at a half-hour or so after two in the morning there was a flashing and a thundering to seaward and a sudden buzzing of CP telephones and the word was passed:

"Condition Black. You may expect shelling from enemy ships followed by counterinvasion."

In Rabaul on November 1 a counterinvasion had been ordered for the Cape Torokina area and then canceled.

Rear Admiral Sentaro Omori had been told to take 1,000 soldiers aboard five destroyer-transports to the American beachhead on Bougainville. Omori assembled his fleet—six big destroyers, the heavy cruisers *Myoko* and *Haguro,* the lights *Sendai* and *Agano*—and took them down to St. George Channel between New Britain and New Ireland. They waited there for the destroyer-transports, which did not show up until half-past ten that night. Already chafing at the delay, disturbed at having been sighted by an American submarine, Omori was further upset to hear that the transports could not make more than 26 knots. Then an American plane dropped a bomb close aboard *Sendai* at eleven o'clock, and Omori

169

asked Rabaul for permission to send back the transports so that he might speed down to Empress Augusta Bay unencumbered and attack the American transports. Permission was granted. Bending on 32 knots, Omori took his warships south.

Waiting below to meet him, knowing he was coming, was Rear Admiral A. Stanton (Tip) Merrill, commanding Task Force 39.

Admiral Merrill had already set minesweepers to work sealing off Torokina with a field of mines. He too had sent his transports away and had taken station about 19 miles off the Cape at the mouth of Empress Augusta Bay—determined "to prevent the entry therein of a single enemy ship."

Merrill had more ships but not as much firepower as the enemy. He had eight destroyers, including the four "Little Beavers" of Captain Arleigh (Thirty-One-Knot) Burke, and the light cruisers *Montpelier, Cleveland, Columbia,* and *Denver.* At about half-past two in the morning of November 2 the pips of the approaching Japanese warships were clearly visible on American radar screens.

"Believe this is what we want," *Montpelier's* combat information center reported, and ten minutes later the battle was joined.

It quickly broke up into three fights, one between the cruisers and two separate destroyer battles. Almost immediately the savage concerted shellfire of Merrill's cruisers struck *Sendai.* It was radar-controlled firing at its best. *Sendai* began to burn brightly, exploding as she burned. Destroyers *Samidare* and *Shiratsuyu* swung violently around to escape the fire that was sinking *Sendai* and collided with one another with a screech of rending steel. They limped home to Rabaul.

Zigzagging violently, making smoke, the American cruiser commanders shifted fire to the Japanese columns centered around *Myoko* and *Haguro.* Again their aim was unerring. The third salvos walked right into them. Destroyer *Hatsukaze* tried to dodge. She swerved between the two big cruisers and shuddered as *Myoko* plowed into her, shearing off two of her tubes, mangling her starboard bow, leaving her to be torn apart and sunk by the American destroyers.

But now Omori's heavies were opening up with eight-inch star-shells and patrol planes were dropping white and colored flares. The American cruisers, unscratched for half an hour, began to receive hits. Eight-inch salvos straddled them. *Denver* received three eight-inch hits forward and began to take in water, but she stayed afloat while the battle became a thing of terrible beauty.

Clouds drifting overhead had become suffused with the light of flare and gunflash. They illuminated the battle as though it were being fought upon a theatrically lighted black pond, and all that flashed and glittered and shone seemed to be magnified by the encircling darkness. There was that quality of slow majesty attendant upon night surface action when great ships move at great speed over great bodies of water. Salvos striking the sea threw up great geysers; they seemed not to leap but to gather themselves upward, to rise in slow-pluming fountains, to catch the red light of burning ships, the green-gold of flame-streaming guns, the jagged orange glinting off swirling black water, to catch it, to make it dazzling with its own phosphorescence—and then to burst apart in a million vanishing sparkles.

It would have been an unreal world, a ghostly one, fantastical, but for the pungent smell of smoke, the constant thundering of the guns and the real crashing of the shells and crying of the stricken.

As the battle continued, Admiral Omori came to believe that he had destroyed three American cruisers. He thought that near-misses straddling them and raising geysers in the air had been torpedo hits. When the American cruisers vanished beneath their own smoke, he believed they had sunk—and he sailed home.

Like Mikawa at Savo, Omori had not gotten in on the American transports. Unlike him he had not sunk an American ship.

It was dawn of November 2 but the Marines inland on Bougainville saw only the murky light of the swamp as they hurried to expand their beachhead. The Twenty-first Marines held in division reserve by Major General Turnage were to be brought in from Guadalcanal, followed by the Army's 37th Infantry Division, representing the corps reserve. In the meantime the Marine combat battalions pushed deeper into the rain forest and expanded the perimeter wide enough to contain the airfield which the Seabees were building. The new line's left rested on the Koromokina Swamp in the west and its right at a point about 2,000 yards east of Cape Torokina. Its over-all width was about 5,500 yards, it was about 2,000 yards at its deepest and something more than 1,000 yards at the norm. Outside it was the rain forest to the north and behind it the waters of Empress Augusta Bay. The Laruma River lay 10,000 yards to the west of it on the left and the crooked Piva River about the same distance east on the right.

Major General Turnage still had the Raiders holding the Mission Trail roadblock—but now only about 400 yards outside the perimeter. Puruata was becoming a supply dump, and little Torokina Island midway between Puruata and the Cape had also been occupied. Turnage also reshuffled his units to place the fresh ones in position to receive the counterthrust he still believed to be impending—either from sea or jungle. In this movement, the left flank had been shortened and the Koromokina Swamp positions held by two battalions had been abandoned. And this would help the enemy in the counter-invasion that was to come.

Lieutenant General Hyakutate had not given up on the idea of counterinvasion by sea. After Admiral Omori sent back the transports the night of November 1, Hyakutate collected 3,000 men from the 17th Division's 53rd and 54th Regiments. They were to go south escorted by another powerful cruiser force which was to sweep the waters clear of Americans and bombard the Marine beachhead while the soldiers went ashore.

The cruisers came down from Truk—*Takao, Maya, Atago, Suzuya, Mogami, Chikuma, Chokai*—the old pros, the big and veteran sluggers of Admiral Kondo's 2nd Fleet. With them came light cruiser *Noshiro*, four destroyers and a sizable fleet train. They came into Rabaul on November 5 to refuel. They considered themselves safe. There were 150 planes on Rabaul's fields. American bases were too far off. There were no American carriers at sea.

But *Princeton* and *Saratoga* had already raced up to Bougainville under cover of darkness. At nine in the morning of November 5 they began to fly off their planes—97 fighters and bombers—and three hours later a torrent of American aircraft thundered up St. George Channel, roared straight through the flak of the flatfooted enemy ships without breaking formation, and then broke off into small groups to begin their work.

The 70 Japanese fighters already airborne to oppose them could not knock down more than 10 of them, and the damage to Kondo's cruisers was enormous. Not one ship was sunk, but few were left in fighting trim. *Takao* was torn apart at the waterline, *Mogami* was sent staggering back to Japan for repairs, *Atago* took three near-misses and a bomb fell down one of *Maya's* stacks and exploded in her engine room. Meanwhile the lights *Agano* and *Noshiro* were also hit and destroyer *Fujinami* was holed by a dud torpedo and *Wakatsuki* ripped open by near-misses.

Then, as the Navy planes flew back to their mother ships, 24 Army Liberators and 67 Lightnings came winging over from New Guinea and the Woodlarks to pound the city itself and tear up the docks.

Yet, with the cruiser force out of action, and the naval phase of the counterattack now almost impossible, a portion of Hyakutate's soldiers was still going to be sent down The Slot on the first run of the Tokyo Express in nearly a year.

Why?

Because the Rabaul planes sent out to hunt *Princeton* and *Saratoga* and their escorting warships thought they had found their quarry between Cape Torokina and the Treasuries. What they had actually found was one damaged LCT under the care of an LCI-gunboat and a PT-boat. The Japanese planes struck. The three little American ships not only beat them off but also shot a few of them down. Next day the world heard this from Radio Tokyo:

"One large carrier blown up and sunk, one medium carrier

173

set ablaze and later sunk, and two heavy cruisers and one cruiser and destroyer sunk."

It was the biggest lie of the Pacific War, the ultimate result of the Japanese custom of making reports wearing rose-colored glasses. Because of it the Tokyo Express sped down to Bougainville the night of November 6. Four destroyers took 475 soldiers down to Koromokina Swamp, the place which would give its name to the brief, bitter battle in which they died.

The men of the Third Battalion, Ninth Marines, rose from their watery sleeping places at dawn of November 7 and saw 21 Japanese barges plodding toward beaches just west of Koromokina Swamp. The boats beached and Japanese soldiers jumped ashore and ran into the jungle. Some of them struck up the Laruma River still farther west of these Marines on the left or western flank. The Japanese planned to get upriver and then turn right or east to work down against the American perimeter.

The main body struck at the Marine left held by the Third Battalion, Ninth. They were stopped. They withdrew into the swamp, and at twenty minutes after eight the Marines attacked.

They too were stopped, for the Japanese had occupied those foxholes and entrenchments abandoned only a few days before when Turnage shortened his lines. They had had more than an hour to improve them, and the Japanese had no equals at digging in.

Now it was stalemate, and during it, a Laruma River patrol led by Lieutenant Orville Freeman opened battle with those Japanese who had marched upriver. Outnumbered, Freeman withdrew. He retreated to the perimeter, setting up frequent rear-guards to ambush the pursuing Japs. It would take him thirty hours to get back to his lines, during which one Marine would be killed and Freeman himself would be wounded. But they would make it.

In the meantime, on that morning of November 7, Major General Turnage called for his reserve.

The men of the First Battalion, Third Marines, had gone

174

into reserve to rest after doing most of the fighting during the Cape Torokina landings. They had been pleased. But now, like the Raiders of Guadalcanal, they were learning that it is often safer to be on the lines than to be behind them where the general can put you to use.

At a quarter past one these men passed through the bogged-down Third Battalion, Ninth. They attacked into a tangle of fern and creeper and giant trees with a mire for underfooting and five yards for visibility. Men shot at movement and when concealed Japanese machine guns spat at them they hurled grenades at the sound.

Sergeant Herbert Thomas threw a grenade in this way, but it was caught by ropelike lianas overhead and dropped back among Thomas and his men. The sergeant threw himself on it and was killed. The men he had saved moved on.

Then a Marine tank came churning through the muck. It swayed as it burst through the undergrowth like a great blind amphibian, the sharp branches of the undergrowth clawing harmlessly at its metal hide, its cannon jerking and spouting flame. Captain Gordon Warner ran alongside the tank. He carried a helmet full of hand grenades, hurling them at Japanese machine-gun nests to spot them for the tank-gunner.

"Fix bayonets!" he roared in the Japanese he had learned years ago. "Charge!"

Betrayed by their own virtues—ardor and obedience—the Japanese leaped erect and charged, coming in a swarm to be obliterated by Marine rifle fire or the hosing of the tank's machine gun.

Six enemy guns were knocked out by Warner and the tank, until the Japanese were gradually thrust from the swamp and a solid Marine firing line had been built up. Captain Warner lost a leg as a result of wounds received in his attack, but he had put the battle on the way to being won. Artillery observers were soon up front calling for the fire which held the line until morning.

Then five batteries of field guns began firing. Machine guns swept the swamp, mortars lobbed in shells, antitank guns blasted away with cannister shot—and the screams of the enemy were audible to the Marines. When the guns fell silent the men of the First Battalion, Twenty-first Marines, moved through the First Battalion, Third, into the swamp and found it as still and silent as a morgue.

Koromokina contained the bodies of 377 Japanese soldiers who had died to kill 17 United States Marines.

It was November 9 and Technical Sergeant Frank Devine was desperate for a story. He was a Marine combat correspondent, one of that corps of professional newsmen who had given up their jobs to march with the Marines and write about them. They were assigned one to a regiment and given the mission of reporting the battle at the cannon's mouth. Their stories went by mail to Marine Headquarters in Washington and were passed on to the press from there.

On that morning of November 9 Devine was soaking wet and he did not have a story in sight.

True, there had been the Battle of the Koromokina Swamp, but that hadn't happened in his sector. True, Major General Roy Geiger had relieved Lieutenant General Vandegrift as commander of the First Marine Amphibious Corps on Bougainville and the Treasuries, but that was a story for the civilian war correspondents (it was a big one, however, for Vandegrift of Guadalcanal was going home to his fourth star and command of the Marine Corps). True again, the first elements of the Army's 37th Division had begun to arrive, but that was the Army combat reporters' beat—and who wanted to write about dogfaces anyway?

Sergeant Devine looked sourly at the sodden sheet of paper in the little typewriter cradled on his knees. He noticed that the machine had already begun to rust and wondered how many days before it would become useless. He wondered what it would be like to wear dry socks and sleep on dry ground. He listened to the rain. He stared and tried to think of something that the folks at home might find interesting, and then he wrote:

"Bougainville, Nov. 1, 2, 3, 4, 5, 6, 7, 8, 9—It rained today."

The fighting on Bougainville had shifted to the Marines' right or eastern flank.

Since November 5, the men of the 23rd Infantry Regiment

176

commanded by Colonel Kawano had been striking hard at the Raiders blocking the Mission Trail. The trailblock held. More, the Marines came out of it to push farther toward a fork about 2,000 yards outside the new perimeter where the Mission Trail joined the Piva Trail, becoming thereafter the Piva Trail. This force, commanded by Colonel Edward Craig, had left the Raiders holding the trailblock behind them and by November 8 had pushed up to a point just below the Mission-Piva confluence. The next morning they would attack past it.

On the morning of November 9 the Twelfth Marines opened up with howitzers. When the barrage lifted, the Marine riflemen attacked—and were struck by Japanese who had waited out the artillery in foxholes.

Again it was grenade for grenade, shot for shot. Tanks were useless. The trail was too narrow and the swamp on either side too deep. The Marines had to attack straight ahead—blindly.

A platoon led by Lieutenant John Sabini was pinned down by an unseen machine gun. Sabini jumped up, shouting, "When they open up on me, fire back!" The Japanese did open up and Sabini was hit. He fell. He jumped up again, still shouting, and was hit again. By then his Marines had spotted the hidden gun and had charged it and destroyed it. The attack slogged forward, 40 or 50 yards an hour.

Downtrail the Japanese came stealthily at the Raiders' roadblock, searching out its defenses. When they had located two foxhole outposts each manned by a pair of Marines with a BAR and rifle, they opened up with heavy machine-gun fire. They filled the air with grenades. The Marines in one of the holes were killed. There was a lull.

In the other hole Pfc. Henry Gurke said to Pfc. Donald Probst, "Look, you've got the BAR and you're more important."

"So?" Probst whispered, his eyes fastened on the green tangle to his front.

"They're using a lot of grenades," Gurke explained. "One of 'em might land in the hole."

Probst nodded in anticipation, and Gurke concluded: "So if one should land in here I'll take it."

177

It was not the time to argue. The enemy was rushing in again and Probst's automatic rifle was chattering and spreading death among them. Then came the somersaulting grenades and the *thud* as one of them plopped between them. It lay there, a dirty hissing container packed with death and Gurke threw Probst aside and dropped upon it.

Pfc. Probst never knew whether or not he heard the muffled explosion for his finger was squeezing the trigger of the BAR his friend had found "important" enough to die for, and the charging enemy was falling back. They returned, again and again, sweeping in on other fronts, but the roadblock still held. The attack up the Piva Trail went forward until, on the morning of November 10, with a brief sharp artillery shoot and the support of 12 low-flying Avengers, the Second Battalion, Ninth, moved out to find that the enemy was gone.

Colonel Kawano had left 550 of his soldiers along the Mission-Piva Trail in fighting that began November 5 and ended November 11, and there were only 19 Marines killed and 32 wounded.

And there was also a posthumous Medal of Honor for Pfc. Henry Gurke.

Life on Puruata was like living on a bull's-eye. This tiny islet 700 yards long and 400 wide was now the warehouse of the Bougainville campaign. The mainland beaches were too narrow and there was no dry coastal plain on which to place food and ammunition dumps. LST's running up to Bougainville had to come to Puruata to unload.

So did the Japanese bombers from Rabaul. It was such an easy trip they could make it regularly. Torokina was only 230 miles from Rabaul, in comparison to the 640 miles which had separated Rabaul and Guadalcanal a year ago.

Japanese bombers plastered Puruata endlessly and made a sleepless hell of the lives of the Marine pioneers and depot companies who were stationed there. By day the bombers were not so bad, for there was always Marine air to intercept them and drive them off.

But at night . . .

At night little Puruata lay like a moonstone embedded

in the dark ocean. Moonlight bathed her coconuts and washed the water breaking on her seaward reef to silver. Moonlight marked her clearly for the enemy bombers, and men who had worked all day ran to man antiaircraft guns or to form stretcher parties to make the inevitable search for the dead and wounded once the bombers had flown away.

Their ears were filled with the wailing and crashing of the bombs and the *whamming* of the antiaircraft guns, and when the fuel dump was set afire or the ammunition depot blew up they rolled the gas drums out of the inferno or darted among the exploding shells to lug ammunition cases to safety.

Even so Puruata never lost its sense of humor, that self-mockery which could make men laugh even while the air around them was whizzing with disintegrating steel—as they did the night Puruata had its third straight raid and a little Marine ran for his foxhole shouting:

"Hang onto your false teeth, girls—they may be dropping sandwiches."

Colonel Kawano had decided to withdraw. He was going to move off the Piva Trail which ran north-south over Bougainville's towering mountains and retreat east over the East-West Trail. He was going to await the arrival of reinforcements.

To gain time to make his withdrawal, Kawano arranged a delaying action at a position he had fortified beforehand. It was in a coconut grove just below the junction where the Piva Trail going north met the East-West going east. It was about five miles outside General Turnage's perimeter. Something less than a company was assigned to hold it. It was a sturdy defense line, well underground, for the men of the 23rd Regiment respected the Marine artillery.

But on the morning of November 13, when Lieutenant Colonel Eustace Smoak's Second Battalion, Twenty-first, attacked through the coconut grove, they came on without their artillery. They were immediately pinned down. E Company led by Captain Sidney Altman was unable to move. Word was sent back to Smoak. He rushed up reinforcing companies and called for the artillery.

Lieutenant Bob Rennie went up the trail to join Major

Glenn Fissel, the battalion's executive officer. He set up his telephone behind a mangrove tree about fifty yards away from the source of all that banging and chattering. He gave his position to the artillery operations officer and said, "Put a round about five hundred yards in front of me."

It went whistling over, but its crash was muffled by the jungle.

"Bring it down two hundred yards," Rennie said.

The whistle was louder, the crash of the shell distinct and reverberating, but it seemed to the left of the battle.

"Another hundred down and you'd better bring it right one hundred yards."

The shell's passage was a scream now, its crash echoing. Rennie glanced at Major Fissel.

"That deflection seem all right, Major?"

Fissel nodded and Rennie spoke again into the telephone.

"Down one hundred. Deflection correct."

There was hardly an instant separating the scream and the *wham*. Rennie glanced again at Fissel. The shells were landing only a hundred yards from the Marine front. It could be dangerous to lower the range, but Fissel nodded, and Rennie's voice was tinged with apprehension as he said:

"Down fifty. Deflection correct."

Now the scream of the shell seemed to begin sooner and stay around longer. The crash shook water from the foliage.

"How was that?" Rennie asked.

Fissel ignored him and shouted uptrail, "Pass the word for someone up there to come back and tell us how those shells are going."

A Marine came back. His face was gaunt and streaked with slime. He shouted, for his ears were still full of the clamor of battle.

"If you come back another twenty-five yards you'll be right on top of those lousy Japs."

Lieutenant Rennie's face blanched. His lips tightened. Twenty-five yards! It was too risky. But he gave the order.

"Down twenty-five."

And now the screams were those of wounded and dying

men, hoarse and trailing in their agony and making no words but only the atavistic sounds of stricken animals.

"Cease fire!" Rennie shouted frantically into the telephone. "Cease fire!"

He knew it, he should never have brought it in that close, and he cursed that Marine for misleading him into bringing death down on his own men. Then another Marine appeared, an officer, and he was angry.

"What in hell's the matter with the artillery? Why'd you cease firing?"

"Aren't we hitting our own men?"

"Like hell you are!" the officer bellowed. "Those are the Japs screaming. Make 'em scream some more—plenty more! My men like to hear it."

So the tension left the lips of Lieutenant Rennie and he smiled as he picked up the telephone and said:

"Belay that last. Fire for effect!"

The shells continued to crash into the coconut grove and when the barrage was lifted, E Company had pulled out of the enemy trap and was able to re-form for the attack which went forward that day and the next until the coconut grove was cleaned out.

The mouth of the East-West Trail had been cleared and the way was now open to pursuit.

7

When Rear Admiral Keiji Shibasaki came out to the Gilbert Islands in August, 1943, to direct the defense of this Central Pacific group about 2,400 miles southwest of Pearl Harbor, he set up headquarters on the islet of Betio. This was the coral speck which the Japanese had renamed Bititu and which the world now knows as Tarawa from the chain of which it is only a part.

For Tarawa is not an island but an atoll, one of those chains of islets created by a great saw-toothed saucer of coral rising from the ocean floor. The broken teeth sticking above water are the islets. Within them, in the hollow of the saucers—enclosed or half-closed by surrounding reef—are lagoons. They are excellent anchorages. Some of the islets are broad enough to support airports. Tarawa Atoll, a triangle with its sides running about 30 miles north-south and its base about 25 miles east-west, formed one of these anchorages. It was accessible through a western channel about six miles above Betio, which was the westernmost islet and the left-hand angle of the triangle. Betio was also just big enough to support an airfield while being too small for enemy maneuver. It became the heart of the defense of Tarawa Atoll, which was itself the key to the Gilberts, and it was fortified by the Japanese as had been no island in history.

Such defenses were the result of the raid on Makin Atoll 105 miles north by Carlson's Raiders in August, 1942. The Makin incursion had had a rich yield of headlines in America, but it had warned Japan of the necessity of defending the Gilberts and of the futility of attempting it on Makin. In September of 1942 an industrious rear admiral named Tomanari Saichiro began fortifying Betio. He built an airfield on the western half of the parrot-shaped islet, on the bird's body, and he made each of Betio's 291 acres bristle with every gun in the Japanese arsenal—all mounted within pillboxes, blockhouses and huge bombproofs of ferro-concrete two stories high. Betio's beaches were girdled by a sea wall made of coconut logs clamped and stapled together. It was from three to five feet in height and stood about 20 feet inland from the water. An American helmet reared above this sea wall would be as clear and helpless as a fly walking down a windowpane. And if the Americans crouched beneath it, Betio's mortars would dye the sands with their blood. The mortars had the beaches registered—and they were behind a formidable array of machine guns and light artillery inter-locked to sweep the lip of the sea wall, and after that the air-field.

There were 62 heavy machine guns and 44 light machine guns—many of them twin mounts—nine 37-millimeter anti-tank guns and the 37's of 14 light tanks dug into the coral sand and camouflaged with palm fronds—to say nothing of the rifles, pistols, grenades and bayonets of the defending troops, to say nothing of the heavier artillery.

Of this there were six 70-millimeter battalion guns, eight more 75-millimeter dual-purpose guns, ten 75-millimeter moun-tain guns, four five-inch dual purpose guns, six 80-millimeter guns, four coast defense guns 5.5 inches in diameter and four eight-inch coastal guns brought to Betio from Singapore. Most of these guns were mounted to fire antiboat along pre-selected fields of fire. They were sighted from concrete-and-coral pillboxes. The five- and eight-inch guns could duel the invading ships. The eight-inchers were placed at each end of the island, two to an end, and served from enormous con-crete ammunition rooms.

To either end of the airfield, east and west, there were tank traps. The field itself was protected by rifle pits and pillboxes, dug in deeply and covered with coconut logs and coral sand and sometimes also with concrete. These firing holes were also interlocked, often served by networks of trenches.

Only the water defenses needed improvement when, eleven months later, Admiral Shibasaki arrived on Betio to relieve Saichiro. The new commander completed these on the south or ocean side by erecting a wicked offshore maze of horned con-crete tetrahedrons. They were wired together, mines were sprinkled among them, and they were so placed as to channel all incoming boats into the point-blank fire of the 70-, 75- and 80-millimeter guns. This was done by mid-September, 1943. Admiral Shibasaki next set his men to placing the same sort of obstacles between the northern or lagoon beaches and the la-goon reef about 500 to 1,000 yards offshore. When this was done, the admiral would have fulfilled his assignment in the Imperial General Headquarters plan called *Yogaki*, or Waylaying Attack. *Yogaki's* purpose was to teach the Americans the prohibitive costs of invading fortified islands. Under it, Shibasaki was to make Betio impregnable while:

Long-range aircraft flew down from Rabaul and Kavieng to bomb the invaders, and then land on Gilberts-Marshalls fields;

Short-range aircraft flew down from Truk by stages to these same airfields to provide aerial defense;

Admiral Kondo's powerful Second Fleet arrived to attack American shipping;

And a heavy force of submarines converged from all directions.

This was the plan, but on September 19 the Americans began hacking away at it.

On that night and the succeeding day the new American carriers *Lexington* and the smaller *Princeton* and *Belleau Wood* made their fighting debut at Betio's expense. Their airplanes shot up the boats needed to carry the tetrahedrons out into the lagoon and they also destroyed much of the cement.

Still, Shibasaki was not dismayed. His gun emplacements had not been harmed. He had had time to make Betio's ocean side impregnable and Tarawa was now on the neap, that seasonal tide when waters are lowest. Shibasaki doubted very much if the Americans would be able to cross the lagoon reef.

So did the Americans; so did a couple of generals named Smith.

The first was Holland M. Smith and he was a major general in command of the Fifth Amphibious Corps. He was six-one, graying, a man with a dandified white mustache and professorial eyeglasses juxtaposed against a big aggressive nose and a tongue that could be blistering and irreverent whenever Marines were being slighted. The Marines called him Howlin' Mad. In legend it was because of what he had said to the men he led on a record-breaking hike through the Philippine jungle in 1906; in fact it was because it fitted his first name and middle initial as much as his temperament.

The second Smith was Major General Julian Smith, the commander of the Second Marine Division. He was soft-spoken, gentle-eyed, fatherly. He rarely lost his temper. But if

Julian Smith was not angry on October 2, 1943, he was at least concerned.

General Julian Smith had come to Pearl Harbor with his chief of staff, Red Mike Edson of Guadalcanal, and had begun to confer with General Holland Smith on the Second Division's assignment to capture Betio. He was worried about the reef and the tides. Even though his men would make their assault from the lagoon side, entering by boat from the western channel, there was a reef there, too. And with the attack occurring during the neap tide, Julian Smith could not be certain of much water over that reef. Tarawa was also visited by "dodging tides" which were sometimes irregularly high, sometimes irregularly low, but Julian Smith did not share Rear Admiral Richard Kelly Turner's confidence that there would be a high-dodger on invasion day. There could be a low one. If there was, Julian Smith's Marines would never get over the reef in their landing boats. They would have to wade inshore from 500 to 1,000 yards out—into a murderous fire. Julian Smith wanted amtracks. Amtracks could climb the reefs and churn ashore. But he had only 75 operable amtracks, which was not enough to get his first waves ashore. He needed at least 100 more.

"All right," said Howlin' Mad Smith. "I'll get 'em for you."

So Julian Smith and Red Mike Edson flew back to Wellington, but when Howlin' Mad Smith spoke to Kelly Turner, Kelly Turner said, "No."

The admiral who commanded the Fifth Amphibious Force said he would not have the amtracks aboard his ships. There was going to be a high-dodging tide off Betio on November 20 and amtracks would not be needed. Howlin' Mad said:

"Kelly, it's like this: I've got to have those amtracks. We'll take a helluva licking without them. No amtracks—no operation."

It was not customary to hand Kelly Turner ultimatums, but this one had the virtue of suggesting Smith's determination. It was finally arranged that of 100 amtracks then in California 50 would be rushed to Samoa where the Second could pick them up after they departed Wellington.

Meanwhile, what about Makin?

Makin would be taken by another general named Smith—

the Army's Major General Ralph Smith, who led the 27th Infantry Division. Intelligence estimated Makin's garrison at a little better than 500 men, though there were actually 900. To take Makin, Ralph Smith was going to use but one of his three regiments, the 165th Infantry.

A third, much smaller operation was planned. This was the seizure of Apamama, a beautiful and historic atoll about 85 miles south of Tarawa. Apamama would not be attacked until November 26, but it would be scouted on November 21 by the Fifth Corps Reconnaissance Company of Captain Jim Jones. These Marines were to sail by submarine from Tarawa the night of November 20, going ashore by rubber boat in early morning to learn the extent of Apamama's defenses. Intelligence believed the atoll to be defended in company strength or more, though actually it was much less.

Intelligence was more accurate in its estimate of 4,500 men on Betio. They had used a unique yardstick to measure it. An aerial photograph had shown numerous latrines built out over the lagoon. Intelligence officers carefully marked the number of holes, and then, knowing that Japanese doctrine was also inflexible in such matters as the ratio of holes to occupants, they made an estimate not very far from the exact figure of 4,836 Imperial Japanese Marines and construction troops.

In assault against them would be only two-thirds of the Second Marine Division's strength, the Second and Eighth Marines with attached troops. The Sixth Marines would be in Corps reserve, on call for either operation. But all of the Second Division's 18,600 Marines were together when they began boarding ship in Wellington in late October under the delusion that they were merely going to run up Hawkes Bay on maneuvers.

Julian Smith had not forgotten how the First Division sailed from Wellington fifteen months ago with newspapers talking of an attack on Tulagi, and he took his own Second out of New Zealand under an elaborate smokescreen. Orders for the "Hawkes Bay Maneuvers" were drawn up. The Royal New Zealand Air Force was solemnly briefed on coverage for these practice landings. Men were told they would be back in camp within a week, and of course they told their girls. The final touch was to arrange with New Zealand firms for the movement of equipment from Hawkes Bay back to the Wellington base.

It was not until the Second sailed from Wellington in late October that the governor general of New Zealand was told the Marines were leaving his country for good. They were going to Efate in the New Hebrides.

It was at Efate that the Second Division made its practice landings, using those 50 new amtracks picked up in Samoa. It was in Efate that a bull-chested, bull-necked, profane colonel named David Shoup was placed in charge of that Second Regiment which was going to lead the way in to Betio. The Second's commanding officer, Colonel William Marshall, became ill in Efate, and Major General Julian Smith named his operations officer, Shoup, to take his place. And it was at Efate, during a meeting attended by Britishers who had lived in the Gilberts, that someone spoke of the difficulty of crossing Betio's lagoon reef on the neap tide.

"Neap tide!" exclaimed Major Frank Holland. "My God, when I told you there would be five feet of water on the reef, I never dreamed anyone would try to land at neap tide. There won't be three feet of water on the reef!"

The Americans were shocked, and a meeting of captains and pilots who had sailed the Gilberts was called. In spite of what Holland had said, it was concluded that there would probably be enough water to float both landing boats and LCM's over the reef.

Which was not true.

But by then all the plans had been made. It was argued that to wait until after November 22, when the spring tides would appear, would also be to risk a coincident west wind which whips up a steep short sea off Betio. Also, the flood of the spring tide would cover Betio's beaches right up to the barricades and there might not be any place to land. Again, each day's delay would mean the arrival of the flood an hour later, and because invasions normally must come at the flood, that meant one hour less daylight in which to seize the beachhead.

Admiral Turner still was willing to gamble on the presence

of a high-dodging tide on November 20, and the great invasion fleet of three battleships, five cruisers, nine destroyers and 17 troop and cargo ships had already begun to assemble. Naval bombardment officers were already predicting what they were going to do to Betio.

"We are going to bombard at 6,000 yards," said one battleship captain. "We've got so much armor we're not afraid of anything the Japs can throw back at us."

"We're going in at 4,000 yards," said a cruiser skipper. "We figure our armor can take anything they've got."

And Major General Julian Smith arose to say, "Gentlemen, remember one thing. When the Marines land and meet the enemy at bayonet point, the only armor a Marine will have is his khaki shirt!"

Then the fleet upped anchor and sailed for Betio.

At Betio more misfortune had befallen the *Yogaki* Plan.

On November 1 the American Marines had landed at Bougainville and troops intended for Shibasaki had been sucked off to the Solomons.

On November 5 the American carriers had made their disastrous strike at Rabaul and had knocked out the cruiser screen of Vice Admiral Kondo's Second Fleet.

On November 11 the American carrier planes came again, destroying many planes on the ground at Rabaul, shooting down something like 90 of them in ensuing dogfights. Many of these were the short-rangers from Truk which had been staged into Rabaul in preparation for strikes at the Marines on Bougainville. Now Shibasaki would not get his aerial cover. More, he had also been informed that the submarine force was badly depleted and he could expect the help of only a few undersea boats in the Gilberts.

By November 13, when the American fleet left Efate, aerial strikes at the Gilberts and especially Betio had risen in fury. American planes were constantly overhead from that date until November 10. On the eighteenth alone, carrier planes dropped 115 tons of bombs. Next day it was 69 tons and three American cruisers and two destroyers hurled 250 tons of projectiles into Betio the same day.

Clearly the Americans believed that they could knock out Betio. Shibasaki did not. He was confident as he moved among the 300 headquarters troops who shared his vast two-story bombproof at roughly the island's center. He knew, and the Americans as yet did not, that only the direct hits of the biggest bombs could destroy most of his positions. His own bombproof he thought impregnable. As Keiji Shibasaki frequently assured his troops:

"A million men cannot take Tarawa in a hundred years."

The men actually coming to take it, in less numbers and time, were in the best of fighting shape, for they were already bitching.

They were openly "beating their gums" over the stench and heat below decks; about the confusion of crossing the International Date Line so often that one week had two Sundays and no Thursday; over being tricked by the "Hawkes Bay Hoax" and not having had the chance to say goodbye in style; about being offered the insult of assaulting an upside-down bird of an island rock while the Third Division was taking Bougainville— which even the Stateside folks had heard of—and the First had sneaked up to New Guinea to try to steal headlines from Dugout Doug; over the tedium of playing endless games of gin rummy, of smoking, of drinking lukewarm coffee that the swabbie messman handed you like he wanted to charge you for it; of washing socks and underwear by tying them to ropes and heaving them over the fantail to be cleansed by the wake from the propeller; of reading paperbacked mysteries, paperbacked westerns, Bibles, histories; and finally of having to be led below daily, platoon by platoon, to dissolve in puddles of their own sweat while the officers rolled down the bulkhead maps and went over their role on Betio—again and again and again.

It was the maps which gave the men the impression of Betio as an upside-down bird. They were of course oriented north, and because the parrot's back was the south coast and the underbelly the north, the bird seemed upside down. The Marines were going to hit this north coast, the underbelly, with three battalions landing in three sectors almost exactly coextensive with the airfield, the bird's head and body. In roughly the center of this was a long pier stretching out into the lagoon, and this gave the impression of the bird's legs.

Attacking on the left or east would be the Second Battalion, Eighth Marines—detached to Colonel Shoup's Second Marines for the assault—led by the red-mustachioed Major Henry (Jim) Crowe, a "mustang" up from the ranks and a commander as energetic as he was enormous. In the center would be the Second Battalion, Second, under Lieutenant Colonel Herbert Amey. On the right or west was the Third Battalion, Second, under Major John Schoettel. Major General Julian Smith would have his three remaining battalions in reserve, for his Sixth Marine Regiment was still detached to Fifth Corps.

The first three waves were to be led into the lagoon by destroyers *Ringgold* and *Dashiell* after the little minesweepers *Pursuit* and *Requisite* had swept the entrance clear of mines. The amtracks would cross the lagoon reef to bring the assault troops ashore at about half-past eight, then return to the reef to pick up reinforcements which would be brought up to it by landing boats.

Julian Smith and his commanders still doubted that there would be enough water on the reef for the landing boats to cross it. Their only consolation was that they had had the forethought to provide themselves with enough amtracks to take in the first three waves. They took no comfort from the message sent them by the Tarawa force's sea commander, Rear Admiral Harry Hill. It said:

"It is not our intention to wreck the island. We do not intend to destroy it. Gentlemen, we will obliterate it."

8

The invasion fleet stood off Tarawa Atoll on the morning of November 20. Seventeen dark shapes slid into position about a mile off the western entrance to the lagoon, a few miles above the islet of Betio. They were the transports.

Below the lagoon entrance were the fire-support ships, battleships *Maryland, Colorado* and *Tennessee* with their cruisers and destroyers. Japan would regret not having attacked old *Maryland* and *Tennessee* in the open sea—where they would have been lost forever—instead of in the shallow waters of Pearl Harbor. They had been salvaged, modernized and sent out to join bombardment forces.

It was about half-past three in the morning. A half-moon flitted in and out of fleecy clouds. It was cool. Marines going down cargo nets into waiting landing boats could feel the perspiration drying on their foreheads.

They came from stifling galleys in which they had dined on steak and eggs, french fried potatoes and hot coffee, a meal as sure to induce perspiration as it provoked dismay from the transport surgeons who would soon be sewing up some of these men.

"Steak and eggs!" a surgeon aboard *Zeilin* exclaimed. "Jesus, that will make a nice lot of guts to have to sew up—full of steak!"

The men were boated now, moving slowly away from the big ships, coming to make the difficult transfer to the amtracks. They made it without accident. The attack lines were forming a quarter-mile off the lagoon entrance. Little *Pursuit* and *Requisite* were darting into the channel to sweep it clear of mines —and at 4:41 A.M. a red star-shell swished into sight high above

191

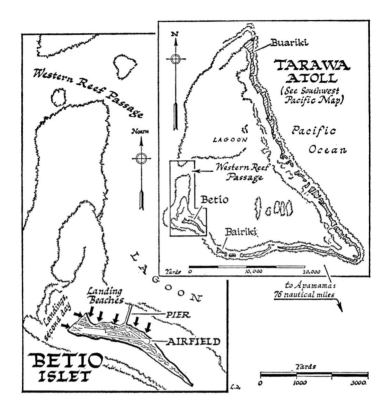

Betio and a half-hour later the Japanese shore batteries opened up.

The American battleships fired back.

Aboard *Maryland* the great long lengths of steel fingered the sky. One of them leaped. Flame spouted from it. A streaking blob of red sailed toward Betio. Marines in their tiny churning boats could watch its progress. They saw no explosion on Betio. The shell was short. Again the great gob of orange flame and the speck of streaking red, and again no explosion. But then dawn seemed to burst like a rocket from western Betio. A great sheet of flame sprang 500 feet into the air, and the explosion

192

which succeeded it sent shock waves rolling out over the water.

Old *Maryland* had hurled one of her 16-inch armor piercers into the ammunition room of the eight-inchers mounted on Betio's western tip. It was perhaps the greatest single bombardment feat of the war, for that shell of more than half a ton had killed men by the hundreds and had detonated hundreds of tons of enemy shells, and utterly wrecked the eight-inchers' blockhouse. And then *Tennessee* and *Colorado* began to thunder. All the battleships were firing in salvos, drifting in and out of their own gunsmoke as they paraded the Betio shoreline. Heavy cruisers belched flame and smoke from eight-inch muzzles. The lights roared away with six-inchers. Destroyers ran in close to send five-inch bullets arching ashore with almost the rapidity of automatic weapons.

Betio was aglow. She was a mass of fires. Great dust clouds swirled above her. Smoke coiled up and fused with them. Fires towered high and lit them with a fluttering pink glare. It seemed that Admiral Hill had been right, that Betio would not greet another dawn. The islet was being torn apart. She was no longer visible beneath that pall, now frowning, now glowing.

Then at forty-two minutes past five the American warships ceased firing. The American carrier planes were coming in, and it would be well to let the smoke clear so that the Dauntlesses and Avengers and the superb new Hellcat fighters could see their targets.

But the air strike did not arrive, and in the interval those "pulverized" Japanese began firing back.

They shot at the transports with five-inchers and those eight-inchers still operative. They drove the transports off, and plowing after them in flight went the amtracks and landing boats loaded with Marines. For half an hour the fleeing transports duck-walked among exploding shells, and then, because the air strike had still not arrived, the American warships resumed fire.

For ten minutes the air was filled with their bellowing, and then with the islet again glowing, the carrier planes came in. Hardly a bursting enemy antiaircraft shell or bullet rose to chastise these strafing, swooping planes, and it seemed that Betio was surely *zemmetsu*. Again she was swathed in smoke.

193

But as *Pursuit* and *Requisite* entered the lagoon through the reef passage, shore batteries on the landing beaches lashed out at them. The minesweepers called for *Ringgold* and *Dashiell*. The two graceful destroyers swept into the lagoon, firing as they came, with amtracks full of Marines churning after them.

A shell struck *Ringgold* to starboard, passing through the engine room. But it didn't explode. Another. Again a dud. Through the smoke and fire ashore *Ringgold's* gunnery officer had spotted the flashes of her tormentor. Her five-inchers swung around and gushed flame. There was a great explosion ashore. The enemy gun's ammunition dump had been hit.

It was getting close to nine o'clock and the amtrack motors were rising to full throttle. The swaying clumsy craft were going into Betio. They were taking harmless air bursts overhead, taking long-range machine-gun fire with bullets rattling off their sides. The wind was blowing Betio's smoke into their faces, blowing the water flat and thin over the reef—but the amtracks were bumping over it and boring in. Now the Marines were ducking low beneath the gunwales, for a volcano of flame and sound had begun to erupt around them and there were amtracks blowing up, amtracks beginning to burn, amtracks spinning around, slowing and sinking—for if they cannot move they sink—and there were amtracks grinding ashore and rising from the surf with water streaming from their sides, with helmeted figures in mottled green leaping from them and sprinting over the narrow beaches toward the treacherous sanctuary of the sea wall; and falling, falling, falling as they ran.

The Scout-Sniper Platoon went into Betio five minutes before the first wave. It was led by a lieutenant named William Deane Hawkins, but hardly any of the platoon's 40 men could remember Hawk's first name. He was just Hawk, lean and swift like a hawk, a man as convinced of victory as he was sure of his own death in battle. Hawkins had joined the Marines with this remark to his closest friend: "I'll see you some day, Mac—but not on this earth." He had come up from the ranks, actually risen, unlike that legion who "come up through the ranks" by marking time as an enlisted man while powerful friends push their commission through channels.

Hawkins and the Scout-Snipers went in to seize the pier extending about 500 yards into the lagoon. It split the landing beaches, and from it those numerous Japanese latrines now filled with riflemen and machine-gunners could rake the Marine amtracks passing to either side.

Hawkins had his men in two landing boats, one commanded by himself, the other by Gunnery Sergeant Jared Hooper. In a third boat were the flame-throwing engineers of Lieutenant Alan Leslie.

They came in and hit the reef. They were held up there just as enemy mortars began to drop among them and drums of gasoline stacked on the pier began to burn. Sniper and machine-gun fire raked the boats. Airplanes were called down on the enemy guns while Hawkins and his men awaited transfer to amtracks. They got them and rode in to assault the pier. They fought with flame-throwers, with grenades, with bayonets. They fought yard by yard, killing and being killed—while the pier still burned—and swept ashore to attack enemy pillboxes.

Like Hector in his chariot, Lieutenant Hawkins stood erect in his amtrack while it butted through barbed wire, climbed the sea wall and clanked among the enemy spitting fire and grenades.

In another amtrack called *The Old Lady* was a stocky corporal named John Joseph Spillane, a youngster who had a big-league throwing arm and the fielding ability which had brought Yankee and Cardinal scouts around to talk to his father. *The Old Lady* and Corporal Spillane went into Betio in the first wave, a load of riflemen crouching below her gunwales, a thick coat of hand-fashioned steel armor around her unlovely hull. Then she came under the sea wall and the Japanese began lobbing grenades into her.

The first came in hissing and smoking and Corporal Spillane dove for it. He trapped it and pegged it in a single, swift, practiced motion. Another. Spillane picked it off in mid-air and

195

hurled it back. There were screams. There were no more machine-gun bullets rattling against *The Old Lady's* sides. Two more smoking grenades end-over-ended into the amtrack. Spillane nailed both and flipped them on the sea wall. The assault troops watched him in fascination. And then the sixth one came in and Spillane again fielded and threw.

But this one exploded.

Johnny Spillane was hammered to his knees. His helmet was dented. There was shrapnel in his right side, his neck, his right hip, and there was crimson spouting from the pulp that had once been his right hand.

But the assault troops had vaulted onto the beach and were scrambling for the sea wall. Though Johnny Spillane's baseball career was over, he had bought these riflemen precious time, and he was satisfied to know it as he called, "Let's get outta here," to his driver and the squat gray amphibian backed out into the water to take him out to the transport where the doctor would amputate his right hand at the wrist.

Pfc. Donald Libby also came in on the first wave. He came in crouching in fear, grimacing in pain. Machine-gun fire had been sweeping his amtrack since it had lumbered up on the reef, and there were bullets in both of Libby's thighs. Then a mortar shell landed in the amtrack, killing all but two men, hurling Libby into the water.

He came to the surface with seven shrapnel fragments lodged in his flesh. He was bleeding heavily, but he hoped the salt water would staunch the flow. He dog-paddled toward his wrecked amtrack. It was canted on its side in the water. Libby grabbed the amtrack's wheel and hung onto it. A life preserver floated by. He seized it and squirmed into it, clenching his teeth against the pain of his movement. He floated behind the amtrack, hardly more than his nose above the surface. At night, if he still had strength, he would try to swim out to the ships.

Lieutenant Commander Robert MacPherson buzzed back and forth over Betio and the lagoon in his Kingfisher observation plane. He was acting as the eyes of Major General Julian Smith aboard *Maryland*. Howlin' Mad Smith was up at Makin with Vice Admiral Raymond Spruance, the over-all commander.

MacPherson peered below him. The muzzles of *Ringgold's* and *Dashiell's* guns were spitting flame and smoke and the little amtracks were bobbing shoreward. Some of them stopped and began to burn. Tiny dots of men leaped on the beach to go clambering over the sea wall and vanish beneath the pall of smoke still obscuring Betio.

The Marines seemed to be attacking in little groups—three or four of them, rarely more than half a dozen—moving behind their NCO's. Here and there a loner struck at the enemy.

Staff Sergeant Bill Bordelon was such a loner. He was one of four Marines to survive the gunning of their amtrack from about 500 yards out. He reached the beach, running low. Behind him were the remainder of his men, dead and dying or drowning. Bordelon had to get the pillboxes that filled the air around these men with whining invisible death.

He prepared his demolition charges.

He sprang erect and went in on the pillboxes, running at them from their flanks because the Japanese used very small gun ports which reduced their field of fire. Twice Bordelon threw and sprinted for cover and each time a pillbox collapsed with a roar. Bordelon primed more charges and ran against a third.

Machine-gun bullets hit him, but he stayed on his feet. He saw the white blocks of explosive sail into the gun port and ducked. The third position was knocked out. Then he seized a rifle to cover a group of Marines crawling over the sea wall.

Bordelon pushed aside a medical corpsman who wanted to treat his wounds. He had heard the cry of "Help!" from the surf. There was a wounded man there. Bordelon dragged him ashore. He ran back into the water to find another wounded man and bring him in. Then, because he was either oblivious of his own wounds, or convinced that he was dying and that there was so little time, Staff Sergeant Bill Bordelon ran again at an enemy position.

And the Japanese gunners saw him coming and shot him dead.

★

The first battalion to reach Betio was the Second Regiment's Third under Major Schoettel. At ten after nine two companies led by Major Mike Ryan reached the sea wall on the right or western beach. They crawled up under its lee, taking fierce machine-gun fire. Major Schoettel was still offshore with following troops. He couldn't get in, and in two hours those companies under the sea wall were cut in half.

At seventeen minutes after nine Major Jim Crowe's battalion hit the beaches on the left or eastern flank. Two of Crowe's amtracks found a break in the sea wall and rolled through, speeding all the way across the airfield's main strip before they were halted. But it was an isolated success. Sea-wall gun ports began to spit death among the Marines on the beach. Snipers picked off head after head raised above the wall. One of Crowe's men strolled down the beach, heedless of the major's angry bellowing to stay low. He grinned impishly at a wildly-gesturing buddy, and then a rifle spoke and the Marine spun and crumpled to the ground, and when he rolled over, face to the smoke-drifted sky, his eyes were bulging from the impact of the bullet which had passed behind them.

"Somebody go get that Jap son of a bitch," Major Crowe yelled. "He's right back of us here waiting for somebody to pass by."

A Marine leaped up on the sea wall. After him came a flame-throwing team, one Marine with the twin cylinders of liquid fire strapped to his back and holding the nozzle out to spray, the other covering him with rifle fire. The Marine beyond the sea wall hurled blocks of dynamite into a pillbox 15 feet inland. There was a roar and clouds of smoke and dust billowed out. A mushroom-helmeted figure darted out the exit. The man with the nozzle squirted. A long hissing spurt of fire struck the Japanese soldier and he flamed like a struck match, shivered and was charred and still.

At the central beach, marked by the burning pier, Colonel Shoup was trying to come ashore to take command of the battle. With Shoup were Lieutenant Colonel Evans Carlson of Makin and Guadalcanal, who had come to Tarawa as an observer; the redheaded Major Tom Culhane, Shoup's operations

198

officer; Lieutenant Colonel Presley Rixey, commander of an artillery battalion; and Commander Donald Nelson, the regimental surgeon. They came to the reef in a landing boat. Shoup hailed an amtrack carrying wounded out to the transports. The wounded were transferred into the landing boat and Shoup's party boarded the amtrack.

It was about ten o'clock, and as the amtrack waddled shoreward, Colonel Shoup listened to radio reports of the carnage on the beaches. On his right, Major Schoettel was still caught out on the lagoon, unable to reach those two companies being chopped up under the sea wall. From Schoettel, Shoup heard this:

"Receiving heavy fire all along beach. Unable to land all. Issue in doubt."

Shortly after ten o'clock Schoettel radioed again:

"Boats held up on reef of right flank Red 1 (the western beach). Troops receiving heavy fire in water."

Shoup immediately replied:

"Land Beach Red 2 (the central sector) and work west."

Schoettel answered:

"We have nothing left to land."

The first message had come out to the ships from the beach. No one could identify the sender. It said:

"Have landed. Unusually heavy opposition. Casualties 70 per cent. Can't hold."

To the Marines of the fourth, fifth and sixth waves waiting beyond the reef in landing boats and LCM's, this meant one thing: they must hurry ashore.

They rode in to the reef and found the water no higher than three feet, and often only inches deep. They looked for the amtracks which were to take them into the battle.

There weren't any.

Eight amtracks had been destroyed as the first wave attacked. Many more of them carrying the next two waves had been knocked out, and others were hit when they tried to back off the beach to return to the reef. Fifteen of them sank the moment they reached deeper water. Major Henry Drewes, commander of the amtrack battalion, had been killed. Nearly all the amtrack gunners were dead. They had dueled the shore guns, but they had been visible and unprotected. The enemy had been neither.

The men waiting outside the reef would have to wade in.

They clambered out of their boats, milled about on the reef while bullets keened among them, and then they jumped off it and began to walk through waist-high water.

The Japanese gunners hung on grimly to their triggers, for now they understood why Rear Admiral Shibasaki had been so confident of repelling the invaders. The Americans were walking along a broad avenue of death. There were so many of them falling they would surely stop coming.

But they waded on, from a quarter-mile out, from a half-mile out—unable even to fire their weapons, for they had to hold them overhead to keep them dry—sometimes stepping into coral potholes and going under, there to lose helmets and weapons.

"Spread out!" the officers cried. "Spread out!"

Pfc. Richard Lund came in with a radio and screamed as a bullet struck him in the right chest and came out his right arm. It spun him around and knocked him under. He arose and walked on. With the radio.

Marines died in the deep water, and died in the shallow surf where gentle waves rolled their bodies along the beaches. They fell like fanned-out decks of cards once they had gained the leftward beach and blundered into the point-blank fire of weapons poked through sea-wall gun ports. They were caught on barbed wire offshore and killed, and here Lieutenant Colonel Herbert Amey, commander of the Second Battalion, Second, met instant death.

Still they came on, even the wounded clinging to the burning pier, working their way in hand over hand. Above them Lieutenant Commander MacPherson gazed in horror from his observation plane, watching the tiny figures wading through the water with rifles held high, watching them vanish, feeling the tears of grief gathering behind his eyes.

But they got inshore, even the wounded, even the dying youth with his chest torn open who fell on the beach and cried for a cigarette.

"Here, I'll light one for you," a Marine said.

"No," the stricken youth gasped. "No time . . . gimme yours . . ."

The cigarette was thrust into his mouth and held there. The youth drew, the smoke curled out his chest—and he died.

There were rifles stuck in the sand of the beaches and there were bottles of blood plasma hanging from them. The bottles were tied to rifle butts with gauze and their little rubber tubes ran down into needles jabbed in the veins of wounded Americans. Corpsmen talked gently to the stricken men, waving the flies away.

The corpsmen and the doctors worked throughout the clamor of battle. They laid the men out on stretchers, giving them plasma and morphine. Marine riflemen guarded them as they worked, for sometimes the Japanese attempted to sneak down to the beaches and throw grenades in among the casualties.

They came out from under the pier or from the latrines or slipped into the water from the hulk of the *Saida Maru*, a freighter which had been knocked over on its side by an American destroyer in the preinvasion bombardments. The Japanese swam to shore through their own fire. One of them appeared in the central sector. He came out of the water brandishing a grenade.

A Marine sentry charged him and bayoneted him in the belly and then shot his bayonet free.

As the doctors worked on, corpsmen loaded the wounded aboard the amtracks which took them to the reef and the waiting landing boats. Men needing immediate care were draped over rubber boats and hauled to the reef by hand.

From the reef the wounded went to the transports, and sometimes they were shelled en route and there would be dead among them by the time they came alongside the ships. On one of these ships a landing boat with a gaping five-inch shellhole in its side was hoisted on deck. The wounded were taken out. But there were three dead Marines. Their bodies were placed in winding sheets and taken to the rail. Chaplain Harry Boer was called. He was a young minister. He had never said burial service before. Marines and sailors removed their helmets and Chaplain Boer spoke:

"We are in the presence of the last enemy, death. We did not know these men personally, but God does—and therefore we commit them unto Him who is the righteous judge of the earth." There was the screech of a plane diving to bomb a Japanese ammunition dump, and the chaplain paused, waiting for the explosion ashore. A sheet of flame rose into the air. The Dauntless had hit the dump. It had also knocked out a Marine tank, but no one aboard ship knew this. They bowed their heads again as the chaplain continued: "It is for us, the living, in the presence of these dead, to devote ourselves more seriously to the task before us. I am the Resurrection and the Life, and he that believeth in Me, though he were dead, yet shall he live."

The white-sheeted figures went over the side. There was a splash. An impersonal voice blared over the bullhorn on the bridge:

"The issue ashore is still in doubt."

It was, and Colonel David Shoup, who was trying so hard to get there, was being struck by savage fire.

Heavy machine-gun fire raked Shoup's amtrack as it neared the beach. The vehicle slewed around and retreated to the end of the pier. It circled to the east or left side and joined a wave of LCM's lightering dual-purpose medium tanks to Jim Crowe's embattled battalion.

Then a pair of Japanese 75-millimeters spoke. *Whang!* *Whang!* One LCM went under with all aboard and another withdrew, sinking.

Colonel Shoup's amtrack again returned to the pier. An exploding mortar shell wounded Shoup in the leg, all but knocking him unconscious. But he was still determined to get ashore, for now he was out of contact with Major Schoettel's battalion on the right.

Schoettel's battalion was attacking, though its leader was still unable to get ashore. Major Mike Ryan had reorganized the two shattered sea-wall companies and struck inland. They were slowly rolling up the enemy, and there were six Sherman tanks coming in to help them.

The tanks left their LCM lighters on the reef and came on through water up to their turrets. Men walking with flags guided them around the treacherous potholes. The Shermans came slowly, leaving wide-spreading V's in their wake, rocking and lurching as their 75's roared. When they reached the beach they found it so littered with dead and wounded they could not pass. They would not crunch over the bodies of their buddies, dead or living, and they backed into the water again to make for the gap which the engineers had blown in Shibasaki's sea wall.

Pfc. Donald Libby wondered if anyone would come for him. The battle had grown fiercer since he had been hurled into the water and had seized hold of his ruined amtrack. Now he could hear the clanging, tooth-rattling *whang* of a Japanese gun and hear the screams of stricken men. Libby was still alone in water now made chalky with dust. He swayed like a beached log, growing colder. . . .

Libby had heard the dreadful slaughter of the Third Battalion, Eighth Marines, as they came to reinforce Major Jim Crowe's battalion on the left.

They came speeding up to the reef five boats abreast. The landing ramps came banging down.

Whang!

The boat farthest right vanished. It had been there and then it was not there.

Whang! A second boat disappeared. One of the coxswains became terrified of approaching the reef. "This is as far as I go!" he cried. His ramp banged down and a full boatload of heavily laden Marines charged off it into 15 feet of water. Many drowned, but still more were able to shuck their loads and swim to the reef, hauling themselves over it oblivious of how it slashed their flesh.

Hardly a third of that first wave reached the beach. Then the second wave of Crowe's reinforcements started ashore. Colonel

Shoup shouted at them from the pier, waving his arms and ordering them to come his way, to take shelter behind the pier and wade to the central beach. They did, but by the time the second wave got ashore it was badly disorganized.

At last Colonel Shoup got in. He set up his command post in a hole dug in the sand behind a pillbox full of Japs. He was 15 yards inland, but he could see almost nothing of the battle for the dust that hung over Betio.

It was everywhere, a cloying caking dust that was thick and clogged in the nostrils, coarse in the throat and clotted in the corners of the eyes. It swirled in dense clouds or sparkled in tiny jewels within those shafts of hot sunlight sometimes made visible by explosions that rent one cloud of dust only to start another.

Into this dust at about noon came the First Battalion, Second. Its men joined the attack in the central sector under Major Wood Kyle. They were also riddled and many of them were deflected toward that right or western flank where Major Ryan still attacked and the tanks rolled toward the sea-wall gap.

Four of the tanks had foundered in potholes, but two of them reached Ryan as he re-formed for a flanking assault through the pillboxes on the western shore. The Shermans rolled over foxholes, blasted pillboxes open with their cannon, and machine-gunned the escaping survivors. Once Lieutenant Ed Bale's *China Gal* met a Japanese light tank in open combat and dueled her. The impact of the Japanese 37's on *China Gal's* hide left the steel lemon-yellow on the inside, but the 75's of the bigger Sherman left the Japanese tank a smoking wreck.

On the left a pair of 37-millimeter antitank guns had been dragged ashore. The boats carrying them had been sunk, but the gunners had rolled their heavy wheeled weapons through the water. They got them up on the beach, but there was still no way to get them over the sea wall. Two Japanese light tanks were seen bearing down toward the lip of the sea wall.

"Lift 'em over!" came the cry. "*Lift* 'em over!"

The 900-pound guns seemed to fly over the wall. There they spoke with sharp authority. One enemy tank lurched around and gushed flame. The other fled.

The Marines on the left had a Sherman tank of their own to force their way across Betio. It was a smoke-blackened, dented hulk called *Colorado* and commanded by Lieutenant Lou Largey. It was the lone survivor of the four which had come into Jim Crowe's sector that morning.

One had been destroyed by an American dive-bomber. Another had been set afire by enemy guns. A third had been hit by the Japanese and had fallen into a hole in which enemy ammunition was piled. It had been there when another American dive-bomber screeched down—even as Chaplain Boer commended the three dead Marines to God and the sea—and it had gone up with the exploding shells. *Colorado* had also been hit and set aflame, but Largey had taken her back to the beach to put out the fire, and by early afternoon *Colorado* was again charging pillboxes.

At half-past one, with all but a single battalion of the reserve committed, Julian Smith was convinced that the critical point had been reached. He asked Holland Smith up at Makin to release the Sixth Marine Regiment to him. If Holland Smith said no, Julian Smith was prepared to gather this last battalion, to collect his bandsmen, specialists, typists and service people, and lead them into the battle himself. Howlin' Mad Smith said yes. Assured now of a fresh and larger reserve, Julian Smith notified the uncommitted First Battalion, Eighth, to stand by for a landing. The men had been boated since before dawn, as had all the Marine combat teams. All that was required was to select the proper place to land. At a quarter of three Julian Smith signaled Shoup asking him if he thought a night landing was possible.

Shoup never got the message, and the First Battalion, Eighth, stayed in their boats.

Someone had come for Pfc. Libby.

The wounded Marine had felt the tide going out and had pushed himself away from his wrecked amtrack. He hoped to float out to the ships on the tide.

Just then someone waded toward him. He wore a Marine's

205

helmet and had a rifle slung across his back. He carried a bayonet in his hand. He came directly toward Pfc. Libby and he called out:

"What state are you from?"

"Maine," Libby gasped. "Where you fr——?"

Pfc. Libby came to his feet in the water, for the bayonet this man was lifting was hooked at the hilt.

The Japanese lunged. Libby threw up his left hand. The bayonet pierced his palm. Libby grabbed the blade with his right hand and wrenched it away. The Japanese fumbled for his rifle. Libby swung. He hit the Japanese behind the ear with the hilt. The Jap moaned and sank into the water. Libby hit him on the forehead as he fell. Then he seized his head and held him under.

Pfc. Libby let go and began paddling weakly toward the reef. Hours later an amtrack found him floating in his life preserver 1,000 yards offshore. His body was wrinkled like a prune and blood still flowed from his torn hands. But he was alive.

Colorado was on the left and *China Gal* was on the right, between them were perhaps 3,500 United States Marines, and the sun was setting behind the tuft of the Betio parrot's head.

Some 5,000 assault troops had come ashore, and of these about 1,500 were already dead or wounded. And now, between that pair of tanks, there were two separate and precarious holds on Betio. The left or eastern foothold, in which Colonel Shoup's command post was located, began at about midway of the north coast and ran west for about 600 yards. It was 250 yards deep at its farthest penetration, roughly halfway across the airfield. Holding this, from left to right facing south or inland, were Major Crowe's Second Battalion, Eighth; the riddled Third Battalion, Eighth; and the First and Second Battalions, Second. The right or western hold was a tiny enclave 200 yards deep and perhaps 100 yards wide which Major Ryan's reorganized Third Battalion, Second had hacked out on the extreme western tip—the bird's beak.

Between Ryan's toehold and Shoup's foothold was a gap fully 600 yards wide stuffed with Japanese men and guns.

Out in the lagoon, still in boats, were the recently alerted

First Battalion, Eighth, and those waves of the Third Battalion, Eighth, which had been unable to get ashore.

Standing west of Tarawa in ships was that Sixth Marine Regiment just returned to Major General Julian Smith. There was no artillery ashore, but Lieutenant Colonel Rixey was preparing to bring in some batteries under cover of darkness.

These were the lines of the Second Marine Division as the dust began to settle and night fell on Betio.

But there were no lines as such; there were groups of Marines who had dug in here or fortified an abandoned pillbox there. There were gaps everywhere. Flanks were dangling. The inland advance of some units could be measured in hundreds of yards, others in scores of feet. Some troops were still trapped beneath the sea wall. In some places the Japanese would need to go only 30 feet to drive the Americans into the sea.

It was a situation made for counterattack, and even the most rear-ranked private among all those embattled Marines knew that just as the Japanese always defended at the water's edge, he always counterattacked at night.

Rear Admiral Keiji Shibasaki had planned to counterattack. He had always believed that his defenses would stop the Americans at the water's edge, and that a strong nocturnal counterblow would finish them off.

But the terrible bombardment which had failed to slaughter Shibasaki's men had knocked out his communications. His men were scattered over the island in strong points and there was now no way of assembling them for the counterattack.

He could attempt to communicate with them by runner, but it was likely the runners would be picked off. Worse, Admiral Shibasaki had not even provided himself with message blanks. There were, of course, dozens of bicycles at his disposal, but bike-riding messengers would only provide these uncouth Marines with jokes as well as targets.

Admiral Shibasaki stayed within his huge bombproof command post. Though his men lobbed mortars into the Marines on the beaches or swam out to the wrecked American boats or the capsized *Saida Maru* to harass them with sniper fire, they did not counterattack. They had killed many Americans that day.

207

Next day they would kill more. Admiral Shibasaki was not cast down by the loss of his communications. Obviously it was the Americans, not the Japanese, who were in a tight spot.

All through the night, cries of "Corpsman!" "Corpsman!" were raised above and below the sea wall. Men wounded during the day, men who fought on while wounded, were dying from loss of blood. And there was a shortage of blood plasma, of bandages.

"Doc" Rogalski had patched up the dozen or so men left of the 40 whom Lieutenant Toivo Ivary had led against the central sector. Ivary's right leg had been shattered by a grenade and he had been shot in the arm. Sergeant Jim Bayer had been shot in the head. Rogalski had fixed up the lieutenant's leg with splints and sulfa and bandaged the sergeant's head. And then, during the morning-long fight to knock out a pillbox looming over the sea wall, he used up the rest of his supplies.

In the afternoon as more wounded were brought back to the beach, Rogalski was forced to take medical kits from the bodies of fallen fellow corpsmen. He waded into the lagoon to strip dead Marines of the little first-aid pouches attached to their cartridge belts and even tore their skivvy shirts off them and ripped them up for bandages.

At last Rogalski could find no more bodies in the black waters of the lagoon. The tide had floated them out.

Faint cries of "Corpsman!" were still being raised along the beach as Rogalski sat, helpless, under the sea wall. Suddenly four amtracks came out of the darkness and crawled up under the sea wall. Rogalski rose expectantly, but then slumped. Marines jumping out of two of them had begun to unload artillery shells or were wrestling howitzer parts over the side. It was then that Rogalski saw the stretcher-bearers and corpsmen jumping out of the other two and he ran to join them, helping them put Ivary and Bayer and the other wounded into the amtracks for the trip to the reef and waiting landing boats.

The amtracks roared away even as wading artillerymen emerged from the water carrying the parts of their dismantled guns on their backs.

208

Beyond the reef, Lieutenant Ivary lay in the landing boat that was taking him to a transport. He turned to Sergeant Bayer.

"I've been wondering for a long time, Sarge—how come they call your home town Dime Box?"

"Dime Box is a pretty little town in Texas, sir," Bayer replied. "An' you know, lying back there under the sea wall I wondered if I'd ever see it again. But it's on the San Antonio Pike, between Giddings and Caldwell. A long time ago it was only a plantation. One of the plantation's mammies would leave a dime in the mailbox every day for the mailman to get her a box of snuff. That's how they come to call my town Dime Box."

Lieutenant Ivary nodded. He could hear voices high above him. He felt the boat being lifted up in the air. He was very weak but he was feeling better already.

"Thanks, Sarge," the lieutenant murmured. "I always wondered."

And as the booms swung the landing boat onto the deck of the transport, ten short-snouted pieces of artillery were made ready hub to hub under the sea wall.

They would be firing at dawn.

The men of the First Battalion, Eighth, had spent the night in boats. They had not come ashore during darkness as Major General Julian Smith had intended, because his message to Colonel Shoup had not been received. On the morning of November 21 Colonel Shoup had called for them to help expand the beachhead in the central sector.

There were by then only 18 amtracks left and the First

Battalion, Eighth, came up to the reef in landing boats. At a quarter after six the ramps of the landing boats banged down, and the Marines began wading in.

From blockhouses on the beach and from the wrecked hulk of *Saida Maru* came a terrible steady drumming of machine-gun fire, and the morning of the second day was worse than the first.

Out on the reef Marines were rescuing wounded comrades and dragging them back to the landing boats. Pfc. James Collins carried one stricken man back. He turned and seized another, a corpsman who had been shot in the shoulder. He lifted him. There was an explosion, and half the wounded man's head was blown off. Collins dropped the lifeless body and waded to the beach in tears. Only three of the 24 men who had been in his boat reached the shore. Only 90 of 199 men in the first wave ever got in.

But the wade-in continued, while Marines of the First and Second Battalions, Second, attacked furiously against the blockhouses that were delivering that awful fire. The pack howitzers lined up hub to hub on the beach were leaping and baying in an attempt to silence the enemy machine guns. The artillerymen were using shells with delayed fuses intended to explode once they had penetrated the concrete, but they were firing to a narrow front and thy could not get them all.

Carrier planes swooped down to strafe and bomb the blockhouses, but the enemy fired on. Dive-bombers pounded the *Saida Maru,* but it still crackled with fire. Marine mortars ashore pounded *Saida Maru,* but the bullets only slackened, they did not stop. It would eventually take a force of dynamite-throwing engineers covered by riflemen to clean out the ship infestation.

Sometimes the Marines sought to veer away from the enemy's field of fire. One platoon slipped off to the right toward the sector held by Major Ryan. They waded into a cove, and they were shot down to a man.

It continued for five full hours, and when Major Lawrence Hays at last got his battalion ashore and reorganized, he found he had lost 108 men killed and 235 wounded. But 600 Marines had survived the wade-in. They were now available for the desperate battle raging everywhere along the western half of Betio. As Colonel Shoup radioed Julian Smith at half-past eleven in the morning:

"The situation ashore doesn't look good."

Earlier that morning, just as the dreadful wade-in began, Shoup had ordered Lieutenant Hawkins to take his scout-sniper platoon against a Japanese position holding five machine guns. It barred the way to the central sector attack with which Shoup hoped to cut Betio in two.

The Hawk gathered his men. He had often said, "I think my thirty-four-man platoon can lick any two-hundred-man company in the world." Now he was going on a company-size mission to prove it. His men moved methodically from gun to gun, laying down covering fire while Hawkins crawled up to the pillbox gun ports to fire point-blank inside or toss in grenades. The guns fell, but not before Hawkins had been shot in the chest. He had already lost blood from shrapnel wounds the day before, but he still resisted the corpsman's suggestions that he accept evacuation.

"I came here to kill Japs, not to be evacuated," Hawkins said. He and his men knocked out three more enemy positions and then Hawkins was caught in a burst of mortar fire and when they carried him to the rear he was already dying.

But he and his men had opened the way for the cross-island attack, an assault which Colonel Shoup held as important as Major Ryan's drive to clear Betio's western beaches for the safe arrival of the reinforcing Sixth Marines.

Still in charge of the battle so long as Julian Smith remained aboard *Maryland*, Colonel Shoup crouched in his command post and listened to telephoned reports, his hand shaking slightly. His CP was still in front of the occupied Japanese pill-box and it seemed to be crowned by a perpetual cloud of dust rising from the attack south across the airfield. Out of the dust just before noon limped the dirtiest Marine Shoup had seen so far. A quarter-inch of grime coated his beardless face while a lock of limp blond hair hung from beneath his helmet. The youth's name was Adrian Strange and he entered the colonel's CP bawling, "Somebody gimme a pack of cigarettes. There's a machine-gun crew out there in a shellhole and there ain't one of 'em's got a butt."

Someone threw him a pack of Camels. Imperturbable, impressed by neither the brass crouching below him nor the bullets buzzing above, Pfc. Strange took one of the cigarettes and lighted it.

"I just got another sniper," he said, grinning. "That's six today, an' me a cripple." He blew smoke. "Busted my ankle steppin' in a shellhole yesterday." The bullets began buzzing as though coming in swarms, and Pfc. Strange sneered, "Shoot me down, you son of a bitch!"—before turning to limp back to the airfield.

Not all the Marines on Betio that day were like Pfc. Strange. A few minutes after he had limped off a tearful young major ran into Shoup's CP crying:

"Colonel, my men can't advance. They're being held up by a machine gun."

Dave Shoup spat in disgust.

"God a'mighty! One machine gun!"

The major turned in confusion and went back to his men, and he had hardly disappeared before there was a sharp *crrrack!* in the CP and Corporal Leonce Olivier yelped in pain. A Jap in the pillbox had poked a rifle out an air vent and shot him in the leg. Someone dropped a grenade down the vent, but no one took comfort from the muffled explosion. The pillbox had walls three feet thick and was probably compartmented inside.

The confused young major came back.

"Colonel, there are a thousand goddam Marines out there on the beach and not one will follow me across the airstrip."

Shoup spat again.

"You've got to say, 'Who'll follow me?' And if only ten follow you, that's the best you can do—but it's better than nothing."

The major departed—for good this time—and the attack across the airfield to Betio's southern coast gained momentum. It reached its objective before dusk, after the Marines occupied abandoned enemy positions and beat off two fierce counterattacks.

Betio was sliced in two and the Marines had possession of most of the airfield, the base which would one day be known as Hawkins Field.

On the left flank, the Marines under Jim Crowe were making slow progress. They were trying to beat down the network of pillboxes and blockhouses surrounding Admiral Shibasaki's bombproof in their sector. It was slow because the men had to go in against an enemy concealed from view. The diving, strafing planes could not knock out these positions. Even Lieutenant Largey's 32-ton *Colorado* was not heavy enough to crush most of them. Largey saw one of his own men fall from his own fire and went back to report in grief to Crowe.

"I just killed a Marine," he said. "Fragments from my 75 splintered against a tree and richocheted off. God damn, I hated for that to happen."

"Too bad," Crowe muttered. "But it sometimes happens. Fortunes of war." He glanced upward at the American planes. "They do it too. One .50-caliber slug just hit one of my men. Went through his shoulder, on down through his lung and liver. He lived four minutes." He shrugged. "Well, anyway, if a Jap ever sticks his head out of his pillbox the planes may kill him."

Over on the right flank, the western toehold, Major Ryan was calling for naval fire to knock out the Japanese positions. Lieutenant Thomas Greene, a naval gunfire spotter, signaled a destroyer and pinpointed Ryan's targets. The destroyer ran in and let go. Another destroyer followed. The men whom Shoup had already called "fighting fools" fanned out behind *China Gal* and another tank to begin their attack. The tanks stopped and one of the tank commanders called out:

"Send us an intelligent Marine to spot the pillboxes for us."

"Hell's fire!" a sergeant snorted. "I ain't very smart, but I'll go."

He went, walking between the tanks, guiding them from pillbox to pillbox, and the western beaches began to fall.

To the east, Dave Shoup heard the report of Ryan's progress

with relief. At a few minutes before four o'clock he turned to Major Culhane and said:

"I think we're winning. But the bastards still have a lot of bullets left."

Then Colonel Shoup put his estimate into the language of official reports, concluding with that terse summary which would become historic:

"Casualties many; percentage dead unknown; combat efficiency: We are winning."

Colonel Shoup's Marines could have told him an hour earlier that the issue was no longer in doubt.

The Japanese had begun to kill themselves.

They had been told that the Americans tortured their captives. More, surrender meant the disgrace of a man's family. So they had begun blowing themselves up, shooting themselves or disemboweling themselves—choosing suicide as the means of immortalizing their spirits among Japan's warrior dead at Yasakuni Shrine. Men found with bayonets thrust up into their vitals lay beside loaded rifles. Grenade suicides with missing hand-and-head or hand-and-chest, or those others who lay down in their bunkers to place rifle muzzles in their mouths while pushing the trigger with their big toe, were often found in places where the attack was only beginning. They had not waited to take a few Marines with them.

Aboard *Maryland* General Julian Smith had given Colonel Maurice Holmes of the Sixth Marines his orders for a pair of landings. One was to be made on the newly cleared western beaches of Betio. The other would be on Bairiki, a little islet just east of Betio. Japanese had been reported attempting to reach Bairiki from Betio's tail. Smith also wanted to place artillery on the islet to batter Betio.

Shortly before five o'clock carrier planes began striking Bairiki, diving at the lone pillbox mounting two machine guns and held by 15 Japanese. Fifty-caliber bullets passed through the gun ports and entered a gasoline can the Japanese had unwisely brought inside with them.

Flames leaped from the position, and the Second Battalion,

Sixth, commanded by big Lieutenant Colonel Raymond Murray, occupied Bairiki without incident.

A few hours later the other landing took place. The First Battalion, Sixth, led by youthful Major William Jones, rode rubber boats in to Betio's western tip. They were embarrassed at the tearful welcome given them by Major Ryan's ragged remnant. They moved through them and dug in.

Up in the central sector Brigadier General Edson had come ashore. Julian Smith had sent Red Mike in to relieve the near-exhausted Shoup. Edson took command at six o'clock and David Shoup resumed control of what remained of his Second Marine Regiment. He had not slept for forty hours and his leg wound was paining him, but he had hung onto those two desperate holds and kept his scattered units fighting.

On the left flank Major Jim Crowe called for naval gunfire against Admiral Shibasaki's bombproof. His men were going to have to go up against it next morning, and he wanted them to go the easy way.

At dusk a destroyer ran in so close to Betio that it seemed it would scrape the bottom of the lagoon. Flame spouted from the muzzles of its five-inchers. . . . Four, five, six rounds— and then the answering crash and flame as the shells struck Admiral Shibasaki's command post. The graceful, slender ship was almost obscured in smoke. Chips of cement flew from the bombproof's five-foot walls, geysers of sand leaped from its roof overgrown with palm trees. Some eighty rounds flashed around it like monster fireflies.

The destroyer stopped firing. Major Crowe shrugged.

"They never hit it squarely," he said, his outer gruffness masking an inner disquiet. "Just almost."

Within the bombproof Rear Admiral Keichi Shibasaki contemplated the shattered bits of the *Yogaki* Plan. He had gotten almost no help, nothing but a submarine or two which had harassed the enemy the night before the invasion. Last night a single plane had flown up from the Marshalls. Tonight he could expect no more. Obviously the Americans had neutralized the Marshalls.

And Tarawa, he knew, was falling.

215

Having felt the lash of the American destroyer's five-inchers, Shibasaki could guess that it would be his bombproof's turn tomorrow. He composed his last message for Tokyo.

"Our weapons have been destroyed," it said, "and from now on everyone is attempting a final charge. . . . May Japan exist for ten thousand years!"

10

Apamama was truly called the Atoll of the Moon.

She was the loveliest of all the Gilberts, a brilliant pale green lagoon caught in a circlet of sun-bathed islets which were themselves clasped by the gleaming white of the beaches—and surrounding it all was the soft blue of the sea. To Apamama in 1889 came Robert Louis Stevenson as the guest of the philosopher-king Tem Binoka; to Apamama three years later came the British Government; and to Apamama in another half-century came two companies of Japanese under a midget of a monocle-screwing colonel.

The colonel departed in 1943 with the airfield done and with some 1,000 handsome, good-natured, lazy Apamamese introduced to the horrors of work. There were only an excitable captain and two dozen Imperials left when, in the early morning blackness of November 21, the 68 Marines of Captain Jim Jones came to Apamama to scout out the atoll's defenses for the November 26 invasion.

They came down from Tarawa the night of November 20, making the 85-mile run southeast aboard the big submarine *Nautilus*. Shortly after midnight *Nautilus* heaved out of the sea and the Marines came up on deck to inflate and launch rubber boats from her stern.

They were struck by rain squalls. Only three of the boats' outboard motors started. One conked out and there were but two left to tow the remaining boats, all bobbing and wallowing now in a wild cross-sea of wind and wave while the current pulled them toward the barrier reef. Two boats were carried off into the darkness. Aboard the others, Marines paddled frantically to avoid being cast up on the boiling reef.

An hour later the wind abated. The two missing boats rejoined the column. Now the only enemy was the current, and three hours later Captain Jones's men were paddling within the comparatively calm waters of the lee shore.

Jones began sending out patrols to scout the islets of Apamama. One of these scouting parties included Lieutenant George Hard, a short, bald Australian who had lived in the Gilberts before the war and knew the people of Apamama. Minutes after the patrol set out, Lieutenant Hard saw and recognized two Apamamese wading to the Marines' islet from another one to the right. Hard and the Marines hid in the bushes, for the Australian had no notion of how the Gilbertese had reacted to Japan's Greater East Asia Co-Prosperity Sphere. When the two men were almost on them, Hard jumped up and called a greeting in Gilbertese.

"Why, my word!" one of them replied in unruffled English. "It's Mr. Hard! But were you wise to come and visit us now, Mr. Hard? The Sapanese are still here."

Hard grinned. So did the Marines when they learned that the Gilbertese pronounce a J as an S. It was a pleasure to imagine the irritation of those numerous Sapanese who spoke English.

Mr. Hard's old friend explained that there were only 25 of these Sapanese now, but that they were well entrenched around a radio station on another islet. They had both heavy and light machine guns, mortars and much ammunition, and their pillboxes on both ocean and lagoon beaches would not be easy to rush.

After Captain Jones heard the news he decided to attack. That night he and his "Recon Boys" spotted the winking of blinker lights at sea. An enemy submarine had come to evacuate the atoll's garrison. But the Japanese couldn't get away.

217

Jones's men had destroyed the motor-powered whaleboat that was to have been their getaway craft, and in the morning the Recon Boys would be out to destroy the Japs as well.

Up north at Tarawa Navy Lieutenant Herman Brukardt and his corpsmen worked through the darkness in a "pillbox hospital." The position had been cleaned out by the Marines and Brukardt had set up an operating room inside. Brukardt was a wisp of a man, black-bearded and seemingly tireless. He had been working throughout the day sewing up the badly wounded. Now, at night, in the light of flashlights held by his corpsmen, Robert Costello and James Whitehead, he worked on.

There was a rifle shot. Brukardt looked up. A wounded Marine pointed grimly into a corner of the pillbox. A Japanese lay there, crumpled in death. He had sneaked into the pillbox while everyone had been absorbed in the operation. Brukardt bent his head again. There was another shot. This time Brukardt didn't bother to look up.

Machine-gun bullets smacked against the pillbox's walls. There were rifle shots. The "walking wounded" outside were beating off a party of infiltrators.

"Next!" Brukardt said softly. One of the corpsmen leaned out the door and cried, "Next!" and a wounded man hobbled quickly across the moonlit clearing while the Japanese rifles made their sharp flat cracking.

"We're out of anaesthetics," one of the corpsmen whispered. Brukardt shrugged. There were things he had to cut and things he had to sew, and they had to be done, with or without the pain.

He worked on. There were sometimes moans, occasionally an uncontrollable sob, but mostly there was silence while the flashlight beams played on his hands and the bullets smacked against the outer walls.

Of 100 men brought to the pillbox hospital only four died.

11

The third day of battle on Betio was businesslike and it was brutal. It had not the horror and transcending courage of the first day, when Marines fought to rescue their stricken comrades, to knock out the guns that struck them. Nor had it the desperation of the second, when men fought to avoid defeat. It had only the cold, wary precision of the clean-up. Men fought to exterminate an enemy gone to ground. They killed not to save or preserve but to destroy. Such unexalted work requires professionals.

The Marines were coldly efficient the morning of November 22 as one battalion attacked east along Betio's spine or southern shore and another struck west into The Pocket.

The Pocket was that 600-yard gap which still separated the original Shoup beachhead from the one which Major Ryan had expanded on the west. At seven o'clock in the morning the First Battalion, Eighth, moved out of the Shoup beachhead to reduce it. The men attacked behind three light tanks, but a suicide-soldier got under one of the tanks with a magnetic mine and blew himself and the vehicle apart. The 37-millimeter guns of the light tanks were unable to do more than chip the pillboxes. By noon the attack had done no more than contain the Japanese strong points, and the half-tracks which had come up to relieve the tanks were driven back by machine-gun fire.

Meanwhile, the First Battalion, Sixth, which had landed on the western beaches the night before, moved rapidly east. Major Bill Jones (whose brother Jim had led the Recon Boys ashore at Apamama) drove his men forward. They were as eager as men can be when attacking a maze of forts concealing a stubborn, skillful enemy. They also had three Shermans and the bulldozers of the engineers to accelerate their attack.

The tanks moved against a front about a hundred yards wide. Fifty yards behind them came the riflemen, spread out and watchful for the appearance of suicide-troopers with their magnetic mines. If a blockhouse or pillbox resisted the Sherman's shells, the tanks waddled on, leaving the position to the riflemen and flame-throwers. If individual assault would not storm the position, it could at least neutralize it while a bulldozer slipped in—its driver crouching behind raised sheltering blade—to seal it off with walls of sand.

At eleven o'clock in the morning the Marines of Jones's battalion had reached the battalions of the Second Regiment, which had fought to the southern shore midway on the bird's back the day before. Jones's men had killed 250 Japanese while taking very light casualties themselves. They moved out along the spine again. By nightfall they had reached the end of the airfield on the southern shore and were dug in looking east toward Betio's tail.

Just to their left and rear, Jim Crowe's men were moving toward them across the ruins of Admiral Shibasaki's bombproof.

The approaches to the bombproof as it faced north toward Crowe's Marines were guarded on the right by a steel pillbox and on the left by a big emplacement made of reinforced coconut logs. At half-past nine in the morning Crowe's mortars began falling on the coconut-log structure.

It blew up with a thundering detonation of flame and somersaulting logs. The puny 81-millimeter mortars had scored a direct hit on what had been an ammunition warehouse as well as bunker.

Then jaunty, battered *Colorado* rolled to the steel pillbox's right. It fired twice, three times, and Shibasaki's bombproof lay open to attack.

Crowe's men moved out, matching shot for shot with the bombproof's defenders but gradually coming in closer. Assault engineers crawled forward led by a tall cheerful lieutenant named Alexander Bonnyman. They gained the sides of the bombproof and forced their way to the top.

The Japanese counterattacked. They came in a fury, for the bombproof was the heart of their defenses. As they charged up the slopes of sand piled atop the building, they ran into Lieutenant Bonnyman. Though they should have overwhelmed him, they didn't. He raked them with carbine fire. They hesitated and Bonnyman charged. "Follow me!" he shouted, and the engineers closed in after him. Bonnyman went down and his Marines went over him and beat the enemy back down the hill. Bonnyman died of his many wounds, but the top of the bombproof had been captured, and as the Japanese began to pour out of its eastern and southern exits they were cut down by riflemen and the scything cannister shot of the 37-millimeter cannon. There were still about 200 left inside, among them Admiral Shibasaki.

Bulldozers heaped sand against the exits and sealed off the gun ports. Marines poured gasoline down the air vents and dropped in hand grenades.

There were muffled explosions and then screams. Jim Crowe's men moved toward Betio's tail to nail down the left flank of the Marines of Major Jones.

Behind them, on the western beaches, the Third Battalion, Sixth Marines, had landed on Betio under Lieutenant Colonel Kenneth McLeod. Also to their rear, at a rough cemetery in about the center of the Shoup beachhead, parties of their fellow Marines were burying the dead.

Bulldozers scooped out long, long trenches three feet deep. Bodies were laid out in rows, without blankets, without ponchos, and the chaplains moved among them somberly, their lips moving with final prayers or the words of last rites. Bodies that had been identified were quickly placed in the trenches. When a trench was full, the bulldozers roared and butted against the piles of sand. It was soggy wet sand, for it was impossible to dig more than four feet on Betio without striking water. The dead were covered over, the trench was rollered smooth—and a new one was dug. Many bodies were impossible to identify. One was brought in, headless, one-armed, a few shreds of flesh dangling from the neck like a slaughtered chicken. Robert Sherrod the war correspondent turned away.

"What a hell of a way to die!" he exclaimed, but a big, red-headed Marine gunner stared him in the eye and replied: "You can't pick a better way."

It was true. Any Marine would prefer being blown apart to the languishing agony of shrapnel or bayonets in the belly, to being left alone to perish in torment.

Many such solitary sufferers were being discovered this third day of battle. Corpsmen wading through the lagoon in search of bodies also found live men lying within wrecked and blackened amtracks. In one of these they found a dozen dead Marines and one who was still breathing.

The man had shrapnel in his head, arms and legs. He had not had food or water since he went down the cargo nets early in the morning of November 20. He had lain in the sun for two days and been broiled like a lobster. His rifle lay with its muzzle pointing up toward his throat and the corpsmen could guess that he had tried to kill himself but had not had the strength to reach the trigger. They spoke to him gently, assuring him that his ordeal was over. He opened his cracked lips and mumbled:

"Water—pour water on me."

Major General Julian Smith was on Betio.

He had left *Maryland* and boarded an amtrack along with Brigadier General Thomas Bourke, his artillery commander. They had gone ashore at the western beach. They had inspected defenses and then gone back aboard the amtrack to move around to Red Mike Edson's command post by water. As they passed The Pocket, where Major Hays's men were battering enemy strong points, machine-gun fire struck the amtrack. The driver was wounded, and the amtrack knocked out. Smith and Bourke had to transfer to another, but they made it in. At four o'clock Smith sent off this discouraging message to Brigadier General Leo Hermle, his assistant division commander:

> Situation not favorable for rapid clean-up of Betio. Heavy casualties among officers make leadership problem difficult. Many emplacements intact on eastern end of the island. In addi-

tion many Japanese strong points to westward of our front lines within our position that have not been reduced. Progress slow and extremely costly. Complete occupation will take at least five days more. Naval and air bombardment a great help but does not take out emplacements.

That night the Japanese themselves improved the situation for Smith, coming out of their emplacements in a boomeranging *banzai* charge.

They struck at Major Jones's First Battalion, Sixth, where it held down the right or southern half of a 400-yard cross-island line. This line was drawn just east of the airfield, where the bird's body ends and the narrowing tail begins. The left or northern half was held by Major Crowe's men.

The attack was made skillfully at first. Some 50 Japanese slipped past an outpost line and at half-past seven had opened a small gap between two companies. They were obviously there to feel out the Marine positions. They tried to draw fire.

But the Marines did not shoot. They struck at the Japanese with bayonets and clubbed rifles and grenades, and while the beach guns and the howitzers on Bairiki converged in a hemming line of fire between the lines, they killed them to a man.

In the interval between this thrust and the second attack, Major Wood Kyle moved a company of Marines into reserve behind Jones while Major McLeod leapfrogged one of his companies forward to fill the gap this movement left. At eleven o'clock the Japanese came again, this time with two 50-man parties. They fired openly, shouting and throwing grenades aimlessly. A score of them came charging at a BAR position held by Pfc. Lowell Koci and Pfc. Horace Warfield. They were clearly silhouetted in the glare of gasoline fires lighted behind them by Marine mortars.

The Marines fired. They ducked down to reload and a Japanese soldier jumped into their hole thrusting with his bayonet. It drove into Warfield's thigh. The Japanese strained to withdraw it, and Koci, a husky 200-pounder, seized his BAR by its muzzle and swung it around like a whip. The butt struck the man behind the head and brained him. His legs thumped the sand as he fell.

Again the artillery cut off retreat for these infiltrating Japanese, and the Marines went about the work of destroying them.

At four o'clock in the morning of November 23, with the moon making a grotesquerie of the coral flats—humping the convex roofs of the pillboxes, squashing the squares of the blockhouses, catching the jagged stumps of coconut trees and drawing them out like giant corkscrews—some 300 more Japanese launched the counterattack which broke their own backs.

They flowed up against the Marine lines yelling and jabbering, and for a time there seemed to be too many of them. Lieutenant Norman Thomas telephoned Major Jones and yelled: "We're killing them as fast as they come at us, but we can't hold much longer. We need reinforcements!" There wasn't time for reinforcement; there was only time for what Jones was sternly commanding:

"You've got to hold!"

While the destroyers *Schroeder* and *Sigsbee* hurled salvo after salvo into the Japanese assembly areas, while the shells of the Marine artillery fell within 75 yards of the front lines, Thomas and his men fought with rifle, bayonet and grenade. By five o'clock the *banzai* charge was shattered. There were 200 dead Japanese within the Marine lines. There were 125 more torn and broken corpses out where the artillery had fallen.

There were now only 500 Japanese left alive on Betio.

12

The men of the Second Marine Division were rushing to victory on the morning of November 23. They were going downhill. The taste of triumph was in the air, and all those who pressed for it moved with a mastery that must have been annihilating to the souls of the enemy.

At seven o'clock, the first of the carrier aircraft plunged to the attack. They bombed and strafed for half an hour. For another quarter-hour, pack howitzers hurled their shells into the tail of Betio. Warships on both the ocean and lagoon sides thundered for the next fifteen minutes, and then it was eight o'clock and time for the riflemen to attack.

"Let's go!" cried Lieutenant Colonel McLeod, and the Third Battalion, Sixth, swept forward with crackling rifles.

They were the freshest troops on Betio. They had not yet fought. They passed through the lines held by Major Jones's Marines—now exhausted from a day and night of constant fighting—and spread out on a two-company front to punch down the length of the narrowing tail. In front of them clanked *Colorado* and *China Gal*—those indestructible Shermans which were still capable of battle—while seven light tanks rolled to either flank.

The attack gathered momentum. It raced forward 150 yards within a matter of minutes. The Japanese defenders fired only fitfully at the onrushing Americans—and then turned their weapons on themselves.

On the left or lagoon side a system of supporting bombproofs slowed one company down. McLeod sent the other company racing down the ocean flank in a bypassing movement. Once they were past the bombproofs, the Marines of this company spread out again. Behind them the bypassed company moved in on the bombproofs, while Lieutenant Lou Largey brought *Colorado* into position. The liquid fire of the flamethrowers began to describe its fiery arc—disappearing through the mouths of the gun ports. Suddenly a door flew open in the biggest of the bombproofs. Perhaps a hundred Japanese rushed out, tumbling over one another in their flight down a narrow exit channel.

Colorado's gun swiveled around and fired.

Fifty, perhaps more, of the enemy were struck to the ground by that shattering shot and soon resistance had ended among the bombproofs.

To the west, in The Pocket, the Marines of Major Hays's

225

battalion and the Ryan-Schoettel battalion were cleaning up. Half-tracks drove among the pillboxes and blockhouses blasting with their 75's, while kneeling riflemen picked off the fleeing enemy. Others hurled shaped charges and grenades. Flame-throwing teams darted up to the entrances and fire gushed from nozzles.

McLeod's Marines were approaching Betio's eastern shore. *China Gal* rumbled among the blockhouses, taking on those that still fired cannon, while the light tanks went after the machine guns and rifles. The Third Battalion, Sixth, was making a slaughter of eastern Betio. The tail was lashing its last. The Marines here killed 475 Japanese with their own losses kept to nine dead and 25 wounded. The enemy was too stunned to fight back.

At one o'clock in the afternoon a dusty, sweating Marine waded into the sea between Betio and Bairiki and stooped to bathe his face in warm water.

Betio had fallen.

13

"The Saps are all dead," the tall young Apamamese said cheerfully on the morning of November 24, and asked for a cigarette. It was given to him, and he began to tell Captain Jim Jones of what had happened to the Japanese since November 22, when Jones attacked their radio station behind the shelling of the submarine *Nautilus*, only to be driven off with one Marine killed and another wounded.

The following day, said the Apamamese, he had gone to the vicinity of the radio station. He had seen that the captain of the atoll garrison was making a speech to about fifteen soldiers who had survived the shelling and the fight. He hid himself and watched.

The captain waved his *samurai* saber and howled.

"We shall kill the American devils!"

He yanked his pistol from its holster and brandished it in the air. It went off accidentally. It struck the captain and mortally wounded him. Then his men began killing themselves. They dug graves and lay down in them and then placed the muzzles of their weapons in their mouths and pulled the triggers.

Captain Jones led his men to the radio station and found that this was so. The Marines finished the burial job the enemy had begun and then the people of Apamama came out of hiding.

There were smiling young men, strong and athletic; eager youngsters more than willing to shinny up trees and throw down coconuts to the Marines; young girls with round bare breasts and straight black hair hanging to their waists and skirts of sail cloth bound tightly around brown hips; and there were old people coming out of the hiding places they had fled to when the shooting began. They came back to their thatched huts to light cooking fires. Shyly, some of the girls began to sing "Brighten the Corner Where You Are."

The Marines looked away. It was not that they were shy. It was just that they were embarrassed. They felt awkward in their clumsy habiliments of war. They felt heavy with themselves and their world, as though they had blundered into some Eden which had not known the serpent.

It was, of course, a romantic notion. But this was the Atoll of the Moon, that Apamama which these Marines would prefer to remember as "The Land of Moonshine."

14

On this same November 24 the Marines were preparing to leave Betio. The transports were already standing into the lagoon with deliberate slow majesty.

The Third Battalion, Sixth, would soon be sailing south to "invade" Apamama and gain that comic celebrity which Marines do not value. The Second Battalion, Sixth, had begun the long hot march up the atoll chain from Bairiki—driving all the Tarawa survivors before them, until, at the northernmost islet of Buariki, they would destroy 175 Japanese against 32 of their own killed and 59 wounded.

But now, on the morning of November 24, most of the Second Division was departing the stench and heat and ruin of Betio. They had killed 4,690 of the enemy and 991 of their own comrades had died or were dying. They had suffered 2,311 men wounded—and many of these would not be fit to fight again. But they had taken Tarawa the untakable, they had done the thing Japan thought impossible. Yet, there was no thought of glory in their minds—of the posthumous Medals of Honor that would come to Hawkins, Bordelon, Bonnyman, of the one that Colonel Shoup would wear—as they came to the beach and stopped and blinked in astonishment.

There was no beach.

The spring tides had come, and the sea flowed up against the sea wall. For a moment there was wonder in the old eyes staring out of young faces. Then they shrugged and clambered aboard the boats. It was all one: high water on the reef also would have meant high water at the sea wall and nowhere to hide.

The boats took them out to the waiting ships while, overhead, roaring airplanes were already beginning to arrive on Hawkins Field. One of them carried Major General Howlin' Mad Smith. He was coming from Makin, which had been taken by about 6,500 soldiers of the Army's 27th Division. They had landed unopposed and killed 445 Japanese combat troops while capturing 104 laborers. They had lost 66 dead and 152 wounded. Howlin' Mad Smith was greeted at the airfield by Julian Smith. Both generals went to division headquarters for the flag-raising.

"Maybe we should have two flags," said Julian Smith. "After all, Tarawa was British once."

"Anybody got a British flag?" Howlin' Mad Smith asked.

Major Holland, the Britisher who had predicted the height of the reef water with such accuracy, rummaged in his bag. He pulled out a pair of underwear drawers and a little Union Jack. He grinned and handed it over. The banners of the two democracies went up the poles and the Rising Sun came down.

The generals Smith began to tour the island. Even Julian Smith, who had been on Betio since November 22, was stunned by what he saw. Both generals understood at last why pillboxes and blockhouses which had withstood bombs and shells had eventually fallen. Within each of them lay a half-dozen or more dead Japanese, their bodies sprawled around those of three or four Marines. Julian Smith's men had jumped inside to fight it out at muzzle range.

Many of the pillboxes were made of five sides, each ten feet long, with a pair of entrances shielded against shrapnel by buffer tiers. Each side was made of two layers of coconut logs eight inches in diameter, hooked together with clamps and railroad spikes, with sand poured between each layer. The roof was built of two similar layers of coconut logs. Over this was a double steel turret, two sheathings of quarter-inch steel rounded off to deflect shells. Over this was three feet of sand.

"By God!" Howlin' Mad exclaimed. "The Germans never built anything like this in France. No wonder these bastards were sitting back here laughing at us. They never dreamed the Marines could take this island, and they were laughing at what would happen to us when we tried it." Howlin' Mad shook his head in disbelief. "How did they do it, Julian?" he began, and then, below and above the sea wall, he found his answer.

Below it as many as 300 American bodies floated on that abundant tide. Above it, leaning against it in death, was the body of a young Marine. His right arm was still flung across the top of the sea wall. A few inches from his fingers stood a little blue-and-white flag. It was a beach marker. It told succeeding waves where they should land. The Marine had planted it there with his life, and now it spoke such eloquent reply to that question of a moment ago that both generals turned away from it in tears.

"Julian," Howlin' Mad Smith went on in soft amendment—"how can such men be defeated?"

15

Battle had begun again on Bougainville.

On November 20, the day the Second Marine Division began landing on Betio, a patrol of the Third Marine Division made the discovery that was to touch off the Battle of Piva Forks.

On the afternoon of that day the Second Battalion, Third Marines, pursued the retreating Colonel Kawano and his 23rd Infantry Regiment through the jungle. The Marines moved east on the East-West Trail, a path about three miles north or inland of Major General Allen Turnage's perimeter at Cape Torokina. A patrol reported reaching a high nameless knoll to the left or north of the trail and about 2,000 yards east of its western terminus. The knoll was the highest ground yet found on Bougainville. It overlooked Empress Augusta Bay and could block the Marines moving east on the trail. It also commanded a big swamp lying south or beneath the trail and occupied by the blocking force under the personal command of Colonel Kawano. Luckily, the knoll was unoccupied.

Lieutenant Colonel Hector de Zayas ordered Major Donald Schmuck to occupy the knoll with F Company. Major Schmuck called a young lieutenant named Steve Cibik.

"There's a knoll of some kind ahead, Steve. It isn't on the maps. No elevation listed. Get your men together and move up on it."

With 35 riflemen and 16 machine-gunners Lieutenant Cibik moved to the knoll. His voice was urgent, for it was getting dark. He told his men to string wire behind them and dig in. He tried to telephone back to the command post, but someone had neglected to connect the wire at the other end.

Cibik and his men passed an anxious but uneventful night, and in the morning, while the mists began to shred over the jungle roof below them, Cibik began sending out patrols.

His men came back excited. They had found empty Japanese positions up ahead. Cibik and his Marines moved out quickly to occupy them. The foxholes were littered with cigarette butts, chopsticks and coconut meat. Cibik guessed that the Japanese had pulled back during the night to avoid Marine artillery fire and that they would return.

The Japanese did return, carelessly. Marine rifles crackled. Mushroom-helmeted figures fell. The others fled. Now Cibik made preparations to hold off the counterattack he expected to follow. He put a machine gun to either flank and a third in the center. A private named Charles Skinner suggested putting a fourth gun out ahead or east of the ridge to surprise the enemy. Cibik agreed and Skinner set up his ambush. Then a section of light mortars came up the ridge. A line was built up to right and left.

But the enemy did not come that night. They came next morning. They blundered into the surprise fire of Private Skinner, the lash of the mortars and the submachine-gun firing of a Marine who had climbed a tree. The attack was broken up, just as Major Schmuck arrived to take command on the knoll that was already being called Cibik's Ridge.

That night 30 more Marines arrived to help stop a second

and heavier attack made the following day, November 23. Cibik's Ridge was taken for good.

Next morning light and heavy field artillery battered the Japanese positions in the swamp. Seven battalions—three of them from the Army's 37th Division—hurled 5,760 shells into the enemy lines. Forty-four machine guns and 21 mortars joined the bombardment.

As the assault battalions moved to the jump-off points, their ears were filled with an incessant roar and rattle. Then there came the sharper, more fearful sounds of the enemy firing counterbombardment. The flashing of their guns was spotted from Cibik's Ridge and within minutes the counterbattery firing of the Marines and soldiers had put them out of action.

The attack went forward. The Marines sloshed through mud up to their calves and broke into a silent swamp. They slogged on. The enemy sent up reserves to counterattack. The Marines met them in toe-to-toe, tree-for-tree fighting that ended in extermination of the counterattackers. So it went throughout this bleak, grim Thanksgiving Day and through the following day, when a fierce charge through a shower of grenades brought death to Colonel Kawano and the remnants of his trail-blocking force.

Reports of enemy losses in the Battle of Piva Forks were conflicting. Some put the dead as high as 1,196, which, together with the Japanese destroyed in the Torokina fighting, would put the 23rd Regiment's dead at 2,014. Other estimates suggested that this figure was highly exaggerated. It probably was, for the 23rd's main body was still intact farther east on the East-West Trail.

More important, Piva Forks enabled General Turnage to expand the Torokina perimeter to roughly 8,000 yards breadth, with Cibik's Ridge and the Piva River now inside its eastern boundary.

This was the new disposition completed by November 26, the day after the Tokyo Express made its last run.

16

The Japanese Army commanders in Rabaul—General Imamura and Lieutenant General Hyakutate—were still not convinced that the enemy's chief objective was Cape Torokina. They believed that the American intention was merely to build a fighter strip there, before moving about 75 miles higher to seize better air bases at Buka Passage off Bougainville's northern nose. Though the Buka airfields had already been made useless to Japan by American bombing, they could still be of use to the enemy in his drive against Rabaul. The Japanese Navy did not agree, but the Army had its way.

On the night of November 24 the Tokyo Express sailed again from Rabaul with 920 soldiers. They were aboard the destroyer-transports *Yugiri*, *Amagiri*, and *Uzuki*, escorted by the big destroyers *Onami* and *Makinami*. The force, commanded by Captain Kiyoto Kagawa, sailed straight for Buka—where Thirty-One-Knot Burke and his Little Beavers were lying in ambush.

American Naval Intelligence had guessed that the Japanese meant to reinforce. On November 24, Admiral Halsey sent this message to Captain Burke:

> Thirty-One-Knot Burke, get this. Put your squadron athwart the Buka-Rabaul evacuation line about 35 miles west of Buka. If no enemy contacts by early morning, come south to refuel same place. If enemy contacted, you know what to do.—HALSEY

Burke led *Charles F. Ausburne*, *Claxton*, *Dyson*, *Converse* and *Spence* north under low-scudding clouds. They came to a 100-mile stretch of squall-dappled sea between Buka and New

Ireland to the west. They waited there, unaware that Captain Kagawa had already completed reinforcement of Buka.

While *Onami* and *Makinami* had stood offshore as a screen, *Yugiri, Amagiri* and *Uzuki* ran in to discharge the troops and also to take aboard 700 aviation troops who had been idle since the Buka fields were knocked out. Then the destroyer-transports rejoined the screen and the entire force made west.

At a few minutes before two in the morning of November 25, the destroyers of Captain Burke sighted these Japanese ships and sent 15 torpedoes streaking toward Captain Kagawa's screen. Then they turned sharp right to avoid counterfire.

Four minutes later Captain Kagawa's lookouts on *Onami* sighted the American fish. Kagawa had thirty seconds to avoid them. It was not enough. He sailed into them. *Onami* blew apart, and a ball of red fire rolled 300 feet skyward from the place where she had been. *Makinami* began breaking in two and was finally pounded beneath the waves by *Spence* and *Converse*.

Aboard *Ausburne,* with *Claxton* and *Dyson* tearing after him, Burke began to pursue the three destroyer-transports frantically hurrying home. They had a good lead, but they couldn't match Burke's 33-knot pace. In a quarter-hour Burke's destroyers had closed the gap from 13,000 yards to 8,000. Burke was exuberant. He radioed Halsey's headquarters at Guadalcanal. "I'm ridin' herd!" he yelled. Being from the Colorado cowboy country, he could not restrain a "Come a Ki-Yi-Yippee, Yippee-Ay!"

Then Burke had a hunch. He zigged his division right for a minute and then zagged back to the previous course. There were three explosions. *Yugiri* had unloaded her torpedoes and they had struck the wakes of Burke's destroyers and exploded.

Burke's destroyers opened up with guns pointing forward. They were coming on hotly, their prows hissing sharply through the black water, and they had no time to maneuver for broadside firing. The blast of *Ausburne's* Number Two mount blew the hatch off Number One mount ahead of it, but the guns continued to fire. Burke began fish-tailing to bring his stern batteries to bear. The fire of all three American destroyers was converging on *Yugiri*. She was circling, burning. At a few minutes after three, while *Amagiri* and *Uzuki* were making their getaway, *Yugiri* went under.

The battle of Cape St. George had ended. The Tokyo Express had run its last, and the Little Beavers of Thirty-One-Knot Burke sailed south without a scratch.

Inside the expanded Torokina beachhead the Seabees had brought off another of those feats of engineering wizardry which the Marines had come to take for granted. The Seabees had built an airfield in the soup of the Torokina swamp. They began it November 9 and at dawn of December 10 the first of VMF-216's Corsairs put down on the completed airstrip. Seventeen came in, followed by a half-dozen Dauntlesses and a Skytrain transport. Within a week Army Aerocobras joined the Corsairs in close-up support against the Japanese on Bougainville. Soon there would be Lightning night-fighters operating from Torokina, which meant the days of Washing-Machine Charley were also numbered. The Navy's Corsairs, the Marines' Venturas and the Army's Lightnings had shown how an intricate system of radar vectoring could put them on Charley's tail.

But more important, Torokina Airfield had brought Rabaul within fighter range. This was the importance of the Seabee's engineering feat, though it was lost on the ordinary Marine in his very real gratitude for the new roads.

It was now possible for a man to walk on Bougainville without having cold wet mud working down within his socks, without hearing the customary *slop-suck, slop-suck* sound of one foot following the other out of foot-high slime. The network of roads hacked out of the jungle by these doughty movers and shakers of earth also meant that the Torokina beachhead was becoming stuffed with food and supplies which would reduce the discomfort of living on an enormous, vile-green lily pad. So the Marines were grateful and on Bougainville they did the Seabees the unrivaled compliment of a kind word for another branch of the United States armed forces. On one of the Seabees' new roads the Second Raider Battalion erected this sign:

235

So when we reach the Isle of Japan
With our caps at a jaunty tilt,
We'll enter the City of Tokyo
On the roads the Seabees built.

It was warm and well-meaning and it made everyone smile. Only later in the war would the Marine smile vanish, but by then it was too late to correct the impression—slyly fostered by the Seabees—that Marines never went ashore anywhere until the Seabees gave them the word that the roads were ready.

17

At the beginning of December Major General Turnage decided to take up a blocking position to the right of the northeast curve of his Bougainville beachhead. He wanted to occupy a series of ridges which began about a half-mile east along the East-West Trail and ran another mile and a half to the west bank of the Torokina River.

There were four of these heights, one called Hill 600 to the south of the trail or beneath it, and three north or above it. These were Hill 1000, next a nameless hill about 250 feet high, then Hill 600A. Turnage struck at the northern hills first.

Hill 1000 was seized by the Third Parachute Battalion in the early part of the month. On December 12 the Twenty-first Marines hit the nameless hill—and quickly called it Hellzapoppin' Ridge for the reception they received.

Hellzapoppin' had sheer slopes on its sides, east and west, and could only be approached from the forward and reverse slopes, south and north. Its crest was a mere 40 yards in width, though it ran 350 yards fore and aft. It was covered with a dense green tangle, in which the Japanese had constructed the usual complex of interlocking holes and bunkers, and giant trees on its summit served as a screen to detonate the mortars which the Marines tried to drop on the heavily fortified reverse slope.

The Twenty-first Marines came at Hellzapoppin' for five days, during which Colonel Evans Ames used every one of his regiment's nine rifle companies in the assault. During this time the Marines also began to develop the tactic of close-up aerial support which would be one of their outstanding contributions to modern warfare, calling on Avenger torpedo-bombers to deliver low-level strafing and bombing attacks within unusually close range of their own lines. But even five days could do no more than bring a purchase on Hellzapoppin's forward slopes, and on December 17 the Marines called for an all-out aerial strike on the still-undented reverse slope.

On that same December 17 a column of unlovely LST's was plodding along the coast of northeast New Guinea, bringing the First Marine Division back to the war.

The final echelons of the First Marine Regiment were coming up from Goodenough Island to Finschhafen and Oro Bay. Here they would join the Seventh Marines, and these two regiments would sail across Dampier Strait to assault Cape Gloucester on the western tip of New Britain.

They would do this for General MacArthur, for the price of frolicking in the fleshpots of Melbourne had been service under his command in the Southwest Pacific area. General MacArthur had placed the First Marine Division in his ALAMO Force and sent it on an operation which would nail down his right flank while he struck farther north in New Guinea, and would also isolate the great Japanese base at Rabaul on eastern New Britain. For Bougainville to the east and the new Japanese airfield on Cape Gloucester to the western end of New Britain would straddle Rabaul.

This was the First Division's mission as it sailed again to battle—as stiff-necked as ever and perhaps a shade more arrogant in the knowledge that it was still going it alone. The men of this division had been on their own since leaving the

States nineteen months ago, and they had come to regard themselves as the proprietors of the Pacific. They had even designed their own uniform while in Melbourne, and it was said of them in Washington: "Any resemblance between the First Division and the remainder of the Marine Corps is purely accidental."

So the hard-nosed First set its sights on western New Britain, while on that same December 17 indelicate Pappy Boyington was treating mighty Rabaul on the eastern tip to its first experience of the fighter-sweep.

It was a simple tactic, one which Boyington had discovered over Kahili two months ago. He had flown over the enemy base and taunted the enemy to come up and fight. When they did the Black Sheep shot them down.

But Boyington had only had four or five planes that time. Now, in early December, with Torokina Airfield bringing Rabaul within 230 miles' range, Boyington proposed to Major General Ralph Mitchell that the fighter-sweep be used on a bigger scale against the 200 or so fighter planes which the Japanese had still operative there. Mitchell agreed.

On December 17 Boyington led 31 Corsairs, 22 Hellcats and 23 of those gaudily painted New Zealand Warhawks from Bougainville to Rabaul.

The slow, low-flying Warhawks went in first and their eager New Zealand pilots ran into a formation of forty Zekes. They shot down five of them before Boyington's main body arrived. The Japanese scurried for home and stayed there.

Again Boyington hurled his taunts, and again came that polite inquiry:

"Major Boyington, what is your position?"

"Right over your effing airport!" Boyington yelled. "Why don't you yellow bastards come up and fight?"

"Why don't you come down, sucker?" the Japanese taunted.

Boyington grinned and led his fighters in a circling, high-low weave designed to confuse the enemy antiaircraft. Still the Japanese refused combat. Boyington and Moe Casey nosed over in a dive. They came in spraying the parked aircraft, always keeping a safe distance from those Japanese machine guns which were so accurate at short range. They climbed back up to 20,000 feet, where the other fighters were stacked.

"All right, you bastards, I was down," Boyington yelled. "How about you coming up?"

Silence.

Exasperated, his gasoline low, Boyington turned and flew back to Torokina.

There were, he told Major General Mitchell, too many Allied planes out that day. The Japanese liked the odds a bit more in their favor. Seventy-six planes of three different types were also too difficult to handle. If the general would let him take up 36 planes—or at least no more than 48—he'd show him some real results.

Mitchell agreed, but it could not be done until the air strikes had flown to Hellzapoppin' Ridge.

Three air strikes flew off Torokina on December 18. The foot Marines marked their front lines with colored smoke grenades. They marked the enemy targets by firing white phosphorous mortar shells. And the pilots dropped their bombs. Hellzapoppin' Ridge was wreathed in smoke. Gradually the gaunt outlines of the ridge became visible, for the bombardment was divesting it of its vegetation and unmasking its defenses.

The First and Third Battalions of the Twenty-first Marines attacked. They moved against the ridge from two sides, but the enemy had come out of his remaining holes once the bombardment was lifted and still held out.

Another air strike.

Six Avengers came roaring over the treetops. They dropped 48 100-pounders on targets within 75 yards of the Marine front. They circled and flew back to strafe at treetop level, and this time the attack was irresistible.

Hellzapoppin' was the last fierce battle of the Third Marine Division on Bougainville. Hill 600A was taken on December 23 and Hill 600 fell on December 27. The following day Major General Turnage turned over his Bougainville lines to Major General John Hodge, commander of the Marines' old friends from Guadalcanal—the Americal Division.

By the end of the year almost all of the Third Marine Division was back at Guadalcanal. They had seized an airfield in the heart of a blackwater jungle, had bought it at the cost of 423 killed and 1,418 wounded. They had counted well over 2,000 enemy bodies and there were probably at least that many more who died from their meeting with the Third Marine Division on Bougainville. Moreover, Torokina Airfield was already mounting the flights of planes that were roaring requiem for Rabaul.

Five days after the fall of Hellzapoppin' Ridge, Major Boyington proved the wisdom of the smaller sweep. He took 48 fighters up to Rabaul and caught 40 enemy fighters in the air. Thirty of them were shot down—12 by the Black Sheep alone, of which Boyington himself got four. For the first time in a year Joe Foss's 26-plane record was in jeopardy.

18

Within the swamp forests of western New Britain was a swamp fox named Iwao Matsuda. He was a major general in the Imperial Japanese Army, a shipping specialist who had come to the vicinity of Cape Gloucester to direct the movement of barges from Rabaul to New Guinea.

The barge movement had become important to Japan after the disaster of the Battle of the Bismarck Sea in March, 1943, when Allied aircraft sank eight transports and four destroyers bringing troops to New Guinea from Rabaul. Thereafter no big ships were risked within range of enemy air power. As had happened in the Solomons, New Guinea began to be supplied by barge.

The barges moved at night, hiding out by day in the numerous coves and creeks of New Britain's irregular northern coast.

They crept around Cape Gloucester at the western tip of the north coast and slipped over to Rooke Island (Umboi) still farther west. From there they made the nocturnal dash across the Dampier Strait to New Guinea.

Major General Iwao Matsuda made Cape Gloucester the midway point of this Rabaul-New Guinea barge movement, but as the thunder of the aerial assault upon Rabaul traveled westward to his own sector, Matsuda saw clearly it would soon be necessary for him to defend the Cape. To do this Matsuda had the 65th Brigade, a mixture of no less than 41 separate detachments and groups ranging in size from four men to 3,365. The war in the Solomons and New Guinea had thrown up many military waifs and orphans on the shores of New Britain and Iwao Matsuda had been made their guardian. He had only two battle-seasoned line regiments—the 53rd Infantry of Colonel Koki Sumiya and the 141st commanded by Colonel Kenshiro Katayama—plus artillery and machine cannon companies and a battalion-size combat outfit called the 51st Reconnaissance Regiment commanded by Colonel Jiro Sato. On December 1, Matsuda listed his strength as 15,018 men, although he actually had something closer to 10,000 to defend western New Britain.

About 3,000 of these under Colonel Katayama were strung out at outposts as much as 40 or 50 miles southeast of the airfield. Another 4,000 were in the Cape Gloucester Airfield vicinity under Colonel Sumiya. The airfield, incidentally, was an area only about two miles wide and a mile deep set in fields of *kunai* grass at the extreme northern tip of the Cape. Cape Gloucester itself formed the northern extremity of western New Britain. It was a nipple of land about 12 miles wide from west to east and rising roughly eight miles higher than the rest of the north coast stretching away east from it. In the indenture thus formed was Borgen Bay. The remainder of Matsuda's men were in this Borgen Bay area or else were with him in his headquarters at Nakarop.

Here Matsuda had a personal residence built 10 feet off the sodden ground. He had a bedroom with a four-poster bed and adjoining bath. He had a fancy kitchen, well stocked with canned delicacies from America, Australia and England. He had cases of *saki* and beer. He had a living room with floors of inlaid wood and pink wicker furniture and he had a record-player. He had a prayer room with an altar window. He had an air raid shelter 30 feet long to which he might descend from his kitchen. General Matsuda had, moreover, the concealment which towering mountain ranges and man-swallowing swamps could give him. Though Nakarop was only a dozen miles south of the airfield, and hardly half that distance inland from Borgen Bay, this was western New Britain. This was a blind, blundering, inconstant place where a man might pass within ten feet of a village or a man and not see either, where rivers changed their courses in a single night because a dozen inches of rain had fallen within half a day, where the soaring mangrove tree which marked this morning's path was gone by noon and the man crushed and hidden beneath its prostrate bulk would be reported missing for a month, or where this afternoon's barricade is carried away by tonight's flood or collapses in tomorrow's earthquake.

New Britain was not, like Guadalcanal, alluring—for she was as unlovely without as she was hideous within. If her interior was a hag of a place, with sunless sinks of swamps and steaming near-equatorial heat, then her exterior was a witch, humpbacked, with great green-black spines of mountains, black-hatted with thundercloud and shrouded with sheets of rain, smoking from the round bowls of volcanoes, and girdled all around by black mud beaches so narrow that a tall man might lie across them with head in jungle and toe in sea.

On this dark island men did not so much think as feel. They felt themselves to be sentient clots stuck in a primeval ooze where everything was soft and squishy to the touch—including the puckering pulp of their own flesh—and it was only when their minds suggested that they, too, were dissolving in this monotonous mush of water and corrupting matter that they would realize they had a mind. Here men struggled to exist, and after that to fight, and here also the Marines would have their first opportunity to maneuver against the enemy. For New Britain was 370 miles long west to east and an average of 40 to 50 miles wide. True, the Marines would be maneuvering only for the airfield and Borgen Bay, but this was still a land mass larger than either Guadalcanal or Bougainville.

Those denunciations delivered since Tarawa—that Marines were capable only of the frontal charge and were careless with men's lives—would receive their reply in the New Britain campaign. On New Britain it was as though Guadalcanal were being reversed, for here were 10,000 Japanese holding a jungle beachhead and airfield against the onslaught of some 19,000 Americans—and here all the superiority of air and sea was as surely American as it had been Japanese at Guadalcanal.

Again Radio Tokyo announced the result in advance. While the First and Seventh Regiments were aboard their destroyer-transports and LCI's, leaving the Fifth in reserve on New Guinea, the Japanese radio was informing the world of how that devil's brood of degenerates and jailbirds called the First Marine Division had been kicked out of Melbourne in disgrace and were now about to be turned loose on Cape Gloucester.

"But I am pleased to add," said the announcer, "that our soldiers are fully prepared to repulse this insolent attempt. The jungles will run red with the blood of the butchers of Guadalcanal."

19

It was Christmas Day in the States, but out on the dark waters of Dampier Strait it was the morning of December 26, and Major General Iwao Matsuda's radios were already sputtering with reports of an invading force circling the Cape and standing off the northern coast a few miles to the east.

At six o'clock the thundering began. Two cruisers and eight

destroyers sailed back and forth, blazing at the shore with orange-yellow bursts while a pair of rocket-firing LCI's daintily picked their way through an opening in the barrier reef. They took up positions to either end of the landing beaches and soon the *swooosh* of their missiles was audible beneath the booming of the guns.

It was still dark, and the Marines assembled on the decks of their destroyers could feel a twinge of pity for the enemy ashore. They knew what it was like to receive naval gunfire. There had actually not been need of a big force of warships, for the bombers of the Fifth Air Force had been pounding Cape Gloucester for weeks. They had dropped 2,000 tons of explosive. During the last few nights Liberators had been circling the airfield, dropping a bomb every six minutes, putting Japanese nerves through the wringer of an American Washing-Machine Charley. Now in the beginnings of a blue day arising roseate behind 6,500-foot Mount Talawe there were more of the big, four-engined Liberators coming back to bomb. Flight after flight of them appeared high in the sky, humming like bees and seeming as small. There was the red winking of Japanese antiaircraft fire, but then the ferocious Mitchells and Havocs—two-engined attack bombers—swooped low with flashing nose cannon and machine guns. There was no more winking.

Men of the Seventh Regiment went over the side of their destroyers into the landing boats. The boats fanned out and headed for a landing beach about five miles east of the airfield. They charged into the smoke being swept seaward by an onshore wind. They vanished. After them went the LCI's, groping for the barrier passage and a quick run-in. They disappeared. The bombardment and bombing lifted. The smoke drifted seaward. The LST's came forward slowly, and then the returning landing boats burst out of the smoke.

They were empty. Their coxswains were grinning and raising jubilant clenched fists. "Landing unopposed," they shouted, and the water began boiling beneath the sterns of the LST's as these unlovely dray-horses of the sea surged forward through the reef passage.

★

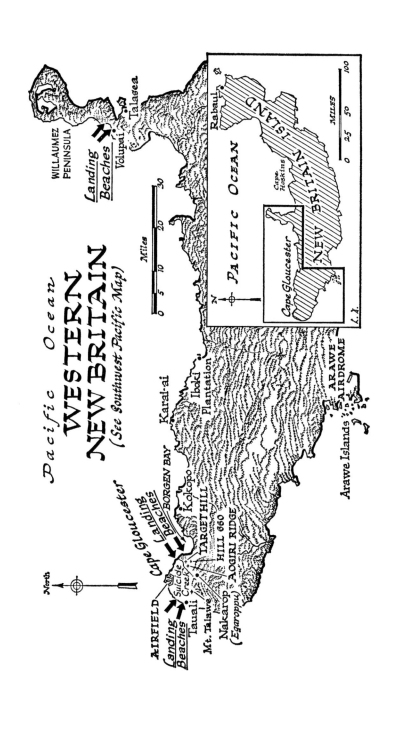

Pacific Ocean

WESTERN NEW BRITAIN
(See Southwest Pacific Map)

Miles

0 5 10 20 30

WILLAUMEZ PENINSULA

Landing Beaches

Volupai

Talasea

North

Cape Gloucester *Landing Beaches*

BORGEN BAY

Karai-ai

Kokopo

TARGET HILL

HILL 660

AOGIRI RIDGE

(Egaroppu)

Nakarop

Mt. Talawe

Tauali

Suicide Creek

Landing Beaches

AIRFIELD

Iboki

Plantation

ARAWE AIRDROME

Arawe Islands

Pacific Ocean

N

Rabaul

NEW BRITAIN ISLAND

Cape Hoskins

Cape Gloucester

NEW BRITAIN

MILES

0 25 50 100

To the southwest, Masters' Bastards were also landing unopposed. They were the men of the Second Battalion, First, and they called themselves that because Lieutenant Colonel James Masters was their commander and because Masters' Bastards had a good rude ring to it.

They landed at Tauali on the extreme west of the Cape, roughly seven miles southwest of the airfield. A swarm of LCI's beached themselves, their ramps banged down—and Masters' Bastards ran ashore. They darted across a man's-length of sunbathed black mud beach and plunged into the murk of the jungle.

They would not see daylight again for two weeks.

They sat there, facing east, blocking the coastal track running from Japanese bases to the southeast of the airfield. They patrolled constantly and killed a few of the enemy and waited for the Japanese to try to force their way through them.

The Seventh Regiment's sector was marked on the map as "Damp Flat."

"It's damp, all right," growled those Marines who were already wading through a hip-deep swamp, already glum with recollection of Guadalcanal. "It's damp clear up to yer ass!"

It was a forest swamp and General Matsuda had not thought any sane commander would land there. He had fortified it lightly, while concentrating his forces to either side of it. When Colonel Julian Frisbie's men landed here they encountered only a few empty coconut bunkers, a pair of untended and unemplaced 75's and a huddling handful of terrified shipping engineers. The Marines overran the beach and swept into the jungle.

On the left, the First Battalion, Seventh, made for a height called Target Hill. They found that the Japanese had abandoned Target Hill during the bombardment, and they occupied the enemy's positions.

On the right the Seventh's Third Battalion sloshed to its designated perimeter.

In the center the Second Battalion crossed the coastal road and drove inland through sporadic sniper fire, only to bog down in the worst of the swamp.

Men moving over what seemed like solid ground were sucked down into waist-high muck, and had to be pulled out. The Marines were floundering, tripped by vines and sometimes thrown down by them. They had to be careful of the numerous shells lying unexploded in the soft mud. They had to clamber over rotten forest giants which had begun to fall during the shelling and were still falling. One man was killed by one. He was the Division's first fatality on Cape Gloucester. Nineteen more men would be killed by New Britain's falling trees, and some 30 others would be badly injured. The Marines were already calling them "widow-makers."

At last the men in the center debouched on dry ground. They moved on, but they had not gone 100 yards before they were in swamp again. They had penetrated to a depth of 1,200 yards.

By a quarter after ten Major General William Rupertus, the Division's new commander, was ashore with his staff and setting up a headquarters. By noon the Third Battalion, First Marines, were landing on another beach about three miles farther west. They wheeled right, marching up the coastal road to attack Cape Gloucester Airfield, another two miles west. By midafternoon Rupertus was calling for the Fifth Marines to come up from New Guinea.

In Rabaul it was believed that the American task force sighted between New Guinea and New Britain on Christmas Night was headed for Arawe on New Britain's southern coast. An Army cavalry regiment had landed against light opposition at Arawe eleven days earlier, and the Japanese believed that the task force was bringing more troops there. Then came Matsuda's call for help on the northern coast.

The officer commanding 63 Zeros and 25 dive-bombing Vals sent aloft from Rabaul quickly changed the target to Cape Gloucester, but his order was not transmitted. The planes flew up to Arawe, found nothing and flew back home again.

At half-past two in the afternoon, however, they were on the target, coming in low and fast on the beached supplies and the second echelons of LST's just arriving from New Guinea. They struck, and the Americans began to make mistakes.

While the Japanese sank the new destroyer *Brownson* and hit others, gunners on the LST's shot down two American bombers and seriously damaged two others—so confusing the Mitchell pilots that they began to bomb and strafe Marines on Cape Gloucester. They killed one man and wounded 14 others before they flew off, and then the Japanese planes headed east for Rabaul and the heavy booming of bombs gave way to the sharp crackling of the fight being made by the Third Battalion, First, on its march to the airfield.

Sergeant Robert Oswald figured he had two good men in the brothers Hansen. They were twins, Paul and Leslie, both privates, sons of a widow who had already lost an older boy in the war. As Oswald's amtrack moved along the road to the airfield Leslie Hansen was on the machine guns with him, and Paul was driving. They were carrying ammunition for the Third Battalion, First.

Up front, one of the companies was raked by bullets coming from a system of four bunkers bristling with machine guns. It was a roadblock. Captain Joseph Terzi and Captain Phillip Wilheit of Company K were instantly killed. Their men deployed. They let go with the newfangled bazooka, but the rockets merely lodged in the soft earth around the bunkers. The flame-throwers wouldn't work. The riflemen deployed and began firing and someone yelled for ammunition.

"Let's go!" Oswald shouted, and Paul Hansen let out the amtrack's clutch and gunned its motor. The gray amphibian came careening up the road with blazing machine guns. Paul Hansen pointed its nose at the nearest bunker, intending to roll over it and cave it in. The Japanese spilled out of the exits and came swarming at the amtrack. Many of them were shot down by Sergeant Oswald and Leslie Hansen, but the rest got to the amtrack before the ground Marines could drive them off. Oswald fell, mortally wounded. Leslie Hansen was dragged from his gun and beaten and stabbed to death. The Japanese turned to take Paul Hansen, but by then he had skillfully rocked the amtrack free and was rolling over the bunker and crushing it while the riflemen closed and polished off the Japanese.

With the blind sides of the remaining bunkers exposed and many of their defenders slain, the Marines quickly overran them with grenades and bayonets.

By then it was late afternoon, and the Marines halted and dug in, just as the first of the monsoon rains broke over their heads.

It came out of the northwest. Men on the beaches struggling to unravel a traffic snarl of 150 abandoned Army six-by-six trucks could see it coming, an opaque gray wall of water marching across the Bismarck Sea. It came with the sound of rolling drums and then it was over the jungle and the water was swishing, streaming, gurgling earthward. It was as nothing these Marines had seen before, this Niagara of a monsoon. It was not a rain storm, a spell of rain—it was a season of it. It was the cloudburst in perpetuity, and it was so constant during the ensuing four months that both Japanese and Americans numbered the dry days of sunshine and cherished their memory.

Already one of the 105-millimeter howitzers of the Fourth Battalion, Eleventh Marines, had sunk together with its prime mover. There were five inches of gun shield, the top of the tractor's vertical exhaust pipe and the tips of its levers above the surface.

In a little while there would be nothing.

Night.
Louie the Louse.
Flares.
Out of their rain-filled holes tumbled Marines, their nerves again pulsing and twanging as though it were Guadalcanal again and there had never been an Australia. But there was no thundering and flashing out at sea. The Marines went back to their holes, already too miserable to be mystified by the inexplicable enemy.

20

Major General Matsuda had to decide whether he was cut in two or whether he had the enemy surrounded.

He chose the latter. It was not because he was a stupid commander, which he was not; it was because on a map this could appear to be the truth. The Americans were in the swamp. They could not maneuver. They were exposed to the very tactics with which Matsuda had hoped to defend the Cape.

While Colonel Sumiya's men held out on the airfield to the west, Colonel Katayama's 141st Regiment would counterattack from the east. Matsuda had already ordered Katayama to call in all his patrols and to march north, leaving only token forces behind to defend his southern garrisons. For Matsuda had accurately concluded that the major assault on New Britain had come in his Cape Gloucester area. The Americans south at Arawe were not to be feared.

But then Matsuda acted on a pair of misconceptions which seemed to be congenital among Japanese Army commanders. He underestimated the enemy's strength and belittled his fighting ability. He put the Marine force down at 2,500—when it was by then actually five times that—and then sent about a thousand men up against it without waiting for Katayama's 141st to arrive from the south.

Matsuda ordered the 2nd Battalion, 53rd, to move from Borgen Bay positions east to the center of the Seventh Marines' position at "Damp Flat." Shortly after midnight the morning of December 27, just as a thunderstorm broke, the Japanese began attacking.

★

Even the howls of the *banzai*-makers were drowned out in the clashing of the clouds, the drumming of the rain, the drawn-out toppling crash of the widow-makers being hurled to earth by the wind, and the treetop explosions of artillery shells. The defending Marines could not fight from foxholes full of water. They lay on top of the ground. It became a blind battle, decided, in the end, by Marine mortars "laid in by guess and by God," and the dawn arrival of a special weapons battery. The Japanese withdrew in the morning, leaving more than 200 dead on the field. There were 25 dead Marines and 75 wounded.

That same morning Pappy Boyington led his Black Sheep up to Rabaul again. Once more the Zeros rose to meet them, and again Boyington's aim was true. He shot one down. He was within one plane of tying Joe Foss's record and he flashed eagerly among the red-balled Zeros. Then oil spurted over his glass hatch. Three times Boyington wound back the hood and tried to wipe the film away, but he couldn't. Exasperated, he turned and flew back to Torokina Airfield. He landed. Someone said it was a shame the oil had prevented his tying Foss's record of 26 planes.

"What's the difference?" Boyington growled. "I couldn't have hit a bull in the ass with a bass fiddle anyway."

But he knew it was not so, and he had wanted that twenty-sixth kill very badly.

The morning of December 28 brought high winds to Cape Gloucester, as well as an earthquake and that rare bird of war: an enemy prisoner.

His name was Corporal Kashida Shigeto and he was taken by the Third Battalion, First Marines, during an action fought at Hell's Point, about a mile east of the airfield. There were a dozen big bunkers there, each occupied by about 20 Japanese soldiers. There were a few 75-millimeter gun emplacements. The Marines threw four Sherman tanks at Hell's Point. One of them rumbled around a bend and ran into a Japanese 75-millimeter gun.

The Japanese gunner ran to his gun and pulled the lanyard.

251

The gun roared and the shell struck the tank and exploded. It left a small dent. The astonished Japanese soldier fled, for the tank had lurched forward and was rolling toward him. Now the other tanks came up, flushing the Japanese out of the bunkers into the fire of following riflemen. One of these riflemen struck his foot on an object in the ground. Looking down, he gazed into the agonized eyes of Corporal Kashida Shigeto. The Marine hesitated. He did not know whether to shoot or to kick the Japanese, but he had plenty of time to decide, for Corporal Shigeto was buried up to his neck. His trench had caved in on him a few moments after he had received a painful wound in the shoulder.

Then to Corporal Shigeto's amazement the Americans began to dig him out. An intelligence officer had arrived just in time to convince the puzzled rifleman that he should neither kill nor kick, that he should in fact be kind. The Marines had learned how kindness could open the lips of Japanese prisoners. Taught to expect torture, Corporal Shigeto was delighted to accept the offer of cheese from a K-ration and an American cigarette. He began to answer questions. His country had not signed the Geneva Convention under which all captured soldiers are to give their name and serial number—and nothing more—nor did Japan tell her soldiers how to act when captured, for surrender was the supreme disgrace. Cave-ins and other forms of accidental surrender were not anticipated, and so the suddenly amiable Corporal Shigeto began to answer his captor's questions with great fervor and detail.

As a result of what he said, General Rupertus did not press his attack to the airfield. He decided to wait until the Fifth Marines arrived in the morning.

Colonel John Selden led the First and Second Battalions of the Fifth Marines into Cape Gloucester shortly after dawn of December 29, landing at the beach where the First Marines had come in. The Fifth's men were brought uproad to the airfield by truck. They dismounted and were deployed wide to the left or south of the road. They were to advance on the airfield through the jungled ridges, while the First rolled up the road.

The assault began and quickly picked up momentum. The

rain stopped. The sun was shining. The roadbound Marines burst from a wood onto the edge of a field of *kunai* grass. Beyond it was the airfield.

Artillery shells screeched overhead and crashed in front of them. The tanks rolled forward, their 75's blasting and machine guns blazing. Riflemen clustered behind them and began moving at a trot. There was the happy barking of a dog. A German shepherd whose Japanese master had fallen at Hell's Point was running out in front. He had taken the point. He was leading them in, and suddenly the troops were grinning with relief, for there was no one on the airfield to oppose them. Corporal Shigeto's reports of thousands of men seemed proven false.

But the Japanese prisoner had actually not exaggerated. Colonel Sumiya and his men had abandoned the airfield. They had also withdrawn from a series of ridges directly south of it, and it was past these empty bunkers that the men of the Fifth Marines moved as they came in on the airfield from their jungle march.

During the darkness of that night the Japanese came back to these bunkers, reoccupied them—and turned the guns toward the airfield below.

It had been a dull damp war at Tauali where Masters' Bastards still sat in roadblock. Patrols moving out from the perimeter ran into occasional brief skirmishes on narrow jungle trails, but then the enemy vanished. Throughout the day of December 29 patrols came in with reports of a silent jungle.

Lieutenant Colonel Masters was worried. That night the men holding his perimeter facing east to the jungle were on full alert. A fierce storm burst on their heads, and at two o'clock the following morning 116 Japanese came charging west down a natural causeway connecting the Marines' ridges with their own.

They came yelling in what might have been a hurricane, and they came with such swift ferocity that they immediately overran one gunpit.

The Marines counterattacked. Gunnery Sergeant Joe Guiliano cradled a light machine gun in his arms and plunged into the dark melee firing from the hip. The Japanese were thrown out of the pit they had taken, but they came back. Guiliano fired again and led another charge. The fight raged on through the wind-whipped darkness, until, in the morning, it had come to the end usually foreordained when a hundred lightly armed men charge a thousand better-armed men holding the high ground. The Marines, whose losses were six killed and 17 wounded, never found out for sure why this detachment from the 53rd Regiment had launched that charge.

There were no officers among the five men taken prisoner, and everyone else was dead.

Up at the airfield a patrol from the Fifth Marines had run into heavy fire from the "deserted" bunkers in the southern ridges. The regiment prepared to return to the ridges, for the Japanese had to be driven from the high ground if capture of the airfield was to be completed. The Fifth began a series of small nasty actions in which the Marines slugged through muck and fire to clear the hills.

By one o'clock on the afternoon of December 30 Major General Rupertus was able to send this message to Lieutenant General Walter Krueger, the commander of ALAMO Force:

> First Marine Division presents to you as an early New Year's gift the complete airdrome of Cape Gloucester. Situation well in hand due to fighting spirit of troops, the usual Marine luck and the help of God—Rupertus grinning to Krueger.

Next day the American flag went up the pole at Cape Gloucester Airfield—and by the time it reached the top it was already limp and dripping. That same day, General Rupertus did what he could to assuage the grief of an American mother. He ordered Private Paul Hansen sent home never to be returned to combat again.

And back in Melbourne the newspapers celebrated the easy victory with the exulting headlines:

OUR MARINES TAKE CAPE GLOUCESTER!

21

Major General William Rupertus began the New Year of 1944 by drawing a perimeter around the airfield and calling upon Brigadier General Lemuel Shepherd, the assistant division commander, to clear out the Japanese holding high ground in the Borgen Bay area.

Borgen Bay was the 10-mile indentation formed by Cape Gloucester on the west and the irregular northern coast jutting out to its east. Along its coast was a series of hills which the Marines wished to hold to guarantee their beachhead.

The eastern flank of this beachhead was represented by Target Hill about six miles southeast of the airfield and about a thousand yards west of the mouth of Borgen Bay. General Shepherd, long considered one of the Marine Corps's foremost tacticians, sent a force into the jungle at Suicide Creek about a mile northwest of Target Hill. The Marines were to cross the stream and swing like a gate southeast through the Borgen Bay hills. Shepherd's plan was simply to hold at Target Hill and hit at Suicide Creek.

While Shepherd's battalions moved into position on the airfield side of Suicide Creek, the Japanese across the stream were building an intricate ambush in a morass. Colonel Kenshiro Katayama, who had arrived from the south coast to take command in Borgen Bay, had conferred with Matsuda at Nakarop, and the swamp fox—who never came within a half-dozen miles of the front—had given him complete control of the battle. It was Katayama who ordered Major Shinichi Takabe to dig in southeast of Suicide Creek with his 2nd Battalion, 53rd.

Katayama had also studied Suicide Creek and Target Hill. He had found that the creek area was impassable for the dreaded American tanks and decided to hold there. Target Hill, however, was open on its seaward side where the coastal road to the airfield ran around it. To recapture the airfield, Katayama decided to hold at Suicide Creek and hit at Target Hill. It was the exact opposite of Shepherd's plan and the guarantor of battle at both points.

The colonel assigned the 2nd Battalion, 141st Infantry, of Major Toyoji Mukai to seize Target Hill. He held Mukai high in his esteem. High in Mukai's esteem was Lieutenant Shinichi Abe, whose 5th Company was chosen to spearhead the attack.

Lieutenant Abe was among the most popular and able young officers in the 65th Brigade. He quickly gathered his platoon leaders and issued orders. The men were to move out from Aogiri Ridge—the Borgen Bay bastion which guarded Hill 660 as well as the approaches to Matsuda's lair—and move to the western face of Target Hill. Artillery, mortar and machine-cannon fire would pin down the Americans while the assault troops and engineers stealthily cut steps in the steep lower slopes of Target Hill. This would make it easier for the 5th Company to strike the Americans fast and hard. Lieutenant Abe also sent a field dispatch to one of his platoon leaders, Warrant Officer Kiyoshi Yamaguchi, who was then moving forward to the attack zone. The message instructed Yamaguchi on the hour of attack and location of the company CP, and it concluded with this admonition:

> It is essential that we conceal the intention that we are maintaining position on Aogiri Ridge. Concerning the occupation of this position, it is necessary that Aogiri Ridge is maintained.

Yamaguchi read it and thrust it into his pocket, unaware of how truly important Aogiri Ridge was to the defense of Borgen Bay and the safety of Iwao Matsuda, not thinking that he might be killed, that the message might be found on him, that the Americans might be able to read it. For Warrant Officer Yamaguchi was in a tearing hurry to get his platoon into position for the attack on Target Hill, which was scheduled for before dawn on January 3.

★

On January 2 the Marines attacked Suicide Creek.

The newly arrived Third Battalion, Fifth Marines, was on the right or west with the Third Battalion, Seventh, on the left. They came up cautiously to the creek's steep banks. Scouts waded across. It was difficult going, for though the creek was but 20 to 30 feet wide and from two to three feet deep and sluggish, its floor was covered with slippery stones. There were also fallen trees which the scouts had to clamber over, but they got across. They slipped into the jungle and soon they were back, waving the main bodies on.

The first platoons crossed and the Japanese struck.

Machine-gun fire swept the Marines from every direction. Marines pitched to the ground or threw themselves down to return fire blindly. It was as though they had been attacked by a battalion of ghosts. They had no notion where their enemy was. They could only hear the bullets whining about them, smacking into trees, cutting leaves, digging up spurts in the mud, sinking into flesh. One platoon was pinned down. A young rifleman was blinded by powder burns. He blundered about, calling, "I can't see—I can't see." Corporal Larry Oliveria grabbed him by the arm. Together, they withdrew. Oliveria paused every few feet to fire, then hefted his rifle and pulled the blinded boy all the way back across the creek as the youth mumbled in a stupor, "I can't see—I can't see."

Some of these platoons crossed Suicide Creek four times, only to be hurled back four times. One platoon came down again to the water's edge. A big husky rifleman stepped into the water. A bullet smacked loudly into his belly.

"Them dirty bastards!" the stricken man mumbled in amazement, and sank into the water dead.

There were wounded Marines stumbling through the water, rolling down the banks, fighting the current that swept them downstream. Men ran out to seize them and pull them to safety and were shot down themselves. Still the fight raged on, a battle incredibly unreal for there was still no sign of the enemy.

At dusk the Japanese very nearly turned the repulse into a rout. About 50 of them followed the retreating Marines across the creek. They crept up the sheltering high banks near an

257

emplacement of four machine guns. The gunners had started to dig their own foxholes. Their guns were untended. If the Japanese could get to them, they could swing them on the Marines and strike a serious counterblow at the entire attack.

They ran for them in a silent rush. They were 30 yards from the digging Marines before someone spotted them and shouted: "Japs!"

Captain Andrew Haldane and Lieutenant Andrew Chisick heard the shout as they spoke to a group of riflemen. They whirled and raced away to intercept.

It was going to be close. Not even the Marines around the guns had much time to lunge for the weapons they had put aside. Some of them had begun to scatter, but many more had joined Haldane and Chisick. A Japanese soldier was first to the guns. He slid into sitting position to fire one of them, and a Marine bayoneted him through his chest. Then the tall men in green closed with the short ones in brown. Some of the Japanese fell. The remainder broke free and ran back across the creek. But now the Marines had their weapons and they cut down 20 of the enemy before the skirmish was over.

They got the guns emplaced as darkness fell. They braced for a nocturnal counterattack. Just before dawn they heard firing to their left, where Lieutenant Abe was attacking Target Hill.

Lieutenant Abe, like so many Japanese soldiers, prepared to go into battle wearing all that he possessed. He pulled on his extra pair of trousers. He put his third shirt over his second shirt and slipped his arms into his raincoat. He stuffed his pack with all his goods and food, and also every document concerning Target Hill which had come his way, and onto the back of this he strapped his rolled overcoat. He hoisted this onto his shoulders. He slung his field glasses over this, buckled on his pistol, seized his sword and his entrenching tool—and called for mortar fire.

The first Japanese mortar shell struck the nose of a ridge held by Captain Marshall Moore's Company A of the First Battalion, Seventh. It instantly killed Gunnery Sergeant Theon Deckrow, but a machine-gunner and a dozen other Marines stayed in line. Soon they detected the sound of digging beneath the mortar barrage. They guessed that the Japanese were cutting steps into the hillside. They waited. The mortar barrage grew in intensity. By five o'clock the Japanese had begun to throw in artillery and 20-millimeter machine cannon, but they missed target and the Marines on the plateau still waited.

At a quarter of six, the red flare rose and the charge began.

The machine-gunner who had stayed at his post after Deckrow's death ran 20 belts of machine-gun ammunition through his gun. That was 5,000 bullets from a single weapon, and there were others firing, as well as mortars exploding among the Japanese coming up the hill. Lieutenant Abe was quickly killed, Warrant Officer Yamaguchi was shot to death, and that Major Mukai who commanded the attacking battalion was driven back into the jungle after Captain Moore heard him screaming orders and brought fire down around him.

What report Major Mukai made to Colonel Katayama is unknown, but the colonel sent this message to Major General Matsuda:

> By the desperate struggle of the officers and men of the Regiment, Target Hill had been captured and the enemy were forced to the water's edge. But, owing to the enemy counterattack with superior forces, we have relinquished it again with much regret.

Of course Target Hill had not been "relinquished," nor had the Marine lines been bent, let alone broken. Close to 200 Japanese were killed or wounded during a two-hour run at the wire, at the expense of three Marines killed and 10 wounded. Target Hill had been so one-sided that Division refused to believe that it had been a well-planned attack with the intention of turning Shepherd's seaward flank. That belief would continue until intelligence officers examined Lieutenant Abe's wellclad body and someone thought to look into Warrant Officer Yamaguchi's pocket.

But even as intelligence officers arrived on the battlefield—angrily shooing the souvenir-hunters away—the clamor of battle had shifted back to Suicide Creek.

★

259

Dawn at Suicide Creek burst from the Japanese mortars. Before the Marines could leap erect to continue the attack on the morning of January 3, the shells were flashing and roaring among them. One young rifleman was decapitated by the direct blast of an exploding shell. Men going forward looked at that sitting headless figure with just the neck from which dogtags dangled and wondered who it might have been.

They went across Suicide Creek, small unit by small unit, sometimes finding and knocking out an enemy gun, but always being thrown back again.

One Marine lay behind a log, firing. "It don't do no good," he muttered, his face ashen. "I got three of 'em, but it don't do no good."

Platoon Sergeant Casimir Polakowski shouted at him angrily: "What the hell you bitchin' about? You get paid for it, don't you?"

The shocked Marine managed a weak grin and continued to fire. Polakowski arose to take his platoon across the creek to rescue another one trapped over there. He saw three of his men killed in rapid succession, returned, ran to rescue a wounded Marine being shot at by a sniper—and was shot in the back.

Lieutenant Elisha Atkins led his platoon of heavy machine-gunners across the water. The enemy gunners allowed half of them to cross, and then the converging fire of six automatic weapons made a screaming, bleeding hell of the others. Some men lay in the water, not daring to move, not even daring to rescue others who lay across trees in full view of the enemy, who called helplessly, over and over, whose blood flowed into the faces of those who dared not move to help them.

Across the bank Lieutenant Atkins lay in a tangle of vines. He had been hit three times and was losing blood fast. Pfc. Luther Raschke found him. He cut him free and tried to drag him back across the creek, but "Tommy Harvard," as the men called Atkins, refused to go.

"Go on," he gasped. "Keep the line moving. Get the men out."

Raschke and Corporal Alexander Caldwell obeyed. They got back in time to hear that the engineers of the Seventeenth

Marines had laid a corduroy road of logs through the swamp which Major Takabe considered impassable.

At last there were tanks coming up to Suicide Creek.

At last there were Corsairs coming up to Rabaul, coming up to one of those wild aerial battles the Marines called "a big hairy dogfight."

Since the December 27 fighter-sweep in which Pappy Boyington had shot down his twenty-fifth plane, there had been no attacks on the dying Japanese base on eastern New Britain. It had rained constantly, while Boyington alternated between badgering others and being badgered. He had but a few days to go on his third and final tour in the Pacific. He hounded meteorological people for the latest word on the weather, and was hounded by war correspondents for the latest word on when he was going to break Foss's record.

On the night of January 2 came reports of clearing weather at last. At dawn of the next day, while Japanese mortars scourged the Marines at Suicide Creek, Pappy Boyington fire-balled his splay-legged fighter down the Torokina strip and circled aloft while his Black Sheep climbed to join him. They pushed the stick forward and roared north.

Over Rabaul 40 to 60 fighters rose to meet them. When they had reached 12,000 feet, Boyington told his fighters to get set. He looked around him.

"Okay," he shouted, "let's get the bastards!"

They went nosing over.

Boyington went down. Captain George Ashmun followed on his tail. They pounced on a pair of Zeros flying at 15,000 feet. Boyington made an overhead run on one of them. From 400 yards away he fired a short burst. The Zero burst into flames.

"You got a flamer, Skipper!" Ashmun yelled, and Boyington grinned in his cockpit. He had shot down as many enemy planes as any other American.

Boyington climbed, Ashmun riding his wing. Again they saw Zeros below. Again they went over, thinking the rest of the Black Sheep were diving after them. They scissored over the Japanese, weaving back and forth over one another, firing short bursts.

Two of the slender, brown, red-balled sausages flamed and fell, but Boyington did not grin this time, for Ashmun's plane was puffing smoke and his wingman was going down in a long graded dive. Behind him came a dozen Zeros converging for the kill.

"Dive, George!" Boyington screamed. "For God's sake, dive!"

There was not so much as a waggled aileron in reply, and the Zeros were taking turns at tail passes.

Boyington slammed in behind them, kicking the rudder back and forth, triggering short bursts. Ashmun's Corsair was now a fiery meteor and was dropping into the sea. But there was another Zero in flames too, Pappy Boyington's twenty-eighth kill—and also his last.

For there was now a pack of Zeros growling on his tail. Boyington threw the stick forward and raced over the ocean at 400 knots. He could see the enemy bullets stitching patterns in his wings. His main gas tank blew up.

It was all over.

Boyington felt as though his body had been hurled into a blast furnace. With his remaining strength he released his safety belt with one hand, seized the rip-cord ring with the other, and kicked the stick hard forward with both feet. He had given his body centrifugal force, made it weigh a ton, and he went flying out the top of his plane. He was only a hundred feet above the water when his chute opened with a spine-snapping jerk, and though he slammed the water hard he was alive and treading water when he surfaced.

The Japanese tried to gun him to death. They played cat-and-mouse for half an hour, one Zero coming in low and pulling out just as another dove in from a different direction. Twenty-millimeter cannon exploded all around Boyington. He was gagging from the sea water he had swallowed as he had played duck-the-apple for the enemy pilots. After two hours of treading water he reached beneath him for the rubber life raft dangling between his legs. He pulled it out and found that it was intact. He inflated it. He climbed aboard and examined himself. His scalp was dangling down over his eyes.

His left ear was half chewed off. His throat was cut and his left ankle torn up. There were shrapnel holes in his hands and his leg ached where it had struck the stabilizer when he was catapulted free. But he was not dismayed. He found himself humming something, and tried to puzzle it out. It was:

If the engine conks out now
We'll come down from forty thou—
And wind up in a rowboat at Rabaul.

The Sherman tanks lumbering up to Suicide Creek were led by a tunnel-blasting bulldozer driven by Corporal John Capito. Capito began cutting down the 12-foot-high near bank, pushing the earth into the stream to form a causeway. A sniper peppered him and Capito was shot in the teeth. Then the Japanese began raking the bank with small-arms fire. Staff Sergeant Keary Lane crawled forward and jumped into the driver's seat. He too was shot. Pfc. Randall Johnson crawled up to the bulldozer. He swung it around between him and the enemy. He began running alongside it, working the controls with a shovel and an axe handle as he cut the bank down. There was now a passage, but it was already getting dark and the crossing would have to be made in the morning.

In that fading light Pappy Boyington paddled his rubber boat toward Rabaul and hoped there was no truth to the line, " 'Cause they'll never send a Dumbo way out here." If there was no rescuing Catalina, there might at least be an American submarine.

A submarine surfaced and it had a big red ball painted on it and in the dimness of dusk Boyington could see the conning-tower hatch pop open and disgorge a dozen short men with odd flat hats. Boyington was brought aboard. His wounds were not treated, but he was offered tea and cookies and given cigarettes. A pharmacist's mate who spoke English said to him: "You don't have to worry about anything as long as you are on this boat."

An hour later the sub docked at Rabaul and Boyington was led ashore tied and blindfolded.

★

It was dark on the Japanese side of Suicide Creek.

Corporal Caldwell and Pfc. Raschke found it hard to see as they crawled down the creek in search of Lieutenant Atkins. They had been given permission to return for their wounded platoon leader, and had brought two riflemen with them for fire cover. They came to the bank where they had last seen "Tommy Harvard" and crawled up it into the underbrush.

They could hear only the rushing of the river and the muttering of the Japanese. Should they go back or should they risk calling out? Caldwell and the riflemen lay in the bushes with covering rifles while Raschke slithered out on the edge of the bank and began calling softly:

"Tommy Harvard . . . Tommy Harvard . . ."

A voice came weakly: "I'm down here."

Raschke stiffened. It could be a Japanese trick. He called out again.

"What's your real name?"

The voice gasped, "Elisha Atkins."

The Marines slid cautiously down the bank. They found Atkins shaking from hours of immersion in the water, weak from the loss of blood. They lifted him up gently and carried him back to their lines.

"God!" Lieutenant Atkins whispered hoarsely. "Am I glad to see *you.*"

22

Aogiri Ridge?

Could there be such a place? There wasn't anything with that name on the map. Even the Melanesians now returning from their mountain hideouts had never heard of it. Nor could you trust them. They were so happy to see the Americans— for the Japanese had latterly treated them wretchedly—that they would smile and bob their heads and say "Yes" to any point fingered out on the map.

Obviously there was such a place, for the message taken from that dead Japanese warrant officer's pocket mentioned it twice, emphasizing its importance, and the documents found in the pack of the deceased Lieutenant Abe indicated that there was at least a full regiment back there somewhere. Also, when the tanks rolled over Suicide Creek on the morning of January 4, they found that the enemy had retreated.

So there should be quite a hatful of Japanese to the southeast, probably around Hill 660.

Was Hill 660 Aogiri Ridge? No. Corporal Shigeto said Hill 660 was called Manju Yama, meaning Sweet Cookie Hill. Maybe it was Hill 150 just to the south of Target Hill. A rough sketch on the message made it look that way, and so the attacking Marine battalions were sent against Hill 150. They took it and found that it was probably not Aogiri Ridge at all.

The attack southeastward continued, with Brigadier General Shepherd still anxious to locate this Aogiri Ridge.

The terrain still favored the Japanese. As the Marine battalions swung like a gate southeastward to Borgen Bay, they plunged into another swamp. The Seventeenth Marines again built corduroy roads and knocked down riverbanks to get the tanks into bitterly-resisting Japanese pockets. At noon on January 7, as the right flank swung through an area 1,000 yards diagonally southwest of Target Hill, Lieutenant Colonel David McDougal of the Third Battalion, Fifth, was wounded. Five hours later his executive officer, Major Joseph Skoczylas, was also hit. Lieutenant Colonel Chesty Puller, still commanding the Third Battalion, Seventh, took over both outfits. Next morning Puller turned the other battalion over to a tall, brawny, square-faced lieutenant colonel with the fanciful name of Silent Lew Walt.

As Walt's men pressed the attack that morning of January 8 they felt the ground rising gently beneath a tangle of vines and creepers. It seemed drier. Though the map insisted they were on level ground, they were in fact beginning to climb steep slopes. They were being swept by interlocking small-arms fire. They did not know it then, but they had found Aogiri Ridge. Nor did they know that there were 37 bunkers ahead, most of them connected by underground tunnels. If one bunker fell and the Marines moved on, it would suddenly erupt again behind them. Walt's men took heavy casualties, and General Shepherd had to rush two reinforcing companies up to Aogiri Ridge. The Marines did not take Aogiri Ridge or even dent it that day. They fell back to their morning positions and dug in.

At dawn of January 9 Walt's men struck out in straight frontal attack again. They couldn't flank the position because its guns could rake either side. They couldn't bypass it, for it would cut Marine communications. They had to strike straight ahead, staggering with fatigue, moving through jungle so thick they could not see 10 yards ahead of them, and all the while being struck by an invisible foe. They faltered, and Walt called for a 37-millimeter cannon.

The 900-pound gun was trundled forward.

"All right," Walt shouted, as he and his runner put their stooping shoulders to one of the wheels. "Who'll give me a hand?"

There was no response, but then Walt tore at the gun with such savage fury that his men leaped in beside him. They pushed the cannon up the steep slope, stopping to fire cannister shot, blasting apart the jungle and clearing a path through the bunkers. Men were killed or wounded but others rushed in to take their place. Up, up it went, bumping and volleying and at last it was atop the ridge, and the hail of its cannister was sweeping among the enemy like shotgun pellets.

The Marines had a hold on Aogiri Ridge.

The Japanese in Rabaul led Major Boyington by rope halter to a hut half a mile from the dock. There they questioned him for twenty-four hours. When he balked, they twisted the ropes around his wrists until he was about to lose consciousness; then they loosened the rope and continued. They did not treat his wounds for ten days. They preferred to punch him in the jaw and beat his legs with rifle butts. They beat him regularly during the six weeks in which they held him prisoner there, for they did not like the American major who had taunted them so derisively, nor did they like the terrible things his comrades were doing to their once-mighty base. Already there was a new light-bomber strip being completed on Bougainville, and Rabaul had only six more weeks to live.

Colonel Katayama had decided to use his last reserve battalion to knock the Americans off Aogiri. It was the 3rd Battalion, 141st, commanded by Major Asachichi Tatsumi. During the darkness succeeding the Marines' conquest of the ridge-top, these men of Major Tatsumi had been gathering on Aogiri's reverse slope. Around midnight of that January 9 they began to chant:

"Marines prepare to die, Marines prepare to die."

At a quarter past one in the morning of January 10 they rushed up the slope screaming and howling, but were swiftly cut down by the Marines who had seized upon the chanting to get ready in the right place. The shattered waves flowed back down the slope and came up again. Once more they were hurled back.

In his foxhole Silent Lew Walt was calling 105-millimeter fire in closer and closer to his lines. He cut through the objections of the artillery officers in the fire-direction centers and called for shells as close as 50 yards to his own men, for the Japanese were obviously under orders to retake Aogiri or die.

A third wave came up and was stopped.

The fourth rushed up led by Major Tatsumi himself. In belted raincoat, with pistol in one hand and *samurai* sword in the other, the battalion commander led two other officers in a dash through the Marine lines. They ran toward Walt's command post where the American commander lay in his water-filled foxhole waiting for them, his .45 automatic pistol in his hand. Two of them fell but Tatsumi came on.

Suddenly two short-round shells struck the treetops overhead and exploded and killed Tatsumi. He fell a few paces from Lieutenant Colonel Walt. Now the Marine machine guns atop Aogiri Ridge were low on ammunition. Walt hurriedly sent men to the rear for ammunition, for he expected a fifth charge. He could hear the enemy chanting again, massing again—and then the ammunition belts arrived. Walt looked at his watch. One minute . . . two . . . three . . . four . . .

They came up again and this time they were broken forever.

Aogiri Ridge had been captured and held, and now it was being renamed. Brigadier General Shepherd climbed the ridge later that morning to look about 2,000 yards southeast to Hill 660, the highest ground in Borgen Bay, lying about seven miles southeast of the airfield. Shepherd spoke to Walt's glassy-eyed Marines and congratulated their leader. He suggested making an American out of Aogiri.

"We'll call it Walt's Ridge," he said.

23

Having found a place that was not on the map—Aogiri Ridge —the Marines on western New Britain now turned to looking for a place marked on the map but impossible to find.

The difficulty was a matter of phonetics.

When the Australians began to map New Britain they often used place names already in use among the Melanesians, translating them phonetically. A tiny village such as Nakarop remained Nakarop. When the Japanese replaced the Australians they made Japanese translations of these English phonetics. Thus Nakarop—the site of Matsuda's lair—became Egaroppu.

The Marines had only lately learned from prisoners that Major General Matsuda was in western New Britain. They heard that he had his headquarters somewhere inland. From enemy maps and documents they correctly guessed that Matsuda was at Egaroppu.

But no one familiar with New Britain—not an Australian planter, not a missionary, not a Melanesian—had ever heard of Egaroppu. Many attempts were made to compare Australian and Japanese maps, but the Japanese maps were so sketchy it was impossible to pinpoint any one interior village. Aerial reconnaissance was useless, for there was nothing to be seen beneath the ubiquitous jungle roof. More, there seemed to be no inland trails from the north coast. The Marines had no way of knowing that Matsuda had linked his headquarters to Borgen Bay in the north by means of a seven-mile trail tunneled through the jungle. Nor did any of their maps show other concealed trails running out Nakarop-Egaroppu's back door to points far east of Borgen Bay.

Even on the morning of January 10, when the importance of Aogiri Ridge as an outerwork of Hill 660 was being grasped, the Marines did not know that they had uncovered the northern trail to that mystifying Egaroppu. Mopping up Aogiri Ridge that morning they crossed a wide firm trail which was found to connect all of Borgen Bay's supply dumps, bivouacs and landing facilities with some point inland. That point inland was the headquarters of Colonel Katayama at a place called Maigairapua. Beneath Maigairapua was Nakarop. But the Marines did not go south along this hidden trail because they were busy cleaning out a nasty pocket between Aogiri and Hill 150.

It was nasty in a very literal sense and it was not crushed, again in a literal sense, until the engineers had built another corduroy road over which four light tanks and a pair of half-tracks were brought up. When the pocket fell, it was found to contain the enemy's biggest supply dump on New Britain.

All that remained was to take Hill 660, on which General Shepherd expected to find the bulk of some 2,500 to 3,000 Japanese estimated to be still in the Borgen Bay area, for many of the 53rd Regiment had slipped out of Cape Gloucester over jungle trails and had joined Katayama's 141st.

In the meantime, Shepherd gave his Marines a rest. The day

after the pocket was crushed and the Second Battalion, First, had marched up to Cape Gloucester from Tauali, the Marines in Borgen Bay spent at their ease in the rain-swept coastal swamps. They read and reread letters from home, then committed them to memory for they had begun to fall apart; they thought of writing letters themselves, but the paper was sodden, their pencils had swelled and burst, the fountain pens had become clogged and their points had separated; they pried apart their pocketknife blades which had rusted together and scraped the mold off their clothing and off their rifles and slung the rifles upside down under their ponchos, while debating whether or not to keep a ruined wrist-watch or heave it into the swamp; they removed their precious cigarettes from beneath their helmets and lit them with matches kept dry inside a contraceptive and smoked them with cupped hands; they badgered their officers for dry socks or a cartridge belt to replace those now decomposing; they ate hot chow of which the rain quickly made a cold wet slop and they were very grateful for the coffee kept hot in covered GI cans— sometimes so hot that it heated the lips of the canteen cups and burned the lips of the drinkers. Then the self-control of men who could joke about jungle rot and dysentery would at last break, because the sudden pain caused them to drop the coffee: "An' now I *am* pissed-off!"

In the morning they cleaned the protective oil off their clips of cartridges, made certain that grenade pins were not rusted tight, and then—after the artillery and mortars had stopped firing and the Fifth Air Force's bombers had flown home—they attacked the steep stern slimy face of Hill 660.

Captain Joe Buckley had been a Marine when practically all the men subordinate to him—and some of those superior to him—were as yet unborn. He had joined the Marines in 1915, and here he was, twenty-eight years afterward, a man close to fifty and a veteran of wars large and small, leading a ragtag bobtail of a force through the jungle of New Britain.

Captain Buckley was going to skirt Hill 660 on its seaward or eastern side and get in behind it. To do this he had a pair of half-tracks, two light tanks, a 37-millimeter gun platoon, about

270

80 riflemen and 40 pioneers who had thoughtfully brought along their bulldozers. There was also a belligerent Army sergeant who had gone AWOL from his service outfit in New Guinea. He had stowed away on an LST and had been gladly welcomed aboard by those Marines with whom he wished to fight.

Early in the morning, with the bulldozer plowing a passage through the barrier of mud, Buckley's motley set out. They were fired at from the Japanese atop Hill 660 but the tanks and half-tracks roared back and the little column sloughed on. By half-past ten in the morning it had skirted the base of Hill 660 and set up a roadblock behind or south of it.

Any Japanese attempting to retreat from Hill 660 would have to move through Buckley's Marines or wade a swamp.

Only occasional snipers hampered Lieutenant Colonel Henry Buse's Marines in their approach march to the foot of Hill 660. The Marines shot them out of the trees, leaving them dangling on their ropes.

Hill 660's slopes were as steep as 45 degrees. They were slimy with rain-soaked, malodorous vegetation and they were swept by enemy fire. The Marines began to climb on all fours, but they were pinned as flat as they could make themselves. Bullets sang above them and they could go no farther. Nor could they withdraw.

Lieutenant Colonel Buse got a platoon of light tanks forward. They laid a covering fire in front of the Marines' noses, and the companies finally came back down the hill as it grew dark.

The next morning, January 14, Buse sent companies around to the right or west of Hill 660, to its inland side. He was probing for a soft spot. His men could never go up that front slope without terrible casualties. Almost to the rear of Hill 660, separated from Captain Buckley by a swamp, the Marines found their soft spot. It was lightly guarded because it was so steep. The Japanese did not think anyone could come up it.

Buse ordered his men up and they went up. They went up in a sudden burst of energy and valor as mystifying as it was marvelous. They clawed up that vertical face of gummy clay and came in on the startled enemy and put him to death among his guns. Those who fled down the hill ran the roaring gantlet of Captain Buckley's men. Those who counterattacked a day later were torn apart in a march and countermarch of mortar shells. And those who survived this slaughter perished in sea or swamp to either side of Buckley's guns, one whole group of them cut down in a daisy chain as they crossed a creek holding hands.

Hill 660 had fallen. Its price had not been high in blood but in hardship, in the ordeal written on the faces of the men who took it and were at last being relieved after twenty-three days in the swamp. They were all dripping hair and smeared red-brown with soil. Mud-stained ponchos or Japanese raincoats hooded their heads against the rain and they walked woodenly, staring straight ahead while mechanically spooning mouthfuls of cold beans from the little ration cans in their hands.

The last of Colonel Katayama's forces in Borgen Bay had been shattered and the colonel had himself gone back to Na-karop-Egaroppu, where General Matsuda was already preparing his getaway. The fighting at Borgen Bay had been as decisive a victory for the First Marine Division as the battle for Cape Gloucester Airfield.

24

Conquest of the Gilbert Islands in November of 1943 had caused the first break in the outerworks of Fortress Nippon. Now, in February of 1944, seizure of the Marshall Islands would start the breakthrough.

The Marshalls sat athwart the Central Pacific about 400 miles north and 650 miles west of Tarawa in the Gilberts.

They guarded all the routes to Tokyo. Directly west or behind them lay the Carolines with the monster air-sea base at Truk and the ocean fort of Peleliu. South and west of them lay General MacArthur's Bismarcks-New Guinea route to the Philippines. North and west of them lay the Marianas with Guam and Saipan, the Volcanos with Iwo Jima, and the Bonins.

Japan by now had no real hope of holding the Marshalls. Even though Premier Tojo still expected to wear down the American will to fight, he planned to do it by delaying in the Marshalls while strengthening the inner ring of defenses—especially at Peleliu, the Marianas and the Bonins.

The Marshalls were admirably suited to delaying action because there were so many of them. There were 36 true atolls —with perhaps 2,000 islets and islands—in this enormous chain running 650 miles on a northwest-southeast diagonal. They had been in Japan's possession since they were seized from Germany in World War One, when Japan was on the side of the Allies and also acquiring such easy German booty as the Marianas, but Japan had not bothered to fortify them in any strength until just before the attack on the Gilberts at Makin and Tarawa.

Now there were six atolls on which she had based airfields. These were Eniwetok, Kwajalein, Wotje, Maloelap, Jaluit and Mili. Of these Eniwetok was the farthest west, closest to Japan. Kwajalein was in the center. Wotje and Maloelap were east and north; Jaluit and Mili were east and south. Vice Admiral Musashi Kobayashi, who was in command of the Marshalls, first began fortifying Wotje and Maloelap, but then came Tarawa, and emphasis was shifted to Jaluit and Mili—closest by far to the new American bases south in the Gilberts. Admiral Kobayashi paid little attention to Kwajalein or Eniwetok. They were fortified, of course, but nothing like the eastern atolls, and nothing at all like Tarawa. Kobayashi expected the Americans to attack on the eastern atolls, more likely on Jaluit and Mili.

Admiral Nimitz chose Kwajalein.

He chose it because by knifing right into the heart of the Marshalls he would bypass all those Japanese outposts on the eastern atolls, and he would make Kobayashi's work there useless. The neutralizing of the bulk of 28,000 troops stationed in the Marshalls could speed up the war by opening both the Central Pacific and Southwest Pacific fronts.

More, Kwajalein Atoll was lightly defended, it had airfields, and its lagoon was the largest in the world. It was 65 miles in length and 18 miles in width within an atoll chain forming a shape best described as a flattened pyramid canted on its right-hand base. Its terminals were Ebadon Islet on the west, the twin islets of Roi-Namur about 40 miles to the east, and then Kwajalein Islet about 45 miles south of Roi-Namur and a bit to the east.

Nimitz was concerned only with Kwajalein Islet in the south, where a bomber field was under construction, and Roi-Namur in the north, where there was an excellent air base.

But Nimitz' commanders—Admirals Raymond Spruance and Kelly Turner, General Howlin' Mad Smith—were concerned about the risks of an operation against Kwajalein.

It could be taken, but afterwards the vast Pacific Fleet which had brought the assault forces to Kwajalein was going to be turned over to Admiral Halsey to cover General Mac-Arthur's proposed landing on New Ireland in the Southwest Pacific. The fleet's withdrawal would leave the men on Kwajalein alone and at the mercy of a ring of hostile airfields, especially Eniwetok with its lines running directly back to Japan. Neither Spruance nor Turner nor Smith wanted to take on Kwajalein without first nailing down some or all of those airfield atolls in the east.

It was then that Admiral Nimitz took a long look at Majuro Atoll nestling almost exactly in the center of that quartet of outer bastions. It was then that Captain Jim Jones took his Recon Boys up to Majuro by destroyer while the greatest invasion fleet yet assembled waited for word of what he found there.

25

Mr. Michael Madison said, "Perhaps you gentlemen would like a drink?" and the Recon Boys of Captain James Logan Jones blinked and wondered if they were back on Apamama.

Though they were not—though they were on Majuro Atoll in the Marshall Islands—it was certainly true that one of this tall half-caste's daughters had just shinnied up a coconut tree and had slid back down grasping a blue *saki* bottle filled with palm toddy. Now she was going up again for more and it looked like Majuro might be better than Apamama.

It was not this for which Lieutenant Harvey Weeks had led a platoon ashore on Majuro's Calalin Islet, for which Lieutenant Leo Shinn had led the point of the platoon in its reconnaissance across the islet. They had come as the scouts of the big invasion force which was to arrive nine hours later. They had left Captain Jones back aboard their destroyer, inflated their rubber boats and passed through the same ordeal of confusion, surf and wind which had nearly swamped them off Apamama. They had talked to the Micronesians and found that there was only a Japanese warrant officer left on the island. That had been on the night of January 30.

Now it was the dawn of January 31 and here was Mr. Michael Madison offering glasses and palm toddy. Actually it was a moment worthy of celebration. The landing on Calalin at eleven o'clock the preceding night represented the first American invasion of soil which Japan had held prior to World War Two, and that "invasion" was made a "conquest" a little later when a Warrant Officer Nagata was surprised and captured.

Nagata said that the 300 to 400 Japanese who once garrisoned the island had been evacuated long ago. This piece of good news was relayed to Captain Jones. After some delays, Jones was able to message Admiral Hill to call off the bombardment of Majuro which had already begun. Luckily only a few shells had fallen, and most of Majuro's valuable installations were unharmed. The 2nd Battalion, 106th Infantry, of the Army's 27th Division could now come ashore unopposed, the work on the first of several airstrips could commence, Majuro Lagoon could be made into an anchorage—and Admiral Chester Nimitz could go ahead with the Marshall Islands conquest which had depended so much on the seizure of Majuro.

26

To bombard Kwajalein Atoll and transport the troops there, Admiral Turner had an enormous fleet of nearly 300 ships, including one big and ten smaller aircraft carriers and seven old battleships.

To make the assault on Kwajalein Islet in the south and Roi-Namur in the north, Major General Howlin' Mad Smith, the expeditionary troops commander, had two full divisions and a brigade. Of this force, Smith would use the Army's 7th Infantry Division against the southern islet and the Fourth Marine Division against Roi-Namur. The brigade, consisting of the orphan Twenty-second Marine Regiment and the remaining two battalions of the 106th Infantry, would be in floating reserve.

It was an overwhelming force, something like 40,000 troops going against Kwajalein Atoll's 8,000 defenders, or whatever number survived the preinvasion bombardment and shelling which was to outdo anything attempted before. The Navy gunfire people had learned from Tarawa that pillboxes could only be knocked out with direct hits from big shells or big bombs, and that these missiles must be armor-piercing. Old battleships such as *Maryland, Colorado, Tennessee, New Mexico, Idaho, Mississippi* and *Pennsylvania* had been found to be ideal for bombardment. They had been schooled in it, had learned how to knock out beach installations with patient, pinpointed fire directed by the Joint Assault Signal Companies (JASCO) whose mission was to put ashore spotters trained in calling down naval gunfire. It had also been learned that neither shells nor bombs will destroy underwater beach defenses. This had to be done by hand, by sailors who volunteered to swim into enemy beaches under covering gunfire and there to explode antiamtrack obstacles or to disarm underwater mines. They formed the Underwater Demolition Teams, and these too would be used for the first time at Kwajalein.

Impressive, too, was the massive preliminary bombing of December-January, during which land-based planes on Makin, Tarawa and Apamama dropped 1,677 tons of explosives on Kwajalein, Wotje, Maloelap, Mili and Jaluit. Carrier-based planes also hit these and other atolls with multiplying fury, sinking ships and damaging cruisers, knocking down planes and destroying them on the ground. Seventh Air Force high-altitude bombing added to the misery of the Marshalls. Then came 6,919 tons of naval shells fired against Marshalls targets for three days preceding and during the invasion. Already, as the American armada separated into Northern and Southern Attack Forces, the bombardment had killed Vice Admiral Michiyuki Yamada on Namur. Already a radioman on Roi-Namur had made this notation in his diary: "Convoy left Pearl Harbor on January 22 to attack us."

A convoy had left Pearl Harbor on that date and it was the Northern Force headed for Roi-Namur. It carried the men of the Fourth Marine Division.

They had sailed from San Diego in California and had paused but a day in Lahaina Roads while their officers went ashore to confer with naval officers. Then they moved on, learning, a few days out of Hawaii, that they were sailing straight from the States to the battleground. Their zigzag course between San Diego and Roi-Namur Islets covered considerably more than the 5,000-mile beeline lying between these points and they began to boast of it; being a brand-new outfit, the Fourth was desperate for things to boast about. They hadn't much, other than that among their ranks were the sons of five Marine generals—including Lieutenant Colonel Alexander Vandegrift, Jr.—and that a private first class named Stephen Hopkins was also the son of Harry Hopkins, the right-hand man of President Roosevelt. Of course, Lieutenant Colonel Evans Carlson of Raider fame was on the division staff, and this was another desperate distinction.

But combat honors? No. Tradition, no. Even the Third Marine Division had a regiment able to claim descent from the Third Marines of World War One. Not so the Fourth. All their outfits were brand-new, born of the Marine Corps' expansion from a 50,000-man prewar force to one now approaching half a million. The Fourth's regiments had double-digit numbers that made them sound like Army outfits—the Twenty-third, Twenty-fourth, and Twenty-fifth Marines, the Fourteenth Marine Artillery, the Twentieth Marine Engineers. The Fourth Division was not nearly as well trained in amphibious operations as was that 7th Army Infantry Division which would take Kwajalein Islet to the south. The Marines themselves had trained the 7th, and the 7th had already been in battle at Attu, but the Fourth had not had much opportunity to train as a unit. Yet, green as it was, it was commanded by one of the most experienced leaders in the Marine Corps, Major General Harry Schmidt.

The sun helmet General Schmidt wore over his scowling face testified to his status as an old China hand. He had been assistant to the Marine Commandant. With Howlin' Mad Smith he had been a pioneer in developing Marine amphibious techniques, and he had worked out a good plan to implement Smith's novel tactic of landing artillery a day before the main body of infantry.

It was a tactic used at Tarawa, when Julian Smith had placed artillery on Bairiki to support troops advancing on

The First Marine Division landed on Guadalcanal, August 7, 1942, but the first major battle came two weeks later. A Japanese force led by Colonel Kiyono Ichiki (left) was annihilated at the mouth of the Tenaru River.

Sergeant Major Vouza of the Solomons Defense Force warned Marines of impending Tenaru assault, crawling to American lines after Japanese captured him, tortured him and left him for dead.

Marines, such as these riflemen crossing the Matanikau River, patrolled the jungle daily on the hunt for Japanese build-ups. Guadalcanal, begun as the first American offensive of World War Two, quickly became a defensive action, with Marines hanging on against Japanese attempts to retake island.

"Pistol Pete" was the nickname Marines gave to Japanese artillery. This 108-mm. rifle was captured at Kokumbona.

Marine stand brought third star and Medal of Honor to Alexander Vandegrift, a major general during the four months he commanded at Guadalcanal.

Whiskers such as Captain Joe Foss's were common among Marine pilots who wrested control of Solomons air from Japanese. With 26 kills, Foss was second-ranking Marine ace of war.

Vandegrift's opponent, Lieutenant General Haruyoshi Hyakutate, was overconfident, fed in his troops piecemeal.

RIGHT: *Lieutenant James (Zeke) Swett became legendary for shooting down seven planes on his first combat flight. Swett's feat was one of many outstanding performances during bitter aerial battle which raged over Solomons for six months after the Japanese quit Guadalcanal in February, 1943.*

RIGHT BOTTOM: *Staff Sergeant Bill Coffeen was a casualty of that fighting. Shot down over waters of The Slot, he spent 70 days wandering through islands. Natives found him floating on raft in delirious state and nursed him back to health.*

The famous Chesty Puller won the third of his five Navy Crosses on Guadalcanal, and was also wounded there.

Manila John Basilone was a machine-gun sergeant in Puller's battalion during night battle in which he won Medal of Honor. Basilone was killed at Iwo Jima more than two years later.

Bougainville in the Northern Solomons was the next big Marine assault, after numerous actions in Central Solomons. On November 1, 1943, landing boats began putting Third Marine Division ashore at Cape Torokina.

LEFT: *Among Marine airmen who helped make Bougainville landing light in casualties was Lieutenant Robert (Butcher Bob) Hanson. He shot down three planes on D-Day, was downed himself, but survived. Hanson had total of 25 kills to his credit when death in action two months later cut short the most phenomenal career of any American flier.*

RIGHT: *Torokina Airfield became the base from which Major Gregory (Pappy) Boyington led his swashbuckling Black Sheep Squadron on the fighter sweeps which helped strangle the big Japanese base at Rabaul. Boyington* (with paper) *was later shot down and imprisoned, but his mark of 28 planes remained tops for Marine aces in World War Two.*

Marines roll drums of oil out of Puruata Island dump that Japanese bombers set afire. Puruata, the storehouse for troops on Bougainville, was bombed night and day.

A machine-gun position in Bougainville rain forest.

Tarawa was next. Second Marine Division hit Betio, chief islet of the atoll, on November 20, 1943; many of them were killed and wounded under the fortified sea wall which surrounded the islet.

On Tarawa there were only the quick and the dead.

Many Marines, such as these riflemen working along pier, had to wade into Tarawa through withering fire. Amtracks, which were to take them ashore from reef a half mile out in lagoon, were knocked out early in the battle.

The sea wall on the second day of battle after the Marines had gradually forced their way into the island's defenses. Colonel David Shoup (above) kept separated and battered Marines together during first critical two days and won Medal of Honor.

These Marines are fighting to take, not a hill, but the top of a Japanese bomb-proof. Japanese admiral inside this fort boasted his defenses were so strong that "a million men cannot take Tarawa in one hundred years." They fell to about 15,000 Marines in less than four days.

RIGHT: *Fatherly Major General Julian Smith (right) commanded the Second at Tarawa. With him is his chief of staff, Colonel Merritt (Red Mike) Edson, the famous Raider leader and a hero of Guadalcanal.*

Many Japanese on Tarawa killed themselves inside their bunkers. Man at left disembowled himself with grenade; man at right put rifle muzzle in mouth and pushed trigger with big toe. Marines regarded Japanese suicides as first sign of enemy collapse.

In December, 1943, the First Marine Division was back in action. Here riflemen wade ashore at Cape Gloucester on New Britain.

War on New Britain was a hellish compound of mud and misery as Marines and Japanese fought each other during monsoon rains in some of the world's foulest jungle.

Strain of battle is etched in face of machine-gunner George Miller as he comes off the line. Lieutenant Colonel Lewis (Silent Lew) Walt (below) helped gain New Britain victory by rallying Marines behind wheeled cannon, which they pushed uphill through enemy fire to storm vital height.

Spectacular explosion on Namur when Marines dynamited what appeared to be enemy blockhouse but was actually warehouse full of torpedo warheads. Only man of attacking squad to survive grim mistake was blown 200 yards into sea.

At Saipan in the Marianas on June 15, 1944, Japanese artillery had the beaches zeroed-in. Drenched Marine was blown from his landing craft. He ducks, with man beside him, to avoid shell fragments.

Big American naval guns always helped the Marines ashore, although this 16-inch shell hurled into Saipan failed to go off. Torn and frayed dungarees of Marine sitting on it testifies to grimness of battle.

Lieutenant General Holland M. (Howlin' Mad) Smith (in helmet) toured battlefield with Admirals King (center) and Nimitz. Smith's Fifth Corps—Second and Fourth Marine Divisions, 27th Infantry Division—took Saipan in 24 days. Marine divisions alone took nearby Tinian, the island from which the world's first atomic bomb was flown to Hiroshima.

Saipan-Tinian gave Marines first contact with civilian populations. Most of Japanese civilians killed themselves, but native Chamorros welcomed the Marines. Here, Sergeant Federico Claveria gives candy to Chamorran child inside internment stockade.

Guam in the Marianas—where Third Marine Division and First Marine Brigade landed July 21, 1944—was another backbreaking fight for men such as this machine gunner weighed down with his weapon's tripod.

Soap and water can be among the fairest fruits of victory: Marine riflemen on Guam wash island's grit off their bodies after fighting is over.

Tiny Peleliu was obscured by smoke and fire of American bombs and shells when First Marine Division assaulted it September 15, 1944.

Marines were immediately pinned down on hot white coral beaches, for Japanese had merely "gone to ground" during bombardment and returned to their guns after it lifted.

A Marine gives his wounded buddy a drink from his canteen. Sometimes temperatures on Peleliu were more than 115 degrees and many men fell of heat exhaustion while attacking what was, in effect, a huge coral rock honeycombed with fortified caves.

America seemed to have everything at Iwo Jima, and these men in new armored amtracks, which could discharge them from the rear, were smiling and confident the morning of February 19, 1945.

But at Iwo—a mere eight square miles of volcanic ash—Lieutenant General Tadamichi Kuribayashi (inset) had prepared the most formidable position in world history. An hour after Marines began landings on beaches below Mount Suribachi (rear) the Japanese began hurling shells into them and the bloodiest, fiercest fight in Marine Corps history was on.

A man always fights alone. This Marine was shot in the head by one of Iwo's numerous and accurate snipers.

The sight of a man helping his wounded buddy to the rear became common on Iwo Jima. Many lives were saved by transfusions of whole blood within a few hundred yards of the fighting.

There were two flag-raisings on Mount Suribachi, and this photograph (perhaps never published before) tells their story. A small flag went up first to signal the fall of Suribachi, highest point on Iwo. But it could not be seen, so a second, larger flag went up. The second raising became the most famous photograph of World War Two, and here it appears in the right background while the camera focuses on the lowering of the first flag, left.

At Okinawa, the largest amphibious assault in history, the Marines had fully developed close air support tactics. This Corsair sends a string of rockets flashing toward a Japanese position.

Okinawa's sea wall didn't have the terrors of Tarawa's, although these Marines weren't sure of that as they scrambled over it on D-Day morning of April 1, 1945.

The Okinawans were in pitiful straits when the Americans landed, and the Marines who found relatively little fighting in their sector—the island's northern half—spent much of their time caring for them.

Okinawans place their ancestors' bones in these hillside tombs, but the Japanese turned them into pillboxes—as the Marines learned when they came south to help the Army divisions crack the main line of resistance.

This Marine is hurling a satchel charge into an enemy cave. Resistance began crumbling after Marines captured Shuri Castle in May.

The Tenth Army was led by Army Lieutenant General Simon Bolivar Buckner, Jr. (left), but after he was killed by Japanese artillery, command passed to Marine Lieutenant General Roy Geiger (right). Geiger, who had been at Guadalcanal, had the honor of announcing the fall of Okinawa, the last battle, on June 22, 1945.

The last Marine landing of World War Two was a peaceful one, as men came ashore to accept the surrender of Japanese forts near Tokyo.

Betio. At Roi-Namur, as well as at Kwajalein Islet, it would be used for that reason and also to force a passage into the lagoon itself. For even the transports were going to go *inside* the lagoon. Unlike Tarawa, where the Marines were boated *outside* the reef, the Americans were going to sail inside Kwajalein Atoll already boated in the bowels of LST's. To enter the lagoon at Roi-Namur—Roi, the air base on the west or left, joined by a causeway to Namur, the supply dump on the right —the Marines must first seize a pair of islets to either side of the lagoon passage below or southwest of Roi.

At eight o'clock in the morning of January 31, even as Mr. Madison of Majuro was regaling the Recon Boys with palm toddy, Rear Admiral Richard Conolly ordered the bombardment of these tiny specks of coral to commence. After the naval guns came the carrier planes, after them came the rocket boats *swooshing* their missiles aloft like flights of arrows, and next the wallowing amphibian tanks—the "armored pigs"— striking the seaward side and blasting away with cannon. A few minutes before ten, the Marines of the Division Scout Company and the First Battalion, Twenty-fifth, were churning ashore.

Most of the few-score Japanese had killed themselves. There were others to be killed during a swift mop-up on both islets, but squalls and a wild surf turned out to be more of an obstacle to the landings than the enemy. Before eleven o'clock Lieutenant Colonel Clarence O'Donnell was able to radio that the islets were secure. An hour later artillery began to come ashore. At the same time minesweepers approached both channels. Moving slowly, almost as though they were butting the mines aside, the stubby little vessels entered the passages while carrier planes swooped over Roi-Namur's lagoon beaches to lay down a covering smokescreen. Slowly, like the rising thunder of a storm, the fury of fire issuing from three battleships, five cruisers and 19 destroyers grew around Roi-Namur. Fires were leaping from Namur's lagoon beaches under the pounding of *Tennessee* and *Colorado*. To the west *Maryland* was hurling steel and fire at Roi and its airstrip. But Admiral Conolly wanted *Maryland* to make sure of Roi's blockhouses.

"Move really close in," he radioed *Maryland*.

The Marines were delighted. This was what they had wanted at Tarawa. Mighty old *Maryland* was less than a mile offshore. Her spotter could *see* the targets. Admiral Conolly had earned his nickname. Henceforth he would be known to Marines as "Close-in Conolly."

The men of the Underwater Demolition Teams were returning to the destroyer *Schley*, reporting their work successful. More Marines were moving across the lagoon to take a trio of islets just below Namur. They were the Second and Third Battalions, Twenty-fifth, led by Lieutenant Colonels Lewis Hudson and Justice (Jumpin' Joe) Chambers. They seized the islets. Artillery was brought ashore here too.

All was in readiness for the next day.

In the morning four battalions of land-based artillery began firing, the bombardment ships hurled the last of 2,655 tons of steel into two islets not a mile-square apiece and the carrier planes bombed and strafed once more. As one Marine cried out exultantly: "This time we've got what it takes! This time we've got everything!"

Everything, as he would soon discover, would have to include the rifle slung over his shoulder.

27

It was a bright pink dawn, but neither Roi nor Namur could be seen in it. Only the narrow white lines of their beaches were visible, with here and there a jagged coconut stump sticking out above the smoke, flames, dust and flying rubble.

The skies became overcast. There were squalls. The lagoon water was choppy and Marines became nauseous in their amtracks. They cursed the hold-up caused by the novelty of bringing the LST's into the lagoon. They had been scheduled to attack at ten o'clock, but now they would not make the 4,000-yard run to shore until twelve o'clock.

They should have been thankful for the delay. By the time they hit the beaches, not a single Japanese officer of consequence was alive to direct the defense of either island. Even as the amtracks formed in line and swept shoreward, a 1000-pound bomb fell on the Namur bomb shelter holding the seven senior officers who had survived the bombardment which killed Admiral Yamada and most of his staff three days ago. It was now every man for himself.

The Twenty-third Marines landed on Roi at exactly noon and raced rapidly inland against almost no opposition. Seventeen minutes later Colonel Louis Jones was jubilantly signaling Major General Schmidt: "This is a pip! Give us the word and we'll take the island." But Schmidt ordered Jones to halt and reorganize while warships shelled the northern half of Roi.

At four o'clock, with tanks leading the way, the Twenty-third swept forward again. A hundred separate skirmishes erupted. Dazed and leaderless, the Japanese fought singly or in small groups. They hid in drainage ditches and fired into the rear of the advancing Marines. They made desperate stands in ruined pillboxes. At one of these Pfc. Richard Anderson pulled the pin of his grenade to throw and the missile slipped from his hands. There was no time to retrieve it. It had been his fault and he compensated for the error by smothering the grenade with his body and was killed. The men whose lives he had saved moved forward.

They raced across Roi's airfield until at six o'clock they had come to the northern beaches on the sea. There they found an enemy trench filled with dead soldiers. The Japanese had placed their rifle muzzles under their chins and kicked the triggers with their big toes. They lay there in precise rows, as though they had been obedient to the last, killing themselves on order.

Roi had fallen to the Twenty-third Marines, but it had also fallen to the bombs and shells of the invasion fleet, to the howitzers set up on the lower islets. The horrible efficiency of that preinvasion bombardment was nowhere more evident than in the desolation of Roi's three-strip airfield.

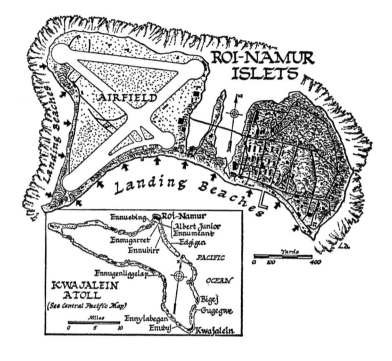

Hundreds of Japanese lay sprawled around it, their bodies horribly mutilated. They were caught in attitudes of flight as though they had been cut down while running for safety. They lay in huge shellholes and in ruined blockhouses. Sheets of corrugated iron were strewn everywhere. Gaunt, denuded concrete pilings stuck out of the ground in rows and the buildings they had held together were heaped about them in rubble. Japanese aircraft littered the airstrips like broken giant birds. There was nothing left, only a handful of doves cooing in a dovecote atop an unharmed radio station, a few little red chickens dashing noisily about, a pig nosing the ruins, and a big white foolish goose which had escaped the invaders' shellfire only to land in their cooking pot.

Roi was the quickest conquest of the Pacific, but across the causeway of Namur there was a real battle going on.

★

"Okay, you liberty-hounds," Sergeant Pappy Meeks had bellowed, "let's go ashore!"

Meeks's platoon had gone charging up Namur's lagoon beach, along with all the other assault platoons of the Twenty-fourth Marines, and had lost contact with headquarters almost immediately. Major General Schmidt's staff had to depend for information on a Douglas dive-bomber which roamed the skies about the battlefield with a major named Charles Duchein in its rear-gunner's seat.

Shortly before noon, immediately after the bombardment lifted, Major Duchein reported Japanese soldiers crossing the causeway from Roi to Namur. At half-past twelve he reported that the Twenty-fourth Marines had landed successfully on Namur, but were running into opposition from pillboxes and blockhouses that were still standing.

Shortly before one o'clock Major Duchein peered down at Namur's eastern shore to see a Marine assault team moving against what seemed to be a giant blockhouse.

But the building was used as a warehouse, and it was stuffed with torpedo warheads.

Lieutenant Saul Stein led his men up cautiously to the big blockhouse on Namur. One of his Marines slipped forward and placed a shaped charge against the side of the building. He ran back and ducked.

The blast tore a hole in the side of the building.

Out the hole, out exits suddenly flung wide, came streams of Japanese soldiers.

Lieutenant Stein's Marines were too surprised to open fire. They were not bewildered. They had heard the Japanese were crazy.

"Throw in some satchel charges," Stein ordered.

They were thrown in.

"Great God Almighty!" Major Duchein roared.

He thought he had seen the island disappear, and his plane had shot up into the air like a rocket. He peered into the dense clouds of smoke billowing in all directions below him, and he yelled again to Headquarters: "The whole damn island's blown up!"

"Are you hurt?" Headquarters inquired.

"Wait a minute," Duchein replied, still trying to see land beneath the smoke. "Stand by a minute."

"Is your plane damaged? Where are you?"

Duchein could hear debris rattling off the bomber's fuselage, but he breathed with relief for he had seen land beneath the smoke, and he answered the question.

"I'm about a thousand feet higher than I was. But the island's still there."

It was, but the warehouse that had held tons and tons of torpedo warheads had vanished completely. Its fragmented remains were still falling on those Marines who crouched in shellholes and craters wondering what had caused that unbelievable rocking roar. They crouched in an inky darkness while whole heads of palm trees, chunks of concrete, bomb and torpedo casings fell from the skies. It seemed an endless rain, and then the smoke drifted away and where there had been a warehouse there was now only a great crater filled with water.

Lieutenant Stein and most of his men were dead, though one man who had been blown 150 feet out into the lagoon was found unhurt. There were 40 Marines killed by the explosion and another 60 wounded. A half-hour later there were more casualties when the Japanese blew up two other blockhouses.

At four o'clock the Twenty-fourth Marines were attacking again, and the Japanese were fighting back.

On the left flank a pillbox pinned down a platoon of Marines led by Lieutenant John Power. The men tried to work up to it to lob in grenades but were driven back. Power charged and was hit in the belly. Covering the wound with his left hand, firing his carbine with the right, receiving two more wounds, he completed his charge. He routed the enemy and fell to his knees, dying. With Pfc. Anderson, Lieutenant Power would receive a posthumous Medal of Honor.

Now the Marines were moving through terrain which made

Namur so much more difficult than Roi. The tanks were stalled by fallen trees and logs, and were laid open to the attacks of Japanese who jumped on them to drop grenades through the visual ports. Captain James Denig and his gunner were killed that way, although a BARman named Howard Smith shot down five of Denig's assailants and risked flaming gasoline and exploding shells in an attempt to save him. The Marine attack slowed down with the approach of night and the order came to dig in.

"Stand by for a counterattack," came the word.

It came in a clear pale moonlit night and the Marines fought individually to contain it. Sergeant Frank Tucker lay behind a tree and shot 38 Japanese dead, firing ammunition brought to him by Pfc. Stephen Hopkins. Tucker received bullets through his helmet, his canteen, his field glasses, while Hopkins received the rifle shot that killed him. Corpsman James Kirby lay in a shellhole between the lines to care for a dozen wounded Marines, saving the life of Pfc. Richard Sorenson, who had fallen on a grenade to save his buddies and would now live to receive a Medal of Honor. Nineteen-year-old Pfc. Jack Brown was killed while his father, Corporal Earl Brown, survived. And then the medium tanks *Jezebel, Jenny Lee, Joker* and *Juarez* rolled up to the front at half-past five in the morning with machine guns and 75's flashing flame and the Japanese attack was broken.

With the full light of day, these four tanks led a counterattack. This was the final lunge which brought death and a posthumous Medal of Honor to Lieutenant Colonel Aquilla Dyess as he put himself at the front of his battalion. The drive ended on Namur's northern shores at some time before noon of February 2 as the tanks rolled up to the edge of a bomb crater filled with Japanese. Corporal Michael Giba looked through *Jenny Lee's* periscope and saw an inflamed Japanese eye. The enemy soldier had jumped on *Jenny Lee,* draped himself over its turret and now he was contemplating Corporal Giba. The Japanese did not seem to know what to do. Corporal Giba reached for a weapon, and the Japanese produced a grenade, pulled its pin, tapped it against the turret to arm it— and then lay down on it.

285

Jenny Lee jumped. Giba heard bullets clattering against *Jenny Lee's* sides. The other tanks were shooting the Japs off his turret. Then all four of them lumbered down into the crater.

It was all over on Roi-Namur. In two more days it was all over at Kwajalein Islet to the south. Eleven days later the Fourth Marine Division sailed east to its new base of Maui in Hawaii, a veteran outfit. The Fourth had secured its objective in twenty-four hours, had lost 190 dead and 547 wounded— and had buried 3,472 enemy troops while taking 264 prisoners.

The camp at Maui was not far from Camp Tarawa, where the Second Marine Division was renewing itself for combat, a battle which the Fourth would join and find more fierce than this. For Admiral Nimitz had his desired bases in the Central Marshalls and American air and sea power were truly neutralizing the other atolls of the chain. Soon the vast and various American panoply would strike west beyond the Marshalls.

But not before the seizure of Eniwetok—"The Land between East and West."

28

Eniwetok was truly a dividing land. The Micronesians had found it so in their long canoe journeys to and from the Carolines in the west and the Gilberts-Marshalls in the east. It had been a stopping place, what the logistics of modern war call a staging area.

Eniwetok was to become a staging area for the United States armed forces. Its numerous islets could hold airfields and receive men and its broad round anchorage could harbor ships. More, lying nearly 3,000 miles west-southwest of Pearl

Harbor, Eniwetok was only 670 miles northeast of Truk and about 1,000 miles southeast of Saipan.

Truk and Saipan would have to be pinned down while Eniwetok was being seized. Truk, being closest, would be hit first—and it would be hit with the swelling power of the Fifth Fleet under Vice Admiral Spruance. Nine carriers under Rear Admiral Marc Mitscher, six big new battleships under Ching Lee, 10 cruisers heavy and light, three full squadrons of destroyers and a special task force of 10 submarines—all of this would strike at the mighty atoll which the Marines called "the Gibraltar of the Pacific."

That would be on February 17.

That same day the orphan regiment of the Marine Corps would be fighting for the airfield on Engebi Islet on Eniwetok Atoll.

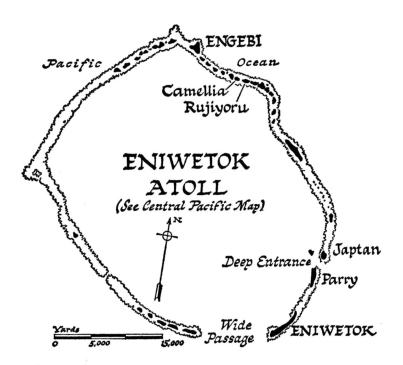

★

The Twenty-second Marines were the waifs of the Pacific. They were an independent regiment formed in early 1942. They had been out of the States eighteen months, but had spent almost all this time on garrison duty in the Samoan Islands, maneuvering in the jungle, making countless landings —training, training, training—and coming down with malaria and that horrible swelling of the legs and genitals called filariasis or elephantiasis, but which the Marines knew as *mumu*. Disease, not bullets, had riddled the Twenty-second and filled it with replacements.

In late 1943 the staging for Kwajalein began and it seemed that Colonel John Walker's regiment would at last see battle. But the Twenty-second wound up with the 106th Army Infantry in that tactical reserve commanded by Brigadier General Thomas Watson. They stood off Kwajalein in their ships while the "boots" of the Fourth Marine Division went ashore at Roi-Namur.

Now it was these very Fourth Division boots who were salty. They hadn't a month overseas yet, but they were already coming around offering to show their scars. It was not pleasant for a grizzled gunnery sergeant of the Twenty-second to be patronized by fuzzy-chinned teen-agers who were still wearing their first pair of GI socks. To them the hash-marked gunnies could not scream, "Yuh chicken-boot—I've worn out more seabags than you have socks!" The boots had only to blink and inquire earnestly:

"You guys seen any action yet?"

But all this would change at Eniwetok.

Up at Engebi Islet at Eniwetok Atoll, Colonel Toshio Yano of the 3rd Battalion, 1st Amphibious Brigade, was completing his battle orders. Colonel Yano calmly expected the invasion of Engebi, for it was the largest of Eniwetok's northern islets and it possessed the atoll's airfield. Also on Engebi were about 1,200 of the 2,586 troops with which Major General Yoshima Nishida was supposed to defend Eniwetok. On the tenth of February, with General Watson's plans for the invasion of

288

Eniwetok already complete, Colonel Yano informed his troops that they could expect to be bombed and shelled and invaded, concluding with this directive:

"Plans must be followed to lure the enemy to the water's edge and then annihilate him with withering firepower and continuous attacks."

It was the inflexible Imperial Staff doctrine of "annihilation at the water's edge" again, but unfortunately for Colonel Yano and his men, the Staff Manual said nothing about what was to be done with *battleships* "lured" to the water's edge.

There *were* battleships almost at the water's edge that windy, overcast morning of February 17.

Great, ghostly, gray shapes—old *Pennsylvania, Tennessee* and *Colorado*—they prowled not a mile off Engebi's beaches with the muzzles of their 14-inch guns streaming flame and smoke.

The entire invading force had entered the lagoon. Rear Admiral Harry Hill had decided to force his way through the southern reef, through Wide Passage, 25 miles directly south of Engebi at the bottom of the lagoon, seven miles northeast of Wide Passage. Minesweepers had cleared a path, sweeping up 28 moored mines in Wide Passage, and then the ships formed column. The little minesweepers led them in, then the destroyers, next the battlewagons and cruisers, finally the transports. They came in with all guns firing, blasting and raking blackjack-shaped Eniwetok Islet on the right at Wide Passage, battering Parry and Japtan Islets to either side of Deep Entrance.

They sailed up the lagoon to Engebi and pummeled her, while Major General Nishida got off this signal from his headquarters on Parry Islet: "Enemy fleet entering the lagoon in large numbers. Request reinforcements." Even if it had been possible to send them, they could never have arrived in time. Already Captain Jim Jones's Recon Boys were going ashore on Camellia and Rujiyoru, two coral specks lying to the east or right of Engebi. Before two o'clock in the afternoon, Jones had reported their capture. By nightfall Company D (Scout) of the Fourth Tank Battalion had captured little Bogon to the left of Engebi, and artillery was ashore and emplaced on these bracketing islands, ready to join the warships at dawn.

That same evening of February 17, "the Gibraltar of the Pacific" had been found to be not an impregnable rock but rather an empty shell.

For years American planners had spoken in awe of Japan's secret base in the Carolines. Truk had been the invincible this and the invulnerable that. No one wanted any part of Truk— not the Army, not the Army Air Force, not the United States Marines. It was the most perfect oceanic fortress that nature could devise. It was a drowned mountain range within a coral reef. The peaks of those mountains formed the numerous wooded islands within vast Truk Lagoon. On four of these islands the Japanese had built airfields and on other islands were naval and administrative centers. All of these islands, and the ships sheltering in Truk Lagoon, were beyond the range of hostile warships forced to stand outside the enclosing coral reef. The Truk Islands were therefore safe against naval surface attack, and assault troops would never get across that reef—if Truk's airplanes ever allowed them to reach it. Truk was only open to attack from the air, but before Kwajalein, airplanes had to fly a long, long way to reach Truk. Before Torokina and Tarawa it was beyond range. By early February, however, the terrible attrition of the Bismarcks and the Solomons had siphoned off much of Truk's air strength. At the same time two Marine pilots—Major James Christensen and Captain James Yawn—had taken Liberator scout planes aloft from Torokina Airfield and flown 850 miles to Truk under cover of freak tropical storms. Upon their return they produced the war's first aerial photographs of Truk, photos which electrified Nimitz' headquarters because they showed the Japanese Combined Fleet anchored in Truk Lagoon.

That had been February 4, the very date on which the Army's 7th Division secured Kwajalein Islet, ending the entire Kwajalein Atoll Campaign. Immediately Rear Admiral Mitscher's three fast carrier groups sped down to Majuro to refuel. On February 12 they were streaking north of Eniwetok to rendezvous with tankers, to join up later with the battleships, cruisers, destroyers and submarines which, with themselves, formed Spruance's Fifth Fleet.

But by then the bird had flown. The eight-rayed flag of the commander in chief, Japanese Combined Fleet, had departed Truk Lagoon forever. Fleet Admiral Koga had not liked the appearance of that American reconnaissance plane and had ordered his big ships back to Tawi-Tawi. He himself sailed to Japan in 63,000-ton *Musashi*.

Yet, as 72 Hellcats rose off the decks of five carriers before dawn of February 17, and as Admiral Spruance led the big warships on a round-the-atoll prowl, there were still two Japanese cruisers, eight destroyers and upwards of 50 merchant ships in and around Truk Lagoon, to say nothing of 365 airplanes and those four airfields which Mitscher's warbirds were coming to destroy.

At sunrise the Hellcats were over Truk and battling 45 Japanese fighters. They shot down 30 of them, formed again and came roaring down to shoot up the aircraft parked on three fields. One exuberant Hellcat pilot spotted a transport plane which had slipped into a safe landing at Param Field. Its occupants were dashing for a concrete slit trench at one end of the field. The Hellcat pilot swooped and blew up the transport. He came back again to try for about 15 fighters parked near the slit trench. He hit a few and tried to spray slugs within the trench but he wasn't able to—which was lucky, for Major Pappy Boyington and six other American fliers were in that trench. The Japanese had been taking them from Rabaul to Japan via Truk, and had arrived in time for the Americans to take a dubious delight in the capabilities of the new Hellcat fighters.

Though Boyington and his companions had been blindfolded, their guards were not at that moment insisting on regulations. The Americans saw the Hellcats chew up about 40 more Japanese planes. They even watched while the Avengers came in with hundred-pound fragmentation bombs, but they ducked for safety with the arrival of Dauntlesses bearing thousand-pounders.

Most of the big bombs were dropped on the ships in the

lagoon. They hit everything afloat, and outside the atoll there were more ships sinking beneath the bombs of the carrier planes or being slashed into shredded steel by the guns of mammoth *New Jersey* and *Iowa,* the heavy cruisers *Minneapolis* and *New Orleans,* and four destroyers. The Japanese sailors fought with customary valor, here a destroyer taking on a battleship, here a subchaser trying to outgun a destroyer, but the results outside the atoll were the same as within. In all, Japan lost two light cruisers, four destroyers, three auxiliary cruisers, two submarine tenders, two subchasers, an armed trawler and an airplane ferry—and 24 merchant ships, of which five were tankers. With smaller craft, a total of 200,000 tons of shipping was lost. Most of Truk's 365 aircraft were either destroyed or damaged, and 75 per cent of the base's supplies ruined.

Against this the Japanese retaliated with a single torpedo-bomber strike. One Kate got a torpedo into *Intrepid,* killing 11 men, wounding 17, and forcing the carrier to retire. With this went 12 American fighters downed, seven torpedo-bombers and six dive-bombers—a total of 29 pilots and crewmen killed. There was not an American ship lost.

It was total, stinging defeat, a source of great bitterness to those Japanese fighter pilots who fought so vainly to prevent it. As had the men of the Bastard Air Force at Guadalcanal, the enemy fliers fought throughout the day flying, returning, re-arming, and flying again. In midafternoon one of them skidded his Zero into a landing at Param Field. He jumped from his plane and ran for the bomb shelters to sit out the strafing attacks until his plane was ready again.

He passed the slit trench in which the seven Americans were crouched and stopped, astonished. He recovered his composure and said quietly, "I am a Japanese pilot." The Americans said nothing, though they wondered if the Japanese was joking. "I am a Japanese pilot," the man said again. He tapped his leather pistol holster ominously. "You bomb here —you die."

The Americans were still not sure, but having survived weeks of torture in Rabaul, expecting more of it and perhaps death in Japan, they were almost beyond caring.

292

"With all the goddamn trouble we got already," Boyington growled, "ain't *you* the cheerful son of a bitch."

There was a bare pause, and then there was the roar of powerful motors, the chilling sound of Hellcat 50-caliber bullets smacking the coral, the tinkling of falling empty cartridges. The Japanese pilot sprinted for the bomb caves, and the Americans were left with another grim joke to sustain them in the bleak eighteen months lying between the present and the day of their liberation in Japan, a liberation which brought Boyington the Medal of Honor and found him still the outstanding Marine ace of all time.

Next morning Admiral Mitscher's planes flew again over Truk's fields, but not a single plane rose to oppose them. The Fifth Fleet sailed east in jubilation.

On that same morning Radio Tokyo spoke to the Japanese nation and the world with unaccustomed candor:

"A powerful American task force suddenly advanced to our Caroline Islands Wednesday morning and repeatedly attacked our important strategic base, Truk, with a great number of ship-based planes. The enemy is constantly repeating powerfully persistent raids with several hundred fighters and bombers, attacking us intermittently. The war situation has increased with unprecedented seriousness—nay, furiousness. The tempo of enemy operations indicates that the attacking force is already pressing upon our mainland."

There had never been such an admission before. It suggested that Premier Tojo's iron grip upon the Emperor and nation was weakening. Within another day there was to be more bad news to hasten the downfall of Tojo's "Manchuria gang."

Engebi was falling.

The Twenty-second Marines attacked bomb-pitted, shell-pocked Engebi two battalions abreast. They ran into Japanese crazed by thirst and maddened by the fury of the bombardment. The battle split off into small separate actions. Sometimes the Japanese fought with knives, leaping into the shell-holes where the Marines had set up their guns, closing with a fury born of desperation. Sometimes they fought out of spider holes, lifting the lids after the Marines had passed, firing into

293

their rear. The inevitable debris of the bombardment clogged the routes of advance, and there were often live Japanese firing machine guns from the ruins. But by four o'clock the Marines had overrun the airfield and General Watson had withdrawn the Third Battalion, Twenty-second, for use against Eniwetok Islet the next day. The other battalions dug in—and spent a restless night.

It was the Twenty-second's first night in combat, and no one had thought to collect all those Japanese and American weapons strewn about the battlefield. The Japanese crept out of their holes, rearmed themselves, and infiltrated. One of them tossed a grenade in a foxhold held by Corporal Anthony Damato and three others. Damato flung himself on the bomb and was killed. He was awarded the Medal of Honor posthumously. Sporadic fighting fluttered on, but by dawn resistance on Engebi had been crushed. Colonel Yano and all but a few of his men were dead, and these others would be mopped up during the day. At dawn, Colonel Walker raised the American flag over Engebi while a private blew "To the Colors" on a captured Japanese bugle.

At dawn of February 19 the two battalions of the 106th Infantry went ashore on Eniwetok Islet. They made slow going at first. General Watson sent in the Third Battalion, Twenty-second. The Marines struck across the islet's waist, the pace of the other battalions quickened, the Japanese spent themselves with individual squad counterattacks during the night, and Eniwetok Islet was secured by late afternoon of February 20.

It remained to take Parry Islet.

Parry was about two miles north of Eniwetok Islet. It formed the southern side of Deep Passage. Across Deep Passage a half-mile farther north was Japtan Islet. To take Parry, the Recon Boys first seized Japtan Islet as a base for artillery. That was on February 21, and on the same day *Pennsylvania* and *Tennessee* stood within a half-mile of Parry's lagoon beaches and pounded the little islet. Next day, with cruisers, destroyers and rocket boats joining the battleships and the Japtan artillery, all three battalions of the Twenty-second Marines attacked Parry.

At half-past seven that night, after Japanese tanks were destroyed in a pitched battle with the Marine mediums, and after naval gunfire destroyed the last pocket and probably also destroyed Major General Nishida, the battle ended with this message from Colonel Walker to General Watson:

"I present you with Parry. Request this unit be relieved for re-embarkation in the morning."

The request was granted. On February 23 the Twenty-second Marines went back aboard ship. They were veterans now. They had lost 184 killed, 540 wounded, and had disposed of roughly 2,000 Japanese. They were going back to Kwajalein, where, with Captain Jones's Fifth Corps Recon Company, with the Scout Company of the Fourth Marine Division, they made dozens of landings to secure the islets of that enormous atoll. Then there was a brief idyll. With other Marines they sang hymns with the Marshallese and walked sentry duty naked but for a tan GI towel swathed about their hips like a Micronesian's *lap-lap*. And they tried very hard to twist their tongues around those unpronounceable islet names—Ennumennent, Edgigen, Enubuj, Gugegwe, Bigej, Ennylabegan. When they met and mastered Ennugenliggelap the campaign in the Marshall Islands was obviously over.

29

The swamp fox of New Britain—Major General Iwao Matsuda —had been prepared to flee long before he was ordered to withdraw.

While the Borgen Bay complex had been falling in mid-January, Matsuda had ordered a Lieutenant Hanahara up to Natamo Point on the eastern edge of Borgen Bay and charged him with a do-or-die defense there. He had also brought

Colonel Jiro Sato up from the south and ordered him to defend the approaches southwest of Nakarop-Egaroppu.

Hanahara, then, held a roadblock between the Americans at Borgen Bay and the mouth of the trail to Matsuda's headquarters. Sato held the high ground between the Americans at the airfield and Matsuda. True, the trails from the south coast were now undefended, but it would take the Americans some time to work all the way around the Cape and come up on Nakarop from the south.

Hanahara and Sato were in place before that January 21 on which Matsuda received a message from Lieutenant General Yasushi Sakai, commander of the 17th Infantry Division at Cape Hoskins—a north coast point midway between Cape Gloucester and Rabaul. Sakai instructed Matsuda to pull the 65th Brigade back to a rallying place called Kokopo, about six or seven miles east of Natamo Point and something like a dozen miles northeast along the back-door trail from Nakarop.

Matsuda left Nakarop by the back door. He sent out his sick and wounded first. Then himself, guarded by Colonels Sumiya and Katayama and the only available combat troops. His artillery followed. If Sato survived, he could come too—but not Hanahara. He was to fight to the death.

Iwao Matsuda was in high spirits as he crossed the headwaters of the Natamo River and encountered Superior Private Toshio Herotsune. He sought to raise Private Herotsune's flagging morale by assuring him that there were strong reinforcements marching even then to the brigade's relief. Then Matsuda vanished into the jungle, bound, not for Kokopo, not for any intermediate rallying place, but for Cape Hoskins some 170 miles east.

The Marines on New Britain were mystified, for the enemy had vanished. No Japanese had been found in force since Hill 660 fell on January 15. The Marines began to hunt the enemy, their search complicated by the fact that he knew the terrain, while they did not, and that he could fight when and where he chose. For every one of the enemy's moves, the Americans would need to counter with a dozen groping moves of their own. They were actually mapping the terrain as they patrolled it, and a day rarely passed without a report of another unmapped trail found through an unknown jungle, over an anonymous mountain, around a nameless swamp. Worse, the Marines had still not located Egaroppu, that place as pregnant with mystery as it was stuffed with vowels. So the war in western New Britain became a huge blind chase, made more nerve-racking by the fact that the pursued was as capable of fight as flight.

A week passed. Once a patrol going south from the airfield was ambushed on Mount Talawe. In the sharp quick fight that followed Sergeant Phil Mottola shot a Japanese. The man screamed in English: "I'm shot!"

"Shot hell!" Mottola yelled. "You're dead!"

With that Mottola finished him off, and the patrol moved on. To run into another ambush. And then another. The closer the Marines got to low ground behind Mount Talawe the stiffer became the opposition. Some attempts to close with the enemy at the points of ambush would find the position abandoned, or sometimes the Japanese would be in pillboxes on cliffs commanding the trails winding down from the hills. From these they fought with mortars and machine guns. Colonel Sato's men were fighting a skillful delaying action.

At Natamo Point east of Hill 660 on the north coast, a patrol was stopped by intense automatic-weapons fire. A captured map showed Natamo Point to be fortified with many machine-gun positions. For two days planes of the Fifth Air Force worked it over, but when the Marines sought to cross the Natamo River they found their way still barred by automatic cannon and artillery. It was not until they had made shore-to-shore landings around the river, called down their own artillery and brought up rockets that they were able to force Lieutenant Hanahara's roadblock.

For such it was. It was the last gate to the northern approaches to Nakarop. Five hundred yards east of Natamo Point the Marines found a wide, unmapped corduroy road. They sent patrols down it. On January 29 the Marines entered their Egaroppu which they at last knew to be Nakarop.

It was empty, and now began an elaborate game of hide-and-seek as Marine amphibious patrols pursued the fleeing

Matsuda. They chased him throughout February, leapfrogging patrols along the coast to all the rallying places.

Matsuda had not tarried at Kokopo. He had gone on to Karai-ai about 20 miles farther east. The Marines landed at Karai-ai and found only the dead and dying. Matsuda had taken a boat. He might be found at Upmadung.

Upmadung?

There had not been so much fun with a word since the Marines had maneuvered in Melbourne Bay aboard a ship called HMS *Manoora*.

But Matsuda had not stayed there, either. While Colonels Sumiya and Katayama had marched off by land, he had taken another boat which eventually landed him at Cape Hoskins.

Behind him, crawling over the trails, eating native dogs and plundering native gardens, starving and suffering, came the wretched, rotting remnant of his brigade. They had been abandoned by their comrades. They were wounded and their flesh stank. Their bodies were covered with fungus infections. There were many of them actually crawling on hands and knees, for their feet were too rotten to support them. They had little idea where they were going. When they had no more strength to move, they lay on the trail. The moment the point of a Marine patrol came into sight they blew themselves up with grenades. There were others too weak to do this and the Marines began to take prisoners.

The Marines had begun to pity the foe, for they had never seen such miserable defeat, and even they became nauseous as they moved along the trails between Borgen Bay and Iboki Plantation, holding their noses against the stink of death.

30

Rabaul, the mighty fortress to which Matsuda's miserable soldiers were crawling, was completely exposed to aerial attack in the last days of February.

The ruinous American strike on Truk had led Fleet Admiral Koga to order all naval planes and pilots out of Rabaul to Truk as reinforcements, and the great base on eastern New Britain was left with a few Army aircraft and an occasional patched-up naval fighter after the January savaging of the fighter-sweeps launched by Marine pilots to the south.

Among these fliers was Butcher Bob Hanson, the lieutenant who had shot down three enemy planes over Torokina on D-Day and had so jauntily survived his own crash. Hanson began his second tour of duty on January 13 with five planes to his credit. Within the following seventeen days he shot down 20 more. Whenever Hanson went up, he shot down at least one Japanese aircraft. On January 30 the last day of that period, Hanson flew up to Rabaul to help strike at newly arrived fighter strength there. Of 21 Japanese planes shot down, Hanson got four. His record now stood at 25 planes. He had another ten days to go on his tour of duty and it seemed likely that he would surpass even Pappy Boyington's mark of 28 planes. But Hanson was not the pilot to play it safe; it was his habit to volunteer for every mission that came his squadron's way—whether a fighter-sweep which could mean more red balls painted on his Corsair's fuselage, or a strafing mission which meant the risk of the black bursts of enemy antiaircraft fire. On February 2 Hanson volunteered for a strafing mission over Cape St. George and he was killed when he was unable to pull out of a run made at typically low altitude. The citation

299

accompanying his Medal of Honor spoke his epitaph: "He was a master of individual combat."

And now, in late February, Rabaul was almost helpless beneath mounting hammer blows. The fighter-sweeps had accounted for the destruction of 863 Japanese planes since the construction of Torokina Airfield and the "milk-run" bombing flights were now beginning. These sorties—Army, Navy, New Zealand and Australian as well as Marine—were launched off the big new fields on Bougainville and Green Island. February also marked the date when the Japanese on Rabaul started to go underground, beginning the first of 350 miles of tunnels and caves for storage and living purposes.

Kavieng, that air-sea base on New Ireland which General MacArthur did not have to invade after all, was also flattened, and Marine bombers of Commander Air Solomons began to sing a new song to the tune of "Oh, Susanna":

> Oh, I went up to Kavieng,
> The maps upon my knees,
> The soup was thick, the night was black,
> No wingtips could I see
>
> The lights went on, they shot at me,
> I swore and heaved a sigh,
> We stayed up there for two damn hours—
> ComAirSols, don't you cry!
>
> *Oh, ComAirSols never cries for me,*
> *Though I go to Kavieng each night*
> *And bomb the enemy.*
>
> We tune in on the radar set,
> Gaze in the crystal ball,
> Geishas smile in the scope—
> We know we're at Rabaul.
>
> This life's a mighty pleasant thing,
> If I depart too soon,
> Please write my epitaph to read:
> "No hits, twelve runs, no moon."

It was these Marine airmen, flying half of all the Allied sorties against Rabaul, shooting down three-fifths of all Rabaul planes destroyed in combat, who were largely responsible for keeping

300

the power of this monster base in check, and the way to new invasions open.

On the twenty-ninth of February, 1,000 troopers of the dismounted 1st Cavalry Division landed in the Admiralty Islands, 250 miles north northwest of Cape Gloucester. It was a reconnaissance-in-force accompanied by General Douglas MacArthur. At the end of that day the troopers had captured the airfield of Los Negros and MacArthur had decided to stay.

Six days later the First Marine Division was staging another invasion of its own, one as well planned as it was unnecessary.

The plan was to invade the Willaumez Peninsula 120 miles east of Cape Gloucester. Why, has never been made clear. It has been argued that Willaumez contained an airfield, but it was in fact only big enough to receive Piper Cubs; or that its seizure would cut off the retreat of Matsuda's survivors, but everyone knew that those poor wretches, if they lived, were already a burden to the enemy; or that, finally, the Marine troops had become dispirited in the miasma of the swamp and needed an offensive operation to revive them—a misconception which seems to afflict many commanders once they pass from company grade to field rank and above. Put plainly: men don't like to fight. They do it for a number of reasons, some of them noble, but not even the men who write Marine propaganda would suggest that the men's morale is raised by finding strongpoints for them to storm. The truth is that in February the First Marine Division possessed all that was useful in western New Britain: the airfield and the Borgen Bay heights guarding it. The Division was also in contact with the Army at Arawe in the south and the enemy had been cut to pieces.

Still, the operation known as the Talasea Landing was ordered, and it was turned over to Colonel Oliver P. ("O.P.") Smith, a man who had a reputation as a planner and who now commanded the Fifth Marines.

Smith decided not to go around the northern tip of the peninsula to get at the airfield on the east coast at Talasea. Most of the 1st Battalion, 54th Infantry, was concentrated there under Captain Kyamatsu Terunuma. Smith preferred coming in the back door, on the west coast at a place called Volupai. This meant a shore-to-shore voyage covering 60 miles from Iboki Plantation to Volupai.

On the afternoon of March 5 the vanguard of some 5,000 Marines climbed into amtracks and the amtracks rolled aboard a group of LCT's. At ten o'clock that night, with torpedo boats leading the way, they sailed east to Volupai. In the morning they attacked under the covering fire of the First Marine Division "Navy" and "Air Force."

The Navy consisted of tanks carried aboard LCM's. Their turret machine-gunners had a clear field of fire and their artillery could blast straight ahead after the ramps were lowered. The Air Force consisted of a Piper Cub observation plane from which Captain Theodore Petras dropped hand grenades, once it became known that Australian Beauforts were weathered in and could not show up to deliver an air strike.

The Marines went in and were hit by mortars. They began to take casualties, but they continued on. Then they ran into flanking fire from Little Mount Worri and halted. They had only five miles to go to Talasea, but it took them three days.

The men who had planned the invasion of Bougainville had chosen Cape Torokina because they estimated that it would take Lieutenant General Haruyoshi Hyakutate three months to mount a counterattack there. They were wrong. It had taken four months.

On March 8 from 100 to 200 artillery shells fell on the perimeter which the Army's Fourteenth Corps held around Torokina's airfields. It was the opening gun in the heaviest artillery bombardment which Japan mounted in all the South Pacific. For months the scattered units of Hyakutate's 17th Army had been toiling over the Bougainville mountain trails to the Torokina assembly point. Field pieces had been laboriously hauled up by hand. Shells had been brought up by hand, too, and it took two men four days to bring up a single hundred-pounder.

On March 8 they were ready. Still using the tactics of Guadalcanal, still smarting from Guadalcanal, Hyakutate told his men:

"The time has come to manifest our knighthood with the pure brilliance of the sword. It is our duty to erase the mortification of our brothers at Guadalcanal. Attack! Assault! Destroy everything! Cut, slash, and mow them down. May the color of the red emblem of our arms be deepened with the blood of the American rascals. Our cry of victory at Torokina Bay will be shouted resoundingly to our native land.

"We are invincible! Always attack. Security is the greatest enemy. Always be alert. Execute silently."

Then, estimating that Major General Oscar Griswold's Fourteenth Corps had only one division, when in fact it had both the 37th and the Americal, Haruyoshi Hyakutate sent 15,000 Japanese up against three times that many Americans.

On March 10 the Fifth Marines broke into Talasea. They had come on through heavy mortar fire and numerous ambushes. They had passed through a unique *banzai* the night the Japanese worked themselves up into a frenzy, and charged off to their own rear. But on March 10 Talasea was theirs, at a cost of 17 Marines killed and 114 wounded, against 150 Japanese dead. The end result of their effort was expressed with succinct eloquence by a mud-stained Marine whom a war correspondent fresh from the States had asked: "What outfit did you relieve here?" The Marine spat disdainfully and said: "The Fifty-fourth Japanese!"

Boredom had set in on Cape Gloucester, wet-blanket boredom. There had been no nocturnal air attacks since mid-February. Except for the Fifth's excursion to Talasea, there had been no action. The storms had begun to subside, though 20 men had been killed so far by the widow-makers and 50 more had been injured, and there had been an Army captain who crawled down a riverbank to drink and had his arm chewed off by an alligator. There had also been three men killed by lightning, and one night a storm turned a brook into a torrent and swept away a battalion's bivouac area. Marines on patrol about 10 miles downcoast awoke next morning to find the battalion's ration of powdered eggs, powdered milk, ten-in-one rations replete with bacon, and even vanilla extract—which would make excellent "jungle juice"—washed up at their feet. They canceled patrolling for the day and gorged themselves.

Otherwise it had been boring since mid-February, and the Marines amused themselves by carving designs on their mess gear, listening to Tokyo Rose, swapping specimens of the highly pornographic propaganda which the Japanese dropped on New Britain, or by launching a counteradvertising campaign against that bitter yellow pill called atabrine which they were forced to swallow three times daily.

Atabrine was a malaria preventative. It had been developed after Japan had cornered most of the world's sources of quinine. It had been introduced in the Pacific at the end of 1942, and in early 1944 on New Britain it had kept the incidence of malaria down to a rock-bottom minimum. But the men did not like atabrine. It was the perfection of bitterness. Many men could not swallow atabrine. It also turned a man's skin yellow, a permanent yellow, many men innocently assumed. There were rumors that it made a man sterile.

Nothing had more power to make atabrine unpopular than this last rumor, and as the number of atabrine delinquents grew, medical people resorted to an advertising campaign which suggested that, so far from being a sterilizer, atabrine actually possessed powers which were at once a compound of monkey glands, Spanish fly and wax from the ear of the queen bee. There were roadside signs of voluptuous nudes accompanied by the legend: "Come Back to This—Take Atabrine." There was, in the school of art which has made the mammary gland the American oriflamme, a picture of a bare-breasted blonde amazon who offered: "Two Reasons Why You Should Take Atabrine." The Marines had become fed up, and they passed off the boredom by producing their own *reductios* of the powers of atabrine. Soon the lines and the bivouacs blossomed with signs such as these:

REACH FOR AN ATABRINE INSTEAD OF A JEEP.

HEMORRHOIDS? GIVE ATABRINE A 30-DAY TRIAL.
WRITE FOR FREE BOOKLET.

STOP EXCESS FALLING HAIR! USE ATABRINE!

And then the entire silly business of sugar-coating the bitter atabrine pill came to an end after the appearance of this taunt:

WHY WEAR A TRUSS? TAKE ATABRINE.

The last nail was being hammered into the coffins of Kavieng and Rabaul. The St. Matthias Islands, the northern-most of the Bismarcks, were coming under attack.

Since the 1st Cavalry's reconnaissance-in-force on Los Negros had been turned into eventual capture of the Admiralty Islands, it had only remained to seize a base north of Kavieng. Once this was done, with American bases to the south on Cape Gloucester and to the west on the Admiralties, the Bismarcks and the Solomons would be completely cut off from the Empire. The St. Matthias island chosen for this maneuver was Emirau. The attacking force was the Fourth Marine Regiment, an outfit now composed of all those Raider units which had been deactivated, once it became apparent that the Raider hit-and-run specialty was no longer of use in the Pacific.

These men were also the heirs of the old Fourth Marine Regiment which had served in China, had barely gotten out of Shanghai before Pearl Harbor—and had arrived in the Philippines in time to fight on Bataan and Corregidor, where they burned their colors and surendered.

The new Fourth Marines went into Emirau on March 20, and because they once were Raiders and had that Raider penchant for songs and slogans, they went in whistling, "Oh, What a Beautiful Mornin'."

It was a beautiful morning on Emirau for there was not a Japanese in sight. There was only a little wooden sign which said, in Japanese: "This island occupied by Imperial Landing Party, January, 1942."

It was not much in the way of material for a new Raider ballad, but it would have to do—at least until April when the Fourth Marines went back to Guadalcanal to hook up with that other loner regiment—the Twenty-second—and form the First Provisional Marine Brigade.

In the meantime Kavieng and Rabaul had been cut off. They

were not aware of it, for they believed in the coming of that mythical "Greater East Asia Annihilation Fleet" which Premier Tojo had invented to keep up the morale of his bypassed bases. But if the Annihilation Fleet could keep up morale, it could not keep the great bases of the Bismarcks in the war.

It was all over at Torokina by March 25. By then the three-pronged assault which Hyakutate had ordered had been shattered by the soldiers of the 37th and Americal Divisions, with considerable help from their artillery. Some 5,000 Japanese soldiers had been killed, and only 263 Americans had died. The long, bloody, toilsome climb up the Solomons ladder which had begun more than nineteen months before at Guadalcanal was at an end. The Slot was now an American canal, Haruyoshi Hyakutate had issued his last battle order and the surviving men of that 17th Army which he had lost twice over were reduced to grubbing for existence in the native gardens of Bougainville.

A similar end soon overtook their counterparts in New Guinea, where units of Lieutenant General Hatazo Adachi's 18th Army were being chopped up and isolated. On April 22 the soldiers of General MacArthur leapfrogged far up the New Guinea coast to land unopposed at Hollandia in Dutch New Guinea, and to move inland to a stiff fight.

By then some 130 miles of New Britain's coast were in Marine hands, Matsuda's 65th Brigade had been all but annihilated, and the last battle had been fought at Linga Linga on March 20. A patrol of the Second Battalion, First, led by that same Charles Brush who had ambushed the vanguard of the Ichiki Detachment on Guadalcanal, ambushed Colonel Jiro Sato's rear-guard. Of the 500 men whom Sato had gathered at Upmadung, not 100 had survived the march, and these were all killed by the Marines. Sato himself died like a soldier, with his sword in his hand at the head of his troops, concluding the delaying action which had enabled Matsuda and half his men to escape. Five thousand Japanese had been killed on New Britain and an unprecedented 500 had surrendered. All this was accomplished at a loss of 310 Marines killed and 1,083 wounded, proof of how low Marines could keep their casualties when maneuver was possible.

By now also the men of the First Marine Division wanted to get away from the Army. In mid-April they awaited the arrival of their relief, the Army's 40th Infantry Division. And yet, when the Army did arrive, there were actually some Marines who were reluctant to leave. That was because the Fifth had found a home at Talasea.

They had found a beautiful grove of tall graceful coconut trees, they had found Bitokara Mission on the high bluffs overlooking blue and breezy Garua Harbor—a place of broad green lawns, of gardens riotous with the vivid blooms of the tropics, of neat white-painted buildings, all dominated by capacious St. Boniface Mission Church. There was also smiling San Remo Plantation and there were even sulphur springs. Some nights the Melanesians would stage "sing-sings" for the American Marines who had been so generous with their cigarettes and had guaranteed many, many years of labor trouble for Australian planters who bought work with "sticks tobac."

"Finding this place," said one Marine, "is like finding Heaven in Hell."

But they were out of Talasea before May, sailing back to the norm of Hell-in-Heaven, the mud and rotting coconuts and rats and bats and dejection of a place called Pavuvu in the beautiful Russell Islands. From Pavuvu some of them went home, for the rotation system developed by the U.S. armed services was at last bringing relief to those men who had been overseas two years or more. But there were more Marines coming out from the States than going in, for there were now five full divisions and a brigade in the field.

On the same twenty-eighth of April on which the last Marine quit New Britain, the Navy struck the blow which would send this striking force charging off in a new direction.

On that day Truk was destroyed.

American carriers stood about 150 miles to the west of the once-fearful base in the Carolines and flew off flights of Hellcats. They swept over Truk to clear the skies for the bombers. They tangled with 62 Japanese fighters and shot most of them down. In two days they destroyed 59 in aerial combat and knocked out 34 on the ground. Truk was left with 12 planes. Though there were no ships of any size in the lagoon, everything afloat there was sunk. Everything above ground on the airfields was knocked down. So thorough was this obliterating blow, so devastated were the Japanese, that the Americans could rescue their downed airmen in Truk Lagoon. A float-plane pilot from *North Carolina* went after three men on a raft there. He capsized in choppy seas, but another of *North Carolina*'s floats came in, took the raft under tow, and taxied out to the waiting submarine, *Tang*, which had patrolled the reef on lifeguard duty. Of 46 Americans shot down, more than half were rescued.

Truk was through. Task Force 58, which had finished it, was already wheeling and steaming north to give Marianas bases a foretaste of the storm which would soon blow up the northwest route to Tokyo.

Guadalcanal, New Georgia, Choiseul, Bougainville, Tarawa, Kwajalein, Eniwetok, New Britain—all those fights in the air, in water, on earth—were now history. Kavieng, Rabaul, Truk —the three terrors of the Pacific—were penned in and chained up.

"The seasons do not change," wrote Vice Admiral Chuichi Hara, the commandant at Truk. "I try to look like a proud vice admiral, but it is hard with a potato hook in my hands. It rains every day, the flowers bloom every day, the enemy bombs us every day—so why remember?"

III. Brisk and Bold

*"They want war too methodical, too measured;
I would make it brisk, bold, impetuous, perhaps sometimes
even audacious."* —Antoine Henri Jomini

1

They were coming out of the lagoons—out of Majuro, out of Kwajalein, out of Eniwetok—coming with a bright white bone in the teeth of their prows.

They sortied out of the reef passages, battleships leading, while the blue sea water boiled white and frothy over the reefs and curled away in the round distance. Escort ships heeled over and broke column, stiffening their strings of signal flags as they bent it on and raced around the others in protective circle. Up ahead were the fast aircraft carriers—16 of these new queencraft of the seas—guarded by seven big new battleships, 13 cruisers and 58 destroyers.

In all there were 800 ships standing out of the lagoons, carrying 162,000 men and all the guns and airplanes necessary to take the Marianas Islands away from Japan.

For this was early June of 1944. It was exactly two and a half years since Vice Admiral Chuichi Nagumo had gathered his armada and sailed for Pearl Harbor, thereby incurring the terrible vengeance now drawing closer to Japan, and Nazi Germany as well. Even as these ships sailed to battle in early June, the greatest amphibious force ever assembled was preparing to cross the English Channel to the beaches of Normandy. And yet, though the Channel force was the greater, it was both American and British and it would sail hardly 20 miles. Here in the Pacific, these Marines and soldiers under Lieutenant General Howlin' Mad Smith were sailing a total of 3,700 miles from the Hawaii staging areas and 2,400 miles from those in Guadalcanal—and every ship but three was American. More, this Pacific force was going to make three separate landings—on Guam, Tinian and Saipan. Saipan would be the first.

Already the assault battalions of the Second and Fourth Marine Divisions had been told that Saipan was their objective. They had learned that this island fourteen miles by six had caves like Tulagi's, mountains and ridges such as those of Guadalcanal and Bougainville, a reef like Tarawa's and a swamp like Cape Gloucester's—while also possessing such novelties as cities, a civilian population of Japanese and Chamorros, and open plains where maneuvering would come under heavy artillery fire. Saipan did not look appealing, and it sounded specially repugnant to those men of the Fourth Division who listened to their battalion surgeon explain some of the island's other defects.

"In the surf," he said with solemn relish, "beware of sharks, barracuda, sea snakes, anemones, razor-sharp coral, polluted waters, poison fish and giant clams that shut on a man like a bear trap. Ashore," he went on with rising enthusiasm, "there is leprosy, typhus, filariasis, yaws, typhoid, dengue fever, dysentery, saber grass, hordes of flies, snakes and giant lizards." He paused, winded, but rushed on: "Eat nothing growing on the island, don't drink its waters, and don't approach its inhabitants." He stopped, smiled benignly and inquired: "Any questions?"

A private's hand shot up.

"Yes?"

"Sir," the private asked, "why'n hell don't we let the Japs keep the island?"

The answer, if the doctor had known, would have been fourfold.

Those islands which an angry Magellan had named Los Ladrones, or The Thieves, in honor of light-fingered Chamorro natives, and which a priest had renamed Las Marianas, in honor of Spain's Queen Maria Anna, were important to the Pacific strategy because possession of them would cut off Truk irrevocably, would pierce Japan's second line of defense, would provide a base to bomb Japan with those huge B-29's now coming off the assembly lines, and might lure the Japanese Fleet into all-out battle.

Saipan was the chief target because it was 1,500 miles from Tokyo and already possessed a good air base in Aslito Airfield to its south and a new one being built in the north at Marpi Point. It was the heart of the Marianas, the headquarters of Japan's Central Pacific Fleet commanded by Admiral Nagumo as well as of that 31st Army which Japan had formed by siphoning off battalions from its celebrated Kwantung Army in China (thereby setting up a pushover for the Russian rush a year later). On Saipan were 30,000 troops, mostly soldiers of the 43rd Division, the 47th Mixed Independent Brigade and the usual clutter of Army detachments and groups under the command of Lieutenant General Yoshitsugu Saito.

Lieutenant General Saito was an aged and infirm man. He had taken over on Saipan after the 31st Army's commander, Lieutenant General Hideyoshi Obata, had departed on a far-flung inspection tour. Saito did not get on with Nagumo, for the hero of Pearl Harbor had been powerless to prevent the steady sinking of Marianas-bound ships by American submarines.

On February 29 the submarine *Trout* sank the transport *Sakito Maru* bound for Saipan with 4,100 troops. Only 1,680 men survived to be shipped on to their destination at Guam. It went on intermittently, this submarine scourging, and as late as June 6 the submarines *Shark*, *Pintado* and *Pilotfish* sank five of seven ships bringing 3,463 soldiers to Saipan, causing the loss of 858 men. Almost as bad was the loss of cement and construction steel with which Saito hoped to emplace his numerous coastal guns. Of this he complained bitterly to Nagumo.

"We cannot strengthen the fortifications appreciably now unless we can get materials suitable for permanent construction," he informed the Central Fleet commander. "No matter how many soldiers there are, they can do nothing in regard to fortifications but sit around with their arms folded. The situation is unbearable."

Nagumo did not think the situation unbearable at all. He

did not think the Marianas would come under attack before November. He was positive, as was Japanese Imperial Headquarters, that the Americans' next step would be along the New Guinea-Philippines axis, probably in the Palaus. For this reason Japan had spent most of her material and energy in fortifying the Palaus, especially a postage stamp of an island named Peleliu. Admiral Soemu Toyoda had assembled the Combined Fleet at Tawi Tawi in the Sulu Sea preparatory for a dash to the Palaus to engage the American invasion fleet in the all-out battle he sought as much as had Toga before him and, before him, Yamamoto.

And so, while General Saito got his abundant artillery in place in the hills, grumbling over his inability to emplace coastal guns to carry out his plan "to destroy the enemy at the water's edge," Vice Admiral Chuichi Nagumo, like almost everyone else in the Army and Navy, kept his eyes fixed on the Palaus.

Lieutenant General Smith, in command of all Marianas ground troops, planned to attack Saipan on June 15. Three days later Guam would be assaulted. Tinian would be taken a few days after the fall of Saipan. That was the over-all plan.

The plan for Saipan called for a two-division assault on the island's western side just south of the coastal city of Garapan. The left or northern beach would be hit by units of the Second Marine Division, now commanded by Major General Thomas Watson, who had earned his second star after Eniwetok. The Fourth Division, still led by the Stolid Dutchman—Major General Harry Schmidt—would strike the right or southern beach. In reserve would be the Army's 27th Infantry Division under Major General Ralph Smith.

While some 700 amtracks carried the assaulting battalions ashore, another force drawn from the Second Division would make a feint at the heavily defended beaches north of Garapan.

Four days before this attacking force dropped anchors off Saipan the planes and guns of the fast carrier fleet began striking the culminating blows of the preliminary bombardment. Three days later, on June 14, the carrier force sent two

314

smaller groups racing north to pin down enemy aerial strength at Iwo Jima and at Chichi Jima and Haha Jima in the Bonins.

That same June 14 Admiral Chuichi Nagumo changed his mind. "The Marianas," he wrote, "are the first line of defense of our homeland. It is a certainty that the Americans will land in the Marianas Group either this month or the next."

But a tank officer named Tokuzo Matsuya figured the ships offshore meant something more immediate and he filled his diary with bitter lamentation.

"Where are our planes?" he wrote. "Are they letting us die without making any effort to save us? If it were for the security of the Empire we would not hesitate to lay down our lives, but wouldn't it be a great loss to the 'Land of the Gods' for us all to die on this island? It would be easy for me to die, but for the sake of the future I feel obligated to stay alive."

And on June 14 the commander of Task Force 58, Vice Admiral Marc Mitscher, got off an exuberant message characteristic of all bombardiers or artillerists captivated by the sound and fury of their cannonading.

"Keep coming, Marines!" he signaled. "They're going to run away!"

2

Saipan burned fitfully beneath a drifting pall of smoke, and yet, she did not seem menacing. She was, along with Tinian, absolutely ringed round by American warships. They sailed back and forth, firing, and some of them lay in the strait between Saipan and Tinian to hurl broadsides at Saipan's southern tip. Others in the strait fired along the beaches which would shortly be swarming with American Marines.

Yet, Saipan was silent, almost dreamlike. The western

beaches were quiet. The peak of 1,554-foot Mount Tapotchau seemed to float on a sea of smoke in the middle of the island. Behind the landing beaches, in their center, the ruined village of Charan Kanoa smoldered, and the blackened smokestack of a wrecked sugar mill seemed to cleave the air like a marker dividing the front. Far to the left, upcoast, lay the city of Garapan, marked only by an occasional ray of sunshine glinting off roofs of corrugated iron.

Above Garapan the Marines of the diversionary force had boarded their landing boats. They were roaring inshore, naval gunfire breathing heavily overhead. They were drawing off a regiment of General Saito's force—but no more. The aged defender of Saipan had guessed that the true effort was coming at Charan Kanoa's beaches, and he had prepared his artillery for it. His guns were emplaced behind Mount Fina Susa, the ridge overlooking Charan Kanoa. They were firing with skill, for they had the water between beaches and reef thoroughly registered, and they had sown it with little colored flags to mark the range.

Counterbattery shells screamed seaward. *Tennessee* was hit. Shells burst on the decks of the cruiser *Indianapolis*, the flagship of Admiral Spruance. But the American warships lashed back. Dive-bombers shrieked down on both islands. The shore batteries were silenced, a flight of 161 Navy bombers came down a staircase of clouds to pound Charan Kanoa once more—and the LST's had run in close to the fringing reef and were disgorging amtracks filled with Marines, discharging also those amphibious tanks or "armored pigs" which would lead the assault in flaming V's.

Halfway inside the 1,500-yard run to the beach the amtracks began to take hits. Officers and men could almost guess the caliber of the next enemy barrage by the color of the flags they passed.

On the right sector attacked by the Fourth Marine Division, riflemen were vaulting from the amtracks and running in low toward Charan Kanoa. Shells were exploding among them. Some of the combat teams remained aboard their amtracks, fighting from them as they swayed inland. But the amtracks were targets for the enemy artillery, as were the

316

SAIPAN
(See Central Pacific Map)

Marpi Point

Tanapag Harbor.
Tanapag Plain

NORTH

Garapan.
SUGARLOAF HILL
The Pimples

MT. TIPO PALE
MT. TAPOTCHAU
DEATH VALLEY

PACIFIC OCEAN

Landing Beaches

HILL 600

Afetna Point
HILL 500
Lake Susupe
Charan Kanoa
MT. FINA SUSA

Kagman Peninsula

MAGICIENNE BAY

Agingan Point

Aslito Airfield (Isely Field)

L.X.

Yards
0   5000

Nafutan Point

amtanks, and soon the Marines preferred to advance on foot toward Charan Kanoa.

On their right, at the southernmost beaches, the assault of the Twenty-fifth Marines had split up into squad-to-squad battles. Lieutenant Fred Harvey led his platoon up the beach. A Japanese officer rushed him, swinging his saber. Harvey parried with his carbine, jumped back and shot his assailant dead. A Marine fell and Harvey seized the man's M-1. With other Marines he closed on three Japanese in a shellhole. Harvey's M-1 jammed. He drove in slashing with the bayonet. A grenade landed. Harvey hit the deck, the explosion picked him up and slammed him down again. He arose helmetless to help finish off the enemy.

So the battle raged, moving steadily inland through the wrecked village, moving over gently rising hills made labyrinthine by hidden caves, spider holes and interconnected dugouts. The Marines and Japanese fought each other among bleating goats, lowing oxen, mooing cows and scampering, clucking chickens. Soon the Japanese soldiers began to fall back behind Mount Fina Susa, and then their artillery fire increased.

On the left the Second Marine Division passed through a rhythmical, flashing hell of artillery and mortars. Every 25 yards, every fifteen seconds of their ride to the beaches, a shell exploded among the amtracks. On Afetna Point in the center of the landing beaches an antiboat gun began clanging. Shore batteries opened up again. Close-in destroyers roared back at them, silencing them. But there were amtracks smoking and burning, there were bloody Marines writhing on their twisted decks. And the antiboat gun was driving the amtracks farther and farther north, forcing some of the battalions to land on the wrong beaches.

Within a few minutes of the arrival of the Marines on the leftward beaches, every one of the commanders of the four assault battalions had become a casualty. Lieutenant Colonel Raymond Murray of the Second Battalion, Sixth, was so seriously wounded he had to be evacuated. Jim Crowe was also badly hit.

The big flamboyant redhead, now a lieutenant colonel, became separated from his men as his Second Battalion, Eighth landed by mistake on another battalion's beach. At half-past nine he moved along the shore with his runner, Corporal William Donitaley. They were fired at by enemy snipers.

Crowe slumped to the earth struck by a bullet which pierced

318

his left lung below the heart and smashed a rib as it came out. Donitaley fell thrashing in a bush, his left side punctured near the kidney. He thought he was dying.

"I'm hit pretty bad, sir," Donitaley gasped. "I guess I'm a goner."

"Goddam it," Crowe spluttered. "Don't talk like that, boy." The act of speaking had caused hot air to puff from Crowe's punctured lung, and he felt blood continuing to gush from his side. Jim Crowe also thought he was a goner.

"I guess they got me too, boy," he choked.

"Goddam it, sir," said Donitaley. "Don't talk like that."

They lay in the bushes, aware of the grim comedy of their exchange, their wounds multiplying under showers of shrapnel thrown down by Japanese artillery treebursts, until they were found nearly an hour later and brought back to an aid station. A corpsman and Doctor Otto Jantan attempted to fix them up, but Japanese shellfire killed the corpsman and wounded the doctor. Crowe was taken out to a transport, where a young surgeon began to cut away his blood-stained clothing.

"Before you do anything else, Doc," Crowe said, "cut off that hanging thumbnail."

"Be quiet, Colonel," the doctor hissed. "You're a very sick man."

"Sick man, hell!" Crowe croaked. "Cut off that thumbnail. It's damned annoying."

The doctor obliged, probably because he wished to humor a man who hadn't much chance to live. But Crowe did live—and his battalion was re-formed by that soft-voiced Major William Chamberlin who was his very opposite. Chamberlin's men wheeled to their right to strike south at Afetna Point, blasting away with shotguns issued especially for close-in fighting. They knocked out the antiboat gun and also reduced those batteries which covered the reef channel where the tanks had been held up.

But by nightfall Afetna Point had not fallen. It was a Japanese pocket almost in the center of the beachhead.

About 1,200 yards behind it, near Lake Susupe, the "armored pigs" were engaging enemy tanks for the first time.

★

Sergeants Ben Livesey and Onel Dickens had halted the amtanks they commanded on the crest of a little, tree-shaded hill. It was ten in the morning and the men were hungry. They jumped out, heated their cans of C-rations, opened them and began to eat.

They heard firing.

Below their hill three Japanese tanks were rolling toward a trio of Marine amtracks mired in the muck of Lake Susupe swamp. The Japanese were between the amtankers and the trapped Marines.

The amtankers jumped back into their armored pigs, buttoned down the turrets and went rocking down the hill and up the road on the Japanese tanks' tail. The Japanese wheeled. One of them stalled.

The 75 in Dickens' tank roared. Flame gushed from the stalled enemy. Then Livesey's 75 spoke. The middle tank jumped and spun off the road. Side by side, Livesey and Dickens moved up on the remaining tank and shot its treads away. The amtank turrets popped open. The Marines jumped out with rifles in hand, and the surviving Japanese crewmen were put to death.

With the Marines they had rescued, Livesey and Dickens returned to their hillcrest. For the rest of the day, the Lake Susupe region was left alone.

Back on the beaches the accuracy of Japanese artillery fire was crowding medical aid stations with casualties. Never before had the Marines encountered such deadly artillery fire, and with about 8,000 men put ashore by nine o'clock in the morning, there was a plenitude of targets for the enemy gunners.

Within the Fourth Division's zone, men dug foxholes to shelter the wounded. One man was brought in with his leg almost blown off between hip and knee. A battalion surgeon amputated it without bothering to remove him from his stretcher. Two more stretcher cases came in, one a private, the other an old-time sergeant. The private said he had to relieve himself. A corpsman seized the sergeant's helmet and handed it to the private. It was the ultimate violation of authority and the sergeant watched in helpless fury, raging:

"That I should live to see the day when a private should do that in my helmet!"

They were taken, both violated and violator, out to the reef and there transferred to landing boats. From there they went to hospital transports already stuffed with wounded and preparing to pull up anchors and sail away. By nightfall the Second Division alone had 238 men killed and 1,022 wounded —and of 355 reported missing few would be found alive. The Fourth Division, though not so badly hit, had already exceeded its casualty rate for the Roi-Namur campaign.

But by nightfall there were something like 20,000 Marines ashore on Saipan. They held a beachhead about four miles wide from its northern down to its southern flank and a mile at its deepest inland or eastern penetration. Within the perimeter, which had both flanks bent back to the sea, were tanks and artillery, as well as Generals Watson and Schmidt, both of whom came ashore in the afternoon.

However, neither division had reached its first day's objective. The Afetna Point pocket still stood between both divisions at the sea, and there was another bulge inland in the unconquered Lake Susupe region.

Among the men, the veterans had ceased comparing Saipan to other battles and were rating it on its own merits. It was clear that Saipan was going to be a thing of dirt and strain, of heat and thirst, of clouds of flies, of clanging steel and splintering rock. It would be a point-by-point advance against an invisible, dogged, slowly retreating enemy—a foe who had already mystified them by whisking away his dead.

So they lay down that night in the ruins of the sugar refinery with which the fast battleships had had such aimless sport—failing even to kill its single occupant, that valorous Japanese soldier who hid in its chimney to call down artillery on the enemy Marines—or they lay down in the muck and stench of pigpens and chicken runs, on the hot smoldering earth of the blackened canebrakes, under the guns of Mount Fina Susa, and beneath the bursting, crashing glare of their own star-shells, illumination so brilliant that it seemed to make the bougainvillaea trees things of airy flame.

Opposite them the enemy was stirring. The counterattack

was preparing. The men of Lieutenant General Yoshitsugu Saito were in high spirits. For everyone in the Marianas seemed to know that the Combined Fleet was coming to the rescue. Admiral Nagumo had told General Saito so. As far away as Guam, Lieutenant Rai Imanishi was writing in his diary: "The Combined Fleet is about to engage the enemy in decisive combat. . . . The enemy has already begun landing on Saipan. Truly, we are on the threshold of momentous occurrences. Now is the time for me to offer my life for the great cause and be a barrier against the enemy advancing in the Pacific Ocean."

Although he would have to wait a month or more for his chance on Guam, Lieutenant Imanishi was right. The Combined Fleet was indeed coming. Admiral Soemu Toyoda had bitten hard on the Saipan bait.

3

On the morning of June 15 the word of the Saipan invasion was flashed by Nagumo to Admiral Toyoda at his headquarters on Japan's Inland Sea. At five minutes to nine that morning, Admiral Toyoda sent this message to all his commanders:

> The Combined Fleet will attack the enemy in the Marianas area and annihilate the invasion force.

Five minutes later, suddenly mindful that it was close to the thirty-ninth anniversary of Admiral Togo's destruction of the Russian fleet at Tsushima, Toyoda bethought himself of the immortal Togo's words on that occasion and flashed them to the Combined Fleet:

The fate of the Empire rests on this one battle. Every man is expected to do his utmost.

It was, to the Japanese mind, the tocsin of total battle. It brought the carriers of Admiral Jisaburo Ozawa up from Tawi Tawi to the narrow waters of San Bernardino Strait, bound for their Philippine Sea rendezvous with a battleship force led by Vice Admiral Matome Ugaki. It brought the Japanese fleet out fighting for the first time since Guadalcanal. Exhilarated by the great news, the Japanese on Saipan attacked all along the line. From dark until dawn there was hardly a moment when enemy shells were not falling on the Marines or the enemy was not probing for the weak spot against which he would launch his full fury. At about eight o'clock on the night of June 15, the Japanese thought they had found a hole on the front held by the command-riddled Second Battalion, Sixth.

At that time, the Japanese began moving down the coastal road from Garapan. They came in columns of platoons, riding tanks, trucks, anything that rolled—coming with the customary clamor of a traveling circus. At ten o'clock they were close enough to attack. Flags were unfurled. *Samurai* sabers flashed and glinted in the moonlight. Someone made a speech. A bugle blared—and the Japanese charged.

A Marine officer picked up a telephone and spoke two words:

"Illumination requested."

It came so swiftly it stunned the Japanese. They had not calculated on the American warships still cruising up and down the west coast. They found themselves outlined from their puttee-taped ankles to the round tops of their mushroom helmets, and they were rapidly cut to pieces in a horizontal hail of bullets, cannister shot, mortar and bazooka shell fragments. They broke and fell back, and then the naval gunfire and Marine artillery burst among them.

The counterattack downroad from Garapan cost General Saito 700 soldiers. It also cost him Garapan, for in the morning General Watson asked the warships and planes to flatten this enemy staging place.

General Saito's plans for driving a wedge into the gap between the Marine divisions was also doomed. Some 200 Japanese who emerged from the gloom of Lake Susupe and struck for the Charan Kanoa pier collided with the men of Lieutenant Colonel John Cosgrove's Third Battalion, Twenty-third. They were destroyed. So also was a three-tank attack launched down the Garapan road just before daylight. June 16 dawned with the Marines still holding what they had seized the day before and preparing to expand it. That same day Admiral Spruance hauled back on the line holding the Saipan bait.

Spruance knew that Ozawa had sortied from Tawi Tawi. Throughout the afternoon and night of D-Day he had been receiving submarine reports of the Japanese approach. At half-past four the sub *Flying Fish* sighted the Japanese carriers debouching from San Bernardino Strait into the Philippine Sea, making dead west for Saipan. An hour later *Seahorse* spotted Ugaki's battleships racing north to the rendezvous area.

On the morning of June 16, Spruance conferred with Admiral Turner and General Holland Smith aboard Turner's flagship *Rocky Mount*. He ordered Mitscher's Task Force 58 to intercept the Japanese, postponed the Guam invasion, promised Smith only two more days of unloading operations, launched prolonged air searches for the enemy, and alerted the old battleships to make nocturnal patrols 25 miles west of Saipan to block any Japanese ships which might elude Mitscher.

In the meantime the escort carriers would continue to give the Marines on Saipan aerial cover and Smith would commit the 27th Division that very day. The conquest of the island was to be pushed forward as rapidly as possible.

Satisfied, Spruance prepared to return to his own flagship *Indianapolis*. Smith stopped him.

"Do you think the Japs will turn and run?"

"No," Spruance said. "Not now. They're out after big game. If they'd wanted something easy, they'd have gone after MacArthur's operation at Biak. But the attack on the Marianas is too great a challenge for the Japanese Navy to ignore."

That attack was going forward with the Second Battalion, Eighth, and the orphan First Battalion, Twenty-ninth Marines, slugging steadily through the Afetna Point pocket. By noon they had cleared it and secured Charan Kanoa pier.

On the right, the Fourth Division's artillery fired shell for shell with the Japanese while General Schmidt marshaled his regiments for a noon attack. With 15 batteries of the Fourteenth Marines ashore, it should have been the pushover that artillery duels with the Japanese had always been. But it was not. Four batteries were knocked out, although the ingenuity of the Division Ordnance Company had them back firing before dusk. One howitzer named *Belching Beauty* took a direct hit which killed or wounded every member of the crew but one. *Belching Beauty* was repaired and firing an hour later. Two others were blown to bits, and the ordnance man gathered up the pieces and made a new gun from them.

Gradually, the Marine artillery asserted its superiority. One by one, the enemy guns were silenced, the last of their rounds killing Lieutenant Colonel Maynard Schultz while he waited at the Twenty-fourth Regiment's CP to receive instructions for his First Battalion's attack.

At half-past twelve the Fourth Division moved out. It slugged ahead slowly. The battalion commanders began calling for tanks. As the Shermans moved up to the front, the Japanese 75's erupted again.

The platoon of Shermans led by Gunnery Sergeant Bob McCard ran into the concentrated fire of an entire battery of 75's. Almost instantly, McCard's tank was cut off from the others and crippled by the converging shells of four enemy guns. McCard battled back with the tank's 75 and machine guns. But the Japanese 75's had the range now. The Sherman was done for.

"Take off!" McCard roared at his crew. "Out the escape hatch!"

One by one, the crewmen lowered themselves through the hatch in the tank's floor, scuttling to safety while McCard hurled grenades from the opened turret. Machine-gun fire raked the tank, wounding McCard. The Japanese charged.

McCard seized a machine gun and faced them a second time alone. He shot 16 of them before they killed him.

The other Marine tanks returned. The stand which won McCard the Medal of Honor had also won the time to coordinate the attack. It went forward, slowly, but by dusk the Marines' lines were firm all along the beachhead. The Fourth Division had a penetration of 2,000 yards across its 4,000-yard front. The Second Division had contented itself with cleaning out the Afetna Point gap, with patrolling, and with consolidating its own left flank facing north toward Garapan. It was well. At dusk, while the 27th Division's 165th Infantry began to come ashore, Lieutenant General Saito ordered the first night tank attack of the Pacific War.

It would strike the left flank sector held by the Jones boy named Bill.

"He may be only twenty-seven, but he's the best damn battalion commander in this division—or any other division."

That was what Colonel Jim Riseley of the Sixth Marines thought of the commander of his First Battalion, Lieutenant Colonel Bill Jones, the Marine Corps' youngest field commander and one so at home in battle he could tell his men, "I'd rather command a battalion in combat than sleep with Hedy Lamarr." Jones was the brother of Captain Jim Jones, whose Recon Boys were then assigned the unglorious mission of guarding the Corps CP in the rear, and he delighted in warning his officers that they must stand at all costs, "because if my brother gets hurt, Mother will never forgive me." This night of June 16-17 they would have to stand against the full brunt of Colonel Hideki Goto's 9th Tank Regiment.

Up in the blackened rubble that was once the city of Garapan, Colonel Goto unbuttoned the turret of his regiment's leading tank. He stood erect. He raised his saber and flourished it over his head. The turrets of the following tanks came open. The commanders, among them that Tokuzo Matsuya who had written so fiercely in his diary two days before, stood erect. They flourished their sabers.

Colonel Goto struck the side of his tank a resounding clank.

His junior officers spurred their metal-mounts forward with similar saber-slaps. The turrets were closed.

The 9th Tank Regiment swept forward.

"Colonel," said Captain Claude Rollen, "it sounds like a tank attack coming. Request illumination."

"Right," said Lieutenant Colonel Jones, and passed the request for illumination back to Colonel Riseley. Then he notified a medium tank company to stand by and got bazookamen from A Company moving over to Captain Rollen's sector. That was at half-past three.

Fifteen minutes later the squeaking, rattling Japanese mediums—the "kitchen sinks" as the Marines called them—burst into Rollen's sector in two waves.

The first wave carried riflemen or light machine-gunners sprawled on the long trunk of the engine compartment or hanging on to the guide rails like firemen. Crewmen led the tanks forward on foot, although here and there a commander stood erect in an open turret, shouting orders and flashing his saber in the crashing glare of the star-shells. Behind the second wave of tanks the bulk of Colonel Ogawa's 136th Infantry Regiment came trotting forward.

The tanks drove into a roaring cauldron of explosions and flashing light. As they were hit and set afire they illuminated other tanks farther back. Sometimes the tanks to the rear stopped. An officer jumped out, waved his saber, made a speech, and climbed back in again. A bugle blared. The tanks came on and the Marine bazookamen tore them apart. Sharpshooters such as Pfc. Herbert Hodges had seven rockets for his bazooka, enough for him to knock out seven tanks. Private Bob Reed got four with four shots, and then, running out of ammunition, he got a fifth by jumping aboard it and dropping in a grenade.

Some of the enemy tanks got in. Two of them rolled over a pair of 60-millimeter mortar positions. Another came up on Captain Rollen, and a rifleman-rider fired just as Rollen attached a grenade to his carbine. The bullet detonated the grenade—and Rollen fell, pinked with shrapnel, his eardrums shattered.

327

Captain Thomas came up to take his place, the same Norman Thomas who had held off the Jap *banzai* on Tarawa. A fourth tank raced up. Its riders shot Thomas dead. They turned to take Sergeant Dean Squires under fire.

But Squires had already blown off the head of the tank's commander. He followed through by tossing a satchel charge in the open turret, finishing both tank and riders.

A fifth Japanese tank penetrated as far back as Colonel Riseley's command post. The commander of the Sixth Regiment had been sitting on a tree stump, smoking a cigar while he watched the battle.

The tank rattled closer. Colonel Riseley removed his cigar.

"Son," he called to his regimental clerk, "get me a bazooka."

Before the man could obey, a Marine half-track clattered up on the tank and set it aflame with its first shell. Thereafter the half-tracks roved like wolves among the Japanese tanks. Each time they fired, a tank burned—until close to 30 had been knocked out. The others fled, and the last of these was sighted going up a distant hill. Its turret could be seen moving among a cluster of houses. The Marines gave the range to an offshore destroyer.

The destroyer fired 20 salvos and the tank burned for the rest of the day—sending up a cloud of oily smoke to mark the limit of the battleground where General Saito had lost another 700 foot soldiers as well as Colonel Goto and most of the 9th Tank Regiment he commanded.

Tokuzo Matsuya had not been killed. He had survived to fill his diary with another lament: "The remaining tanks in our regiment make a total of 12. Even if there are not tanks, we will fight hand to hand. I have resolved that, if I see the enemy, I will take out my sword and slash, slash, slash at him as long as I last, thus ending my life of twenty-four years."

It was no boast but a prediction, and by the morning of the third day there were already 3,500 Marine casualties to give it force. June 17 brought more than 500 more casualties in a slow, gouging attack which extended the beachhead north about a thousand yards and up to 2,000 yards east or inland. The inland successes, however, also served to lengthen the Lake Susupe bulge between divisions. The Japanese had hidden in Susupe's marshes, and the Marines who went in after them with heavy machine guns and mortars sank up to their waists in muck. It would be many days before Lake Susupe was cleared.

On the right or southern front the Fourth Division's gains were followed by the entry of the 165th Infantry on the Marine right flank. The 165th would attack Aslito Airfield in southern Saipan the following day.

On the extreme edge of the left or northern flank, the Second Marines under Colonel Walter Stuart moved cautiously upcoast in a column of battalions until a point 1,000 yards below Garapan had been reached. They were to sit there until southern Saipan had been cleaned out.

Out on the ocean Kelly Turner was already taking the transports and cargo ships away from Saipan to empty blue seas many, many miles to the south and east. There they joined all the ships and men of the Guam invasion force, circling, circling, circling, to the extreme disgust of the troops, until word arrived of the victory or defeat of Mitscher's Task Force 58.

And at a point about 500 miles west of the Philippines, the fleets of Admiral Ozawa and Ugaki rendezvoused and refueled, and were now streaking east for Saipan, their scout planes conducting searches many hundreds of miles before and around them, hunting for the American fleet.

Tracking the Japanese for Admiral Spruance was a submarine called *Cavalla*. She was making her first cruise. She had sighted Ozawa's carriers astern at dusk. Commander Herman Kossler had quickly turned tail and put 15,000 yards between them and *Cavalla*. It turned dark, but Kossler could still see the vast silhouette of a monster carrier.

"Christ!" Kossler swore. "It looks like the Empire State Building."

Then Kossler had been forced to take *Cavalla* down. She submerged 100 feet and Kossler and his men tried to count the screws of the ships passing overhead in a half-hour-long procession. They counted 15, but Kossler thought that was too low.

Cavalla surfaced and got off her report to Spruance. She

went down again for two hours. When she surfaced, shortly before midnight, she had lost contact.

On Saipan in the early morning of June 18 the Japanese had received a message from Premier Hideki Tojo. It said:

> Because the fate of the Japanese Empire depends on the result of your operation, you must inspire the spirit of the officers and men and to the very end continue to destroy the enemy gallantly and persistently. Thus alleviate the anxiety of our Emperor.

Back flashed the message of Colonel Takuji Suzuki, the 43rd Division's chief of staff. It said:

> Have received your honorable Imperial words and we are grateful for boundless magnanimity of Imperial favor. By becoming the bulwark of the Pacific with 10,000 deaths we hope to requite the Imperial favor.

At daylight, Lieutenant General Saito began burning his secret documents preparatory to moving his headquarters farther north from the American invaders even then breaking out of their beachhead.

By the night of July 18 the Fourth Marine Division had struck straight across the island to the shores of Magicienne Bay—"Magazine Bay" as it would be forever called—while beneath them the 27th Division's 165th Infantry had overrun Aslito Airfield.

All was gradually shaping up for the drive to the north planned by Lieutenant General Howlin' Mad Smith, who had set up headquarters at Charan Kanoa the day before. Smith now had three divisions on Saipan and he hoped to attack to the north on a three-division, cross-island front. He already had seen to the emplacement of his corps artillery—30 155-millimeter "long toms" and howitzers which would fire in support of the assault—but he would not launch the clean-up drive until Mount Tapotchau in the center of the island was seized.

★

Cavalla was going down again. A night-flying Japanese plane had sighted the American sub and Commander Kossler was submerging. It was three o'clock in the morning of June 19.

At seven o'clock *Cavalla* was up again—but once more an enemy plane spotted her and drove her down. Something was stirring. Kossler could guess it from the number of enemy planes abroad. At ten o'clock he brought *Cavalla* up. Again the Japanese planes menaced him.

Cavalla went down. Kossler decided to wait fifteen minutes. . . .

Albacore was cruising at periscope depth and Commander J. W. Blanchard was peering into the glass.

He started. There was a big carrier, a cruiser and the tops of other ships about seven miles away—and that carrier was big! It was *Taiho*, the carrier Commander Kossler had first sighted and the biggest flattop that Japan was able to float. She was 33,000 tons, brand-new, and she flew the eight-rayed, single-banded flag of Admiral Ozawa. She was launching planes, for Ozawa's attack on the Americans was already begun.

Commander Blanchard retracted his periscope and made plans to attack. He calculated the range and ordered a spread of six torpedoes prepared. Then something went wrong with the torpedo data computer. The "Correct Solution" light refused to flash—and *Taiho* was fast moving out of range.

Blanchard upped periscope and fired by sight.

Then he sent *Albacore* plunging down deep and awaited the arrival of both the enemy destroyers and the sound of a torpedo explosion.

They came swiftly—three destroyers and one great explosion.

Blanchard was disappointed. He could never hope to sink the biggest enemy carrier he had ever seen with a single torpedo.

The quarter-hour had passed and *Cavalla* was up to periscope depth.

There were four planes on the starboard bow. But they did not molest *Cavalla*. Kossler watched. He saw the mast of a de-

331

stroyer over the horizon. He moved to his right. He saw the mast of a carrier. She was taking on planes. She was not as big as the monster he had seen last night, but she would still rate around the 22,000-ton *Shokaku* class. Wanting to be sure she was Japanese, Kossler came in closer.

"Goddam!" he exploded when the ship's flag came into view. "It's the Rising Sun—big as hell!"

Cavalla began firing torpedoes. She got four off in rapid succession and another pair as she began to submerge.

Going down, Kossler heard three of his fish hit. And then he heard and felt the wrath of the Japanese depth-charges. For two hours the enemy worked *Cavalla* over, while above the surface mighty *Shokaku* was a holocaust of burning gasoline and exploding bombs.

At about three o'clock in the afternoon *Cavalla's* sound gear picked up monstrous water noises. Kossler and his crewmen heard great concussions.

"That damn thing is sinking," Kossler said.

He was right. One of *Shokaku's* bomb magazines had exploded and the big ship fell apart and sank.

A single torpedo hit did not alarm Admiral Ozawa, nor should it have. *Taiho* was much too big, much too modern, to be so easily knocked out.

But aboard her was a damage-control officer who was not very experienced, and after *Albacore's* fish had ruptured one of *Taiho's* gasoline tanks, the damage-control officer ordered all ventilating ducts turned on full blast while the ship tore ahead at 26 knots. He hoped to blow the fumes away, but he only succeeded in distributing them. He filled *Taiho* with gasoline fumes, and also the vapors of the crude petroleum then being used for fuel, and he turned her into an enormous floating gas-bomb. All that was needed was friction.

It came at half-past three. *Taiho's* flight deck blew up, her hangar sides blew out and her bottom blew down. She rolled over on her left side and sank by the stern, taking with her many airplanes and all but 500 of her 2,150 officers and men. Among those who survived were Admiral Ozawa and his staff.

Carrying the admiral's flag and a framed portrait of the

Emperor, Ozawa and his staff were ferried by lifeboat to the destroyer *Wakatsuki*. From there Ozawa moved to *Zuikaku,* and it was aboard this carrier that he received the first of those terrible reports that bore upon his head like hammer blows. Not only was *Taiho* lost and *Shokaku* sunk, but his airplanes and aviators were being torn to bits in the battles which the Americans would derisively name "The Marianas Turkey Shoot." That day alone Ozawa lost 330 planes, against 30 American craft destroyed—the most resounding single day's defeat in the history of aerial warfare. Next day he lost a third carrier, *Hiyo*, plus two tankers, and seven more of his ships were damaged. The airfields on Guam were turned into rubble by the American bombers. He himself was forced to flee toward Okinawa, with Admiral Ugaki following.

There was no rescue at Saipan. In the log of the commander who opened battle June 19 with 430 aircraft on his decks, there was this ominous entry on the night of June 20:

"Surviving carrier air power: 35 aircraft operational."

The disaster had been even greater. With scout planes and land-based air losses added in, Japan's defeat in the Battle of the Philippine Sea totaled 476 airplanes destroyed and 445 aviators killed. American losses were three ships damaged and 130 planes lost—80 of these during night landings at the conclusion of the pursuit of the Japanese—and 76 airmen dead.

No nation had ever been so badly beaten in the skies. But Tokyo was already telling the world of the customary magnificent victory, just as Lieutenant General Saito had been telling Tokyo of the splendid successes being scored in the hot, shell-blasted hills south of Mount Tapotchau.

4

During the first four days of the fighting on Saipan it was a rare Marine who had not felt himself slammed to earth by concussion or had not heard the whine of flying steel and rock or the nasty peening of the bullets, for the Japanese holding the foothills masking Mount Tapotchau in central Saipan were fighting with tenacity and skill.

In those first four days the First Battalion, Sixth, lost all but two of its captains and Lieutenant Colonel Bill Jones concealed his grief in the grim joke that to save these two, "I guess I'd better bust 'em down to second looey."

In the Fourth Marine Division's sector, the eastern half of the island, a battered rifleman also made a sardonic estimate of the first ninety-six hours.

"Three times in the past four days," he said, "my wife has been almost a rich woman. I could see them counting out my insurance money ten dollars at a time and the wife riding downtown in a new Packard roadster with a spotlight on each side."

The following four days were equally harrowing, especially for the Third Battalion, Twenty-fifth Marines, under Lieutenant Colonel Justice Chambers.

Chambers was known as Jumpin' Joe for his exuberant style in the field. He looked a bit like a buccaneer, big and raw-boned, with a cut-down bayonet knife dangling from his cartridge belt alongside a .38 revolver stuck in a special quick-draw holster. Under his left armpit was a .45 shoulder holster. If it were not true that Jumpin' Joe had used these weapons, as a Raider captain under Red Mike Edson, at Kwajalein, and latterly on Saipan, the effect might have been a caricature of what is supposed to be a type of Marine commander.

But Jumpin' Joe was genuine, as were the men who called themselves Chambers' Raiders and who spent the last half of their eight days on the line overrunning the defenses around Hill 500. The hill was actually a clutter of rocky peaks which commanded most of southern Saipan and which also covered the approaches to Mount Tapotchau. It was about a mile inland ·from the eastern coast. It was pocked with caves filled with machine guns carefully sighted in on the flat, approaching plain.

Chambers got his men across the plain and up to the base of the hill by laying down a covering smokescreen. Before they attacked, the hill's defenses were showered by 4.5-inch rockets fired by rocket trucks, just appearing in the Pacific War. Then Chambers' men charged. Hunched, bent-over figures shadowy in the thinning smoke, they went up Hill 500 while artillery shells walked briskly up the slopes ahead of them. Six machine guns gathered in a single cave raked them, but by midafternoon they had taken Hill 500.

"We lost fifty men, but we came a'hellin' and took our objective," Jumpin' Joe Chambers said.

Of these 50 casualties, only nine were killed, although there were more that night when the Japanese counterattacked, waving knives and bayonets lashed to poles—"idiot sticks" as the Marines called them.

In the morning Lieutenant Colonel Evans Carlson joined the battalion as a division observer while Jumpin' Joe led his men farther north toward Tapotchau. In two days they had overrun Hill 500's peaks and were debouching into a valley beyond.

There they walked into a trap. Machine guns to either side began chattering and mortars could be seen rising from a clump of woods to the front. Pfc. Vito Cassaro, Chambers' radioman, was hit almost immediately. Chambers and Carlson went out to rescue him and bullets made smacking sounds in someone's flesh.

"I'm hit," Carlson gasped.

The famous Raider leader had been shot in the leg and another bullet had shattered an arm. He was dragged to safety, along with Cassaro, and placed on a stretcher.

"Last time I was wounded was the First World War," he told Chambers. "If I can keep 'em that far apart I'll be all right."

He was carried to the rear, still chomping on his foul pipe while he dictated a memo covering the location of a new division command post. Behind him, as Chambers' Marines pulled out of the valley pocket, it was seen that there was still a wounded man lying out in the open. He was unconscious. His crumpled body made a fine aiming reference for the Japanese gunners in the woods beyond. Each time someone crawled out for him, a spate of bullets drove him back.

Then the tanks arrived. A Sherman commanded by Lieutenant Robert Stevenson lumbered out into the valley with bullets spanging harmlessly off its steel hide. The Sherman straddled the unconscious Marine. It rolled forward and obscured him.

"Open the escape hatch and drag him in," Stevenson ordered.

It was done, the man was saved—and the other tanks joined Stevenson to lead the advance. Half-tracks and 37's also came up. The emplaced Japanese began to withdraw.

"Come get us, Marines," they cried.

"Take your time, boys," the Marines replied. "We will."

The Japanese began blowing up positions and supplies. They blew up an ammunition dump near the battalion CP and the blast knocked Jumpin' Joe Chambers unconscious.

He was taken to the rear while Major Jim Taul took command, but the moment Chambers had regained consciousness he was on his feet and demanding the return of his weapons.

"But you can't go back there, sir," said the battalion surgeon. "You're a casualty."

"Casualty, hell!" Jumpin' Joe exploded. "You'll have to lock me up if you want to keep me here."

Chambers returned to his battalion, but to his ill-concealed annoyance, and to the unconcealed delight of Major Taul, the objective had already been taken. All along the line by late afternoon of June 22, the Fourth Division had gained 2,000 yards. On the left the Second Division held half of Mount Tipo Pale and was prepared to strike Mount Tapotchau itself about 600 yards northeast.

By nightfall of this eighth day of battle about six of Saipan's 14 miles in length were in American hands. This represented most of the southern half of the island, although there was still a Japanese pocket down at Nafutan Point on the southernmost tip of the east coast. The Japanese on Nafutan—about 500 of them—had been bypassed in the rush to take Aslito Airfield. They were now hemmed in by the 27th Division's 105th Infantry, which was preparing to clean out the point.

Elsewhere on Saipan the engineers had made rapid progress on improving the airfield—now called Isely Field after the Navy flier who was killed in preinvasion attacks on it—and they were hauling supplies from the Charan Kanoa beachhead about three miles to the northwest by means of a narrow-gauge railway formerly employed in the Charan Kanoa sugar industry. Isely Field was fit to receive squadrons of Army P-47 Thunderbolts assigned to Saipan combat patrol and scheduled to arrive the following day. Out on the bay the battleship *Maryland* was holed on her port side by a Japanese aerial torpedo strike launched the afternoon of June 22. She would have to return to Pearl Harbor.

The next day, June 23, the three-division attack to the north planned by Howlin' Mad Smith at last got going. The 27th Division—less its 105th Infantry still south at Nafutan Point —went into the line between the Second Marine Division on the left and the Fourth on the right.

The Fourth again made good gains, although the attack was still a matter of climbing another mountain to behold another mountain. The division's chief objective this day was Hill 600, guarding the entrance to Kagman Peninsula, which stretched east into Magicienne Bay for about three miles. The Marines of the Fourth took Hill 600 and renamed it Hot Potato Hill for the fierce hand-grenade fight which won it. Then they swerved right or east to bite deep into Kagman Peninsula. They could have gone farther, but the 27th Division in the center was unable to move because of resistance met in a crackling lowland called Death Valley. The Fourth halted and dug in, for the lag in the center had exposed its left.

On the left of the three-division front the Second Division's Marines began struggling up the cruel steeps of Mount Tapotchau—blundering through a jumble of limestone crags, lava heads and coral ridges, gullies, gulches and ravines, all piled one upon another as though kicked together, all exposed to the direct rays of a hot sun. All around Tapotchau were caves and subterranean forts from which Japanese artillery had attempted to destroy the Marines on the beaches. The short tan men of Nippon were still fighting from these, at closer, more accurate range now, and still invisibly.

Against them, against the slashing madness of Tapotchau itself, came the Sixth and Eighth Marine Regiments. They came without tanks, jeeps or bulldozers—for there was not even so much as a trail up the mountainside. They came warily, sending out probing patrols, waiting for the sound of firing which would signal that the patrol had found the enemy, and then going forward on foot, climbing.

But they advanced. And then, finding their right flank exposed by the 27th's failure to make any appreciable gains, they too halted and dug in.

In the morning both the Second and the Fourth Marine Divisions moved out. But the 27th in the center was again slow, again unable to get through Death Valley. For the second straight day the attack was slowed down, and Lieutenant General Holland Smith relieved Major General Ralph Smith of his command of the 27th Division. The Army's Major General Sanderford Jarman, who was to have been Saipan's military governor, took Ralph Smith's place. The pace of the attack began to quicken, but by nightfall there were still long vertical gaps between the Marine divisions ahead on the flanks and the 27th behind them in the center.

That night the Japanese counterattacked the Second Division's front in the Tapotchau hills, coming in greatest strength against a machine-gun post held by Pfc. Harold Epperson with Corporal Malcom Jonah and Pfc. Edward Bailey. It was very dark. The Marines could barely make out the bulk of a dense wood about 50 yards away.

It was out of the wood that the Japanese came, running straight at Epperson's pit. The young gunner opened fire. The short shapes began to fall. One of them seemed to crumple right under the muzzle of the gun. Epperson fired on. Suddenly the figure under the gun came alive. The Japanese jumped up. He tossed a grenade into the pit.

Pfc. Epperson threw himself on it and was killed.

He had saved the lives of his comrades and they were able to fight on and break up the attack—and he had won a posthumous Medal of Honor.

The following day—June 25—Mount Tapotchau's peak was placed under direct assault.

Since June 22 the orphan First Battalion, Twenty-ninth, had been driving up a jumbled valley which ran between two ridges to Tapotchau's crest. They had fought forward under Lieutenant Colonel Rathvon (Tommy) Tompkins, who had taken over after Lieutenant Colonel Guy Tannyhill had been wounded. They had been joined by the Second Battalion, Eighth, led by Jim Crowe's executive, Major Chamberlin.

On June 25, Chamberlin and Tompkins conferred with Colonel Clarence Wallace, commander of the Eighth, and got up a plan to take Tapotchau.

While Tompkins' men went up the valley, Chamberlin's battalion was to attack along the ridge, where the bulk of enemy opposition could be expected.

But it was the valley that was nastiest. Tompkins' men ran into rough terrain and a stubborn enemy, while Chamberlin's Marines were moving swiftly along the heights, advancing as far as a 50-foot cliff which crowned Tapotchau like a top hat. Chamberlin sent a patrol up the cliff. The men returned with the report that the crest of Tapotchau seemed unoccupied.

The patrol's return coincided with the arrival of Tommy Tompkins from the valley below. He brought with him a platoon from the Division Scout Company, for he had become convinced that a frontal attack up the mountain was impossible. He took the Scouts up the steep side of Tapotchau's top hat. They were all but exhausted by the rigor of that climb, but at eleven o'clock in the morning there was no longer anything above them.

They broke into the clear, into the open where their helmets touched the sky, and all around them rolled the vast smoking, glinting, glittering, moving panorama of an ocean island under assault from the sea. They stood at almost the exact center of Saipan, with the northern extremity of Marpi Point on the west coast seven miles in front of them and the southern tip of Nafutan Point slanting the same distance to the rear on the east coast.

Tompkins ordered the Scouts to hold the crest while he returned to the valley to get his battalion. They occupied a 12-foot-square dugout abandoned by the enemy during the day's shelling. They fought from it to hold off repeated Japanese thrusts at them, while all around Tapotchau the ridges shook to furious Marine onslaught calculated to pin the Japanese main body down while Tompkins' men came up from the valley single-file.

At dusk, Tompkins and his men clawed their way up to the crest—where the Scouts had killed 40 Japanese while losing three of their own men. They, too, dug in. They hurled back the inevitable nocturnal counterattack, holding Tapotchau even as destroyers and rocket boats offshore shattered an attempt to reinforce southern Saipan by barge.

On the same night, Lieutenant General Saito began to tell Tokyo the truth about what was happening on his island. He signaled the chief of staff in Tokyo:

> Please apologize deeply to the Emperor that we cannot do better than we are doing. However, because of the units sunk at sea, the various forces have no fighting strength, although they do have large numbers.
>
> There is no hope for victory in places where we do not have control of the air and we are still hoping here for aerial reinforcements.
>
> Praying for the good health of the Emperor, we all cry, "Banzai!"

The aerial reinforcements for which Saito still hoped would never come. Only the day before, Vice Admiral Joseph (Jocko) Clark's carrier force had raided Iwo Jima and destroyed 95 fighters and bombers at a loss of six Hellcats. On the very day of Tapotchau's fall, June 25, another American carrier force struck hard at air bases on Guam and Rota.

There was nothing for this ailing and aged commander to do but to retreat north and await the end made so clearly inevitable to him by the constant presence of those circling, booming American warships.

5

The Japanese cornered on Nafutan Point were preparing to break out of the trap.

Since the capture of Isely Field on June 18, these 600 soldiers of the 47th Brigade's 317th Infantry Battalion had been holed up on their stern-browed peninsula—endlessly pounded by offshore American warships or battered by artillery supporting the American 105th Infantry blocking their escape route north. On the night of June 26, having eaten the last of their food and drunk their water, they prepared to make a break-out born of desperation. Their commanding officer, one Captain Sasaki, issued this final order:

"Casualties will remain in their present positions and defend Nafutan Point. Those who cannot participate in combat must commit suicide. The password for tonight will be *Shichi Sei Hokoku* [Seven Lives to Repay Our Country]."

Shortly after midnight, Sasaki's men slipped down from their high caves and stole through the outposts of the 105th Infantry. Many of them wore American uniforms, most of them were half-crazed with thirst—and all were bent on destroying Isely Field before wheeling east to Hill 500, where Captain Sasaki imagined brigade headquarters to be.

On Hill 500, most of Jumpin' Joe Chambers' men were already asleep.

The battalion had been placed in reserve, along with the remainder of the Twenty-fifth Marines, and ordered back to the hill they had captured on June 20.

Men such as Pfc. Tom McQuabe and Pfc. Bill Cramford—a BAR team holding down a foxhole outpost to the south or rear of Chambers' command post—could hear the sound of sporadic firing to the north and be grateful for the chance to rest behind the lines.

Captain Sasaki's band had gotten past the American soldiers. By two o'clock in the morning they had penetrated about a mile to the north. They blundered into the 2nd Battalion, 105th Infantry's command post and fought a savage close-in fight, inflicting 24 casualties on the soldiers while losing 27 of their own men. Then they swept on to Isely Field, reaching it a half-hour later.

The Japanese set one P-47 on fire and damaged a few others, before they were beaten off by a counterattack of Seabees and Marine engineers. Sasaki's men turned right and headed for Hill 500, about three miles above them. It was getting light.

"Japs!"

Tom McQuabe and Bill Cramford yelled the warning with a single astonished voice, even as they saw the short men slipping through the half-light toward Hill 500.

The Japanese replied by hurling a grenade which landed in the Marines' outpost foxhole and wounded McQuabe. Cramford got his BAR going, shooting off three clips before he, too, was wounded—and the Japanese rushed past screeching, *"Shichi sei hokoku!"*

Huddled in a hole beneath a strip of galvanized iron, Pfc. Jim Ferguson and Pfc. Ed Martin heard the shrieking and the sound of gunfire. Ferguson knocked aside the roof with the muzzle of his tommy gun. A helmeted Japanese stared down at him. Ferguson shot him dead with a stream of .45 slugs. Now Sasaki's men—many of them armed with only "idiot sticks"—were hacking wildly at the Marines. One of them bayoneted Pfc. Robert Postal—but Postal killed him with a rifle shot as he struggled to withdraw the blade. Another knocked Pfc. Jim Davie down with a shovel. A third charged Pfc. Ken Rayburn with a lowered bayonet. Rayburn's carbine jammed. He seized a pick mattock and hurled it into the Japanese's stomach.

While Chambers' men quickly recovered from the surprise of finding the "front" to their rear, the rest of the Japanese were battling with the artillerists of the Second Battalion, Fourteenth Marines.

The American uniforms they wore helped them get close to the artillerymen between Isely Field and Hill 500. The Marines let them come, mistaking them for an Army patrol scheduled to appear at about that time.

By the time a sharp-eyed Marine yelled, "Those ain't doggies, those are Japs!"—it was almost too late. But the machine guns set up by the artillerymen to protect their guns opened up quickly. The battle raged on for most of the morning, until the men of the Fourteenth Marines had killed 143 of the attackers and lost 33 killed and wounded themselves, and the Twenty-fifth Marines had come down from Hill 500 and cleaned out the remainder of Sasaki's band.

It had not been anything like "seven lives to repay our country." It had been a massacre. And as the men of the Twenty-fifth turned to march back to Hill 500, they stopped to watch a Japanese bomber trying to get down through the storm of antiaircraft fire puffing over Isely Field.

"Blow up, you son of a bitch!" a Marine yelled.

The bomber did blow up, and a yell of fierce delight rose from the throats of thousands of Americans who had been watching the plane's descent. Then the crackling of small arms and the booming of artillery signaled that the attack to the north was still running into enemy resistance.

6

Even with Tapotchau captured, the attack to the north could not become an all-out lunge until the three divisions had spent some time shifting, pinching out, and tidying up the front.

In the days between the mop-up of Nafutan Point on June 27 and resumption of full-scale attack on July 1, the Fourth Marine Division on the right or eastern flank had to clean out Kagman Peninsula before it pushed still farther north.

In the center the 27th Infantry Division still had difficulty moving, and General Jarman relieved one of his regimental commanders. By July 1, however, the 27th had drawn even with the Marines on both flanks and had also received a new commander—Major General George Griner.

On the left the Second Marine Division held fast on the coast beneath Garapan while it hit slowly through The Pimples, the four hills north of Tapotchau. Once The Pimples had been passed, the Second would hurl one regiment into Garapan—now flattened by naval gunfire—while the other units swung left or northwest into Tanapag Harbor just above the city.

Also during this interval the Guam invasion was postponed and the Third Marine Division was sent back to Eniwetok Lagoon while the First Marine Brigade was held in floating reserve. Saipan had been much too tough to allow the Guam landings to proceed. The Japanese had fought with a doggedness and skill which had slowed the American advance beyond expectation. Without water, forced to chew leaves and eat snails or hunt big tree frogs, the Emperor's soldiers had made the invaders' life a hell of exploding shells and flying rock splinters.

344

But the invaders had also taken a fierce toll among the defenders and Howlin' Mad Smith was confident that his renewed assault would quickly overrun the northern half of Saipan. On June 29, Smith and General Watson of the Second Division went up to Mount Tapotchau to study the terrain Watson's men would be attacking two days later. It was nearly their last look at any terrain, for Japanese mortars began crashing around them. They jumped from their jeep and ran for a foxhole, waiting there until the barrage stopped—and then quickly departing Tapotchau.

Next day a fierce American mortar barrage produced the same effect upon Lieutenant General Saito. He pulled back to his sixth and last headquarters, another cave, and the main body of his troops began retreating north to new positions.

The following day—July 1—the Second Marines attacked Garapan and found hardly a building intact in a city that had once housed 15,000 people. Hanging everywhere among the ruins, making a poignance of the desolation, were thousands of bright silk *obis*, the sashes which Japanese women bind about their midriffs and which the women of Garapan left behind in their flight to the north. Only occasional snipers hidden beneath scraps of iron roofing, or machine guns holed up in ruined buildings, delayed the first day's advance of the Third Battalion, Second, commanded by Major Harold Throneson. But during the night 200 Japanese slipped back into Garapan's rubble to set up machine guns.

Throneson's men routed them next day after vicious fighting. By dusk the Marines held the lower half of the city. A command post had been set up on "Broadway" across the street from the ruined Bank of Taiwan and alongside a Spanish-style Catholic Church which was one of the few buildings still undamaged. Some of the Marines went in. They paused, shocked. Up on the altar was a plaster statue of Christ with the face blown away.

Underneath Sugar Loaf Hill in the foothills to the right or east of Garapan the face of a young Marine had been blown away. An enemy gunner had shot him as he slithered forward over a rock. The bullet tore off the top of his head and sent his helmet clanging against the rocks. Blood spattered on a nearby sergeant.

"Goddam it, Mac!" the sergeant roared to everyone with hearing. "Let's go up and get those bastards!"

They went up, hanging onto stone knobs with one hand, hurling grenades with the other—sometimes shot from their holds and dropped to the boulders below—but going up, up and over, cleaning out the caves and taking Sugar Loaf Hill.

Then they descended on Garapan to the west. They fought into Royal Palm Park and gaped at the 40-foot stone shaft supporting the figure of a Japanese statesman. He wore western dress. He was 10 feet tall.

"Hell's fire!" a Marine swore with fervent irreverence. "This must be the guy that told 'em they was bullet-proof!"

The conquerors of Tapotchau and The Pimples were coming down from the mountains. Their faces were smeared with dirt and grimy with beard stubble. Their dungarees were stiff with sweat and dried earth. Their hands were black. They were walking as wooden men with leaden feet. But now, those dull sunken eyes were beginning to gleam. For they had seen the blue beckoning water of Tanapag Harbor, and the tanks had begun to lead them down the last hills to the canefields below.

And there were the Japanese—running.

They were being flushed from their foxholes by the roaring 75's of the Shermans. They were in full view, and the Marines were rushing down the hill, dropping to their knees, firing, jumping up and running forward to fire again, their gaunt faces suddenly alive with victory, their eyes glittering with a fierce joy.

They came down the hill and swept through the canebrake and halted a few hundred yards short of the harbor, while to their left rear the Marines in Garapan began attacking up to them.

"Slaughterhouse is back!" a Marine sergeant in Garapan yelled, and the men of the Third Battalion, Second, understood him to mean that Lieutenant Colonel Arnold Johnston had returned to command them. Johnston had brought the battalion

346

into Saipan, had been wounded twice and then evacuated. But now, on the morning of July 3, he had rejoined the outfit and taken over from Major Throneson.

"Crazy Gyrene bastard!" the sergeant swore. "He's dead but he won't lie down. He's back there stompin' around on one gimp leg and a Jap cane."

He was, and Lieutenant Colonel John Easley had also come back for the attack to the harbor. He had been wounded on D-Day while leading the Third Battalion, Sixth, ashore. There were many men in the ranks like Johnston and Easley fighting up to Tanapag with bandaged bodies, helping to overrun the few snipers standing between themselves and the big seaplane base the Japanese had built there.

They reached it just before dusk. It was deserted. There were only the darkening burned-out bulks of eight Kawanishi four-engined bombers. There was only silence and offshore the black silhouettes of the transports they had not seen since June 15.

The Marines waded out into the harbor and bathed their faces.

"Son of a bitch!" one of them exclaimed. "If tomorrow ain't the Fourth of July!"

7

There was no longer any hope for either Lieutenant General Yoshitsugu Saito or Vice Admiral Chuichi Nagumo or the men they commanded. Their food and ammunition were spent—as were their bodies—and by July 5 they held only the northern third of Saipan. The airfield which Saito and Nagumo had ordered completed at Marpi Point was now a shambles.

"General Saito is not going to get away in an airplane if

we can help it," said Howlin' Mad Smith on July 5, and the American artillery wrecked the little field. Shelling also had destroyed communications between Nagumo and Saito, and yet, on July 6, these separated commanders had come to the same conclusion: it was now time for the *samurai* or nobleman to make the final gesture.

In the early morning of that date, tired old General Saito gathered his staff in his cave. He was a pathetic figure. His beard was long and matted. His clothing was stained. All of his strength had deserted him and to sustain him he had only the last resource of that deep Oriental despair which is the other side of the coin of pride.

"I am addressing the officers and men of the Imperial Army on Saipan," he wrote in his final message.

> For more than twenty days since the American Devils attacked, the officers, men and civilian employees of the Imperial Army and Navy on this island have fought well and bravely. Everywhere they have demonstrated the honor and glory of the Imperial Force. I expected that every man would do his duty.
>
> Heaven has not given us an opportunity. We have not been able to utilize fully the terrain. We have fought in unison up to the present time but now we have no materials with which to fight and our artillery for attack has been completely destroyed. Our comrades have fallen one after another. Despite the bitterness of defeat, we pledge, "Seven lives to repay our country!"
>
> The barbarous attack of the enemy is being continued. Even though the enemy has occupied only a corner of Saipan, we are dying without avail under the violent shelling and bombing. Whether we attack or whether we stay where we are, there is only death. However, in death there is life. We must utilize this opportunity to exalt true Japanese manhood. I will advance with those who remain to deliver still another blow to the American Devils, and leave my bones on Saipan as a bulwark of the Pacific.
>
> As it says in Battle Ethics, I will never suffer the disgrace of being taken alive, and I will offer up the courage of my soul and calmly rejoice in living by the eternal principle.
>
> Here I pray with you for the eternal life of the Emperor and the welfare of our country and I advance to seek out the enemy. Follow me!

But if those valiant, suffering Japanese foot-soldiers had indeed followed General Saito there would have been no *banzai*.

For the aged commander of Saipan sat down to a farewell feast of canned crabmeat and *saki*. At ten o'clock he had finished. He arose and said:

"It makes no difference whether I die today or tomorrow, so I will die first. I will meet my staff at Yasakuni Shrine."

He walked slowly to a flat rock. He cleaned it off and sat down. He faced the misty East and bowed gravely. He raised his glittering *samurai* saber in salute and cried, "*Tenno Heika! Banzai!*" He pressed the point of his blade into his breast and the moment he had drawn blood his adjutant shot him in the head.

In another cave on Saipan at about the same time, Nagumo of Pearl Harbor sent a bullet crashing into his brain by his own hand.

Tonight the Japanese would follow their leaders' orders, without their leaders.

On that same July 6 Holland Smith visited 27th Infantry Division headquarters and warned Major General Griner that a *banzai* would probably come against his men that night or early the next morning.

Smith had long anticipated a strong enemy counterstroke south along the coastal flat on the island's western shore. It was for this reason that he had kept his left or northern flank strong during seizure of the beachhead, and the fact that all the strong Japanese counterblows had been made there had confirmed his judgment. For this reason also he had ordered Major General Watson to keep the Second Marine Division's west flank strong during the attack north.

But now the 27th Infantry Division had taken over the entire west or left flank, for on July 5, as his attack began moving on a front narrowing away to the northeast, Smith had reduced his commitment to two divisions. The Second Marine Division went into reserve, and the alignment became 27th on the left or west and Fourth Marine Division on the right or east. In the 27th's sector was Tanapag Plain, about three miles northeast of Garapan.

It was because Tanapag Plain was a lowland made for counterattack, as well as because the hemmed-in enemy could be expected to make his unfailing reaction to such predicament, that Smith came to Griner to warn him of impending *banzai*. He also cautioned him to be sure his battalions were tied tightly to each other's flanks.

But as night fell on July 6 the 105th Infantry Regiment which held the Tanapag Plain had not buttoned up its front. Its left-to-right alignment by battalions was 2nd, 1st and 3rd —the last tying in with the 165th Infantry on high ground to the right or east of Tanapag Plain.

Between the 1st Battalion in the center and the 3rd on the right was a gap of 300 yards—and north of it the Japanese had begun to mass.

> *Across the sea, corpses in the water.*
> *Across the mountain, corpses in the field.*
> *I shall die for the Emperor.*
> *I shall never look back.*

The Japanese were singing as they massed, singing *Umi Yukaba*—the martial air which had been broadcast throughout Japan the day Premier Tojo announced the attack on Pearl Harbor. That had been December 8, 1941, and this was the black early morning of July 7, 1944. The hero of Pearl Harbor was dead, Tojo's own iron rule was beginning to crack, and yet, here were between 2,000 and 3,000 Japanese promising to die in sea and field and forming ranks to do it.

Down the coastal plain they swept. They rolled like a cattle stampede against the lines of the 2nd and 1st Battalions, 105th, and they cut them off and overwhelmed them. They found the gap between the 1st and 3rd Battalions, 105th, and thundered through it.

Army artillery pounded them, Marine guns bayed—but still they swept over those army battalions, for there were so many of them. They had come determined to die and they made the American soldiers fight for their lives. Some soldiers shot so many Japanese that bodies clogged their fields of fire and they had to move their guns. Others shot themselves out of ammunition and fought with their hands. The 105th's left and center was cut up into pocket after pocket. Lieutenant Colonel William O'Brien of the First Battalion tried to rally his men and was killed firing a heavy machine gun from a jeep. Sergeant Tom Baker of the same outfit was wounded and refused to leave the lines when his unit withdrew. He asked to be propped up against a tree. He was. By morning he was dead, but there were eight lifeless Japanese around him, and he was awarded a Medal of Honor along with O'Brien. Throughout the morning the fighting swirled within and around the lines of these two battalions. Their remnants were forced to form a hasty perimeter on the water's edge. They were driven into the sea, by their own artillery as much as by enemy fire, and had to be rescued by small boats. In all, the 1st and 2nd Battalions, 105th, suffered a total of 668 casualties.

Meanwhile, the Japanese who had shot the gap during the night burst in a howling flood on the startled gunners of the Third Battalion, Tenth Marines. The gunners lowered their 105's to point-blank range. They cut their fuses to 150 yards, to 100 yards. But still the enemy charged. The gunners disarmed their howitzers and fell back into a covered-wagon defense. They too fought on through the morning, helped by men from brother artillery battalions—Marines such as Pfc. Harold Agerholm, who singlehandedly evacuated 45 wounded men until he fell from the wound that would make his Medal of Honor posthumous—and then the turrets of the 106th Infantry's counterattacking tanks came into view.

Then also on this morning of July 7 the Japanese hospitals disgorged and the *banzai* became a ghoul's parade.

They came down the plain hobbling and limping, amputees, men on crutches, walking wounded supporting one another, men in bandages. Some had weapons, most brandished idiot sticks or swung bayonets, others were barehanded or carried grenades. Behind them some 300 of their comrades who had been unable to move had been put to death. And now these specters, these scarecrows, were coming down Tanapag Plain to die. They were requited.

By nightfall of July 7 the beaches of Tanapag Harbor were clogged with Japanese dead. Next day the Second Marine

Division came out of reserve to mop up the area, and a tank sergeant named Grant Timmerman won a Medal of Honor by smothering a grenade with his life to save his crew. Fighting fluttered on throughout that night, but by morning of July 9 the mop-up was finished and men were beginning to make the count of enemy dead that reached nearly 2,500. Gunnery Sergeant Claude Moore of the First Battalion, Second Marines, was among them.

Sometimes Gunny Moore bent over to count, and once, as he did, there came a shot from a sniper in a cave. Moore went down bawling his dismay. A corpsman rushed up to assuage the gunny's wounded posterior. He knelt down and gasped.

"Damned if it didn't go in and out both cheeks!"

A beatific smile chased the grimace of pain from Gunny Moore's face.

"Four Purple Hearts," he breathed. "And all with the one bullet!"

Several hours later—at four in the afternoon—the Second, Twenty-fourth and Twenty-fifth Marines drove up to the island's northernmost extremity at Marpi Point. They reported they could see nothing in front of them but blue sea.

Saipan had fallen, and now the Japanese civilians began to make the final gesture.

Marpi Point was a high plateau. It rose 220 sheer feet from the shore above a clutter of cruel coral rocks. Its seaward face was honeycombed with caves. At Marpi Point had gathered half of Saipan's civilian population, together with the surviving remnant of its military defenders, and here, throughout the afternoon and night of July 9, throughout the following day, there occurred an orgy of self-destruction which sickened those Marines who were powerless to halt it.

Surrender pleas broadcast from sound trucks, the entreaties of the Marines themselves, the pleading of prisoners—both civilian and military—nothing could deter these Japanese civilians in the horrible slaughter of themselves and their families.

Men and women jumped hand in hand from the cliff onto the rocks. Fathers stabbed or strangled their babies to death, hurled their tiny forms over the cliff, and threw themselves after them. Soldiers prodded groups of civilians out of the caves, posed arrogantly before them, and blew themselves apart. Cowed, the civilians also committed suicide.

On the beaches below, one boy of about fifteen paced irresolutely over the rocks. He sat down and let the water play over his feet. A roller gathered out on the sea. He awaited it stoically. It broke over his body, it swept him away. He lay face down in it—and then, suddenly, frantically, unable to restrain the youth of his life, his arms flailed the water.

But it was too late. He lay inert. His trousers filled with water, and he sank.

Not far away, three women sat on a rock combing their long black hair. They stood erect. They joined hands and walked slowly out into the sea.

A father, mother and three children had also walked into the water. But they had come back to the rocks. A Japanese soldier in one of the caves shot the father. The soldier fired again and hit the woman. She dragged herself along the rocks but the sea seized her and floated her out in a spreading stain of blood. The sniper took aim on the children. A Japanese woman ran across the beach and carried them away.

The sniper strode out of his cave, preening himself, and crumpled under the concentrated firing of a hundred Marine weapons.

Sometimes the Marines were able to rescue a child, and then an entire squad of men would rush about for dried milk to placate the squalling infant whose mother had chosen to leap alone. One big Marine squatted in the road brushing flies from the face of a dazed six-year-old girl, while the tears streaked his earth-stained cheeks.

Along the reefs to the west of Marpi Point, knots of Japanese soldiers had gathered to commit suicide. An amtrack full of Marines approached one group, just as six men knelt down and an officer backed off to draw his saber from its scabbard. The Marines called to him to surrender. He swung. He hacked off four heads, and as the Marines approached the reef, he and the two remaining men charged. The Marines cut them down.

Underneath Marpi Point, 100 soldiers emerged from the caves to frolic on the rocks. They bowed ceremoniously to the Marines above. They stripped and ran into the sea. They came out and put on their clothes. Their leader distributed hand grenades. One by one, they blew themselves up.

By July 10, the waters off Marpi Point were incarnadine and so clogged with bodies rolling on the swells that small American ships could not run into shore to rescue civilians from the soldiers who held them. Nor could they have come ashore if the waters had been clear, for the soldiers had begun to snipe at them and the rocket boats and minesweepers were forced to turn their guns on the caves.

It was then that a naked woman in the last stages of childbirth waded into the water to drown herself and her child.

Eight days after this ultimate expression of the horror of *Bushido*, the very high priest of the cult—Premier Hideki Tojo —was himself fallen. The loss of Saipan, the catastrophe of the Battle of the Philippine Sea, had broken the power of the man who led the Empire into the war. He was forced to resign on July 18, although this disgrace did not shame him into the final gesture made by his misguided followers on Marpi Point. Hideki Tojo chose to live, until the Americans came to Japan and he was convicted as a war criminal and hung.

Saipan had cost a total of 14,111 American casualties— 3,674 soldiers, 10,347 Marines—while destroying all but 1,000 prisoners of the island's 30,000 defenders. But Saipan also caused changes as important as the fall of Tojo. After Saipan, Japan was within bombing range of air bases which she could not neutralize, as she would do in China; she had no more

354

carrier air power; and the inner works of Empire lay open to attack. The force of the blow struck by the Americans was measured in anguish by Fleet Admiral Osami Nagano, supreme naval advisor to the Emperor. Hearing of Saipan's fall, Nagano held his head and groaned:

"Hell is on us."

Back in San Diego, California, during this July of 1944, the new Fifth Marine Division had completed training and was preparing to shove off for Camp Tarawa in Hawaii.

On Pavuvu Island in the Russells, staff officers of the First Marine Division were drawing plans for the assault on a little island which was spelled Peleliu and pronounced "Pella-loo."

In Eniwetok Lagoon the long wait was ending for the men of the Guam invasion force.

And in the narrow waters between Saipan and Tinian, on that very night of July 10, while Marpi Point still shook to the last of the suicide cave explosions, there were a pair of destroyers discharging Captain Jim Jones and his Recon Boys into rubber boats.

Tinian, three and a half miles to the south of Saipan, had to be taken. Its seizure, along with the reconquest of Guam, would consolidate the Marianas. More, Tinian held an excellent airdrome with two 4,700-foot runways and there were three more being built. Though Tinian was but 10½ miles long and a maximum of five miles wide, it had enough level ground to make it the chief B-29 base in the Pacific.

But Tinian had very few landing beaches. The only ones known to be suitable for invasion, opposite Tinian Town on the island's southwest coast, were also heavily defended. The Marines dared not risk them.

That was why the Recon Boys of Captain Jones—together with sailors of two Underwater Demolition Teams—had come into the strait between Saipan and Tinian. They were looking for unguarded landing beaches on Tinian's northern nose.

In two groups, one bound for the western beaches, the other for those on the east, they paddled softly to within 500 yards of their objectives. Then they slipped into the water and swam the rest of the way, floating silently past parties of Japanese engaged in mining work.

They found that the eastern beaches were a wicked labyrinth of boat-blocks, underwater mines and barbed wire, set among natural obstacles of boulders, potholes and 20-foot cliffs. But on the west were two narrow beaches to either side of a cliff. One was 60 yards wide, the other 150 yards.

It did not seem possible to land a regiment, let alone two full Marine divisions, on such abbreviated beaches, but they were judged acceptable by the new Fifth Corps commander, Major General Harry Schmidt.

Schmidt had taken over after Lieutenant General Smith had been made commander, Fleet Marine Force, Pacific. Schmidt had handed his Fourth Division over to the aristocratic Major General Clifton Cates, a veteran of World War One and a regimental commander on Guadalcanal. The Fourth would be in assault while the Second Marine Division sailed down to Tinian Town to make a feint off the fortified southwest beaches. Then the Second would turn around and land behind the Fourth.

Schmidt was making an armored battering ram of that Fourth Division. He gave it the Second's tanks and artillery, and he would send it in with all of Saipan's guns banging away. The Marines would move from shore to shore in landing boats. The invasion was scheduled for July 24, which was three days after the assault on Guam.

"Guam? Goddamit, man, these men have had Guam until it's been comin' out their ears!"

So spoke a Marine officer to a war correspondent, and he

356

spoke the truth. For weeks and weeks on end these men of the Third Marine Division and First Marine Brigade had looked at maps of Guam and listened to lectures on it. They knew by heart, now, that Guam had been American for forty years before the Japanese landed there on December 10, 1941; that this peanut-shaped island 32 miles long and four to eight miles wide was the biggest and most populous of the Marianas; and that its Chamorro inhabitants were deeply loyal to the United States, for which fidelity—including their reluctance to learn Japanese or to use the official new name of Omiya Jima, "Great Shrine Island"—they had come under fierce persecution, their schools and churches closed, their priests tortured and murdered, their men beheaded for so much as a smile at the sight of a U.S. plane. The Marines also learned that the general objectives of their assault were all on Guam's west coast—the former U. S. Navy Yard at Piti, the old Marine barracks and airfield on Orote Peninsula, Apra Harbor and the coastal city of Agana. By the time the news of the fall of Saipan reached them, they had become so familiar with their individual objectives that they talked of them with the familiarity of home-town landmarks.

News of Saipan's fall, however, did not immediately release the Guam invasion force from the slack-jawed tedium of shipboard life in Eniwetok Lagoon. The high casualties suffered at Saipan had impressed Major General Roy Geiger, the Guam commander. He thought he would need about 40,000 troops to overwhelm the 19,000 men comprising the Japanese 29th Infantry Division and other units commanded by Lieutenant General Takeshi Takashina. Geiger asked for and was given the 77th Infantry Division then in Hawaii. It would take two weeks for the 77th to reach Eniwetok, but Geiger did not chafe at the delay. It meant that Guam would receive fourteen full days of naval and aerial bombardment—the heaviest preparation of the war—and there would also be time for the Underwater Demolition Teams to clear the landing beaches.

Geiger planned landings on either side of Apra Harbor, just as the Japanese had landed. Major General Allen Turnage's Third Division would land above Apra on the north. Below it, on the south, the First Brigade was to come ashore under

Brigadier General Lemuel Shepherd of Cape Gloucester fame. When the two outfits joined, all of Guam's military facilities would have been enveloped, and the way would be clear for the First Brigade to push out on Orote Peninsula to the west. The 77th Division would be in reserve.

And while that 77th Division was sailing for Eniwetok, the men who were already there had turned the lagoon into a floating slum. All over the weather decks of the LST's the Marines had set up tents, or slung ponchos and spread tarpaulins between themselves and the blistering sun. Their bedding was strewn everywhere. Men gasped in the heat and scratched prickly rashes. They made betting pools on the number of days they would be aboard ship before they landed (those holding numbers 48 to 52 were the winners) and they imposed careful cigarette rationing on themselves, while giving the clothes they wore fewer and fewer washings, for they had begun to fray.

Each day officers herded these bored and enervated Marines together and took them ashore in landing boats. They ran up to the reef and piled out. They waded ashore. They walked over the little islets and felt the burning coral through the thinning soles of their boondockers. Then they waded out to the reef again and went back to the ships—to ennui relieved only by a surprisingly inexhaustible supply of ice cream or an occasional good joke.

Such as that morning on which a group of Marines waded back to their boat:

"Anyone here from Texas?" one of the coxswains called.

A corporal brightened and pushed back his helmet.

"Ah'm from Lubbock," he said, his voice proud and expectant.

The coxswain grinned impishly.

"You can swim out, mate," he said.

They were laughing, too, on Pavuvu.

Chesty Puller had contributed another Pullerism to his legend. He had been made a full colonel and had taken command of the First Marine Regiment. And then some comfort-loving clod of a quartermaster officer had issued Chesty Puller's men sleeping pads. They were all of a half-inch thick and to the comfort-hating Puller they were as corrosive and beguiling as the soft voices of sirens in the ears of Ulysses' men. Chesty Puller ordered the pads gathered up and thrown into the bay.

"Goddamit," he raged, "are they trying to make sissies out of my men?"

There were rubber boats standing off Tinian's southern shore. There were 12 of them. They were filled with Japanese officers. Among them was a huge figure. Vice Admiral Kakuji Kakuda was more than six feet tall and his bulk of more than 200 pounds was big even by Western standards. By all standards, bald and burly Kakuda was a coward and a drunk.

He was the commander of the First Air Fleet on Tinian, but Kakuda could no more command than he could stop swilling *saki* or scheming for his own safety.

On this night of July 15 he had collected his headquarters staff and begun to paddle south toward Aguijan Island and the rendezvous he had arranged with a Japanese submarine. But the sub did not show up.

Admiral Kakuda paddled back to Tinian. He tried again for three more nights. Still the submarine did not appear. On the night of July 20 an American gunboat almost sent Kakuda's rubber-boat flotilla to the bottom. The admiral retired in dismay. He hastened to a well-armored dugout on the eastern side of the island, and was never heard from again.

That was on July 21, the day the Americans came back to Guam.

10

There had been a typhoon scare.

Admiral Spruance had asked Close-in Conolly if he planned to postpone the Guam landings to avoid the typhoon headed his way. But Conolly's weather officer assured him that July 21 would be a perfect day for landings.

It was. It dawned clear and slightly overcast, with a light wind and calm sea, and in that dawn a voice came over the bullhorns of the transport ships.

"Men, this is General Geiger. The eyes of a nation watch you as you go into battle to liberate this former American bastion from the enemy. Make no mistake, it will be a tough, bitter fight against a wily, stubborn foe who will doggedly defend Guam against this invasion. May the glorious traditions of the Marine *esprit de corps* spur you to victory. You have been honored."

The general's voice ceased. "The Marines' Hymn" crashed out and the men began to go over the side.

It was an unusual D-Day morning, almost a theatrical one, but the Marines wanted Guam badly. Some of the NCO's and officers going over the side had served there. Many of them had buddies among the 153 Marines who were taken prisoner when Guam surrendered. The recapture of Guam would heal an old hurt.

At eight o'clock the Third Division's first wave had made the transfer from landing boats to amtracks. The men crouched low as the ungainly craft fanned out and roared ashore, heading for those beaches lying between the "devil's horns" of Adelup Point on the left, Asan Point on the right. At eight-twenty an air observer reported:

360

"The rockets are landing and giving them hell. Good effect on beach. Landing craft seem to be about one thousand yards from beach."

Seven minutes later came this report:

"First wave two hundred yards from beach."

Naval gunfire lifted and began pounding targets inland. At eight thirty-three the air observer reported:

"Troops ashore on all beaches."

The Marines had returned to Guam, and already, the sands below the bleak white face of Chonito Cliff were streaked crimson with their blood.

About six miles to the south, underneath Orote Peninsula, which formed the lower land arm of Apra Harbor, the First Brigade attacked with both regiments abreast. And heavy as the Guam bombardment had been, it had not knocked everything out. Japanese 75's and 37's were firing as the men of the Fourth and Twenty-second Marines rode their amtracks shoreward. Before the amphibians had waddled up on the sand, 24 of them were knocked out. Casualties mounted, and there was no one to care for them. Doctors and corpsmen were the heaviest hit. One battalion's aid station took a direct hit from a 75 which killed and wounded all but one man.

Corpsman Robert Law saw a shellburst spread eight Marines around him. One of the men had a shattered leg and his life's blood was spouting carmine from it. Law gave the man morphine. The man smiled and asked for something to hold. Law shoved clods of earth into his hands. He pulled out his combat knife and began to amputate the leg. The Marine squeezed the clods of earth to dust. But he made no sound. Law bandaged the stump. When he glanced up, the Marine smiled at him again. Then he sank into unconsciousness.

On the left, the Twenty-second Marines under Colonel Merlin Schneider were charging toward the rubble of Agat Village. Captain Charles Widdecke began to lead his company around Bob's Hill, a mound overlooking the town. Machine-gun fire knocked them flat. They took cover in a trench. They dug in, expecting to stay there for the night. Down a trail straight toward them marched a dozen Japanese carrying the very

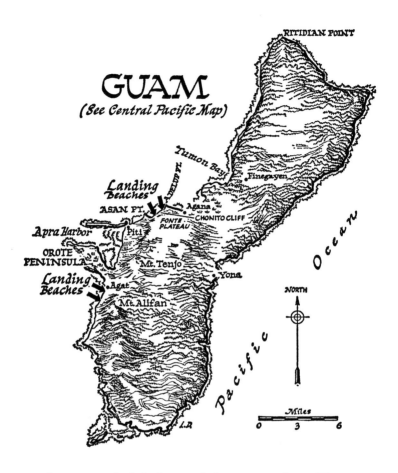

GUAM

(See Central Pacific Map)

RITIDIAN POINT

Tumon Bay

Finegayen

Landing Beaches

ASAN PT.

Agana

CHONITO CLIFF

FONTE PLATEAU

Piti

Apra Harbor

OROTE PENINSULA

Mt. Tenjo

Yona

Landing Beaches

Agat

Mt. Alifan

Pacific

Ocean

NORTH

Miles

0   3   6

machine guns which had pinned the Marines down. There was the crackling of American guns. The Japanese were slammed to earth and the way to the village was clear.

On the right, Colonel Alan Shapley's Fourth Marines drove toward Mount Alifan, about 2,000 yards inland. They passed through a grove of palm trees and concealed snipers. Sherman tanks led them through a maze of pillboxes and blockhouses. They sprinted through the slippery muck of a rice paddy, leaping across its myriads of tiny interlacing streams. They ran the gantlet of machine-gun fire and mortar shells, they threaded

362

the strong points of Alifan's foothills while the lumbering tanks bucked and roared and sealed off cave after cave, and by nightfall they held a beachhead a mile deep.

Behind that beachhead, "The Old Bastards" were wading ashore.

They were not really so old, these dogfaces of the 77th Division's 305th Infantry Regiment. But they were in their late twenties, something like an average of four to six years older than their youthful comrades in the First Marine Brigade.

They had to wade into the southern beaches from the reef simply because the Marine amtracks had suffered heavy losses and they had none of their own. Fortunately, the young bastards ahead of them were busily cleaning out the enemy. The soldiers had only the discomfort of waist-high water and occasional potholes to hinder their walk ashore. The entire regiment was on land by nightfall, the last to arrive being its commander, Colonel Vincent Tanzola, who was saved from being stranded on the reef when a rubber boat drifted by. He grabbed it and paddled ashore.

The southern force had the situation in hand.

"Our casualties about 350," General Shepherd signaled General Geiger at half-past six. "Critical shortage fuel and ammunition all types. Think we can handle it."

But up north, the Third Division was fighting hard for its beachhead.

By noon of July 21, there were two battalions of the Twenty-first Marines atop the central height which frowned down on the Asan-Adelup beachhead.

Colonel Arthur Butler had discovered a pair of defiles to either side of the hill. He sent a battalion up each of these passes while a third battalion swept the ground below the cliff.

It was a fight all the way up, the men of the ascending battalions all but melting under the combination of fierce heat and the long debilitating weeks aboard ship. Gasping for breath, their dungarees dark with sweat, they tumbled among the rocks and boulders and lay where they fell. NCO's and officers dragged them erect and sent them climbing again—to be savaged by crisscrossing Japanese machine-gun fire or blown to bits by the grenades which the enemy rolled among them.

But they reached the top, linked up, and drove forward.

On their right, the Ninth Marines were moving swiftly through easier terrain, and lighter resistance. They attacked with artillery firing in support, for the northern landings had been such near-perfection that there were 105's ashore by noontime. They had been brought over the reef in "ducks"— those amphibian trucks developed by the Army—and unloaded by A-frames mounted on accompanying ducks. By midafternoon Chonito Cliff had been overrun in the center and the right.

But on the left the Third Marines were being torn apart.

The steep sheer seaward face of Chonito Cliff winked with the muzzle-blasting of Japanese machine guns as the Third moved beneath it toward Adelup Point. The Japanese pulled back only after the Point had fallen, and then the most savage fighting of the Guam campaign began. It was here that the Third Marines lost 815 killed and wounded within forty-eight hours, among them two Medal of Honor winners—Pfc. Leonard Mason, who died destroying a pair of machine-gun posts, and Pfc. Luther Skaggs, whose leg was shattered as he took command of a mortar section and led it forward to annihilate a Japanese pocket.

It took four days for the Third Marines to clean out their sector and make contact with the Twenty-first Marines on their right. It also took four days for all of the division's regiments to drive forward and establish the Asan-Adelup beachhead to a depth of about a mile and a width of 6,000 yards. By then, the First Brigade to the south had expanded the Agat beachhead, had turned its sector over to the 77th Division and had marched north to the mouth of Orote Peninsula and sealed off the Japanese there.

By then also Lieutenant General Takashina was satisfied that the Americans at Asan-Adelup had all their supplies and equipment ashore and that he could now destroy them at one blow as he had planned to do. Takashina had already begun to assemble his units on the Fonte Plateau just east of the Asan-Adelup perimeter. His suicide troops had infiltrated the Marine lines with explosives strapped around their waists or stuffed in packs. They were, in effect, human bombs. Their mission was to destroy the American artillery, tanks and transport.

"The time has come," Takashina told his commanders, "to solve the issue of the battle at a single stroke by an all-out counterattack."

That was on July 24, the day when the time had come for Tinian, 130 miles to the north.

11

Short and sweet—this one will be short and sweet.

That was what the Marines of the Fourth Division thought as they stood on the rain-swept decks of the LST's taking them to Tinian's northwestern beaches. It was a dream as old as Tulagi, and even though the realities had been the extremes of the long black night of Guadalcanal or the scarlet short hell of Tarawa, Marines going into battle still looked about them eagerly for signs that this time it was true.

Off Tinian the morning of July 24 the fact that the fight would be short seemed guaranteed by the streamlined combat issue the men carried. Packs, bedding rolls and gas masks had been left on Saipan. Besides their weapons, the men had only a can of rations, a spoon, a pair of clean socks and a bottle of mosquito lotion—all stuffed in a pocket.

"Hell's bells!" a Marine swore. "It's a silly picnic kit!"

That Tinian would also be sweet seemed to be indicated by that panoply of American might ringing the island with steel and booming guns. Battleships and cruisers, five escort carriers and three of the big ones, Army and Marine fighter squadrons, Army bombers already operating from Isely Field on Saipan, 156 big field pieces massed hub to hub and firing from southern Saipan—all this was arrayed against that lovely flat checkerboard of canebrakes and rice paddies that was northern Tinian. And America's newest weapon was being tried out for the first time. Some planes were dropping napalm bombs, those tanks of jellied gasoline which the fliers accurately called "hell-jelly." Gushing flame clouds were mushrooming everywhere beneath the smoke, setting the northern canebrakes afire and flushing out concealed Japanese, burning buildings in Tinian Town.

Unknown to these Marines exulting in their nation's power there was another reason why Tinian might be short and sweet: the quarrel between Colonel Kiyochi Ogata, commander of the 50th Infantry Regiment, and Captain Goichi Oya, commander of the 56th Naval Guard Force. Between them they commanded slightly more than 9,000 soldiers and sailors, and between them there rankled that endless rivalry of the Anchor and the Star. Its bitterness was manifested by the diary entries of one of Ogata's artillerymen, who wrote:

9 March—The Navy stays in barracks buildings and has liberty every night with liquor to drink and makes a great row. We, on the other hand, bivouac in the rain and never get out on pass. What a difference in discipline!

12 June—Our AA guns (Navy) spread black smoke where the enemy planes weren't. Not one hit out of a thousand. The Naval Air Group has taken to its heels.

15 June—The Naval aviators are robbers. . . . When they ran off to the mountains, they stole Army provisions. . . .

25 June—Sailors have stolen our provisions. . . .

6 July—Did Vice Admiral Kakuda when he heard that the enemy had entered our area go to sleep with joy?

On the Navy side, Captain Oya never let his men know that with Vice Admiral Kakuda abstaining from everything but *saki*, command on Tinian had passed to Colonel Ogata. Cap-

Landing
Beaches

Airfield No.1

North

Airfield No.3

Faibus San
Hilo Point

PACIFIC

OCEAN

Philippine Sea

Airfield No.2

Airfield No.4

Tinian Town

TINIAN
(See Central Pacific Map)

Yards

0   2000   4000

L.A.

tain Oya's plans to defend Tinian Town were independent of those made by Colonel Ogata for the rest of the island. It was at Tinian Town that the southwestern beaches had been heavily fortified under Oya's direction, and here, too, Oya had concentrated the bulk of the island's coastal guns, which, being naval, belonged to him.

At about half-past seven in the morning of July 24, while the Fourth Marine Division sailed toward Tinian's northwest beaches, Captain Oya ordered his six-inch guns to open up on the big American warships guarding the men of the Second

Marine Division as they boarded landing craft and roared toward Tinian Town in a feigned invasion.

Oya's gunners had a splendid target in old *Colorado*, only 3,200 yards offshore, and they hit the big battleship 22 times before she could get out of range. *Colorado* lost 43 men killed and 198 wounded—many of them Marines on duty at the antiaircraft guns. Six hits on the destroyer *Norman Scott* killed her skipper, Commander Seymour Owens, and 18 other sailors while wounding 47 more. But then the Japanese guns were spotted and knocked out by a rain of American salvos.

Still, Captain Oya was elated. He had stopped the Americans. He could see their landing boats veering, turning, churning back to their mother ships. The enemy Marines were reboarding their transports. They were sailing north, with their warships.

It was then about nine o'clock, and it was then that Captain Oya received word that the Americans had landed up in the northwest and were pouring over narrow beaches there in incredible speed and volume. And all of Captain Oya's guns were sited to fire to seaward. He was out of the fight. From now on, it was up to Colonel Ogata.

Colonel Ogata had also been hoodwinked by that feint off Tinian Town. By the time he had realized that the true landing was being made over those undefended northwest beaches, it was too late for him to move troops there.

Battalion after battalion of the Fourth Marine Division burst from the bellies of the LST's and went racing shoreward. Full 533 amtracks—all the Fifth Corps could muster—brought them inland while the LCI rocket boats raced ahead and darkened the sky with showers of rockets. Even the 140-millimeter cannon which Colonel Ogata had set up in Faibus San Hilo to the right or south of the beachhead were knocked out by battleships which fired armor-piercers into the cliff face above them and tumbled both guns and emplacements into the sea.

Only land mines which the Japanese had concealed between high- and low-water marks survived to defend these narrow beaches against the attacking Americans. Three amtracks were demolished by these, and many others were forced to bring

368

their boatloads around to the coral ledges. But the Marines jumped up on the ledges, and that marvelous swift surge swept inland.

At ten minutes to eight, the Marines landed. A half-hour later they had their beachheads. Before nine o'clock, there were reserve battalions speeding in from the sea. Then there were tanks punching inland, artillery was being brought in, and the assault troops were fanning out and sweeping aside the light resistance of Colonel Ogata's startled defenders. Here was a pocket of 50 Japanese fighting out of crevices in the cliff ledges, there a pair of blockhouses the bombardment had missed—but they fell, and the beachheads were bought at a cost of 15 Marines killed and 225 wounded.

Throughout the afternoon, Colonel Ogata sought desperately to reinforce his surprised northern sector. He tried rushing up small party after small party from the south, but the American planes spotted and scattered them. Two of Ogata's tanks were knocked out while moving up. Many of his soldiers who sought cover would not venture forth again until night. They had been pounded for months as had no troops of the Empire, and now they were terrified of the "hell-jelly" bombs filling the air with gouts of sticky flame.

By midafternoon the Marines had knifed inland to well over a mile. They could have gone farther, but General Cates was content with a defensible beachhead. At half-past four, still offshore in an LST, for he had no wish to add to the congestion of those narrow beaches, Cates ordered his regiments to halt, to tie in their flanks, to string barbed wire, to dig in. They nailed down a beachhead 2,900 yards wide and about 1,700 deep at its farthest penetration west. It rested on all the best terrain. Its flanks curved back to a sea filled with friendly ships. It had been seized at a cost of 77 Marines killed and 470 wounded. And it held 15,614 Marines.

And Colonel Ogata was going to strike it. Outnumbered, his communications all but knocked out, his units scattered, his very authority being constantly challenged by the orders of Captain Oya to his south, Colonel Ogata was still going "to destroy the enemy at the beach."

Even though the Americans were off the beach, he would

carry out that plan of "annihilation at the water's edge" which so many Japanese commanders seemed to conceive concurrent with their own conception. In fact, he had already instructed his units to counterattack at two in the morning.

At exactly that hour on the morning of July 25, about 600 screaming Japanese struck at the left flank held by the Twenty-fourth Marines. They were annihilated.

A half-hour later the first of a series of strong thrusts began against the Twenty-fifth Marines in the center. About 200 Japanese found an opening at the boundary between this regiment and the Twenty-fourth. They poured through. They met muzzle-blasting artillerists and counterattacking riflemen. They were killed to a man.

At half-past three the third and final assault fell on the Twenty-third Marines to the right. It was blown to bits. Five tanks were destroyed. At dawn, astonished Marines saw Japanese bodies flying 15 feet into the air. The wounded were blowing themselves up with magnetic mines—an end at once more powerful and spectacular than the customary hand-grenade suicide.

That dawn was also the end of Colonel Ogata's defense of Tinian.

Strewn all around the Fourth Division's perimeter were the bodies of 1,241 Japanese soldiers and sailors. At least another 700 had been wounded. With a single stroke, Ogata had deprived himself of perhaps a quarter of the best troops which had survived the first day's assault. He could do nothing else but fall steadily south until he and all but 255 of his command were destroyed.

That took seven more days, with the Second Marine Division joining the attack. On July 25, the Second moved in behind the Fourth. It cleaned out the northern end of Tinian, then wheeled to move down the eastern half of the island. Second on the left, Fourth on the right, General Schmidt's attack rolled south with the impetuosity which had not been possible on Saipan. On July 31, Tinian was declared fallen. On that night, Colonel Ogata himself fell—machine-gunned to death on Marine barbed wire—while leading the last *banzai*. There was mopping-up to follow, during which Pfc. Robert Wilson sacrificed his life for his friends by falling on an enemy grenade, winning the Medal of Honor. There was also a replication of the suicidal horrors of Marpi Point. But Tinian was the masterpiece of island war. Only 327 men had died and 1,771 had been wounded in securing Saipan's southern flank and in seizing some of the finest bomber sites in the Central Pacific. It would indeed have been better if none had died and none had suffered, but such perfection is possible only against men of straw.

By all the real and cruel standards of war, Tinian was amphibious assault mastered at last, the problem of how to land on a hostile, fortified island finally solved—and then made perfect by Colonel Ogata's back-breaking *banzai*.

12

Marines of the Third Division and First Brigade had been taught everything there was to know about Guam—except that it was the Japanese liquor locker of the Central Pacific.

Guam had whisky by the small pond, it had rivers of *saki*, it had lakes of beer by the uncountable case. It had, in this sea of intoxicants, the answer to a question which had puzzled Marines since the first *banzai* was broken at Tulagi on the night of August 7, 1942. That was:

Are they drugged or are they drunk?

On Guam the night of July 25 the Japanese to the north were buoyant with booze, while those in the south were riproaring drunk.

On the southern or Agat beachhead, the Japanese troops led by Commander Asaichi Tamai had been driven west on Orote Peninsula by the First Marine Brigade. On the morning of July 25 the brigade sealed off the mouth of the peninsula.

The Marines dug in, Fourth Regiment on the left, Twenty-second on the right.

Tamai made a desperate effort to evacuate his troops by water. Barges put out into Apra Harbor from Orote's north coast. But Marine artillery on the mainland and on Cabras Island in the harbor blew them to bits. That happened at five o'clock in the afternoon. A few hours later, with the advent of a black night, while a daylong drizzle changed to a downpour, Tamai's officers began passing out the whisky.

Six miles to the north, outside the Asan-Adelup beachhead held by the Third Marine Division, the drinking did not begin until midnight.

At Asan-Adelup the attack was not going to be the drunken suicide-rush brewing on Orote. This was to be the well-planned "single stroke" with which Lieutenant General Takashina hoped to "solve the issue of the battle." *Saki* would be used to inflame the ardor of the troops, but not until after they had reached their assembly areas on the Fonte Plateau east of the American lines. Six battalions from the 45th Brigade, the 18th Regiment and other units—about 5,000 men—began moving out at about ten o'clock under cover of Japanese artillery and guided by red flares. After they had assembled, patrols went out to probe for weak spots in the American line.

They found gaps. By July 25 the Third Division's line was about a mile deep and five miles wide, and it was held by only 7,000 riflemen. The alignment had the Third Marines on the left (with the detached Second Battalion, Ninth), the Twenty-first in the center, and the Ninth (less that detached Second Battalion) on the right. Between the Twenty-first and the Ninth was a gap 800 yards wide and held by a mere scouting unit. Many of the rifle companies were understrength. One Japanese patrol found a soft spot in the Marine left-center held by the First Battalion, Twenty-first, and another one of 50 soldiers ran into the Marine scouts in the 800-yard gap and drove them back.

There was now a broad undefended avenue running to the American rear, and in its path, 200 yards inland from the beach, was the Division Hospital.

Already many of the wounded in the hospital were stirring

uneasily to hear the sound of Japanese artillery shells exploding around the batteries of the Twelfth Marines a few hundred yards to the left or north.

Not far from the hospital a young artilleryman of the Twelfth Marines felt a terror that is the palsy of the soul.

He had crawled into a cave to take cover from the Japanese shells. He had gone to sleep. He had awakened to find someone sitting on him. He felt for his carbine. Someone was sitting on that. There were perhaps a half-dozen of these intruders. He could hear the clinking of their canteens and smell the sour reek of *saki*, could hear the soft jabbering of their voices, could feel on the man astride him the hard round shape of a magnetic mine.

A squad of Japanese infiltrators had crept into his cave and were sitting there awaiting the daylight—when they would depart to attack the Marine guns.

It was eleven o'clock at night on Orote Peninsula, and an indescribable clamor had erupted in a mangrove swamp outside the right front of the First Marine Brigade.

"Listen at 'em," a Marine hissed to his foxhole buddy. "Damn if it don't sound like New Year's Eve in the zoo!"

The Japanese were screaming, singing, laughing, capering— they were smashing empty bottles against the big mangroves and clanging bayonets against rifle barrels.

Hoarse voices cried, "The Emperor draws much blood to-night!" Others rose in fits of cackling presumed to be terrifying. Some tossed grenades, yelling, "Corpsman! Corpsman!" or "K Company withdraw!" If they had hoped to unnerve the Marines or to goad them into giveaway fire, they had less than success. Their uproar only helped artillery observers call down a restraining fire on the edge of the swamp, while carefully registering all the Japanese avenues of approach with the combined guns of the brigade, the corps, and the 77th Division —as well as with the light and heavy mortars and 37's of the front-line companies.

At five minutes before midnight, a Japanese officer staggered out of the swamp. He waved a saber in one hand, a big flare in the other. Stumbling into view behind him, wielding their rifles and light machine guns, as well as pitchforks, idiot sticks, baseball bats and broken bottles, came his *saki*-mad followers.

A Marine spoke into a telephone:

"Commence firing!"

Maniacal voices began bellowing over the mouth of Orote Peninsula. The ground shook. Flares cast their ghostly light. Puttee-taped legs, khaki-clad arms, went flying through the air. The ground to the left front became a slaughter-pen. Within it the Japanese began to run amuk. They screamed in terror. Those who survived fled back into the mangroves, where the Marine artillery pursued and punished. Between midnight and two in the morning, 26,000 shells were poured into the swamp.

Forty-five minutes later another *banzai* began on the far right flank with the cry of, "Marines, you die!"

The Japanese rushed in among the Marine foxholes, where flares and star-shells displayed them in all their drunken madness. They reeled about. They tossed grenades into foxholes with the giggling cry, "Fire in the hole!"—and lurched crazily on. They clambered over heaps of their own dead to jump into the holes with the Marines, to die there—and often to kill as they died. Waves of attackers following them were caught in a crossfire and cut to pieces. Morning showed 400 Japanese bodies strewn in front of this position. On the First Brigade's left, a single platoon killed 258 Japanese without the loss of a single man.

Commander Tamai's attack had failed utterly.

But up in the north, Lieutenant General Takashina's counter-attack was breaking through.

Takashina's grand *banzai* came in three columns, and it was only the first—and strongest—of these which had no success.

This stroke was made around midnight by the full force of the 48th Brigade on the left of the American line, the sector held by the Third Marines reinforced by the Second Battalion, Ninth Marines. It was against this last battalion that the 48th Brigade struck.

But the 48th never got through.

Seven times the Japanese attacked the American left, and seven times they were hurled back.

The fight raged for ten hours and was not spent until around nine in the morning of July 26. Before it was over the Second Battalion, Ninth Marines, was cut in half—but its men had killed 950 Japanese. Captain Louis Wilson of F Company was wounded three times, but stayed to rally his men and win a Medal of Honor. Once the bull-chested Wilson ran 50 yards in front of his lines to rescue a helpless Marine. As the battle began to go against the enemy, he gathered 17 men and led them in a rush on high ground commanding his own position. Thirteen of those men fell, but Wilson and the others took the hill.

In the morning they pursued the retreating Japanese from there, moving through assembly areas cluttered with empty bottles and *saki*-sour canteens.

Takashina's second column was formed by the 2nd Battalion, 18th Regiment, led by Major Chusa Maruyama.

Maruyama brought his men up to the soft spot discovered by the probes of earlier patrols. It was held by a 50-man company of the First Battalion, Twenty-first Marines, and stood at the left-center of the American line. At four in the morning of July 26, Maruyama ordered his men to throw grenades.

They fell in a hissing volley behind and among the Marines.

"Wake up, American, and die!" the Japanese yelled, and rushed.

So tightly were they bunched, so oblivious were they to the death that swept among them, that they overwhelmed that undersized company and ripped a hole in the lines. The flanking Marine companies bent back their flanks. The left held by Captain William Shoemaker's A Company beat back Maruyama's attempts to widen the hole. Shoemaker went among his men. "If we go, the whole beachhead goes," he told them. But a rumor swept the lines. Company A was being ordered to withdraw, some men whispered. Shoemaker heard it. He leaped to his feet, a big man bulging at the seams of his captured Japanese raincoat. His voice roared out in the dark.

"By God, we hold here!"

They held. On the right of the opening, Captain Henry Helgren's C Company was also holding. Both outfits began pouring an enfilading fire into Maruyama's men racing through the narrow hole. The Japanese were dashing for the beach and the massed American equipment back there. Some of them ran with land mines in their hands. Others had packs stuffed with 20 pounds of explosives or had charges strapped to their legs or wound around their waists. The Marine fire struck them and the rain-swept blackness was illuminated with blinding white flashes as these human bombs blew up. But many others got through, sweeping down on Marine tanks parked to the rear.

They attacked the tanks with their bare hands. They kicked them, beat upon them with their fists, backed off and fired useless rifle rounds against them—all in an effort to get at the crewmen within—Marines who were even then swiveling machine guns to shoot the squat tan men off each other's tanks with the aplomb of cows mutually switching flies off one another's backs.

Unable to destroy the tanks, Maruyama's men ran farther down the draw. They came to the cliff, destroyed two platoons of Marine mortars, and began attacking the First Battalion's CP, their drunken yells and the booming of their grenades counterpointing the shouts and firing of a pick-up force of Marine cooks, clerks and communicators which had been assembled to counterattack them. The CP fight—in which Maruyama was killed—ended at daylight with the destruction of the Japanese soldiers who had broken through.

Up at the opening which they had torn in the Marine line, Captain Shoemaker and Captain Helgren were counterattacking. They fought back across the hole, slamming it shut like a pair of swinging doors. A company of engineers and three weapons platoons were sent to reinforce them. They arrived just before Maruyama's reserve struck at the restored line in a second thrust.

Howling, stumbling, waving sabers, bayonets and long poles, the Japanese rushed at Shoemaker's and Helgren's men and were destroyed.

The left-center of the Marine line was now safe.

376

★

The third column of Takashina's *banzai* was formed by the 3rd Battalion, 18th Regiment, under Major Setsuo Yukioka. Shortly after Maruyama's stroke began, at about a quarter after four in the morning, Yukioka's men struck a company of the Twenty-first Marines on the center-right. They captured two machine guns, but then the Americans re-formed and drove them out. Yukioka took his battalion sliding along the Marine front, and it was then that they blundered into that 800-yard gap between the Twenty-first Marines in the center and the Ninth Marines on the right.

They swarmed through, following lantern-bearing scouts.

A Marine roadblock began firing on the right flank of the Japanese column, and Yukioka's men wheeled right and over-ran the roadblock. They moved farther to the rear, the main body setting up a position on high ground behind the Third Battalion, Twenty-first, the men of the demolition squads continuing to move down the ravines toward the beach and the Division Hospital.

The Japanese soldiers on the high ground began striking the rear of the Third Battalion, Twenty-first, commanded by Lieutenant Colonel Wendell Duplantis. Duplantis asked Division for artillery. It was refused, for it might fall on friendly troops. Instead, Company L was taken out of the Ninth Marines reserve and ordered to counterattack Yukioka.

The Marines let loose a shower of grenades, charged—and routed the Japanese on the hill.

But to the rear of that hill, toward the sea, Yukioka's demolition squads were slipping down the ravines toward the Division Hospital. They were tipsy and they were swigging the last of the *saki* in their canteens. Some were already in the throes of hangover. They moved on, their ranks augmented by the suiciders creeping from the caves in which they had spent the night. One such group came out reeling drunkenly, unaware that they had spent the night sitting on a terrified American who had by now lost his mind. They joined up. They came to a high hill overlooking the American hospital tents. They could see the sea only a few hundred yards west.

It was half-past six in the morning, and they started down the hill.

A wounded Marine coming east from the hospital to rejoin his outfit on the front saw the short men in khaki slipping and sliding down the hill. He turned and wide-legged it back to the hospital, bawling:

"The Japs are coming! The Japs are coming!"

Corpsmen and patients grabbed weapons and flung themselves behind cots or cartons of plasma. Some of the walking wounded jumped from their cots and ran for the beach. A cook wounded the night before leaped erect, naked, and hobbled for safety.

The Japanese came with a yell and a shower of grenades. Corpsmen and patients fired back. A doctor absorbed in an operation glanced up as shrapnel whistled through the tent canvas. He sent his corpsmen outside to fight and continued the operation.

Meanwhile, at Division Headquarters, a few hundred yards to the right of the hospital as it faced the front, Colonel George Van Orden began rounding up another pick-up force. Every available man behind the lines—Seabees, MP's, combat correspondents, truck drivers—was collected and led toward the hospital, where the Japanese were driven back into a jumble of hills.

Then Colonel Van Orden's force turned to a methodical mopping-up of all the terrain between the sea and the front lines. It was grisly work, relieved only by the fact that the Japanese began to blow themselves up. Here and there a new method of suicide appeared. Enemy soldiers took off their helmets, placed a primed grenade on top of their heads, replaced the helmet—and awaited oblivion with folded arms.

By noon it was all over.

By nightfall it was clear that General Takashina had lost 3,500 soldiers, exclusive of the Orote losses. He had lost 95 per cent of his commissioned officers and 90 per cent of his weapons had been destroyed. He had so many wounded that their presence was weakening morale. He had no hope of help either by sea or by air, and American power in those elements was battering him ceaselessly. His men had killed only 200 of the enemy, while wounding 645 more, and the Third Marine Division was already prepared to come out fighting on Fonte Plateau. There was nothing for Takashina to do but withdraw. He had staked all on that grand *banzai*, but in the words of the man who opposed him, Major General Allen Turnage:

"It was a grand victory for us."

13

Two days after General Takashina's grand *banzai* had been shattered, the general was himself dead. He was machine-gunned by Marines breaking out of the Asan-Adelup beachhead. Command passed to elderly Lieutenant General Hideyoshi Obata, the commander of the Marianas defenses who had been caught on Guam when the Americans landed.

On that same July 28, the 77th Division completed patrolling to the south, came up north, took Mount Tenjo, and linked up with the Third Marine Division's right flank. Also that day, Brigadier General Shepherd's First Brigade struck out along Orote and drove into the old Marine Barracks. They found a cigar box holding prewar Post Exchange receipts, a star-spangled pillow which a Japanese soldier had made from the blue field of the American flag, and a bronze plaque. The rest was rubble. They drove on, to take the airfield and to herd the last of Commander Tamai's 3,500 men onto Orote's eastern tip.

On July 31—the day General MacArthur's approach to the Philippines reached its terminus on Sansapor Point in western New Guinea, the date of the Allied breakout from the Normandy beachhead in France—the First Brigade came to the end of Orote Peninsula. The Brigade had fought a bitter battle since the landing at Agat, the sweep north, the fighting left-turn onto Orote. Their dead and missing numbered 431, their wounded 1,525. But they had buried 3,372 Japanese and taken only three prisoners. Now a squad had come upon the last living enemy soldier on Orote.

He was a forlorn scrimp of a man, small even for his race, and his tattered blouse and breeches were much too large. But there was an easiness about him that puzzled the Marines who took him captive. Many times Japanese prisoners had become ashamed of having surrendered and asked for a knife to commit *hara-kiri*. Yet this soldier seemed almost eager to be taken away. A Marine interpreter spoke to him.

"Why did you surrender?"

"My commanding officer told us to fight to the last man."

The Marine's eyebrows rose.

"Well?"

The Japanese soldier's eyebrows also rose—in wounded innocence—and he exclaimed:

"I am the last man."

The same day, Guam's two-division attack to the northeast began with the Third Marine Division on the left, the 77th Infantry on the right. The Marines were moving against Agana, the city which stood on the island's western shore at the narrow waist where the Guam peanut twists east and north. There was no opposition in Agana. The city had been ruined by American bombing and naval gunfire called down on General Takashina's artillery concentrations there. Its Chamorro population had fled into the bush days before the invasion, after American warplanes dropped leaflets advising them to do so.

A squad of Marines moved warily through Agana's streets, now silent and powdery with dust. They passed what had once been a neat little cemetery, now debauched by naval shelling. Huge 14-inch shell craters pocked it and its crosses and headstones were a jumble of jagged pieces. One of the Marines shook his head.

"Even the dead can't rest in peace," he said.

★

On the right flank, Major General Andrew Bruce's 77th Infantry Division also moved ahead with no opposition. The only hindrances were the roughness of the terrain, the heat, and nagging swarms of flies and mosquitoes.

Then, at a jungle place called Yona, the soldiers found a concentration camp filled with Chamorros.

There were 2,000 of them, cheering, weeping, laughing, singing. They had been living in lean-tos and thatched huts built in the mud to either side of a sluggish stream. They had had little food, no medical care. They were clothed in rags. They were weak, racked by continual coughing fits—victims of malnutrition, malaria and tuberculosis. Their bodies were sticks of bones and their olive skin was drawn drum-tight. But this thirty-first of July was the day they had awaited for nearly three years. When they saw the American soldiers coming through the trees they hobbled to their feet with glad cries.

They sang "The Marines' Hymn"—for they remembered the Marines—but the soldiers of the 3rd Battalion, 307th Infantry, didn't mind that at all. They began to sing a song of their own underground, composed especially for this date and memorized in face of every threat of reprisal.

> *Early Monday morning*
> *The action came to Guam,*
> *Eighth of December,*
> *Nineteen forty-one.*
> > *Oh, Mr. Sam, Sam, my dear Uncle Sam,*
> > *I want you please come back to Guam.*
>
> *Our lives are in danger—*
> *You better come*
> *And kill all the Japanese*
> *Right here on Guam.*
> > *Oh, Mr. Sam, Sam, my dear Uncle Sam,*
> > *I want you please come back to Guam.*

Such scenes were repeated all the way up the island, while General Geiger drove his attacking divisions forward.

There were battles along the way. On August 3 the Ninth Marines reached a place called Finegayen near Tumon Bay on the west coast. On that morning a good-humored youth with a flashing white smile and the name of Frank Witek said to his friends, "I think this is my day." It was surely so, although Pfc. Witek did not see its end. He fought tigerishly in the attack at Finegayen, exposing himself repeatedly to cover his squad. He shot 16 of the enemy. But as so often happens to the brave, he made his last charge and fell dead. As does not so often happen, he won the Medal of Honor. The next day the gallant Captain Shoemaker fell. He was sitting beside the road when a Japanese 75 shell swooshed in and blotted out his life. "All the good ones go," a Marine said sadly, unashamed of the tears streaking his dusty cheeks. Next day Finegayen fell. Two days later, on August 7, General Geiger put the First Brigade on the line. With the brigade on the left, Third Marines in the center, 77th on the right, the assault rolled north until it reached Ritidian Point on August 10 and Guam was declared conquered.

But the southward streaming of the Chamorros did not stop. A Civil Affairs Section had been set up to care for them. Stockades were built. Captured Japanese food was issued. Some Chamorros came to the stockades to eat, to regain a little strength, to find a bayonet or a machete and slip back into the northern hills for vengeance. But most of them stayed, among them an emaciated old man with snow-white hair. He came to the stockade and introduced himself as Gaily R. Kamminga, a former member of the Guam Congress. He found old friends among some of the Navy officers who had landed with the Marines. He showed them a little pillow he was carrying. It was the only article of comfort which the Japanese had allowed him to take to the penal camp. Suddenly he ripped it open. Inside it was a faded American flag which had flown over the Piti Naval Yard the day of the Japanese invasion.

Down at Orote a new American flag flew over the rubble that had once been the Marine Barracks. It had been raised on July 29. General Geiger had been there, with his chief of staff, Colonel Merwin Silverthorn. General Shepherd had spoken quickly, while shells whistled east toward Orote's tip.

"On this hallowed ground," Shepherd said, "you officers and men of the First Marine Brigade have avenged the loss of our comrades who were overcome by a numerically superior enemy three days after Pearl Harbor. Under our flag this island again stands ready to fulfill its destiny as an American fortress in the Pacific."

Colonel Silverthorn stepped forward.

"Hoist the American colors," he commanded.

Old Glory fluttered up the pole.

"To the Colors!" commanded Geiger.

A Marine blew the quick-sweet, slow-sad notes on a captured Japanese bugle.

The Marines saluted.

It had cost 7,800 Americans killed and wounded—839 soldiers, 245 sailors, 6,716 Marines—but Uncle Sam had come back to Guam.

14

HOTEL ATOLL
No Beer Atoll
No Women Atoll
Nuthin' Atoll

The sign had been raised outside a billet on Kwajalein Atoll. But, like that "PAVUVU RIFLE AND GUN CLUB, WHERE LIFE IS A THIRTY CALIBER BORE," it had its cousins by the dozen from Camp Tarawa in Hawaii to the newly built Second Marine Division encampments on Saipan.

Tedium had taken hold in the Pacific. Except on Guam, where the Third Marine Division was still mopping up, life had become an unutterable yawn. The blaze of battle had flickered out and would not flare up again until mid-September.

There were occasional thrilling spectacles, such as that of the morning of August 28 at Eniwetok, when Admiral Halsey took Task Force 38 out of the lagoon for a westward-ranging strike at the Palaus, later to swing north and strike at Mindanao in the Southern Philippines. But generally there was a lull. There had not even been much news from Europe since the announcement that the Allies had landed in Southern France on August 15.

On Pavuvu, it was a time when the men of the First Marine Division "trained" by walking around and around their tiny rattrap of an island, one outfit marching clockwise, the other counterclockwise, so as not to clog the single coastal road, exchanging cordial insults as they passed each other, cursing the pervasive odor of rotten coconut and those constantly falling nuts which made it necessary to wear helmets at all times— either when going to chow for that unvarying "rest and rehabilitation" diet of powdered eggs, spam and dehydrated potatoes, or when watching a grade-B movie in what was hopefully called an "open-air theater" but was actually a clearing in which men sat on fallen logs and watched a screen, yelling like sex-starved satyrs the moment any human being in skirts skipped, swished or staggered across it. There was no beer issue on Pavuvu for the men, as there was in the plush Army and Navy bases on surrounding islands. But the men of the First knew how to strain a bottle of after-shave lotion through a loaf of bread to make it palatable; they could cook up inebriate delights with raisins, sugar and coconut milk, or vanilla extract stolen from the galley—and those men invalided across the bay to the naval hospital on Banika could be counted upon to return with stores of medical alcohol bought with battle souvenirs. So supplied, the men could drink and sing.

The coffee that they give us, they say is mighty fine,
It's good for cuts and bruises, in place of iodine.
　　I don't want no more of the U. S. Marines,
　　Gee, but I wanna go home.

They say when you're enlisted, promotions are mighty fine,
Well, I'm a goddam private, I been in over nine.
　　I don't want no more of the U. S. Marines,
　　Gee, but I wanna go home.

The bedsacks that they give you, they say are mighty fine,
Well, how in hell should I know, I never slept in mine.

The officers they give us, can stand up to the worst,
You find 'em every weekend, shacked up with a nurse.
I don't want no more of the U. S. Marines,
Gee, but I wanna go, right back to Quantico,
Gee, but I wanna go home.

There was little of such diversion on Saipan-Tinian. The Fourth Marine Division had already departed, sailing back to its old base on Maui in the Hawaiian Islands, and leaving the Second Marine Division sole proprietors of islands made dismal by the August monsoon and mosquitoes carrying dengue or "breakbone" fever. There were also close to 1,000 Japanese still holed up in the hills, and there were Marines being killed in cleaning them out. But for the Second's veterans, as with those of the First Division, there was the blessed rotation system which was taking many of them home. Close to 1,300 Marines who could claim service back to Guadalcanal were shipped Stateside. Some of their comrades painted gold stars on their tents in sardonic mockery of the American penchant for taking bows. If a man's school, church, community, club, factory or office could put his name on a plaque headed, "Our Men in Service," why couldn't a man's squad commemorate his entry in the ranks of the rear-echelons? So they put up signs like this:

WE HAVE A BOY STATESIDE.

Back at the Second's old Camp Tarawa in Hawaii, the new Fifth Marine Division was getting accustomed to training overseas—adjusting to such novel nuisances as censorship. But there was one private who had cause to bless the censor. He had received a note: "Letter at mail desk. Name on envelope Dorothy, name on letter Bettye. Check and if correct, mail."

The last of the Marine divisions—the Sixth—was being formed on Guadalcanal. Its nucleus was the First Brigade and its commander was the brigade's old leader, but Lemuel Shepherd now wore the twin stars of a major general. To the brigade's Fourth and Twenty-second Marines—units of which had fought at Guadalcanal, Makin, Bougainville and Eniwetok —was added the Twenty-ninth Marines. The First Battalion, Twenty-ninth, had captured Mount Tapotchau on Saipan, but its Second and Third Battalions were newly formed in the States.

Though the Sixth Marine Division also got an artillery regiment, the Fifteenth, it got almost none of the specialists characteristic of Marine amphibious divisions of the past. For the Fleet Marine Force, Pacific, had been divided into two corps— the Third under Major General Geiger, the Fifth under Major General Schmidt—and all the special functions were now taken over by the corps. A Marine division was now streamlined to about 18,000 men, although the First, scheduled for a one-division landing, remained at a strength of above 20,000.

Training of the new Sixth Division began in late August with the arrival of the First Brigade from Guam, and it was made difficult by the Guadalcanal base commander's insistence that Marine divisions furnish 1,000 men daily for base working parties. It had been to avoid this typical harassment of line divisions by rear-echelon generals that the First Division had been assigned to its private "little-ease" on Pavuvu.

To some of the Sixth's veterans who had known Guadalcanal in the days of the Tokyo Express and Pistol Pete or Washing-Machine Charley, the island had become a placid fat cow of a place with its officers' clubs, its hospitals, its warehouses, its roads and piers and libraries and theaters and indoor mess halls and quonset huts, its battalions of military police required to guard its Red Cross girls and nurses and to enforce the numerous regulations clattering off the typewriters of those ubiquitous clerk-typists who had become the new heroes of Guadalcanal. The Marines did not like it there, nor could they take the new Guadalcanal seriously when, at night, with the open-air theaters going full blast, the MP's got around to playing air-raid-precaution.

"Put those goddam lights out!" an MP called to a Marine driving a jeep one night.

The driver obeyed. But he happened to be a general's driver, and the general said evenly:

"Put those goddam lights back on."

The driver obeyed.

"Put those goddam lights *out!*" the MP shrieked.

"I *can't,*" the Marine yelled back. "I got the goddam general with me!"

If late August and early September meant a time of lull to the Marines on the ground, it marked the end of the doldrums for the Marines in the air. They would soon get the escort carriers from which they would launch close-up aerial support of their foot-slogging comrades. They would also send 17 squadrons into the Philippines to place this tactic at the service of Army divisions. And the "forgotten war" they had been fighting over the Marshalls would be over.

Having shown how to knock out a base at Rabaul, the Marine fliers had been assigned a repeat performance over the by-passed atolls of Wotje, Maloelap, Milli and Jaluit. Resistance had been fierce at first. Thirty-six planes had been shot down. But then the fearful accuracy of such dive-bomber pilots as Major Elmer (Iron Man) Glidden—who set the record of 107 combat dives in the Pacific—gradually eliminated the Japanese antiaircraft guns and the Marshalls mission became a boring "milk run."

All of the glory, all of the glamour, had moved westward with the invasion timetable. Except for the Marshalls siege and the occasional appearance of squadrons flying by stages to the Marianas, life on Eniwetok, Kwajalein and Majuro could be the perfection of tedium. It was worse at Tarawa, now the backwater of the Pacific War.

Only the cemetery on Betio served to remind the atoll's garrison of the savage four-day battle fought there less than a year before. It was a place of shining coral and slender white crosses, surrounded by a neat coconut-log wall which the Seabees had built. Here a lieutenant colonel lay between privates. Here was so often the word "Unknown." And here, on a white plaque raised above the cemetery gate, was inscribed the sadly beautiful epitaph which Captain Donald Jackson wrote for his comrades.

To you, who lie within this coral sand,
We, who remain, pay tribute of a pledge,
That, dying thou shalt surely not
Have died in vain.
That when again bright morning dyes the sky
And waving fronds above shall touch the rain,
We give you this—that in those times
We will remember.

II

We lived and fought together, thou and we,
And sought to keep the flickering torch aglow
That all our loved ones might forever know
The blessed warmth exceeding flame,
The everlasting scourge of bondsman's chains,
Liberty and light.

III

When we with loving hands laid back the earth
That was for moments short to couch thy form,
We did not bid a last and sad farewell
But only, "Rest ye well."
Then with this humble, heartfelt epitaph
That pays thy many virtues sad acclaim
We marked this spot, and, murm'ring requiem,
Moved on to westward.

Westward they had moved, until, by mid-September, 1944, full 40 degrees of longitude lay between Tarawa and another coral island called Peleliu.

15

The Palau Islands, of which Peleliu was one of two chief bastions, were to be held at all costs.

Imperial General Headquarters had made this clear to Lieutenant General Sadae Inoue when he had taken command there in March. For the Palaus, a series of volcanic islands inside a coral reef 77 miles long and 20 wide, provided the anchorage and air bases no longer available at Truk. They were only about 550 miles east of the Southern Philippines.

In March, Imperial General Headquarters had wrongly guessed that the Americans would strike the Palaus and not the Marianas. The Japanese had expected General MacArthur's invasion of the Philippines to take precedence over the Marianas route to Japan. Having used the Palaus to stage their own Philippines invasions of 1941, it seemed to them likely that the Americans would want them for the same reasons in 1944.

After the surprise at Saipan, after the disaster of the Battle of the Philippine Sea and the agony of the Marianas losses, Headquarters regarded a Palaus invasion as inevitable. So did Inoue. The commander of the "Palau Sector Group," which also included Yap and Ulithi Atolls, decided to make his defense so tenacious as to gain months of time during which the Empire could recover from the air and fleet losses of the Marianas fighting.

To do this he withdrew all troops from Ulithi and began concentrating his 30,000 to 40,000 men in the Palaus, in little Peleliu just inside the southern end of the reef, and on big Babelthuap just within the northern end. Another island, Angaur, was 10 miles south of Peleliu but outside the reef. It got only about 1,400 men.

Peleliu got between 10,000 and 11,000 men—the 2nd Infantry Regiment, a battalion of the 15th Infantry, a battalion of the 54th Independent Mixed Brigade, a Naval Guard Force and a tank battalion—all commanded by Colonel Kunio Nakagawa. Most of these units were from the 14th Infantry Division, Inoue's own outfit and the nucleus of his force. It was a proud old division with a service record running back through four years in Manchuria to the Russian War. In General Inoue and his chief of staff, Colonel Tokechi Tada, at Babelthuap, and in Colonel Nakagawa at Peleliu, the 14th Division possessed three of the finest officers in the Japanese Army.

Such ability was reflected in the "Palau Sector Group Training for Victory" plan issued by Inoue on July 11. It began:

"Victory depends on the officers and men of the entire army concentrating on our thorough application of recent battle lessons, especially those of Saipan."

Less than startling to Western ears, this was unorthodox in Japan. For years the doctrine of defense had been simply and inflexibly "annihilation at the water's edge." Hold the beach and you hold all. More, the invading American Marines had not been in the habit of allowing anyone to survive to challenge it. But there had been a few officers who escaped from Saipan, where General Saito's artillery had punished the Americans. They came to Inoue's command. They passed along their observations. The result:

"If the situation becomes bad we will maintain a firm hold on the high ground and prevent the enemy from establishing or using an air base by a daring guerrilla warfare with our artillery."

Peleliu was made for such defense.

It was six miles long south-north and two miles wide at its broadest west-east. It was shaped like a lobster's claw. It was, in fact, a pair of peninsulas joined on the east coast about one-third up its length. On the east coast were shoals and mangrove swamps and a series of islets extending the lower prong eastward. On the west were narrow beaches of white coral sand, fortified and defended in the accustomed manner. Both coasts were encompassed by the reef surrounding all the Palaus but Angaur. In the south was Peleliu's excellent airfield, one which

390

had been in use since before the war. Rising above it and running north about two miles was a low wooded ridge which the Japanese called the Momiji Plateau, which the Micronesians called Umurbrogal Mountain and which the American Marines would call Bloody Nose Ridge.

It was this high ground which made Peleliu so perfectly adaptable to defense-in-depth, for it was neither ridge nor mountain but an undersea coral reef thrown above the surface by a subterranean volcano. Sparse vegetation growing in the thin topsoil atop the bedrock had concealed the Umurbrogal's crazy contours from the aerial camera's eye. It was a place that might have been designed by a maniacal artist given to painting mathematical abstractions—all slants, jaggeds, straights, steeps and sheers with no curve to soften or relieve. Its highest elevation was 300 feet in the extreme north overlooking the airfield-islet of Ngesebus 1,000 yards offcoast there. But no height rose more than 50 feet before splitting apart in a maze of peaks and defiles cluttered with boulders and machicolated with caves. For the Umurbrogal was also a monster swiss cheese of hard coral limestone pocked beyond imagining with caves and crevices. They were to be found at every level, in every size— crevices small enough for a lonely sniper, eerie caverns big enough to station a battalion among its stalactites and stalagmites.

It was here that Colonel Nunio Nakagawa and his engineers set to work widening, improving and fortifying the caves. When Colonel Nakagawa reported to General Inoue on Babelthuap that Vice Admiral Itou was interfering with his work, Inoue sent Major General Kenjiro Murai down to Peleliu. He was not to take command, he was only, in that friction between the Anchor and the Star, to match rank with Admiral Itou. Beneath the cover of this stalemate, Nakagawa continued his fortifying, and by the end of August he had 500 caves completed.

Nearly all were connected by interior tunnels. Most had entrances on more than one level and all had entrances on both sides of the mountain. Log-and-sandbag barricades protected the entrances, and their tunnels ran only a few feet inside the mountain before turning sharply to escape both direct gunfire and the terrible American flame-throwers. Some of the caverns were five and six stories deep. They contained barracks and kitchens. If the top of the Umurbrogal were to be lifted off, some of these tunnel networks would appear like monster H's or series of E's laid back to back. And this would be repeated for five and six levels down.

Within these caves Colonel Nakagawa placed all of his artillery except his coastal guns, all of his mortars and also the new 200-millimeter rocket-launchers just received from Japan. The guns fired from cave mouths equipped with sliding doors of armored steel. They could hit the beaches, the airfield to the south and Ngesebus to the north. They were protected by squads of riflemen and machine-gunners firing through the slits of natural crevices. All of these strong-points were covered by interlocking fire. For the Americans to attack one of them would be to bring down the fire of two or three others on them, to say nothing of those which would remain silent until the Americans advanced under the delusion that they had knocked out the entire system. Then, as Hercules had found with Hydra, they would find the beheaded stump sprouting two fresh heads to bite at them.

The Umurbrogal was the Pacific's masterpiece of defensive engineering, and it was going to be manned by a new Japanese warrior. For Lieutenant General Inoue's training plan instructions had also killed the *banzai*. Inoue had agreed that "We are ready to die honorably," but he had also gone on to suggest, in that imprecise language which was as great a military drawback as the *banzai* itself, that mere dying was not enough. It had to have that exotic Western thing: purpose. Otherwise: "We must preserve personnel and ordnance." Nor was "spiritual power" any longer vaunted over material power.

"It is certain that if we repay the Americans (who rely solely upon material power) with material power it will shock them beyond imagination. . . ."

Unlike the crimson imagery with which commanders such as Haruyoshi Hyakutate urged the Japanese soldier to eat three of the American devils with each morning's bowl of rice, this remark had the quality of reality. A bursting shell, as Saipan had shown, did have more effect than a *banzai* scream. Clearly,

General Inoue agreed with Napoleon's cynical dictum that "God is on the side of the heavy artillery." In a Japanese paraphrase, he said:

"Heavenly aid on the road to victory falls only to those commanders who have a thorough control of command. . . ."

Nor did Inoue fear naval gunfire. He told his men:

"Without concerning ourselves with the great explosive bursts or the strong local effect of naval firing, the destructive power wrought upon personnel is not very great. . . . Aerial bombardment is almost identical. . . . By observing very carefully the activity of enemy planes and the bombs while they are falling, avoiding thereby instantaneous explosions, and by taking advantage of gaps in bombardment in order to advance, it can cause no great damage."

In proof, Inoue ordered his men to practice crawling through the bombs dropped during the light American raids of the spring and summer. But he ordered them to the antiaircraft guns when Admiral Halsey's warbirds struck at the Palaus from Task Force 59 carrier decks on September 6 through September 8. When the bombardment force of battleships and cruisers showed up under Rear Admiral Jesse Oldendorf in the pale moonlight of early morning, September 12, all Palau troops got under cover.

At Peleliu, Colonel Nakagawa left about a battalion south of the airfield, perhaps another battalion along the western beaches, while withdrawing the rest of his men and tanks into the Umurbrogal.

Up at Babelthuap, General Inoue prepared to receive the main American attack.

It was his only mistake.

16

The American plan in the waning summer of 1944 was to commence the invasion of the Philippines by stages.

The first stage was to open the gates: Morotai on New Guinea in the west, Peleliu-Angaur in the Palaus on the west. This would be followed by invasion of Yap on October 5, and after that, the seizure of Ulithi.

Then, in mid-November, General MacArthur would land on Mindanao in the Southern Philippines. Victory here would lead to December invasion of Leyte in the Central Philippines.

By March of 1945 the American forces in the Pacific would combine to secure either Luzon in the Northern Philippines, or to capture Formosa and ports on the China Coast. On either of these land masses the necessary large bodies of troops could be staged for the final assault on Japan.

Then the tides of war began shifting and the plan changed.

The Japanese in China launched their inevitable attacks on American air bases there and the Fourteenth Air Force had to retire from its forward fields. Soon the Japanese would make the China coast difficult to invade. For these reasons, and because no more American troops could be spared from Europe, the Formosa-China route to Japan was about to be canceled out.

And then, on September 13, Admiral Bull Halsey made his electrifying discovery that Japanese air power in the Philippines was on its last leg. On September 12, the carriers of Task Force 58 stood within sight of the mountains of Samar in the Central Philippines. They flew off 2,400 sorties. They destroyed 200 enemy planes. They sank ships. They bombed installations. They roved with such impunity that Halsey suggested to Admiral Nimitz, and thence to the Joint Chiefs of Staff, that all the Palau, Yap, Morotai and Mindanao landings be called off in favor of an immediate bold thrust into Leyte in the Central Philippines.

But General MacArthur was already headed for Morotai aboard the cruiser *Nashville*—and the ship was maintaining radio silence. Two days of messages shooting back and forth among Nimitz in Hawaii, the Combined Joint Chiefs of Staff attending the Octagon Conference in Quebec, and Lieutenant General R. K. Sutherland speaking for MacArthur in New Guinea produced these changes:

Instead of landing on Mindanao in November and then on Leyte in December, MacArthur would go directly to Leyte in October.

The Yap landing would be called off, and the Twenty-fourth Corps would be used at Leyte instead.

The Morotai landing by the 31st Infantry Division would go forward as planned, as would the landings on Angaur, Ulithi and Peleliu. The last three, considered necessary to obtain the air bases and anchorage which Admiral Nimitz wanted to support the Philippine landings, were to be made by troops of the Third Corps under Major General Geiger; the 81st Infantry (Wildcat) Division to hit Angaur and after that Ulithi, the First Marine Division to take Peleliu.

Peleliu, it had been known for months, was going to be a tough nut. The Marines had asked for heavy preinvasion bombardment there. And yet, off Peleliu on September 14, Admiral Oldendorf got off this message from his bombardment force:

"We have run out of targets!"

That same day, correspondents and unit commanders aboard the transports broke open sealed envelopes given them by Major General Rupertus, still commanding the First Marine Division. They read that Peleliu would be tough, like Tarawa, but also just as short.

It would take, said General Rupertus, something like four days.

17

On the morning of September 15 the First Marine Division struck at Peleliu's western beaches three regiments abreast.

On the left or north was the First Marines, using the code word *Spitfire;* in the center opposite the airfield was the Fifth or *Lonewolf;* on the right moving against the southern tip was the Seventh or *Mustang.*

The Marines were almost gay going in, for General Rupertus' prediction of four days had made them cocky, but once their amtracks had bumped over the fringing reef, once Colonel Nakagawa's thousand-eyed mountain stuffed with men and guns had begun to flash, they stopped calling to one another, stopped throwing kisses, stopped wagging four confident fingers. They ducked beneath the gunwales and began to pray.

"Playmate, this is Spider. The First Waves are on the beach. Repeat: The first waves are on the beach. Over."

"Spider, this is Playmate. What resistance do they seem to be meeting? Over."

"Playmate, this is Spider. Hard to tell much through this smoke. Over."

All that could be seen to shoreward was a great pall of twisted, drifting smoke, sometimes suffused with a pinkish glare by the shivering of flames beneath or within it. It was a fiery Moloch of a cloud, created by the thundering of the great naval shells exploding beneath it, the clash-crashing of thousands of rockets and the whuffling thump of the bombs which screaming dive-bombers dropped through it. It was so impressive that the skipper of Colonel Chesty Puller's transport

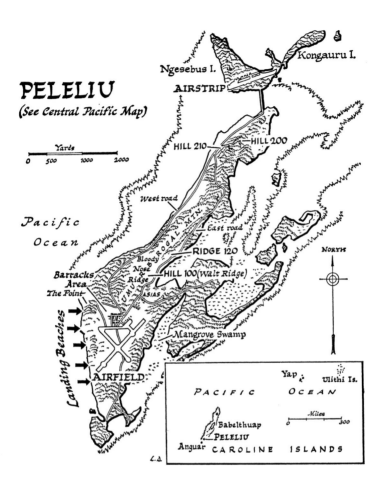

PELELIU

(See Central Pacific Map)

rushed up to the veteran Marine commander as he began to go over the side to join his men.

"Coming back for supper?" he called out cheerfully.

"Why?" Puller growled.

The skipper waved an airy hand shoreward.

"Hell, everything's done over there. You'll walk in."

"If you think it's so easy," Puller snapped, "why don't you come on the beach at five o'clock? We could have dinner together and maybe you could pick up a couple of souvenirs."

397

Then *Spitfire's* commander went ashore, losing all of his communications amtracks on the way.

"Playmate, this is Spider. Resistance moderate to heavy, I'd say. There are amtracks burning on the reef. Repeat: There are amtracks burning on the reef. Over."
"Spider, this is Playmate. Where are our front lines?"
"Lines well inland on the right and center, but left of Spitfire is still on beach. They seem to be pinned down. . . . I'm going lower to try and see what's to their front. . . ."

They were pinned down. The Marines of Captain George Hunt's K Company, First, had come in jauntily singing, "Give My Regards to Broadway," until the amtracks began to lurch and odd bumping, strangling noises against their sides signaled the arrival of Japanese mortars. The Marines fell silent, their faces paling beneath the outlandish streaking of their camouflage paint. Captain Hunt's amtracks crunched ashore, his men jumped out—and they were struck from their left by a terrible enfilading fire.

On that left stood The Point, a mass of coral rising 30 feet from the sea, a natural fort made of crevices, boulders and pinnacles, fortified at its base with five pillboxes of ferro-concrete, sprinkled with others protected by coral-and-concrete roofs six feet thick, and salted with spider holes. Within the pillboxes were heavy machine guns and one of them held a 47-millimeter antiboat gun.

Even now that gun was dropping shells among the First Marines on the beaches. For The Point stood on the division's extreme left or northern flank and it had the First's landing zone clearly in view beneath it. Over a rocky corridor between The Point and the sea, the Japanese could launch a counterattack almost any time they chose. Clearly, The Point must fall.

Captain Hunt ordered two platoons up against it. They turned left from the coconut grove and attacked. They were riddled. Hunt called battalion.

"We're pretty well shot up and there's a gap between my two assault platoons. I'm throwing the first platoon in to take The

Point. The goddam naval gunfire didn't faze the Japs! We need stretcher-bearers!"

"All right, bub," said Major William McNulty. "I'll have L Company fill in the gap. I'll send up everybody I can spare with stretchers."

But L Company did not plug the gap, nor did A or B Company from the First Battalion, nor were the stretchers able to reach the stricken during that incredible and impetuous assault which did, in fact, storm The Point.

The wounded had to be taken out by amtracks running the gantlet from the sea. When they had departed, there were Captain Hunt and Lieutenant Bill Willis and 30 men—all alone atop The Point.

"Playmate, this is Spider Two. Spider One has been shot down. Lonewolf is on the edge of the airfield in several places. Mustang making good progress, too, but resistance is heavy behind Spitfire's beaches. Over."

"Spider Two, this is Playmate. How are things on the reef now? Over."

"Damned bad! Boy, the stuff's sure hitting the fan now! There's about twenty amtracks burning off the Spitfire beaches and I make about eighteen off Mustang's. They got that one enfiladed, too."

"Spider Two, th——"

"Ow, I see 'em! Six of 'em with a field gun! Request permission to attack. Over."

"Spider Two, this is Playmate. Your request: Negative."

"Please? Just one little strafing?"

"Spider Two, this is Playmate. Negative. Repeat: Negative. You're supposed to be an aerial observer. Stay in the air and observe. Over."

"Oh, goddamit it to hell. . . ."

On the heavy cruiser *Portland* a gunnery officer had also seen the Japanese field piece. He watched through glasses as a great steel shutter swung open in the face of a hill, as tiny figures trundled out a gun, as it fired, as the men pulled it back inside the cave and the steel door swung shut again.

399

The gunnery officer had the target spotted.

"Fire!"

A full salvo of eight-inch armor-piercers screamed shore-ward. The hillside flashed and smoked.

The shutter swung open again.

The field piece was run out again, it spoke again, it was withdrawn again.

Four times more *Portland's* eight-inchers breathed flame and smoke rings, four times more the cave-gun fired, and at last the gunnery officer shook his head in grieving futility and said:

"You can put all the steel in Pittsburgh on that thing and still not get it."

From the division's right flank—the beaches south of the airfield where the Seventh Marines were landing, where Spider Two had seen all those burning amtracks—Colonel Herman Henry Hanneken sent the command ship that most ominous message of an amphibious invasion:

"Assault waves are wading ashore."

The Seventh had come in to a deadly subsea garden sown with antiboat mines, antiboat barriers, antitank mines, and antitroop mines—above which sprouted a wicked black tumbleweed of barbed wire—and all planted to channel attacking boats and wading Marines into preregistered mortar and artillery fire.

From reef to water, smoke and flames rose from burning amtracks while ammunition popped around them. The white coral sands of the beaches ashore were pocked with shellholes and these were filled with Marines in mottled green dungarees and helmets. And there were limbs and heads and pieces of flesh flying through the air; there were men staggering about in the last throes of death, their lives spouting crimson from severed faces or stumps of arms; there were files of men erased from sight in the water by obliterating shellbursts; there were bullets clipping the wavelets and Marines falling with heavy splashes among them.

Then there were Sherman tanks coming ashore, plodding carefully in the wake of the few remaining amtracks, stopping whenever the amtracks became waterborne in coral potholes, waiting until a safe path could be scouted. The Shermans got ashore, only to be blocked by beach mines.

One of the tank commanders unbuttoned his turret. He scouted the mined beach on foot. He led his tank through it, trailing toilet paper to lead the others through. They lumbered inland at the point where the Seventh's left flank joined Colonel Harold "Bucky" Harris' Fifth or *Lonewolf* in the center.

"Playmate, this is Spider Three. Enemy tanks forming in Target Area 134-R. . . . Enemy tanks supported by infantry crossing airfield to attack Lonewolf. . . ."

The Japanese tanks came in a cavalry charge.

They emerged from a cluster of concrete buildings which formed the Japanese headquarters and barracks area on the northern edge of the airfield. They approached as Japanese artillery on the ridge to their rear began to fire, and when they reached the edge of the airfield, the drivers stepped on the gas and the tanks sped over the crushed-coral surface at 30 miles an hour, leaving the infantry far behind. They charged on a southwest diagonal for the left-center juncture of the First and Fifth Marines.

They went whizzing past the front of the Second Battalion, First, about a baker's dozen of them, their little wheels spinning within their treads, their guns barking. Snipers rode their engines or were slung to the rear in camouflage nets. They took a terrible flanking fire. Snipers were picked off one by one and the men in the nets shot to death and left lolling like dolls stuffed in Christmas stockings.

One tank butted a Marine amtrack in its rear, but another amtrack butted the Japanese rear. Caught, the Japanese tankers popped out of their turret and were cut down by rifle fire.

Then the Marine tanks arrived, an American rocket-firing plane swooped low over the airfield, and the work of destroying the Japanese tanks was begun.

The Japanese infantry, witnesses to that annihilated charge, withdrew.

401

The Seventh Marines moved east across the island, and turned to their right to face south and close off Peleliu's southern tip.

The Fifth Marines drove across the southern edge of the airfield to reach the east coast.

The First was able to keep its right flank tied in with the Fifth's left, but its own left was splintered into three segments.

Night began to fall on Peleliu, and up on The Point, where K Company was still cut off, Lieutenant Willis whispered to Captain Hunt:

"There's one thing that can be said for our situation. We'll be able to kill some more of the bastards."

That night they did not kill as many as they thought they would, for the single thrust that the enemy made was quickly repulsed. Hunt thought it was only a sharp probing attack.

In the morning, Hunt found that the probing attack had actually been a skillful infiltration-in-force—and all along the line the Marines could sense that the Japanese on Peleliu seemed a breed vastly different from their brothers of Guadalcanal and New Britain.

Four days?

It looked more like forty.

18

It was the Seventh Marines who were first to test the tenacity of Japan's new defensive fighter. On the blazing hot morning of September 16, the Seventh's First and Third Battalions began their drive to clean out southern Peleliu.

They were contested by the elite 3rd Battalion, 15th Infantry, which Colonel Nakagawa had left behind, and all the way they encountered copious supplies of those targets which the bombardment force claimed to have exhausted. Pillboxes, casemates, bunkers, rifle pits, trenches, and here and there a blockhouse—they were still standing, still spitting death and defiance. If they had not been fixed to fire seaward over the eastern beaches, the ordeal of the Seventh to the south might have rivaled the slaughter impending in the north. But the Marines were able to strike at the Japanese rear and flanks.

All the while the enemy stayed holed-up. Soon the Marines found themselves harassed by the tactic of "passive infiltration" which General Inoue had recommended in his training plan. Swarming along their underground tunnels, the Japanese reoccupied pillboxes which the Marines thought they had knocked out. They attacked the Marines from the rear. They popped up out of unsuspected cavemouths. Where they held high ground, they ran out entrances on one side of their ridge while the Marines pumped explosives or swished flame into it. Then they ran back in again and resumed fighting.

The attack south became a grinding, three-day push, but the Seventh's two battalions gradually herded the enemy before them into a pair of tiny, pillbox-studded promontories. It was here on the third day that Pfc. Arthur Jackson launched a one-man attack. He charged pillbox after pillbox, spraying automatic fire, hurling white phosphorous grenades and explosives brought up by other Marines, moving from point to point in an astonishing singlehanded foray which wiped out 12 pillboxes and brought death to 50 Japanese—as well as the Medal of Honor and a lieutenant's commission to Pfc. Jackson. On the afternoon of September 18, the surviving Japanese jumped in the water in hopes of swimming to the islets on the Peleliu lobster-claw's lower prong. They were picked off by riflemen. Colonel Hanneken reported to General Rupertus:

"The Seventh Marines' mission on Pelelius is completed."

In the first light of September 16 Captain Hunt's men on The Point beat off the Japanese attack launched by the force which had infiltrated during the night. They hung on to their vital height until other Marines reached them and Captain Hunt's band was firmly tied into the line.

In the meanwhile, the front of the First and Fifth Marines

403

was plugged and straightened everywhere and the two regiments wheeled across the northern edge of the airfield to face the Umurbrogal rising above it.

The Marines crossed the airfield with the temperature at 110 degrees. Heat rose from the surface of the runways in shimmering, visible waves. Bullets hummed among the Marines and struck them down. They went across standing up—for there was no place to hide on this cruel table-top—and they walked or ran, scattered, hundreds of men, but each to himself alone. Men were falling of water poisoning, sickened by water floated ashore in oil drums from which the oil had not been thoroughly cleansed. All along this line steadily straightening from west to east and swinging north there rose the shrill calls of "Corpsman! Corpsman!" and the hoarser cries for blood plasma or water, the lesser calls for salt tablets.

Amtracks answering these calls had to run the gantlet of the reverberating hell which Colonel Nakagawa's concealed guns were making of the airfield. They had to go careening up Purple Heart Run from the beach to the airport, zigzagging wildly over Silver Star Run from airfield to ridge.

At the end of the day the line was straight. But the Umurbrogal was not yet quite reached, although the Marines had already a hint of the confidence of the men who held it. They had found a Japanese propaganda leaflet, which said:

> American brave soldiers!
> We think you much pity since landing on this ileland. In spite of your pitiful battle we are sorry that we can present only fire, not even good water. We soon will attack strongly your Army. You have done bravely your duty.
> Now, Abandon your guns, and come in Japanese military with white flag (or handkerchief), so we will be glad to see you and welcome you comfortably as we can well.

There were no takers.

"There they are! They're comin' in at us!"

It was ten o'clock at night, and the cries of alarm rose all over The Point. They rose as 350 Japanese charged furiously at Captain Hunt's men, now supported by Marines on the right as well as with mortar and artillery fire and the illumination of naval flares.

"Give 'em hell!" Hunt bellowed. "Kill every one of the bastards!"

"Klopf! Cut loose! Fire until I tell you to stop."

"LaCoy, LaCoy—"

"Yes?"

"Let 'em have it! Traverse the whole line and keep firing!"

"Kill! Kill!"

"Artillery falling short!"

"Goddamit, Klopf! Lift the range 200 yards."

"Short rounds! We're raising it now!"

"Who's there, who's there?"

"It's LaBerge, LaBerge."

"Who's there, I say—I'll shoot!"

"It's LaBerge, goddamit, don't you know me? I'm LaBerge!"

Bang!

"Are you satisfied now, you son of a bitch, you did shoot me?"

"They're coming around the flank in the water! Bring that gun down to the beach."

"LaCoy—drop some rounds along the beach 50 yards in front of us."

"There they are, there they are—let 'em have it!"

"They're duckin' in the niches! Don't let 'em get away. Use thermite grenades!"

"Oh, my God! Oh, Jesus, lookit 'em. Lookit 'em burn! Even in the water. . . . Y'hear 'em?"

After the last ammunition belt had gone off like a string of firecrackers, after the last scream had subsided, there were no more sounds of battle on The Point. Captain Hunt's Marines had held. Of 235 who had landed on September 15, there were 78 left on the morning of September 17 where K Company was relieved.

19

On the Sunday morning of September 17 the southern third of Peleliu—where the island is broadest and the airfield is located —was in American hands. The Seventh Marines were cleaning out what few enemy remained within this sector, while above them the Fifth Marines began to move up the east coast to the mouth of the lower peninsula or prong and the First Marines struck headlong at the Umurbrogal.

The First attacked across a three-battalion front. On the left the Third Battalion had good going along West Road running like a corridor between sea on the left, Umurbrogal on the right. They had to slow down. They were outdistancing the First Battalion on their right.

One of those enormous blockhouses missed by the bombardment force had halted the First Battalion. It had reinforced concrete walls four feet thick and was supported by 12 surrounding pillboxes and a maze of tunnels. The Marines marked time while old *Mississippi* steamed in to hurl her 14-inch armor-piercers and high-capacity shells into it. The blockhouse shuddered and began to fly apart. Those Japanese who attempted to escape it were cut down. The Marines of the First Battalion rolled through the remaining pillboxes and fought through a tiny dense jungle. They came to the ridges.

On their right, the Second Battalion was the first to reach the Umurbrogal's outpost hills. They went up against Hill 200, while the Japanese field pieces ran in and out of cover to strip them of supporting Shermans and amtanks, to knock out the amtracks coming up with supplies, and then to fire point-blank among the climbing riflemen, even then being raked with small-arms fire.

Up, up, up, fighting in an oven of 112 degrees, climbing the cruel slashing coral, clawing over razorbacks, flopping behind boulders to gasp for breath, shinnying up the pinnacles, rolling down steep inclines to escape the bullets and grenades, crawling back up it again to re-form and attack once more, and all around the clanging hell of the enemy artillery and mortars, the cries for water and plasma, and over and over again: "Pass the word for stretcher-bearers, pass the word for stretcher-bearers."

But they went up, sometimes having to slide back down to retake "fallen" caves which had erupted with killing fire again. They took the first height of the Umurbrogal, and found that to their left above them was another. It was Hill 210, just that much higher than Hill 200, and down from it plunged a terrible rain, while up from the wooded ravine between ridges flashed a matching fire.

The men of the Second Battalion, First, "dug in." That is, they gathered coral rocks and piled them between themselves and the enemy fire. Then they lay down on the unyielding rock, feeling its intense heat through dungarees slashed and torn by the ordeal of their climb.

But they had driven a deep salient into the enemy's lines and had covered the Fifth Marines to their right against possible flanking fire. The cost?

"We're up here," reported the single company commander who had survived. "But we're knee-deep in Purple Hearts."

In the morning, there were more casualties all along the line, for the Second Battalion's salient in fact had made a shallow W of the entire front from west to east coast. The Japanese took advantage of the W and hammered hard at its joints, counterattacking and shooting the gaps where they found them. Hill 200 shook to constant battle, and Colonel Puller was forced to take G Company from the Second Battalion, Seventh, given him as a reserve, and rush it up to bolster the line. The Marines held, and in the morning of September 18, the attack went forward in an attempt to straighten out the W. It went forward at seven o'clock with the thermometer already rising to 115 degrees, and each man issued a dozen salt tablets and two canteens of water to resist the Umurbrogal's horrible heat. The guns of both armies had stripped the battleground of all shade. Everything lay open to the sun, which hung in the sky like a burning ball above a jumble of blinding white coral rubble. The Marines were lying out on this like fish gasping on a skillet. The enemy was in his caves, cool and covered.

Marines dropping of heat exhaustion were helped to the rear to be revived with intravenous feedings of normal saline. Then they returned to battle, their camouflage nets pulled out from beneath their helmets and hanging over the back of their necks like the *kepis* of the French Foreign Legion.

In this heat, Chesty Puller roamed his command post stripped to the waist, his pipe stuck in one corner of his mouth while he issued his orders from the other. Puller had already relieved his badly mauled First Battalion and placed the Second Battalion, Seventh, in the center of his line. He had fed 115 men from the First Pioneer Battalion into the other depleted battalions. His own regiment's casualties were 1,236, not counting combat fatigue or heat exhaustion, or about one-third—and most of these were among Marines of the line. But Puller was optimistic, as was Major General Rupertus. High ground had been reached the day before, had been held during the night, and now the enemy collapse was imminent.

It had always happened that way. Once the Marines had fought into dominating terrain, Japanese resistance had weakened until it had been utterly broken by a last *banzai*. Although there had been no *banzai* as yet, there was no reason not to expect one.

Nor could Puller or anyone else conceive of the depth of the position under attack. There had been a few uneasy reflections on the 35 unmapped caves which the First Battalion had been forced to knock out the day before, but no one dreamed that so many hundreds more awaited them in the higher ridges, as no one doubted the efficacy of the naval gunfire, artillery and air strikes preceding each assault, laying bare more and more of the Umurbrogal's ugly white pate.

But on this September 18 there were so many more caves, so many more troops and guns in those higher ridges that the attacks of the Second Battalions, Seventh and First, were quickly fragmented center and left. Though the object was to pinch out the Japanese on Hill 210 inside the first V of the W, the Marines were attacking in every direction of the compass, for they were under fire from every direction. It was a bloody scramble of squads or platoons, with here and there a surviving officer rounding up the remnants of a company and leading them on until the Hill 210 bulge was erased. And the Japanese in surrounding ridges retaliated by bringing down such a murderous fire on the Second Battalion, First, and by mounting a series of counterattacks so savage that Lieutenant Colonel Russell Honsowetz reported that he might not be able to hold.

"What d'yuh mean, cain't hold?" Puller roared. "You're there, ain't you, Honsowetz?"

Then, while a smoke barrage was laid down to conceal Honsowetz' position, Puller ordered B Company out of the First Battalion reserve to a point forward and right of besieged Hill 200. B Company went up it in a rush. But it was only an isolated ridge. It did not relieve much of the pressure on the Second Battalion, First. B Company pushed on. They came to a system of peaks and palisades called The Five Sisters, a complex running transverse to the entire Umurbrogal. They attacked it.

They were hurled to the ground.

They had come to the heart of Colonel Nakagawa's infernal mountain, and because they had been stopped so abruptly by what had seemed a single, roundhouse punch, they gave it the name which would describe the entire Umurbrogal—the name of Bloody Nose Ridge.

They did not take it that day, nor that month, nor the next. It was to be the final pocket of Japanese resistance on Peleliu, and it would not fall until November 25.

In the meantime, the First's attack had fared better on the flanks. The Third Battalion had moved again on the west or left coast, and again had to halt to mark time. On the right flank, the Second Battalion had sent troops over the low ground between Hill 200 and the village of Asias on the east. They tied in with the left-flank company of the Fifth Marines. Between this company and the rest of the Fifth lay a deep swamp which would divide them until a new phase of the offensive began on September 23.

By dusk, that uncomfortable W formation had been erased. Puller's command at Bloody Nose Ridge now held the enemy in a very shallow U. The regiment's casualties, exclusive of those of the attached troops, were now at 1,500, or half its strength. But the report to Division said that although gains were slight, "the center of Japanese resistance has been detected and the weakest spots probed."

"Let's go git killed on that high ground up there!" the red-haired sergeant yelled, and he and his men went up the sides of Bloody Nose Ridge and many of them were killed.

That was the morning of September 19, when the First Regiment's Second Battalion was broken on that evil coral complex and the First Battalion all but disappeared.

Everything was hurled against the ridge's sheer southern face—all the big guns of land and sea, along with aerial bombs, tank weapons, bazookas, flame-throwers, mortars and machine guns and the hand-weapons of attacking riflemen. And Colonel Puller had also reinforced the Second Battalion with the Division Reconnaissance Company and Company C of the First Battalion. All that the First Battalion had left in reserve was A Company, plus a machine-gun platoon composed of men from the Battalion Intelligence Section, cooks, clerks and jeep drivers. In Lieutenant Colonel Honsowetz' Second Battalion command post, an ominous sequence of orders and reports began:

0545 Heavy mortar fire fell all through our lines during the night. Lieutenant Mercer was killed and his platoon hit hardest.
0605 Enemy rockets firing on E Company lines.
0610 Mortars notified to fire on rocket launchers in 141U.
0715 F Company reports enemy mortars falling on our lines, requests amtracks to evacuate wounded.
0745 The attack is proceeding.
0752 Enemy artillery shelling front lines heavily.
0805 FROM REGIMENT: "Practically all dead enemy officers are booby-trapped. Use caution."

0815   Observation Post requests naval gunfire and bombing on east side of island at Phase 0-4 line.

0818   Heavy enemy artillery fire on Observation Post. Stretcher-bearers and corpsmen dispatched as requested.

0850   Tanks moving forward.

0902   FROM F COMPANY: "I have approximately 60 men left and four officers including myself. Lieutenant Russo has three pieces of shrapnel in his back. Lieutenant Maples has been wounded in the shoulder. We are still in the fight."

0915   Observation Post requests that more tanks be rushed forward. But runners sent to bring tanks forward report no tanks in entire area between Command Post and Observation Post.

0117   G Company reports that they are hitting caves with 37-millimeter armor-piercing and high explosive. Will require tanks with 75's before they can advance.

0930   C Company and G Company being committed up the draw to get into 141U.

0940   Mortar fire commencing on target.

1100   Advance stopped. All companies and Observation Post pinned down under heavy mortar barrage.

1105   E Company reports they have only one effective squad due to exhaustion and heat prostration.

1110   TO REGIMENT: "We need more men to continue the advance." FROM REGIMENT: "Will furnish A Company to support you.

1130   A company moving forward. They report they have 56 men.

1200   G Company radio operator wounded. Replacement sent forward.

1212   Command Post under mortar barrage.

1220   Attack continues at 1230.

1245   F Company requests 15 stretchers and as many bearers as available.

1250   F Company requests that tanks be sent forward. They are receiving heavy machine-gun fire and are having heavy casualties and only tanks can clear the way.

1300   G Company requests permission to withdraw. The men are dropping from exhaustion and our casualties are great from heavy machine-gun fire and mortars. The position is untenable.

    FROM BATTALION: "How far will you have to withdraw?"

411

FROM G COMPANY: "To the reverse slope of the hill to avoid fire."

FROM BATTALION: "Do not withdraw any farther than absolutely necessary. We will lay smoke to cover your change of position."

1302 TO A COMPANY: "What situation is G Company in? Can you go forward at all?"

FROM A COMPANY: "No."

1310 TO FIRST BATTALION SICK BAY: "Please send all available ambulances and stretchers to our Command Post."

1320 A Company reports that the Second Battalion, Seventh, is pinned down to the left and cannot cross the ridge.

1325 TO A COMPANY: "You will advance at once across the ridge to relieve pressure on the line."

FROM A COMPANY: "We cannot move out. There is heavy machine-gun fire raking the entire ridge."

TO A COMPANY: "It is necessary that you move out at all costs. I am giving you a direct order. You will move out at once. If you move in small rushes your casualties will not be great."

1345 All contact lost with A Company. Second Battalion, Seventh, has taken hill to the left.

1350 SITUATION: Troops and Observation Post are pinned down by machine-gun fire and mortars in front of Hill 100. All available firepower is being brought to bear on this sector.

1420 FROM F COMPANY: "I must have more men to continue the advance. I am having heavy casualties."

1425 All available men in the Command Post who can be spared ordered forward. Twenty-four men moving out.

1440 TO E COMPANY: "Move up in support of F Company."

1450 Pioneers have been sent forward as support for F Company.

1455 A Company has reported to Observation Post for further orders. They have six men and one officer (of original 56).

1505 G Company and E Company have been withdrawn.

1515 Five of 24 men from Command Post knocked out by mortar fire on the way to the lines.

1530   Flame-throwing tanks on way to support F Company.

1531   TO MORTARS: "Extend fire into 143E."

1540   TO MORTARS: "Cease firing."

1550   FROM G COMPANY RADIO OPERATOR: "Lieutenant Fournier has just been killed. But I think I can get the machine gun that got him if I can get a bazooka."

1555   FROM G COMPANY RADIO OPERATOR: "Machine-gun nest knocked out. Am awaiting orders."

1558   Captain Tiscornia has reported back from hospital ship and is being sent forward to take over G Company. Lieutenant Maples killed in F Company. F and G Companies combine under Captain Tiscornia. Lieutenant Burke wounded and evacuated.

1750   The Third Squad of the Fourth War Dog Platoon moving up to support G Company.

1755   Assault continued on entire front on Hill 100.

1759   C Company reports they have taken Hill 100.

It was not called Hill 100, but Walt Ridge, this vital height which Captain Everett Pope and 90 men of C Company had been assaulting since noon. It stood well north of Bloody Nose Ridge, dominating the East Road and the swamp lying between the First and Fifth Regiments. If it were taken, Bloody Nose Ridge might be hit from the rear. Lieutenant Colonel Honsowetz ordered Pope's company to seize it, with the Division Reconnaissance Company following in support.

Pope's men moved through the swamp to attack. They were driven back. They moved to their left along East Road, following it until it formed a causeway across a large sinkhole. Pope called for tanks to lead them over the causeway. One tank slipped off the left side, another off the right.

"We'll have to cross in squad rushes," Pope ordered.

413

They crossed. With mortars and machine guns in support, they drove up to the crest of Walt Ridge, and it was at one minute before six o'clock that they reported it seized.

From then on, C Company was struck at from every side. They were shelled, machine-gunned and counterattacked. They fought with rocks and with fists. They struggled with their assailants and hurled them bodily over the cliffs. They held, but at dawn there were only Captain Pope and 16 others alive, and of these only nine had enough strength to fight. It was because of Pope's leadership that there were any left at all, and for this he won a Medal of Honor. But on the morning of September 20, Pope had to bring his men down from the hill which would be renamed Walt Ridge later in the fight.

The combined First-Second Battalion then attempted to retake Walt Ridge, and was shattered in a relentless crossfire. It was the First Regiment's last bolt. Colonel Nakagawa jubilantly signaled Lieutenant General Inoue:

> Since dawn the enemy has been concentrating their forces, vainly trying to approach *Higashiyama* [Walt Ridge] and *Kansokuyama* [Hill 300] with 14 tanks and one infantry battalion under powerful aids of air and artillery fire. However, they were again put to rout, receiving heavy losses.

Bloody Nose Ridge had cut the First's battalions down to half the size of companies, had reduced some companies to less than a squad. In the combined First-Second Battalion, with its attached units from Division, there were not 100 effectives by the end of the day.

In hard figures of killed and wounded, the First Marines had lost 1,749 men, and there were additional hundreds made noneffective by heat exhaustion, water-poisoning, combat fatigue or blast concussion. But they had killed 4,000 Japanese and had taken 10 defended coral ridges, three big blockhouses, 22 pillboxes, 13 antitank guns and 144 defended caves—one-third of Peleliu's armament, two-fifths of its defenders. It would require four regiments to take the rest.

But it required only two small hospital transports, *Pinckney* and *Tryon*, to take the First's survivors back to Pavuvu. Even on the way out to the ships, misfortune overtook them. It was a

414

high sea. The edge of a typhoon was moving toward Peleliu. Some of the ducks were swamped, though no one was lost. Weary, dirty, dripping, the Marines climbed over the rails—to be met by clean dry eager sailors.

"Any souvenirs?" an officer asked a Marine.

The Marine stood examining him in silence. He patted his behind.

"I brought my ass outta there, swabbie," he said. "That's the only souvenir I wanted."

20

Early reports of the slaughter under Bloody Nose Ridge had convinced Major General Roy Geiger, the Third Corps commander, that Peleliu would not be the whirlwind conquest predicted by Major General Rupertus.

Geiger saw very quickly that reinforcements would be needed. But General Rupertus was reluctant to use Army troops which became available after the 81st Infantry (Wildcat) Division took Angaur in three days. Although resistance on Angaur was to continue for another month, only two of the 81st's regiments were needed to contain it. Thus a third regiment was free to enter the bigger battle on Peleliu.

On September 21, Geiger came to Rupertus headquarters on Peleliu and told him he thought the First Marines should be relieved and that he was considering bringing an Army regiment into the battle. Rupertus became alarmed. He asked Geiger not to take such action, and he assured the Third Corps commander that Peleliu would fall in another day or two.

Geiger disagreed. He told Rupertus to prepare to evacuate the battered First and also to receive reinforcements from the 81st Division.

Then Geiger asked Major General Paul Mueller, the 81st's commander, to detach his 321st Infantry Regiment for assignment to the First Marine Division on Peleliu. The 321st's soldiers came into the island on September 23—the same day on which their brother doughfoots of the 323rd Infantry landed unopposed on Ulithi—and they marched up West Road to relieve the Third Battalion, First Marines. The following day the 321st turned right to strike at the western face of the Umurbrogal Pocket.

The next day, the twenty-fifth, the Fifth Marines launched a drive around the western side of The Pocket into northern Peleliu—the upper prong of the lobster's claw.

Colonel Harris' battalions marched rapidly out of the eastern peninsula—the lower prong of the claw—crossed the island south of the Umurbrogal and then turned right or north to move up West Road. They passed through the 321st to drive into enemy territory.

That night, Colonel Harris bent both his flanks back to the sea. He was all alone, holding a solitary beachhead. The Japanese counterattacked three times, savagely. They were beaten off. On the morning of September 26, the Marines raced farther north. They left the Umurbrogal behind, overran a radio station, crossed the junction of West and East Roads, and came up on the left of L-shaped Amiangal Mountain. Here they encountered cave systems so constructed that Marine tanks could fire point-black into entrances and be struck by fire which *continued* to come out the same cavemouth. Here the Marines could seize a hill, sit on it to rest or smoke, and smell the rice and fish being cooked by the enemy four or five stories beneath them. Here, too, they made skillful use of the tank-dozer which had been developed by fitting a Sherman tank with a bulldozer blade and using it to seal off caves under fire.

On September 27, while the Fifth began attacking east to seal off the northern tip of Peleliu, the 321st made the maneuver which cut off the Umurbrogal Pocket.

Captain George Neal of the 2nd Battalion, 321st, formed a task force of seven Sherman tanks, six amtracks, one amtrack flame-thrower and 45 riflemen. He led them up West Road, came to the captured junction and turned down East Road on a southward run that brought his force up behind the enemy. When Task Force Neal came up against Hill 100 and killed 15 Japanese in a brief fight, the Umurbrogal Pocket was contained.

Above Neal's force, the Fifth had been caught between two fires.

On their right, they had come up against the biggest cave on Peleliu. It housed 1,000 men and occupied all of the island's northernmost ridge. Its seaward tip loomed over the road, here so narrow as to allow only a single tank to pass. Its face was freckled with cavemouths. The moment a tank nosed around its snout, it was struck. The moment infantry sought to crawl along the road they were hit from cavemouths on the right and from Japanese gunners across the 1,000-yard strait on Ngesebus and its adjoining isle of Kongauru to its right or east.

The Marines called for naval gunfire on Kongauru. They brought land-artillery fire down on Ngesebus, firing smoke-shells every fourth round to disconcert the enemy while nine Sherman tanks rolled into range to fire nothing but smoke. Then they sent five armored amtracks wallowing into the strait. The amtracks sailed 300 yards, wheeled, swiveled their guns around and poured a terrible flat fire into the cavemouths. While they did, Shermans swept along the road and around the snout with infantry following. Following them came an amtrack flame-thrower, which doubled back to burn out the cavemouths.

That happened on September 27, the day after Major Robert (Cowboy) Stout brought the white-nosed Corsairs of Squadron 114 into Peleliu.

Now, the Marine fliers would get their first chance to show how well they had developed that tactic of close-up support first used at Hellzapoppin' Ridge on Bougainville. Cowboy Stout's low-chargers were to support the Third Battalion, Fifth, during the invasion of Ngesebus on September 28.

The Marines crossed the strait in amtracks, after an hour of naval gunfire, aerial bombing and shelling by corps and division artillery. Two hundred yards from the beaches, the Corsairs roared over them and began to strafe. They kept it up until the Marines were but 30 yards from the shore, and they struck at levels so low the terrified Japanese were unable to defend the beaches. The landing was made without a single casualty, although 50 Japanese were killed or captured in coastal pillboxes.

At three o'clock in the afternoon—six hours after the assault began—all but a few hundred yards of Ngesebus had fallen. The rest, with the airfield and adjoining Kongauru Islet, was in Marine hands. There had been 28 men lost.

The next day Major Stout's fliers were strafing and bombing up and down the Umurbrogal Pocket, helping the Seventh Marines hammer where the First Marines had left off. Day after day, Corsairs made the fifteen-second run from airfield to Bloody Nose Ridge to drop tanks of napalm on the Japanese, banking and landing to rearm without having bothered to retract landing gear.

"The enemy plan," Colonel Nakagawa reported to General Inoue, "seems to be to burn down the central hills post to ashes by dropping gasoline from airplanes."

But as the typhoon edged nearer and sullen rains fell on Peleliu, Colonel Nakagawa began to experience less difficulty with napalm and soon had trained his men to keep very low whenever the Corsairs were flying over The Pocket. So the Corsairs began to drop unfused tanks of napalm, leaving it to the attacking Marines to set them alight when they chose by dropping white phosphorous shells on them. When the typhoon's rains did come they were a blessing to Nakagawa's remnant. The Japanese had begun to run out of water. Now they trapped enough in underground cisterns to last for months.

Meanwhile, the Seventh Marines had relieved the 321st of their sector in the west, had held there and begun a steady drive from the north and east. They fought against an enemy maintaining an extraordinary discipline. Marines could move through a draw conscious of hundreds of hostile eyes focused on them, and not be fired at. But when they attempted to get a tank through the draw, or tried scaling the ridges—then it fell in fury. At night, the Japanese swarmed from their caves as infiltrators. They caused little trouble to veteran Marines, but they killed many souvenir-hunters. Sailors and service troops who wandered up to The Pocket in search of souvenirs or thrills oftentimes never came out of it alive. Some were even impressed as riflemen by Marine commanders who needed reinforcements and were not fussy about how they were obtained. There were also Marine airmen and service troops who came up to The Pocket for the express purpose of fighting.

Still Nakagawa held out. As September turned into October, his men had inflicted so many casualties on the gradually advancing Seventh Marines that their ranks were almost as badly depleted as the First's had been. On October 4, with the two most vital of the eastern ridges in their hands, the Seventh Marines made their last attack. The Third Battalion tried to take Baldy Ridge, hoping thus to drive a deep wedge from the east. To get at Baldy, L Company struck at Ridge 120 to its left or south. From this, they hoped to strike Baldy in the flank and rear. A force of 48 men took Ridge 120 with ease. They turned to drive at Baldy and found they were in a trap.

The Japanese struck at these exposed Marines from Baldy and a ring of strong-points, hitting them with small arms, machine guns, cannon and mortars. Gunnery Sergeant Ralph Phillips fell dead at the first machine-gun burst. Men were falling everywhere. Big 230-pound Lieutenant James Dunn attempted to lead the men down the ridge's sheer face. He was hanging on to rocks when machine guns chugged across the draw and dropped him to his death on the boulders below.

Now the bullets were spanging among the Marines as they crawled wildly for cover. Some of the wounded urged their comrades to leave, others begged them to stay. A corpsman jumped erect.

"Take it easy!" he called. "Bandage each other. Get out a few at a time."

Then he fell dead.

Down in the draw, Captain James Shanley watched the slaughter of his men in horror. He bellowed to the men of K Company on his left.

"For God's sake, smoke up that hill!"

K Company's Marines began hurling smoke grenades into the

419

ravine between their own positions and Ridge 120 to their front and right. Wind wafted a billow of phosphorus over the stricken platoon on the ridge crest. Captain Shanley called for a tank. It came up the draw, but was halted by the boulders. It could not strike at the Japanese, but it became a rallying point for the men on the ridge who were even then pulling out under the smoke.

Some of them jumped and ran to the tank. But there were still six wounded on the ridge, guarded by three Marines and one of the three corpsmen who had not been killed. The wounded urged the able to leave.

"You've done all you can for us," one of them sobbed. "Get outta here."

The unharmed Marines rolled their stricken comrades over the ledge. They fell among the boulders. One man's foot caught in a vine and he hung there until a comrade kicked it free. Above them, a trio of Marines who had been playing dead jumped to their feet and ran for the ledge. One was killed but the others jumped to safety.

In the draw, two wounded men stumbled toward the tank. One of them put his arms around his friend and half-carried him forward. They could not make it. They sank to the ground, and Japanese bullets spurted around them.

Captain Shanley shook off a lieutenant's restraining hand and ran out to get them. He seized one man in his arms, ran back to the tank with him, laid him down—and ran out again. But a mortar shell exploded behind Captain Shanley and he fell, mortally wounded. Lieutenant Harold Collis ran to rescue Captain Shanley. He fell beside him, dead.

Now there was more smoke drifting over the ledge. More of the unharmed Marines jumped to safety. They ran across that terrible draw and only a few survived it. Two who did ran back to rescue the wounded. They were killed.

And then dusk began to veil that tableau of tragedy. Of the 48 men who went up Ridge 121, only 11 came back down— and six of these were wounded. The Seventh Marines could also fight no more. Their casualties were 1,497, nearly matching those of the First.

It was up to the Fifth Marines to crush less than 1,000 Japanese still living in the constricted Umurbrogal Pocket. They relieved the Seventh on October 6. But the valiant arrogant Fifth, the regiment that had been blooded in Belleau Wood, could not do it either. By October 15, they too were exhausted and their casualties of 1,378 were also nearly 50 per cent.

On that date, with the assault phase on Peleliu ended, with about 500 of Nakagawa's men still holding out in a pocket about 400 yards at its widest east-west, about 600 yards at its longest north-south, command on Peleliu passed to Major General Paul Mueller of the 81st Division. There began then a grim, step-by-step reduction that would last a month and would be fought with bulldozers and explosives and bombs and napalm as much as by foot soldiers with hand guns.

For now the need for speed no longer existed at Peleliu. Five days after the Army took command, General MacArthur's soldiers began landing at Leyte in the Philippines. Two days more marked the beginning of the Battle of Leyte Gulf, the struggle which was the greatest naval battle in history, bringing death to the Japanese Navy and establishing America as the greatest sea power afloat, while also marking the passing of the battleship and introducing that strange new *banzai* with wings called *kamikaze*.

On October 12, the first of the B-29's landed on Saipan. On November 24, the first B-29 bombing raid was flown from there to Tokyo. On that same night, when the thunder of the monster American bombers could be heard above the Ginza, Colonel Nakagawa and Major General Murai killed themselves on Peleliu. They had destroyed the colors of their commands and they had no one left to command.

Kunio Nakagawa and his men had inflicted a total of 6,526 casualties on the First Marine Division, of whom 1,252 were killed. They also killed 208 and wounded 1,185 soldiers of the 81st Division. They had made the oldest and most battle-experienced of all the Marine divisions fight for their lives—fight for each other's lives. In that recurring and noblest phenomenon of the Marines' war, Lieutenant Carlton Rouh, Corporal Lewis Bausell, Pfc. Richard Kraus, Pfc. John New, Pfc. Wesley Phelps and Pfc. Charles Roan all threw themselves on enemy grenades to save their comrades. Lieutenant

Rouh survived his wounds to receive his Medal of Honor. The others did not.

Out of this Peleliu which gave General MacArthur his secure right flank, which obtained Admiral Nimitz' anchorage and air base, came the new phenomenon of the war, the Japanese soldier fighting with head as well as heart. Colonel Kunio Nakagawa had shown the world that in place of the fiction of the Japanese warrior irresistible on offense stood the hard fact of the world's most tenacious defensive fighter immovable except in death.

There were many more of them. As one who had been overpowered on Saipan snarled to the conquerors who would not let him kill himself: "You may have this island, but back there is the Empire."

Against these new warriors, into the heart of this Empire, the Marines would now go charging.

IV. And No More

God and the soldier
  All men adore.
In time of trouble
  And no more;
For when war is over
  And all things righted
God is neglected
  The old soldier slighted.

—Inscription carved in a
stone sentry box on Gibraltar

1

It was early 1945 and the Marines had had their second breather.

They had fought and won seven major actions in 1944, but apart from two artillery battalions fighting in the Philippines, Marine ground forces had not fired a shot since the Fifth Marines came down from the Umurbrogal in mid-October.

They needed the respite—for the battered First Division to recuperate from Peleliu, for the new Fifth to shake down in Hawaii, for the Third to fill its ranks and train the newcomers by sweeping Guam of its remaining Japanese soldiers, for the Second and Fourth to renew themselves with replacement drafts from the States, for the Sixth to twist the regimental rivalries of the loner Fourth, Twenty-second and Twenty-ninth Marines into the single strand of divisional pride.

And now there were six full Marine divisions in the field, two corps, a full army, some 200,000 men; the largest, the most successful, the most experienced body of amphibious assault troops the world has known. Before this force, invincible since Guadalcanal, lay two final targets: Iwo Jima and Okinawa.

Iwo and Okie—the first a bare eight square miles of desolate crag and volcanic ash lying 760 miles south of Tokyo, the second an irregular island 60 miles at its longest, two at its narrowest and 18 at its broadest, but lying only 375 miles below southernmost Japan.

Iwo would come first, for Iwo was already urgent.

425

2

The B-29 Superforts which had been flying from Saipan to Tokyo since November 24 had been suffering severe losses. Japanese antiaircraft fire was savage. There were many fighter planes left to defend the Japanese home islands, and some would ram a Superfort if they could not shoot it down. And there was no chance of surprise because Iwo-based radar warned the homeland in time to fly off fighter protection.

Worst of all was the long 1,500-mile flight home. Crippled Superforts unable to fly more than a few hundred miles from Tokyo fell into the sea and were lost with their crews. Those which fell between Iwo and Saipan might be reached by Dumbo rescue planes, but if the crews were saved, the enormously expensive B-29's were surely lost.

With Iwo Jima in American hands, the Superforts could fly much closer to Tokyo undetected, they could be escorted over the Japanese capital by Iwo-based fighters, and men shot down off the very shores of Japan might even hope for the arrival of Iwo-based rescue planes. Most important, any Superfort capable of flying halfway home could be saved by an emergency landing at Iwo. With the eventual use of Iwo Jima as a regular stop-off on return flights, smaller gasoline-loads would make possible bigger bomb-loads. Iwo's own raids on the Marianas would cease, bringing about the release of Marianas-based fighters for use elsewhere, and possession of the island would nail down the right or eastern flank of the Okinawa operation.

Such was the importance and urgency of Iwo Jima in early 1945. Rarely before had an objective been so clearly necessary. Perhaps never before had so much counted on the seizure of such a no-count place.

426

It was only 4½ miles long, 2½ miles wide, this Iwo Jima or Sulphur Island. It was a loathsome little cinder clog, a place black and charred and shaped like a lopsided pork chop. To Major Yokasuka Horie, who had come to it in late 1944, the place was an abomination. It was "only an island of sulphur, no water, no sparrow and no swallow. . . ." Major Horie's detestation of Iwo was evident in what may stand as one of the world's most original defense plans, the one he submitted to his superior, Lieutenant General Tadamichi Kuribayashi.

"Now we have no fleet and no air forces," Major Horie's plan stated. "If American forces will assault this island it will fall into their hands in one month. Therefore it is absolutely necessary not to let the enemy use this island. The best plan is to sink this island into the sea or cut the island in half. At least we must endeavor to sink the first airfield."

General Kuribayashi rejected the plan. After a few more disagreements with his staff officer, he transferred Major Horie to Chichi Jima, 160 miles to the north. Tadamichi Kuribayashi was like that: curt, stern, cold—one of those moon-faced, pudgy men who are all ruthless energy and driving determination. The troops did not like him. They had no girls of the "comfort troops," no *saki*, only duty. They called him a martinet. But Tadamichi Kuribayashi was something more than that: he was a perfectionist.

He had begun his career in the cavalry, the elite service of the Japanese Army. In 1938 and 1939 he was a colonel commanding the 7th Cavalry Regiment during action in Manchuria. In 1940 he was promoted to major general and given the 1st Cavalry Brigade. Two years later he was transferred to Canton and made chief of staff of the 23rd Army. He was called to Tokyo in 1943 on the ineffable assignment of reorganizing the Guards Brigade into the 1st Imperial Guards Division. And Tadamichi Kuribayashi had met the Emperor. Not many Japanese below cabinet rank are so favored, but Tadamichi Kuribayashi was going out to command at Iwo Jima, and Iwo Jima was in the very Prefecture of Tokyo.

He reached his unlovely black pork chop in June, 1944, taking over the usual mixture of Army and Navy troops which would eventually reach 21,000 men and of which his own

109th Infantry Division formed the nucleus. He sent the civilians back to Japan and grimly told his troops that it looked like a fight to the death. For comfort, he issued the Iwo Jima Courageous Battle Vow. It said:

> Above all else we shall dedicate ourselves and our entire strength to the defense of this island.
> We shall grasp bombs, charge the enemy tanks and destroy them.
> We shall infiltrate into the midst of the enemy and annihilate them.
> With every salvo we will, without fail, kill the enemy.
> Each man will make it his duty to kill 10 of the enemy before dying.
> Until we are destroyed to the last man, we shall harass the enemy by guerrilla tactics.

The Vow may have sounded like the same old *Bushido,* but there was a new and coldly logical mind behind the defense plan which Kuribayashi drew up.

Like any good plan, it took utmost advantage of Iwo Jima's unusual terrain. Unlike many plans, it had the genius of placing the right number of men at the right points. Lieutenant General Kuribayashi had hit on the great secret of proportion. Luck had given him the 21,000 men which was all that he needed and had also spared him the confusion of a crowd. With this force, with his engineers, with all the guns and ammunition he needed, with a sufficiency of stored water and the materials of fortification, he was going to make Iwo Jima into a fixed position at least unsurpassed in modern military history.

At the southwest end of this southwest-northeast-slanted island—at the very tail of the pork chop—stood Mount Suribachi, a dead volcano humping 550 feet above the sea. Here General Kuribayashi stationed from 1,500 to 2,000 men in a semi-independent position. Between Suribachi and the point north where the chop bellies out to Iwo's extreme width of 2½ miles was a flatland of volcanic ash about 1½ miles wide and two miles long. Here was the island's finest airfield, Airfield Number One. Here General Kuribayashi put only light infantry defenses, for here, either to west or to east, were Iwo's only landing beaches. Here the enemy would have to come, and once the enemy was ashore, with his vehicles and ammunition and stores piling up behind him, with his boats coming ashore by the literal thousands, here would fall all the fire of Kuribayashi's guns sited on Suribachi to the south and the high Motoyama Plateau to the north.

How many guns?

12	320-mm. spigot mortars	17	75-mm. field guns
22	150-mm. trench mortars	24	70-mm. battalion guns
4	15-cm. coast defense guns	70	90-mm. or 81-mm. mortars
4	14-cm. coast defense guns	380	50-mm. heavy grenade dischargers (knee mortars)
9	12-cm. coast defense guns		
12	12-cm. short coast defense guns	54	47-mm. antitank guns
30	12-cm. dual-purpose guns	15	37-mm. antitank guns
		4	40-mm. antiaircraft machine guns
6	10-cm. dual-purpose guns	213	25-mm. machine guns
5	8-cm. dual-purpose guns	9	23-mm. antiaircraft machine guns
18	7.5-cm. dual-purpose guns	4	20-mm. machine guns
		168	13-mm. machine guns
1	150-mm. howitzer	30	tanks dug in as pillboxes
4	120-mm. howitzers	61	flame-throwers
6	10-cm. howitzers	350	heavy machine guns
4	90-mm. howitzers	480	light machine guns
5	75-mm. pack howitzers	200	rocket launchers
		10,000	rifles

Though the 320-millimeter spigot mortar was bizarre—its 675-pound shell bigger than the firing cylinder and fitting over and round it, its life no more than half a dozen rounds, its erratic projectile feared as much by its crew as by its intended victims—it could nevertheless make a monster bang. And when 60,000 Marines became packed onto tiny Iwo Jima, it would be difficult for it to be harmless. The rockets, varying in size from 550 to 200 pounds, were likewise more noisy than nasty. But the rest of that fearful armament could have ferocious effect, and Kuribayashi had emplaced these guns in an elaborate system of caves and concrete blockhouses.

Where Peleliu had 500 caves, Iwo Jima had 1,500—most of them on the Motoyama Plateau rising north of Airfield Number One. Where Tarawa had blockhouses and pillboxes of ferro-concrete, Iwo Jima also had them—five-foot walls, ten-foot ceilings, sandbagged, humped around with 50 feet of sand and piggy-backed with machine-gun turrets—but Iwo Jima also had them invisible. Tarawa's had been above ground, for the water level was only four feet. Iwo had no bottom, and up in the north it had a tunnel system surpassing the Umurbrogal's. Kuribayashi had already set his men to work digging the first links of an underground network to total some 30 miles. Construction was around the clock. Every man worked three hours on, five off, or as long as was necessary to dig a minimum three feet. They worked wearing gas masks to filter out the fumes from Iwo's numerous sulphur wells. Some places were so hot with sulphur that the men could cook a pan of rice over them in twenty minutes. But Kuribayashi got only about four miles of this master tunnel system finished before the Marines came, although he still had many miles of completed tunnels and interconnected caves below the ridges and among the rocky gorges of the two cross-island defense systems he had completed in the northeast.

The first of these two barriers was the main one. It began on the Motoyama Plateau about a mile northeast of Airfield Number One and the narrow ashen neck on which Kuribayashi hoped to annihilate the Americans. Both of its flanks were on the sea and its center was anchored on Airfield Number Two, located at almost the exact middle of the island. This line was actually a belt of mutually supporting positions about 1,000 yards in depth, southwest-to-northeast. The second line, not as deep or as formidable, began a mile or so northeast of the first. The second line's flanks were also on the sea, while uncompleted Airfield Number Three, a mile directly northeast of Airfield Number Two, represented its center. Behind the second line, in the last mile or so of northeastern Iwo, were

430

more defenses—all made menacing by fantastic terrain. Such terrain could conceal the communications center located just south of Kita. It was a fortress with five-foot walls and ten-foot roof, a single room 150 feet long and 70 feet wide, housing 20 radios, reached only by a 500-foot tunnel about 75 feet underground—the tunnel's entrance cleverly hidden between two small hills.

Nor would the gunners popping out of this monster Chinese-box of a defense be the usual bad shots the Marines had encountered across the Pacific. Kuribayashi made sure of this in training characterized by this order:

"It is necessary to eliminate completely the idea that firing results are satisfactory if shells merely fall in the enemy area. We must without fail score direct hits on the targets."

The general was also that rare thing among Japanese officers —he was security-conscious. He set up eight different defense sectors, each with a plan of its own, none aware of the others'. If the *Bushido* code made it impossible for Kuribayashi to instruct his men on what to say when captured, he could at least guard against the inevitable by giving them nothing to talk about. There were also plans for defense against possible airborne attack, for the destruction of roads, for the digging of numerous ditches to guard against the American tanks Kuribayashi feared so much, and, finally, for encouraging the troops to disregard the devastating aerial and surface bombardment which preceded the American attacks.

"We must strive to disperse, conceal, and camouflage personnel, weapons and materiel, and make use of installations to reduce damage during enemy bombing and shelling. In addition we will enhance the concealment of various positions by the construction of dummy positions to absorb the enemy shelling and bombing."

All this was done. Even the firing ports of the pillboxes were made small and angled so that nothing could enter them but a grenade thrown from a few feet away or a hand-gun fired point-blank. If this cut down the field of fire, it made little difference—there were so many pillboxes supporting each other.

431

When the Seventh Air Force launched its seventy-two day pounding of Iwo Jima, Kuribayashi's men stayed out of sight and dug their ditches all the deeper.

When the long thick shapes of the American bombardment ships slid out of the darkness on the morning of February 16, the Japanese refused to be goaded into firing back and giving away the position of the coastal guns. Even though they had smokeless powder, they refused. Only when the swimmers of the Underwater Demolition Teams came into the eastern beaches on February 17 did they open up. They thought the invasion had begun, and big guns on the cliffs to the north began shooting at the covering gunboats. It was their only mistake and they paid for it dearly. Those vital guns were knocked out and left dangling down the cliff faces.

Otherwise, Lieutenant General Tadamichi Kuribayashi calmly observed the destruction of pillboxes on the eastern beaches and heard reports of the gradual loss of much of his communications. He had expected the last, and had prepared for the first. The Americans would come ashore thinking his armor knocked out. Their planes would fly away. Their naval gunfire would lift. They would see only the terraces of volcanic ash which sea and wind had piled a few dozen yards inland at heights up to 15 feet. They would struggle beyond these. Then they would see the flatland with its hummocks of sand.

But the hummocks would turn out to be hidden guns and the armor supposedly knocked out would begin the slaughter already celebrated in the Iwo Jima Garrison Song.

Where dark tides billow in the ocean
A wink-shaped isle of mighty fame
Guards the gateway to our empire:
Iwo Jima is its name.

We brave men who have been chosen
To defend this island strand
Filled with faith in certain triumph
Yearn to strike for Fatherland.

Thoughts of duty ever with us,
From dawn to dusk we train with zeal,

Bound by Emperor's commanding
To bring the enemy to heel.

Oh, for Emperor and homeland
There's no burden we won't bear.
Sickness, hardship, filthy water
These are less to us than air.

Officers and men together
Work and struggle, strive and trust,
Till the hated Anglo-Saxons
Lie before us in the dust.

3

The hated *Anglo-Saxons?*

Though there were indeed many men of that racial strain among the force forming to come against Iwo Jima, the Japanese who had mistakenly assumed at the war's outset that their chief opponents were to be the British Army and Navy had again erred in identifying the foe.

They were Americans. There were Anglo-Saxon names such as Erskine or Gray or Chamberlain. But there were others such as Schmidt or McCarthy or Stein or LaBelle or Basilone, and there was that commonalty of the Smiths which could be any or all of these.

Chief of the Smiths was old Howlin' Mad, now a gruff lieutenant general of sixty-three years. He was commander of the expeditionary troops mounting out for Iwo, a position which was purely titular. Kelly Turner commanded at sea and Major General Harry Schmidt would be in charge ashore once the Fifth Corps had landed. Smith sought to explain his presence with the quip: "I guess they brought me along in case something happens to Harry Schmidt."

Actually, he was along because the admirals wanted him to be. Smith and his staff were the most experienced amphibious commanders in the Pacific. Even so, the admirals' admiration for Smith did not preclude a recurrence of the dispute over the volume of preinvasion bombardment to be delivered by the Navy.

The Navy planned three days of preinvasion shelling timed to coincide with the Fast Carrier Forces' first strikes on Tokyo. These raids would neutralize enemy homeland air strength. If they began, say, four days before the invasion, and were interrupted in two days or less by either bad weather or enemy resistance, then Japan would have enough time to recover from them and strike American shipping at Iwo. If they began only three days before the landings, as planned, and were interrupted in two days or less, then Japan would not have enough time to recover. The Navy's other reason for restricting the preinvasion bombardment to three days was that this was sufficient and that anything beyond it would be subject to the law of diminishing returns.

The Marines, still mindful of how little was knocked out at Tarawa and Peleliu, as well as how much was destroyed at Roi-Namur, made four separate requests for extended shelling, one of them asking for ten days of it.

The Navy refused, for the reasons cited, the most telling of which was the one concerning the law of diminishing returns. Three days' shelling did get the Marines safely ashore. After that they had to go against Kuribayashi's masterly defenses the only way possible: on foot with a hand weapon. Events proved that nothing else but target pinpointing by troops *ashore* could have knocked out those positions. But at the time of the Marine requests no one suspected the extent of Iwo's fortifications. Smith and Schmidt honestly believed that more bombardment would reduce casualties. That was why there were tears in Howlin' Mad Smith's eyes when he met the press off Saipan on February 16, told them there would probably be 15,000 casualties and said: "We have never failed, and I don't believe we shall fail here."

Harry Schmidt also spoke, scowling heavily to conceal his inner tension. "The landing force is ready for combat," he said.

434

"We expect to get on their tails and keep on their tails until we chop them off."

It was Schmidt who had done most of the planning for the Iwo assault, but the man who had contrived the masterpiece at Tinian had found no lonely unguarded beaches on Iwo Jima. Here it was either east beaches or west beaches with only the forecasts of wind and tide to suggest which might be easier. Schmidt chose the east. The Fourth Division would go in on the right or north, the Fifth Division on the left.

Commanding the fledgling Fifth was Major General Keller Rockey. He had been Assistant Commandant of the Marine Corps before taking over his division a month after it was activated in January, 1944. Though big Keller Rockey's outfit was new to battle, neither he nor many of his men were. Rockey had fought in World War One and could wear the French *fourragere* won in Belleau Wood. He was leading Marines such as Manila John Basilone, the man who had won his Medal of Honor holding off the Sendai on Guadalcanal.

Sergeant Basilone could have spent the rest of the war making War Bond tours in the States. "But it was like being a museum piece," he explained, when his astonished new buddies in the Fifth asked what had possessed him to come back to the islands. "I kept thinking of how awful it would be if some Marines made a landing on Dewey Boulevard on the Manila waterfront and Manila John Basilone wasn't among them."

So Sergeant Basilone and other veterans such as Corporal Johnny Geddings—the parachutist whom Brute Krulak had called "The Pineapple Kid" on Choiseul—were back leading untried youths like Pfc. Jacklyn Lucas or Corporal Tony Stein.

Stein was a youth of unusual good looks, and he was tough and bold as well. He had passed the time in Hawaii learning to use a special weapon he had devised. It was an air-cooled machine gun stripped from a wrecked Navy fighter. It was called a stinger. Stein had it with him as he left Camp Tarawa with the Twenty-eighth Marines and the regiment began boarding its ships.

Stowed away aboard another ship was young Jacklyn Lucas. He was not yet seventeen. He had enlisted at fourteen, lying about his age. It was easy to believe he was older, for he was a young bull at five feet eight inches and 200 pounds. Jacklyn Lucas had been in the brig twice already. The first time for fighting; the second for being absent without leave, for being in possession of a case of beer which was not his, for beating up the MP who sought to shut off his frolic. Two sentences of thirty days' bread-and-water were enough to convince Lucas that he was stuck in a "chicken outfit." He went down to the docks where his cousin was boarding ship with the First Battalion, Twenty-sixth Marines. He went aboard with them. On January 10, 1945, his own outfit—the Sixth Base Depot in Hawaii—declared him a deserter. But Jacklyn Lucas couldn't care less. He was off to Iwo to fight with the Fifth Marine Division.

The Fourth Marine Division was also mounting out of Hawaii to fight at Iwo Jima. It had been only a year since the Fourth sailed straight to Roi-Namur from the West Coast, but the division was already as salty as outfits that had "been out" three times that long. It still had its old salts, men as radically different as Jumpin' Joe Chambers, the hell-for-leather leader of Third Battalion, Twenty-fifth; as tight-lipped, taciturn Captain Joe McCarthy, still commanding Company G of the Twenty-fourth Marines with a Silver Star from Saipan and two battle stars to his credit; and as little Sergeant Ross Gray, still moving quietly along with Company A of the First Battalion, Twenty-fifth. They called him Preacher Gray. He had studied for the ministry. He read his Bible constantly. He had held church services before the guns of Roi-Namur had ceased and been a carpenter on Saipan until his buddy was killed. Then he changed. He volunteered to fire a BAR on Tinian and now the Preacher was going to lead a platoon on Iwo.

Commanding such men was the oldest salt of them all. Major General Clifton Cates had been in Belleau Wood and had come out of France loaded with American and French decorations. He commanded the First Marines the night the Ichikis shuffled off to annihilation at the Tenaru; he had commanded the Fourth Division when it was the spearhead at Tinian. He was a leader of invincible aplomb. His division had drawn the toughest assignment of landing on the right beneath the guns of the northeastern cliffs.

"You know," Clifton Cates said slowly to a war correspondent, "if I knew the name of the man on the extreme right of the right-hand squad of the right-hand company of the right-hand battalion, I'd recommend him for a medal before we go in."

As the Fourth was making the 3,800-mile voyage to Iwo, the men of the Third Marine Division on Guam prepared to follow in floating reserve—under the new commanding general they called "The Big E."

Graves Erskine had been Lieutenant General Smith's chief of staff. Now, at forty-six, already wearing two stars, he led a division. His men had named him well, not so much for his physique, which was strong, but for the strength of his will, for the disciplined intelligence evident on his handsome face. In France during World War One, Erskine had taken a patrol of 38 men into no man's land and had come back with four. His commanding officer said: "Go back out there and throw a rock at that machine gun so it will shoot at you and then we can knock it out." Erskine went back and threw the rock. He was soft-voiced and his smile could be gentle, but his eyes were green and cold. He was stern. On Guam, he had court-martialed artillerymen for firing short rounds that killed Marine riflemen. But he had the respect of his men—of men such as Sergeant Reid Carlos Chamberlain.

He had been Lieutenant Chamberlain once. That was in the Philippines, where he had fought as a guerrilla for a year and a half. Before that he had been a corporal with the old Fourth Marines. He had fought on Cavite, Bataan, Corregidor. Five hours after The Rock fell, suffering from malaria and multiple wounds, he made his escape by boat to Mindanao. He joined the guerrillas. He was commissioned a second lieutenant in the U.S. Army, then a first lieutenant. In 1943 a submarine took him to Australia. He was flown to the States to receive a Distinguished Service Cross for what General MacArthur described as "extraordinary heroism." He could have remained there to take the bows he deserved, but he resigned his Army

437

bars in exchange for a Marine sergeant's stripes and requested
combat duty. They sent him to the Third Division. There he
trained with those men who marched over dusty roads bellowing the song they had composed to the tune of "McNamara's
Band."

> Right now we are rehearsing for another big affair,
> We'll take another island, and the Japs will all be there.
> And when they see us steaming in, they'll take off on the run.
> They'll say, "Old pal from Guadalcanal, you didn't come
>   here for fun."

Training ended and the Third boarded ship to join the armada of 495 vessels "steaming in" to Iwo with the "Anglo-Saxons." And yet, when the assault Marines did go ashore on February 19, some of them had in their pockets copies of the prayer of a seventeenth century Anglo-Saxon general. One of the chaplains had given them cards bearing Sir Jacob Astley's plea before the Battle of Edgehill in 1642:

O Lord! Thou knowest how busy I must be this day:
If I forget Thee, do not Thou forget me.

4

It was a bright clear day.

Superforts were bombing, Hellcats were strafing, all the warships and rocket ships were thundering, but Iwo Jima lay deathlike and quiescent—Mount Suribachi squatting toadlike to the south, the black beaches and hummock-speckled sands silent and menacing in the center, the jumble of ridges and hills vaguely visible north.

"Very light swells," broadcast Vice Admiral Turner's flagship *Eldorado*. "Boating: excellent. Visibility: excellent."

It was a day made for invasion and the Marines went roaring in.

They hit the beaches at about nine o'clock and within an hour both divisions had all their assault battalions ashore and fighting.

One hour.

That was all that Tadamichi Kuribayashi gave the American Marines. Then his gunners struck at the invaders with all the fury of their formidable armament. Shells shrieked and crashed among the invaders, every hummock spat automatic fire and the very beaches erupted with exploding land mines. But the American Marines had had the opportunity to move inland from 200 to 300 yards and that was all they needed.

On the left flank, the Fifth Division was battling to carry out its mission of crossing the island.

"C'mon, you guys," Manila John Basilone called to his machine-gunners. "Let's get these guns off the beach."

They sprinted inland, sinking above their ankles in that hot loose sand, the soles of their shoes turning warm, the calves of their legs protesting against the unfamiliar strain—but Manila John would never see Dewey Boulevard again. A mortar shell crashed in his very footprints and Basilone died with four other Marines.

Below one of the highest terraces barring the path of tanks and amtracks, young Lieutenant Norman Brueggeman jumped erect and shouted to his men:

"If you want to win this war let's get the hell up there!"

He swung an arm at the top of the terrace, and fell dead —while his men crawled and clambered over the sands and swept inland. In their ears, in everyone's ears, was the constant crashing of enemy shells, the sighing of bullets, the soughing of the big projectiles, the whizzing of shrapnel. Concussion lifted them and threw them down. They dug foxholes for cover, but the buckshot-sand slid down and filled them in. No hummock could be trusted. A captain sat on one and called out an order to advance. The blasting of a five-inch gun beneath him knocked him unconscious.

Still the attack on the left pressed forward, and with the passage of every new obstacle a new Marine hero was born— too often in his death.

Captain Dwayne (Bobo) Mears went after a pillbox blocking his company's advance. He knocked it out, but a bullet opened a gash in his neck. He waited until it could be bandaged. He moved on. Another bullet tore through his jaw. Blood poured from the ragged hole. He kept on. At last he sank to his knees, his huge vitality ebbing from his big body. Bullets dug spurts of sand around him. A private tried to hide him from sight of the enemy.

"Get the hell out of here," Mears gasped. "I'll be all right."

440

The corpsmen found him, but he died aboard ship.

Tony Stein did not die until he had fought perhaps the most incredible single fight of the landing. Weighted with ammunition and his stinger, Stein covered his entire company as it moved into position. When it was pinned down, he jumped erect, drawing fire and spotting the enemy guns. Alone, he struck at pillbox after pillbox, killing 20 Japanese. He ran out of ammunition. He threw off his helmet, shucked his shoes, and sprinted back for more bullets. He did this eight times, each time pausing en route to help a wounded Marine to an aid station. At last the Japanese forced his platoon to pull back. Stein covered their withdrawal. Twice his stinger was shot from his hands. But he retrieved it and fired on—until at last the inevitable bullet found him and he died.

It was with such men that the Fourth Division bucked across the island, cutting off Mount Suribachi to the left— while to the rear of both divisions the Japanese gunners made a bloody, burning, smoking shambles of the beachhead. For perhaps two hours after the Japanese had opened up, only a few landing craft were able to pierce that curtain of fire drawn along the shore. Tanks in lighters, amtanks and amtracks sank or blew up on the beaches.

Early in the invasion Lieutenant Henry Morgan brought his tank, the *Horrible Hank*, into the left-flank beaches—only to have its lighter founder and sink in the surf. Morgan radioed his commander: *"Horrible Hank* sank." He went on to have two more tanks blown out from under him. Many of the vital Shermans were stalled before the terraces. They could neither climb nor find traction in the loose sand. Amtanks were forced to back out into the surf to take pillboxes under fire from the water. Bulldozers were needed to cut paths through the terraces. Marston matting was needed to build hasty roadways of steel mesh. But that could not be done until the Fourth Division on the right stormed the high ground from which much of the Japanese fire was coming.

On that extreme right for which Major General Cates had shown so much respect, the "ghouls"of Jumpin' Joe Chambers had fought into their Gethsemane. They called themselves "ghouls" for the ghostly antiflashburn cream they had smeared on their faces in anticipation of close work with demolition charges. But the cream was not proof against bullets and shell fragments as Chambers led them against the high ground above a rock quarry. They took it. They beat off Japanese attempts to throw them off, but they had only 150 front-line men left when the First Battalion, Twenty-fifth, relieved them that night. By nightfall, the regiment had suffered 35 per cent casualties, but the right flank was nailed down, and on the left of the Fourth Division's zone the Marines of the Twenty-third Regiment had fought up to the eastern edge of Airfield Number One.

Sergeant Darrell Cole got them there as much as anyone. He led his machine-gun section toward the field and into a network of pillboxes and a storm of fire. He knocked out two positions with hand grenades himself. A trio of pillboxes pinned his men down. Cole directed a torrent of machine-gun fire on the nearest to silence it. The Japanese retaliated with grenades. Cole counterattacked. He slipped forward, armed with a pistol and one grenade. He tossed his bomb and withdrew to get more. He attacked again, hurling grenades—again running back. Still, the Japanese fired. Cole struck a third time. He knocked out the Japanese strong point, and then a bursting grenade snuffed out his own life.

Casualties were mounting, and the reinforcing regiments had hunched their shoulders and come ashore. They came in riddled, forming on a battlefield more horrifying than any in the memory of the oldest salts. Death had been violent on Iwo Jima. Few indeed were the corpses not mangled. Some were cut squarely in half. Legs and arms lay everywhere, rarely within less than 50 feet of the body from which they had been torn. It was as though the owner of a toy factory had gone berserk and strewn handfuls of heads and limbs over a miniature island. Except for the puttee-tapes of the Japanese or the yellowish leggings of the Americans, it was hard to identify the fallen of either side. From it all rose the intensifying reek of death. It had cost the Marines 2,420 casualties to take a beachhead 4,000 yards wide from south to north, 1,000 yards deep at the left where the island had been crossed, 400 yards deep on the right. Of these casualties, close to 600 were surely dead and there were more dying.

During the night there were more casualties under the methodical onslaught of Japanese artillery. The big Japanese rockets also appeared, although they turned out to be harmless. They invariably overshot their marks and landed in the open sea, after first having terrified the Marines by passing overhead with a horrible blubbering noise, trailing showers of red sparks. The Marines soon grew contemptuous of the rockets, calling them "Bubbly-wubblies." But the Marines were not so derisive of the enemy artillery, especially the fire falling on the beachhead from Mount Suribachi to the south.

This was Iwo's highest ground. Atop Suribachi the Japanese could look down the Americans' throats. The volcano would have to be taken.

Big Colonel Harry Liversedge was called "Harry the Horse" both for his size and his galloping style of attack. He had commanded a Raider regiment on New Georgia, and now he led that Twenty-eighth Regiment which had landed on the extreme left flank and cut off Suribachi from the rest of Iwo Jima.

On February 20, the second day of battle, Liversedge's men faced south toward the volcano and attacked.

They struck down-island, two battalions abreast, while warships, rocket boats and land artillery pounded Suribachi's approaches. Although the shelling knocked out some pillboxes, it merely unmasked the presence of many others—and the Marines had to go in on foot with dynamite and flame-throwers. There were also Navy and Marine fighters slashing the volcano's slopes in strafing runs or dropping tanks of napalm, but the fire-bombs merely flamed and went out. There was nothing to catch fire.

The Marines gained only 200 yards. Their casualties grew. The wounded were taken to the beaches, where wine-colored bottles of whole blood swung like strange blossoms on up-ended rifles, and they were loaded aboard amtracks.

The amtrack *Mama's Bathtub* took six maimed Marines

443

aboard and wallowed into the sea with a roar as a Japanese rocket slobbered in from Suribachi. Corporal Bruno Laurenti and Pfcs. William Seward and Alex Hebert had been making round-trip runs since the day before. They were groggy from want of sleep. Laurenti sent *Mama's Bathtub* churning out to a mercy ship. It was dark when they reached it, but they discharged their burden. Laurenti wheeled the amtrack around and made for his LST. The ship's jaws were clamped tight-shut and the skipper would not open them during darkness and a mounting sea.

Mama's Bathtub came about and headed for the shore. Halfway in, a huge wave struck the amtrack, and she nearly capsized. Her engine sputtered and died. She began to drift. She floated eight miles out to sea. A Higgins boat came along and took her in tow but the rope broke. The Higgins boat turned to go ashore for another rope.

"We'll come back," the coxswain called.

They did not. Laurenti got the motor going just enough to idle the bilge pumps and keep the pontoons from filling with that sea water which would sink them. *Mama's Bathtub* began to drift faster. The tiny craft pitched and tossed. The three Marines passed an LSM. They shouted at it, flashed lights, waved signal flags. The LSM chugged on unheeding. It was nearing midnight and it was getting very cold. Iwo Jima is in the North Pacific and this was February. In the bright moonlight the darkly gleaming obsidian waves seemed mountainous. Behind them, they could see rockets exploding in the sky.

They were not rockets, but flares. The commander of Suribachi had fired them after he had signaled his general, "We should rather like to go out of our position and choose death by *banzai* charges," and Kuribayashi had curtly answered, "No." So the Suribachi garrison stayed under cover and sent up flares marking the American lines. Down from the northern ridges came a whistling rain of shells—and the Twenty-eighth Marines passed a night almost as bad as the day.

In the morning, with 40 fighters and bombers harrying the volcano, supported by tanks, half-tracks, naval gunfire and field artillery, Harry the Horse's regiment pressed slowly for-

444

ward until by nightfall all lower pockets had been reduced and the base of Suribachi had been reached on both coasts.

That same morning, the trio of chattering Marines in *Mama's Bathtub* sighted a destroyer. They signaled. They were seen. The destroyer came carefully alongside and threw them a line. They were towed back to their mother-ship, and helped aboard, exhausted. They staggered below and sank into sleep, while behind them *Mama's Bathtub* sank beneath the surface of an angry sea.

The weather had turned bad at Iwo.

Wind and waves were broaching supply craft on the beaches, leaving them helpless targets, capsizing some of them.

On the morning of February 22, as the Twenty-eighth Marines attacked three battalions abreast, a drizzling rain began to fall. It turned into a downpour and Suribachi's ashes became a clutching gray paste, a sticky goo which fouled rifle breeches and made them impossible to fire except on single-shot. Drenched, exhausted, the Marines moved around the base of the volcano, to either side, fighting all the way. Corporal Dan McCarthy alone shot 20 Japanese. Sergeant Merritt Savage killed seven as he led his platoon in a charge. One Marine was charged by a saber-swinging Japanese officer. He seized the sword, wrenched it away with dripping hands and cut off the officer's head. Another Marine jumped alone into a blockhouse and killed its 10 occupants before he died. Corpsmen crept up to the muzzles of the enemy guns to treat wounded Marines. Sergeant Charles Harris paddled a rubber raft out in the rocky surf to come in among the enemy bullets and rescue two Marines lying helpless on the west side of Suribachi.

By dusk Suribachi was surrounded.

All but a 400-yard strip on the west coast was in Marine hands. Already it had become obvious that the Japanese defenders were cracking. A language officer had come forward with a loudspeaker to broadcast surrender appeals. Shortly after, the Marines saw Japanese leaping to their deaths from the lip of the crater. It was a sure sign.

"At dawn," said Harry the Horse, "we start climbing."

★

They started at dawn and went right up.

Sergeant Sherman Watson and Pfcs. Ted White, George Mercer and Louis Charlo climbed to the summit without spotting a single Japanese. Watson reported back. Lieutenant Colonel Chandler Johnson of the Second Battalion made a decision. He rounded up a 40-man patrol under Lieutenant Harold Schrier.

"If you reach the top," Johnson said, "secure and hold it." He handed Schrier a square of colored cloth. "And take this along."

It was an American flag. Lieutenant George Wells had brought it ashore from the transport *Missoula*.

Schrier's patrol picked its way up the northern or inner slope of the volcano. They climbed through the debris of shelled positions, through an eerie silence. Battle sputtered to their rear, but here there was no sound. They worked past the Japanese defenses and came to the crater where they spread out and charged.

Nothing—nothing but the lava pit yawning beneath their feet.

Suribachi had fallen.

At half past ten the American flag was raised above it, flown from a hollow pipe someone had found and jammed between rocks. It was raised by Schrier and Sergeants Ernest Thomas and Henry Hansen, by Corporal Charles Lindberg and Pfc. James Michels. It fluttered while Sergeant Louis Lowery photographed the event, and Pfc. Jim Robeson snorted, "Hollywood Marines!" and wisely kept a wary eye peeled for Japanese.

They came. Even as the tiny flag brought forth a cheer from the Marines below, an enraged Japanese jumped from a cave to heave a grenade. He was shot dead. An officer charged waving his sword. He was shot into the crater.

"Let's go!" Schrier called. "We haven't got any time to waste around here. Let's get back to work."

For the next four hours fierce fighting raged at every level of Suribachi, but by half-past two the volcano was fairly secure, and it was then that the most dramatic picture of World War Two was recorded.

446

From below Suribachi the Marines could barely see the little 54-by-28-inch flag. One of them went aboard LST 779 beached near the eastern base of the volcano. He borrowed a big flag 96 by 56 inches and took it up Suribachi. Joe Rosenthal of the Associated Press saw him going, and followed with his camera. When Rosenthal reached the summit he saw six men raising the new flag. They were Pfc. Ira Hayes, Pfc. Franklin Sousley, Sergeant Michael Strank, Corpsman John Bradley, Pfc. Rene Gagnon and Corporal Harlon Block. Rosenthal photographed them in that order, left to right—and the great battle photograph of American arms had become history.

The flag had risen at Iwo Jima, and although the inevitable scoffers of the inevitable postwar reaction have spit on the event as "a phony," there was very little fakery about the death which shortly overtook Sergeant Strank, Corporal Block and Pfc. Sousley, or in the wound of Corpsman Bradley. Nor was the first flag-raising a piece of stagecraft any more than the subsequent deaths of Sergeants Hansen and Thomas and Pfc. Charlo, or the wounds suffered by Pfcs. Robeson and Michels. The flag went up in the first place because the sight of it would cheer Marines below who knew that the Japanese looked down their throats so long as they held the highest land on Iwo. When the first flag proved too small to be seen, a second and bigger flag went up. This raising was photographed by Rosenthal with no attempt to stage it—else why everyone's face away from the picture and thus unidentifiable for the newspapers?—and it turned out to be superb. The fact that the famous flag-raising was the second, not the first, no more affects its place in history than the fact that the Suribachi flag-raising was itself intermediate to the first flag-raising on Guadalcanal and the last on Okinawa. The facts were that Suribachi fell because American Marines suffered and died to conquer it, and that some of them raised flags above it to proclaim the victory.

It was the second, famous flag which was seen by Secretary of the Navy James Forrestal as he stepped on the warm soil of Iwo Jima, just as it was caught and flung by the strong north wind whipping Suribachi's crest. Forrestal had followed the battle aboard the command ship *Eldorado*. Now he was standing on the battleground, with Lieutenant General Smith beside him. He saw the flag unfurling and he turned to Smith.

"Holland," he said, "the raising of that flag on Suribachi means a Marine Corps for the next five hundred years."

To the Marines slowly slugging into the First Belt in the north, the news came over the loudspeaker used by the beachmaster to direct unloading operations. The speaker blared:

"Mount Suribachi is ours. The American flag has been raised over it by the Fifth Marine Division. Fine work, men."

Those who could, turned dust-rimmed staring eyes to their rear. They squinted and saw the flag. They looked to the north once more, the loudspeaker blared again:

"We have only a few miles to go to secure the island."

The young-old eyes blinked.

"Only," one Marine repeated. *"Only . . ."*

5

All but three of the 26 Medals of Honor awarded to Marines and their Navy corpsmen on Iwo Jima were won in that nightmarish up-island battle which began the day the Twenty-eighth Marines swept south to Suribachi and the rest of the assault troops slugged north into General Kuribayashi's First Belt.

That was on February 20 and on that day young Jacklyn Lucas saw his first and last combat. He moved with three other men in the Fifth Division's strike up the western coast. They came to a ravine and were ambushed. The air was filled with enemy hand grenades. One landed among the four Marines. Lucas dove over his comrades to smother it with his body. Just as another grenade landed . . .

He pulled this one to him and he had begun to think, "Luke, you're gonna die," when the bombs exploded and his own hoarse trailing scream rose above the roar. The three other Marines attacked and forced the enemy position. Lucas was left for dead behind them, but seven months later he was well enough to receive his Medal of Honor.

On that same day Captain Robert Dunlap was leading his company against a steep, cave-pocked cliff commanding the western beaches. The Japanese pinned them down. Dunlap crawled forward for 200 yards while the bullets sang above him. He spotted the enemy guns, crawled back, relayed the information to naval gunfire and artillery observers, crawled up again and spent two days and nights among the enemy's rocks —calling down the fire which did most to knock out the guns and secure the western beaches. He, too, won a Medal of Honor.

On the right flank the Fourth Division fought a fierce battle to overrun Airfield Number One as well as to push deeper into the cliffs north of the landing beaches. The airfield fell by nightfall of the first day, but the high ground along the east coast was not so swiftly seized. Here it was flesh and blood and will opposing steel and concrete; here captains commanded battalions, lieutenants and sergeants led companies, corporals and privates rallied platoons. Here there were also Medals of Honor won—by Jumpin' Joe Chambers, who was wounded leading his last attack; by Captain Joe McCarthy, who gathered a picked band of Marines to take a vital ridge in a hand-grenade charge; by little Sergeant Ross Gray, taking six pill-boxes and 25 Japanese soldiers before he fell fatally wounded. Hundreds of other Marines received their mortal wounds in this bitter three-day advance through the eastern anchor of General Kuribayashi's First Belt.

But on the fourth day, February 23, the very day on which the flag flew over Suribachi and the loudspeaker voice prattled of "only" a few more miles to go, the Fourth Division made its biggest gains. The Marines broke into the ridges at the point where the pork chop bellies out. They seemed to have pierced Kuribayashi's inner line, but they had actually reached The Meatgrinder.

★

By February 23 the Marines began to suspect that they had made no beachhead on Iwo Jima because Iwo was all beachhead. The familiar rhythm of break-in, break-out, breakthrough would not be repeated here. Lieutenant General Smith had said: "We will be ready for an early counterattack in one of three places. We welcome a counterattack. That is generally when we break their backs."

But there had been no counterattacks and it was the Americans whose backs were breaking on the rock of the Japanese center.

A regiment of the Third Division had been committed there on February 21. The Twenty-first Marines, veterans of the big *banzai* on Guam, dashed again and again at the center just below the southwestern tip of Airfield Number Two. Small breakthroughs often became disasters. Penetrating Marines were raked from the flanks, chewed up—sometimes wiped out. Tanks that butted through were knocked out by guns blasting from interlocking pillboxes, or were hoisted on the spouting fireballs of exploding land mines. Engineers crept forward on their knees, probing the black sand for the kettle-shaped killers which the Japanese had buried so abundantly, but they couldn't find them all. Nor could Marines with flame-throwers and dynamite knock out all the pillboxes. Corporal Hershel Williams won a Medal of Honor by blasting or burning out position after position, but there were 800 pillboxes in this sector 1,000 yards wide and 200 yards deep.

Yet, the center had to move. It was holding up the Fifth Division on the left and the Fourth on the right. When Major General Erskine came ashore with Major General Schmidt on February 23 he ordered the Twenty-first Marines forward the next day "at all costs."

Lieutenant Colonel Wendell Duplantis had commanded the Third Battalion during that wild night on Guam when Major Yukioka's suicide troops had shot the gap and surrounded his command post. Now, on Iwo Jima, Duplantis was awaiting the tanks which would lead his battalion forward at nine o'clock.

450

But the tanks didn't show.

"Attack must proceed without the tanks," he signaled his company commanders.

Captain Clayton Rockmore led out I Company and fell dead with a bullet through the throat. Captain Dan Marshall took over.

Captain Rodney Heinze led out K Company and fell wounded. Lieutenant Raoul Archambault took over.

Archambault urged K Company's Marines forward, into the first line of pillboxes, the wind-blown sand pelting their faces like buckshot. Hurling grenades, they sped through it. They found the Japanese in their trenches and jumped in among them. They jabbed them with bayonets, chased them down those corridors, jumped out again and swept on.

The charge changed to a rush. Far ahead of I Company, the men of K Company were running past mounds of pillboxes and up the slope leading to Airfield Number Two. Marine tanks had entered the fight behind them and were pouring into the hole—mopping up.

Now the riflemen in their baggy green dungarees were flowing across the airfield with a yell. They crossed it raked and struck by bullets. Marines fell, but the others went over the airfield and up to the crest of a 50-foot ridge just on its northern side.

And then, by one of those errors common to war, Marine artillery fire began to fall on them.

Lieutenant Archambault took K Company back down the hill. The shelling stopped. Archambault took them back up. The Japanese drove them off again.

Now I Company was driving through the hole, coming up to the northern edge of the airfield, but now both companies were being struck on their exposed flanks. Still, Archambault led his Marines forward once more. They started up the ridge and a wave of Japanese infantry rose from a gully on its reverse slope to come pouring over the crest and down among them.

The Marines stood back-to-back in ankle-deep sand, fighting with knives, bayonets, clubbed rifles, shovels and fists. In a few minutes the banging and screaming had subsided and there were 50 dead Japanese at the foot of the ridge.

I Company came up and both outfits began digging in. They had come through Kuribayashi's rugged center "at all costs," and now their orders were: "Hold at all costs."

They did. Next day the Third Division's entire attack flowed through the hole these companies had punched. The Ninth Marines went into battle. They slugged slowly up to vital Hill 199 overlooking the airfield, making the kind of fight immortalized in Admiral Nimitz' remark that on Iwo Jima, "uncommon valor was a common virtue."

To win a Medal of Honor in this advance a man's daring and shrewdness must surely be blessed by the fortunes of war. Only this or the direct intervention of the Almighty could have kept Private Wilson Watson alive as he stood in plain view on top of a ridge line to hold off an entire Japanese company with his BAR. Watson got up there by knocking out a pillbox alone. He came down after he shot 60 Japanese and his ammunition ran out. That was on February 27—the day that the up-island advance at last encompassed Hill 199 and the very heart of Kuribayashi's First Belt had been pierced. Airfield Number Two had been conquered except for a few yards on its extreme northeastern tip. Southern Iwo Jima was now American and the growl of the bulldozer was already audible on Airfield Number One.

But on the left flank the Fifth Division had been brought up short in an evil pocket known as Hill 362, while on the right the Fourth had entered The Meatgrinder.

The Hill, the Amphitheater, and Turkey Knob were the three knives of The Meatgrinder.

The Hill, or Hill 382, was the highest ground on northern

Iwo. It rose about a hundred yards east of the northern end of Airfield Number Two. About 600 yards beneath it was the Amphitheater. Just east of the Amphitheater was Turkey Knob. Within this complex was Iwo's communications center and a maze of crags, rocks and outcroppings from which the Japanese had kept the Marines under observation since the landings.

Tanks buried to their turrets guarded all natural approaches. Antitank guns poked their snouts from scores of cavemouths. There were 75-millimeter antiaircraft guns and twin-mount artillery pieces with muzzles lowered to fire point-blank—and everywhere was a multiplicity of heavy and light machine guns. The Hill, the Amphitheater and Turkey Knob were also mutually supporting. Artillery and mortars could be brought down on all or any of them.

The Meatgrinder, hard shell of this iron nut of an island, could only be taken by storming all its points at once.

Up against The Hill went the Twenty-third Marines. The Twenty-fourth took on the Amphitheater. The Twenty-fifth moved on Turkey Knob.

At the Hill the Marines reached the summit with amazing ease. And then the Japanese struck them to the ground and kept them there with a murderous fire. It even came from the rear, for the Marines' rush had carried them past a system of well-hidden pillboxes. The Marines came down from The Hill under cover of a smokescreen. The same thing happened the next day, even though Pfc. Douglas Jacobson attended to the pillbox system—knocking out 16 positions and a tank with his bazooka and killing 75 Japanese to win the Medal of Honor.

It happened also down at the Amphitheater and on Turkey Knob behind it. It seemed the Marines could take these heights almost at will, and then be sorry for taking them. The Japanese withdrew each time it became clear they could not hold. Then they called for their artillery and mortars. When the Marines were forced to withdraw at dusk, the Japanese returned.

For seven days—from February 25 to March 3—the Marines were torn on the knives of The Meatgrinder, taking casualties so great that on a single day the Fourth Division used 400 pints of whole blood. Casualties among the doctors and corpsmen were also fierce, and there were many feats of impromptu medical skill as well as of courage among them. Corpsman Cecil Bryan rushed to aid First Sergeant Fred Lunch when a shell fragment shattered Lunch's windpipe. Bryan seized a section of yellow-rubber transfusion tubing from his pack. He cut off a six-inch length. He inserted it within Bunch's torn throat and carried him to an aid station, saving both his life and his power of speech.

Gradually, the battering of the Marine attacks began to break Japanese resistance. Four days after the battle began, there was a shift of regiments. The Twenty-fourth relieved the Twenty-third in front of The Hill, while still-fresh units of the Twenty-third went down to the Amphitheater and Turkey Knob. One position after another on The Hill was hammered into powder. Caves were sealed, observation posts blown up. At Turkey Knob a 75-millimeter howitzer was hauled to the front to deliver point-blank fire into a blockhouse. Men with demolitions crawled up to it to blast holes in its walls. A flame-throwing tank rolled up a path cut by tank-dozers to pour hissing streams of flame through the holes. Turkey Knob fell. So, too, did the Amphitheater by the sixth day of fighting.

On the seventh, E Company of the Twenty-fourth Marines all but disappeared. But its remnants, having survived a half-dozen company commanders, joined the remnants of F Company and a platoon remaining from a company of another battalion and went up The Hill under Captain Walter Ridlon. They stayed there.

The Meatgrinder was utterly broken on March 3, though it had cost the Fourth Marine Division thousands of casualties. The division's losses were now 6,591 men killed and wounded, and its fighting capacity was down 30 per cent.

In the center, the Third Division slashed through the First Belt with a series of slanting attacks, finally breasting it, overrunning the half-completed Airfield Number Three and coming up short against Kuribayashi's Secondary Line.

On the left, Hill 362 still resisted the Fifth Division. If this western height was only 20 feet lower than its bigger brother in The Meatgrinder, it was only that much less costly. Marines burned the Japanese out of their caves by rolling gasoline drums inside and shooting them aflame, by hanging over cliff ledges to lower explosives on ropes—which the Japanese often cut—and by bringing up rocket trucks to loose showers of missiles on the infested hillside.

Three of the men who helped raise flags over Suribachi died on Hill 362. Lieutenant Colonel Chandler Johnson, the commander who had ordered Old Glory flung to the winds on the volcano's summit, also was killed there.

The Pineapple Kid died, too. Corporal Geddings volunteered to help evacuate wounded. He gave his helmet to a stricken Marine. Ten minutes later a shell fragment struck him in his now-exposed neck and killed him. Four more Medals of Honor were won on Hill 362: by Sergeant William Harrell holding off a squad of Japanese infiltrators; by Gunnery Sergeant William Walsh, Corporal Charles Berry and Pfc. William Caddy throwing themselves on grenades and dying to save their friends.

Hill 362 fell on March 1, after holding out to the last man. The final defender killed himself. He came out of a cave and tapped his grenade on his helmet to arm it. The Marines who saw him ducked back, thinking he meant to throw it. There was a silence and the Marines raised their heads above the rocks again.

The Japanese soldier was crouched with the grenade to his ear, as though listening. It had not exploded.

He tapped it again and listened. No sound.

He tapped it a third time and listened. It went off.

None of the Marines thought it grimly comic. None thought it sad. They merely turned to glance at those western beaches which the fall of Hill 362 now made secure and wondered if the skipper would be able to get hot chow up to them.

7

It was March 4 and General Kuribayashi was signaling Tokyo for help. He had already told Imperial Headquarters: "I am not afraid of the fighting power of only three American Marine divisions, if there are no bombardments from aircraft and warships." Now he was calling for his own aircraft, his own warships. "Send me these things, and I will hold this island," he said. "Without them I cannot hold."

He would not get them, although Japan had tried. On February 21 the *kamikazes* had made a major attack on the American warships surrounding the island. Suicide planes came in at dusk and sank the escort carrier *Bismarck Sea*, badly damaged big *Saratoga* and sent her limping home to Pearl Harbor, and damaged the escort carrier *Lunga Point*, plus a cargo ship and an LST.

None of the planes of this Second Mitate Special Attack Force ever returned to base.

That was all the help that Kuribayashi got from a homeland beginning to reel beneath the intensified raids of the American B-29's. The night before Kuribayashi's last appeal Japan had been raided again, and on that very morning of March 4 one of the returning Superforts was frantically trying to contact Iwo Jima. At last Sergeant James Cox heard a voice crackling over his radio.

"This is Iwo. What is your trouble?"

"Iwo, this is Nine Baker Able. We are running low on gasoline. Can you give us a bearing to Iwo?"

"Course 167 for 28 miles. Do you prefer to ditch offshore or try to land on the strip?"

"We prefer to land."

456

Sergeant Cox switched off his radio. He watched the tiny cinder draw closer to the big bomber's nose. He looked over the side as Lieutenant Raymond Malo circled the smoking, flashing little island in two wide circles—the narrow runway sliding out of his field of vision each time. The third time Lieutenant Malo hit the runway squarely. The big silvery bomber rolled 3,000 feet before it came to a halt.

Lieutenant Malo and Sergeant Cox grinned to hear the cheering of the Marines outside the plane.

The first B-29 had landed on Iwo Jima. It was the forerunner of 2,251 Superforts, which, with 24,761 crewmen, would make safe landings on Iwo before the war ended. Already, with the battle for Iwo not yet over, the value of Iwo had been made evident.

Even though Major General Erskine's Third Division had overrun Airfield Number Three more than two-thirds of the way up the island, they had not been able to knock out a pocket of savage resistance holed up in blockhouses about 200 yards below the field at Motoyama Village.

It was decided to flank it, to strike at Hill 362-C, which stood above and behind it, for the Third Division was trying desperately to break through Kuribayashi's Secondary Line to the northeastern beaches. This was to be done while the Fourth Division continued to clean out all resistance in the eastern bulge of the pork chop. The Third was to drive to the sea above the Fourth, then face north and press up the island's right flank while the Fifth marched up the left. Below them, in the bulge, the Fourth would be whittling away at the enemy.

The decision to make the flanking movement on Hill 362-C a night attack was made by General Erskine. He had come to realize how skillfully the Japanese had adapted themselves to American attacks. When Marine artillery and naval guns began the fire preceding each morning's attack, the Japanese scampered down to their deepest caves to wait it out. When it ceased, they ran back up to their guns to receive the Marines, inflicting heavy casualties—killing men such as the brave Sergeant Reid Chamberlain. The Japanese had done this so often they had it mastered to the point of split-second timing, and they had practially nullified the effect of preparatory shelling.

On the morning of March 7, an hour and a half before daylight, the Ninth Marines attacked without artillery. Three battalions faced almost directly east. The left or northernmost battalion was to take Hill 362-C, the others were to slip into the heart of the Japanese defenses and strike them at daylight.

At five in the morning, with a whistling wind hurling cold rain in their faces, they slipped out. There was not a shot fired. There was not a hand raised against them. The battalions on the lower or right flank reported moving 200 yards without detection. They were ordered to take another hundred.

The left-flank battalion came upon the enemy asleep in their emplacements, and wiped them out. Jubilantly, the Marines reported they had taken Hill 362-C. But they had not. In the darkness they had mistaken Hill 331 for their objective, and now it was daylight and those two battalions in the center and right had been spotted and pinned down.

They fought back throughout that day. The men in the center were hit so savagely that companies were reduced to barely more than squad strength. By nightfall Lieutenant Wilcie O'Bannon commanded less than 10 men—all that was left of F Company. He held them together on a mound 300 yards within the Japanese strong-point, while directing mortar fire by radio. But the Japanese opened with countermortars and O'Bannon's radio fell silent. Lieutenant Colonel Robert Cushman ordered tanks to the rescue. Thirty-six hours after the dawn attack began, the tanks ground over the rubble to the mound where O'Bannon and four other men lay fighting.

They straddled them to drag them inside the escape hatches. And Company E under Captain Maynard Schmidt fared just slightly better in the same sector. They had seven men left.

On the right, there were also companies cut off among the jumble of rocks and crags, out in front of pillboxes passed during the darkness. Here Lieutenant John Leims risked death three times to save his men—once crawling 400 yards through enemy fire to lay communications wire from his cut-off company to the battalion command post, and then, after skillfully pulling his company back out of the trap, twice more crawling up to the abandoned ridge to rescue wounded Marines—and for this he received the Medal of Honor.

Such desperate heroics throughout that tragic March 7 made it appear that the night attack had ended in disaster.

But it had not. Other companies had been fed into the fighting on the center and the right, and here it was found that the Marines had penetrated the outer works of a formidable bastion which would be known as Cushman's Pocket and would fall only after eight evil days of fighting. On the north, the men who had taken Hill 331 fought doggedly on to take their original objective—Hill 362-C—which rose directly in front of them. They took it, but only because their surprise assault had taken Hill 331. It was there that the Japanese had concentrated their fortifications.

By nightfall, all the highest ground on the Motoyama Plateau was in Marine hands—and from it the end was in sight.

There were other proofs that the Japanese had begun to crack: They had begun to commit suicide. Over on the left flank a hundred enemy soldiers holed up inside a ridge blew themselves up—as well as a company of Marines who had occupied the ridge.

The night of the next day came the battle's only *banzai*, another sign of Japanese desperation. A thousand Japanese tried to break the Fourth Division's lines on the right flank. They tried to infiltrate to gain Airfield Number One, where they would blow up equipment with the charges wound around their waists. But they were blown up themselves. The Marines killed 784 of these human bombs. It was the only break of the

Iwo Jima campaign—784 Japanese who could have exacted a fearful price within their caves and pillboxes had come out to be killed easily.

The following day, March 9, a patrol of the Third Division reached the northern end of Iwo Jima. They clambered down the rocky cliffs to the sea. They filled a canteen with sea water and sent it back to Major General Schmidt, inscribed: "For inspection, not consumption."

Iwo Jima had been traversed in eighteen days.

That night Tadamichi Kuribayashi sent his first melancholy message to Tokyo.

"All surviving fighting units have sustained heavy losses. I am very sorry that I have let the enemy occupy one part of Japanese territory, but I am taking comfort in giving him heavy damages."

He was indeed doing that. Even though resistance was subsiding, there were still many Japanese holed up in individual pockets. In the eastern bulge, where the Fourth Division had been gathering momentum since the *banzai*, there were numerous hold-out pockets. One of them was believed to be the headquarters of Major General Sadasui Senda, commander of the 2nd Mixed Brigade which had opposed the Fourth. To him Major General Clifton Cates addressed a surrender appeal broadcast from loudspeakers. He said:

"You have fought a gallant and heroic fight, but you must realize the Island of Iwo Jima has been lost to you. You can gain nothing by further resistance, nor is there any reason to die when you can honorably surrender and live to render valuable service to your country in the future. I promise and guarantee you and the members of your staff the best of treatment. I respectfully request you accept my terms of honorable surrender. I again appeal to you in the name of humanity— surrender without delay."

But Senda did not surrender. Nor was his body found when, by March 16, there was nothing but corpses opposing the Marines in the eastern bulge. The Fourth Marine Division had conquered again—but it had suffered casualties of 9,098 men, of whom 1,806 had been killed. That was half the division's strength. In fourteen months' time, this splendid division had fought three major battles and had suffered casualties almost equal to its strength—17,722 dead and wounded Marines. In three more days the battered Fourth would sail for Hawaii, never to enter battle again.

But the brother Third and Fifth Divisions still had fighting to do in the west sector commanded by Colonel Masuo Ikeda. On March 16 General Erskine made his own surrender appeal. It was addressed to Colonel Ikeda and typed in English on one side of a paper, written in Japanese on the other. It said:

> Our forces now have complete control and freedom of movement on the island of Iwo Jima except in the small area now held by the valiant Japanese troops just south of Kitano Point. The fearlessness and indomitable fighting spirit which has been displayed by the Japanese troops on Iwo Jima warrants the admiration of all fighting men. You have handled your troops in a superb manner but we have no desire to completely annihilate brave troops who have been forced into a hopeless position. Accordingly, I suggest that you cease resistance at once and march, with your command, through my lines to a place of safety where you and all your officers and men will be humanely treated in accordance with the rules of war.

General Erskine entrusted the message to two captured enemy soldiers. He gave one of them a walkie-talkie radio and instructed him to tell his countrymen that he had taken it from enemy Marines after a harrowing fight. On the message, Smith said that the Japanese soldiers had been taken captive while lying unconscious in their foxholes. The two men set out to pass a day and a night divided between lying to their countrymen and dodging the shell-bursts of both armies. One of them actually reached the cave occupied by Colonel Ikeda and got a sergeant friend to take the note in to him. But then, the resourceful prisoner got cold feet. He slipped away. He rejoined his companion and spent the next day spotting targets for the Marine artillery.

The two Japanese returned to the Marine lines the night of March 17, but to those of the *Fifth* Division. To their great indignation they were seized and treated as common pris-

461

oners. An American officer asked them in Japanese how they got the walkie-talkie.

"An American general gave it to me," the boldest of them replied, adding stiffly: "I demand to be taken to my commanding officer."

The interpreter grinned.

"Oh, yeah? Who's he?"

The Japanese soldier stiffened and rapped it out rat-a-tat-tat.

"Major General Graves Erskine," he said, and the interpreter was just startled enough to call the Third Division's command post.

"Well, I'll be damned," he said after the grin had faded from his face. "Yes, *sir!* I'll bring them right over!"

General Erskine's attempt had also failed, and now it was up to the Fifth Division to clean out the rocky, Japanese-infested gorge lying south of Kitano Point. Here were the remnants of Colonel Ikeda's 145th Infantry, here were block-houses commanding all the entrances, and here was General Kuribayashi himself.

It was the most grinding work of the grimmest battle in Marine history. One blockhouse withstood endless shelling as well as demolition attempts with 40-pound shaped charges. The Marines cleaned out the surrounding positions and by-passed it, leaving it to the tank-dozers to seal off its air vents and cave it in with five 1,600-pound dynamite charges.

Then the tank-dozers caught up with the riflemen moving through the gorge. One of them began shoving out a path for the Sherman tanks to follow. Suddenly a single Japanese soldier scrambled out of a cave and ran at the tank-dozer with a satchel charge.

The driver swung his tank sharply to face the charging Japanese. He raised his blade high in the air. It paused there. Then it dropped to cut the assailant in two.

To the astonishment of the men in the waiting Sherman tanks, the tank-dozer's turret came open. The driver popped out. He ran back to the tanks, while bullets whined and clanged off rock and steel. He hammered on the side of one of them, until someone answered him through a fire port.

"Did you see what that Nip bastard tried to do to me?" he called. "That does it, brother—I've *had* it!"

He turned and walked out of the gorge.

But the next day he was back again, sealing off caves, clearing roads for the killer-tanks as the attack in the gorge ground forward. That was on March 21. That night General Kuribayashi was still alive, for he got off a message to Major Horie on Chichi Jima.

"We have not eaten nor drunk for five days. But our fighting spirit is still running high. We are going to fight bravely to the last."

Three days later, Major Horie's radio crackled again.

"All officers and men of Chichi Jima—goodbye."

Silence.

The following night on Iwo Jima some 300 figures arose from caves, from the ruins of pillboxes and blockhouses in that last northwest pocket. Many of them carried swords, for there were numerous officers among them. Most of them carried explosives. They slipped down to the western beaches and they fell on men of the Army Air Corps' VII Fighter Command based there.

They had come upon those Americans least trained to fight on foot in the dark, and they took a fearful toll. Then they raced on to the bivouac of the Fifth Marine Pioneer Battalion, and here they were brought up short against a hastily organized defense line, and were struck to the ground by a counterattack led by Lieutenant Harry Martin. The counterstroke broke them, though Lieutenant Martin himself did not live to receive his Medal of Honor.

In the daylight of March 26 there were 223 Japanese bodies counted on the western beaches, 196 of them in the Fifth Pioneers' area. The Marines looked eagerly for the body of Tadamichi Kuribayashi, for they had heard it was he who had led this last lash of the Japanese tail on Iwo Jima. Like Senda's, it was never found.

But there were the bodies of more than 5,000 Marines to be buried in grim testimony to the skill and tenacity with which Tadamichi Kuribayashi and 21,000 Japanese warriors had defended the Emperor's front gate. In all, 5,885 United States Marines were killed on Iwo, or in the air above or sea around it. There were also 17,272 Marines wounded, 46 Marines missing and surely dead, 2,648 Marines felled by combat fatigue —as well as 738 dead and wounded Navy doctors and corpsmen.

The Fifth Division had more Medal of Honor men to bury. Platoon Sergeant Joseph Julian lost his life charging pillboxes, Pfc. James LaBelle and Private George Phillips had thrown themselves on grenades to save their comrades, Lieutenant Jack Lummus had died leading his men, Corpsmen Jack Williams and John Willis had perished protecting wounded Marines. They were all buried in the shadow of the volcano their division had captured. In the hospitals far from Iwo Jima Private Franklin Sigler and Corpsman George Wahlen recuperated from wounds suffered while helping stricken comrades. They too would receive Medals of Honor. So the fledgling Fifth was blooded now with 8,563 casualties in its first and only fight—and the Fifth buried its dead at the base of Mount Suribachi while taps blew sad and solitary over the drifted ash dunes.

Higher up the island the Third and Fourth Divisions buried their dead in adjoining cemeteries. Already the men had carved memorials out of Iwo's sandstone and decorated the graves of their friends with carved crosses and Marine emblems. Some had made inscriptions:

REACH DOWN, DEAR LORD, FOR THIS MARINE WHO GAVE
HIS ALL THAT WE MIGHT LIVE.

MONTY—A GOOD MARINE WHO DIED IN DEED BUT NOT IN VAIN.

And then this single stark cry of anguish:

BUT GOD— FIFTEEN YEARS IS NOT ENOUGH!

Marines came to the cemeteries from their bivouacs to stand or kneel in prayerful farewell before they took ship to sail away from this dark ugly curse of an island. Major General Erskine spoke to them, commemorating all the fallen.

"Only the accumulated praise of time will pay proper tribute to our valiant dead. Long after those who lament their immediate loss are themselves dead, these men will be mourned by the Nation.

"They are the Nation's loss!

"There is talk of great history, of the greatest fight in our

464

history, of unheard-of sacrifice and unheard-of courage. These phrases are correct, but they are prematurely employed.

"Victory was never in doubt. Its cost was.

"The enemy could have displaced every cubic inch of volcanic ash on this fortress with concrete pillboxes and blockhouses, which he nearly did, and still victory would not have been in doubt.

"What was in doubt, in all our minds, was whether there would be any of us left to dedicate our cemetery at the end, or whether the last Marine would die knocking out the last Japanese gun and gunner.

"Let the world count our crosses!

"Let them count them over and over. Then when they understand the significance of the fighting for Iwo Jima, let them wonder how *few* there are. We understand and we wonder— we who are separated from our dead by a few feet of earth; from death by inches and fractions of an inch.

"The cost to us in quality, one who did not fight side by side with those who fell can never understand."

There would be more crosses for the world to count, more stars, more plain headboards for those nonbelievers who also fell—and the cost to the nation in quality would increase.

On March 26, the day the fighting at Iwo Jima was declared ended, an Army division landed at a place called Kerama Retto.

Okinawa, the last battle, had begun.

No one expected Okinawa to be the last battle.

To both sides the inevitable fight for this chief and largest island of the Ryukyu chain was to be but prelude to the titanic struggle on Japan itself. To America it meant seizure of the last steppingstone to Nippon. To Japan it was to be the anvil on which the hammer blows of a Divine Wind would destroy the American fleet.

This was still the chief object of Japanese military policy—this destruction of American sea power. It was sea power which had brought the Americans through the island barriers, had landed them at Iwo within the very Prefecture of Tokyo, was now bringing them to within less than 400 miles of Kyushu in southern Japan. Only sea power could bring about the invasion of Japan, something which had not happened in the three thousand years of Nippon's recorded history, something which had been attempted only once before.

In 1570 a Mongol emperor massed a great amphibious force on the Chinese coast. Japan was ill prepared to repel the invaders, but a *kamikaze*, a Divine Wind, sprang up in the shape of a typhoon and it scattered and sank the Mongol fleet.

In early 1945, nearly four centuries later, a whole host of Divine Winds was blowing out of Nippon. They were the suicide bombers of the Special Attack Forces, the new *kamikazes* who had been so named because it was seriously expected that they too would destroy an invasion fleet.

They had been brought into being by Vice Admiral Takejiro Onishi. He had led a carrier group during the Battle of the Philippine Sea. After that aerial disaster, he had gone to Fleet Admiral Toyoda with the idea of organizing a corps of flyers to crash-dive loaded bombers into the decks of American ships. Toyoda agreed. He sent Onishi to the Philippines. There, in August, 1944, Onishi began organizing *kamikazes* on a local and spontaneous basis. Then came the Palau and Philippines invasions. On October 15, Rear Admiral Masafumi Arima tried to crash-dive the American carrier *Franklin*. He was shot down by Navy fighters, but the Japanese High Command told the nation he had succeeded in hitting the carrier, and had thus "lit the fuse of the ardent wishes of his men." The first organized attack of the *kamikaze* came on October 25 at the start of the Battle of Leyte Gulf. Suicide bombers struck blows savage enough to startle the Americans and make them aware of a new weapon in the field against them, but not enough to stun them. Too many *kamikaze* missed their targets and were

466

lost, too many were shot down. Of 650 *kamikaze* sent out in the Philippines, about a quarter of them scored hits—but mainly on small ships. The High Command, still writing reports in rose-colored ink, still keeping the national mind carefully empty of news of failure, announced hits of almost 100 per cent. The High Command did not believe this, of course. The High Command guessed privately at hits ranging from 12 to 50 per cent, but the High Command also assumed that nothing but battleships and carriers had been hit.

So the *kamikaze* was born in a storm of enthusiasm and anticipated glory. A huge *kamikaze* corps was organized in the homeland under Vice Admiral Matome Ugaki. By January of 1945 they were a part of Japanese aerial strategy, if not the dominant part. So many suiciders would be ordered out for an operation, to be joined by so many fighters and bombers. Often the duty of the fighters would only be to protect these six-plane units of suiciders; the duty of the bombers would be to guide them to the targets.

They needed to be guided because they were often a combination of old, stripped-down aircraft and young, hopped-up flyers. Admiral Ugaki did not use his best planes or his best pilots, as Admiral Onishi had in the Philippines. Ugaki considered this wasteful. He considered that the spiritual power of "the glorious, incomparable young eagles" would compensate for their own lack of flying skill as well as the missing material power of obsolete aircraft from which even the instruments had been removed. To this end, as well as to inspire the nation, the *kamikaze* were hailed as saviors. They were wined, dined, photographed and fondled. Many of them attended their own funerals before taking off, or climbed into the cockpit with legs made wobbly by the exuberance of farewell feasts. It did not seem to occur to the Japanese that the *saki* drunk at such inspiring leave-takings might influence the purpose, as well as the aim, of the *kamikaze*. It did not, because the *kamikaze* had so thoroughly captivated them. It was this very deep, this very real faith in the *kamikaze's* second coming which dictated how the battle on Okinawa would be fought.

Okinawa was to hold out as long as possible to make the supporting American fleet a target as long as possible.

This was the order which Major General Isamu Cho took down to Lieutenant General Mitsuru Ushijima in January of 1945.

They had served together in Burma, Ushijima as an infantry group commander, Cho as chief of staff of the Southern Army. They had returned to Japan together, Ushijima to become Commandant of the Japanese Military Academy, Cho to serve on the General Military Affairs Bureau. They had come to Okinawa together, Ushijima to command the Japanese 32nd Army, Cho to be his chief of staff. And they were as unlike as two men could be.

Lieutenant General Ushijima, graying, a senior officer in line for full general, was a man of great presence and serenity, capable of inspiring his subordinates, capable of seeing his own incapacities. To fill these he had chosen Major General Cho, a firebrand of fifty-one years, already in line for his second star, a planner and an organizer, strict but resourceful, aggressive, and so invincible in argument as to be unpopular.

Since August of 1944, when Ushijima had taken command on Okinawa, the two men had been anticipating Tokyo's orders to fight the kind of battle which would bleed the Americans white. Their plans were reflected in the 32nd Army's battle slogans:

> *One Plane for One Warship*
> *One Boat for One Ship*
> *One Man for Ten of the Enemy or One Tank*

Fulfillment of the first slogan was up to the *kamikaze*, for General Ushijima had little air power based on Okinawa's five airfields.

The second would be handled by nautical Divine Winds of the Sea Raiding Squadrons. They were enlisted youths fresh out of high school, trained to ram explosive-stuffed motorboats into American ships. There were about 700 suicide boats hidden in the Ryukyus, and about 350 were only about 15 miles west of southern Okinawa in the islets of the Kerama Retto.

The third stricture was left to a force of about 100,000 men, of whom about a fifth were conscripted from an Okinawan population of nearly half a million people. The great bulk of these men were concentrated in the southern third of Okinawa's 485 square miles, where a fantasia of cliffs and caves made formidable defensive terrain.

Here Ushijima began to build a line facing north like a broad arrowhead. Its point rested on the heights surrounding Shuri and Shuri Castle, the city and citadel of Okinawa's ancient kings. Its flanks swept back to the sea on either side, through a jungle of ridges to the chief city of Naha on the west or left, through similar hills back to Yonabaru Airfield on the right. It was the Naha-Shuri-Yonabaru line. It held the bulk of Ushijima's fighting men—the 62nd Division which had served in China, the 24th Division, and the 44th Independent Mixed Brigade. To its left on Oroku Peninsula jutting into the sea west of Naha were about 3,500 Japanese sailors and 7,000 Japanese civilians under Vice Admiral Minoru Ota. Roughly 3,000 soliders of the 2nd Infantry Unit under Colonel Takehiko Udo held the wild, uninhabited northern half of Okinawa—that part which Ushijima under the urging of Cho had chosen not to defend. Nor would Ushijima attempt to defend the Hagushi Beaches in west central Okinawa. He would defend the Minatoga Beaches to the south because they were in the rear of his Naha-Shuri-Yonabaru line, but he would defend almost nothing north of that line, except, of course, its approaches. He would not even defend Yontan and Kadena Airfields to the east of the Hagushi Beaches. These would be wrecked the moment the Americans appeared by a special force drawn from the *Boeitai,* the Home Guard of about 20,000 men which Ushijima had ruthlessly called up from among the Okinawan males of between twenty and forty. The wrecking crew was called the *Bimbo Butai,* or Poor Detachment, by those Japanese soldiers whose loathing of Okinawa and all things Okinawan had already become a problem to General Ushijima.

There was indeed little to love about the Great Loo Choo, as Okinawa was called when Chinese influence was great enough to give the entire chain its original name of the Loo Choos

469

or "bubbles floating on water." Japanese military power and Japanese difficulty in pronouncing the letter L changed it to Ryukyus in 1875, but even the Divine Emperor could do nothing about those floating bubbles. Neither Eritrea nor the Belgian Congo is more humid than Okinawa, and the Great Loo Choo's skies are capable of pouring out 11 inches of rainfall in a single day. Its people, of mixed Chinese, Malayan and Ainu blood, are among the most docile in the world.

The Okinawans have no history of war. They neither make nor carry arms, a fact which filled Napoleon with enraged incredulity in the early nineteenth century, and which, in the mid-twentieth, led the Japanese to regard the Okinawans as an inferior race. Apart from those schoolteachers trained in Japan, Okinawans were disdained as good for nothing but farming their tiny plots of sweet potatoes, sugar cane or rice. So spurned, they resented their masters and clung doggedly to their Chinese culture.

"The houses and customs here resemble those of China," a Japanese private wrote in his diary. "They remind one of a Chinese town."

Christ, Allah and Buddha had been to Okinawa with venturesome European and Malay sailors, with Chinese culture—but the people still practiced a primitive animism while worshipping the bones of their ancestors. These were placed in urns kept within lyre-shaped tombs sprinkled over plains and low hillsides. Many tombs within the Naha-Shuri-Yonabaru line had also been fitted with machine guns and cannon, and strengthened by those diggers and drillers of Ushijima's unwilling *Boeitai*.

Conscription of the *Boeitai* had unwittingly led to one of the chief complaints among Ushijima's soldiers: the lack of fresh vegetables. There hadn't been enough adult males around to produce the normal vegetable crop that fall and winter, and Tokyo was shipping in bullets, not beans.

"I cannot bear having just a cup of rice for a meal with no side dishes at all," a soldier wrote. "Our health will be ruined."

The lament was raised frequently elsewhere, and Ushijima took account of it by urging his men to "display a more firm and resolute spirit, hold to the belief of positive victory, and

470

always remember the spirit of martyrdom and of dying for the good of the country."

By way of consolation, the general issued each man a pint and a half of sweet-potato brandy, proclaimed a temporary amnesty for drunkards and promised another issue on April 13, when the Emperor Hirohito would become forty-four years old. That had been in January, just before General Ushijima dispatched General Cho to Tokyo on a flying visit.

Cho came back in late January. He reported that Ushijima's defense plans dovetailed with Imperial Headquarters strategy and that he had been able to dispel some doubts about the decision not to defend the Hagushi Beaches. Cho was also elated by a secret report on the *kamikaze* which he had seen. The attacks of 26 of Admiral Ugaki's six-plane units had brought about instantaneous sinking of one American battleship, six carriers and 34 cruisers. Even the clearheaded Cho had been blown overboard by the Divine Wind. He got out an inspirational message for the 32nd Army's top commanders. It said:

"The brave ruddy-faced warriors with white silken scarves tied about their heads, at peace in their favorite planes, dash out spiritedly to the attack. The skies are slowly brightening."

But the skies were rather darkening with the airplanes of the American Fast Carrier Forces which began striking the Great Loo Choo late that month. After the raid of January 22, a Japanese superior private wrote in his diary:

> While some of the planes fly overhead and strafe, the big bastards fly over the airfield and drop bombs. The ferocity of the bombing is terrific. It really makes me furious. It is past three o'clock and the raid is still on. At six the last two planes brought the raid to a close. What the hell kind of bastards are they? Bomb from six to six!

They were "hard-nosed bastards," these Americans, and there were more and bigger ones coming—both at the Ryukyus and Japan, both by air and by sea. Naha was being pounded to rubble and the wolf packs of the American submarine service were littering the floor of the China Sea with sunken cargo vessels and drowned soldiers.

471

"The enemy," wrote another private, "is brazenly planning to destroy completely every last ship, cut our supply lines and attack us."

The "enemy" was also hurling neutralizing thunderbolts at the homeland. Giant B-29's had begun to strike Tokyo, Nagoya, Osaka and Kobe in 300-plane raids. On March 9 the Superforts came down to 6,000 feet over Tokyo to loose the dreadful fire-bombs which burned up a quarter of a million houses, made a million persons homeless and killed 83,793 others. Neither Hiroshima nor Nagasaki would equal the carnage of this most lethal air raid in history.

Throughout February and March, while the Marines were conquering Iwo Jima, land- and carrier-based air struck again and again at the Great Loo Choo. Superforts began to rage all over the Ryukyus. Okinawa was effectively cut off from Kyushu in the north, Formosa in the south. On March 1, while the Fast Carrier Forces were returning to Ulithi from their third strike at Japan, there were so many planes strafing, bombing and rocketing Okinawa that pilots had to get in line for a crack at a target. Lieutenant General Mitsuru Ushijima was impressed.

"You cannot regard the enemy as on a par with you," he told his men. "You must realize that material power usually overcomes spiritual power in the present war. The enemy is clearly our superior in machines. Do not depend on your spirits overcoming this enemy. Devise combat method based on mathematical precision—then think about displaying your spiritual power."

Ushijima's order was perhaps the most honest issued by a Japanese commander throughout the war. It was *Bushido* revised, turned upside down, but the revision had been made too late.

10

There were 1,300 ships and perhaps another 300 left behind in the anchorages. Some of the ships were new, some came from the West Coast and were sailing 7,200 miles to battle, putting in at island battlegrounds whose names they bore, staging up through the latest battlegrounds at Ulithi, Leyte and Saipan. They roved boldly about that Pacific Ocean which was now an American lake, for Manila had fallen on February 24 and only the mighty battleship *Yamato* had survived the holocaust of Leyte Gulf. There were British vessels present, a fast carrier force of 22 warships, for in Europe the gate had been left open at Remagen, American troops were over the Rhine, and the old queen of the waves was sending help to the new lord of the seas.

Fleet Admiral Nimitz was still in over-all command in Hawaii as he had been when the Japanese were stopped at Midway, when the long charge began at Guadalcanal. Admiral Spruance commanded the Fifth Fleet, and there was the saltiest salt still giving orders to the expeditionary force. Vice Admiral Richmond Kelly Turner had brought the Marines to Guadalcanal and now, nearly three years later, still roaming his flagship bridge in an old bathrobe, still a profane perfectionist with beetling brow and abrasive tongue, a matchless planner who would also not scruple to tell the coxswain how to beach his boat, Kelly Turner was bringing the Tenth Army to Okinawa.

A newcomer to the Central Pacific led the ground troops: Lieutenant General Simon Bolivar Buckner, Jr., "the old man of the mountain," the son of the famous Confederate general of that name and rank, himself a product of the strictest Army

473

training, a big man, ruddy-faced, white-haired, strong for the physical conditioning of troops. He had served four years in Alaska and the Aleutians and had built up the Alaskan defenses. He had hoped to lead the invasion of Japan through the North Pacific, but the thrust from the Aleutians was never made. It was coming from the center, and Simon Bolivar Buckner was called down to lead it—commanding that Tenth Army which was in fact only a new number for seven veteran divisions which had made the assault possible.

These were the 7th, 27th, 77th and 96th Infantry Divisions making up Major General John Hodge's Twenty-fourth Corps, and the First, Second and Sixth Marine Divisions of Major General Roy Geiger's Third Corps.

The 27th, which had seen action at Makin and Saipan and was still commanded by Major General George Griner, would be in Tenth Army reserve. The 77th of Major General Andrew Bruce—those "Old Bastards" who had waded ashore at Guam and gone on to Leyte—were to start the battle for Okinawa.

On March 26 the 77th's soldiers began taking the islands of the Kerama Retto, destroying the lairs of Ushijima's suicide boats. They also occupied those reef islets of Keise Shima which the Marines of Major Jim Jones' Reconnaissance Battalion had scouted in night rubber-boat landings. On these islets went the 155-millimeter long toms of the 420th Field Artillery Group. They began laying down a galling fire on southwestern Okinawa, especially in the vicinity of the Hagushi Beaches.

These beaches were to be taken with the Marines on the left or north, the soldiers on the right. Nailing down the right flank was the spearhead team which Hodge had used in the Philippines—the 7th, led by Major General Archibald Arnold and blooded at Attu, Kwajalein and Leyte, and the 96th of Major General James Bradley, also a veteran of Leyte. Once these two divisions were ashore, they were to capture Kadena Airfield, drive east across the island's waist and then wheel south to attack abreast in that direction.

Geiger's Third Corps would capture Yontan Airfield, drive east cross-island and turn north to overrun that half of Okinawa. This would be done by the Sixth and First, while the

Second made a feint off those southern or Minatoga Beaches which General Ushijima had so carefully fortified.

Covering the landings would be the biggest bombardment force yet assembled—10 old battleships, 10 cruisers and scores of destroyers and gunboats—as well as the far-ranging new battleships and fleet carriers of the Fast Carrier Forces, the flying buffer of the British task force in the southern Ryukyus, the Navy's minesweepers and Underwater Demolition Teams, the big bombers of the Twentieth Air Force, and the Tenth Army's own Tactical Air Force made up chiefly of Marine flyers and commanded by a Marine—Major General Francis Mulcahy.

Okinawa was to be the biggest battle of the Pacific, with 548,000 Americans of all services involved, as well as history's greatest amphibious assault, with an attack force of 183,000 men, of which 154,000 were in the actual combat divisions.

Okinawa would also crown the unique mission of the Marine Corps, one which began after the Allied disaster at Gallipoli in World War One had convinced most military thinkers that hostile and fortified shores could not be overcome by invasion from the sea. The Marines disagreed. They insisted amphibious assault could be successful and developed the craft and techniques to make it so. They also trained the Army in this speciality, which was to be needed in Europe as well as the Pacific. The Army's first three amphibious divisions— the 1st, 3rd and 9th—were trained by Marines. Those very infantry divisions going into Okinawa—the 7th, 77th and 96th —were Marine-trained, while the 81st Division which Lieutenant General Buckner was holding in area reserve in New Caledonia had also been taught by Marines. And the Tactical Air Force led by Major General Mulcahy was to put into the air an overwhelming number of Marine pilots especially trained in the Marine tactic of close-up aerial support.

It was also fitting, in this last battle of the war, that the First Marine Division, which had launched the long counteroffensive, should be in at the kill. The First had a new commander, Major General Pedro del Valle. He had relieved Major General Rupertus, who went back to the States to die in his bed. Del Valle was a Puerto Rican who had gone through

Annapolis and had served with Italy's Marshal Badoglio as an observer in Ethiopia. Hot-tempered—with dark brows the equal of Admiral Turner's—he was quick-witted as well, an artillerist whose guns had saved the First at Guadalcanal so that the hard-noses could go on to fight at New Britain and Peleliu.

There was the Second Marine Division, which had also come a long way from Guadalcanal, had passed through bloody Betio in Tarawa and fought the grinding fight on Saipan. Major General Thomas Watson still led the Second, and he had broken in 8,000 replacements by setting them to mopping-up Japanese stragglers in the Marianas. The Second's battalions would make the feint off southern Okinawa. They had done it so well at Tinian, they were being asked to do it again; but even so, there were frequent growls about how come the upstart Sixth was going into the assault on the left of the First.

If the Sixth was new in number, it had a faultless, veteran staff and command under Major General Lemuel Shepherd. It had men such as Brute Krulak, the sawed-off dynamo who had made so much smoke at Choiseul and was now a lieutenant colonel in charge of operations. It had 70 per cent veterans and only two of its battalions had not yet been in battle. The Sixth was "gung ho," and veterans of other outfits might have been startled to find that the division with a silver Crusader's sword for its emblem harbored such seemingly passé types as the Glory Kid. He was a brawny red-haired corporal of twenty years and his name was Donald (Rusty) Golar. He had fought with the Twenty-second Regiment on Guam and won a Bronze Star. "I'm a storybook Marine," Golar said. "I'm lookin' for glory and I'm lookin' for Japs." There were glory-boys from the ranks of collegiate football, too. In the Fourth Regiment commanded by Colonel Alan Shapley, one of the Naval Academy's finest athletes, there were enough football stars to field two All-American teams. Lieutenant George Murphy of the Twenty-ninth Marines had been captain of the Notre Dame team.

These were the troops of the Third Corps, with their artillery battalions and engineers, their tanks and Navy corpsmen. In all, there were 85,246 of them, nearly as many as the

88,515 soldiers of the four-division Twenty-fourth Corps, for the three Marine divisions, having anticipated heavy casualties early in the battle, were bringing their replacement battalions to Okinawa with them.

Yet, there was hardly any talk of casualties as the great convoy flowed up the curve of the world. Most of the conversation was about The Deadly Habu, a snake something like a cobra which Intelligence reported abundant on Okinawa. Intelligence even had pictures of The Deadly Habu, and because it was indeed a venomous-looking reptile, the habu soon joined the immortal Marine menagerie of the goony-birds of Midway, the pissing-possum of Guadalcanal, the New Zealand kiwi, the lunatic-lunged kookaburra of Australia and the indecent snow-snake of Iceland. The men spoke so much of the habu they almost forgot the Japanese, although officers would frequently "hold school" on the importance of their objective to the war effort.

"From Okinawa," one lieutenant told his platoon, "we can bomb the Japs anywhere—China, Japan, Formosa . . ."

"Yeah," a sergeant mumbled, "and vice versa."

It was true, of course, that the Japanese had 65 airfields on Formosa to the south and 55 on Kyushu to the north, as well as a few dozen scattered throughout the southern Ryukyus, but such discouraging information is not normally disseminated among the troops. More pointed and helpful information came from veterans such as Corporal Al Biscansin of the Sixth Division, who offered this earnest advice to the boots:

"When you aren't moving up or firing, keep both ends down! The GI Bill of Rights don't mean a thing to a dead Marine."

The GI Bill rivaled the habu as a topic of conversation, for a surprising number of these young men intended to go to college when the war was over. They even expected that great event to happen soon.

"Home alive in '45," they said, a happy revision of Guadalcanal's gloomy estimate of "The Golden Gate in '48." They sang "Goodbye, Mama, I'm off to Okinawa," and joked about the latest dreadful estimates of American disaster broadcast by Radio Tokyo.

The Japanese had already made the mistake of believing that

477

the five American carriers damaged by *kamikaze* during the March 18-19 strikes against Japan would prevent early invasion of Okinawa. Because of this, the *kamikaze* were caught unprepared when the Kerama Retto landings began. Only Ushijima's handful of planes on Okinawa and scattered suicide units from Japan were able to intervene, and though they did extensive damage, it was nothing like the broadcast reports. On March 28 the Marines heard Radio Tokyo announce the sinking of a battleship, six cruisers, seven destroyers and one minesweeper, and then the voice of an American-educated announcer simpering:

"This is the Zero Hour, boys. It is broadcast for all you American fighting men in the Pacific, particularly those standing off the shores of Okinawa . . . because many of you will never hear another program. . . . Here's a good number, "Going Home" . . . it's nice work if you can get it. . . . You boys off Okinawa listen and enjoy it while you can, because when you're dead you're a long time dead. . . . Let's have a little juke-box music for the boys and make it hot. . . . The boys are going to catch hell soon, and they might as well get used to the heat. . . ." Then, having described the varieties of death instantly impending for "the boys off Okinawa," the voice concluded: "Don't fail to tune in again tomorrow night."

Two days later the voice was somber. "Ten American battleships, six cruisers, ten destroyers, and two transports have been sunk. The American people did not want this war, but the authorities told them it would take only a short while and would result in a higher standard of living. But the life of the average American citizen is becoming harder and harder and the war is far from won. . . ."

Two more days and Radio Tokyo had lost its audience: "The boys off Okinawa" had gone ashore.

That was on April 1—Easter Sunday, April Fool's Day, or L-Day as it was called officially. The L stood for Landing, but the Marines who hit the Hagushi Beaches with hardly a hand raised to oppose them had another name for it.

They called it Love-Day.

11

The *Bimbo Butai* had broken and fled at almost the first salvo of American guns. The airfields at Yontan and Kadena were left intact, and there were only a few mortars and a handful of riflemen to oppose the hordes of Americans circling offshore beneath overcast skies.

They came in.

On the northern beaches the Marines had anticipated another Tarawa in the reefs barring their passage, in the three-foot sea wall just back of the beaches. But high water bore them over the reefs and they had merely to clamber up the sea wall to get past it.

Only the inevitable confusion of putting 50,000 fighting troops ashore on a beachhead eight miles long hindered the invasion of Okinawa. All along the line the incredible landing was going forward with unbelievable speed.

By midmorning the Sixth Marine Division had reached Yontan Airfield and was moving across it, while the First Marine Division on the right struck out rapidly for Nakagusuku Bay on the east coast, chopping up the remnants of the demoralized *Bimbo Butai*. Many of these reluctant soldiers threw off the hated Japanese uniform and melted out of sight among their own people. Many true Japanese soldiers who were scattered throughout the landing area also put on dirty blue Okinawan kimonos and turned guerrilla, but there were not enough of these sniping irregulars to do more than badger the advancing Marines. They brushed past them, exulting in the pacific bliss of Love-Day.

A half-hour after the first of the Sixth Division's riflemen had swept inland, the Division's tanks were ashore. They

479

rolled over beaches blessedly free of mines, while behind them came the bulldozers to cut passage through the terraces. American mechanical energy was everywhere moving and shaking, transforming the beachhead, while up front the Marines were succumbing to the Great Loo Choo's pastoral charm. They were rounding up the shaggy little Okinawan ponies found ambling along narrow dirt roads.

"Ya-hoo! I'm Captain Jinks of the Horse Marines!"

It could have seemed an April Fool's Day joke, even though here and there a Marine was being shot. In the battalion aid stations along the beaches, the doctors looked almost frustrated.

Out on the command ships among the forests of masts and fluttering signal flags, steady reports of bloodless advance had produced an atmosphere first of disbelief, then relief, then wary suspicion. At noon, Major General Shepherd moved his Sixth Division Headquarters ashore with the smiling remark:

"There was a lot of glory on Iwo, but I'll take it this way."

Shepherd's staff sailed shoreward past hospital ships lying lonely and unattended by an invasion's customary swarming of casualty boats. In one of the new LST-hospitals assigned to the First Marine Division, the ship's surgeon was impatient. Since the moment the assault amtracks had rolled down the ramp, sailors had been at work transforming the ship. All the litter left behind by the Marines was heaved over the side. The tank deck was hosed down. Rows of cots were set up inside it. Outside the big yawning bow doors a company of Seabees rigged a pontoon-pier for casualty boats. All was accomplished in less than two hours. The surgeon strode out on the pier. He could see columns of Marines vanishing behind the sea wall. But there was no return traffic. He turned anxiously to a corpsman.

"No boats, no wounded?"

"Nothing yet, sir."

The surgeon shrugged and went back inside the LST. In a moment he was outside again, for he had heard a motor.

A Marine was stepping onto the pier from a casualty boat.

"What's wrong with you, son?"

The Marine held up a spouting finger stump.

"One of my buddies let one go and shot the top of my finger off."

The surgeon peered at it, ordered it dressed.

"What's happening in there, son?"

"Don't ask me, Doc. All I know is everybody's goin' in standin' up."

The surgeon sighed. He glanced shoreward again, turned and went back inside the ship to eat lunch. He came out. Still no return traffic. He called to his solitary patient, "C'mon, son, let's go make you a new finger. We've got plenty of time to do it in."

That was Love-Day on Okinawa, a most fortuitous eight hours of daylight during which the Tenth Army captured two airfields and a beachhead eight miles long and three to four miles deep—all at a cost of 28 killed, 27 missing and 104 wounded. Only a few of the dead or missing was from either of the assaulting Marine divisions—but 16 of them were from that Second Marine Division which had drawn the soft assignment of making the feint off southern Okinawa.

Down there a *kamikaze* crash-dived LST 884 with 300 Marines aboard her. The ship burst into flames. Ammunition began to explode. The LST had to be abandoned temporarily. Eight Marines were killed, eight were missing and 37 were wounded. Another *kamikaze* put three holes in destroyer *Hinsdale* and the stricken ship had to be towed away by fleet tugs. The departure may have prompted General Ushijima's report of having forced the enemy to withdraw "after being mowed down one after another."

Up north, though, there were 50,000 of the enemy on Okinawa. Objectives which were expected to require three or more days and many lives were firmly in American hands. At Yontan Airfield that dusk of April 1, there were bulldozers clearing away wrecked planes and General Ushijima's clever dummies of sticks and stones. Already an airplane was touching down. But it had a red ball on its fuselage. It came in as bulldozers stopped and men hopped quickly to the ground. Marines heating their rations stood erect and walked quietly toward the landing strip. The Zero swung seaward and turned back to a smooth landing.

The pilot wriggled out of his parachute pack. He climbed down. He walked toward the Marines. He stopped. Between that moment in which he reached for his pistol, and the next when he slumped to the runway, riddled, an expression of indescribable horror had passed over his face.

"There's always one," a Marine said, shaking his head ruefully—"there's always one poor bastard who doesn't get the word."

482

12

It was the morning of April 2. The Marines were awake, stamping chilled feet, amazed to see their breath making vapor puffs while they drew their newly issued wool-and-gabardine field jackets tighter around them. It was something less than 50 degrees, it would not go above 60, but it was nippy enough to chill the thinned blood of men with years in the tropics behind them.

They moved out rapidly along the narrow roads, passing through peaceful fields sprinkled with little thatched farmhouses, each sheltering behind stone walls or bamboo windbreaks. They gathered momentum, the Sixth Division striking swiftly for Zampa Cape in the north to seize the site for Admiral Turner's badly needed radar station, the First speeding east across island for Nakagusuku Bay.

"Off and on!" the sergeants shouted. "Let's keep moving!"

"You there—whattaya keep looking behind yuh for?"

"I can't help it, Sarge—I keep feelin' somebody's gonna slug me from behind."

It was a common sensation, as Love-Day turned into Honeymoon Week at Okinawa. Only the Sixth Division was running into any kind of opposition, and this in ambushes or isolated attacks on scattered strong-points—battles real enough to the few men who died or were wounded in them, but not in large enough volume to deter the Sixth's swift advance.

The First Division was having a picnic. Major General Del Valle called a press conference in the afternoon and told the newsmen: "I don't know where the Japs are, and I can't offer you any good reason why they let us come ashore so easily.

We're pushing on across the island as fast as we can move the men and equipment."

They were, and in two days of "fighting" the First Division's casualties totaled three dead and 18 wounded. Next day, the Division's jubilant Marines were standing on the eastern sea wall overlooking the bay and the Pacific Ocean. They had severed the island. That same day, scouting parties turned sharply right and swept out onto the narrow finger of the Ketchin Peninsula, traversing it without opposition. With the Tenth Army lifting all restrictions, the First Division rapidly secured all the east coast between Yontan and the Ishikawa Isthmus, that narrow neck of about two and a half miles which lay two-fifths of the way up Okinawa's 60-mile length. In four days, the First had taken territory expected to require three weeks of heavy fighting.

Above these Marines, the Sixth Division was sealing off the base of the isthmus preparatory to its drive north. The First would clean up behind the Sixth, and also attend to the problem of the Okinawan refugees now clogging the roads.

There were so many of them: women with babies at their breasts; children without parents; grizzle-bearded ancients hobbling along with bent backs, leaning on staffs and carrying pitiful small bundles representing all that the war had left them, that terrible war which had also robbed them of the authority of their beards and had exposed them to Japanese mockery and American pity; and the old white-haired women who could not walk, who merely squatted in the road, shriveled, frail, hardly bigger than monkeys, waiting to be carried, waiting for the kind Marine who might stop and stick a lighted cigarette between their toothless gums.

They were a docile people, and now they were terrified because the Japanese had told them the Americans would torture them. They were frightened also because they knew that among them were Japanese soldiers disguised as civilians. But their fear vanished with gentle treatment, with the policy of carefully searching all males between fifteen and forty-five— to discover many a knife or cartridge belt beneath a smock— and of placing all of these within prisoner-of-war camps. Soon

484

the Okinawans were speaking openly of their hatred for the Japanese, their loathing for the Reign of Radiant Peace.

"*Nippon ga maketa*," they said. "Japan is finished."

But Nippon was neither *maketa* nor *zemmetsu*. Nippon had at last recovered from the American carrier strikes at the homeland and was about to hurl her thunderbolts with characteristic suicidal fervor. On April 6 hundreds of *kamikaze* came roaring down from the north, and trailing after them in the spreading white majesty of her mighty bow wave came nothing less than a suicide battleship.

She was the *Yamato*, the mightiest warship ever built, the most beautiful battleship afloat and the last capital ship left to Japan.

Yamato had survived Leyte Gulf where her sister ship, *Musashi*, had not. *Yamato* could outshoot anything in the U.S. Navy. She had nine 18.1-inch guns firing a projectile weighing 3,200 pounds a distance of 45,000 yards, compared to the 2,700-pound shell and 42,000-yard range of the American 16-inchers. She displaced 72,809 tons fully laden, and drew 35 feet. She was 863 feet long and 128 in the beam. She could hit 27.5 knots at top speed or cruise 7,200 miles at 16 knots. And she was sortying out of the Inland Sea for Okinawa with only enough fuel in her tanks for a one-way voyage.

If soldiers and tanks, fliers and airplanes, sailors and boats could be enrolled in the ranks of the suiciders, it was logical that admirals and dreadnoughts should follow. There were three admirals coming with *Yamato*, and the light cruiser *Yahagi* and eight destroyers. There might have been more of them and more warships, but Admiral Toyoda could scrape up only 2,500 tons of fuel for the venture. Toyoda also had only 699 planes, half of them *kamikaze*, to hurl against the Americans in the aerial phase of the attack. He had hoped to have 4,500, but American strikes on the homeland had crippled aircraft production and had also destroyed many planes on the ground.

Still, Toyoda hoped for great things from the *kikusui*, or "floating chrysanthemums," which was the name given to 10 massed *kamikaze* attacks planned for Okinawa. His hopes for the Surface Special Attack Force led by Vice Admiral Seichi Ito aboard *Yamato* could not have been other than forlorn. He gave the great ship only two fighter planes for cover.

Yamato shoved off from Tokuyama at three-twenty on the afternoon of April 6, exactly twenty minutes after the first of the *kikusui* dove on the American ships off Okinawa.

On that morning of April 6 the Fast Carrier Forces were discovered by Japanese scout planes in the northern Ryukyus. Some 100 fighters and bombers were brought down on them.

Later in the day American air patrols flying off Okinawa's now-operable airfields were drawn off into battle with Japanese fighters sent down in advance of the *kamikaze*.

At three o'clock, with the way cleared for them, the suiciders struck. They dove on the destroyers of the radar picket screen and among the forests of masts in the Hagushi Anchorage. Some 200 came for five hours until darkness veiled the targets or magnified the death pyres of American ships.

Destroyers *Bush* and *Calhoun* went down, the minesweeper *Emmons*, LST *447*, and the ammunition ships *Logan Victory* and *Hobbs Victory*. Nine other destroyers were damaged, as were four destroyer escorts and five mine vessels. Up north, the carrier *Hancock* and two destroyers of the Fast Carrier Forces were hit.

It was an impressive day's work for the first sally of the *kikusui*, even though they had lost 135 planes. But the *kamikaze* reports were as usual exaggerated, dovetailing with those from the 32nd Army claiming 30 American ships sunk and 20 more burning. Such bloated estimates helped inflate the spirits of *Yamato*'s 2,767 officers and men as the sleek dreadnought tore through the night, making for the Inland Sea's southeastern gate at Bungo Strait.

There had been a ceremony. At six o'clock, all men and officers not on duty had been broken out on deck. A message from Admiral Ozawa was read:

"Render this operation the turning point of the war."

The men sang the National Anthem, gave three *banzais*

486

for the Emperor, and returned to quarters. At ten o'clock, *Yamato* was in the Pacific Ocean—racing down Kyushu's eastern shores with her consorts gathering about her, shooing the American submarine *Hackleback* away, swinging to starboard off Kyushu's southern nose to sail west through Van Diemen Strait into the East China Sea.

Admiral Ito was taking the Surface Special Attack Force on a big swing west-northwest in hopes of pouncing on the Americans off Okinawa at about dusk of the next day.

But *Hackleback* had already alerted Admiral Spruance and shortly before half-past eight the next morning a scout plane from *Essex* spotted the Japanese force just southwest of Kyushu, less than 400 miles above Okinawa.

Patrol planes began taking off from Kerama Retto.

At ten o'clock, *Yamato*'s pathetic pair of fighter escorts flew back to Japan.

At ten-thirty Rear Admiral Morton Deyo was ordered to take six battleships, seven cruisers and 21 destroyers north and place them between the approaching Japanese warships and the American transports. At almost the same moment the patrol planes found *Yamato* sailing at 22 knots in the middle of a diamond-shaped destroyer screen, with cruiser *Yahagi* trailing behind. The big planes shadowed the naked enemy fleet like vultures.

"Hope you will bring back a nice fish for breakfast," Admiral Turner signaled Admiral Deyo.

The commander of the intercepting force seized a signal blank and pencil to write his reply. "Many thanks, will try—" An orderly handed him an intercepted message. Scouts of the Fast Carrier Forces had found the enemy. Three groups totaling 380 planes were preparing to strike. "Will try to," Deyo concluded, "if the pelicans haven't caught them all!"

The "pelicans" had.

At half-past twelve the American warbirds were over the target. Ten minutes later two bombs exploded near *Yamato*'s mainmast. Another four minutes and a torpedo had pierced her side. At the same moment destroyer *Hamakaze* stood on her nose and slid under, and *Yahagi* took a bomb and a fish and went dead in the water.

There was a respite.

The Americans came again at half-past one and planted five torpedoes in *Yamato's* port side. Water rushed into boiler and engine rooms and great *Yamato* began to lean to port. Rear Admiral Kosaku Ariga, *Yamato's* captain, ordered counterflooding in the starboard boiler and engine rooms. Ensign Mitsuru Yoshida attempted to warn the men there. Too late. They were sacrificed.

Still *Yamato* listed, and she had but one screw working. Her decks were a shambles of cracked and twisted steel plates. Her big guns would not work. The watertight wireless room was filled with water, and an explosion had wrecked the emergency dispensary and killed everyone inside.

At two o'clock the final attack began.

Hellcats and Avengers plunged from the skies to strike at the hapless ship. *Yamato* was shaken fore and aft and the entire battleship shuddered violently. Communications with the bridge were cut off, the distress flag was hoisted, the steering room became flooded, and with the rudder jammed hard left, mighty *Yamato* sagged over to a list of 35 degrees.

"Correction of list hopeless!" the executive officer cried.

Down came the Americans for the death blow.

"Hold on, men!" Ariga shouted. "Hold on, men!"

Bombs were striking around and upon *Yamato*, raising a giant clanging, flinging waves of roaring air across her decks, jumbling men together in heaps. Out of one pile crawled highranking staff officers. Admiral Ito struggled to his feet. His chief of staff arose and saluted him. The two men regarded each other solemnly. Ito turned, shook hands with each of his staff officers, wheeled and strode into his cabin, either to embrace death or await it—the world will never know which. Admiral Ariga rushed to save the Emperor's portrait, but met death instead.

Yamato was dying slowly, like the giant she was. Her decks were nearly vertical, her battle flag all but touched the waves, explosions racked her monster body, her own ammunition began blowing up—and all around her were her sister ships in death agonies. *Yahagi* was sinking, *Isokaze, Hamakaze, Asashimo* and *Kasumo* had received their death blows.

At twenty-three minutes after two *Yamato* slid under, a full day's steaming from Okinawa.

Japan had lost her navy, the suicide battleship had failed, and it was now up to the *kamikaze* and the men of Lieutenant General Mitsuru Ushijima.

13

In the north of Okinawa, Ushijima's men seemed to have melted away from the pelting up-island advance of the Sixth Marine Division—the "Striking Sixth" as the men of General Shepherd's freshly blooded outfit were calling themselves.

The Sixth swept up both coasts, a regiment to either side, making giant strides daily. Tanks loaded with grinning riflemen rolled up the dusty roads unimpeded but for an occasional sniper, a clumsy roadblock which bulldozers or the tanks themselves could knock aside, or here and there an obviously freshly planted land mine.

On April 8 the tanks came to the mouth of the Motobu Peninsula, a wild headland jutting to the west or left flank of the Marines. Here the Marines discovered why it was they had come so swiftly up the island.

On Motobu were gathered almost all of the 2,000 remaining soldiers of Colonel Udo's northern defense force. They were holed up on 1,200-foot Mount Yaetake, among the usually well-chosen and well-fortified labyrinth of cave-eaten ridges, cliffs, gorges, steep hills and rocky corridors—well supplied with guns, prepared to fight to the end.

The Marines moved in. They pushed cautiously around the coastal roads, their engineers swiftly building bridges over the ruins of those demolished by the Japanese or trucking in loads of rock and dirt to fill tank-traps blasted at the foot of cliffs or out in the rice paddies. By April 13 they had driven the Japanese back onto the crest of the Yaetake stronghold. They were prepared to attack in a pincers, three battalions to begin a fighting climb from Motobu's west coast, two to strike from the east.

That was a Friday the thirteenth on Okinawa. With first light, these Marines of the Sixth Division were startled, then grief-stricken to hear the bullhorns of the ships offshore blaring:

"Attention! Attention! All hands! President Roosevelt is dead. Repeat, our supreme commander, President Roosevelt, is dead."

Swiftly the news reached men out of earshot. They were stunned. Many of them cried, most of them prayed. Many of these youths had known no president other than Franklin Delano Roosevelt. They had truly loved him, had depended on him—how much they did not know until they heard that he was dead. Nor could they turn for solace to company officers, barely a few years their seniors. They could only ask: "What do we do now?"

Memorial services might be possible on ships even now flying the flag at half-mast, but the Marines on Motobu could do nothing but move out.

The Yaetake attacks became a week-long nightmare against a phantom enemy. Everywhere in the hills were small groups of Japanese clustering around a Hotchkiss heavy machine gun and the usual proliferation of Nambu lights. Marines might grenade these nasty spitting nests, might call down exact mortar fire, but then, in the succeeding rush, might find nothing but a trail of blood to suggest that anyone had struck at them.

"Jeez!" a Marine swore. "They've all got Nambus, but where the hell are they?"

On April 15 naval gunfire and close-up air strikes grew stronger. More artillery was brought in. Artillery observers went forward, among them a battery commander and his spotter, Pfc. Harold Gonsalves. The commander lived because Gonsalves hurled himself on a Japanese grenade to save him—

and win the Medal of Honor. More and more guns lashed at Yaetake.

Next day the Marines drove deeper into the Japanese complex. Corporal Richard Bush led a squad forward on the right flank of the three-battalion line striking at Yaetake's eastern mass. The face of the opposing ridge erupted with gunfire. Bush's squad went up and over it to drive the Japanese out, to score the first breakthrough. But Bush was badly wounded. He was pulled back to a cluster of protecting rocks where other men lay. A grenade sailed in. Bush pulled it to him. He saved the other wounded and he also lived, to join that amazing company of Marines whose Medals of Honor testified to the toughness of their bodies. Through the hole his squad had cut, through other holes along the line, the fight marched upward—swirling up in the mountains where it became as much a matter of supply as killing the enemy.

Marines toiled up hills with five-gallon cans of water on their backs and bandoleers of rifle-clips or grenades slung crisscross about their bodies. Battalion commanders going up to inspect the lines brought a water-can or a mortar shell along with them.

It was four days before the Marines burst into Colonel Udo's headquarters to discover this mimeographed sheet intended for their eyes:

NEWS OF NEWS

No. 1

Saturday, April 14

PRESIDENT ROOSEVELT DIED A SUDDEN DEATH

To the men of the Sixth Marine Division!

We take it a great honor to speak to you for the first time. We are awfully sorry to learn from the U.P. telegraph that the life of President Roosevelt has suddenly come to its end at 3:30 P.M. on April 12. It seems to be an incredible story in spite of its actual evidence.

Men of the 6th Marine Division, particularly men of the 15th and 29th Marines and the 3rd Amphibious Corps, we express our hearty regret with you all over the death of the late President. What do you think was the true cause of the late Presi-

dent's death? A miserable defeat experienced by the U.S. forces in the sea around the island of Okinawa! Were this not the direct cause leading him to death, we could be quite relieved.

We do not think that the majority of you have exact knowledge of the present operations being carried out by the U.S. forces although a very few member of you must have got a glympse of the accurate situation.

An exceedingly great number of picked aircrafts carriers, battleships, cruisers and destroyers held on her course to and near the sea of Okinawa in order to protect you and carry out operations in concert with you. The 90% of them have already been sunk and destroyed by Japanese Special Fighting Bodies, sea and air. In this way a grand "U.S. Sea Bottom Fleet" numbering 500 has been brought into existence around this little island.

Once you have seen a "Lizard" twitching about with its tail cut off, we suppose this state of lizard is likened to you. Even a drop of blood can be never expected from its own heart. As a result an apopletic stroke comes to attack.

It is a sort of vice however to presure upon others unhappiness. This is why we want to write nothing further.

It is time now for you, sagacieus and pradent, however, to look over the whole situations of the present war and try to catch a chance for reflection!!

The Marines went on to conquer the rest of Motobu, securing the peninsula on April 20. Above them, the Sixth Division's Twenty-second Regiment had reached Okinawa's northernmost point. The biggest battle in the northern sector was over.

The Sixth spent the rest of April patrolling and pursuing those Japanese who had fled Yaetake and turned irregular, using wardogs to scent the enemy and bark a warning. They even found that natural enemy of whom they had had such ample, ominous warning.

"Lookit the snake I just killed. It's one of them habu!"

"Hoo-what?"

"Habu, the snake they was all talkin' about before we landed."

"What're yuh gonna do with it?"

"Do with it! With the slop they been feeding us on this

492

screwy island? I'm gonna cut it into fillets and then I'm gonna fry it and eat it!"

Marines of the First Division were not quite so desperate. They were, in fact, still celebrating the Honeymoon, extending it for the duration of the month of April.

Many of the division's battalions built bivouacs complete with gravel paths, showers and mess halls. The men went to abandoned Okinawan homes to remove the sliding panels which separated the rooms. They used them for foxhole covers or to build shanties. Everybody had a pet—a pony, a goat, even one of those numerous Okinawan rabbits which might have escaped the pot. There was an open-air theater at Division Headquarters and there all the clerks and typists gathered nightly to play leapfrog until it was dark enough for a movie. This was not battle as the First had known it. But the men said, "Peace—it's wonderful!" They were so enchanted by Lilac Time that they brewed jungle juice out of their rations, drank it from "borrowed" lacquer ware—one of Okinawa's few crafts—and began to harmonize.

They sang all the old favorites such as "The Wabash Cannonball" or "Birmingham Jail," as well as that vast repertoire of bawdies and unprintables collected or composed by local bards during three years of tramping the Pacific. There was a new printable one for Okinawa, and it went:

> Oh, don't you worry, Mother, your son is
>   safe out here.
> No Japs on Okinawa, no saki, booze or beer.
> Your sons can't find no Nips, so we're going
>   back on ships.
> But don't you worry, Mother, cause we're going
>   on another.

But they were not. The honeymoon was ending. They were staying on Okinawa and going south, down to that Naha-Shuri-Yonabaru line which had stopped the Army's Twenty-fourth Corps.

493

14

The honeymoon had been brief for the Twenty-fourth Corps —hardly more than a weekend.

The day after Love-Day, while the Second Marine Division made another feint off southern Okinawa, the Twenty-fourth's soldiers raced across the island. Next day they turned south, 7th Division on the left flank, 96th on the right. Their advance seemed to be as effortless as the Marine thrust in the north.

But on April 4 they found resistance "stiffening."

It grew stiffer daily until, on April 8, "greatly increased resistance" was reported. They had come into the outerworks of Ushijima's barrier line. Three days later they were stopped cold beneath one of the Pacific War's most furious and skillful artillery barrages. A regiment of the 27th Division—now ashore while the Second Marine Division was sailing back to Saipan—was ordered in with the 96th Division on the right.

On April 12 the Japanese launched a land-air counterattack. Another massed *kamikaze* raid struck at American shipping that day, and in the night the 32nd Army attacked all along the line. The Japanese were repulsed, but they came again the following night. They were stopped again, with losses totaling 1,594 men.

It seemed that the time for the American breakthrough had arrived. Major General Hodge planned a powerful thrust with three divisions abreast. It was scheduled for April 19.

In the interval, the 77th Division, assisted by Major Jones's Recon Battalion, moved to seize Ie Shima just off the western tip of Mobotu Peninsula. Ie was a good-sized island and had an airfield. The 77th landed on April 16 and fought a savage four-day battle, killing 4,706 Japanese while losing 258 soldiers

494

killed or missing and 879 wounded. Among the 77th's dead was the most famous and beloved civilian who ever marched with the dogfaces: the correspondent Ernie Pyle.

Pyle was killed going up front again. Back at Ulithi, as he shoved off to join the First Marine Division, with whom he landed at Hagushi, another newsman called out jokingly, "Keep your head down, Ernie," and Pyle had snorted, "Listen, you bastards—I'll take a drink over every one of your graves." But Pyle's grave was dug on Ie Shima and over it his new comrades in the Pacific placed the inscription: "On this spot the 77th Infantry Division lost a buddy, Ernie Pyle, 18 April 1945."

It was the following day that General Hodge's grand assault began. With the 7th Division on the left, 96th in the center, 27th on the right; with six battleships, six cruisers and nine destroyers firing on call; with 650 Marine and Navy planes flying close-up support or scourging enemy supply and assembly areas; with 27 battalions of artillery massed and hurling everything from 75-millimeter to eight-inch shells all along that five-mile front—the Twenty-fourth Corps attacked.

And it began to measure gains by the yard.

The Army infantry had come to its own Peleliu or Iwo Jima. It had come to defenses against which enormous massed fires, from sea, land or air, were often hardly more useful than a smokescreen. Bombardments might get them close to such positions, but only ardor could overrun them. Only the impetuous foot-soldier slashing in with his hand weapons and using tanks, explosives and aimed flame can succeed in a war against armed and resolute moles. The naval shell's flat trajectory, the bomb's broad parabola, the artillery projectile's arc, even the loop of the mortar, cannot chase such moles down a tunnel. If they can occasionally collapse the tunnel and the whole position with a direct hit—a rare feat—they have knocked out only one spoke of the wheel. But the wheel still turns, and in the absence of that military miracle—direct hits *on call*—the man on foot has to go in. With his tanks, if he can.

In southern Okinawa on that April 19 the soldiers of the Twenty-fourth Corps found it tough to take the tanks along. Up-and-down terrain and Ushijima's careful preparations had made it so. Not long after the 27th Division moved out on the right, a company of tanks ran into a trap at Kakazu Ridge. Mortar spreads and the fire of machine-gun infiltrators cut them off as they sought to pull out of a pass. Without covering infantry, they were defenseless against antitank guns and hurled satchel-charges. Only eight of 30 tanks came out of the Kakazu action. In one day, the 27th had lost almost a third of its armor.

It was not so disastrous in the center and on the left, but the attack was nevertheless slow. During twelve days of see-sawing battle toward the Naha-Shuri-Yonabaru line, the front did not advance two miles. In spots it failed to make a mile. The situation called for fresh, veteran troops, and on April 27 Lieutenant General Buckner ordered the First Marine Division to stand by. The next day he put the entire Third Corps of Marines on alert. The First Division would enter the line on the west on May 1, relieving the 27th. The 27th would move north as garrison troops, relieving the Sixth Marine Division, which would also come south. In the meantime, the 77th Division would relieve the battered 96th. By May 7 the line would be divided between two full corps, Twenty-fourth on the left or east, Third on the right. In that order the divisions would be: 7th Infantry, 77th Infantry; First Marine, Sixth Marine.

On April 30 the men of the First Marine Division stopped harmonizing. They knocked down their shanties and trucked to the south. On May 1 they entered the line. They began patrolling, realigning, marking time until the Sixth came down to take up the slack on their right.

Two miles southeast of them, in a dimly lighted tunnel underneath Shuri Castle, the fiery Isamu Cho was preparing their annihilation.

The top commanders of the 32nd Army had come to the tunnel at the summons of Lieutenant General Mitsuru Ushijima. They sat on canvas chairs at a rough flat table covered with maps. Around them the stones of the tunnel glistened with sweat. Water from the moat surrounding medieval Shuri Castle seeped through crevices and dripped on the earthen floor. Sometimes the dim light glinted off the glasses worn by all these men or danced on the collar stars of the numerous generals present.

Isamu Cho, now wearing the double stars of a Japanese lieutenant general, sat near Lieutenant General Ushijima. Cho stared arrogantly into the questioning gaze of Colonel Hiromichi Yahara, the 32nd's senior staff officer and operations chief. Yahara, outspoken, persuaded by neither the rank nor the rhetoric of Isamu Cho, had raised the single voice of protest against the abortive counterattack of April 12-13. He was alone again in opposing the present plan for a massive counterstroke put forward by Cho and his friend, Lieutenant General Takeo Fujioka, commander of the 62nd Division. Even Lieutenant General Tatsumi Amamiya, no admirer of the boastful Fujioka, supported the plan—for it would put his untested 24th Division into battle at last. Major General Kosuke Wada, who led the 5th Artillery Command, was for it, too. He agreed with the others that the 32nd Army had made an achievement unprecedented in Pacific warfare: it had preserved its main body intact after a month of fighting the Americans. Yahara had said bluntly that this was only because there had been no costly counterattacks, and also because the Americans had not yet hurled their full strength against the Naha-Shuri-Yonabaru line.

The argument had raged for days, with much bitterness and acrimony between commanders of the 62nd and 24th Divisions. Concurrently with dissent among the top command had come discontent among the troops. The Emperor's birthday had passed without the promised issue of sweet-potato brandy. The American attack, though slow, was inexorable. For thirty days these men had arisen every morning to look from the heights of their bastion upon bays and anchorages choked with American ships. The Divine Winds had not blown them away. It was difficult even for Japanese soldiers to believe that the American fleet held the bottom half of the ocean—nor could they fail to complain about being left to fight alone only one day's sail from the homeland.

The situation was difficult, and now, on the night of May 2, Mitsuru Ushijima, a general cast in much the same formal mold as his opponent, Simon Bolivar Buckner, had called for final presentations. Then he would say, "I decide."

497

Isamu Cho arose. It was true, he said, that the Americans had not thrown in all their strength. But they were doing so now. There was a new Marine division in the line, the First, the hated butchers of Guadalcanal. The moment to destroy this fresh power was opportune. Strike them now and annihilate them before the Americans can grind down to the main line. Careful, full-scale counterattack, not the foolish splendor of the *banzai*, would do it. There must be help from the *kamikaze*, then massed artillery fire with the troops attacking all along the line. The fresh 24th would be hurled at the center, would open a hole through which the 44th Brigade would pour in a thrust to the west coast. Then the 44th would wheel south and the First Marine Division would be isolated, then annihilated. Twenty-fourth Corps would be rolled up. There should also be counterlandings on both flanks. The 26th Shipping Engineer Regiment would embark from Naha in barges, small boats and native canoes to strike the rear of the Marine division. Later, the youths of the 26th, 28th and 29th Sea Raiding Squadrons would cross the reef and wade ashore to help the engineers. A similar counterlanding would strike the rear of the 7th Infantry Division on the east. It was a good plan, detailed, realistic. Even Colonel Yahara could agree that Cho's tactics were excellent. It was his strategy that was bad.

"To take the offensive with inferior forces against absolutely superior enemy forces is reckless and will only lead to certain defeat," Yahara said. "We must continue the current operation, calmly recognizing its final destiny—for annihilation is inevitable no matter what is done—and maintain to the bitter end the principle of a strategic holding action. If we should fail, the period of maintaining a strategic holding action, as well as the holding action for the decisive battle for the homeland, will be shortened. Moreover, our forces will inflict but small losses on the enemy, while on the other hand, scores of thousands of our troops will have been sacrificed in vain as victims of the offensive."

Yahara sat down.

It was now up to Ushijima.

He nodded to Cho.

The attack would begin at dawn on May 4. Before that, the

flank counterlandings would be launched. Before them the artillery would commence, and before everything would come the *kamikaze*.

The Japanese aerial assaults began at six o'clock on the night of May 3. Once again, the bombers sought to get at the rich pickings in the Hagushi Anchorage, but 36 of them were shot down and the rest forced to unload at high altitude, with little damage. Only the suicide-diving *kamikaze* broke through. They sank destroyer *Little* and an LSM, while damaging two mine-layers and an LCS. After midnight, 60 bombers struck Tenth Army rear areas, coming in scattering "window" or streamers of metal foil to cloud radar screens with blips of nonexistent aircraft. Terrible antiaircraft fire rose in criss-crossing streams of light, as though a million narrow-beamed searchlights were aimed into the night, and the bombers dropped their loads aimlessly—though some of them landed in a Marine evacuation hospital.

An hour later Marine amtanks guarding Machinato Airfield on the west coast fired at voices on the beach. American cruisers, destroyers and gunboats on "flycatcher" patrol shot at squat Japanese barges sliding darkly upcoast from Naha. The barges lost their way. Instead of landing far enough north to take the Marines in their rear, they veered inshore and blundered into the outposts of B Company, First Marines.

The Japanese sent up a screeching and gobbling of battle cries and the surprised Marines sprang to their guns. All up and down the sea wall the battle raged, with Marine amtracks waddling out to sea and coming in again to grind the Japs to pieces between two fires. Some 500 Japanese died in this futile west-flank landing.

The east-flank landings came to the same annihilating end. Navy patrol boats sighted the Japanese craft. They fired at them and turned night into day with star-shells. Soldiers of the 7th Division's Reconnaissance Troop joined the sailors to complete the destruction of 400 men.

At dawn, the main attack began.

It went straight to the doom which Colonel Yahara had predicted. Wave after wave of the 24th Division's men shuffled forward to death in that gray dawn, moving among their own artillery shells, taking this risk in hopes of getting in on the Americans. But the soldiers of the 7th and 77th Divisions held firm—while American warships, 16 battalions of division artillery and 12 battalions of heavier corps artillery plus 134 airplanes, smothered the enemy in a wrathful blanket of steel and explosive. Ships as big as the 14-inch-gunned *New York* and *Colorado*, as small as gunboats with 20-millimeter cannons, ranged up and down the east coast firing at the Japanese on call.

Across the island, the *kamikaze* dove again on ships in the Hagushi Anchorage, again falling on the luckless small vessels of the radar picket screen. With them were the *baka* or "foolish" bombs, those piloted, rocket-fired suicide missiles flown to the target area beneath the bellies of twin-engined bombers. When a *baka*'s pilot had sighted his victim, he was released from his mother plane with a swooshing of rockets. The *bakas* were well named. Clumsy, with low fuel capacity and piloted by ill-trained suiciders, they seldom hit anything. This May 4 one of the *bakas* hit the light mine-layer *Shea* and set it temporarily on fire. But the *kamikaze* sank two more destroyers, *Luce* and *Morrison,* as well as two LSM's, while damaging the carrier *Sangamon,* the cruiser *Birmingham,* another pair of destroyers, a minesweeper and an LCS. Again, they failed to get at the cargo and transport ships. And they lost 95 planes.

Ashore, Isamu Cho's massive counterthrust was being broken by that very material power for which Mitsuru Ushijima had shown such great respect. Much of the Japanese assault died a'borning. Sometimes the Japanese closed, but rarely. There were seesaw battles up and down some of the ridges held by the 77th, but they ended with the soldiers either in command of their previous position or holding new ground farther inside the Japanese territory. One battalion of the Japanese 24th Division got behind the 77th on the left, but it was annihilated by a reserve battalion of the 7th Division in a three-day fight. Otherwise the 24th Division never punched that hole through which the 44th Brigade was to race and isolate the First Marine Division.

And the First began attacking on the morning of May 4. Even

as the soldiers on their left bore the brunt of Cho's big sally, these Marines were battling toward the key bastion of Shuri to the southeast. They scored gains of up to 400 yards. Next day they attacked again, once more pushing the Japanese back —even though their advance was made more costly by the fact that they were up against rested battalions of the Japanese 62nd Division which had not joined the counterassault. By the night of May 5 the Marines had picked up another 300 yards, and by that night also Lieutenant General Isamu Cho's massive stroke had been completely shattered. Those two days of fighting had cost the Japanese 6,227 dead. The 7th and 77th Divisions had lost 714 men killed or wounded while holding the line, the First Marine Division had taken losses of 649 men in the more costly business of attack. Next day the First gained another 300 yards, and added a fourth Medal of Honor winner to its rolls since coming into the line on May 1. Corporal John Fardy had smothered a grenade with his life, as had Pfc. William Foster on May 1 and Sergeant Elbert Kinser on the fourth. Two days before that Corpsman Robert Bush had risked his life to give plasma to a wounded officer, driving off a Japanese rush with pistol and carbine, killing six of the enemy and refusing evacuation though badly wounded.

There would be more Medals of Honor won in the days to come. The First Division by that night had come against Ushijima's main line, as had the soldiers on their left. In front of the First was the western half of the Shuri bastion. To their right was Naha, and this would be assigned to the Sixth Marine Division next day. In the sector of both these Marine divisions were systems of interlocking fortified ridges such as those encountered on Iwo Jima. Nor would the way be made easy here by further counterattack.

A change had taken place at Shuri Castle. In tears, Lieutenant General Ushijima had promised Colonel Yahara that from now on he would listen to no one but him. The Ushijima-Cho relationship had ended in the recrimination of a red and useless defeat. Isamu Cho argued no longer. He became stoic.

From now on, said General Cho, only time stood between the 32nd Army and ultimate destruction.

501

15

Time, yes—time for 60,000 men of the 32nd Army to set a high
price on their ultimate destruction, for the *kamikaze* to strike
and stagger an American fleet as none had been shaken before,
for the Great Loo Choo to pour out some 15 inches of water
during seventeen days of storm and torrential rain, for the
Japanese to attempt airborne raids on the airfields, and for the
month of May to become a mad compound of mud, misery and
death.

Even as General Geiger's Third Corps took over the western
half of the Tenth Army's front, the rains came rushing down
with an intensity reminiscent of New Britain. By late afternoon
of May 7 they had begun to make that mud which was nowhere to be matched, which was to become a factor in the
down-island attack.

Okinawa mud was everywhere, in the ears, under the nails,
inside leggings or squeezed coarse and cold between the toes.
It got into a man's weapon, it was in his food and sometimes
he could feel it grinding like emery grains between his teeth.
Whatever was slotted, pierced, open or empty received this
mud. Wounds also. Men prayed not to get hit while rain
fell and made mud. It embarrassed the bulldozer and made
pick-and-shovel men of those haughty tank Marines. Some days
it denied the Americans the use of roads altogether, and Marines
attacking Shuri only a few miles from base had to be supplied
by air-drop. Some days it was hardly possible to walk in it.
Two strides and a man's shoes were coated, two more and
they seemed as though encased in lead, another two and it
was easier to slip out of the shoes and walk barefooted. Engi-

502

neers around the airfield threw their shoes away, working with sacking drawn over bare feet and tied around the knees.

It was this mud which bogged down the entire Tenth Army on the eighth of May, the day on which smeared and dripping soldiers and Marines received the splendid news that Germany had surrendered.

"So what?" they snorted.

The death of Hitler and the fall of the Third Reich had as much meaning to them as the pardon of one condemned man might have to another still under sentence. General Ushijima and the Japanese 32nd Army were their only concern, and at that very moment Ushijima was taking advantage of the rain to strengthen his flanks while his men were reminding the Americans of reality by striking them with deliberate artillery shots fired from carefully husbanded guns and shells. Ushijima reinforced his strong-points over a 40-foot-wide concrete highway running east-west behind his barrier line. He settled down to that grim war of attrition urged on him by Colonel Yahara, and because of this, as well as the rain, the attack to the south moved slowly on the following day, May 9.

As it did, the *kamikaze's* scourging of the invasion fleet rose to almost that pitch of destruction predicted for it by the Japanese High Command. Nowhere was the ordeal more terrible and sustained than among those small ships of the radar picket line.

Here, perhaps mistaking destroyers for battleships and minesweepers for cruisers, the *kamikaze* and the *baka* struck in massed hundreds. Men were horribly burned. They were blown into the ocean, either to drown or pass agonizing hours awaiting rescue and the ministrations of a corpsman. Those who survived the suiciders' screaming dives went for days on end without sleep, their nerves exposed and quivering like wires stripped of insulation. Men in the boiler rooms worked in fierce heat. The superheaters built to give quick pressure needed for sudden high-speed maneuvering under aerial attack were often kept running three or four days at a time, though they had been made for intermittent use. It had to be that way, for the war off Okinawa was war at a moment's notice. Very little time separated that moment when radar screens clouded with pips and the next when the *kamikaze* came plunging through the ack-ack.

Following them down were those Marine Corsair pilots who had come to Okinawa to fly close-up support but had been called to the rescue of the radar picket line instead. Even with ammunition expended, they rode the suiciders down, forcing them away from their targets and into the water—even going after them with their propellers, as Lieutenant Robert Klingman did in the battle of the frozen machine guns.

That was the dogfight fought at over 40,000 feet among a Japanese two-seater Nick fighter and two Corsairs piloted by Klingman and Captain Kenneth Reusser. On combat air patrol over Ie Shima on May 10 they spotted the vapor trail of the Japanese at 25,000 feet. They chased him, climbing steadily from 10,000 altitude until, after a pursuit of 185 miles, firing off most of their ammunition to lighten their load, they caught up with the Nick at 38,000 feet.

They closed.

Reusser shot up all his ammunition in damaging the Japanese's left wing and left engine. Klingman bored in to within 50 feet and pressed his gun button. His guns were frozen. He drove in, his propellers whirling. They chopped up the rudder and left it dangling. In the Nick's rear cockpit the gunner was banging his fists on his own frozen guns. The Corsair's big propellers chewed on. Klingman turned and came back for another pass. He cut off the rudder and loosened the right stabilizer. He was running out of gas. He decided he didn't have enough to make Okinawa anyway, and turned for a third pass. He cut off the Nick's stabilizer. The plane went into a spin and at 15,000 feet it lost both wings and plunged into the East China Sea.

Klingman started down, losing his oxygen at 18,000 feet, and his power at 10,000. But he landed at Kadena Field, dead-stick and on his belly, his wings and fuselage sewn with bullet holes and pieces of the destroyed Nick in his cowling.

Next day Klingman's fellow pilots were whirling among 150 Japanese planes that struck the radar picket lines, coming to

504

the aid of little destroyers *Evans* and *Hugh W. Hadley* in one of the classic ship-airplane battles of World War Two.

For an hour and a half without letup *Evans* and *Hadley* fought off 50 *kamikaze*. *Hadley* alone shot down 23 of them while *Evans* claimed 15. The Marines from Yontan and Kadena knocked another 19 out of the skies. Commander Baron Mullaney of *Hadley* called for Marines to help him. Back came the squadron leader's answer: "I'm out of ammunition but I'm sticking with you." He did, flying straight into a flurry of 10 *kamikaze* coming at *Hadley* fore and aft, trying to head them off—while other Marines of his squadron rode down through the ack-ack with stuttering guns. They were not always successful, for both of these tough little ships took four *kamikaze* hits apiece. But they survived to be towed to that anchorage in Kerama Retto which had become a vast hospital ward for stricken and maimed American ships, and there Commander Mullaney could write this tribute to the Yontan and Kadena fliers: "I am willing to take my ship to the shores of Japan if I could have these Marines with me."

But the commander's ship would be a long time repairing, as would dozens of others which had limped or been towed to Kerama Retto. It had been because of this terrible loss among picket ships, as well as mounting casualties among the big vessels of the fleet, that Admiral Turner had asked General Buckner to speed up his drive to the south. Buckner had agreed. He had set May 11, the very day of *Hadley's* ordeal, as the date for the Tenth Army to attack all along the line.

On that day the attack rolled forward in massive frontal assault. In its numbers and in the fact that it was being fought on foot, it was similar to those great offensives in France during World War One. But in its terrain and in the quick splintering off of its actions it was as unlike France as battle could be. It was mountain warfare on the broad scale. Each of these four divisions in line were fighting for a specific height: the refreshed 96th Infantry, which had relieved the 7th Infantry on the left, struck out for Conical Hill; the 77th Infantry fought for Shuri Castle; the First Marine bucked at Shuri Heights; and the Sixth Marine marched on the Sugar Loaf.

★

Like the terrible Meatgrinder of Iwo Jima, the Sugar Loaf of Okinawa was not one hill but a complex of three. Coming down from the north the men of the Sixth Marine Division saw Sugar Loaf as an oblong of about 50 feet in height, protected to its left rear by the Half-Moon and to its right rear by the Horseshoe, a long ridge stuffed with mortars. Commanding their approach from the left was Shuri Heights, also stuffed with gunners and many of them able to hit Sugar Loaf.

To attempt to get at Sugar Loaf was to be hit by the others. To strike at the others was to be hit by Sugar Loaf. But this was not suspected until the main position was reached on the morning of May 14, after a fighting crossing of the Asa River and steady grinding down of smaller hills guarding the approaches.

On that May 14 most of the morning was spent evacuating Marines stricken while crossing the flat open ground approaching that harmless-looking loaf of earth. In the afternoon a charge with supporting tanks was driven back when three of four tanks were knocked out and artillery from Sugar's front, left-rear and rear fell among the riflemen. A second assault before dusk reached Sugar Loaf's base. But of 150 Marines from the Second Battalion, Twenty-second, who began it— only 40 reached the hill. They were exhausted. They were out of supplies. It was getting dusk. Suddenly, the enemy stopped firing. The men realized that someone was speaking to them. It was Major Henry Courtney, the battalion's executive officer.

"If we don't take the top of this hill tonight," he was saying, "the Japs will be down here to drive us away in the morning. The only way we can take it is to make a *banzai* charge of our own. I'm asking for volunteers."

There was hardly a pause before the Glory Kid stepped forward, grinning.

"I hate to sound like a guy in a dime novel," said Corporal Rusty Golar, "but what the hell did we come here for?"

There were 19 other volunteers from this exhausted remnant and there were 26 fresh men who appeared carrying supplies. Major Courtney took these 45 Marines up Sugar Loaf under cover of darkness, heaving grenades as they went, digging in under the protection of their own mortars. From the Horseshoe and Half-Moon came machine-gun fire and mortar shells, while grenades came up at them from the reverse slope of Sugar Loaf. At midnight, Courtney heard the enemy gathering below. He decided to strike them.

"Take all the grenades you can carry," he whispered. "When we get over the top, throw them and start digging in."

They went out, behind Courtney. They heard the major shout, "Keep coming, there's a mess of them down there!" and then they heard the explosion of the mortar shell that killed him. They answered with grenades of their own, hanging on to Sugar Loaf while all of the Japanese positions struck at them, while a cold rain swept in from the East China Sea, until the mists of the morning showed that there were only 20 men left of the 46 who had come up the night before.

In that mist Rusty Golar, the self-styled Storybook Marine, fought the battle he had always sought. He had set up his light machine gun on the right flank of Sugar Loaf. With daylight, the Japanese on Horseshoe Hill to his right opened up on him. Golar fired back. The Japanese on Half-Moon to the left opened up. With a deep, booming "Yeah!" Golar swiveled his gun to rake Half-Moon.

Back and forth it went, the whip-sawing Japanese fire, the booming "Yeah!" of the Glory Kid and his own alternating bursts. It went on while Sugar Loaf's defenders were gradually whittled to a handful and men trying to bring up ammunition were killed or wounded, until only Golar and a few others were left alive. By then the Glory Kid's machine-gun belts had all been fired. He drew his pistol, yelling, "Gotta use what I got left." He emptied it twice more. He threw it at the caves below and began scurrying about the hillcrest to gather grenades from the bodies of dead Marines.

"Still need some more stuff to throw at those guys," he yelled at Private Don Kelly, one of the few men still alive on the ridge. He threw. He found a loaded BAR in the hands of another fallen Marine, seized it, jumped erect and fired it until it jammed.

"Nothin' more to give 'em now," he bellowed to Kelly. "Let's get some of these wounded guys down." He bent down and easily picked up a stricken Marine. "I'll have you in sick bay in no time," he said. He walked toward the rear edge of Sugar Loaf. A Japanese rifle cracked. Rusty Golar staggered. He put the wounded man down carefully. Incredulity was written on his broad whitening features. He walked to a ditch. He sat down, pushed his helmet over his face and he died.

Soon the Japanese mortars were bursting on the crest of the Sugar Loaf, driving the Marines off. Japanese crawled from their caves at the foot of the reverse slope and began creeping to the crest again.

It was on the crest that they collided with a relief platoon of 60 men led by Lieutenant George Murphy. The Japanese met the Marines at bayonet-point and in a hand-grenade battle and were driven back. But to hold Sugar Loaf was to hold a lease on death. Little clouds of dust and mortar smoke eddied over it. Murphy contacted Captain Howard Mabie and asked for permission to withdraw. Mabie ordered him to hold, but Murphy could not. He had heard too many of his men scream. He covered them as they crawled down the hill. He picked up a wounded Marine and brought him down. A mortar struck him in the back. He let the Marine fall, turned to empty his pistol at the Japanese—and fell mortally wounded.

Captain Mabie brought his company forward to cover Murphy's survivors. He signaled battalion: "Request permission to withdraw. Irish George Murphy has been hit. Has 11 men left in platoon."

The reply came two minutes later: "You must hold."

Five more minutes, and Mabie had rejoined: "Platoon has withdrawn. Position was untenable. Could not evacuate wounded. Believe Japs now have ridge."

They did have it. They held onto it through that day and the next, clinging to Sugar Loaf while the entire complex quivered beneath the combined air-sea-land barrages which preceded the Marine assaults, hurling back each attack exactly as they had repulsed the first. But on May 17 an end run turned Sugar Loaf's left flank.

An almost imperceptible depression had been observed running north and south between Half-Moon Hill to the left and Sugar Loaf. It was not actually a valley, but Japanese fire on Marines who had wandered into it had not been heavy or accurate. General Shepherd, up on the lines now, decided to move an entire regiment—the Twenty-ninth—through this tiny chink in Sugar Loaf's armor. Two battalions would go through to strike at Half-Moon Hill, holding there to support another battalion moving against the left face of Sugar Loaf which their own assault was expected to unmask.

The battalions went forward under a fierce barrage. Half-Moon Hill was hit. Sugar Loaf was attacked. Three times a company of Marines charged to Sugar Loaf's crest. Each time they were driven off. They surged up a fourth time and won. But they had no more ammunition. None could be brought up to them. It was heartbreaking. They had to go down, giving up the vital height taken at a cost of 160 casualties.

Next day they went up to stay.

Four days of full-scale attack, the hammering of two Marine regiments and supporting arms, had worn the complex's defense thin. Sugar Loaf was ready to fall.

Captain Mabie brought his assaulting company up to the edge of the low ground opposite the hill. Artillery and mortars plastered the crest, while three tanks slipped around the left flank. The barrage stopped. The Japanese rushed from their caves below the reverse slope to occupy the crest. The tanks took them under fire, surprised them and riddled them.

Rocket trucks raced down from the north, bumping and swaying over a saddle of ground, stopped, loosed their flights of missiles, whirled and careened away with a whine of changing gears and a roar of wasted gasoline—just avoiding the inevitable Japanese artillery shells crashing in behind them. The rockets made Sugar Loaf's hillsides reel and reverberate as though a string of monster firecrackers had been set off. Artillery began again. The Marines sprinted over the field and up Sugar Loaf, one platoon taking the right face, peeling off its fire teams, another sweeping up on the left. They met on the crest, formed and swept down the reverse slope, killing as they went. Back came the message:

"Send up the PX supplies. Sugar Loaf is ours."

Next day the fresh Fourth Marines relieved the fought-out

Twenty-ninth. Marines such as Private Harry Kizirian, a man so big his buddies called him "The Beast," could rest and have their wounds cared for. Kizirian had three, all received at Sugar Loaf. The Sixth Division's total casualties for the battle were 2,662 killed and wounded, with another 1,289 knocked out by battle fatigue. But the fall of Sugar Loaf had set Ushijima's western flank to crumbling. During the next three days, the Fourth Marines drove deeper and deeper into the complex, while throwing back a counterattack in battalion strength. They turned to take Half-Moon Hill, to nail down their left flank preparatory to the drive down-island into Naha. Artillery struck them. It came plunging from the left. It was on Shuri Heights.

The Sixth Marine Division could not strike into the Naha flank of the Japanese line until the First Marine Division polished off Shuri Heights in the center.

The First Marine Division was "processing" its way south.

This was the cold, impersonal term coined by Major General del Valle to describe the cold, grim warfare his Marines were fighting en route to Shuri Heights.

Along that way lay Dakeshi Ridge, Dakeshi Town, Wana Ridge, Wana Draw—those bristling rough places which only the "processing" of tank–infantry–flame-thrower teams could make smooth. These four places were the sentinel forts guarding the northwest way into the heart of the Naha-Shuri-Yonabaru line at Shuri Castle. Moving down against them, its regiments leapfrogging one another all along the pitiless way, the First Marine Division was exposed to almost constant fire from its left flank and struck unceasingly from its front. The deeper the advance, the more numerous and formidable became the defenses-in-depth, the more difficult the terrain.

On May 11 the First began bucking at Dakeshi Ridge and Dakeshi Town. Both fell after a seesaw three-day battle, the Americans plodding forward by day, the Japanese counterattacking by night. Platoons took a position at the cost of three-fourths of their men, then tried to hang on with the survivors. Sometimes they could not. Daylight sometimes meant a fresh attack to recover ground surrendered during the night. In

Dakeshi Town the Marines found a labyrinth of tunnels, shafts and caves, with snipers everywhere among the ruins—crouching behind broken walls, hidden in wells or cisterns. But Dakeshi Town also fell and on May 14 the First Marine Division entered Wana Draw.

Wana Draw was a long, narrowing ravine running east to Shuri. It was formed by the reverse slope of Wana Ridge on its left and the forward slope of another ridge to the right. All its low, gently-rising ground was covered by gunfire, from its mouth 400 yards wide to the point at which, 800 yards east, it narrowed sharply between steep cliffs under the heights of Shuri.

Although neither Shuri nor Shuri Castle was in the zone of the First Marine Division, but rather in the 77th Division's, the plunging fire that fell from them was meant for the First Division's left flank. It was necessary for the First to face left, or east, and attack up Wana Draw—both to remove that thorn from its flesh and to knock out those powerful positions menacing the entire western half of the Tenth Army front. Any attack south past Shuri would be struck in both flank and rear.

On May 14, the day on which Major Courtney led the charge on Sugar Loaf which was to bring him the Medal of Honor, the First Marine Division began "processing" Wana Draw.

A few tanks slipped into the ravine. They probed for the caves. Antitank fire fell on them. Supporting riflemen took the Japanese gunners under fire. Suicide troops rushed the tanks hurling satchel-charges. Again the supporting riflemen protected the tanks. But sometimes the antitank guns knocked out the tanks, sometimes the Japanese infantrymen drove the Marine riflemen back, sometimes the satchel-chargers blew up a tank. But when the tanks did gain a foothold, then the more vulnerable flame-throwing tanks rumbled in. They sprayed the hillside with fire, particularly those reverse slopes which could not be reached by bombs or artillery.

Squads of foot Marines went in after them, men with bazookas, flame-throwers, hand grenades, blocks of dynamite —peeling off, team by team, taking cave after cave, crawling up to them under the protective fire of riflemen kneeling in the mud. More and more men went into Wana Draw. Day after day the Division bucked against this barrier, but soon there were whole companies working up the slopes, "processing" caves and pillboxes, calling down their mortars and rifle grenades on the machine guns and mortars sure to be nesting on the reverse slope. It was war at its most basic, man-to-man, a battle fought by corporals and privates. And these were the men who won the Medals of Honor while the First Division processed its way into Shuri: Private Dale Hansen, using a bazooka, a rifle and hand grenades to knock out a pillbox and a mortar position and kill a dozen Japanese before he lost his own life; Pfc. Albert Schwab, attacking machine guns alone with his flame-thrower, silencing them even as he perished; Corporal Louis Hauge, doing the same with grenades, and also dying. With these men were their indomitable comrades of the Navy Medical Corps, men such as Corpsman William Halyburton, who deliberately shielded wounded Marines with his own body until the life leaked out of it.

This was the fight for Wana Draw, that elemental bloodletting which took place while the very elements howled about these struggling men in muddy green floundering up the forward slopes, these men in smeared khaki sliding down the reverse slopes. At night, under cover of smokescreens, the men in khaki crept forward again to close with the men in green, to fight with bayonets and fists and strangling hands. But the men in khaki were losing the fight for Wana Draw. The Marines drew closer to Shuri. The soldiers of the 77th Division on their left were thrusting toward Shuri and Shuri Castle from the eastern gate. On the east flank the 7th Infantry Division was back in the line and smashing into Yonabaru; the Sixth Marine Division was again on the march to Naha on the west. All along the line division and corps artillery were battering Ushijima's strong points, the Tenth Army's Tactical Air Force roved over the battlefield at will—and the warships of the fleet were slugging away with the most formidable supporting fire yet laid down in the Pacific, for they had caught the hang of pasting those reverse slopes which land-air pounding could not reach.

Ushijima's barrier line was buckling.

On the night of May 22, while Marines of the Sixth Division

crossed the Asato River and the Division was poised to break into Naha, there was another conference under Shuri Castle. Lieutenant General Ushijima had decided to retreat. He could no longer hold his Yonabaru-Shuri-Naha line. He would have to withdraw south of the Yonabaru-Naha valley, abandoning even that fine cross-island road. Where to? Should it be the wild, roadless Chinen Peninsula on the east coast, or southernmost Kiyamu Peninsula? The wrangle began. In the end, the Kiyamu was chosen because of the strength of the Yaeju-Yuza Peaks and the honeycombs of natural and artificial caves which could accommodate the entire 32nd Army for its final stand.

Next day Ushijima began reinforcing his flanks again to hold off the Americans while his withdrawal began, but he was too late to prevent the turning of the west flank at Naha. The Sixth Division burst into the city's ruins and began its reduction.

Ushijima still counterattacked the 7th Division on the east flank at Yonabaru, trying to relieve the pressure there, but the 7th's valiant dogfaces held fast.

A nocturnal *kamikaze* raid hurled at Okinawa shipping to coincide with Ushijima's land strikes was shattered, with 150 planes shot down in exchange for the loss of the destroyer-transport *Bates* and one LSM, plus damage to eight other ships.

The most ferocious display of antiaircraft power yet seen in the Pacific broke up a daring airborne attack on Yontan and Kadena Airfields. It was an unusually clear night and there were thousands of witnesses to this small savage setback which the suicide spirit was able to inflict on the Americans.

Perhaps 20 twin-engined bombers came gliding through a fiery lacework woven by American antiaircraft gunners. Eleven of them fell in flames. The rest, except one, fled.

That solitary Sally bomber skidded on its belly along one of Yontan's runways. When it stopped, eight of 14 men of the Japanese 1st Air Raiding Brigade were dead in their seats, but six of them were alive, tumbling out the door, coming erect and sprinting for parked planes while hurling heat grenades and phosphorus bombs. They blew up eight airplanes, damaged 26 others, destroyed two fuel dumps housing 70,000

513

gallons of gasoline and killed two Marines and wounded 18 others before they were finally hunted down and killed.

In the morning the Tenth Army was still grinding down toward the heart of Ushijima's defense in Shuri Castle. Marines of the First Division in Wana Draw began to draw swiftly closer to the city and its heights to their east. They began to notice Japanese sealing off caves and quitting the draw. At noon of May 26 Major General del Valle asked for an aerial reconnaissance over the Yonabaru-Naha valley. He had a hunch the Japanese were pulling back from Shuri, trying to sneak out under cover of a heavy rain.

A spotter plane from the battleship *New York* reported that the roads behind Shuri were packed. Between 3,000 and 4,000 Japanese were on the rear-march with all their guns, tanks and trucks. In thirteen minutes, despite rain and bad visibility, the warships of the fleet were on the target. Soon 50 Marine Corsairs were with them, rocketing and strafing, and every Marine artillery piece or mortar within range had its smoking muzzle pointed toward the valley. They killed from 500 to 800 Japanese and littered the muddy roadways with wrecked vehicles.

Three days later the Marines took Shuri Castle.

It was not supposed to be theirs to take; it was the objective of the 77th Division, the very plum of the Okinawa fighting, but the First Marine Division took it anyway.

General del Valle sent a battalion of the Fifth Marines climbing into Shuri on May 29. He wanted to get around and behind the Japanese still holding out in Wana Draw. The First Battalion quickly stormed Shuri Ridge to the east or left of the draw—so quickly that Lieutenant Colonel Charles Shelburne asked permission to go on to the castle 800 yards east. Del Valle granted it. The 77th Division was still two days' hard fighting from the castle, and the chance was too good to ignore. The light defenses around Shuri might be only a temporary lapse.

Company A of the Fifth Marines under Captain Julius Dusenbury began slogging east in knee-deep mud. Inside Captain Dusenbury's helmet was a flag, as had become almost customary among Marine commanders since Suribachi. While the Marines marched, del Valle was just barely averting the

77th's planned artillery and aerial strike on Shuri Castle—and then Dusenbury's Marines overran a party of Japanese soldiers and swept into the castle courtyard, into the battered ruins of what had once been a beautiful palace with curving, tiered roofs of tile. They ran up to its high parapet and over this Captain Dusenbury flew his flag.

Shuri Castle, the key bastion of the Okinawa defenses, was in American hands—and if the 77th Division was irritated, if the Tenth Army was displeased, the soldier who commanded the Americans on Okinawa could not be entirely annoyed. The flag which Captain Dusenbury of South Carolina flew was the flag of Simon Bolivar Buckner's father. The Stars and Bars, not the Stars and Stripes, waved over Okinawa.

Two days later Old Glory was in its rightful place. General del Valle sent a party with the standard of the First Marine Division, the one that had flown over Guadalcanal, New Britain and Peleliu.

Now, above Shuri Castle not far from the spot where Commodore Perry had hoisted the American flag a century ago, the most victorious flag of the Pacific was caught and flung in the breeze.

The Japanese retreating to the south could see it. They fired on it, missing. They kept firing, for they understood that the terrible power it symbolized was already massing to come south and destroy them.

16

It was the month of June, the month of Ushijima's last stand.

Lieutenant General Buckner had redisposed his Tenth Army for the final heave of the war. On the west or right flank the Marines' sector had been narrowed. The Sixth Marine Division was going to make a shore-to-shore amphibious assault on the Oroku Peninsula in the southwest, and the First Marine Division had not the strength to cover the entire Third Corps front.

The Third Corps, in fact, was depleted. With the Second Marine Division sent back to Saipan—rather than kept afloat as a *kamikaze* target—Major General Geiger had not been able to rest either the First or the Sixth. He had no reserve, and the divisions themselves had tried to maintain battle efficiency by resting one regiment while the other two attacked. But it could not always be done. So the Third Corps needed troops, and soon the Eighth Regiment of the Second Marine Division would be brought into Okinawa to furnish them. But not until after the Eighth had finished capturing islands to the west of Okinawa to give Admiral Turner long-range radar and fighter-director stations.

The Twenty-fourth Corps was in better shape. Major General Hodge had three divisions—exclusive of the 27th on garrison in the north—and had been able to rest one while the other two were attacking. Only infrequently, as in the final days before Shuri, were all three in the line. But from June 4 onward the Twenty-fourth Corps was grinding down on the Yaeju-Yuza Peaks where most of the 32nd Army's remnants had holed up. Even General Ushijima was here, conducting the last stand from his headquarters cave just above the ocean.

The Yaeju-Yuza's caves were crammed with men, and also with misery. There were many sick and dying. Some caves had become reeking pest-holes. As many as 40 men lay in some of these hillside holes. At times a doctor or a corpsman came around to ask how they felt. They could do little more. They had no supplies. Men died from wounds not considered serious. Filth accumulated. The rain drummed outside, water streamed into the caves and the wounded nearly drowned. The smell was so overpowering that men could hardly breathe.

Still Ushijima was determined to fight on with so many of his men in such affliction. He shared the fanaticism of those Army die-hards who were even then, in that month of June, attempting to wreck the peace party which the new premier,

516

Baron Kantaro Suzuki, was forming with the secret encouragement of Emperor Hirohito. Tokyo had been savaged twice more, on May 23 and 25, and the Emperor was now genuinely dismayed by the slaughter among his people.

But General Ushijima and General Cho, resuming their old relationship, were capable of no such dismay. The fight was to be to the finish, and on June 4 the Tenth Army shuddered and drove forward.

On that date the Sixth Marine Division's spearheads shoved off from Naha to make the last Marine amphibious assault of World War Two. Again the amtracks, the wallowing sea waves, the naval gunfire thundering overhead, the shores of the objective winking and spouting smoke—and in they went to conquer three-by-two Oroku Peninsula in a whirling ten-day battle. Again beaches, coral pinnacles, caves, hills, tunnel systems, 5,000 last-ditch Japanese to be killed, an admiral to be driven to suicide, and again death and wounds for Marines— 1,608 of them. Oroku was the Pacific War in microcosm—even in its Medals of Honor: Private Robert McTureous attacking machine guns firing on stretcher-bearers and losing his life to save his buddies; Corpsman Fred Lester continuing to treat wounded Marines while dying of his own wounds. But Oroku fell; it ended with Admiral Ota committing *hara-kiri* and it ended in a rout. On June 13 the Japanese threw down their arms and fled toward the mainland in the southeast. They could not escape. The First Marine Division had driven past the base of the peninsula and sealed it off. The Japanese began surrendering.

Beneath Oroku, the First Marine Division had broken through to the south coast. Okinawa had been sliced down the middle, but more important to those weary, hungry Marines who did it was the sea outlet to which amtracks could now bring supplies. The men had been a week on reduced rations, slogging through the mud which made supply nearly impossible.

On the eastern flank the 7th and 96th Infantry Divisions were also nearing the southern coast. Lieutenant General Buckner had already made a surrender appeal to Ushijima. He had had a letter dropped behind the lines. It said:

The forces under your command have fought bravely and well, and your infantry tactics have merited the respect of your opponents. . . . Like myself, you are an infantry general long schooled and practiced in infantry warfare. . . . I believe, therefore, that you understand as clearly as I, that the destruction of all Japanese resistance on the island is merely a matter of days. . . .

The letter was dropped on June 10. It reached Ushijima and Cho on June 17. They thought it hilarious. How could a *samurai* surrender? A *samurai* can only kill himself.

Ushijima and Cho had already resigned themselves to *harakiri* by that seventeenth of June, for by then all was over. On the west flank the First Marine Division was battling through Kunishi Ridge while the Sixth had again come into line on the right and was racing for Ara Point, the southernmost tip of Okinawa. In the east, the 96th Division was finishing off resistance in the Yaeju-Yuza Peaks, and the 7th Division's soldiers were closing in on the 32nd Army's very headquarters.

There was nothing left, save the satisfying news next day that the American who had insulted them with a surrender offer was himself dead.

Simon Bolivar Buckner had come down to Mezado Ridge to see the fresh Eighth Marine Regiment enter battle. The Eighth had come to Okinawa on June 15, after seizing Admiral Turner's radar outposts, and was attached to the First Division. As had happened in the beginning at Guadalcanal, when another regiment of the Second Division was attached to the First, so it was happening in the end at Okinawa.

Colonel Clarence Wallace sent the Eighth Marines in at Kunishi Ridge. They were to attack in columns of battalions to seize a road, to split the enemy in two, to carry out General del Valle's plans for a decisive thrust to the sea. Lieutenant General Buckner joined Colonel Wallace on Mezado Ridge at noon. He watched the Marines for about an hour. They moved swiftly on their objective. Buckner said:

"Things are going so well here, I think I'll move on to another unit."

Five Japanese shells struck Mezado Ridge. They exploded

518

and filled the air with flying coral. A shard pierced General Buckner's chest and he died within ten minutes—knowing, at least, that his Tenth Army was winning.

Command went to Roy Geiger, senior officer and about to be promoted to lieutenant general. The grizzled white bear who had been at Guadalcanal in the beginning was leading at the end on Okinawa.

That came three days later.

On June 21 a patrol from the Sixth Marine Division reached a small mound atop a spiky coral cliff. It was the tip of Ara Point. Beneath them were the mingling waters of the Pacific Ocean and the East China Sea.

A few more days of skirmishing and a reverse mop-up drive to the north remained. When these were over, and the last of the *kamikaze* had been shot down, the Japanese 32nd Army was no more, with roughly 100,000 dead, and, surprisingly, another 10,000 surrendered. American casualties totaled 49,151, with Marine losses at 2,938 dead or missing and 13,708 wounded; the Army's at 4,675 and 18,099; and the Navy's at 4,907 and 4,824. There was little left of Japanese air power after losses of 7,800 planes, against 763 for the Americans; and the sinking of *Yamato* and 15 other ships meant the end of Nippon's Navy. Though the American Navy had been staggered with 36 ships sunk and another 368 damaged, there were still plenty left to mount the fall invasion of Kyushu from Okinawa.

So the Great Loo Choo fell to the Americans after eighty-three days of fighting. A few hours after the Marine patrol reached Ara Point, Major General Geiger declared organized resistance to be at an end.

That night Mitsuru Ushijima and Isamu Cho wrote final messages and prepared to kill themselves.

"Our strategy, tactics, and techniques all were used to the utmost," Ushijima signaled Tokyo. "We fought valiantly, but it was as nothing before the material strength of the enemy."

Cho wrote: "22nd day, 6th month, 20 year of Showa Era. I depart without regret, fear, shame, or obligations. Army Chief of Staff; Army Lieutenant General Cho, Isamu, age of departure 51 years. At this time and place I hereby certify the foregoing."

519

Precise to the end, Isamu Cho arose and vested himself in the white kimono proper for *hara-kiri*. He joined General Ushijima, who was dressed in full uniform. They sat down to the last banquet, while the roof of their cave shook to the muffled sounds of American grenades exploding above. Behind them, at the mouth of the cave, they could see moonlight shimmering on the sea. They finished eating and drank off toasts of Scotch whisky. They arose.

"Well, Commanding General Ushijima, as the way may be dark, I, Cho, will lead the way."

"Please do so. I will take along my fan, since it is getting warm."

They strolled out to the ledge above the sea, General Ushijima calmly fanning himself. They bowed in reverence to the eastern sky. They sat on a white sheet spread over a quilt.

A hundred feet behind them were the American soldiers. They began hurling grenades, unaware that Ushijima and Cho were so close to them.

First Ushijima, then Cho, bared their bellies to the upward thrust of the ceremonial knife, while the adjutant stood by with his saber, awaiting the sight of blood.

Two shouts, two sword flashes, and it was done—and the moon began sinking beneath a sea turning polished black.

17

And when he gets to Heaven,
To Saint Peter he will tell:
"One More Marine reporting, sir—
"I've served my time in Hell!"

It was everywhere behind them, this glorious rough epitaph. It had been pinpricked out on a mess pan nailed to a rough cross among the rots and stinks of Guadalcanal. It had been carved into coconut logs forming that dreadful sea wall at Tarawa. Men had spelled it out with cartridges pressed into the damp black earth of the Bougainville rain forest, or scrawled it beneath Stars of David rising from leveled *kunai* fields in New Britain. Makin knew it, and the hyphenated coral islets of Roi-Namur in the vast atoll of Kwajalein. Eniwetok, Choiseul, New Georgia, and a dozen forgotten islands where only a handful fell. Marines who lived to sail away from Saipan and Tinian, or from Guam, had left this farewell there in memory of those who did not sail. It had fallen from heat-shrivelled lips on Peleliu, had followed the flag that rose at Iwo Jima, and been scratched on a punctured helmet perched on a bayonet stuck in Okinawa mud.

It was the salute of the brave living to the braver dead, it was a Marine's sad, sardonic "so long" to a fallen buddy. And yet it was also the epitaph of the mighty island empire that was once Japan's, for the men who earned or wrote these lines were also the men whose long sea charge had now brought that very "Hell" to within 350 miles of Japan herself.

And they were ready to resume the charge. Six Marine divisions were again in training, again preparing for battle, on the sixth of August, 1945, when a great silvery airplane named *Enola Gay* rose from that very Tinian Island which had been the masterpiece of Marine warfare. It flew to Hiroshima to drop its horrible mushrooming egg. Three days later The Bomb was dropped again—on Nagasaki.

Five more days and Japan surrendered.

Sixteen more days, the thirtieth of August, and transports were sliding through the dawn mists into Tokyo Bay. They carried men of the Second Battalion, Fourth Marine Regiment. The ships anchored off Futtsu Point, where massive stone forts flew white flags of surrender. For the last time came the order:

"Land the landing force."

For the last time came the roaring run inshore, the salt sea spray in the face, the firmer hold on rifle slings; for the last time the grinding of steel keels on beaches, the lurching halt, the banging fall of the ramp and the buckskin-shod feet pelting through surf and sand.

521

For the first time, Nippon had been invaded. The men in green were forming orderly ranks on Japanese soil and marching on the silent forts to receive the surrendered arms of Japanese soldiers.

The long charge was over and there would be no more epitaphs.

BIBLIOGRAPHICAL
NOTE

Because this book has been written in a narrative style which might have been defeated by the use of footnotes, I have chosen to explain what needs to be explained, as well as to list a selected bibliography, in this Note.

To begin, all the persons herein are real and their names are real. Middle initials have been dropped because I find letters more ambiguous than numerals and have used only those which have significance, such as the M which explains how Holland M. Smith came to be called Howlin' Mad or the P which gave Colonel Oliver P. Smith his nickname of "O.P." General Roy Geiger's middle initial S, however, has even less meaning than, say, the number 3—and it will be remembered that George Washington, Julius Caesar and Napoleon Bonaparte, to name a few generals, did not use middle initials.

The ranks mentioned here are those held at the time and all distances are given in statute miles, usually rounded off to the nearest zero or hundred to avoid an impression of exactness. Casualties—always very difficult to determine with accuracy —are normally those given in the excellent battle monographs published by the Marine Corps Historical Branch. When these books failed to list casualties for a particular action, I have fallen back on the equally fine histories prepared by the Army's Office of the Chief of Military History. Almost all the accounts of naval battles, together with ship and naval aircraft losses, are based on the nine volumes of Samuel Eliot Morison's *History of U.S. Naval Operations in World War II* which deal with the Pacific War.

Generally these three sources—the Marine monographs, the Army histories (written, incidentally, by civilian historians), and the Morison volumes—provide the bones of military history on which I have attempted to lay the flesh of men speaking and acting. All three have also been rich in quotations from captured Japanese diaries or battle orders, and I must say frankly that *Strong Men Armed* could not have been written if these works had not all been published by 1960. Before then, without a research staff of my own, I would have been bogged down in literal tons of classified documents at the various headquarters around Washington and Arlington.

Japanese sources were works such as *Kogun, the Japanese Army in the Pacific War,* by Saburo Hayashi with Alvin D. Coox, my authority for the statement that Japanese staff officers struck each other in the quarrel over Guadalcanal or that the Japanese originally expected to have to fight the British more than the Americans; the two volumes of *U.S. Strategic Bombing Survey, Interrogations of Japanese Officials,* a work abounding in background information concerning Japan during the war and also surprisingly productive of "human interest" material; or *The Divine Wind,* by Rikihei Inoguchi and Tadashi Nakajima, with Roger Pineau, which explains much of the philosophy of the *kamikaze.*

Fletcher Pratt's *The Marines' War* and *The Island War* by Frank O. Hough, both outline works on the Marines in the Pacific, helped chart a course for the author, while *The U.S. Marines and Amphibious War,* by Jeter A. Isely and Philip A. Crowl, was the source of much information on logistics or the technical aspects of the Pacific. For facts and figures on Marines in the air I have quarried Robert Sherrod's exhaustive *History of Marine Corps Aviation in World War II,* and have gone to John A. DeChant's *Devilbirds* for accounts of individual flying feats or for ballads such as those sung at the Hotel de Gink.

Other sources were division histories, memoirs, personal-

524

experience narratives, maps, pictures, citations, on-the-spot books of the civilian war correspondents, war anthologies, magazine articles—from news and general magazines as well as from professional periodicals such as *Marine Corps Gazette, Leatherneck, Infantry Journal* or *U.S. Naval Institute Proceedings*—verifiable newspaper clippings and Marine combat correspondents' reports, as well as my own experiences as a scout and machine-gunner with the First Marine Division in all that outfit's campaigns but Okinawa.

I have drawn on this last, and also on numerous interviews with famous Marines while gathering material for other books and articles, in telling such stories as that of the tongue-tied Marine who could not pronounce the password on Guadalcanal, or of Chesty Puller booting a reluctant rifleman into action. In the first incident, the author was the sentry who demanded the password, while the second comes from a conversation with Lieutenant General Puller one wintry afternoon in Saluda, Virginia.

Also, I have frequently quoted men in the midst of battle, to name a typical few: Colonel David Shoup on Tarawa, an unidentified sergeant under Peleliu's Bloody Nose Ridge, Captain William Shoemaker on Guam, Sergeant Phil Mottola on New Britain, or Red Mike Edson at Guadalcanal. These remarks came, respectively, from Robert Sherrod's *Tarawa*, Russell Davis' *Marine at War*, Alvin M. Josephy's *The Long and the Short and the Tall*, a story filed by Sergeant Hans R. Johansen, and *The Old Breed*, George McMillan's History of the First Marine Division. Mr. McMillan's book, incidentally, along with the late Major Hough's monograph, *The Assault on Peleliu*, insists that there were no snipers riding the Japanese tanks annihilated in the D-Day attack at Peleliu. I have said there were, because I saw them and shot at them, as did many of my comrades. Major Hough's authority was my own battalion commander, who was quite properly some distance behind the battle, whereas Mr. McMillan's is a tank colonel who went over the battlefield after the fight was over. Certainly there were no snipers on the tanks by then; they'd been shot off or pulled down from their slings of camouflage netting.

I cite this discrepancy between myself and two authors whom I respect only by way of indicating that I have usually preferred the account of a man who has been in the battle to that of another who has not, even if that other person happens to be the commander of the unit involved. It is the man who is on the spot who makes judgments that must be exact, if only because he risks his life on them. A Marine sees a bulky object on the back of a speeding tank and he must judge whether it is an enemy soldier or merely, say, a roll of camouflage cloth. If it's a soldier then the Marine runs the risk of being shot before he can attack the tank, and so he must shoot the soldier first. If it is only cloth, then the Marine can throw his grenade right away. Marines who make bad judgments at such times rarely survive to confuse writers.

On the other hand, I have been wary of those inflated "I-was-there" accounts which proliferated in the press during the war. Stories which suggest that the hair on the chest of the typical Marine grew to a ferocious twelve-inch length have had no part in this book, nor have I trusted those accounts which overestimate a single man's actions. Often the most gallant deeds turn out to be futile, or nearly so, if all results are to be measured in victory or defeat. But gallantry or valor—to this writer's mind—are beyond such yardsticks. Because of this, and because valor and gallantry have been so frequently belittled in the reaction of the postwar era, I have named every one of the Marine Medal of Honor winners and paid particular attention to those who consciously and deliberately sacrificed their lives to save others. The French writer Albert Camus says "heroism is not much, happiness is more difficult," and tells us in *The Fall* that modern man is incapable of forgetting himself for even a few seconds; the book and motion picture *They Came to Cordura* shows Medal of Honor winners as connivers of base motivations who are not nearly so noble as their major who hid in a ditch during battle; and Pappy Boyington, a Medal of Honor winner himself, concludes his *Baa Baa Black Sheep* with the remark: "Just name a hero and I'll prove he's a bum." These three, and many others, are answered by the dozens of Marines who fell on enemy grenades to save the lives of their buddies. This is heroism, which is something more than natural courage, though it is often confused with it.

While being wary of exaggeration, I have also suspected almost all that is fanciful or gives off the aroma peculiar to the post-battle campfire. One of my buddies (not a source for this book) used to say of such tales: "Certainly, I believe this story. I made it up myself!" These are what Marines call "sea stories." They are popular, though seldom believed, and they are unmistakable. One of these, I am sure, is the widely accepted story of the Battle of Coffin Corner on New Britain, where Sergeant Joe Guiliano counterattacked the enemy with a cradled machine gun. The story goes that Guiliano's men kept calling for him by name and that the Japanese, mistaking the name for an American battle cry, began shouting it themselves—thus bringing the formidable Guiliano into their midst. Unfortunately for the story's reputation, the name Guiliano has one of those L's which the Japanese pronounce as R, and there is no version speaking of the enemy calling for "Guiriano." Even if this difficulty did not exist, the story seems a bit too salty.

Official accounts of Marine operations have also been received with a cocked eyebrow, and such Marine errors as the first Matanikau operation, the useless Talasea landings or General Rupertus' reluctance to use Army troops at Peleliu have been described for what they were. However, I have also avoided taking sides in any controversy, and have presented the famous quarrel over Marine General Howlin' Mad Smith's dismissal of Army General Ralph Smith on Saipan only as an actual event. If even so little seems prejudicial to Ralph Smith's case, then I refer the reader to *The Campaign in the Marianas,* written by Philip A. Crowl, a former Navy officer, for the Army's Office of Military History. Chapter X, pages 191-201, gives, in my opinion, the fairest presentation of what happened and makes the calmest judgment.

Army operations, incidentally, are not described in detail, even when they are conjoined to those of the Marines—as at Okinawa, the Marianas, or the Solomons—because this is the

527

story of the Marines' war. This book's account of Guadalcanal, for instance, is ended on December 9, 1942, the day command passed from the Marines to the Army. What happened between then and February 9, when the island was secured, can be found in *Guadalcanal: The First Offensive*, by John Miller, Jr., a Marine who fought at Bougainville and who is now the Deputy Chief Historian, Office of the Chief of Military History.

Most of the human touches in this book come from division histories, memoirs, biographies and anthologies, and the stories of Marine combat correspondents. There might have been more of them, except that my attempt to go through nearly a hundred cartons of combat correspondents' material at Marine Headquarters was defeated by the discovery that the stories were on file by correspondents' names. Since all were undated and rarely identified the battlefield—as censorship required—the only person who could have made use of them was he who knew the battles through which every combat correspondent had passed as well as which one was being described then. This, like the name of the Unknown Soldier, is known but to God.

A few small alterations or deliberate maintenance of misconceptions need explanation. I have spelled the Japanese word for wine as *saki* rather than *sake*, realizing that the general reader would probably pronounce the latter to rhyme with cake, rather than with rocky, as it should. I am aware, of course, that *saki* is the Japanese word for a point of land, just as I know that *take* means mount and that in speaking of Mount Yaetake on Okinawa I am committing a redundancy. But the Marines always called it Mount Yaetake, just as they still talk of the Battle of the Tenaru on Guadalcanal even though Army maps have proved that the fight was fought on the Ilu. In this book it remains Tenaru, and if there is criticism from historians, I prefer this to having a Marine friend write: "Can't you even remember the names of the battles we were in?" For similar reasons the body of water separating Guadalcanal from Florida and other islands is called Iron Bottom *Bay*, rather than Iron Bottom Sound as historians now call it. No one in my memory ever called it anything but "the bay,"

528

although it is actually neither bay nor sound but a channel and was known as Sealark Channel before the war. Also, jaw-breaking Navy Medical Corps ratings such as Pharmacist's Mate Second Class and, worse, the mystifying abbeviation PHM 2/C, have been avoided simply by using the title "Corpsman" for all these men who served with the Marines.

It is hoped that readers will grant that numerous drama-tizations such as the last few minutes aboard the sinking bat-tleship *Yamato* or the suicidal end of Generals Ushijima and Cho on Okinawa or the words which Colonel Hiromichi Ya-hara spoke beneath Shuri Castle have their basis in historical fact. The first comes from Morison's *Victory in the Pacific*, Volume XIV of his series, which quotes a surviving ensign named Mitsuru Yoshida; the second from Japanese prisoners of war quoted in *Okinawa: The Last Battle*, by Roy E. Apple-man, *et al;* the third from *Okinawa Operations Record* and the *Yahara Interrogation* quoted in *Okinawa: Victory in the Pacific*, by Major Charles S. Nichols, U.S.M.C., and Henry I. Shaw, Jr.

Mr. Shaw, incidentally, kindly consented to check my man-uscript for accuracy. He has spent the last decade researching and writing histories of the Marines in World War Two, and there are few people so well qualified to hunt for error or to detect the apocryphal. I am most grateful to him, both for helpful suggestions and corrections. Those mistakes that re-main here are, of course, mine.

Before I conclude, let me acknowledge my debt to the Ma-rine Corps and to its commandant, General David M. Shoup, as well as to Colonel James E. Mills, head of the Division of Information, and to Lieutenant Colonel Philip N. Pierce of that division's media section. The staff of the Marine Historical Branch commanded by Colonel Thomas G. Roe has been of invaluable assistance with its customary grace and generosity, especially Mr. D. Michael O'Quinlivan, head of research and records. Although Mr. Robert D. Loomis, my editor at Random House, is already aware of my gratitude, the reader should know that if this book is consistently clear and all signposts are plainly marked, this is chiefly to the credit of his advice and criticism.

Finally, all that is subjective or impressionistic here—and I admit there is much of it—comes from my own experience in the war. This I regard as my warrant for having written this story in this way.

ROBERT LECKIE

Mountain Lakes, New Jersey
September 4, 1961

SELECTED
BIBLIOGRAPHY

APPLEMAN, ROY E., *et al. Okinawa: The Last Battle*. ("U.S. Army in World War II.") Washington: Government Printing Office, 1948.

ARNOLD, ARMY GEN. H. H. *Global Mission*. New York: Harper & Bros., 1949.

AURTHUR, 1ST LT. ROBERT A., *et al. The Third Marine Division*. Washington: Infantry Journal Press, 1948.

BARTLEY, LT. COL. WHITMAN S. *Iwo Jima: Amphibious Epic*. (Marine Corps Historical Monograph.) Washington: Government Printing Office, 1954.

BLAKENEY, JANE. *Heroes: U.S.M.C.* Published by author, 1957.

BLANKFORT, MICHAEL. *The Big Yankee: A Biography of Evans Carlson*. Boston: Little, Brown and Co., 1947.

BOGGS, MAJOR CHARLES W., JR. *Marine Aviation in the Philippines*. (Marine Corps Historical Monograph.) Washington: Government Printing Office, 1951.

BOYINGTON, COL. GREGORY. *Baa Baa Black Sheep: An Autobiography*. New York: G. P. Putnam's Sons, 1958.

BAYLER, LT. COL. WALTER L. J., and CARNES, CECIL. *Last Man off Wake Island*. Indianapolis and New York: The Bobbs-Merrill Co., 1943.

CANNON, M. HAMLIN. *Leyte: The Return to the Philippines*. ("U.S. Army in World War II.") Washington: Government Printing Office, 1954.

CASS, BEVAN G. *History of the Sixth Marine Division*. Washington: Infantry Journal Press, 1948.

CONDIT, KENNETH W., and TURNBLADH, EDWIN T. *Hold High the Torch:*

A History of the Fourth Marines. (Marine Corps Historical Monograph.) Washington: Government Printing Office, 1960.

CONN, STETSON, and FAIRCHILD, BYRON. *The Framework of Hemisphere Defense.* ("U.S. Army in World War II.") Washington: Government Printing Office, 1960.

CONNER, HOWARD M. *The Spearhead: History of the Fifth Marine Division.* Washington: Infantry Journal Press, 1950.

CROWL, PHILIP A. *Campaign in the Marianas.* ("U.S. Army in World War II.") Washington: Government Printing Office, 1960.

CROWL, PHILIP A., and LOVE, EDMUND G. *Seizure of the Gilberts and Marshalls.* ("U.S. Army in World War II.") Washington: Government Printing Office, 1955.

DAVIDSON, ORLANDO R., et al. *The Deadeyes: The Story of the 96th Infantry Division.* Washington: Infantry Journal Press, 1947.

DECHANT, CAPT. JOHN A. *Devilbirds: The Story of United States Marine Corps Aviation in World War II.* New York: Harper & Bros., 1947.

DEVEREUX, COL. JAMES P. S. *The Story of Wake Island.* Philadelphia and New York: J. B. Lippincott Co., 1947.

ESPOSITO, COL. VINCENT J. (chief ed.). *The West Point Atlas of American Wars,* Vol. 2. New York: Frederick A. Praeger, 1959.

FELDT, COMMANDER ERIC A., R.A.N. *The Coastwatchers.* New York and Melbourne: Oxford University Press, 1946.

FOSTER, CAPTAIN JOHN M. *Hell in the Heavens: The True Combat Adventures of a Marine Fighter Pilot.* New York: G. P. Putnam's Sons, 1961.

FULLER, MAJ. GEN. J. F. C. *The Second World War.* New York: Duell, Sloan and Pearce, 1949.

GOLDBERG, ALFRED (ed.). *A History of the United States Air Force, 1907-1957.* Princeton: D. Van Nostrand, 1958.

GREENFIELD, KENT ROBERTS (ed.). *Command Decisions.* ("U.S. Army in World War II.") Washington: Government Printing Office, 1960.

HALSEY, FLEET ADML. WILLIAM F., and BRYAN, LT. CMDR. J., III. *Admiral Halsey's Story.* New York: McGraw-Hill Book Co., 1947.

HAYASHI, SABURO, with COOX, ALVIN D. *Kogun: The Japanese Army in the Pacific War.* Quantico, Va.: The Marine Corps Association, 1959.

HEINL, LT. COL. ROBERT D., JR. *The Defense of Wake.* (Marine Corps Historical Monograph.) Washington: Government Printing Office, 1947.

————. *Marines at Midway*. (Marine Corps Historical Monograph.) Washington: Government Printing Office, 1948.

HEINL, LT. COL. ROBERT D., JR., and CROWN, LT. COL. JOHN A. *The Marshalls: Increasing the Tempo*. (Marine Corps Historical Monograph.) Washington: Government Printing Office, 1954.

HOFFMAN, MAJOR CARL W. *Saipan: The Beginning of the End*. (Marine Corps Historical Monograph.) Washington: Government Printing Office, 1950.

HOUGH, LT. COL. FRANK O., *et al*. *Pearl Harbor to Guadalcanal*. ("History of U.S. Marine Corps Operations in World War II.") Washington: Government Printing Office, 1958.

HOUGH, LT. COL. FRANK O., and CROWN, MAJ. JOHN A. *The Campaign on New Britain*. (Marine Corps Historical Monograph.) Washington: Government Printing Office, 1952.

HOUGH, MAJOR FRANK O. *The Assault on Peleliu*. (Marine Corps Historical Monograph.) Washington: Government Printing Office, 1950.

————. *The Island War: The United States Marine Corps in the Pacific*. Philadelphia and New York: J. B. Lippincott Co., 1947.

HOWARD, CLIVE, and WHITLEY, JOE. *One Damned Island after Another: The Saga of the Seventh Air Force*. Chapel Hill: University of North Carolina Press, 1947.

HUNT, CAPTAIN GEORGE P. *Coral Comes High: A Company on Peleliu*. New York: Harper & Bros., 1946.

INOGUCHI, CAPTAIN RIKIHEI, and TADASHI, CMDR. NAKAJIMA, with PINEAU, ROGER. *The Divine Wind: Japan's Kamikaze Force in World War II*. Annapolis: U.S. Naval Institute, 1958.

ISELY, JETER A., and CROWL, PHILIP A. *The U.S. Marines and Amphibious War*. Princeton: Princeton University Press, 1951.

JOHNSTON, RICHARD W. *Follow Me!: The Story of the Second Marine Division in World War II*. New York: Random House, 1948.

JOSEPHY, ALVIN M., JR. *The Long and the Short and the Tall: The Story of a Marine Combat Unit in the Pacific*. New York: Alfred A. Knopf, 1946.

KENNEY, GEN. GEORGE C. *General Kenney Reports*. New York: Duell, Sloan and Pearce, 1949.

KING, FLEET ADML. ERNEST J., and WHITEHILL, CMDR. WALTER M. *Fleet Admiral King: A Naval Record*. New York: W. W. Norton & Co., 1952.

LEAHY, FLEET ADML. WILLIAM D. *I Was There*. New York: Whittlesley House, 1950.

LODGE, MAJ. O. R. *The Recapture of Guam.* (Marine Corps Historical Monograph.) Washington: Government Printing Office, 1954.

LOVE, EDMUND G. *The 27th Infantry Division in World War II.* Washington: Infantry Journal Press, 1949.

MARSHALL, LT. COL. S. L. A. *Island Victory: The Battle of Kwajalein Atoll.* Washington: The Infantry Journal, 1945.

MCMILLAN, GEORGE. *The Old Breed: A History of the First Marine Division in World War Two.* Washington: Infantry Journal Press, 1949.

———, *et al. Uncommon Valor: Marine Divisions in Action.* Washington: Infantry Journal Press, 1946.

MERILLAT, CAPTAIN HERBERT L. *The Island: A Personal Account of Guadalcanal.* Boston: Houghton Mifflin Co., 1944.

MEYER, ROBERT, JR. (ed.). *The Stars and Stripes Story of World War II.* New York: David McKay Co., Inc., 1961.

MILLER, FRANCIS TREVELYAN. *History of World War II.* Philadelphia: Universal Book & Bible House, 1945.

MILLER, JOHN, JR. *Cartwheel: The Reduction of Rabaul.* ("U.S. Army in World War II.") Washington: Government Printing Office, 1959.

———. *Guadalcanal: The First Offensive.* ("U.S. Army in World War II.") Washington: Government Printing Office, 1949.

MILNER, SAMUEL. *Victory in Papua.* ("U.S. Army in World War II.") Washington: Government Printing Office, 1957.

MONKS, JOHN, JR. *A Ribbon and a Star: The Third Marines on Bougainville.* New York: Henry Holt & Co., 1945.

MORISON,* SAMUEL ELIOT. *The Rising Sun in the Pacific.* (*History of United States Naval Operations in World War II,* Vol. III.) Boston: Little, Brown and Co., 1959.

———. *Coral Sea, Midway and Submarine Action.* (*History of United States Naval Operations in World War II,* Vol. IV.) Boston: Little, Brown and Co., 1960.

———. *The Struggle for Guadalcanal.* (*History of United States Naval Operations in World War II,* Vol. V.) Boston: Little, Brown and Co., 1959.

———. *Breaking the Bismarcks Barrier.* (*History of United States Naval Operations in World War II,* Vol. VI.) Boston: Little, Brown and Co., 1960.

———. *Aleutians, Gilberts and Marshalls.* (*History of United States Naval Operations in World War II,* Vol. VII.) Boston: Little, Brown and Co., 1960.

* All Morison volumes cited are revised editions.

————. *New Guinea and the Marianas.* (*History of United States Naval Operations in World War II,* Vol. VIII.) Boston: Little, Brown and Co., 1960.

————. *Leyte.* (*History of United States Naval Operations in World War II,* Vol. XII.) Boston: Little, Brown and Co., 1958.

————. *The Liberation of the Philippines.* (*History of United States Naval Operations in World War II,* Vol. XIII.) Boston: Little, Brown and Co., 1959.

————. *Victory in the Pacific.* (*History of United States Naval Operations in World War II,* Vol. XIV.) Boston: Little, Brown and Co., 1960.

MORTON, LOUIS. *The Fall of the Philippines.* ("U.S. Army in World War II.") Washington: Government Printing Office, 1953.

MYERS, LT. COL. MAX (ed.). *Ours to Hold It High: The History of the 77th Infantry Division in World War II.* Washington: Infantry Journal Press, 1947.

NAVAL HISTORY DIVISION. *Naval Chronology, World War II.* Washington: Government Printing Office, 1955.

NICHOLS, MAJ. CHARLES S., and SHAW, HENRY I., JR. *Okinawa: Victory in the Pacific.* (Marine Corps Historical Monograph.) Washington: Government Printing Office, 1955.

O'SHEEL, CAPT. PATRICK, and COOK, STAFF SGT. GENE (eds.). *Semper Fidelis: The U.S. Marines in the Pacific.* New York: William Sloane Associates, Inc., 1947.

PIERCE, LT. COL. PHILIP N., and HOUGH, LT. COL. FRANK O. *The Compact History of the United States Marine Corps.* New York: Hawthorn Books, Inc., 1960.

PRATT, FLETCHER. *The Marines' War.* New York: William Sloane Associates, Inc., 1948.

PROEHL, CARL W. *The Fourth Marine Division in World War II.* Washington: Infantry Journal Press, 1946.

RENTZ, MAJ. JOHN N. *Bougainville and the Northern Solomons.* (Marine Corps Historical Monograph.) Washington: Government Printing Office, 1948.

————. *Marines in the Central Solomons.* (Marine Corps Historical Monograph.) Washington: Government Printing Office, 1952.

ROBSON, R. W. *The Pacific Islands Handbook, 1944.* New York: The Macmillan Co., 1945.

SHERROD, ROBERT. *History of Marine Corps Aviation in World War II.* Washington: Combat Forces Press, 1952.

————. *On To Westward: War in the Central Pacific.* New York: Duell, Sloan & Pearce, 1945.

————. *Tarawa: The Story of a Battle.* New York: Duell, Sloan & Pearce, 1944.

SMITH, GEN. HOLLAND M. *Coral and Brass: Howlin' Mad Smith's Own Story of the Marines in the Pacific.* New York: Charles Scribner's Sons, 1949.

SMITH, ROBERT ROSS. *The Approach to the Philippines.* ("U.S. Army in World War II.") Washington: Government Printing Office, 1953.

STILWELL, GEN. JOSEPH W., and WHITE, THEODORE H. (ed.). *The Stilwell Papers.* Philadelphia and New York: William Sloane Associates, Inc., 1948.

STOCKMAN, CAPTAIN JAMES R. *The Battle for Tarawa.* (Marine Corps Historical Monograph.) Washington: Government Printing Office, 1947.

The War Reports of General of the Army George C. Marshall, General of the Army H. H. Arnold, and Fleet Admiral Ernest J. King. Philadelphia and New York: J. B. Lippincott Co., 1947.

TREGASKIS, RICHARD. *Guadalcanal Diary.* New York: Random House, 1943.

United States Navy, *Medal of Honor, 1861-1949.* Washington: 1950.

United States Strategic Bombing Survey (Pacific), Naval Analysis Division. *The Campaigns of the Pacific War.* Washington: Government Printing Office, 1946.

————. *Interrogations of Japanese Officials,* 2 vols. Washington: Government Printing Office, 1946.

WILLIAMS, MARY H. (compiler). *Chronology 1941-1945.* ("U.S. Army in World War II.") Washington: Government Printing Office, 1960.

ZIMMERMAN, MAJ. JOHN L. *The Guadalcanal Campaign.* (Marine Corps Historical Monograph.) Washington: Government Printing Office, 1949.

CHRONOLOGY OF THE
WAR IN THE PACIFIC

Only the major events of the Pacific War are listed in this chronol‑
ogy. All dates are those obtaining in the place where the events
occurred, which, in the vast majority of occurrences in the Pacific,
happens to be the East Zone, or one day later than our own time.
The few which took place this side of the International Date Line
(180th Meridian)—West Zone time—are marked with an asterisk.
Also, to relate the Pacific to the war against the Axis Powers, a few
of the important dates from Europe and Africa are carried in paren‑
thesis.

1941

7 December*—Japanese bomb Pearl Harbor; Japanese surface force
    raids Midway Island.

8 December—First Japanese air attacks on Wake, Guam, Philip‑
    pines; Hong Kong bombed; Thailand conquered.

8 December*—U.S. declares war on Japan.

9 December—Japanese land in Malaya.

10 December—Guam falls to Japan.

11 December*—U.S. declares war on Germany and Italy.

22 December—Japan invades Borneo to open Netherlands Indies
    Campaign.

23 December—Wake Island falls to Japan.

25 December—Hong Kong falls to Japan.

537

1942

23 January—Japanese invade New Britain, New Ireland, the Solomons.

24 January—U.S. Naval force batters Japanese troop convoy in Battle of Makassar Strait.

(26 January—First U.S. troops reach Northern Ireland.)

1 February—Gilberts and Marshalls bombed by U.S. carrier forces.

4 February—Allied fleet battered in Battle of the Java Sea.

16 February—Singapore falls to Japan.

8 March—Japan invades New Guinea (Lae, Salamaua, Finschhafen).

9 March—Java falls to Japan concluding Netherlands Indies Campaign.

9 April—Bataan falls to Japan.

18 April—Shangri-La raid (Army bombers flying off U.S. carrier decks) strikes Tokyo, other Japanese cities.

4-8 May—Battle of the Coral Sea turns back Japan from invasion of Port Moresby in New Guinea, vital to defense of Australia.

7 May—Corregidor surrenders to Japanese.

12 May—Last of U.S. troops surrender in Mindanao; Japanese declare Philippines secure.

3 June*—Japan bombs Dutch Harbor in Alaska, occupies Kiska and Attu in the Aleutians.

3-6 June—Japanese Navy decisively defeated by U.S. Navy in Battle of Midway; Japan loses initiative in Pacific War.

28 July—Japanese begin overland drive on Port Moresby from base at Buna-Sanananda.

7 August—U.S. Marines land at Tulagi-Guadalcanal (Guadalcanal secured 9 February 1943).

8-9 August—U.S. Navy staggered in Battle of Savo Island, withdraws from Tulagi-Guadalcanal.

17 August—U.S. Marines raid Makin Island.

(19 August—Canadian and British troops raid Dieppe in France.)

5 September—Australians halt Japanese attempt to invade Milne Bay in New Guinea.

14 September—Germany opens Siege of Stalingrad.)

3 October—U.S. Marines occupy Funafuti in Ellice Islands.

(*24 October—British Eighth Army opens El Alamein drive in Egypt.*)

(*8 November—British and American troops land in North Africa.*)

12-15 November—Japanese repulsed in Naval Battle of Guadalcanal; crisis is passed ashore.

9 December—Command on Guadalcanal passes to U.S. Army.

1943

23 January—Australian-U.S. counterattack recaptures Buna-Sanananda from Japanese.

(*23 January—Tripoli falls to Allies.*)

9 February—Japanese resistance on Guadalcanal ends.

20 February—U.S. occupies Russell Islands.

2-4 March—Allied land-based planes inflict decisive defeat on Japanese attempt to reinforce New Guinea, sinking entire convoy in Battle of the Bismarck Sea.

11 May—U.S. Army attacks Attu(secured 30 May).

(*11 May—German resistance in North Africa broken.*)

21 June—U.S. Marines land at Segi Point, New Georgia, opening Central Solomons Campaign (campaign concluded 25 September).

(*9 July—Allies land in Sicily.*)

15 August—U.S.-New Zealand forces land on Vella Lavella in Northern Solomons.

(*3 September—Italy surrenders.*)

(*9 September—Allies invade Italy.*)

2 October—Australians retake Finschhafen in New Guinea.

27 October—New Zealanders land in Treasury Islands.

28 October—U.S. Marines make feint landing on Choiseul.

1 November—U.S. Marines assault Bougainville (airfield area at Cape Torokina secured 21 December).

5 November—First U.S. carrier strike at Rabaul.

20 November—U.S. Marines assault Tarawa (secured 23 November)

15 December—U.S. Army troops land at Arawe in New Britain.

26 December—U.S. Marines assault Cape Gloucester (airfield area secured 15 January 1944).

1944

1 January°—Lieutenant General (later General) Alexander Vandegrift made Commandant of Marine Corps.

2 January—U.S. Army makes surprise landing at Saidor, begins drive up New Guinea coast.

(*27 January—Anzio beachhead seized in Italy.*)

31 January—Majuro Atoll in the Marshalls, first prewar Japanese territory, seized.

1 February—U.S. assaults Kwajalein Atoll (Marines at Roi-Namur, secured 2 February; Army at Kwajalein Islet, secured 4 February).

17 February—U.S. Army, Marines assault Eniwetok Atoll (secured 23 February).

(*21 February—Russians lift Siege of Stalingrad.*)

29 February—Admiralty Islands reconnaissance begins (islands captured 18 March).

6 March—Marines assault Talasea on New Britain (secured 8 March).

8 March—Japanese counteroffensive on Bougainville launched, smashed for good 24 March.

20 March—Marines land on Emirau.

22 April—U.S. Army lands at Hollandia and Aitape in New Guinea.

(*4 June—Allies enter Rome.*)

(*6 June—Allies invade France in Normandy landings.*)

15 June—U.S. Marines land at Saipan (island secured 9 July).

19 June—Japanese Navy decisively defeated by U.S. Navy in Battle of Philippine Sea; Japan's carrier power all but destroyed.

21 July—U.S. Marines assault Guam (secured 10 August).

24 July—U.S. Marines on Saipan assault nearby Tinian (secured 1 August).

30 July—U.S. Army's New Guinea drive ends on Sansapor Point.

(*31 July—Allies break out of Normandy.*)

(*15 August—Allies invade southern France.*)

540

15 September—U.S. Marines assault Peleliu (secured 12 October); U.S. Army troops seize Morotai.

17 September—U.S. Army assaults Angaur (secured 20 September).

23 September—Ulithi seized as advanced Naval base.

20 October—U.S. Army lands on Leyte to open Philippines Campaign.

(*21 October—Aachen, first city inside Germany, falls to U.S. troops.*)

23-26 October—U.S. Navy destroys remnants of Japanese Navy in Battle of Leyte Gulf.

24 November—U.S. Army Air Corps delivers first B-29 raid on Tokyo.

(*16 December—German counterstroke opens Battle of the Bulge, Germans stopped 30 December.*)

1945

9 January—Luzon in Northern Philippines invaded.

(*17 January—Russians capture Warsaw.*)

16-17 February—First U.S. carrier raids on Tokyo Bay.

19 February—Marines assault Iwo Jima (secure 26 March).

24 February—Manila falls.

(*7 March—U.S. troops take Remagen Bridge and cross Rhine.*)

10 March—Mindanao in Southern Philippines invaded.

9-10 March—U.S. B-29s fire-bomb Tokyo at night in most savage air raid in history (including later atomic bombings).

1 April—U.S. Marines, Army troops land on Okinawa (island secured 22 June).

(*28 April—Mussolini put to death by Italian partisans.*)

1 May—Australians invade Tarakan Island, Netherlands Indies (secured 19 May).

(*1 May—Death of Hitler.*)

(*2 May—Fighting in Italy ends.*)

(*7 May—Germany surrenders.*)

10 June—Australians and Dutch land on Borneo.

22 June—Okinawa capture marks end of ground fighting in Pacific.

14 July—U.S. begins first surface fleet bombardment of Japan.

30 July—Japan refuses Potsdam ultimatum.

6 August—World's first atomic bomb dropped on Hiroshima.

8 August—Russia attacks Japan.

9 August—Atomic bomb dropped on Nagasaki.

14 August—Japan accepts surrender terms.

2 September—Japanese surrender signed in Tokyo Bay.

MARINE MEDAL OF
HONOR WINNERS IN
WORLD WAR TWO

NAME	RANK	DATE	PLACE	STATE
* Agerholm, Harold Christ	Pfc.	7 July 1944	Saipan	Wisconsin
* Anderson, Richard Beatty	Pfc.	1 Feb. 1944	Kwajalein	Washington
* Bailey, Kenneth D.	Major	12-13 Sept. 1942	Guadalcanal	Oklahoma
Basilone, John	Sergeant	24-25 Oct. 1942	Guadalcanal	New Jersey
†* Bauer, Harold William	Lt. Col.	May-Nov. 1942	South Pacific	Nebraska
* Bausell, Lewis Kenneth	Corporal	15 Sept. 1944	Peleliu	Dist. of Colum.
* Berry, Charles Joseph	Corporal	3 March 1945	Iwo Jima	Ohio
* Bonnyman, Alexander, Jr.	First Lt.	20-22 Nov. 1943	Tarawa	New Mexico
* Bordelon, William James	Staff Sgt.	20 Nov. 1943	Tarawa	Texas
† Boyington, Gregory	Major	Oct. 1943- Jan. 1945	Solomons	Washington
Bush, Richard Earl	Corporal	16 April 1945	Okinawa	Kentucky
‡ Bush, Robert Eugene	HA 1/c	2 May 1945	Okinawa	Washington
* Caddy, William Robert	Pfc.	3 March 1945	Iwo Jima	Massachusetts
* Cannon, George Ham	First Lt.	7 Dec. 1941	Wake	Michigan
* Cole, Darrell Samuel	Sergeant	19 Feb. 1945	Iwo Jima	Missouri

* Denotes posthumous award
† Denotes Marine aviation personnel
‡ Denotes Navy Medical Corpsmen serving with Marines
§ Denotes U.S. Coast Guardsman serving with Marines

NAME	RANK	DATE	PLACE	STATE
* Courtney, Henry Alexius, Jr.	Major	14-15 May 1945	Okinawa	Minnesota
* Damato, Anthony Peter	Corporal	19-20 Feb. 1944	Eniwetok	Pennsylvania
† DeBlanc, Jefferson Joseph	First Lt.	31 Jan. 1943	Solomons	Louisiana
Dunlap, Robert Hugo	Captain	20-21 Feb. 1945	Iwo Jima	Illinois
Chambers, Justice Marion	Lt. Col.	19-22 Feb. 1945	Iwo Jima	West Virginia
* Dyess, Aquilla James	Lt. Col.	1-2 Feb. 1944	Kwajalein	Georgia
Edson, Merritt Austin	Colonel	13-14 Sept. 1942	Guadalcanal	Vermont
†* Elrod, Henry Talmage	Captain	8-23 Dec. 1941	Wake	Georgia
* Epperson, Harold Glenn	Pfc.	25 June 1944	Saipan	Ohio
* Fardy, John Peter	Corporal	7 May 1945	Okinawa	Illinois
* Fleming, Richard E.	Captain	4-5 June 1942	Midway	Minnesota
† Foss, Joseph Jacob	Captain	Oct.-Nov. 1942	Guadalcanal	South Dakota
* Foster, William Adelbert	Pfc.	2 May 1945	Okinawa	Ohio
† Galer, Robert Edward	Major	Sept.-Nov. 1942	Guadalcanal	Washington
* Gonsalves, Harold	Pfc.	15 April 1945	Okinawa	California
Gray, Ross Franklin	Sergeant	21 Feb. 1945	Iwo Jima	Alabama
* Gurke, Henry	Pfc.	9 Nov. 1943	Bougainville	North Dakota
†* Halyburton, William David, Jr.	PHM 2/c	19 May 1945	Okinawa	North Carolina
* Hansen, Dale Merline	Private	7 May 1945	Okinawa	Nebraska
†* Hanson, Robert Murray	First Lt.	Nov. 1943-Jan. 1944	Solomons-Rabaul	Massachusetts
Harrell, William George	Sergeant	3 March 1945	Iow Jima	Texas
* Hauge, Louis James, Jr.	Corporal	14 May 1945	Okinawa	Minnesota
* Hawkins, William Dean	First Lt.	20-21 Nov. 1943	Tarawa	Texas
Jackson, Arthur J.	Pfc.	18 Sept. 1944	Peleliu	Oregon
Jacobson, Douglas Thomas	Pfc.	26 Feb. 1945	Iwo Jima	New York
* Julian, Joseph Rodolph	Pl. Sgt.	9 March 1945	Iwo Jima	Massachusetts
* Kinser, Elbert Luther	Sergeant	4 May 1945	Okinawa	Tennessee
* Kraus, Richard Edward	Pfc.	3 Oct. 1944	Peleliu	Minnesota
* LaBelle, James Dennis	Pfc.	8 March 1945	Iwo Jima	Minnesota
Leims, John Harold	Second Lt.	7 March 1945	Iwo Jima	Illinois

544

NAME	RANK	DATE	PLACE	STATE
‡* Lester, Fred Faulkner	HA 1/c	8 June 1945	Okinawa	Illinois
Lucas, Jacklyn Harrell	Pfc.	20 Feb. 1945	Iwo Jima	North Carolina
Lummus, Jack	First Lt.	8 March 1945	Iwo Jima	Texas
* Martin, Harry Linn	First Lt.	26 March 1945	Iwo Jima	Ohio
* Mason, Leonard Foster	Pfc.	22 July 1944	Guam	Ohio
* McCard, Robert Howard	Gun. Sgt.	16 June 1944	Saipan	New York
McCarthy, Joseph Jeremiah	Captain	21 Feb. 1945	Iwo Jima	Illinois
McTureous, Robert Miller, Jr.	Private	7 June 1945	Okinawa	Florida
§* Munro, Douglas Albert	Signal. 1/c	27 Sept. 1942	Guadalcanal	Washington
* New, John Dury	Pfc.	25 Sept. 1944	Peleliu	Alabama
* Owens, Robert Allen	Sergeant	1 Nov. 1943	Bougainville	South Carolina
* Ozbourn, Joseph William	Private	30 July 1944	Tinian	Illinois
Paige, Mitchell	Pl. Sgt.	26 Oct. 1942	Guadalcanal	Pennsylvania
* Phelps, Wesley	Private	4 Oct. 1944	Peleliu	Kentucky
* Phillips, George	Private	14 March 1945	Iwo Jima	Missouri
‡ Pierce, Francis, Jr.	PHM 1/c	15-16 March 1945	Iwo Jima	Iowa
Pope, Everett Parker	Captain	19-20 Sept. 1944	Peleliu	Massachusetts
* Power, John Vincent	First Lt.	1 Feb. 1944	Kwajalein	Massachusetts
* Roan, Charles Howard	Pfc.	18 Sept. 1944	Peleliu	Texas
Rouh, Carlton Robert	First Lt.	15 Sept. 1944	Peleliu	New Jersey
* Ruhl, Donald Jack	Pfc.	19-21 Feb. 1945	Iwo Jima	Montana
* Schwab, Albert Earnest	Pfc.	7 May 1945	Okinawa	Oklahoma
Shoup, David Monroe	Colonel	20-22 Nov. 1943	Tarawa	Indiana
Sigler, Franklin Earl	Private	14 March 1945	Iwo Jima	New Jersey
Skaggs, Luther, Jr.	Pfc.	21-22 July 1944	Guam	Kentucky
† Smith, John Lucian	Major	Aug.-Sept. 1942	Guadalcanal	Oklahoma
Sorenson, Richard Keith	Private	1-2 Feb. 1944	Kawajalein	Minnesota
* Stein, Tony	Corporal	19 Feb. 1945	Iwo Jima	Ohio
† Swett, James Elms	First Lt.	7 April 1943	Solomons	California
* Thomas, Herbert Joseph	Sergeant	7 Nov. 1943	Bougainville	West Virginia

545

NAME	RANK	DATE	PLACE	STATE
° Thomason, Clyde	Sergeant	17-18 Aug. 1942	Makin	Georgia
° Timmerman, Grant Frederick	Sergeant	8 July 1944	Saipan	Kansas
Vandegrift, Alexander Archer	Maj. Gen.	Aug.-Dec. 1942	Guadalcanal	Virginia
† Wahlen, George Edward	PHM 2/c	26 Feb. 1945	Iwo Jima	Utah
† Walsh, Kenneth Ambrose	First Lt.	Aug. 1943	Solomons	New York
° Walsh, William Gary	Gun. Sgt.	27 Feb. 1945	Iwo Jima	Massachusetts
Watson, Wilson Douglas	Private	26-27 Feb. 1945	Iwo Jima	Arkansas
Williams, Hershel Woodrow	Corporal	23 Feb. 1945	Iwo Jima	West Virginia
†° Williams, Jack	PHM 3/c	3 March 1945	Iwo Jima	Arkansas
†° Willis, John Harlan	PHM 1/c	28 Feb. 1945	Iwo Jima	Tennessee
Wilson, Louis Hugh, Jr.	Captain	25-26 July 1944	Guam	Mississippi
° Wilson, Robert Lee	Pfc.	4 August 1944	Tinian	Illinois
° Witek, Frank Peter	Pfc.	3 August 1944	Guam	Illinois

MARINE CORPS ACES
IN WORLD WAR TWO

NO.	NAME	NUMBER OF PLANES SHOT DOWN
1.	Boyington, Gregory	28*
2.	Foss, Joseph J.	26
3.	Hanson, Robert M.	25
4.	Walsh, Kenneth A.	21
5.	Aldrich, Donald N.	20
6.	Smith, John L.	19
7.	Carl, Marion E.	18½
8.	Thomas, Wilbur J.	18½
9.	Swett, James E.	15½
10.	Spears, Harold L.	15
11.	Donahue, Archie G.	14
12.	Cupp, James N.	13
13.	Galer, Robert E.	13
14.	Marontate, William P.	13
15.	Shaw, Edward O.	13
16.	Frazier, Kenneth D.	12½
17.	Everton, Loren D.	12
18.	Segal, Harold E.	12
19.	Trowbridge, Eugene A.	12
20.	DeLong, Philip C.	11⅙
21.	Bauer, Harold W.	11
22.	Sapp, Donald H.	11
23.	Conger, Jack E.	10½
24.	Long, Herbert H.	10
25.	DeBlanc, Jefferson J.	9

* Includes 6 planes shot down with Flying Tigers in China.

NO.	NAME	NUMBER OF PLANES SHOT DOWN
26.	Magee, Christopher L.	9
27.	Mann, Thomas H., Jr.	9
28.	Overend, Edmund F.	9*
29.	Thomas, Franklin C., Jr.	9
30.	Loesch, Gregory K.	8½
31.	Morgan, John L., Jr.	8½
32.	Snider, William N.	8½
33.	Case, William N	8
34.	Dobbin, John F.	8
35.	Gutt, Fred E.	8
36.	Hernan, Edwin J., Jr.	8
37.	Hollowell, George L.	8
38.	Kunz, Charles M.	8
39.	Narr, Joseph L.	8
40.	Post, Nathan T.	8
41.	Warner, Arthur T.	8
42.	Yost, Donald K.	8
43.	Baker, Robert M.	7
44.	Brown, William P.	7
45.	Caswell, Dean	7
46.	Crowe, William E.	7
47.	Haberman, Roger A.	7
48.	Hamilton, Henry B.	7
49.	Jensen, Alvin J.	7
50.	McClurg, Robert W.	7
51.	O'Keefe, Jeremiah J.	7
52.	Owens, Robert G., Jr.	7
53.	Pittman, Jack, Jr.	7
54.	Reinburg, Joseph H.	7
55.	Ruhsam, John W.	7
56.	Wade, Robert	7
57.	Williams, Gerard M. H.	7
58.	Mullen, Paul A.	6½
59.	Durnford, Dewey F.	6½
60.	Dillard, Joseph V.	6½
61.	Axtell, George C., Jr.	6
62.	Baird, Robert	6
63.	Bolt, John F., Jr.	6
64.	Chandler, Creighton	6
65.	Conant, A. Roger	6
66.	Dillow, Eugene	6
67.	Dorroh, Jefferson D.	6
68.	Drury, Frank C.	6
69.	Fisher, Don H.	6

548

NO.	NAME	SHOT DOWN
70.	Fraser, Robert B.	6
71.	Freeman, William B.	6
72.	Hall, Sheldon O.	6
73.	Hundley, John C.	6
74.	Jones, Charles D.	6
75.	McManus, John	6
76.	Percy, Gilbert	6
77.	Pierce, Francis E., Jr.	6
78.	Pond, Zenneth A.	6
79.	Presley, Frank H.	6
80.	Shuman, Perry L.	6
81.	Stout, Robert F.	6
82.	Terrill, Francis A.	6
83.	Valentine, Herbert J.	6
84.	Vedder, Milton N.	6
85.	Hansen, Herman	5½
86.	Hood, William L.	5½
87.	Kirkpatrick, Floyd C.	5½
88.	Lundin, William M.	5½
89.	Payne, Frederick R., Jr.	5½
90.	Sigler, Wallace E.	5½
91.	Alley, Stuart C., Jr.	5
92.	Baldwin, Frank B.	5
93.	Braun, Richard L.	5
94.	Carlton, William A.	5
95.	Davis, Leonard K.	5
96.	Dawkins, George E., Jr.	5
97.	Doyle, Cecil J.	5
98.	Drake, Charles W.	5
99.	Elwood, Hugh McJ.	5
100.	Farrell, William	5
101.	Finn, Howard J.	5
102.	Fontana, Paul J.	5
103.	Ford, Kenneth M.	5
104.	Hacking, Albert C.	5
105.	Kendrick, Charles	5
106.	Laird, Wayne W.	5
107.	McCartney, Henry A., Jr.	5
108.	McGinty, Selva E.	5
109.	Olander, Edwin L.	5
110.	Phillips, Hyde	5
111.	Poske, George H.	5
112.	Powell, Ernest A.	5
113.	Ramlo, Orvin H.	5

NO.	NAME	NUMBER OF PLANES SHOT DOWN
114.	Scarborough, Hartwell V., Jr.	5
115.	Scherer, Raymond	5
116.	See, Robert B.	5
117.	Synar, Stanley	5
118.	Weissenberger, Gregory J.	5
119.	Wells, Albert P.	5
120.	Yunck, Michael R.	5

INDEX

551

552

Conolly, Rear Adm. Richard, 279, 280, 360
Converse, destroyer, 233, 234
Cooley, Lt. Col. Albert, 69
Coral Sea, 63
Cory, Lt. Ralph, 39
Corzine, Pfc. James, 59
Cosgrove, Col. John, 324
Costello, Corpsman Robert, 218
Courtney, Maj. Henry, 506, 507, 511
Cox, Sgt. James, 456, 457
Craig, Col. Edward, 177
Cram, Maj. John, 86-88
Cramford, Pfc. William, 342
Crane, Capt. Edgar, 24, 25
Crowe, Maj. Henry, 190, 198, 202, 203, 205, 213, 215, 220, 221, 223, 318, 319
Culhane, Maj. Thomas, 198, 214
Cushing, destroyer, 121, 122
Cushman, Lt. Col. Robert, 458

Damato, Corp. Anthony, 294
Dampier Strait, 237, 241, 243
Dashiell, destroyer, 190, 194, 197
Davie, Pfc. James, 343
Davis, Maj. Leonard, 78, 86
Deckrow, Gy. Sgt. Theon, 258
De Gink, Hotel, 151
del Valle, Maj. Gen. Pedro, 475, 476, 483, 510, 514, 515, 518
Denig, Capt. James, 285
Denver, cruiser, 170, 171
Devine, Tech. Sgt. Frank, 176
Deyo, Rear Adm. Morton, 487
de Zayas, Lt. Col. Hector, 231
Diamond, Gy. Sgt. Lewis, 40
Dickens, Sgt. Onel, 320
Donitaley, Corp. William, 318, 319
Dooley, Capt. George, 122
Drewes, Maj. Henry, 199
Duchein, Maj. Charles, 283, 284
Duncan, destroyer, 80
Dunlap, Capt. Robert, 449
Dunn, Pfc. Harry, 66-68
Dunn, Lt. James, 419
Duplantis, Lt. Col. Wendell, 377, 450
Dusenbury, Capt. Julius, 514, 515
Dutch East Indies, 3
Dyess, Lt. Col. Aquilla, 285
Dyson, destroyer, 233, 234

Easley, Lt. Col. John, 347
Eastern Solomons, battle of the, 49

Edson, Lt. Col. Merritt, 19, 52, 53, 54, 55, 57, 58, 60, 61, 75, 76, 129, 185, 215, 222
Efate, 187, 188
Egaroppu (*see* Nakarop)
Eldorado, flagship of Adm. Turner, 439, 447
Emirau, 305
Emmons, minesweeper, 486
Empress Augusta Bay, 160, 167; battle of, 169-171
Engebi Islet, 287; capture of, 288-290, 293-294
Eniwetok, 273, 286-290, 308, 311, 355, 357, 383
Eniwetok Islet, 293, 294
Enola Gay, B-29 bomber, 521
Enterprise, carrier, 111, 123
Epperson, Pfc. Harold, 338, 339
Erskine, Maj. Gen. Graves, 437, 457, 461, 462, 464
Espiritu Santo, Island of, 63, 85
Essex, carrier, 487
Evans, destroyer, 505
Evans, Pvt. "Chicken," 100

Fardy, Corp. John, 501
Ferguson, Pfc. James, 342, 343
Fiji Islands, 4, 9, 14, 15
Fissel, Maj. Glenn, 180
Fletcher, destroyer, 121, 122
Fletcher, Vice Adm. Frank Jack, 14, 18, 32, 49
Florida Island, 9, 17, 22, 31, 103
Flying Fish, submarine, 324
Formosa, 394, 472, 477
Forrestal, Secretary of the Navy James, 447, 448
Foss, Capt. Joseph, 78, 81, 104, 135, 240, 251, 261
Foster, Pfc. William, 501
Fournier, Lt. Joseph, 413
Franklin, carrier, 466
Freeman, Lt. Orville, 173
Frisbie, Col. Julian, 246
Fubuki, destroyer, 80
Fujinami, destroyer, 173
Fujioka, Lt. Gen. Takeo, 497
Furumiya, Col. Masajiro, 99, 100, 106, 112
Furutaka, cruiser, 33-35, 80

Gagnon, Pfc. Rene, 447
Galer, Maj. Robert, 73, 88
Gaston, Pfc. James, 106, 108
Geddings, Corp. John, 435, 455

Mercer, Lt. Frank, 410
Mercer, Pfc. George, 446
Merrill, Rear Adm. A. Stanton, 170
Michels, Pfc. James, 446, 447
Mikawa, Rear Adm. Gunichi, 33-35, 61, 123
Miller, Maj. Charles, 23
Miller, Pvt. Russell, 22, 24
Mindanao, 394, 395
Minneapolis, cruiser, 292
Mississippi, battleship, 277, 406
Missoula, transport, 446
Mitchell, Maj. John, 141, 142, 143
Mitchell, Maj. Gen. Ralph, 238, 239
Mitscher, Rear Adm. Marc, 141, 143, 287, 290, 293, 315, 324
Mogami, cruiser, 172, 173
Monssen, destroyer, 121, 122
Montpelier, cruiser, 170
Moore, Sgt. Claude, 352
Moore, Pfc. Eugene, 26, 27
Moore, Capt. Marshall, 258, 259
Morgan, Sgt. Butch, 81, 82, 119
Morgan, Lt. Henry, 442
Morotai, 394, 395
Morrison, Pvt. Jack, 66-68
Morrison, destroyer, 500
Mottola, Sgt. Philip, 297
Mount Austen (*see* Grassy Knoll)
Mount Suribachi, 428, 429, 439; capture of, 443-448; flag-raising on, 446, 447
Mueller, Maj. Gen. Paul, 416, 421
Mukai, Maj. Toyoji, 256, 259
Mulcahy, Maj. Gen. Francis, 475
Mullaney, Cmdr. Baron, 505
Munda Airfield, 140, 141, 153, 157, 160
Munro, Donald, 72
Murai, Maj. Gen. Kenjiro, 391, 421
Murakamo, destroyer, 80
Murphy, Lt. George, 476, 508
Murray, Lt. Col. Raymond, 215, 318
Musashi, battleship, 291, 485
Mutsuki, destroyer, 49
Myoko, cruiser, 88, 169, 170

Nagano, Fleet Adm. Osami, 355
Nagara, cruiser, 121
Nagasaki, 472, 521
Nagata, W. O., 275
Nagumo, Vice Adm. Chuichi, 3, 41, 90, 93, 311, 313-315, 322, 347, 349
Nakagawa, Col. Kunio, 390-393, 396, 402, 404, 414, 418, 419, 421, 422
Nakaguma, Col. Jiro, 75, 90, 94, 95

Nakarop, 241, 242, 255, 268, 269, 272, 296, 297
Nashville, cruiser, 395
Natsugumo, destroyer, 80
Nautilus, submarine, 216, 226
Neal, Capt. George, 416, 417
Nelson, Cmdr. Donald, 199
New, Pfc. John, 421
New Britain, 138, 159, 169, 237, 240-242; campaign on, 242-272, 295-308
New Caledonia, island of, 55, 91
New Georgia, 139, 149, 150, 160, 308
New Guinea, 14, 138, 140, 159, 173, 237, 240, 241, 243, 247, 273, 306, 314, 379
New Ireland, 169, 274
New Jersey, battleship, 292
New Mexico, battleship, 277
New Orleans, cruiser, 292
New York, battleship, 500, 514
New Zealand, 8
Nimitz, Fleet Adm. Chester, 91, 273, 274, 277, 395, 422, 452, 473
Nishida, Maj. Gen. Yoshima, 288, 289, 295
Normandy, 311, 379
North Carolina, battleship, 63, 308
Noshiro, cruiser, 172, 173
Noumea, port of, 81, 91, 98, 147

O'Bannon, destroyer, 121, 122
O'Bannon, Lt. Wilcie, 458
Obata, Lt. Gen. Hideyoshi, 313, 379
O'Brien, destroyer, 63
O'Brien, Lt. Col. William, 351
Oda, Capt., 92
O'Donnell, Lt. Col. Clarence, 279
Ogata, Col. Kiyochi, 366-371
Ogawa, Col., 327
Oka, Col. Akinosuke, 74, 90, 94, 96, 105, 107-109
Okinawa, 333, 425, 447; conquest of, 465-485, 489-520
Oldendorf, Rear Adm. Jesse, 393, 395
Oliveria, Corp. Lawrence, 257
Olivier, Corp. Leonce, 212
Omori, Rear Adm. Sentaro, 169-172
Onami, destroyer, 233, 234
Onishi, Vice Adm. Takejiro, 466, 467
Orote Peninsula, 357, 358, 361, 371-374, 379, 380
Oswald, Sgt. Robert, 248
Ota, Vice Adm. Minoru, 469, 517
Owens, Sgt. Robert, 165-166
Owens, Cmdr. Seymour, 368

560

Manufactured by Amazon.ca
Acheson, AB